The Pivot of Civilization
In Historical Perspective

by

Margaret Sanger

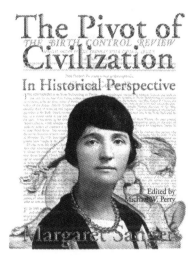

Other Books from Inkling

Dachau Liberated: The Official Report by The U. S. Seventh Army

Released only days after the concentration camp's liberation, this was one of the first post-war reports to describe Nazi crimes against humanity. The original was typewritten and is extremely rare. Now, for the first time, it has been typeset and published as a book. This edition includes all the original text and photographs plus a detailed index and stark combat artist sketches made the day after the camp's liberation. The report includes a description of the camp's organization, interviews with inhabitants in the town of Dachau, moving extracts from a diary kept by one of the inmates, and the transcript of an interview with a woman who claimed to have been the mistress of Auschwitz's infamous commandant, Rudolf Hoess.

ISBN: 1-58742-003-1

Eugenics and Other Evils by G. K. Chesterton

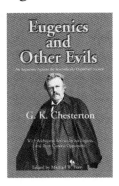

In the early decades of the twentieth century, eugenics, the scientific control of human breeding, was a popular cause within enlightened and progressive segments of Western society. Few dared to criticize it and fewer still had the courage to launch a sustained attack on what the *New York Times* had praised as a wonderful "new science." Perhaps the boldest of that brave few was the talented British writer, G. K. Chesterton. In words that proved chilling accurate, he warned that, "the creed that really is proclaimed not in sermons but in statutes and spread not by pilgrims but by policeman—that creed is the great but disputed system of thought which began with Evolution and has ended in Eugenics."

ISBN: 1-58742-002-3

Theism and Humanism by Arthur J. Balfour

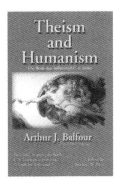

In 1962, *Christian Century* magazine asked C. S. Lewis to name the books that had most influenced his thought. Among them was this book, the published version of British Prime Minister Arthur Balfour's popular Gifford Lectures at the University of Glasgow. "My desire," Balfour wrote, "has been to show that all we think best in human culture, whether associated with culture, goodness or knowledge, requires God for its support, that Humanism without Theism loses more than half its value." Long out of print, the book that Lewis once praised as "too little read," is now available to all who are intrigued by the relationship between science and religion.

ISBN: 1-58742-005-8

The Pivot of Civilization
In Historical Perspective

The Birth Control Classic

by
Margaret Sanger

Edited by
Michael W. Perry

With Articles by Others Including:

Victoria Woodhull Martin, H. G. Wells, G. B. Shaw, Theodore Roosevelt,
Ellen Key, Henry Goddard, G. K. Chesterton, Charlotte Perkins Gilman,
Archbishop Patrick Hayes, and Oliver Wendell Holmes, Jr.

Inkling Books   Seattle   2001

Original Dedication and Epigraph

To Alice Drysdale Vickery

Whose prophetic vision of liberated womanhood has been an inspiration.

"I dream of a world in which the spirits of women are flames stronger than fire, a world in which modesty has become courage and yet remains modesty, a world in which women are as unlike men as ever they were in the world I sought to destroy, a world in which women shine with a loveliness of self-revelation as enchanting as ever the old legends told, and yet a world which would immeasurably transcend the old world in the self-sacrificing passion of human service. I have dreamed of that world ever since I began to dream at all." —Havelock Ellis

Library Cataloging Data

Sanger, Margaret (1879–1966)

The Pivot of Civilization in Historical Perspective: The Birth Control Classic

Editor: Perry, Michael W. [Wiley] (1948–)

279 p. 7.5 x 9.25 in. 235 x 191 mm.

Includes: 43 chapters, 42 graphics, 1 appendix and an index

ISBN 1-58742-004-X (paper)

LC 00-107135

Keywords: Sanger, Margaret; Birth Control; Eugenics; Immigration; Feminism; Race Suicide

HQ766 S33 2001

301.3

Inkling Books, Seattle, WA Internet: http://www.InklingBooks.com/

Published in the United States of America on acid-free paper

First Edition, First Printing: April 2001

Contents

Preface

Time magazine's remarkable account of Margaret Sanger's life, published the week after her death on September 6, 1966, illustrates why this book was written.

Family planning by contraception was the cause, Margaret Sanger was its champion. Half a century ago, when she raised the banners of her lonely crusade, she was lacerated from the pulpits as a "lascivious monster" bent on "murdering" unborn children. Birth control, a phrase she herself invented, was unmentionable, immoral and illegal. It was a federal crime merely to send information about it through the mails. She was arrested eight times. Her zeal led to the breakup of her first marriage. Yet when she died last week of arteriosclerosis in Tucson at the age of 82, her vision had been realized beyond her dreams. Birth control, which to her meant the right of every woman to control the size of her own family, had become accepted in the U.S. and was spreading rapidly throughout the world.[1]

What is remarkable about that account is that virtually everything this respected news magazine said about her life (but not her death) was not only false, it was easily demonstrated to be so.

Some of the mistakes are minor. Sanger didn't coin the term "birth control," much less get everyone to talking about a topic previously "unmentionable." She merely publicized it as an easy way to refer to a something that had been an obsession of the nation's 'chattering classes' for over a decade. In fact, the first 17 chapters in this book quote extensively from magazine articles and books that predate Sanger's active public life and each touches, directly or indirectly, on the subject. In addition, Sanger's crusade was not only far from lonely, it soon elevated her into the ranks of that 'enlightened and thoughtful' class of people who consider their opinions superior to those of the general run of humanity.

Other mistakes are a bit more serious. Her marriage was not destroyed by her "zeal" for the cause. Her first husband did jail time for promoting birth control before she did. Like most spouses, he simply couldn't cope with her sexual promiscuity. That matters, because in that era a critical part of the debate over birth control centered on whether it would encourage promiscuity. Catholics claimed it would. Liberals—though they may have known otherwise—denied any such link. Sanger's own behavior hints at what we now know is true, that the Catholics and their religious allies were right. In fact, the organization that Sanger founded, Planned Parenthood, now gets large sums of public money to counter with chemistry a teen lifestyle it helps to promote. That's a bit like a tobacco company getting a federal subsidy to treat lung cancer.

Then there is the much more serious matter of abortion. Alas, in its endless pursuit of fashion, upper-Manhattan style, *Time* misplaced a pair of quotation marks. They were put around "murdering" rather than "unborn children." The pretense that what lives in the womb was of an uncertain nature was not yet dogma. Sanger's conservative religious critics got it wrong, *Time* told us, when they claimed that Sanger wanted abortion legalized. Birth control, everyone who was anyone then knew, was intended to prevent what many 1960s liberals were still calling the "evil of abortion." As propaganda, it was clever. At the time of Sanger's death, federally funded family planning was being promoted as a counter to abortion rather than its prelude. But the blunder also illustrates that *Time*'s staff was as foolish as Sanger's Catholic and Fundamentalist foes had been shrewd. Time, alas, has not been kind to *Time*.

It is true that you can find quite a bit of material to back up *Time*'s claims in the pages of Sanger's own magazine, *Birth Control Review*. In the March, 1925 issue, for instance, a physician and board member in the American Birth Control League said: "Not only has Birth Control nothing in common with Abortion, but it is a weapon of the greatest value in fighting this evil."[2] The following

---

1. "Every Child a Wanted Child," *Time* (Sept. 16, 1966), 96.

year the magazine would explain: "Birth control is not abortion. Abortion is the taking of life after conception; Birth Control is the prevention of conception."[3]

Earlier on, Sanger did call for abortion. In 1915, Marie Stopes, Sanger's British counterpart, wrote to her while gathering signatures of prominent people to induce President Wilson to intervene in Sanger's prosecution for sending her 1914 magazine, *Woman Rebel* through the mail. "I am getting on with my letter to your President," she wrote, "but it is slower and more difficult than I expect[ed] chiefly because of what you said about abortion. If *only* you had left that out!"[4] Sanger did not need anyone to teach her to lie, but she did need to know when to lie, hence the quotes above. Like similar remarks by some politicians, they weren't to be taken seriously. When the time came, her zeal to get rid of undesirables would have been more than enough to cross the conception gap.

Those who read Sanger carefully can sense that she saw abortion complications and deaths as little more than a tool to batter her "puritanical" and "masculine-minded"[5] opponents. In a 1946 letter, she described that technique when she explained how she handled Catholics: refusing to be on the same platform with them, "saying they were vulgar," and her primary technique—"Attack. Accuse them of all the evils on earth, including abortions and war."[6] Her oft-repeated claim that birth control would do away with abortion was nonsense. Even today's much better technologies haven't done that.

In the late 1930s, this deception may have become more difficult to maintain. It was true that in a February 1938 speech in Tucson, Sanger did claim that the birth control movement, "has advocated definite means to eradicate abortion,"[7] and in May of the next year she'd write "Destroy" on a letter from someone with the Abortion Law Reform Association in London.[8] But in the fall of 1939, a colleague named Clarence Gamble was in contact with her about an African folk remedy that he claimed had produced abortions "in 13 out of the 15" pregnancies.[9]

In his grim tale of totalitarian rule, *1984,* George Orwell would blast the British left ("Engsoc" in the novel is English socialism) for the speed with which it could not only shift its opinion, but deny that it had ever believed what it had recently been saying. *Time*'s shifting stance on Sanger and abortion illustrates just that sort of behavior. Much as a totalitarian state has a Big Brother who can do no wrong, progressive thought has 'brave pioneers' who serve humanity by defying convention. That is the 'story' that journalists and biographers are expected to write, often in defiance of the facts.

For virtually all Sanger's adult life, the politically correct story was that abortion was an 'evil' created by 'reactionaries' opposing the spread of birth control. At a superficial level that might seem true. A survey of writings on birth control and similar topics from late nineteen century to about 1960 just might find feminists and their allies more likely to profess a deep concern for the fate of children as yet unborn than their opponents.[10] Only the more astute would notice that the "potential child" they championed was merely a symbol for the improved humanity they intended to breed. In the end, they could not maintain a pretense so out of line with their beliefs. Abortion fit all too well with the 'might makes right' mindset of evolution, just as the belief that a person is a person no matter how small, weak, or unwanted fits with Judeo-Christian beliefs.

But this book is not about legalized abortion. Except for a few radical feminists, particularly in Germany, it wasn't a major issue during the period of time covered by this book—from the 1870s until the early 1930s—so it won't be a major issue in this book. Honestly or dishonestly, virtually all those involved in the debates we will cover professed a horror of abortion. Charlotte Perkins Gilman, perhaps the premier feminist intellectual of the early twentieth century, portrayed it as something so terrible it could exist only because men forced it on women.

2. Benjamin T. Tilton, "Birth Control as a Prevention of Abortion," *Birth Control Review* (Mar. 1925), 71.

3. "Birth Control Primer," *Birth Control Review* (Jan. 1926), n.p.

4. Marie Stopes to Margaret Sanger, Sept. 15, 1914, Sanger/Smith microfilm, S01:0459.

5. For example: Margaret Sanger, "Birth Control or Abortion?" *Birth Control Review* (Dec. 1918), 3.

6. Margaret Sanger to Anna Jane Phillips Shuman, 1946. Sanger/Smith microfilm, C08:0143.

7. Margaret Sanger, speech to the Mother's Health Center, Tucson, Arizona, Feb. 8, 1938, Sanger/Smith microfilm, S71:0975.

8. Janet Chance to Margaret Sanger, May 12, 1939, Sanger/Smith microfilm, S16:0805.

9. Clarence Gamble to Margaret Sanger, Oct. 31, 1939. Sanger/Smith microfilm, C06:1068. The correspondence went on for about a year, but Sanger seemed more interested in a Hungarian spermatoxin that had been tested on "about a hundred women and numerous rabbits." She hoped the idea could get further testing using money intended for "the colored problem in the South." Sanger to Gamble, Nov. 5, 1939, Sanger/Smith microfilm, C06:1069. Though the letter has no obvious racist 'smoking gun,' the fact that she was discussing Southern blacks probably explains why it was headed, "Confidential for C.J.G."

10. For an example, see Chapter X, "The Century of the Child," by Ellen Key, a Swedish feminist.

The central focus of this book is on something quite different. We will be looking at the motivations that drove Sanger, the birth control movement, and its many allies. This is where the story gets *very* interesting. While progressive movements can be ruthless at covering up evils they did in the past, they are often quite candid (at least among themselves) about the currently fashionable causes they champion—even causes that later come to be regarded as great evils. Eugenics, a kissing cousin of birth control, is a good example.

One reason is arrogance. Believing themselves right, they lack the restraint that most of humanity displays. They fail to ask themselves, "But is what I believe so certain that I must force my agenda on others?" In this book you will find writer after writer discussing not whether he and his sort has the right to decide who has children—that is assumed as a matter of course—but what criteria and techniques ought to be used by a few intent on making that decision for the many. Eugenists advocated one set of criteria, liberals and socialists slightly different rationale, and feminists such as Sanger yet another. Each had its own axe to grind, but that axe is inevitably being sharpened to be used on the reproductive powers of others. Their minds can follow no other paths.

In recent years, the growing weight that all-too-obvious fact has made it increasingly difficult in the academic world to portray Sanger as a champion of women's rights. Where biographers and historians go from there often depends on their political beliefs. Those on the left blame Sanger's contacts with large capitalists such as the Rockefellers, neglecting to mention that all her life Sanger drew warm support from socialists and liberals. Others claim, rather belatedly, that a woman who was long championed as a feminist was never really one. Again they get it wrong. Sanger made an excellent case for why feminists should support restrictions on other women's childbearing that remains as persuasive today as it was in the 1920s.

The result has been a muddle, with various groups from that period being confused with one another. Race suiciders, eugenists, Social Darwinians, and birth controllers are all jumbled together with the beliefs of one attributed to another. As a result, some of the worst offenders remain uncriticized, while the more benign are targeted as bigots.

In their histories of birth control, two deservedly well-respected scholars make the first mistake, misattributing the same quote to Sanger. Both claim that in the May 1919 issue of *Birth Control Review* Sanger wrote, "More children from the fit, less from the unfit—that is the chief issue in Birth Control."[11] Anyone who knew Sanger would know that the first clause would *never* pass her lips. Her life was dedicated to preventing just that sort of "cradle race." Make sure the unfit have fewer children— "Yes!"—she would say. But there must be no pressure on *her* class to have more children. The quote they both misattribute was taken from an *American Medicine* editorial that Sanger reprinted and represents what eugenists were saying. Though Sanger disagreed vehemently with the "positive" measures eugenists advocated, they were allies and had to be humored. In the long run, she knew she had little to fear from eugenists. Their zeal for pressuring the 'better' sort of people to have more children was so anemic that many of them had few or no children.

The final position for those wanting to whitewash Sanger is less than impressive. In Sanger's day, we are told, almost everyone was a bigot and a racist. Sanger, for all the goodness of her heart, was caught up in her culture and could not escape. Under such reasoning, Sanger, once considered a radical of radicals, wasn't radical enough. Again, the truth lies elsewhere. The great bulk of Americans never adopted the nasty attitudes that drove Sanger and her supporters. While certainly not perfect, they simply weren't that prejudiced.

An excellent example is an oft-reprinted 1904 book entitled *The Laws of Sex Life and Heredity or Eugenics*. Not only was this Ohio-published book more candid about many sexual matters than Sanger typically was (demolishing the illusion that the era was sexually repressed), but the eugenics it advocated was far milder and vastly more tolerant than what you will be reading in this book. True, the publisher did seem to have been reading the nation's elite press. He opens the book briefly warning of the dangers of "feeble-mindedness." But none of that reappears in the text. (Feeble-minded isn't even listed in the index.) Instead, the book presents a point of view congenial to religious conservatives, including the Women's Christian Temperance Union, which endorsed it. Readers are assured that the "law of inheritance" is "not an invariable one," and "its force must not be overestimated."[12] Health problems are not only regarded as predominately environmental, they are treated as something the average person can handle. There is no call for

---

11. The references are David Kennedy, *Birth Control in America*, 115; and Linda Gordon, *Woman's Body, Woman's Right*, 281. Both books are well worth reading. The article Sanger did publish in *American Medicine* was reprinted two pages earlier.

12. T. W. Shannon, *The Laws of Sex Life and Heredity or Eugenics*.(Marietta, Ohio: S. A. Mullikin, 1917), 3, 235. The book's old fashioned frankness about sex led Doubleday to republish it in 1970.

scientific dictates or new religions of the sort that appealed to Sanger and her colleagues.

So keep in mind as you read *The Pivot of Civilization in Historical Perspective* that the attitudes you see displayed here were held only by an affluent, educated, and well-connected few who were obsessed with improving the world by manipulating the birthrates of others. Obvious as it may seem to those who read the articles collected here, the average Americans of that day did not grasp what Sanger's real agenda was. Her claims about giving poor mothers 'choice' was enough to cloud their more tolerant minds. Because they did not think someone else's family size was any of their business, they had trouble believing anyone else would be obsessed with such things. They were wrong, tragically wrong.

History is clear about one thing. In the era covered by this book, open cultural and genetic intolerance was far more common among the progressive-minded than among the religious conservatives who were Sanger's most vocal opponents.[13]

You get taste of that in an article in the *New York Times* on the last Thursday of February, 1924. A Rev. Charles Francis Potter of the West Side Unitarian Church, the paper said, was announcing his plan for "a new, all-American Bible." In a chilling prelude to what would soon be happening in Germany, this very liberal clergyman made it clear that there would be no place within its pages for foreigners, and particularly not for "the literature of a Semitic nation of 2,000 years ago." He went on to add: "If we are to have the Bible taught in our American schools, let it be the American Bible." Did the *Times* go to a liberal to counter this nasty bit of anti-Semitism? No, they went to Dr. John Straton, the city's best known fundamentalist preacher.[14] As we see, many

on the political left felt threatened by waves of immigrants bringing in their tradition-minded culture and more than a few of those immigrants were religious Jews.

The *Times* choice of a religious conservative to defend other cultures and races wasn't a fluke. In July of the following year, *Forum* magazine published an article by the famous fundamentalist politician, William Jennings Bryan, entitled "Mr. Bryan Speaks to Darwin." In the same issue, their "Toasts" section described a lecture by the Rev. William R. Inge, a friend of Sanger and the Anglican church hierarchy's boldest birth control supporter. As they began describing what the Rev. Inge had said, the magazine noted, "it would be difficult to find in all Christendom a greater contrast between the beliefs of two men both professing the same faith" than Bryan and Inge.[15]

They zeroed in on the critical difference. At that time Bryan was evolution's best known foe. In contrast, Inge was "a confirmed evolutionist" and "a believer in the possibility of improving the human race through eugenics." The political labels given the two men reflect this difference. Bryan's championing of ordinary people earned him the title, "The Great Commoner." In contrast, Igne's elitist whining about social ills gave the well-known Dean of St. Paul's Cathedral in London the nickname the "Gloomy Dean."

In his lecture, Gloomy Dean Inge championed themes we will encounter repeatedly in this book. There was, for instance, the issue of 'old stock' Americans being overwhelmed by waves of inferior immigrants: "America, I am afraid, is becoming less Anglo-Saxon every year. . . . I know the new immigration laws are designed to protect the old tradition, and I hope they will preserve the dominance of the northern European stock. I don't mean just the English—many Englishmen are not particularly desirable—but the Scandinavians, the Dutch, and the better sort of Germans, also."

At that point, this champion of northern European supremacy was challenged by a representative from another group that opposed birth controllers, Rev. Cornelius C. Clifford, pastor of a Roman Catholic church in New Jersey. "I am puzzled to know," Clifford asked, "upon what biological ground your assumption of a superior northern type rests, and, if you will pardon me, I do not believe it has a leg to stand on." Refusing to back down, Inge replied that, "I doubt whether southern Mediterraneans are desirable people to introduce into this country." Or be permitted to have large families once

---

13. It is easy to suspect that the same pattern continues today despite rhetoric about "diversity" and "pluralism." Why are some so obsessed with a topic that most Americans find boring? And why isn't "pluralism" given its correct meaning—one in which laws concerning marriage and education are decided by ethnic and religious groups rather than society as a whole?

14. "Plans New Bible for America," *New York Times* (Feb. 28, 1924), 21. The day before, the *Times* gave Potter's Jew-free 'new bible' front-page coverage. Like Inge, described next, Potter had ties to Sanger. In November of that year, she would invite him to speak at a meeting she was holding. (Sanger to Francis Potter, Nov. 11, 1924, Sanger/Smith microfilm, C03:0225.) There is also a link to evolution. Potter attended the Scopes Monkey trial and promoted himself as an expert on evolution and religion. For pointing me to the 'new bible' controversy, I am indebted to Carlton J. H. Hayes, *Essays on Nationalism* (New York: Macmillan, 1926), 121–122.

15. "Toasts," *Forum* 74 (July 1925), n. p. Inge described himself as a Liberal.

they arrive, we might add. It's easy to see why Inge and Sanger got along so fabulously.

Forum got it exactly right. The difference between Bryan and Inge hinged on their views about evolution. The "biological ground" of Inge's assumption was evolution. It is true that Darwin's basic theory did not in itself prove that the 'Germanic' race was superior to a 'Mediterranean' one. But it did claim as scientific truth that some human groups were 'fit' and others 'unfit.' Instinctively, evolution's true believers sought to discover the 'holy grail' of their secular religion—which is which? Once on that path, what grouping is more biologically apt than race or, within races, economic classes? From belief in evolution to zeal for eugenics, sterilization or birth control was but a small step.

In contrast, for those whose worldview was essentially biblical—the old Jewish one—all the measures of fitness that so impressed their foes, a comfortable financial state, alleged intelligence, artistic genius and the like, were simply not that important. In Chapter XXI, we will see a quote that sums up the contrast: "Heredity! Heredity! The word has rung in my ears until I am sick of it. There is just one heredity in this world of ours—we are the children of God." Harvard's Edward East might sneeringly dismiss that as no more than a "burst of emotion," but its implications, if rejected, are enormous.[16]

Deprived of a theistic reason for attaching genuine value *all* to human lives, the alternatives are bleak. We can claim, with the crudest of Social Darwinians, that rights belong only to those who can defend them—as Justice Holmes does in Chapter XXIII. Or we can develop some sort of criteria that gives an illusion of value: intelligence, foresight, efficiency or whatever. This book is filled with the champions of that point of view. All share the same flaw—the criteria is relative. Whether it is silly, like Nazism's fascination with blue-eyed blonds, or more complex, involving intelligence tests and measures of professional success, the criteria always measures some against others. "Intelligent" always means "more intelligent than." As Inge's remarks indicate, that sort of thinking can take a nasty turn, particularly when attention turns to immigration or differing birthrates. Modern evolution has replaced its original belief in the importance of mere survival with a more nuanced one involving the

16. In *Theism and Humanism*, Arthur J. Balfour suggested that those who trace human beginnings to naturalistic causes (as East did) have trouble explaining how *any* human belief is more than instinct and emotion. From the evolutionary perspective, our minds are not tools designed to lead us to the truth, but organs, arising by accident, that give us the guile to defeat larger and fiercer foes.

number of surviving offspring. He who dies with the most living offspring wins the evolutionary game. The result is an almost uncontrollable urge to squelch the birthrate of others.

A disclaimer needs to be added to the above. The danger does *not* lie in a vague assent to evolutionary theory. Much more is required. Several of those in this book got it right when they wrote of founding a new religion. It is only when belief in evolution becomes the central, defining dogma of one's life that serious problems develop.

The resulting thought process isn't hard to follow. Evolution splits each species into fit and unfit. Who belongs to each? As we will see, therein lies much nastiness. Next comes evolution's attempt to put an optimistic spin on a nature that seems "red with tooth and claw." To do that, the death of the unfit is linked to progress—the ones who die *ought* to die. Any glorification of death has chilling implications, especially when a mindset develops that this progress-inducing natural culling is no longer taking place. What if virtually every child born now grows to reproductive adulthood? Evolution, it seems, has come to an end. Does that mean biological progress has stopped? Certainly. Is evolutionary disaster upon us? Quite possibly. What can be done to prevent this disaster? That's what most of those in this book discuss. You find the roots of this sort of reasoning in the very last words of Charles Darwin's *The Origin of Species*.

> Thus, from the war of nature, from famine and death, the most exalted object of which we are capable of conceiving, namely, the production of the higher animals, directly follows. There is a grandeur in this view of life, with its several powers, having been originally breathed by the Creator into a few forms or into one; and that, whilst this planet has gone cycling on according to the fixed law of gravity, from so simple a beginning endless forms most beautiful and most wonderful have been, and are being evolved.

Note how Darwin praised his new theory, referring to its "grandeur" and to the "most beautiful and most wonderful" results it created. Good, he was saying, could come out of the twin evils of "famine and death."

But is that really true? Exactly who benefits by evolution? Does the slow-footed little bunny who is devoured by a better evolved wolf? Obviously not. But, you say, how about the speedier bunny who does evade the wolf, at least until he grows old? Again the answer is a clear no. The same process that evolves the bunny also evolves the wolf. The result is a biological 'arms race' with no real winners. The deadly race between predator and prey merely moves a faster pace.

Viewed from the perspective of individuals within a species, evolution seems to have only victims. Who are the winners? Darwin and his kin certainly are. As the tellers of this grand story, they win our adoration. That was and remains one of evolution's chief attractions within the scientific community—one that blinds them to just how gruesome their tale really is.

Another winner are those who, like Darwin, see themselves at the apex not just of the "higher animals" but of humanity itself. But, as we have noted, that is where the nastiness begins. Follow Darwin and you can find beauty in the survival of the fittest only by growing indifferent (or worse) to the deaths of the unfit. In the end what is idealized and even worshiped is an abstraction, an ever-evolving, ever-improving, almost god-like humanity. To that abstraction living, breathing people must be sacrificed. Some see beauty in that. Others find it monstrous.

At this point a few cautions are appropriate. Yes, many of the ideas advanced in this book do sound quite silly today. Virtually no American alive claims, with Inge, that southern Italians make bad citizens. Nor do we hear much about the threat of rapidly multiplying feeble-minded people. Though more than a few undoubtedly still think that way, population control replaced eugenics as the rhetoric of choice in the 1950s and 1960s.

The shift is easy to track. In 1962, Alan Guttmacher, former vice-president of the American Eugenics Association, assumed the presidency of Planned Parenthood. Soon, a 'population bomb' hysteria (and later rhetoric about environmental doom) was driving public policy. In 1969, a medical news magazine revealed what was really going on when it quoted Guttmacher warning that if "voluntary means" did not achieve the desired goals, "Each country will have to decide its own form of coercion and determine when and how it should be employed. At present, the means available are compulsory sterilization and compulsory abortion. Perhaps some day a way of enforcing compulsory birth control will be feasible."[17] Think of women being dragged into a medical clinic and forcibly sterilized or aborted and you capture his intent. Beneath the rhetoric about "choice" their real agenda was just that ugly.

17. "Outlook," *Medical World News* (June 6, 1969), 11. "Voluntary means" could include manipulating circumstances to pressure undesired groups into having fewer children. Compulsory means are those that can be imposed efficiently on the unwilling. The arrival of long-term injectable contraceptives such as Depro Provera closed the only gap in the technological arsenal.

"But," you may say, "Planned Parenthood is about giving women reproductive choices. How can the second most important individual in the organization's history talk about compulsion. The evening news, my local paper, and anyone who is anyone tells me that. You could get a hundred Noble Prize winners to sign a paper stating just that. After all they call themselves 'prochoice' don't they."

Yes, 'prochoice' singular, not 'prochoices' plural. The distinction is *extremely* important. Coercion, one step short of compulsion, means that you narrow someone's choices, so those targeted feel that they have only one option—not having a child. That's what Sanger intended, as we will see repeatedly in the portions of this book she wrote, so why should it be surprising that Guttmacher felt the same? And, whether you have heard it or not, Sanger's bigotry is old news. Academically, the issue was settled very quietly during the 1970s. And in that silence lies truth. If Sanger was so anti-choice, why hasn't she been properly demonized by the "prochoice" movement? And why haven't they praised the "religious right" for the role it played in blocking what Sanger intended to do to our parents and grandparents?

Instead, the sorts of people who once championed Sanger's cause now focus on damage control. Any awareness of Sanger's real agenda is to be confined to as small a circle as possible. As dramatic as the events in this book are, don't expect them to become the theme of a hard-hitting network documentary. Even more important, the general population must kept from realizing that from certain perspectives—feminist, liberal and socialist— what Sanger was trying to do is not only reasonable but absolutely necessary. That is precisely why those groups supported her so enthusiastically. Doubt that? Then read on. In this book we will let them explain, in their own words, why they intend to control—with whatever level of coercion was necessary—just who has children. In fact, most of the text of this book is theirs. To ensure that what they say is not ripped out of context, they are allowed to go on for page after page explaining what they believe in great detail. As unpleasant as it is, they have as much right to be understood as you and I have a right to understand them and what they intended to do.

With that I leave you with this book to read in the hope that you will find it as stimulating to read as it has been to edit.

—Michael W. Perry, Seattle, March 21, 2001

I

The Martyrdom of Man

1872

Winwood Reade

English Novelist

Our religion therefore is Virtue, our Hope is placed in the happiness of our posterity; our Faith in the Perfectibility of Man.

EDITOR

In early October of 1921, Margaret Sanger wrote Eden Paul, editor of a 1917 book, *Population and Birth Control,* to ask him to join a birth control conference she planned for November. (Chapter XIX is from Paul's book.) In his reply, Paul explained why he could not attend. Referring to both himself and his wife, he told her, "to be quite frank—we regard birth control as (at the moment) a side issue. Like alcoholism, venereal disease, and half-a-dozen other matters we might name, it is of great importance to the welfare and happiness of the human race. But unless another, more urgent, and more vital problem is rightly solved in the near future, we do not think that what Winwood Reade termed the Martyrdom of Man will end except by man's extinction, or than mankind in the future will have any happiness or welfare worth considering."[1]

Paul dismissed those "who are hostile to birth control on what are termed 'moral' grounds'" as "obviously living in the Middle Ages" because they believe that the spread of birth control would lead to increased promiscuity, particularly among the young. He also gave a hint at what he did consider important when he mentioned "a glimmer of dawn in the East"—undoubtedly a reference to the then newly born Soviet Union. (In Chapter 7 of *Pivot,* Sanger described Eden and Cedar Paul as "two convinced Communists.") He closed his letter with encouraging words for the beleaguered Sanger: "Birth control is an important element in 'man's control of nature.' As such, it has come

to stay—if in other respects man makes good his claim to be the Master to Things."

As Paul had pointed out, Sanger's movement was but one element in a much broader agenda—an agenda that had enlightened mankind taking god-like charge of its destiny and becoming the "Master of Things." These words are deceptive. An abstraction—man (or in Sanger case, woman)—conceals the fact that a few intend to control the births of the many.

In this chapter, we present extracts from *The Martyrdom of Man,* the book that Paul mentioned to Sanger.[2] It certainly ranks among the oddest of books. It was first published in 1872 by Winwood Reade (1838–75), a vain and dogmatic English novelist so lacking in talent that the introduction to a 1926 edition of *Martyrdom* didn't hesitate to expose his faults. Yet there was something about *Martyrdom* that appealed to a certain mindset. As a novelist, Reade had difficulty seeing books survive past the first edition. Yet *Martyrdom* demonstrated remarkable staying power, remaining in print decade after decade. The quotes here come from an edition printed some 65 years after the book first came out, an American release based on the twentieth-fourth English edition. Few books survive so many editions over so many years.

Why did some find *Martyrdom* appealing? First, because it gave them a universal history of mankind from an evolutionary perspective. Decades after it came out, H. G. Wells copied the idea with his enormously successful *The Outline of History.* But the second reason was more important. Temperamentally, Reade was ideal for this sort of book. Like Wells, his characters were little more

---

1. Eden and Cedar Paul to Margaret Sanger, Oct. 16, 1921. Sanger/Smith microfilm, S02: 38–39. Sanger also published their letter in *Birth Control Review* (April 1922), referring to them as "English Writers of Short Stories."

2. A prominent feminist intellectual, Charlotte Perkins Gilman, would also commend Reade's book (Chap. XXII).

than tools of his ideas. One commentator described Reade's novels rather bluntly: "They show no gift of characterization, and in the whole series there appears no personage whose personality seems real to the eyes of the most indulgent reader. Nor is there any reason to suppose that his characters were any more real or lifelike to their creator. He seems to have regarded them throughout as a set of puppets into whose mouths he could thrust the opinions that he wished to lay before the public."[3] A novelist who treated his characters as puppets was the ideal author for a non-fiction work that treats read people not as Christianity would have them, as "degenerated angels" created in the image of God, but as "elevated apes" (his terms) who can, if properly managed, achieve "The Perfectibility of Man." People as the raw material for something greater, that was an idea many on the left—including Margaret Sanger—found appealing.

Throughout its history, the movement Sanger helped found has been torn between a Reade-like mystical idealism about a perfected humanity and a pragmatic realism that sought—often ruthlessly—to see that the world remained populated, as much as possible, with those who looked and thought much like themselves. This chapter and several others illustrate the first point of view. The chapters on race suicide and elite birthrates illustrate the second. Readers can find both points of view in *The Pivot of Civilization.*

Winwood Reade, *The Martyrdom of Man* (New York: E. P. Dutton, 1872). Page numbers are given in square brackets after the text quoted [ ].

—§§§—

God made all men equal is a fine-sounding phrase, and has also done good service in its day; but it is not a scientific fact. On the contrary, there is nothing so certain as the natural inequality of men. Those who outlive hardships and sufferings which fall on all alike owe their existence to some superiority, not only of body, but of mind. [6-7]

—§§§—

There is a certain class of people who prefer to say that their fathers came down in the world through their own follies than to boast that they rose in the world through their own industry and talents. It is the same shabby-genteel sentiment, the same vanity of birth which makes men prefer to believe that they are degenerated angels rather than elevated apes. In scientific investigations, such whims and fancies must be set aside. . . . And when it is

3. From F. Legge's introduction to Winwood Reade, *The Martyrdom of Man* (New York, E. P. Dutton, 1872, 1926), xxi.

fully realised and understood that the genius of man has been developed along a line of unbroken descent from the simple tendencies which inhabited the primeval cell, and that in its later stages this development has been assisted by the efforts of man himself, what a glorious futurity will open to the human race! [351–52]

—§§§—

The popular theory is this:—The world was made by a Great Being; he created man in his own image; and therefore his mind is analogous to that of man. But while our minds are imperfect, troubled by passions, stained with sin, and limited in power, his mind is perfect in beauty, perfect in power, perfect in love. He is omnipotent and omnipresent. . . . The soul of the poorest creature in the streets and the soul of the greatest philosopher or poet are equal before the Creator; he is no respecter of persons; souls are measured only by their sins. But the sins of the ignorant will be forgiven; the sins of the more enlightened will be more severely judged. [461]

—§§§—

But it is when we open the Book of Nature, that book inscribed in blood and tears; it is when we study the laws regulating, the laws productive of development, that we see plainly how illusive this theory that God is Love. In all things there is cruel, profligate, and abandoned waste. Of all the animals that are born a few only can survive; and it is owing to this law that development takes place. The law of Murder is the law of Growth. Life is one long tragedy; creation is one great crime. [464]

—§§§—

The abolition of this ancient and elevated faith [Christianity]; the dethronement of God; the extinction of piety as a personal feeling; the destruction of the Image made of golden thoughts in the exquisite form of an ideal Man [Jesus], and tenderly enshrined in the human heart—these appear to be evils, and such undoubtedly they are. We can do nothing that is exclusively and absolutely good. . . . No useful inventions can be introduced without some branch of industry being killed and hundreds of worthy men being cast, without occupation, on the world. All the mental revolutions are attended by catastrophe. [473]

—§§§—

We do not wish to extirpate religion from the life of man; we wish him to have a religion which will harmonise with his intellect, and which inquiry will strengthen, not destroy. We wish, in fact, to give him a religion, for now there are many who have none. We teach that there is a God, but not a God of the anthropoid variety, not a God who is gratified by compliments in prose and verse, and whose attributes can be catalogued by theologians. God is so great that he does not deign to have personal relations with us human atoms that are called men. Those who desire to worship their Creator must worship him through mankind. Such, it is plain, is the scheme of Nature. [479]

—§§§—

Our religion therefore is Virtue, our Hope is placed in the happiness of our posterity; our Faith in the Perfectibility of Man. A day will come when the European God of the nineteenth century will be classed with the gods of Olympus and the Nile; when surplices and sacramental plate will be exhibited in museums; when nurses will relate to children the legends of the Christian mythology as they now tell them fairy tales. [480]

—§§§—

With one faith, with one desire they will labour together in the Sacred Cause—the extinction of disease, the extinction of sin, the perfection of genius, the perfection of love, the invention of immortality, the exploration of the infinite, the conquest of creation.

You blessed ones who shall inherit that future age of which we can only dream; you pure and radiant beings who shall succeed us on the earth; when you turn back your eyes on us poor savages, grubbing in the ground for our daily bread, eating flesh and blood, dwelling in the vile bodies which degrade us every day to a level with the beasts, tortured by pains, and by animal propensities, buried in gloomy superstitions, ignorant of Nature which yet holds us in her bonds; when you read of us in books, when you think of what we are, and compare us with yourselves, remember that it is to us you owe the foundation of your happiness and grandeur, to us who now in our libraries and laboratories and star-towers and dissecting-rooms and workshops are preparing the materials for human growth. . . . All men indeed cannot be poets, inventors, or philanthropists; but all men can join in that gigantic and god-like work—the progress of creation. [481–82]

Editor: To illustrate how ideas like Reade's influenced Sanger, the following is from a magazine she edited, *Birth Control Review* (Jan. 1918, 11). In Sanger's day these ideas were championed by those who considered themselves "advanced."

Superman Arise

by Gertrude Boyle

Woe-lined Womb of Now,
What man art thou delivering forth?
What being doth issue from the loins of War!

Lo, Superman arise!—
Shod in iron,
Helmed in spirit,
Winged with flame.
Rejoice! Rejoice!—
The world has broken its shackles;
Humanity at last burst its chains!
Rejoice! flesh-entombed man is resurrecting;
Shedding the cerecloth of ages;
Freeing self from bondage of ignorance,
From the dust of oppression;
Eons man has been matter-enslaved!

Behold, Superman advancing upon chaos and night!—
Slaying with sword of spirit
The monsters of discord and darkness,
Scorching their evil with wings of flame.
Beware oppressors, his pinions of fire,
Through earth, through hell they shall burn his way!

Rejoice O Earth! O Heavens!
Superman is risen!
Toward Godhood he's winging his way!

—§§§—

Editor: What was this mystic vision of a Superman that drove Sanger to publish verses and (as we see later) inspired George Bernard Shaw to write a play? The best known champion of the Superman was a once fashionable German philosopher named Friedrich Nietzsche. In his *The Story of Philosophy,* Will Durant, a friend of Sanger's,[4] extracted the essence of the Superman from Nietzsche's *Thus Spake Zarathustra.* Note in particular the last line. It summarizes all too well the sort of idealism that drove Sanger and those like her.[5]

---

4. Will Durant to Margaret Sanger (Nov. 1, 1921). Sanger/Smith microfilm, S02:0051. Durant was responding to a survey from Sanger. Taking up a theme popularized by the 1901 article in Chapter VII, the famous historian added: "To offset the so-called 'yellow peril,' it would only be necessary to raise the quality of our own people by better education and to spread birth-control knowledge abroad so as to decrease the quantity of peoples whose unchecked reproduction threatens international peace." For Durant, as for Sanger, the world's problems came from *other* people having too many babies.

5. One link from Nietzsche to Sanger is easy to trace. Sanger was heavily influenced by Havelock Ellis, an English writer on sex and eugenics. In a tribute to Ellis published by Sanger, the author noted that Ellis's "study of Nietzsche was the first to appear in England: it remains the best, the most perceptive and the most judicious." See: Hugh de Sélincourt, "Havelock Ellis: A Great Humanist" *Birth Control Review* 6 (Feb. 1922), 5.

Nietzsche's Superman

Dead are all Gods; now we will that superman live. . . .

**I teach you the superman. Man is something that shall
be surpassed.** What have ye done to surpass
him? . . .

What is great in man is that he is a bridge and not a goal:
what can be loved in man is that he is a *transition*
and a *destruction*.

I love those who do not know how to live except in per-
ishing, for they are those going beyond.

I love the great despisers because they are the great ador-
ers, they are arrows of longing for the other shore.

I love those who do not seek beyond the stars for a reason
to perish and be sacrificed, but who sacrifice themselves to earth in order that earth may some day
become superman's. . . .

It is time for man to mark his goal. It is time for man to
plant the germ of his highest hope. . . .

Tell me, my brethren, if the goal be lacking to humanity,
is not humanity itself lacking? . . .

**Love unto the most remote man is higher than love
unto your neighbor.**[6]

—§§§—

Editor: We now turn to another well-known writer who
believed similar Nietzschean ideas about humanity as a
work-in-progress and the need to create the god-like
Superman.

The Voice of Destruction

In our talks he put these ideas before me in a rather
more materialistic form.

"Creation is not yet at an end," he said. "At all events,
not so far as the creature Man is concerned. Biologically
regarded, man has clearly arrived at a turning-point. A
new variety of man is beginning to separate out. A muta-
tion, precisely in the scientific sense. The existing type of
man is passing, in consequence, inescapably into the biological stage of atrophy. The old type of man will have
but a stunted existence. All creative energy will be concentrated in the new one. The two types will rapidly
diverge from one another. One will sink to a sub-human
race and the other rise far above the man of today. I might
call the two varieties the god-man and the mass-animal."

---

6. Will Durant, *The Story of Philosophy* (New York: Simon &
Schuster, 1926, 1927, 1933), 313. Durant understood fashion
and strove to keep up with it. His chapter on Nietzsche was
longer than his chapters on Aristotle or Plato.

That, I commented, was very reminiscent of Nietzsche
and his superman. But I had always taken all this as meta-
phorical.

"Yes," Hitler continued, "man has to be passed and
surpassed. Nietzsche did, it is true, realize something of
this, in his way. He went so far as to recognize the superman as a new biological variety. But he was not too sure
of it. Man is becoming God—that is the simple fact. Man
is God in the making. Man has eternally to strain at his
limitations. The moment he relaxes and contents himself
with them, he decays and falls below the human level. He
becomes a quasi-beast. God and beasts, that is what our
world is made of.

"And how simple, how elementary it all becomes! It is
constantly the same decision that has to be made, whether
I am faced with new political decisions to be made or
with problems of the reordering of our social system. All
those who cut themselves off from our movement, who
cling to the old order, die away and are doomed. **But
those who listen to the immemorial message of man,
who devote themselves to our eternal movement, are
called to a new humanity.** Do you now appreciate the
depth of our National Socialist movement? Can there be
anything greater and more all-comprehending? Those
who see in National Socialism nothing more than a political movement know scarcely anything of it. It is more
even than a religion: it is the will to create mankind
anew."

Now, I said, I began to realize the deeper significance
of his Socialism. It was the preparation for a division of
humanity into the new *Herrenmensch,* the man of the
élite, of the dominant few, and the *Herdenmensch,* the
man of the herd. The new masses were, in the political
field, the first indication of what Hitler called the atro-
phying type of humanity.

Hitler agreed. "Politics today is, literally, the frame of
destiny. Don't you agree that the process of selection can
be accelerated by political means?"

"We certainly can't breed the superman," I replied.
"But, strictly speaking, what do we mean by breeding?
Simply selecting." That, after all, was all that we farmers
did, I told him. If a variety turned up, we kept it alive,
deliberately selected it for propagation, and so hurried on
the natural process. In scientific language, we sought for
the homozygous plus-variation and cultivated it. "This,
after all, is all that breeding amounts to, and I can conceive that a particular political system might make possible a process of human selection."

"Exactly so," said Hitler brightly. "You have put it
well. Politics today is completely blind without a biologi-

The Pivot of Civilization in Historical Perspective

cal foundation and biological objectives. Only National Socialism has recognized this. My policy is not a national policy in the conventional sense. It draws its criteria and its objectives from a complete and comprehensive recognition of the essential nature of life."

"But you can only assist nature. You can only shorten her path when she chooses to grant you the new variety. All the breeder can do is to foster and propagate mutations when they appear."

"The new man is among us! He is here!" exclaimed Hitler. "Now are you satisfied? I will tell you a secret. I have seen the vision of the new man—fearless and formidable. I shrank from him!"[7]

—§§§—

EDITOR

Herman Rauschning, the man who published the conversation above, was an exceptional individual. Initially, a prominent supporter of Hitler, the persecution of Jews led him to break with the party, flee Germany for an Oregon farm, and publish several books graphically describing Nazi ideology from the inside.

As Hitler's closing remarks about a "fearless and formidable" new man hint, the Nietzschean Superman contained two distinct ideas. One envisioned a new *race* of biologically superior creatures who were as different from us as we are from apes. The other focused a new type of *individual* who would regard with contempt the 'slave morality' of the past and act as he chose, in defiance of traditional morality and particularly the Christian religion.

---

7. Hermann Rauschning, *The Voice of Destruction.* (New York, G. P. Putnam's Sons, 1939), 245-48.

In her first book, *Woman and the New Race* (1920) and in this book (1922), Sanger would advocate—more practically than Nietzsche—the first idea. Birth control and sterilization (but not yet abortion) were tools to prevent the "new race" from being forced into a "cradle race" with rapidly breeding inferiors (Hitler's "mass-animal").

Sanger was also aware of the first idea, which might be called the Super Rebel and expressed it in her defunct 1914 magazine, *Woman Rebel* with its defiant motto, "No Gods, No Masters." There she proclaimed: "The Right to be lazy. The Right to be an unmarried mother. The Right to destroy [abortion]. The Right to create. The Right to love. The Right to live."[8] It was in its June, 1914 issue that she was the first to publicly use the term "birth control" in a paragraph was a screech against, "the parasitic institutions" that "thrive upon the exploitation of poverty—that Stupidity and Ignorance and Slavery are the foundations of Church, State and Business."[9]

Historians and biographers who contrast the Sanger of 1914 and that of the 1920s are right to sense a change. But the change was not as radical as they assume. She merely shifted her stress from one Nietzschean theme—a god-like self—to another—a god-like race—returning to the strident, individualistic rhetoric of the former when it suited her purposes. After all, the two themes weren't incompatible. The superior could be free to live as they chose, only if the inferior were kept from swamping the world with their tainted offspring. That distinction lay at the heart of Sanger's worldview.

---

8. Margaret Sanger, "On Picket Duty" *Woman Rebel* 1 (Mar. 1914), 3.

9. Margaret Sanger, "Suppression" *Woman Rebel* 1 (June 1914), 25. In general, she proclaimed the 'right' to be irresponsible.

II

Malthusianism, Darwinism, and Pessimism

1879

Francis Bowen

In the struggle for existence between different classes of human beings, it is the lower classes which survive, because they are more prolific than those above them; while the upper classes, just in proportion to the degree of their elevation, either increase slowly, or tend to die out altogether. And this victory of the lower classes in the battle for life is a survival, not of the fittest, but of the unfittest, so that it constantly tends to a deterioration of the race instead of contributing to its improvement.

EDITOR

In this article, we encounter again a belief in human perfectibility by human scheming. This author linked the idea to the French Revolution of a century earlier and its belief that a perfect society or utopia was possible. Interestingly, Thomas Malthus intended his pessimistic ideas about the pressure of population to be a weapon *against* all such utopian ideas. That changed in 1859 when Charles Darwin's new theory hit the progressive-minded world like a bolt of lightning. (So much so that Karl Marx wanted to dedicate his monumental *Das Kapital* to Darwin.) Why? Because in one brilliant stroke, Darwin gave gloomy Malthus a positive spin. The Malthusian death toll, he told us, was not impartial. Disproportionately, it struck down the 'unfit,' thus slowly but steadily improving all living things including humanity. Yes, Darwin said, it was true that Malthus + Population equals Starvation, War and hence Pessimism. But the world was more complex than that. Malthus + Population + Natural Selection equaled Progress and a New and Improved World including a Better Humanity. That spelled optimism.

Or so it seemed in 1859. As the century drew to a close, however, the optimism that had greeted Darwin's theory began to be tempered by a growing pessimism and even fear. At least in the industrialized world, humanity seemed to have made itself immune to the horrors Malthus had chronicled and Darwin had praised. The 'unfit' were not longer dying by the thousands. In fact,

death tolls in all segments of society had declined dramatically. What was even worse for the progress-minded, the more 'fit' elements were having few, if any, children. The result was, as the author of this chapter aptly put it, "Malthusianism, Darwinism *and Pessimism*." It was that pessimism which brought out the darker side of Malthus and Darwin. The disturbing implications of that pessimism are the focus of this book.

Francis Bowen, "Malthusianism, Darwinism, and Pessimism." *North American Review* 129 (Nov. 1879), 447–72.

—§§§—

The doctrine of the perfectibility of the human race was first systematically taught by a school of philosophical radicals toward the close of the last century. It was a natural outgrowth of the extravagant hopes that were created by the earlier stages of the French Revolution. Condorcet, while he was in hiding in order to escape the fate of the Girondists, showed the firmness of a philosopher by writing his *Sketch of the Progress of the Human Mind,* in which he predicted the removal of all social and political evils, and the establishment of peace, virtue, and happiness over the whole earth. He was arrested before the work was completed, and escaped the guillotine only by a self-inflicted death. In England, William Godwin published, in 1793, his "Political Justice," in which he advocated the same doctrines that Condorcet had taught, and almost with equal peril to himself; since the Government and the populace at that period, as Dr. Priestley found to his cost, showed little mercy to those who were accused of holding revolutionary opinions. Godwin attributed nearly all the vices and misery with which society is afflicted to bad government and bad laws. Reform these, he said; do away with the institutions of property and marriage, which are based on monopoly and fraud, establish the equality of all men, and all wars and contentions will cease, and the spirit of benevolence, guided by justice, will distribute equitably the bounteous fruits of the earth among all persons according to their several needs.

In 1798, as an answer to Godwin's "Political Justice," the Rev. T. R. Malthus published his *Essay on the Principle of Population, or a View of its Past and Present Effects on Human Happiness.* This work had early and great success; it formed the basis on which, in great part, during the first half of the present century, the English science of political economy was constructed. Of course, it was deeply imbued with pessimist opinions. The author's purpose was to show that the principal evils with which human society is afflicted are ineradicable, having their root in human nature itself, so that they are sure to break out anew, and with increased virulence, after any temporary alleviation. Misery and crime, he argued, are not produced to any considerable extent by laws and institutions of man's device, and certainly are not curable by them. Poverty and want are their chief source, and these are the inevitable results of over-population and the consequent struggle for existence. A blind and insatiable craving urges man to multiply his kind, and the necessary consequence of gratifying this impulse is, that the increase of the population has a constant tendency to outrun the means of subsistence. At present, some restraint is put upon this increase by prudential considerations, since most persons consider the irremediableness of marriage, and fear to create an obstacle to their success in life by burdening themselves with the support of a family. Let us suppose, then, that this restraint is taken away by a removal of all the causes which now render it an act of imprudence for either sex to gratify their natural inclinations. Let us suppose that property is equally distributed; that marriage is no longer an indissoluble tie; that wars and contentions have ceased; that unwholesome occupations and habits of life no longer prevail; that medical skill and foresight have stamped out all preventable diseases; that the people no longer congregate in great cities, those nurseries of vice and disease, but are distributed over the face of the country, and are engaged chiefly in healthful agricultural operations; and that the community, as Plato recommended, undertake the whole care, and support, of all the children that are born, instead. of

allowing them to become a particular burden to their parents. Is it not evident that, under such circumstances, population would multiply more rapidly than ever, and that there would soon be, not only a lack of food, with a swift return of all the evils consequent, upon poverty and famine, but even a want of standing-room for the multitudes claiming place upon the surface of the earth?
"How small, of all that human hearts endure,
That part which kings and laws can cause or cure!"

For the law is common to the vegetable and animal kingdoms, the human race included, that the rate of increase, however slow or rapid it may be, must operate in the way of a geometrical ratio. The same causes which double a population of one thousand will double a population of one thousand millions. For example: a given rate of increase between 1790 and 1800 added only 1,200,000 to the white population of this country; between 1830 and 1840 the same rate of increase added 3,600,000. Our population was more than doubled between 1790 and 1820; it was again more than doubled between 1820 and 1850. But the former doubling added less than five millions to our numbers, while the latter one added over ten millions; and the next doubling, in 1880, will have added considerably more than twenty millions. Inevitably then, if the population increase at all, it must increase in the way of a geometrical progression—that is, as the numbers 1, 2, 4, 8, 16, etc.

But the means of subsistence, at best, can not possibly be made to increase faster than in an arithmetical ratio—that is, as the numbers 1, 2, 3, 4, 5, etc. The surface of the earth affords only a limited extent of ground, and this is of various degrees of fertility, large portions of it being hardly cultivable at all. By putting more ground in cultivation and improving the modes of agriculture, it is conceivable that, within twenty-five years, the quantity of food should be doubled. But it is not conceivable that more than this should be accomplished; that is, that the second twenty-five years should make a *larger* addition to the existing stock than was obtained during the former period. Hence, under the most favorable supposition that can be made, beginning with an annual product equal to one million bushels of wheat, at the end of the first quarter of a century this might be raised to two millions, at the end of the second quarter to three millions, and at the close of the third period to four millions.[1]

Of course, the population can not actually outrun the supply of food, though it is constantly, as it were, striving to do so and battling for the ground. It is restrained, first, by what Malthus calls the *preventive* check, which consists in the exercise of moral restraint whereby some persons repress their natural inclinations, and either do not marry at all, or postpone the time of marriage till comparatively late in life. This check keeps down the increase of number through diminishing the proportion of births. Where this fails to operate to a sufficient extent, the second, or *positive* check *must* come into play, by increasing the number of deaths, through insufficient nourishment, overcrowding, disease, and crime. Vainly does private munificence or public liberality seek to remove the proximate causes of these evils. Interference only does harm. Leave the poor alone, then, say the Malthusians, to be chastised by fever, hunger, and misery into a sense of their obligation to society to refrain from increasing their own numbers. The more numerous the family of the pauper, the less claim he has to relief; his own sufferings and that of his family must be his punishment, for thus only can his neighbors be taught prudence.

Editor: Bowen then explained the popularity of Malthusianism during the first half of the nineteenth century, not only among "Tories and the landed gentry, but with the Whig *doctrinaires* generally, the wealthy manufacturers, and especially the philosophical radicals of the Benthamite [utilitarian] school." In an interesting anticipation of Sanger's movement almost a century later, during the 1830s these radicals tried to promote birth control in large cities. But the Irish famine of the next decade would cause Malthusians to question how useful their beliefs were. The ruthless application of Malthusian ideas, it seemed, led not only to depopulation but to a decline in a nation's economic and military power as the healthier and more talented immigrated to more fertile lands.

But the triumph of Malthusianism lasted only for about, half a century, and its decline and fall have been even more rapid than its rise. The tide turned about the time of the famine in Ireland in 1846–47, and the consequent fearful exodus from that unhappy island, which, in less than ten years, deprived it of full one fourth of its population. In 1845 the number of persons in that country was estimated at 8,295,000, and they were increasing with considerable rapidity. In 1851 the population was only 6,574,278; and in 1871 it was less than five and one

---

1. Editor: Malthus argument was little more than an appeal to plausibility. In practice, because virtually everything we eat multiplies faster than we do, the rate at which our food supplies can increase is not only also geometric, its doubling period is far smaller. The other limit, the amount of productive land or sea available, is dependent on many factors and cannot be predicted by simplistic math.

half millions, being a diminution of nearly thirty-five per cent. The Malthusians themselves were appalled at such a result. For the evil did not stop with the immediate diminution of numbers; as usual in such cases, it was chiefly those who were in the flower of life, the healthy and the strong, who emigrated, leaving behind them the aged, the feeble, and the diseased. Hence the people at home deteriorated in vitality and working power even in a higher ratio than their decrease in numbers. At the same period there was also a great emigration, though by no means to an equivalent extent, from England, and especially from Scotland, where the great land-owners had acted on Malthusian principles by depopulating their vast estates, unroofing the cottages over their tenants' heads, and thus compelling them to ship themselves beyond sea. Then came the great trials of the Crimean and the Indian mutiny, with the attendant difficulty of recruiting the army, so that the country awoke to a knowledge of the truth that, in banishing their people, they were drying up the sources of their productive power and their military strength.

Editor: The author then explained that Malthus went wrong when he did not anticipate the enormous productivity gains made possible by the industrial revolution or the new food supplies opened up by world trade.

The actual limit to the growth of the population of any country is not the quantity of food which it alone is capable of producing from its own soil, but the quantity which it is able and willing to purchase from other lands. Practically, then, the only limit for it is the number, which the entire surface of the whole earth is capable of feeding. The world is far from being over-peopled yet, and the amount of food which it can produce is so immensely in excess of the present demand that any deficit in the supply cannot reasonably be anticipated for thousands of years to come. . . .

. . . . Hence, civilized nations, let them multiply as fast as they may, do not direct their energies chiefly to the raising of food, but to the acquisition of wealth. And, for the attainment of this end, any increase of their numbers, far from being an obstacle, is a help; for if there are more mouths to be fed, there are also more hands to feed them with. An increase of population is *pro tanto* an increase of productive power, and it makes no difference whether the article produced is food or a commodity immediately exchangeable for food. One pair of hands, if allowed fair play, can more than satisfy the demands of one stomach, so that there will always remain a surplus for the gradual accumulation of wealth.

Editor: Malthus's mistake did not end there. He had argued that overpopulation, with its accompanying famine and disease, would reduce the numbers of the poor. Nineteenth century observers noted a different effect, one that the elite on the eastern seaboard of the U.S. would soon find alarming.

On examining the facts in the case more closely, it will always be found that it is not the excess of population which causes the misery, but the misery which causes the excess of population. Hopeless poverty makes men imprudent and reckless, and leads them to burden themselves with a family because they can not be worse off, and there is no possibility of improving their condition. . . .

. . . . But the facts prove beyond all question that the increase of any class of people is in inverse proportion to its wealth and social rank—that is, to the amount of sustenance which it can easy command. Universally the law is, that the numbers of the poor increase most rapidly, of the middle classes more slowly, and of the upper or wealthier ones either not at all or so slowly as hardly to be perceptible. . . .

. . . . The continued and increasing opulence of the landed gentry of England is chiefly attributable to this cause; since the diminution of their numbers tends, of course, to the concentration of their estates. Celibate or childless lives are common among the younger sons of the nobility and gentry, while they are very infrequent in the class of artisans and laborers. Even here, in the eastern part of the United States, the sons in educated and wealthy families marry later in life, and have fewer children, than those in the classes that live by handiwork; while the Irish laborers are the most prolific of all.

Editor: In his most interesting observation, the author concluded that at the very time when Malthusian ideas were being rejected by economists, they were taken up by biologists as the foundation for a bold new theory. Originally, Darwin's theory was given an optimistic spin. This author sees nothing but pessimism in it.

Singularly enough, in 1860, at the very time when this gloomy doctrine of "a battle for life" had nearly died out in political economy, most of the authorities upon the subject having quietly abandoned it as an indefensible speculation, it was revived in biology, and made the basis in that science of a theory still more comprehensive and appalling that than which had been founded upon it by Malthus. Among the countless forms of vegetable and animal life which are developed through the hereditability of casual variations from the ancestral type, "a strug-gle for existence" is constantly going on; and it is a necessary consequence of this struggle that the fittest forms—that is those whose organs are best adapted to their surroundings—should survive, and that the others, the comparatively unfit, should perish. "The struggle for existence among all organic beings throughout the world," says Mr. Darwin, "inevitably follows from their high geometric powers of increase"; and he adds, "This is the doctrine of Malthus applied to the whole animal and vegetable kingdoms." Hence, every improvement, however slight, in the adaptation of any species to its environment tends inevitably and mechanically, as it were, to make that species a victor in the battle with all its competitors not possessing such improvement. . . .

Then we only have to recur to the facts which have disproved Malthusianism as a principle in political economy in order to find in them also a complete refutation of Darwinism. In the struggle for existence between different classes of human beings, it is the lower classes which survive, because they are more prolific than those above them; while the upper classes, just in proportion to the degree of their elevation, either increase slowly, or tend to die out altogether. **And this victory of the lower classes in the battle for life is a survival, not of the fittest, but of the unfittest, so that it constantly tends to a deterioration of the race instead of contributing to its improvement.** . . .

But all these advantages, and the improved organization which is founded upon them, if considered as means and helps toward a victory of the upper classes in the battle for life, are as nothing when compared with the one signal advantage under which these classes labor, that the birth-rate among them, through their own fault, is very low, so that they increase slowly or not at all. . . . Those who are rich and high in the social scale are too dainty in their appetites. They prize too highly the luxuries, the social advantages, on which they have been fed. They will not imperil their position by contracting a hasty or otherwise imprudent marriage, or by cumbering themselves with an inconveniently large family. In countries where the distinctions of rank are so strongly defined and deeply rooted as to appear insurmountable, many are contented to lead lives of licentious celibacy, because they dread social more than moral death. **And everywhere, the men of affluence and culture, the highly born and highly bred—the Brahmans of society, as Dr. Holmes calls them—prize the refinements of life, and the gratifications of the social and artistic tastes, more than the homely comforts and enjoyments which any one may have who can induce some good-natured woman** to share them with him. . . . The poor have a much narrower range of enjoyments open to them than the rich; the comforts of domestic life are about the only ones that are easily accessible to the lowly; and who can wonder that these are early sought and highly prized? . . . .

. . . . It is the inherent vice of an aristocracy of wealth and intellect, who are intent upon nothing so much as the adoption of any efficient means for preserving the superiority of their class above the vulgar. But it is a suicidal policy; for, while it has a deceptive semblance of strengthening the position and influence of individual families, through preventing these advantages from being parceled out among too many heirs, it is destructive of the best interests of the class as a whole, and must soon lead to its entire extinction. **Civilization can not be kept alive and transmitted undiminished to posterity, if the members of the educated classes think it a burden to have large families, and if even the women prefer to find some other vocation in life than that of bearing children and educating them.** If a process of what the Darwinites would call "negative selection" is to go on, if only the creatures of a lower type are freely to propagate their kind, the average level of the species must be lowered, and a general deterioration of society is inevitable. Persons of wealth, culture, and refinement, instead of adopting the selfish policy of Mainländer, and taking care only for their personal redemption from the ills of life; should seek rather to transmit by inheritance their high qualities of mind and character to a future generation, and teach their children how to use these personal advantages in continuous efforts to promote the civilization and ennoble the type of humanity. If they do not fill the vacant places on the earth's surface, these will soon be occupied by the progeny of the ignorant and the debased, who in this respect are the dangerous classes of society.

EDITOR

Thus you have, by 1879, a clear statement of the sort of reasoning that would drive Margaret Sanger and her birth control movement some four decades later. Whether Malthus and Darwin were right about plants and animals was not important for, as this writer noted, those principles were no longer relevant to human populations. Modern humanity's triumph over its environment is so complete that the relative advantages of 'fit' over the 'unfit' no longer apply. While the children of the 'unfit' poor may die at a higher rate than those of the 'fit,' that difference is small compared to the much higher birthrates of the 'unfit' and the stubborn unwillingness of the 'fit' to have more than the smallest of families.

Note his mention of educated women intent on "finding some other vocation in life than that of bearing children and educating them." Warnings that the 'unfit' were reproducing faster that the 'fit' put such women in a difficult position. Their belief in evolution, progress and their own superiority created social pressures to have more children. But their desire for active careers and busy social lives made them want to keep their families small. In retrospect, we can see that the only way out of this dilemma lay in the fact that the trouble lay in the *relative differences* between the two birthrates rather than their *absolute numbers.* If these women could come up with a scheme to drive *down* the birthrate of 'unfit' women, they could continue to have small families and retain their own 'reproductive freedom.' That issue from a feminist perspective is in Chapter IV, "The Rapid Multiplication of the Unfit." But in the next chapter we look at closely related fears stimulated by America's high immigration rates. Ironically, while British intellectuals were upset that the better sorts of Irish were immigrating to American, their American counterparts were outraged at the 'inferior' quality of the Irish who were coming here and, it was alleged, forcing down the birthrate of the nation's older and better 'stocks.' Nothing, it seemed, could make these pessimistic people happy.

In the end, a wide expanse of political thought from the 'old money' establishment to the most radical of feminists and socialists would reach a general consensus about how to solve the problem that Malthus had raised and Darwin had been unable to solve. Malthus + Many Deaths was no longer possible, and they now believed that Malthus + Darwin + Unrestricted Reproduction + Few Deaths was a recipe for disaster. But Malthus + Darwin + Selective Reproduction could restore humanity's upward path. With reproduction under their control they could claim—perhaps a little too loudly to be believed— that they were championing low death rates even among the unfit whose existence they otherwise deplored. After all, the fewer children poor mothers had, the lower in infant mortality rate. Their opponents could even be slandered for wanting babies to die. Very clever!

In the next chapter we look at immigration. In the United States of the late nineteenth century it was widely believed that the problem of differential birthrates between the 'fit' and 'unfit' was being made worse by our high rates of immigration. The fact that so many of those immigrants were Irish gave the movement to limit births an anti-Catholic taint that remains to this day.

—§§§—

III

Immigration and Degradation

1891

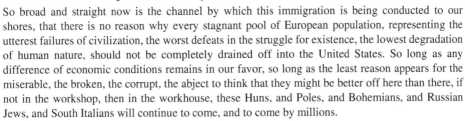

Francis A. Walker

Superintendent of the Census, 1870 & 1880

So broad and straight now is the channel by which this immigration is being conducted to our shores, that there is no reason why every stagnant pool of European population, representing the utterest failures of civilization, the worst defeats in the struggle for existence, the lowest degradation of human nature, should not be completely drained off into the United States. So long as any difference of economic conditions remains in our favor, so long as the least reason appears for the miserable, the broken, the corrupt, the abject to think that they might be better off here than there, if not in the workshop, then in the workhouse, these Huns, and Poles, and Bohemians, and Russian Jews, and South Italians will continue to come, and to come by millions.

EDITOR

When the birthrate of America's 'old stock' natives began to decline in the latter half of the 1800s, several explanations were offered. In this 1891 magazine article by a former Superintendent of the Census, first the Irish and then Eastern and Southern European immigrants are blamed. Once that explanation was accepted, the solution was obvious. Immigration must be restricted.

Notice Walker's remark about "leaving the Africans out of account." He and others *were* monitoring the nation's black population statistics every bit as closely as they were those of the Irish, Italians and Russian Jews. Similar attitudes toward blacks existed, but the issue would not become a matter of concern until the migration of blacks north (from World War I on) began to extend their presence outside the rural South, the curtailment of European immigration in 1924 began to slow white population growth, and the decline in black death rates which accompanied the end of overt racism made traditionally high black birthrates all the more alarming. The result was an obsession to collect and evaluate our nation's racial statistics that continues up to this day. That, however, is a subject for another book.

Francis A. Walker, "Immigration and Degradation."
Forum 11 (Aug. 1891), 634–44.

—§§§—

To me, as a student of the American census, the statistics of the foreign elements of our population have had a peculiar interest. To note the first appearance, in the web of our national life, of these many-colored threads; to watch the patterns which they formed as they grew in numbers during the successive stages of our development, was always a fascinating study. But, curious and even instructive as are inquiries into the varying aptitudes, as to residence and occupation, manifested by the several foreign nationalities represented among us, or into their varying liabilities to different forms of disease, of physical infirmity, or of criminal impulse, I shall confine myself in this paper to speaking of the influence exerted by our foreign arrivals upon the native population in the past, and to considerations arising upon the contemplation of the overwhelming immigration of the present time. . . .

Now, it is to be freely admitted that between 1850 and 1870 the rate of increase in the pre-existing population of this country fell sharply off; and that between 1870 and 1890 that decline has gone on at an accelerated ratio. From the first appearance of foreigners in large numbers in the United States the rate of increase among them has been greater than among those whom they found here; and this disproportion has continually, ever since, to increase. But has this result been due to a decline in physical vitality and reproductive vigor on that part of the population which we call, by comparison, American, or has it been due to other causes, *perhaps to the appearance of the foreigners themselves?* This is a question which requires us to go back to the beginning of the nation. The population of 1790 may be considered to have been, in a high sense, American. It is true that (leaving the Africans out of account) it was all of European stock; but immigration had practically ceased on the outbreak of the Revolution, in 1775, and had not been renewed, to any important extent, at the occurrence of the first census; so that the population of that date was an acclimated, and almost wholly a native population. Now, from 1790 to 1800, the population of the United States increased 35.10 per cent, or at a rate which would have enabled population to be doubled in twenty-three years; a rate transcending that maintained, so far as is known, over any extensive region for any considerable period of human history. And during this time the foreign arrivals were insignificant, being estimated at only 50,000 for the decade. Again, from 1800 to 1810 population increased by 36.38 per cent. Still the foreign arrivals were few, being estimated at only 70,000 for the ten years. Again, between 1810 and 1820 the rate of increase was 33.07 per cent, and still immigration remained at a minimum, the arrivals during the decade being estimated at 114,000. Meanwhile the population had increased from 3,929,214 to 9,633,822.

I have thus far spoken of the foreign arrivals at our ports as estimated. Beginning with 1820, however, we have custom-house statistics of the numbers of persons annually landing upon our shores. Some of these, indeed, did not remain here; yet rudely speaking we may call them all immigrants. Between 1820 and 1830, population grew to 12,866,020. The number of foreigners arriving in the ten years was 151,000. Here, then, we have for forty years an increase, substantially all out of the loins of the four millions of our own people living in 1790; amounting to almost nine millions, or 227 per cent. Such a rate of increase was never known before or since, among any considerable population, over any extensive region.

About, this time, however, we reach a turning point in the history of our population. In the decade 1830–40 the number of foreign arrivals greatly increased. Immigration had not, indeed, reached the enormous dimensions of these later days. Yet, during the decade in question, the foreigners coming to the United States were almost exactly fourfold those coming in the decade preceding, or 599,000. The question now of vital importance is this: Was the population of the country correspondingly increased? I answer, No! The population of 1840 was

almost exactly what by computation it would have been had no increase in foreign arrivals taken place. Again, between 1840 and 1850, a still further access of foreigners occurred, this time of enormous dimensions, the arrivals of the decade amounting to not less than 1,713,000. Of this gigantic total, 1,048,000 were from the British Isles, the Irish famine of 1846-47 having driven hundreds of thousands of miserable peasants to seek food upon our shores. Again we ask, Did this excess constitute a net gain to the population of the country? Again the answer is No! Population showed no increase over the proportions established before immigration set in like a flood. In other words, as the foreigners began to come in larger numbers, the native population more and more withheld their own increase.

Now, this correspondence might be accounted for in three different ways: (1) It might be said that it was a mere coincidence, no relation of cause and effect existing between the two phenomena. (2) It might be said that the foreigners came because the native population was relatively declining, that is, failing to keep up its pristine rate of increase. (3) It might be said that the growth of the native population was checked by the incoming of the foreign elements in such large numbers.

The view that the correspondence referred to was a mere coincidence, purely accidental in origin, is perhaps that most commonly taken. If this be the true explanation, the coincidence is a most remarkable one. In the June number of this magazine, I cited the predictions as to the future population of the country, made by Elakanah Watson, on the basis of the censuses of 1790, 1800, and 1810, while immigration still remained at a minimum. Now let us place together the actual census figures for 1840 and 1850, Watson's estimates for those years, and the foreign arrivals during the preceding decade:

	1840	1850
The census	17,069,453	23,191,876
Watson's estimates	17,116,526	23,185,368
The difference	–47,073	+6,508
Foreign arrivals during preceding decade	599,000	1,713,000

Here we see that, in spite of the arrival of 599,000 foreigners during the period 1830-40, four times is many as had arrived during any preceding decade, the figures of the census coincided closely with the estimate of Watson, based on the growth of population in the pre-immigration era, falling short of it by only 47,073 in a total of

17,000,000; while in 1850 the actual population in spite of the arrival of 1,713,000 more immigrants, exceeded Watson's estimates by only 6,508 in a total of 23,000,000. Surely, if this correspondence between the increase of the foreign element and the relative decline of the native element is a mere coincidence, it is one of the most astonishing in human history. The actuarial degree of improbability as to a coincidence so close, over a range so vast, I will not undertake to compute.

If, on the other hand, it be alleged that the relation of cause and effect existed between the two phenomena, this might be put in two widely different ways: either that the foreigners came in increasing numbers because the native element was relatively declining, or that the native element failed to maintain its previous rate of increase because the foreigners came in such swarms. What shall we say of the former of these explanations? Does anything more need to be said than that it is too fine to be the real explanation of a big human fact like this we are considering? To assume that at such a distance in space, in the then state of news-communication and ocean transportation, and in spite of the ignorance and extreme poverty of the peasantries of Europe from which the immigrants were then generally drawn, there was so exact a degree of knowledge, not only of the fact that the native element here was not keeping up its rate of increase, but also of the precise ratio of that decline, as to enable those peasantries, with or without a mutual understanding, to supply just the numbers necessary to bring our population up to its due proportions, would be little less than laughable. To-day, with quick passages, cheap freights, and ocean cables, there is not a single wholesale trade in the world carried out with this degree of knowledge, or attaining anything like this point of precision. in results.

The true explanation of the remarkable fact we are considering I believe to be the last of the three suggested. The access of foreigners, at the time and under the circumstances, constituted a shock to the principle of population among the native element. That principle is always acutely sensitive alike to sentimental and to economic conditions. And it is to be noted, in passing, that not only did the decline in the native element, as a whole, take place in singular correspondence with the excess of foreign arrivals, but it occurred chiefly in just those regions to which the new-comers most freely resorted.

But what possible reason can be suggested why the incoming of the foreigner should have checked the disposition of the native toward the increase of population at the traditional rate? I answer that the best of good reasons

can be assigned. Throughout the north-eastern and northern middle States, into which, during the period under consideration, the new-comers poured in such numbers, the standard of material living, of general intelligence, of social decency, had been singularly high. Life, even at its hardest, had always had its luxuries; the babe had been a thing of beauty, to be delicately nurtured and proudly exhibited; the growing child had been decently dressed, at least for school and church; the house had been kept in order, at whatever cost, the gate hung, the shutters in place, while the front yard had been made to bloom with simple flowers; the village church, the public schoolhouse, had been the best which the community, with great exertions and sacrifices, could erect and maintain. **Then came the foreigner, making his way into the little village, bringing—small blame to him!—not only a vastly lower standard of living, but too often an actual present incapacity even to understand the refinements of life and thought in the community in which he sought a home.** Our people had to look upon houses that were mere shells for human habitations, the gate unhung, the shutters flapping or falling, green pools in the yard, babes and young children rolling about half naked or worse, neglected, dirty, unkempt. Was there not in this, sentimental reason strong enough to give a shock to the principle of population? But there was, besides, an economic reason for a check to the native increase. The American shrank from the industrial competition thus thrust upon him. He was unwilling himself to engage in the lowest kind of day labor with these new elements of the population; he was even more unwilling to bring sons and daughters into the world to enter into that competition. For the first time in our history the people of the free States became divided into classes. Those classes were natives and foreigners. Politically the distinction had only a certain force, which yielded more or less readily under partisan pressure, but socially and industrially that distinction has been a tremendous power, and its chief effects have been wrought upon population. Neither the social companionship nor the industrial competition of the foreigner has, broadly speaking, been welcome to the native.

It hardly needs to be said that the foregoing descriptions are not intended to apply to all of the vast body of immigrants during this period. Thousands came over from good homes; many had had all the advantages of education and culture; some possessed the highest qualities of manhood and citizenship.

But let us proceed with the census. By 1860 the causes operating to reduce the growth of the native element, to which had then manifestly been added the force of important changes in the manner of living, the introduction of more luxurious habits, the influence of city life, and the custom of "boarding," had reached such a height as, in spite of a still-increasing immigration, to bring the population of the country 310,503 below the estimate. The fearful losses of the civil war and the rapid extension of habits unfavorable to increase of numbers, make any further use of Watson's computations uninstructive, yet still the great fact protrudes through all the subsequent history of our population that the more rapidly foreigners came into the United States, the smaller was the rate of increase, not merely among the native population separately, but throughout the population of the country as a whole, including the foreigners. The climax of this movement was reached when, during the decade 1880-90, the foreign arrivals rose to the monstrous total of five and a quarter millions (twice what had ever before been known); while yet, population, even including this enormous re-enforcement, increased more slowly than in any other period of our history, except, possibly, that of the great civil war.

If the foregoing views are true, or contain any considerable degree of truth, foreign immigration into this country has, from the time it first assumed large proportions, amounted not to a re-enforcement of our population, but to a replacement of native by foreign stock. That if the foreigners had not come, the native element would long have filled the places the foreigners usurped, I entertain not a doubt. The competency of the American stock to do this it would be absurd to question in the face of such a record is that for 1790 to 1830. During the period from 1830 to 1860 the material condition of existence in this country were continually becoming more and more favorable to the increase of population from domestic sources. The old man-slaughtering medicine was being driven out of civilized communities; houses were becoming larger; the food and clothing of the people were becoming ampler and better. Nor was the cause which, about 1840 or 1850, began to retard the growth of population here, to be found in the climate which Mr. Clibborne stigmatizes so severely. The climate of the United States has been benign enough to enable us to take the English short-horn and greatly to improve it, as the re-exportation of that animal to England at monstrous prices abundantly proves; to take the English race-horse and to improve him to a degree of which the startling victories of Parole, Iroquois, and Foxhall afford but a suggestion; to take the English man and to improve him too, adding agility to his strength, making his eye keener

and his hand steadier, so that in rowing, in riding, in shooting, and in boxing, the American of pure English stock is to-day the better animal. No! **Whatever were the causes which checked the growth of the native population, they were neither physiological nor climatic. They were mainly social and economic; and chief among them was the access of vast hordes of foreign immigrants, bringing with them a standard of living at which our own people revolted.**

Opinions may differ widely on the question whether the United States have, as a whole, gained or lost by so extensive a replacement of the native by foreign elements in our population. But whatever view may be taken of the past, no one surely can be enough of an optimist to contemplate without dread the fast rising flood of immigration now setting in upon our shores. During the past ten years, five and a quarter millions of foreigners entered the ports of the United States. We have no assurance that this number may not be doubled in the current decade. Only a small part of these new-comers can read, while the general intelligence of the mass is even below what might be assumed from such a statement. By far the greater part of them are wholly ignorant of our institutions, and, too often, having been brought up in an atmosphere of pure force, they have no sympathy with the political ideas and sentiments which underlie our social organization; often not even the capability of understanding them.

What has just now been said would, of course, have been true in some degree of the body of immigrants in any preceding period. But the immigration of the present time differs unfortunately from that of the past in two important respects. The first is, that the organization of the European railway and the ocean steamship service is now such as to reduce almost to a minimum the energy, courage, intelligence, and pecuniary means required for immigration; a result which is tending to bring to us no longer the more alert and enterprising members of their respective communities, but rather the unlucky, the thriftless, the worthless. The second characteristic of the immigration of the present, as contrasted with that of the past, is that it is increasingly drawn from the nations of southern and eastern Europe—peoples which have got no great good for themselves out of the race wars of centuries, and out of the unceasing struggle with the hard conditions of nature; peoples that have the least possible adaptation to our political institutions and social life, and that have thus far remained hopelessly upon the lowest plane of industrial life. So broad and straight now is the channel by which this immigration is being conducted to our shores, that there is no reason why every stagnant pool of European population, representing the utterest failures of civilization, the worst defeats in the struggle for existence, the lowest degradation of human nature, should not be completely drained off into the United States. **So long as any difference of economic conditions remains in our favor, so long as the least reason appears for the miserable, the broken, the corrupt, the abject to think that they might be better off here than there, if not in the workshop, then in the workhouse, these Huns, and Poles, and Bohemians, and Russian Jews, and South Italians will continue to come, and to come by millions.**

Has not the full time arrived when the people of the United States should set themselves seriously to consider whether the indiscriminate hospitality which has thus far cheerfully been exercised, should not be, it least for a while, withheld, to give the nation opportunity to digest and to assimilate what it has already received; whether justice, if not to ourselves, then to our posterity, does not require that the nation's birthright shall no longer be recklessly squandered; whether we are not under obligations, as the inheritors of a noble political system, to "see to it that the Republic sustains no harm" from an invasion in comparison with which the invasions under which Rome fell were no more than a series of excursion parties? For one, I believe that the United States have, by a whole century of unrestricted hospitality, and especially by taking in five and a quarter millions of foreigners during the past ten years, fully earned the right to say to all the world, "Give us a rest."

—§§§—

Gross Little Aliens

I have yet to meet an observer who does not rate the North Italian among us as more intelligent, reliable, and progressive than the South Italian. . . . Yet only a fifth of our Italians are from the North. It is the backward and benighted provinces from Naples to Sicily that send us the flood of "gross little aliens" who gave Henry James, on revisiting Boston, the melancholy vision "of a huge applied sponge—a sponge saturated with the foreign mixture and passed over almost everything I remembered and might still have recovered."[1]

—EDWARD A. ROSS, UNIVERSITY OF WISCONSIN, 1913

---

1. Edward A. Ross, *The Old World in the New* (New York: Century, 1913, 1914), 101. Ross, a friend of Sanger's, will reappear in Chap. VII.

IV

The Rapid Multiplication of the Unfit

1891

Victoria C. Woodhull Martin

Feminist and U.S. Presidential Candidate

The best minds of to-day have accepted the fact that if superior people are desired, they must be bred; and if imbeciles, criminals, paupers, and otherwise unfit are undesirable citizens they must not be bred.

EDITOR

Victoria Woodhull Martin's (1838–1927) feminist credentials are impeccable. She was the first woman to run for the U. S. Presidency (1872). Her leftist credentials are equally beyond doubt. Her magazine, *Woodhull and Claflin's Weekly* brought the *Communist Manifesto* to America. She also held what were then termed 'advanced' ideas, including equal sexual standards for men and women (meaning an equal lack of standards). Children, she believed, ought to be raised communally rather than by their parents. It was a convenient philosophy for someone whose life was a confusing maze of divorces and remarriages. She also had close ties to Cornelius Vanderbilt, the railroad magnate and one of the nation's wealthiest men, and eventually married into the British upper class—illustrating the often close but rarely commented upon link between the very wealthy and those with radical social ideas. Only the rich can buy their way out of the harm those ideas create.

In her 1938 autobiography, Margaret Sanger described nineteenth century radicals such as Martin: "Eugenics, which had started long before my time, had once been defined as including free love and prevention of conception. . . . Recently it had cropped up again in the form of selective breeding, and biologists and geneticists such as Clarence C. Little, President of the University of Maine, and C. B. Davenport, Director of the Cold Spring Harbor Station for Experimental Evolution, had popularized their findings under this heading"[1] Those men were eugenists—people who believed that society should encourage superior people to have large families and ensure that inferior people had few or no children. Sanger may have been indulging in humor at their expense. The eugenists of Sanger's day were the sort who got excited crossing blue flowers with pink in their gardens. Some were so out of touch with reality that they thought all society had to do to keep to 'unfit' from having children was to ban their marriage. Sanger was pointing out that eugenics had an unconventional past. Many of its early adopters lived in communal societies (such as Oneida) where sex with anyone was expected, but childbearing was restricted to selected individuals. Though not as radical as some, Martin was in that long-forgotten movement.

As we see in this chapter, Martin's remarks run counter to the oft-repeated claim that as an oppressed group, women (meaning feminists) stand up for the powerless. Few men in her day showed open hatred for so many. Disabled children, the "pauper class,' the "ominous" birthrate of American blacks, and the "spectre" of Asian "hordes" were all targets of her liberated wrath. One month before her death she was delighted when the U.S. Supreme Court ruled that women less fortunate than her could be sterilized without their consent.

Victoria C. Woodhull Martin, *The Rapid Multiplication of the Unfit.* (London, 1891). Page numbers are given in square brackets after the text quoted [ ].

—§§§—

1. Margaret Sanger, *Margaret Sanger, An Autobiography* (New York: W. W. Norton, 1938), 374.

It is said that one in every five of the population of London does die or is destined to die in a hospital, the workhouse, or pauper lunatic asylum. *Pari passu* with this statistical statement the cry is growing louder for more public institutions to house the incapable, and it is urged that all stigma should be removed from them.

In visiting one of these institutions a short time since, in one of the wards I saw a little child moving about with the aid of a chair, its body being too big and heavy for its legs; in another ward a nurse, who was carrying a baby covered with scrofulous sores, asked me if I would adopt it. The baby had no one to claim it and they were only waiting to find someone who would take charge of it. There were cases of hip disease, some had been successfully operated upon. There was one with spina bifida. The doctor took great pride in showing me a child on whom he had just operated for hare-lip; my attention was drawn to the success he had had in delivering a mother of an idiotic baby. What is the destiny of these children? They require able-bodied nurses from their birth, and able-bodied physicians to spend their valuable time over them. They are scarcely ever able to shift for themselves, they are a care all their lives, and at last swell the ranks of the one in five who die in the hospital, the workhouse, or pauper lunatic asylum.

The relationship between the abnormal palate and the brain is being recognized by all physicians who have made any study of the subject. They are consequently enabled to predict that in all probability the child with cleft palate will either be semi-idiotic, a criminal, or a lunatic, especially if subjected to the stress of poverty or adverse conditions, in any case will add to the burden already heavy laid on the community by the incapable. And the chances are they will be among the five who will die in the workhouse, hospital, or pauper lunatic asylum.

The following extract I copied from a paper:—

> A woman named Abigail Cochrane, who has just died at Kilmalcolm at 84 years of age, was a pauper from the cradle to the grave. She was born in Greenock in 1807, and was imbecile from her earliest youth. It is estimated that she cost the public purse between £2000 and £3000.

As in the case of Abigail Cochrane, each one of our human failures adds a considerable item to the burden, already large, put upon the healthy useful citizens. [11-13]

—§§§—

Many are so deficient in sensibility that although afferent impulses may be started by the most beautiful pictures, sculpture, divine strains of music, noble and humane examples, in fact the most sublime combinations of nature and art, they will awaken no response, they will arouse no efferent processes of noble thoughts and actions. This accounts for the fact that certain persons only take pleasure in vulgar low resorts and the companionship of coarse people. They seek their affinities. The saying is, that a man is known by the company he keeps; in other words, his nervous system is similarly developed.

If we study the nervous system of the pauper class, we find that instead of their nervous energy being economically expended, there is lavish, uneven and wasteful expenditure which is of no great benefit to the individual nor to society. They are organically deficient; they inherit defective, ill-regulated nervous systems, or their nervous systems become badly adjusted through irregular habits, bad training, or diseases. They are incapable of sustained effort. They prefer jobs to regular work, spasmodic efforts to work for a few hours or days, and these efforts are followed by a reaction of utter inability to make further exertion. They can assign no reason why any sustained effort is wearisome to the last degree. These characteristics are symptomatic of retrogression, or they are the reappearance of a more primitive type.

There are savages who will work hard to collect material things, and then will debauch and idle away weeks and months until the pangs of hunger compel them to make another effort to work. In this we have the simplest condition of economic pressure. It is said that the special characteristic of the savage is that he has no thought for the morrow. He eats until he can eat no more, then goes hungry until he finds more food. These very characteristics we see exhibited among our own savages. I saw a poor man, who said he was hungry and had been given some bread and cheese, eat until his hunger was appeased and then throw the bread and cheese which remained into the street; he could not or did not realize that in a few hours he would be hungry again. I have frequently seen bread thrown away by such and lying in the street. To them bread had been given once, it would be given again, or they would go hungry until the pangs of hunger compelled them to make a further effort to procure more. It is a waste of words to say that these individuals are paupers because they have not been careful, thrifty, and temperate. We might lecture for hours to them on the advantages of industry, we might urge our plea with the fervour of a divine oracle, the afferent impulses we give rise to arouse no response in those torpid brains. For our plea to have an effect they must be given new nervous systems and healthy rich blood, in other words, they must not be bred. It is characteristic of those organically defective that it is the voluntary part of their nature which is most affected. They have not the *will* to make any exertion, they fall into the conditions which circumstances place them. With the offspring of parents suffering from fatigue or other poison, compulsory education may be enforced, but our efforts will not be repaid by healthy useful individuals unless they spring from a healthy source.

Political economists [Malthusians] have said that the conscientious, the right-minded, will not marry until they are in a position to do so, and herein is the *crux* of the social problem. The more highly developed human beings yield less and less readily to the dictates of sexual passion alone. They judge and consider consequences. They profit by the experiences of others and therefore avoid doing that which will bring sorrow to those whom they love. High motives deter the fit from marrying until they are in a position to do so. **Among the better classes marriage is being deferred more and more, the standard of living is becoming higher among them, and more time is given to education, whereas the unfit who are not deterred by any qualms of conscience or apprehension of consequences go on multiplying. And as the more highly developed are not perpetuated, or if perpetuated it is in fewer numbers, the thoughtless, improvident, degenerate, and diseased, multiply upon us.**

An educated man made the remark a short time ago, "The cause of so much misery among the poor to-day is over-population, it is their reckless indulgence in large families. I am too poor to marry, I can't afford to have a family, I wish I could, and yet I am called upon to pay taxes to educate and help to support others' paupers." Here is a man who was accustomed to a certain standard of living, and who therefore did not care to have offspring who would not have the same advantages as he had had, or to have a family who might become a burden on others. An example of the conscientious not marrying until he could afford it, a result which is most disastrous in its effects on the quality of the human race

A man may possess a noble character and have a magnificent physique, but if he do not perpetuate these qualities they do not survive. A man may be diseased, stupid or reckless, but withal he marries and raises a large family: his qualities are perpetuated, but it is not the survival of the fittest. Many men break their health down by overwork, and the terrible strain is seen in the physical condition of their children. Many men have not over exerted themselves, and have had no scruples about living on the charity of their relations or friends, and hence their children do not suffer from the depleted physical condition of

their fathers; but are these children the survival of fittest? Moral checks which would appeal to the superior intellectual mind, do not influence the unfit. In the majority of cases they have not a nervous system sufficiently developed to appreciate these motives.

A great many seem to think that interference with marriages of the unfit will only give greater opportunities to races, lower in the scale of development who are multiplying so fast, to overcome and conquer the more advanced races. We have an example of this in the rapid multiplication of the negroes in America, who at some not far distant day will outnumber and overrun the whites if the rapid increase be not checked. Eventually, if America is owned and governed by negroes, would it be the survival of the fittest? The outlook is as ominous in Europe.

Mr. Raines states in his census of the population of India, that the returns show an increase of thirty millions in the population in ten years, the total being 285,000,000. Add to this number 400,000,000, or probably more in China, and it looks as if these vast hordes may yet overrun and wipe out Western civilization. With this spectre looming up in the distance it is considered a dangerous policy to advocate any theory which would tend to limit the population of Western nations. The argument holds good if we wish simply to limit the numbers of the population of the fit, but has no application with regard to the marriages of the unfit. An American child brought up in China, if it had a defective nervous system, will demonstrate it in China; and a Chinese child brought up in Europe, if born of diseased parents, will demonstrate its hereditary condition here. We find often that physical causes, not numbers, determine whether races shall be conquerors or conquered. Stamina often gives the victory to a race. Generalship indicates superior development of the general.

But in any attempt to raise the standard of humanity, to aid evolution, we must take into consideration that it is not the survival of the fittest, but the survival of the unfit by means of their rapid multiplication in societies as presently organized. [14–20]

—§§§—

To sum up some of the principal causes in the rapid multiplication of the unfit, we may class them under two heads, namely, Physiological and Psychological.

Among the probable Psychological causes are:—

(1.) The more intelligent the individuals the more they think of consequences and the less likely are they to be influenced by sexual passion alone. Later marriages among the upper classes with the result of having fewer children, and if too long deferred the marriages are infertile. The improvident therefore would marry first and would rear the largest number of offspring. The sense of responsibility develops [develops] with age, but the very poor marry at very early ages.

(2.) Among the unfit easier modes of becoming acquainted, less prudery, more freedom in the intercourse of the sexes.

(3.) The mystery and secresy [secrecy] which envelopes these natural functions, too often create a morbid desire which often leads to masturbation and other practices.

(4.) Marriages among the upper classes for money and position, or the marriages of those who have not sufficient opportunities under our present social decrees to seek and find a more suitable partner.

(5.) The sexual passion excited by the intermingling of the sexes in overcrowded tenements; whole families often sleeping in one room. A lady who has a home for girls to help them through their first confinement, and to save first offenders, if possible, said: "It is appalling the number of girls who come here who have been seduced by their own brothers." [33–34]

—§§§—

The best minds of to-day have accepted the fact that if superior people are desired, they must be bred; and if imbeciles, criminals, paupers, and otherwise unfit are undesirable citizens they must not be bred.

The first principle of the breeder's art is to weed out the inferior animals to avoid conditions which give a tendency to reversion and then to bring together superior animals under the most favourable conditions. **We can produce numerous modifications of structure by careful selection of different animals, and there is no reason why, if society were differently organized, that we should not be able to modify and improve the human species to the same extent.** In order to do this we must make a religion of the procreative principle. Our girls and boys must be taught how sacred is the life-giving principle. The most wonderful of all the forces at work throughout nature.

Our young men and women should realize the purpose for which they are uniting in the holiest bond of physical life. And by this means we would have inaugurated the upper million and the lower ten. Any social conditions which tend to transpose these terms are subversive of the true interests of humanity.

EDITOR

On May 2, 1927, in a decision entitled *Buck v. Bell* the U.S. Supreme Court ruled that the forced sterilization of men and women in state institutions was constitutional. *The New York Times* had no problem with the ruling. Two of its headlines hinted at the politically correct opinion to hold: "Right to Protect Society" and "Justice Holmes Draws Analogy to Compulsory Vaccination in Woman's Case."[2] Even more significant, the paper signaled that the issue was not a matter for debate by burying it deep within the paper next to an article about another court's decision to bar the use of "chain coupons" in "silk stocking sales."

Equally revealing was a story the paper carried five days later. Britain was at that time debating a bill that would give women the right to vote, and a reporter located the famous feminist who wrote the book quoted in this chapter to discover her view on forced sterilization. The elderly Martin (she would die just over a month later) used the opportunity to comment on two of her pet causes, sex education and eugenics. We now look at that article.

Says Voting at 25 is 'Young Enough'
Mrs. Woodhull Martin Supports the British Franchise Bill to That Effect

BRIGHTON, England, May 7 (AP)—Mrs. Victoria Claflin Woodhull-Martin, the first woman candidate for the Presidency of the United States in 1872 and long a fighter for equal suffrage, believes 25 is young enough for men and women to obtain the franchise. . . .

. . . . Time has not dimmed the eyes of this spirited woman who, with her sister, the late Lady Cook, formerly Tennessee Claflin, was the first woman broker in New York and lectured and published *Claflin's Weekly* in support of equal suffrage and eugenics before they both came to England. . . .

Mrs. Martin, who wrote and lectured for thirty years on eugenics, remarked that she was pleased to read that the Virginia Eugenics law had succeeded in establishing the right to sterilize the feeble-minded.

"I advocated that fifty years ago in my book, *Marriage of the Unfit,*" she said. "I am also glad that parents are now beginning to instruct their adolescent children in the facts of life. My sister, Tennessee, and I were mercilessly slandered fifty years ago when we dared to advocate women's emancipation and discussed eugenics in America, but time has proved that we were right."[3]

—§§§—

2. "Upholds Operating on Feeble-Minded." *New York Times* (May 3, 1927), 19.
3. "Says Voting at 25 is 'Young Enough.'" *New York Times* (May 8, 1927), pt. 2 p. 6.

V

Anticipations

1901

H. G. Wells

Science Fiction Writer

To the multiplying rejected of the white and yellow civilisations there will have been added a vast proportion of the black and brown races, and collectively those masses will propound the general question, "What will you do with us, we hundreds of millions who cannot keep pace with you?"

When most people think of H. G. Wells, they think of the talented nineteenth-century author such science fiction classics as *War of the Worlds, Time Machine,* and *Invisible Man.* But there was another Wells who is not as well known—the twentieth-century writer of highly politicized books that today are only read by the most die-hard Wells fans. Since the Wells who wrote the introduction to the original edition of *The Pivot of Civilization* was the later Wells, it makes sense to examine what he believed in order to discover why he supported Sanger and the birth control movement.

Anticipations

The first book that the politicized Wells wrote was his 1901 *Anticipations and Other Papers.* It retained the science fiction flavor of his earlier writings by looking forward to the dawn of the twenty-first century and the birth of a socialist World State speaking one language and ruled by a scientifically trained elite. To create this World State, he wanted, "an open conspiracy of intellectuals and willful people against existing institutions and existing limitations and boundaries."[1] More astute readers soon spotted what institutions Wells intended to destroy: traditional families, private property, genuine democracy, and any public role for religion. All offered potential centers of resistance to his scientific utopia.

Wells believed that his open conspiracy had already begun among those left aimless and disconsolate by "the collapse of the old Liberalism" who needed something new to believe in. He also felt that it had begun to touch America's wealthy "legacy-leaving class." It is here that his much praised powers of observation get interesting. Advocates of big government often claim that ordinary people need powerful government to protect them from the evils of big business. Wells had noted the very opposite, that a particular kind of big business—the brutal and allegedly efficient world of global cartels and market-controlling trusts—were quite similar to his World State. In *Anticipations* Wells poked fun at those who thought socialism would arrive when workers "with a little demonstrating and balloting" take power away "from the capable men in charge." More likely, he said, "that a confluent system of Trust-owned business organizations, and of Universities and re-organised military and naval services may presently discover an essential unity of purpose, presently begin thinking a literature, and behaving like a State."[2] Forgetting the role of the military (which tends to follow rather than lead political change) and substituting for turn-of-the-century monopolists the giant foundations they founded, his prediction has proved remarkably accurate.

At this point, racism entered Wells' grand scheme. He claimed that his World State would begin with a "great federation of white English-speaking peoples" who would "protect or dominate or actually administer most or all of the non-white states of the present British Empire, and in addition, much of South and Middle Pacific, the East and West Indies, the rest of America, and the larger part of black Africa." He believed that around "the year 2000," his English-speaking state, the "first of the three powers of the world," would begin to

---

1. H. G. Wells, "Introduction to the 1914 Edition of 'Anticipations'" in H. G. Wells, *Anticipations and Other Papers* (New York, 1924), 279.

2. *Anticipations,* 237–40. This military reorganization could refer to a multi-national military force (p. 226). Obviously, Wells needed the "dominated races" disarmed, so they would be unable to oppose his World State.

display a "intelligent sympathy" with the idea of uniting its ruling whites and "dominated races" with a similar French-speaking European state and "probably the Yellow state" of Eastern Asia. From its position of power, the English-speaking state—with "at least a hundred million sound-bodied and educated and capable [white] men"—would be able to dictate terms of a union, "by which the final peace of the world may be assured for ever."[3] That was the book that set Britain to talking and would, as we will see in the next chapter, draw praise from some of the nation's most prominent socialists.

In his later books, Wells realized that his World State would not become popular outside the English-speaking world unless he made it appear less racist and more multi-cultural. So token members of other races were conspicuously inserted into a ruling "Samurai" elite, displaying trivial differences in dress and lifestyle, but not challenging its basic assumptions. Wells had discovered "diversity" and "multi-culturalism."

Wells never solved the real problems his World State raised. Why, for instance, should the people of the earth peacefully submit to one distant government rather than a more responsive local one? Why should they agree to one language, one set of laws and the unrestricted rule of his robed Samurai, however technically skilled they might appear? Most important of all, how could the world be kept united without continual civil war—typically the worst sort of war? And how could restless populations be pacified without squelching free speech? The Gestapo-like central card file of Wells's *A Modern Utopia,* located in Paris and containing the thumb print, prior history, and current address of everyone on the planet was not enough. To survive, Wells' World State would need a large army, a brutal secret police, and much more.

In those days, the deep-seated racism of Wells and those who believed like him was in the open for all to see. In his 1934 *Experiment in Autobiography* Wells was quite candid about that.

> It was made a matter of general congratulation about me that I was English . . . and my mind had leapt all to readily to the idea that I was a blond and blue-eyed Nordic, quite the best make of human being known. . . . We English, by sheer native superiority, practically without trying, had possessed ourselves of an Empire on which the sun never set, and through the errors and infirmities of other races were being forced slowly but steadily—and quite modestly—toward world dominion. . . . In those days I had ideas about Aryans extraordinarily like Mr. Hitler's. The more I hear of him the more I am convinced that his mind is almost

the twin of my thirteen year old mind in 1879; but heard through a megaphone and—implemented. I do not know from what books I caught my first glimpse of the Great Aryan People going to and fro in the middle plains of Europe . . . **Their ultimate triumphs everywhere squared accounts with the Jews, against which people I had a subconscious dissatisfaction because of their disproportionate share of Holy Writ.** I thought Abraham, Isaac, Moses and David loathsome creatures and fit associates for Our Father, but unlike Hitler I had no feelings about the contemporary Jew.[4]

Whatever Wells may have felt about Jews as a youth—he obviously linked his hostility toward them to his hatred of Christianity—it is clear that as a world-famous writer he had little good to say about them. In *Anticipations* he described many of them as "very ugly," "intensely vulgar in dress and bearing, materialistic in thought, and cunning and base in method," and favoring their own people "against the stranger"[5] (as do virtually all groups). But when Wells wrote that his World State would treat the Jew "as any other man," he was telling the truth. His future society would judge all individuals, races and classes by the same brutal standard. It would permit those who pass to continue to reproduce. On the other hand:

> It will, I have said, make the multiplication of those who fall behind a certain standard of social efficiency unpleasant and difficult, and it will have cast aside any coddling laws to save adult men from themselves. It will tolerate no dark corners where the people of the Abyss may fester, no vast diffused slums of peasant proprietors, no stagnant plague preserves.[6]

In short, the Jew would be judged by the same rules as others but special attention would be paid to accusations that, "the Jew is incurably a parasite on the apparatus of credit." When the World State ended the loaning of money at interest (the essence of capitalism), it would test, in proper evolutionary fashion, if Jews could adapt to a new environment. "If the Jew has a certain incurable tendency to social parasitism, and we make social parasitism impossible, we shall abolish the Jew; and if he has not, there is no need to abolish the Jew."[7] Like many liberals, Wells did seem to believe that Jews would adapt and believed that adaptation would lead to their disap-

---

3. All quotations from *Anticipations,* 226.

4. H. G. Wells, *Experiment in Autobiography* (New York, 1934), 72–74. Much like the feminist Gilman (Chap. XXII), Wells' anti-Semitism was linked to a hatred for the Bible.

5. *Anticipations,* 273.

6. *Anticipations,* 272.

7. *Anticipations,* 272–73.

pearance "in a century or so" as a "physically distinct element in human affairs."[8] This cultural genocide certainly differed from Hitler's more violent schemes, but it offered no comfort to those Jews (or any other group) who wanted to retain their own unique identity in defiance of the World State. In particular, Wellsian multiculturalism had no tolerance for Judeo-Christian culture.

Viewed globally, Wells's ideas about genocide were more than cultural and not much different from those of Stalin and Hitler. In *Anticipations* H. G. Wells wrote of the "many processes" that have been "outside human control or controlled unintelligently and superstitiously" which his scientific elite would take "in hand." In one chapter Wells described his loathing for "small agriculturalists" (meaning farmers) everywhere because they were "as hopelessly immovable a thing as the forces of progressive change will have to encounter." He then launches an attack on them.

> At the Cape of Good Hope, under British rule, Kaffirs [a disparaging term for African blacks] are being settled upon little inalienable holdings that must inevitably develop in the same direction, and over the Southern States the nigger squats and multiplies. It is fairly certain that these stagnant ponds of population, which will grow until public intelligence rises to the pitch of draining them, will on a greater scale parallel in the twentieth century the soon-to-be-dispersed urban slums of the nineteenth century.[9]

Given Wells' socialism, he may have been almost as angry about African and Southern blacks acquiring their "little inalienable holdings"[10] as he was about the fact that they are thus able to 'squat and multiply' in modest comfort. His attitude illustrates just how quickly progressive thought degenerates into ugly racism when those hindering progress are seen in racial terms.

Sanger on Wells

The event of my visit to London in 1920 was the beginning of my friendship with H. G. Wells. . . . Wells had ranged every field of knowledge, had dared to invade the sacrosanct precincts of the historian, the economist, and the scientist and, though a layman in these fields, had used his extraordinary gifts to interpret the past and present and even prophesy the future; in novel after novel he had shocked England by championing women's right to a freer life. . . . We in the United States were just beginning to be affected by sociological concepts. . . . Now here was Wells giving a fresh picture of what could be if man had an ideal system of society that was workable. . . . On my lecture tour of 1916 his name had been on everybody's lips. . . . I believed he had influenced the American intelligentsia more than any other man. . . . For good reason countless faithful friends had attached themselves to Wells, and he indulged in his varied, intricate, and unpredictable personality a capacity for loyally loving both individuals and humanity.[11]

—MARGARET SANGER, 1938

Women's "Liberation"

For more than half a century, Sanger dedicated herself to the deceptively simple proposition that access to a safe and reliable means of preventing pregnancy is a necessary condition of women's liberation and, in turn, of human progress. . . . Since her death the rebirth of a vigorous feminist movement has given new resonance to her original claim that women have a fundamental right to control their own bodies. . . . She has become an occasional scapegoat of extremists opposed to abortion or of black militants, who insist that family planning is genocidal in intent.[12]

—ELLEN CHESLER, *WOMAN OF VALOR*, 1992

A further hint of the terrifying extent of Wells' World State came when he described what would happen just after the year 2000 as hundreds of millions of people around the world wait to hear if the newly formed World State would allow them to have children.

To the multiplying rejected of the white and yellow civilisations there will have been added a vast proportion of the black and brown races, and collectively those masses will propound the general

8. *Anticipations*, 274.

9. *Anticipations*, 83.

10. Editor: In Chap. XVIII the Catholic Chesterton wanted every family to have a house and garden of its own to better withstand the pressures Wells and his sort wanted to apply.

11. Margaret Sanger, *Margaret Sanger, An Autobiography* (New York: W. W. Norton, 1938), 268. There's no reason to take Sanger's praise seriously. Any good biography of Wells describes how he mistreated those close to him, particularly his two wives. His ideas were liked by those who wanted to impose their vision on humanity and by women eager for promiscuity. But he had no love for people other than as tools to shape the future. Even his correspondence with Sanger tended to be hastily written notes such as that in November of 1921, when he told her that birth control was necessary for "any better social or international order" and that her work was "of primary importance among progressive movements." Sanger/Smith microfilm, S02-0064.

12. Ellen Chesler, *Woman of Valor* (New York: Simon & Schuster, 1992), 11. Much nonsense has been written by Sanger's admirers.

question, "What will you do with us, we hundreds of millions who cannot keep pace with you?"

. . . . It has become apparent that whole masses of human population are, as a whole, inferior in their claim upon the future to other masses, that they cannot be given opportunities or trusted with power as the superior peoples are trusted, that their characteristic weaknesses are contagious and detrimental in the civilising fabric, and that their range of incapacity tempts and demoralises the strong. To give them equality is to sink to their level, to protect and cherish them is to be swamped in their fecundity.[13]

With these words, Wells became one of the first scientific writers to advocate global population control—today an all too progressive cause. According to him, controlling births would be how the World State would rid itself of "rejected" whites and Asians as well as the "vast proportion of the black and brown races." Expressed in numbers, Wells intended to reduce the world population of black and brown people to a small fraction of its present size. At the same time that it was checking "the procreation of base and servile types." the World State would ensure of the procreation of those who were "fine, efficient and beautiful"[14] Do not forget that in a Wellsian World State there would be no place to flee from birth controllers, no distant corner where "rejected" races and individuals could simply raise a family in peace. In a world like ours—where nation states still exist—that same mindset opposes treating reproductive persecution (such as forced birth control and abortion in China) as grounds for refugee status. Again, we are to have no refuge from population controllers.

In addition to the doomed black and brown races, there were those among the white race that Wells termed the "People of the Abyss." These were people who had been adequately productive in less advanced times but were now "thrown out of employment by machinery, thrown out of employment by the escape of industries along some newly opened line of communication to some remote part of the world, or born under circumstances that give them no opportunity of entering the world of active work." They were, in Wells' grisly words, "bulky irremovable excretion" and "gall stones of vicious, help-

less, and pauper masses." As part of his deeply ingrained hostility toward historic Christianity, he recognized that there was a "growing class of energetic people" intent on using "religious acquiescence and light moral reforms"[15] to help such people find new work, but he felt their efforts would make "little on no difference." He believed that simply eliminating the underclass was far easier and certainly more scientific. In Darwinian terms, these were the "unfit" standing in the path of progress.

Feminist of Feminists

One afternoon I was invited to a tea arranged by Henrietta Rodman, Feminist of Feminists, in her Greenwich Village apartment. Wells was particularly sanctified among her group and I must be all right if he approved.[16]

—MARGARET SANGER

Mankind in the Making

Wells' ideas did not remain confined to British readers. In 1902, he published a series of articles in *Cosmopolitan* magazine and those articles resurfaced in 1903 as a book, *Mankind in the Making*. In both he focused on practical steps that government could take to limit births among segments of society that he and many *Cosmopolitan* readers did not like.

A century later, the book has an all too modern ring to it. The key to Wells' scheme lay in making parenting "improbable and difficult" by ensuring that "the burden of parental responsibility" was not "lightened a featherweight." Brutal government regulations would be turned on parents. The "Rights of the Parent" over their child's education would be severely curtailed. Government overseers would establish "a minimum standard" that parents must meet. When parents failed to meet that standard, "the child should be at once removed from the parental care, and the parents charged with the cost of a suitable maintenance—which need not be excessively cheap." Parents who failed to keep up those high payments would be "put into celibate labour establishments" until they paid their parental debt. This, you might recall, is the Wells that Greenwich Village feminists doted over and Sanger praised as "loving," the very Wells who had told them all this in their adored *Cosmopolitan*. Of course, they knew that none of this applied to *them*.

---

13. *Anticipations*, 241–42, 250. Note Wells' remark about "civilising fabric." Seen as inferior but prolific, the great "mass" of the black and brown races threatened Wells' grand vision. By making birth control the "pivot of civilization" the Sanger of 1921 had a practical way to end the "fecundity" that alarmed Wells in 1901. Sanger 'pioneered' little. But she did display a crude sort of 'courage' in saying what many were thinking.

14. *Anticipations*, 256–57.

15. *Anticipations*, 70–71. The then-new Salvation Army was an example of this attitude.

16. Margaret Sanger, *Margaret Sanger, An Autobiography* (New York: W. W. Norton, 1938), 187. Wells signed a 1915 letter supporting Sanger's work.

Reforms giving the impression of compassion would also be used. A deliberately high "Minimum Wage" would strain "these people out," ensuring that they would be unable to get jobs. "Our raised standards of housing, our persecution of overcrowding" (urban planning) would sweep out "the rookeries and hiding-places of these people of the Abyss. They would exist, but they not multiply—and that is our supreme end." In short: "Everything would converge to convince these people that to bear children into such an unfavorable atmosphere is an extremely inconvenient and undesirable thing."[17] Though he sometimes pretended to care about poor children, Wells was supremely unconcerned about what his brutally "unfavorable atmosphere" would do to children who, though targeted for elimination, still managed to get born. To get rid of bad heredity, he was willing to create a hideously degrading environment. His counterparts are still around today.

A Modern Utopia

For the rest of Wells' life population control remained one of his obsessions. In his 1905 *A Modern Utopia,* he dealt with it on a global scale. According to him, "the Utopia of a modern dreamer" must be different from those "planned before Darwin quickened the thought of the world."[18] Unlike the static utopias of the past, the modern utopia was to be dynamic, each stage in human development leading to one yet higher. A taste of just how ruthlessly his new order would pursue that goal came when Wells explained what it would not do.

> There would be no killing, no lethal chambers. No doubt Utopia will kill all deformed and monstrous and evilly diseased births, but for the rest, the State will hold itself accountable for their being. . . . Lives that statesmanship has permitted, errors it has not foreseen and educated against, must not be punished by death.[19]

The limit on killing—except for newborn babies—is hardly reassuring. The Nazi genocide, after all, began in the fall of 1939 with a secret order from Hitler allowing physicians to kill a Leipzig child born blind and lacking one leg and part of an arm.[20] In a short time the new order would be ruthlessly practical enough to realize that if a problem justified killing a baby, it also justified killing an adult.

Wells' rationale for restraining the killing was not impressive. True, he did display the usual liberal belief in environmental determinism. Criminals, including murderers, were not to be put to death because: "Crime and bad lives are the measure of a State's failure, all crime in the end is the crime of the community." But if people are so much a product of the state that even their crimes are not their fault, why attach any value to them at all, and why keep them alive at great expense? Factories, after all, dispose of their defective products at will, and a misbehaving human is far more trouble than a leaky teapot.

In *Anticipations,* Wells' racial and class bigotries were in the open for all to see. The bulk of the world's brown and black races were slated for elimination along with troublesome segments of the white and yellow races. In *A Modern Utopia* the bigotry was more subtle. Wells claimed that "every race of this planet earth is to be found in the strictest parallelism there, in numbers the same— only, as I say, with an entirely different set of traditions, ideals, ideas and purposes."[21] Implied though never said, this meant that an African black man may now father children (if he keeps under his race's quota), but he cannot raise them as Christians or Muslims lest the old traditions continue. Along with freedom of religion, freedom of speech appears to have been sacrificed to maintain population quotas. President Theodore Roosevelt's zeal for large families will be discussed in Chapter VIII, but here is what Wells said would be done to those who promoted parenthood in the wrong places.

> What, for instance, will Utopia do with Mr. Roosevelt? There drifts across my inner vision the image of a strenuous struggle with Utopian constables, the voice that has thrilled terrestrial millions in eloquent protest. The writ of arrest, drifting loose in the conflict, comes to my feet; I impale the script of paper, and read—but can it be? "attempted disorganization . . . incitements to disarrange . . . the balance of the population.[22]

Even the seeming tolerance of Wells' newly discovered racial quotas was dubious. Exactly whose racial birthrate would set the standard that the others must match to maintain the proper ratios—the French whose birth rate had been low for two generations, the British whose birth rate had been falling since the 1870s, the Germans whose birth rates began to fall about 1904, or races with high birth rates and falling death rates? It is

17. H. G. Wells, *Mankind in the Making* (New York, 1904), 27, 92, 94, 102–03. Chesterton blasted this agenda when he discussed socialism in Chap. XVIII.

18. H. G. Wells, *A Modern Utopia* (New York: Charles Scribner's Sons, 1905), 7.

19. *A Modern Utopia,* 129.

20. Hugh Gregory Gallagher, *By Trust Betrayed* (New York, 1990), 47. Liberals seemed to have a similar distaste for less-than-perfect births. See Chap. XXI.

21. *A Modern Utopia,* 23. This utopia exists, not on earth in the future, but on a parallel planet, identical to ours in every respect but its political and social organization.

22. *A Modern Utopia,* 26–27.

easy to suspect that Wells intended for the birth rate of the rest of the world to be lowered to West European levels. Hints come when he describes "beautiful regions" such as the Alps where children will "remit taxation" while in other places "the presence of children will be taxed." In fact, he says: "the statesman of utopia will constantly adjust and readjust regulations and taxation to diminish the proportion of children reared in hot and stimulating conditions."[23] It is no accident that these tropical regions are precisely where most of the world's black and brown people live or that, in Wells' day, it was taken as a given that whites could not adapt well to the tropics. Like many present-day population control agendas, Wells' program was loaded with a built-in bias.

Wells also provides an excellent illustration of an all too common trait in the progressive mindset—an unwillingness to accept responsibility for evil deeds when the reasons that inspired those deeds are no longer fashionable. He might grudgingly admit to a bit of Hitler-like bigotry in his undeveloped "thirteen year old mind in 1879." But admitting to the same faults at a more enlightened age was a different matter. The result is easy to predict. In his hugely successful *The Outline of History* (1920) he pointed out that the "immediate effect" of evolution on "the prosperous and influential classes . . . was very detrimental indeed." He went on to say, "Prevalent peoples at the close of the nineteenth century believed that they prevailed by virtue of the Struggle for Existence, in which the strong and cunning get the better of the weak and confiding." (He was describing Social Darwinism.) He even put blame on a fellow writer:

> It was quite characteristic of the times that Mr. Kipling should lead the children of the middle and upper-class British public back to the Jungle, to learn "the law," and that in his book *Stalky and Co.* he should give an appreciative description of the torture of two boys by three others, who have by a subterfuge tied up their victims helplessly before revealing their hostile intentions.[24]

But it was Wells himself who was a leading champion of a brutal application of Darwin's ideas, writing in 1899:

> What, unless biological science is a mass of errors, is the cause of human intelligence and vigor? Hardship and freedom: conditions under which the active, strong, and subtle survive and the weaker go to the wall; conditions that put a premium upon the loyal alliance of capable men, upon self-restraint, patience and decision.[25]

Evolutionary arguments for imperialism went out of style after World War I and Wells, ever sensitive to progressive fashion, no longer openly promoted them. But evolution as interpreted by his scientific elite remained at the center of his agenda as did the ultimate imperialism, a World State. The novelist George Orwell noted just that in a 1941 article, "Wells, Hitler and the World State."

> If one looks through nearly any book that [Wells] has written in the last forty years one finds the same idea constantly recurring: the supposed antithesis between the man of science who is working towards a planned World State and the reactionary who is trying to restore a disorderly past. In novels, utopias, essays, films, pamphlets, the antithesis crops up, always more or less the same. On the one side science, order, progress, internationalism, aeroplanes, steel, concrete, hygiene; on the other side war, nationalism, religion, monarchy, peasants, Greek professors, poets, horses.[26]

Evolution as a Creed

Evolution has become not merely a theory but a creed, not merely a conception by which to understand the universe, but a guide to direct us how to order our lives.[27]

—DAVID G. RITCHIE, 1901

Wells and Sanger

Wells would have a direct and even intimate connection to American politics. In 1914, Margaret Sanger fled to Europe to avoid federal prosecution for *Woman Rebel,* a radical magazine that she had tried to send through the mails. H. G. Wells and a number of other prominent Englishman sent a letter to President Woodrow Wilson on her behalf. On a later visit to England, Sanger repaid the favor handsomely. H. G. Wells' illegitimate son, Anthony West, described their meeting.

> In May 1920 my father ran into a woman who seemed to be the perfect material for one of those casual affairs licensed by his understanding with [his second wife] Jane. She was a New York parlour radical . . . and had become more widely known for standing trial and serving a prison term for advocating the unrestricted sale of contraceptives in defiance of a federal law banning the dissemination of birth control information. Liberated in the modern sense, she was on the loose in England for a

23. *A Modern Utopia,* 46–47.
24. H. G. Wells, *The Outline of History* vol. 4, (New York, 1920, 1921, 1922), 112–14.
25. H. G. Wells, *Three Prophetic Novels* (New York, 1960), 288.
26. George Orwell, "Wells, Hitler and the World State," reprinted in *Collected Essays* (London, 1946), 163. Forty years refers to the period from *Anticipations* on.
27. David G. Ritchie, *Darwinism and Politics* (New York: Charles Scribner's Sons, 1901), 2.

summer's lease, nerving herself to take, after a three-year delay, the legal steps that would end an unsatisfactory marriage by divorce. When it is added that Margaret Sanger was also a pretty woman, grey-eyed, auburn-haired, trimly built and fairly overflowing with high spirits and physical energy, it will be seen why my father jumped at the chance of having an affair with her. No complications could come out of an affair with her.[28]

Two years later in 1922, Wells would contribute his well-established fame to Sanger's growing notoriety by writing the introduction for the first edition of this book, *The Pivot of Civilization*. In it he awarded Sanger a place in his open conspiracy, noting that she quite lucidly, "sets out the case of the new order against the old." Sanger's agenda was one dear to his heart, birth control used to artificially restore the evolutionary balance between superior and inferior. Sanger said exactly that in a 1921 article written for publication by a liberal group in Japan.

> Nor can we comfort ourselves with the reflection that the struggle for existence will serve to improve the race, that the strong, the capable and the intelligent will survive and that the weaklings and those of inferior mind and body will be eliminated. The struggle for existence does not have these results in human society. Artificial restraints of civilization and law prevent the struggle from being a fair trial of strength and endurance, such as it still may be among wild animals. . . .
>
> . . . From any and every point of view, we find that man cannot trust to the blind forces of nature for the improvement of his race: but that if he desires improvement he must use his intelligence and his will power and win it for himself.[29]

Throughout her life, Sanger continued to praise Wells. In a speech given in his honor at the Waldorf-Astoria in October 1931, she spoke (with typical exaggeration) about how his letter had saved her from "the possibility of spending 45 years in a Federal prison."[30] Later, in an October 1950 speech to the organization she founded,

Planned Parenthood, she called him her "good, dear friend" and quoted something he had told her during "his last unhappy years."

> Mankind is not the privileged favorite of mother nature and in spite of all my lifelong optimism it now seems to me that the Universe is utterly bored by the whole species of mankind. I can see the human race sweeping along the stream of fate to defeat, degradation and final extinction. Mankind is likely to breed itself clean out of existence.[31]

According to Sanger, Wells went on to express his belief that without birth control the future would be "absolutely lost." For him, birth control was the key to the new world order that he had spent almost half a century promoting. It would enable scientific planners to dictate who became parents. Whether the arguments used were based on quality (eugenics) or quantity (population control), the purpose remained the same. Evolutionary "stagnant ponds" must be drained in order to prevent a dismal future much like that he envisioned as a young man in *The Time Machine*.

The Road to Freedom

It was Wells who helped to free us—even before he knew my womanly charms! It revealed him: . . .

Warm-hearted and chivalrous in his love for mankind, and a veritable dynamo of energy in directing misguided humanity along the road to Freedom.

No knight ever set out with higher ideals and a nobler love of mankind than did H. G. Wells. Though he has lived to see some of his darkest fears converted into harsh facts, yet I believe that he will live to see some of his dreams come true.[32]

—MARGARET SANGER, WELLS DINNER, 1931

H. G. Wells and Joseph Conrad

Perhaps the most telling criticism of Wells came from the pen of another of the twentieth century's great writers, Joseph Conrad. Their friendship began accidentally. In May of 1896, Conrad wrote to the unsigned reviewer of one of his books only to discover that the reviewer was the already famous Wells. An unequal friendship developed between the two men, one famous and one not yet famous. At first, even making allowances for that inequality and the necessity to please someone who could

28. Anthony West, *H. G. Wells, Aspects of a Life* (London, 1984), 83. The prison sentence actually resulted from a conviction for her Brownsville birth control clinic.

29. Margaret Sanger, "For Kaizo, Japan, 1921." Sanger/Library of Congress microfilm, LOC 130:13f, 2-3. One title that Sanger suggested was, "Birth Control and Selective Evolution." In *My Fight for Birth Control* (p. 238), Sanger described the Kaizo group as "liberal intellectuals" who "published a radical monthly called *Reconstruction.*"

30. Margaret Sanger, "Mrs. Sanger's Speech at the Wells Dinner," October 23, 1923, Waldorf Astoria" Sanger/Library of Congress microfilm, LOC 131:133. The long sentence was absurd, though some of her audience no doubt believed her.

31. Margaret Sanger, "Address by Margaret Sanger" given to the Planned Parenthood Federation of America, October 25, 1950. Sanger/Library of Congress microfilm, LOC 130:28f, p. 2.

32. "Mrs. Sanger's speech at the Wells' dinner, Oct. 23, 1931." In Sanger/Library of Congress, LOC 131:133.

make or break him as a writer, Conrad seemed quite taken with Wells' books, claiming in one early letter that he was "held by the charm of their expression and their meaning. I surrender to their suggestion . . . and I am convinced by the logic of your imagination so unbounded and so brilliant."[33]

By 1902, however, doubts began to intrude. Responding to a lecture that Wells had given on "The Discovery of the Future," Conrad stressed his "rooted idea" that "The future is of our own making." Wells, he suggested, should have stressed that more, if indeed that was his view.[34]

Between 1902 and 1904 Wells revealed more clearly how he believed the future was to be made, first in a series of articles on "Mankind in the Making" serialized in *Fortnightly Review* (Britain) and *Cosmopolitan* (United States) and later in a book with that same name. In the fall of 1903, having seen a copy of what Wells had written, Conrad wrote a letter in which he tried to convince himself that, "Our differences are fundamental but the divergence is not that great." He illustrated his point by drawing two sets of lines. In the first pair, the W (for Wells) line wiggles up and down, sometimes crossing the C (for Conrad) line, but never diverging far from it. That, Conrad said, was what their "convictions are like." In the other, which he said did not illustrate their convictions, the two lines diverge rapidly apart never to return together.[35] A few days later, Conrad wrote again. Trying to be helpful, he warned Wells that he had begun to address a "select circle . . . leaving the rest of the world outside the pale." He also warned that he will be accused of wanting to create an elite "who look at the world as a breeding place."[36] Of course that was exactly what Wells

wanted to do and by the end of 1903, Conrad seems to have realized that, at one point telling Wells, "There is a cold jocular ferocity" about how he handled mankind "that gives me the shudders sometimes."[37]

Throughout his life, Conrad retained many of the beliefs of his childhood in Catholic Poland. By 1906, he was no longer trying to reconcile his beliefs with those of Wells. Like others, Wells linked his desire to set up a scientific elite who would determine who could have children with his desire to abolish all codes of sexual behavior. In a novel entitled *In the Days of the Comet,* Wells used the passing of the earth through the tale of a comet to 'sexually liberate' society. After reading it, Conrad wrote Wells: "The day of liberation may come or may never come. Very likely I shall be dead first. But if it does come that'll be the day on which I shall marshall my futile objections as to the matters treated in this book."[38]

Perhaps in a last bid to sustain their friendship, Conrad dedicated his 1907 *The Secret Agent* to Wells, but no correspondence between them after it was published has survived. In early 1918, Conrad would explain to Hugh Walpole, another writer, that his final quarrel with Wells had centered on their differing views about humanity, and that he had told Wells: **"The difference between us, Wells, is fundamental. You don't care for humanity but think they are to be improved. I love humanity but know they are not!"**[39]

Those three sentence sum up, perhaps better than anyone else has, what was fundamentally wrong with how Wells, Sanger and many others viewed the world. In the next chapter, "Man and Superman," we examine the deceptions that Wells' and his socialist allies used in their schemes to 'improve' humanity.

—§§§—

33. Conrad to Wells, May 25, 1896. In Frederick Karl and Laurence Davis, ed., *The Collected Letters of Joseph Conrad,* Vol. 1 (Cambridge, 1983), 282. Conrad's first letter is on page 278.
34. Conrad to Wells, undated. *Collected Letters,* Vol. 2, 386.
35. Conrad to Wells, Sept. 19, 1903. *Collected Letters,* Vol. 3, 62.
36. Conrad to Wells, Sept. 25, 1903. *Collected Letters,* Vol. 3, 63–64.

37. Conrad to Wells, Nov./Dec., 1903. *Collected Letters,* Vol. 3, 79.
38. Conrad to Wells, Sept. 15, 1906. *Collected Letters,* Vol. 3, 356.
39. Rupert Hart-Davis, *Hugh Walpole* (New York, 1952), 168.

VI

Man and Superman

1901

Fabians: George Bernard Shaw
Sidney & Beatrice Webb

The Fabian Society provides leadership for the British Left

It is fortunate when one happens to believe in one's own arguments: one always does so in a fashion, the most one does is to suppress the qualification.... As a matter of fact, with regard to administration work, we plunge without hesitation on to the position of an advocate pledged only to display the arguments which tell in favour of the cause we believe in. —BEATRICE WEBB

Despite his talent and world fame, H. G. Wells could not carry out his agenda alone. Creating a scientific World State where births were regulated according to evolutionary principles required what he called an "open conspiracy" of the like-minded.

Strange as it sounds, they came to him on bicycles. In turn-of-the-century England and for all too brief a time bicycles were the height of fashion. Since keeping a horse and carriage was expensive and the primitive automobile had yet to enter mass production, the new safety bicycle was at the peak of its popularity as sensible transportation for adults as well as children. So it was not surprising that early in 1902 one of the more significant political events of the twentieth century took place when a Mr. and Mrs. Webb appeared H. G. Wells' home, "riding upon bicycles from the direction of London."[1]

It was Wells' *Anticipations* that prompted Sidney and Beatrice Webb to mount their bicycles. Their visit's importance lay in the fact that the Webb couple were intellectual leaders in the Fabian Society.[2] Later Wells would claim that before they came he "knew scarcely more of the Fabian Society than I did of the Zetetic Society."[3] Whether that was true or not, Wells' alliance with them united one of the world's most influential writers with a group that, though small in size, has had a enormous impact on British politics. During the 1970s the *Encyclopaedia Britannica* would note that, though the Fabian Society's membership had never been greater

than 8,400, "generally nearly half of the number of Labour members of Parliament in the House of Commons and a majority of the party leaders are Fabians." In Britain, Fabians provide the intellectual elite for the political left. They also provide the left around the world with a model for achieving power that, unlike communism, does not rely on revolution or military conquest. In fact, their name comes from Fabius, a Roman general whose motto was 'slow but sure.' Of course Fabians also stress that when the time was right, Fabius could strike quickly and ruthlessly.[4] And, as we will see, Fabians provide the left with a model of how to achieve their ends by the most devious of means.

As shocking as may sound to those who believe the political left to be untainted by racism (merely because it accuses others of the fault), the Webbs agreed with virtually everything Wells had written in *Anticipations*. When Sidney Webb first wrote Wells in December of 1901, he

---

1. H. G. Wells, "Introduction to the 1914 Edition of 'Anticipations'" in H. G. Wells, *Anticipations and Other Papers* (New York, 1924), 279.

2. In addition to her later ties to the Fabians through Wells, Shaw and others, when Sanger arrived in England in 1914 she carried a letter of introduction to the Fabians and gave a speech at Fabian Hall on July 5, 1915. (Her 16 pages of handwritten notes from that speech are in the Margaret Sanger papers at the Library of Congress, L129:0167.) She mentions the Fabians twice in her 1938 autobiography (122, 170). In her *My Fight for Birth Control*, Sanger claimed (true or not) that her Fabian Hall speech led the British feminist, Marie Stopes, to realize that the "knowledge of contraception" was important (104).

3. *Anticipations*, 279.

4. That ruthlessness can best be seen in Sidney and Beatrice Webb's praise of Stalin's murderous dictatorship in their 1935 *Soviet Communism: A New Civilisation?*

referred to himself as "an immensely interested reader" who greatly admired Wells' new book.[5] His disagreements were minor. There was the matter of the ruling elite. Sidney Webb had no problem with Wells' idea of a world run by a scientific elite. Rule by experts was and is the very essence of the Fabian left. Like many enlightened and progressive thinkers, both Wells and Sidney saw the great mass of humanity as mere objects to be manipulated or, as Sidney told Wells in that first letter:

> But all experience shows that men need organsing as much as machines, or rather, much more; that the making of such arrangements, and constant adjustments, as will ensure order, general health and comfort, and maximum productivity, among human beings, is a professional art in itself—not consciously studied in England, where we do much instinctively, but recognized in India, and deliberately studied in Germany.[6]

But Sidney Webb complained that Wells saw his "trained professional expert . . . too exclusively as an engineer, a chemist or an electrician." The scientists that Fabians wanted to put in charge included, "the trained administrator, the expert in organising men—equipped with an Economics or a Sociology which will be as scientific, and as respected by his colleagues of other professions as Chemistry or Mechanics." In short, the Fabians wanted a world in which the behavior of people was as well understood and as carefully controlled by social scientists as the behavior of electrons is by physicists.

There is grave danger in what Sidney Webb said. Modern science is rooted in a demystified world, in a nature that is merely a thing created by God, a thing whose behavior can be studied and controlled as part of the dominion that man was commanded to have over nature in the Bible. But during the nineteenth century something went wrong with that idea. As Sidney's remark illustrates, as the idea that man was created in the image of God began to fade, man himself became part of the machinery. Socialism all too loudly claimed to be responding to social problems created by the Industrial Revolution. But in practice it simply carried that revolution to its logical conclusion, making men as much a part of the machinery as steam engines and cotton looms.

Two of the great horrors of twentieth century flow from that mistake. At the core of communism (international socialism) lay a system of economics that saw history as a clash between classes. At the core of Nazism (national socialism) lay a system of biology that saw history as a clash between races (in evolutionary terms, competing subspecies). In both, ordinary people were captive to forces that science could describe and that dictated how men must behave. Evolution turned men into animals, socialism into machines. Historically, it has proved all too easy to merge the two ideas into one.

Both Wells and his Fabian allies had what they mistakenly believed to be a kinder, gentler version of that same mechanistic, scientific worldview. In Wells' books the World State is not created by blood-soaked revolutions as in Marxism nor is it the result of brutal wars as in Nazism. Wells at least claimed that it would be created, "by the sheer power of naked reasonableness, by propaganda and open intention, by feats and devotions of the intelligence."[7] That was not all that different from the Fabian plan to conquer the world one sociological tract and municipal water board at a time. Like Marxism and Nazism, people were still things, but the manipulation would be more far more subtle and deceptive. It is that deceptiveness which links Wells and the Fabians to Margaret Sanger and her movement.

In *Anticipations,* Wells clearly understood that at one level this "development of mechanism," as he called his determinism, made his call for an "open conspiracy" meaningless. "In the abstract world of reasoned science," he said, "all things exist now potentially down to the last moment of infinite time" and "rigidly predestinate [the] scheme of things in space and time." If people are merely bio-chemical machines, then all of human history is already determined and no room is left for human choice. Wells covers over this problem by noting that "in the real world of sensory experience, will is free, just as new sprung grass is green, wood hard, ice cold and toothache painful."[8] But no amount of verbal semantics can conceal the fact that science also tells us that our senses deceive us. Intense cold, for instance, can feel like burning heat. For mechanistic science, even our sense of freedom is an illusion. In practice, those who adopt this attitude apply Wells' argument for free will only to themselves and treat their foes and those they wish to manipulate as captives of forces beyond their control. Since people are already

---

5. Sidney Webb to H. G. Wells, Dec. 8, 1901. In Norma Mackenzie, ed., *The Letters of Sidney and Beatrice Webb*, vol. 2: *Partnership, 1892–1912* (Cambridge, 1978), 144.

6. *The Letters of Sidney and Beatrice Webb*, vol. 2, 144. "India" refers British imperial rule, "Germany" to something far more disturbing. In his 1922 *Eugenics and Other Evils*, G. K. Chesterton warned of the grave danger posed by Germany's "modern craze for scientific officialism." Those who worry about a German tendency to obey orders without question should examine Chesterton's warning. Those who want British parallels can look to the Fabians.

7. *Anticipations*, 282.

8. *Anticipations*, 248, 246.

determined by something else, it is perfectly acceptable for others—controllers, planners or an all-powerful state—to make them to behave differently for their own good, the good of society, or to achieve some distant goal.

Giving Orders

Beatrice Potter [Webb] was born in 1858 in Gloucester, into a class which, to use her own words, "habitually gave orders."[9]

—*ENCYCLOPAEDIA BRITANNICA*, 1977

That was exactly how Fabians felt about the ordinary working people they claimed to represent. For much of her life Beatrice Webb kept a diary filled with perceptive insights into how she and her fellow Fabians thought. An entry in late December of 1894 is particularly interesting because she spent that Christmas with her two sisters and the husbands of the three were almost a microcosm of British politics. Beatrice's husband Sidney was the leading Fabian intellectual. Another husband, Alfred Cripps, was a wealthy Tory who opposed welfare programs but was willing to let the great mass of the British people live their lives as they saw fit. The final husband, Leonard Courtney, was an economist whose classical liberal views were similar to modern libertarianism. It was Leonard who stimulated Beatrice's thinking.

> To Leonard the means whereby you carry through a proposal, the arguments with which you support it, are as important as the end itself. And to do Leonard justice he is a democrat at heart, in that he honestly desires that the government of the country should be a reflection of the free desires and views of the whole body of the people. Possibly he is more of a democrat than we [Fabians] are ourselves; for we have little faith in the "average sensual man," we do not think that he can prescribe the remedies. It is possibly exactly on this point that Leonard feels most antagonism to our opinions. We wish to introduce into politics the professional expert—to extend the sphere of government by adding to its enormous advantages of wholesale and compulsory management, the advantage of the most skilled entrepreneur.[10]

Beatrice's "entrepreneur" was not someone who had invested his own money in a new business and was thus not accountable to others for how he ran it. Instead, she was speaking of its bureaucratic equivalent, an expert with the "enormous advantages" a government position offers—the ability to force everyone else to obey his will—with absolutely no accountability to the public. He was an "entrepreneur" only in the sense that he would put into place new (Fabian) ideas. Anyone who has been frustrated by presumptive judges, inflexible bureaucrats, unresponsive school officials and the like has had the misfortune to encounter a Fabian "entrepreneur." Science and specialized training would replace blood and breeding as the rationale for aristocracy, but the world was to remain divided into powerful lords[11] and powerless serfs. At times, Fabians could be surprisingly candid about their intentions. In January of 1894, Sidney Webb gave a speech to the Fabian Society in which he said:

> What we Fabians aim at is not the sub-division of property, whether capital or land, but the control and administration of it by the representatives of the community. It has no desire to see the Duke of Bedford replaced by five hundred little Dukes of Bedford under the guise of enfranchised leaseholders . . . It has no vain dream of converting the agricultural labourer into a freeholder, farming his own land, but looks to the creation of parish councils, empowered to acquire land for communal ownership, and to build cottages for the labourers to rent.[12]

Sidney went on the call this "securing the great end of equality of opportunity to every citizen." In practice, this meant that virtually everyone would be reduced to equally abject dependence upon an all-powerful state and its favored bureaucrats. George Orwell expressed this mindset brilliantly in *Animal Farm* when "All animals are equal" was amended to add "but some animals are more equal than others." That came at the point when the pigs (socialists) began to carry whips. Fabians saw themselves as "more equal" and intended to be with ones with the whips.

An important question arises. If the Fabian leadership had, as Beatrice so often pointed out, such an enormous contempt for the average working Briton, how have they

9. Beatrice Webb also combined in her person three groups often seen as hostile. She was born into the wealthy, old-moneyed class. As a young woman she was chosen to manage Herbert Spencer's literary legacy and thus that of Social Darwinism, with its grim call for a ruthless, economic 'survival of the fittest.' Instead, she became a Fabian socialist and worked for a state-managed economy. In reality, all three have one critical idea in common, a belief that a few should habitually give orders to the many.

10. Beatrice Webb, *Our Partnership* (New York, 1948), 120. The diary entry is for Dec. 29, 1894.

11. This can be taken literally. In 1929 Sidney Webb became Baron Passfield and acquired a seat in the House of Lords.

12. Sidney Webb, "Socialism: True or False," (Jan. 1894). In *Our Partnership,* 106. G. K. Chesterton was a fierce foe of such ideas, believing every man should own his own home and garden. See his *Eugenics and Other Evils,* Chapter 12.

been able to dominate a Labour party dependent on the votes of millions of working-class men and women? The answer lies in how its leaders express their contempt. Rather than simply say, "You are losers and need us to run your lives," they say, "Your failures are due to capitalism. Let us run things and you will be better off." (In the U.S. race is used the same way.) By creating scapegoats and stirring up hatred and envy, they can treat people as incompetent without openly saying so. By creating a fiction that big government is needed to restrain big business (or religion), they are able to use big government to dominate virtually everyone. It is a clever trick.

Fabians also concealed their agenda behind a smokescreen of statistics, incremental legislative changes, and administrative reforms that most people incorrectly interpreted as showing a desire to make government better and more efficient. As Beatrice Webb put it, her fellow Fabians "were, indeed, far more extreme in their opinions and projects than their phrases conveyed to the ordinary citizen."[13] This tactic of deception was, she said, called a "policy of inoculation—of giving to each class, to each person, coming under our influence, the exact dose of collectivism that they were prepared to assimilate."[14] Having little respect for most people, Fabians felt no need to be honest with them. It was an attitude they shared with many in this book, including Sanger. The hidden meaning Sanger and her followers gave to "choice" (discussed later) was every bit as deceptive as that the Fabians gave to "equality."

In his autobiography, Wells referred to this lying as "Fabian understatement" and gave an example from 1907 when he and some other socialist candidates were charged with being hostile to marriage and the family life. At that time it was politically useful to deny the charges and that is what Wells did, claiming that socialism was neutral on topics such as marriage and divorce, that neither Catholics nor Protestants need worry about what it might do. Writing in 1934, however, Wells saw no reason to continue that lie and bluntly said:

> Socialism, if it is anything more than a petty tinkering with economic relationships is a renucleation of society. The family can remain only as a biological fact. Its economic and educational autonomy are inevitably doomed. The modern state is bound to be the ultimate guardian of all children and it must assist, replace, or subordinate the parent as supporter, guardian and educator; it must release all human beings from the obligation of mutual proprietorship, and it must refuse absolutely to recognize or enforce any kind of sexual

ownership. It cannot therefore remain neutral when such claims come before it. It must disallow them.[15]

Even then, Wells was not fully honest. He might claim to free individuals from slave-like relationships. As a womanizing husband and an indifferent father, Wells cared little for marriage or family responsibilities. But Wells had his eyes set on something bigger. He wanted to replace the "mutual ownership" of families with the ownership of everyone (particularly children) by an all-domineering state.

Socialism and Sexual Rebellion

The free-love charge was a constant thorn to the birth controllers. Margaret Sanger was frequently accused of free loveism, and always denied it. The origins of birth control as a women's movement were in free love. Some socialists not only recognized this but thought it best to accept that legacy, trying perhaps to redefine it. Those who took this view were inclined to the perception that youth involved in sexual rebellion might be an important socialist constituency.[16]

—LINDA GORDON, 1976

Fabians were not the only ones thinking this way. At that time British liberalism was splitting. Some liberals remained true to the classic liberal principles of limited government and individual rights. Beatrice referred to them as, "the other school of Liberalism . . . extremely distasteful to us: we disagree with them on almost every point of home and foreign policy." On the other hand, the new liberals—those Wells called state liberals—agreed with much of the Fabian agenda. They were in the process of taking over the name liberal, not because they believed in freedom from the state, but because they needed a cover for their almost pathological obsession with creating dependence in order to control. In 1906, a leader of the old liberals denounced the new with these words:

> But the state invites us every day to lean upon it. I seem to hear the wheedling and alluring whisper, "Sound you may be; we bid you be a cripple. Do you see? Be blind. Do your hear? Be deaf. Do you walk? Be not so ven-

---

13. *Our Partnership,* 107.

14. *Our Partnership,* 122.

15. H. G. Wells, *Experiment in Autobiography* (New York, 1934), 404–05. State control of child rearing is precisely what Gilman institutes in her feminist utopia (Chap. XXII). No "sexual ownership" means widespread promiscuity and easy divorce, lest a man and woman unite for life to resist the state's indoctrination of their children. It is easy to combine that sort of increasing state power with the illusion that lives are becoming more free (meaning less responsible).

16. Linda Gordon, *Woman's Body, Woman's Self* (New York: Penguin, 1976), 243.

turesome. Here is a crutch for one arm; when you get accustomed to it, you will soon want another—the sooner the better." The strongest man if encouraged may soon accustom himself to the methods of an invalid; he may train himself to totter, or to be fed with a spoon.[17]

About these new or state liberals Beatrice wrote: "These men have helped us with our undertakings, they have been appreciative of our ideas, and socially pleasant to us. They have no prejudice against our views of social reform: while their general attitude towards the Empire as a powerful and self-conscious force is one in which we are in agreement." Beatrice was describing the beginning of the alliance between a liberalism that wanted to enmesh everyone in a debilitating web of welfare programs and a socialism still further left that was so expansive that the state took over most of the functions of society and reduced most people to cogs in a vast machine. Both intuitively understood that the difference between the them was a matter of degree rather than kind. Both still do.

Beatrice Webb's frustration with the new liberals lay in what she felt was their lack of cleverness. Both the new liberalism and Fabian socialism needed to radically weaken existing institutions—religion, family, local communities and private property—in order to make the state more powerful. The Fabians had no problem with that for, as Beatrice noted, "we are not against the policy of a 'clean slate.' We want to be rid of all the old ideals and enthusiasms." But she was upset that liberals were exposing these plans by talking about them. To counter that, Beatrice wrote, "we want to stamp out the notion that the world can be bettered by abolition of some of the existing institutions." Like their socialism, to be achieved by gradual means, the Fabians wanted eliminate or radically alter everything that stood in their way. But they wanted to achieve radical results by gradual means. Change was to be made so slowly and carefully that most of the population would not realize what was being done to them. Any time a critic pointed out the larger agenda, the "notion" was to be stamped out with vehement denials. What the controversy died down, the creeping would resume. Devious but very clever.

Beatrice gave examples of how Fabians intended to keep the form while destroying the substance. Ireland was to remain in union with England but governed so cleverly that the Irish would no longer demand independence. The House of Lords was to remain, but only as a figurehead deprived of real power including "non-intervention with national expenditures—all collectivism coming under this head." The Anglican Church would remain the established church of England, but "science and secular ethics and any other form of intellectual activity that may seem desirable" (such as the arts) would so well-endowed by government that they could counter any lingering church influence. In short, the Fabians intended, "to set people to work to build up new tissue which may in time take the place of the old."[18] New institutions more amenable to manipulation would replace old ones that shielded people from an all-powerful state. Elsewhere, Beatrice gave an example of just such a replacement when she noted that one idea the Fabians had started, "the dominance of the National Union of Teachers over the borough councils"[19] had been taken up by the teacher's union itself. The more power that this "new tissue" (the teachers' unions) developed, the less influence parents would have over their child's education, a goal dear to the heart of Fabians and their modern liberal allies.

Beatrice closed one diary entry by describing her recent first meeting with Wells. She noted that, like them, Wells, "has no great faith in government by the 'man in the street' and, I think, has hardly realised the function of the representative as a 'foolometer' for the expert."[20] That final comment hints that Fabians judged the foolishness of an idea by observing political representatives who were responsive to public opinion. Since Fabians believed that most citizens were unfit to govern, a politician who listened to them was a "foolometer."

In *Our Partnership* Beatrice devoted several pages to describing how, in order to "get things done in what one considers the best way," she and her husband engaged in what she called "intrigue." Since "there is no such thing as spontaneous public opinion;" she says, "it has to be manufactured from a centre of conviction and energy." She explained how:

> It is fortunate when one happens to believe in one's own arguments: one always does so in a fashion, the most one does is to suppress the qualification. Is that "debasing the currency" or is it not the whole truth? As a matter of fact, with regard to administration work, we plunge without hesitation on to the position of an advocate pledged only to display the arguments which tell in

17. Thomas C. Mendenhall and others, *The Quest for a Principle of Authority in Europe 1715 to Present* (New York, 1948), 365. Taken from E. P. Cheyney, *Readings in English History* (Boston, 1922), 774–75. The speaker was the Earl of Rosebery (1847–1929).

18. The Beatrice Webb quotes are from *Our Partnership*, 228–29. The diary entry is Jan. 20, 1902.

19. *Our Partnership*, 260.

20. *Our Partnership*, 231.

favour of the cause we believe in. In our scientific work, however, we honestly seek to tell the truth, the whole truth, and nothing but the truth; a distinction in standards which puzzles and perplexes me.[21]

Her husband knew why. The scientific work would be read by few and understood by even fewer. It did not matter if its evidence went against the intended policy. The prestige of doing the research would lend authority to dishonest advocacy. This was especially true with the press, since the typical journalist combines a near-complete ignorance of science with a worshipful awe of it as the source for all truth. Beatrice gave a disturbing example of just how Sidney shaped "public opinion" during a 1937 debate over reforming London's schools. A letter to the editor of the *Daily Mail* from Sidney had prompted an invitation to meet with the newspaper's staff.

> He was ushered in and found Harmsworth looking amazingly youthful, seated in conference with four still more boyish-looking assistant editors. Harmsworth asked several sharp questions, and then said, "Very well, Mr. Webb, we'll do it. But we don't know anything about the subject. You must come in every night at 11 P.M. for a week, and see that we say everything just right." Needless to say, S.W. jumped at the chance, and for a week sat with Thomas Malowe, who was then the chief acting editor, and corrected the reports and paragraphs on London education. "I never revealed to anyone," he laughingly said, years afterward, "that one of my experiences had been to edit the *Daily Mail* for a week."[22]

Getting to edit a newspaper in secrecy was unusual. More often when reporters "don't know anything about the subject" they simply find authorities whose views they echo without question. Reporters probably never realized, for instance, that to get an "unemployment scheme" passed the Webbs concealed its faults and underestimated the expense involved or that Beatrice dealt with her guilt over that by noting, "Only one does not like to mislead the public, even for its own good!"[23] For Fabians and their allies, lies and deceptive statistics were simply a way to manipulate public opinion and force legal and social change. Once the changes were put into effect, there was little danger of the news media exposing those lies. Doing so would reveal its own woeful incompetence.

If this developing alliance had been merely anti-democratic, elitist, and obsessed with increasing governmental power, it would have been bad enough. But there was a darker underside to that agenda than simply an obsession with controlling the lives of others and creating ever more intrusive bureaucracies. An entry in Beatrice's diary in January of 1903 revealed just what that was. George Bernard Shaw, the famous playwright and another prominent Fabian, had just spent "three delightful evenings" reading his new play, *Man and Superman,* to a small group of his friends including Sidney and Beatrice Webb.

> Then I am so genuinely delighted at his choice of subjects. We cannot touch the subject of human breeding—it [the time] is not ripe for the mere industry of induction, and yet I realise that it is the most important of all questions, this breeding of the right sort of man. G.B.S's audacious genius can reach out to it.[24]

Beatrice was excited about Shaw's play because it exposed the public to an idea that many on the left supported but could not yet aggressively advocate, the idea of breeding "the right sort of man." Behind Beatrice's reasoning lay yet another clever deception. Those with leftist views often exaggerate the importance of the arts, treating artists as secular prophets who are morally superior to ordinary people. The artists, in turn, provide the initial shock to move the public in the proper direction however vile. If criticism arises, the artist can retreat behind cries of 'censorship' assured of support by those who are covertly using his art to spread their ideas. Once the cries die down, the next small step is taken. When the public no longer protests an idea like controlled breeding as art, then a Fabian-like group can create what Beatrice called an "industry of induction" to put the idea into practice. Until then, all claims that any such an idea is envisioned will be loudly denied. The masses simply have no right to know what is intended. Their thinking is to be as rigorously controlled as their reproduction. All too often the deception works.

Shaw's *Man and Superman* was subtitled "A Comedy and a Philosophy." The play itself is a light, romantic comedy with only a few allusions to breeding the race "to heights now deemed superhuman."[25] Shaw even made fun of his own ideas. In a scene that takes place in a dream, the devil warns, "Beware of the pursuit of the Superhuman: it leads to an indiscriminate contempt for the Human" and prophesies that, "the 20th century will

---

21. *Our Partnership,* 260.
22. *Our Partnership,* 257–58.
23. *Our Partnership,* 454.

24. *Our Partnership,* 256–57. The diary entry is for Jan. 16, 1903. Sidney seems to have found Shaw's Superman unappealing. He may have been objecting to Shaw's belief that a new sort of man would have to be bred for socialism, delaying the already lengthy process.
25. George Bernard Shaw, *Man and Superman* (New York, 1903), 637.

run after this newest of the old crazes when it gets tired of the world, the flesh and your humble servant."[26] Serious as he was about the idea, Shaw recognized that for many of the shallow people who attended his plays the pursuit of the Superman was merely a passing fad.

The play had a direct link to Wells' *Anticipations.* In an introductory letter, Shaw claimed that his Superman was a dramatization of, "H. G. Wells's anticipation of the efficient engineering class which will, he hopes, finally sweep the jabbers out of the way of civilization."[27] But the real 'philosophy' of the play came at the end of the published version in a *Revolution's Handbook,* allegedly written by John Tanner, the play's cynical, Shaw-like character. The first chapter of this book-within-a-play is aptly entitled "On Good Breeding." The God of the eighteenth century, Shaw says, was the "god of the lazy and incapable" unwilling to help themselves. In the nineteenth century, it was decided that "there is indeed no such god; and now Man must take in hand all the work that he used to shirk with an idle prayer." (This taking in hand was what Sanger meant by "choice"—a few choosing for the many.) According to Shaw, that work must include the breeding of man much as the wolves have been breed into domesticated dogs for, "what can be done with a wolf can be done with a man."[28]

Shaw found foes to the Superman in private property and marriage. Property, by dividing humanity into small cliques based on wealth, prevents all sorts of odd matings ("a duke to a charwoman") and would "postpone the Superman for eons."[29] Those who protest that such odd matings are unlikely to produce good marriages miss Shaw's next point, that marriage itself is a barrier to the Superman. Congenial marriages are not necessarily the best breeding pairs, so breeding and companionship must be separated. With typical Fabian deception, however, Shaw advocated keeping the word marriage around but altering its meaning: "the absolute confidence of the public in the stability of the institution's name, make it all the easier to alter its substance."[30] Shaw hints that family life will need to be manipulated in a similar fashion, suggesting that the results of all those out-of-wedlock matings could be cared for by a "human stud farm (piously disguised as a reformed Foundling Hospital)."[31] Children would become wards of the state and a father's influence reduced to zero: "We have taken the minds of his children out of his hands and put them into those of our State schoolmaster. We shall presently make their bodily nourishment independent of him."[32]

In a later book, Shaw recognized that the more orthodox churches would oppose these attempts to control human breeding. In his 1928, *The Intelligent Woman's Guide to Socialism and Capitalism* he brutally framed the population issue as it would exist under socialism. There would be only two alternatives: either "putting the superfluous babies into a bucket" and drowning them like cats or making "it a severely punishable crime for married couples to have more than a prescribed number of children." Church opposition to such policies would be dealt with brutally, whether, "the State would simply ignore the Churches or pass a law under which their preachers could be prosecuted for sedition would depend wholly on the gravity of the emergency, and not on the principles of liberty, toleration, freedom of conscience, and so forth."[33] This attitude lies at the heart of the modern left's hatred for the "religious right." The slander used against them is merely the first step a process intended to crush all dissent. It also undergirds the push to make homosexuality an acceptable lifestyle since homosexuals, typically unencumbered by children or grandchildren, have little interest in protecting the rights of parents. The more of them around, particularly if their relationships are treated as "family," the weaker the traditional family becomes.

It is easy to see in all this (and in the similar ideas of Wells) the ramblings of a promiscuous old man eager to fill his life with sexual variety unburdened by the responsibilities of marriage or fatherhood. It is equally easy to understand why bored and decadent fad-seekers would find a vicarious thrill in tasting such ideas. But that does not explain why someone as straitlaced as Beatrice Webb believed that "breeding the right sort of man" was the "most important of all questions." The answer lies in the sort of person that socialism needs in order to rule. Revolutionary (Marxist) socialism was forced to become violent and kill tens of millions of people because those it ruled refused to become cogs in their machinery. In a rambling and difficult-to-follow argument, Shaw claims that Fabian socialism will be different. It will take the time to create people to fit its machinery. Shaw begins by

---

26. *Man and Superman,* 648.

27. *Man and Superman,* 506–07.

28. *Man and Superman,* 691.

29. *Man and Superman,* 694.

30. *Man and Superman,* 697. The same can be said of homosexual marriages.

31. *Man and Superman,* 726. Nazism did precisely that with illegitimate births to S.S. men.

---

32. *Man and Superman,* 728. Shaw refers to working fathers as "riff-raff" with no right to influence government policy. The same mindset excludes fathers from abortion decisions.

33. George Bernard Shaw, *The Intelligent Woman's Guide to Socialism and Capitalism* (New York: 1928, 1931), 459.

answering one of the most intriguing questions in politics, why wealthy people are attracted to socialism and its close kin, welfare state liberalism.

> But why are Fabians well spoken of in circles where thirty years ago the word Socialist was understood as equivalent to cut-throat and incendiary? Not because the English have the smallest intention of studying or adopting the Fabian policy, but because they believe that the Fabians, by eliminating the element of intimidation from Socialist agitation, have drawn the teeth of insurgent poverty and saved the existing order from the only method of attack it really fears.[34]

Wealthy people, Shaw says, like Fabian socialism because does not go to the poor calling for a bloody revolution like Marxism. He goes on to explain that revolutionary socialists were right in one respect. Given human nature as it now is, any attempt to take away property would require a great deal of violence. By not calling for revolution, Fabians were hinting that they had no intention of inflicting real harm on the wealthy. (This is hardly surprising, since Beatrice Webb and her husband lived well on the large fortune she inherited from her father, a railroad executive.) For much the same reason, welfare state liberalism had a great appeal to the rich. Its reforms 'drew the teeth' from poverty and created a dependency on government that prevented revolution.

But Shaw went a step further and offered an argument that makes violent revolution pointless: "we may as well make up our minds that Man will return to his idols and cupidities, in spite of all 'movements' and all revolutions, until his nature is changed."[35] Pure socialism, Shaw claimed, will come but only after generations of controlled breeding intended to prepare a New Man willing to accept it. Reassuring words to those who wanted to enjoy their wealth in the here and now. There will be no revolution in which the masses displace the old financial or new scientific elites because the size and sorts of people in the population will be strictly managed by those on top. Left unsaid is the fact that two types of men would have to be created: a small ruling elite, bred and trained to rule, and a far larger group bred and conditioned to be as passive and obedient as domesticated animals.[36]

In his anti-utopia novel, *Animal Farm,* George Orwell was aware of this agenda. When the personified animals on the farm revolt and drive out their human owner, Mr.

Jones (capitalism), they become a small socialist state in which all animals are proclaimed equal. But things soon become very unequal. Rule passes to a pig elite backed up by vicious dogs. For most animals, life on the farm becomes harder than it was under Mr. Jones. The only animal who seems fitted to the new system is a horse described this way: "Boxer was an enormous beast, nearly eighteen hands high, and as strong as any two ordinary horses put together. A white stripe down his nose gave him a somewhat stupid appearance, and in fact he was not of first-rate intelligence, but he was universally respected for his steadiness of character and tremendous powers of work."[37] Socialism's New Man must bear a striking resemblance to the unfortunate Boxer.

Coming up with a practical scheme to breed human nature for passivity has proved difficult. Crude attempts to do so have focused more on environment than heredity and targeted for elimination two groups who fail to meet the requirements—the underclass and religious conservatives. The underclass fails because, though it is passive (or at least powerless to resist), it is not properly obedient. It may like rhetoric about redistributing wealth from the rich to the poor, but it prefers present pleasures to the long and drawn out labor of building socialism. Religious conservatives are even worse. At their best, they refuse to be passive about issues such as marriage, family or reproduction and insist on obeying a higher authority.

Sidney Webb touched on the problem of the underclass in a jargonistic 1896 Fabian tract entitled. "The Difficulties of Individualism." According to him, the individualism of unrestrained nineteenth-century capitalism has "difficulties" handling social problems because it "promotes extreme inequality in the distribution of the annual product of the united labors of the community." Difficulties in the distribution of wealth, in turn, result in two forms of "malproduction." One is well known and loudly trumpeted by the advocates of socialism and the welfare-state: "the preparation of senseless luxuries [for the rich] whilst there is need for more bread [for the poor]." The other is less well known but even more important: "the breeding of degenerate hordes of a demoralized residuum unfit for social life."[38]

Both those statements by Sidney Webb—the breadless poor and the breeding hordes of unfit—are in the same sentence. Historically, those who have been most eager to expand the size of government have also been those who often use the most derogatory language about ordinary

---

34. *Man and Superman,* 710.

35. *Man and Superman,* 712. Throughout this book, we'll see this theme about changing human nature repeated over and over.

36. The first group will be mentioned, in a less radical framework, in Chap. XI. This idea was one of the main points in Aldous Huxley's anti-utopia, *Brave New World.*

37. George Orwell, *Animal Farm* (New York, 1946), 2–3.

38. Sidney Webb, "The Difficulties of Individualism," Fabian tract 69, (London, 1896), 6.

people and are the most eager to get rid of the socially troublesome groups through ugly schemes to control who has children. In his first letter to Wells, Sidney Webb—as Britain's leading leftist intellectual—had no problem with that agenda. He merely suggested that: "The 'People of the Abyss,' in this country at any rate, need not be any large mass."[39] Read carefully, however, it is obvious that Webb was primarily interested in saving from planned oblivion only that portion of the Abyss whose people "will play no small part in that administration, that organization of man to which I have referred." The rest, the non-bureaucrats, could be done away with.

Other than that minor limitation, Sidney Webb was as interested in controlling who had children as he was in controlling a city's water supply. In May of 1905 the Fabians appointed a subcommittee to study Britain's birthrate. The following year Sidney released its widely publicized report. Much of what it had to say was expected and was quite similar to American articles we will be reading later in this book. Britain was going through changes similar to those that triggered a 'race suicide' scare in the United States. After carefully adjusting for population changes, the report concluded that 200,000 fewer babies had been born in England and Wales in 1901 than would have been born had the birth rates of 1871 continued without change.

But the Fabian's real interest centered on who was still having babies. Using London as an example, the study pointed out that the greatest decline in births was occurring among the affluent "servant-keeping class." (The Webbs lived in a large home with two servants.) The district with the greatest decline in births (36 per cent) was the one with the largest number of servants. The one with the smallest decline (12 per cent) also had the fewest household servants. The Fabians located the cause in what they delicately called "the deliberate regulation of the marriage state." Sidney went on to point out that there were, from a Fabian perspective, serious problems with the current situation. The growing population "vacuum," he said, would make it impossible to keep out the "alien immigrant" (echoing similar fears in the U.S.). He also warned that, left unchecked, the high birthrates of immigrants and the underclass would change the nation's character. With the substitution of Irish Catholics for Italian Catholics, his list was almost identical to the one that was creating alarm among the New England elite and, in the American West, fears of a 'yellow peril.'

In Great Britain at this moment, when half, or perhaps two-thirds, of all the married people are regulating their

families, children are being born to the Irish Roman Catholics and the Polish, Russian and German Jews, on the one hand and to the thriftless and irresponsible—largely the casual laborers and the other denizens of the one-roomed tenements of our great cities—on the other. Twenty-five per cent of our parents, as Professor Karl Pearson keeps warning us, is producing 50 per cent of the next generation. This can hardly result in anything but national deterioration; or, as an alternative, in this country gradually falling to the Irish and the Jews. Finally, there are signs that even these races are becoming influenced. The ultimate future of these islands may be to the Chinese![40]

Sidney Webb's solution was just the sort often dreamed up by social planners, a complex set of social and economic incentives to encourage the right sort of women ("especially those of the fine type") to have more children while discouraging others. It also illustrates why Fabians and their ideological kin wanted the government to run social services and schools. Only with that level of control could experts carefully adjust rewards and punishments to achieve the desired results, encouraging some to have larger families while punishing others for exactly the same behavior.

To give but one example of the potential that this social control offered, Sidney Webb wanted to encourage "the best members of the middle and upper artisan classes" to have more children by increasing funding for "secondary, technical and university education." At that time it did not suit the Fabians to reveal their hostility toward Christianity,[41] so in his report, Sidney expressed the hope that his economic programs would encourage the birth of children that result from the "mystical obligations" of the "religious-minded."[42] But if their agenda took an anti-religious turn, government-funded education would make it quite easy to ban support for religious schools, creating a double burden on religious parents. They would be forced to pay taxes to support secular schools but would be unable to benefit from those taxes. The opposite tactic could also be used; tax money could

39. *Letters of Sidney and Beatrice Webb*, vol 2, 144.

40. Sidney Webb, "The Decline in the Birth-rate," Fabian tract 131, (London, 1906), 16-17. The previous quotes are from pages 4-5. Sanger quotes this tract in Chap. 9.

41. The Fabian tract on the birthrate was numbered 131. Tract number 133, "Socialism and Christianity," begins with a claim that "socialism is the necessary result of a sound Christianity." Rev. Percy Dearmer, "Socialism and Christianity," tract 133, (London, 1907), 3.

42. "The Decline in the Birth-rate," 19. He may have meant mystical "life force" religious ideas rather than historic Christianity. For an example, see Chap. X.

be used to control private schools. In 1896 Beatrice wrote that her husband was "not against helping voluntary or denominational schools in return for a measure of control, which is bound to grow."[43] At times the bigotry did slip out. The next year Beatrice quit the Manchester Conference of Women ("sensible and God-fearing folk") because they refused her demand that what she called "religious rites"—prayers before business meetings—be eliminated.

Sidney closed his report on the birthrate with a call for a "sharp turn" in policy to "avoid degeneration of type—that is, race deterioration, if not race suicide." (We take up race suicide in the next chapter.) Though they would later have a parting of the ways—partly because Wells, a sexual predator, was seducing the young daughters of prominent Fabians—both Wells and the Fabians continued to agree on one thing. The state must dictate who has children. Given their obsession with control, they had no choice. If the government runs a nation's economy and its social programs, it must also regulate its most important input—babies.[44]

Wells, Shaw and the Webbs illustrate how easy it was for political radicals to reconcile eugenics with liberalism, socialism or any other large and intrusive form of government. Reproduction simply becomes another area that the government plans and controls. But many 'establishment' eugenicists and businessmen were interested in merely preserving the status quo and far less eager to expand government. For such men, socialism appeared to be an enemy since it claimed to provide for all, fit and unfit. As they had with Wells, Sidney and Beatrice Webb again served as bridge builders. In September of 1910 a meeting occurred that was an ominous warning of things to come. The scene was a summer school sponsored by the Fabian Society. Attending as a eugenicist was a Dr. C. W. Saleeby. Beatrice described what happened.

> Perhaps one of the most important results of the School is the alliance between ourselves and Dr. Saleeby. The eugenicists have always been our bitter opponents on the ground that all attempts to alter environment are not only futile, but positively mischievous, as such improvements in environment diminish the struggle for existence and retard the elimination of the unfit. Eugenics have, in fact, been used as an argument against Socialism. Dr. Saleeby, who is one of the most prominent of the apostles, now joins not only the National Committee but the Fabian Society. We spent two days talking with him and eventually proved to him that changes in the environment were a necessary accompa-

niment to even negative eugenics, whereas positive eugenics can only be brought about by collective control and collective expenditure.[45]

In 1910, many eugenicists still had their eyes fixed on their old ideal, a state of nature in which failure led to death or fewer offspring (negative eugenics), while success led to health and many offspring (positive eugenics). As a result, they were suspicious of anything (such as socialism) that reduced the struggle for existence. Malthus had warned that a political system could become so benevolent it would be destroyed by the sheer *quantity* of people it produced. Though he was much less prone to speak out, Darwin had said much the same about the *quality* of people. By providing treatment for once fatal diseases, science was eliminating evolutionary selection. People who once died now lived.

But the problem went beyond declining death rates to what was, for these people, the chilling spectre of rising birth rates or increasing numbers of inferior people. If either socialism or the welfare state accomplished their publicly stated goals, the living conditions of the poor would improve dramatically. They would get better access to medical care, better living conditions and better paying jobs. They would thus be able to have more children and the children they had would be more likely to live to reproductive adulthood. If, as many eugenicists and socialists believed, the poor were inherently less talented than the affluent and better educated, then the evolutionary quality of the human race would decline. Some old school eugenists might long for the old days when poor babies died near the stench of open sewers, but no self-respecting socialist could advance such ideas. Yet, with the exception of the more dogmatic Marxists, socialists believed in both Malthus and Darwin.[46]

Paradoxically, the solution to the problems that were thought to be created by socialism were found in yet more socialism. The very evolutionary theory that both eugenicists and socialists put so much faith was proving to be almost infinitely flexible, capable of rationalizing virtually any social policy. (The vagueness of evolution is one of its chief attractions and primary flaws.) It could be used to justify an unregulated economy approximating a jungle-like state of nature (Social Darwinism). But it could also justify a highly centralized economy such as socialism or welfare-state liberalism.

When the nineteenth century began most industries were small and decentralized, often little more than

---

43. *Our Partnership*, 132.
44. An English socialist explains their reasoning in Chap. XIX.

45. *Our Partnership*, 460.
46. Sanger deals with Marxist opposition to Malthus and birth control in Chap. 7.

home-based crafts. By the century's end, industries such as steel and oil had grown enormously. They now spanned continents and employed tens of thousands of workers. Their efficiency and economy of scale drew much praise. Even their centralized control was said to be proof of the evolutionary principle that the higher an organism evolved, the more centralized its nervous system. Big was not only good, bigger was better.

Some said that the same principle was true of society. Much as the more evolved species had a highly centralized nervous system, so the more 'evolved' societies were said to need a highly centralized political system. The more laws a society had, the larger its bureaucracies and the more centralized the power of its government, the 'higher' it was. Once this idea was accepted, it was obvious that the crisis that had been created by the loss of natural selection could only be remedied by planned and scientifically controlled selection. (Their usual term for this was "intelligent.") Now that Nature no longer decided who lived and reproduced, Man (meaning a self-appointed elite) must make the proper decisions. That is why the language of such people is so filled with terms based on 'control' and 'plan"—birth control and planned parenthood being two of their favorites.

Looked at from another angle, this meant that Darwin's original model for progress—a fierce, jungle-like struggle—must be replaced by one much like a scientifically managed farm. Man the predator must become Man the domesticated animal. From this perspective, Malthus and Darwin were no longer a problem. Instead, they provided yet another rationale for what socialists and liberals like best, manipulating people.

Margaret Sanger provided a perfect example of just this sort of manipulation in her *My Fight for Birth Control*. In late autumn of 1913, she, her husband, and their three children sailed for Europe. Their first stop was Glasgow, where friends told them they could study the marvels of socialism in action at the city level. Here is her description of what she found.

> I went the rounds of the markets, the schools, the playgrounds, the laundries, bakeries and at last the houses. The excellent living quarters for the workers were held as an example for the rest of the world. For so many rooms, so much light, so many people to a square foot, no overcrowding allowed. For a one-child family, so many rooms; for a two-child family, so many more; three—and there the story closes.
>
> "Well," I asked," what happens when they have five or six children?"
>
> "Oh, they can't live here," replied the attendant. "They must live elsewhere."

> "But where?" said I. Conversation ceased. I was looked upon as a trouble-maker and not encouraged to look further."

Undeterred, Sanger did look further, only to discover that large families were forced into sub-standard housing far from socialism's wonderful public laundries and bakeries. Did Sanger protest this cruel way of dictating family size. Hardly. Her conclusion demonstrated that she fully understood and agreed with what the Fabians were doing even before she began her campaign for birth control. Those who look for a point at which the early Sanger—said to be concerned about the poor—was replaced by the later and evil Sanger, need look no further than this watershed event.

> Then I came face to face with the facts, and realized that only a controlled fertility in human beings can maintain any progress. No system of society depending for its continuation on intelligent humans can stand long unless it encourages the control of the birth rate and includes contraceptive knowledge as a right. Without it no system, no matter what its ideals, can withstand the overpowering force of uncontrolled, unrestricted fecundity. I was convinced of this when I left Glasgow.[47]

There was a final reason why both socialism and liberalism had to control births, one that had little to do with Malthus and Darwin. In order to produce future citizens who thought the way they wanted, both political systems must strip parents of the right to oversee their child's education. But the long-term effects of that policy were potentially disastrous. The more independent and responsible parents would resist encroachments on their rights and, if necessary, have fewer children in order to ensure that they had the resources to fight this loss of power (for example, with private schooling). That might cut down on religious troublemakers, but it would also reduce other productive elements. On the other hand, irresponsible parents might move in the opposite direction. Deprived of yet another parental burden, they would be all the more inclined to produce large families for the state to rear and train. The result would be more children from the very

---

47. Margaret Sanger, *My Fight for Birth Control,* 64. Sanger's description of Glasgow's housing policy was vague. Probably, more than two children gave working families no larger accommodations, and after several children, they were tossed out, allegedly to prevent "overcrowding." This pressure to have two children or less—at a time when the replacement birthrate for the British poor was about four children—meant that city officials intended to force on the working class a below-replacement birthrate leading over time to extinction—slow genocide.

people that the progressively inclined did not want to see become parents. That was bad, very bad.

Malthus had warned that utopias lead to overpopulation. In private, Darwin suggested that social improvements might bring racial degeneration. Socialism's reply was that was true only if those who ran society did nothing to control the quantity or quality of the population. Since they intended to do both, the improved living conditions that they doled out would cause no harm. Socialism and eugenics could be reconciled and human progress assured.[48]

In the United States, people with similar attitudes were coming to much the same conclusion, often with advice from Britain. In the fall of 1924, Margaret Sanger received a letter from Shaw that she would later quote. In it Shaw suggested that, "Birth control should be advocated for its own sake, on the general ground that the difference between voluntary, irrational, uncontrolled activity is the difference between an amoeba and a man; and if we really believe that the more highly evolved creature is the better we may as well act accordingly."[49]

With Fabian duplicity, Shaw didn't say who would be exercising that control, but Sanger would in a 1925 address to a Kiwanis Club that, given the nature of her audience, made no reference to socialism and spoke instead of the cost of keeping alive "the Diseased, Defective, Delinquent and Dependent." Her words suggest something very chilling—but no doubt true—that for those who considered themselves "enlightened" the debate was over, births must be regulated in some fashion or disaster would follow.

> It has already become the universal opinion of the most enlightened statesmen and scientists that population must be controlled. It must be controlled, not only because of the pressure of numbers upon the food supply, but because of the quality of the race as well.[50]

In the rest of her speech Sanger made it clear that she and the other "enlightened" wanted the government to do that controlling. And, like her Fabian counterparts in Britain, she would use "understatement," meaning lies, to conceal her true agenda from those she targeted (obviously not these Kiwanis). That explains the seeming contradiction we see in her writings between her loudly professed concern for overburdened poor mothers and her zeal to remove all such people from the face of the earth. Like Fabians, she did not hesitate to lie in order to achieve her goals. In truth, her loudly professed concern for poor mothers was utterly bogus. In the chapters that follow, we will examine precisely why Sanger and her American colleagues believed as they did.

—§§§—

48. For more detail see Chap. XIX.
49. Margaret Sanger, *Margaret Sanger, An Autobiography* (New York: W. W. Norton, 1938), 372.
50. Margaret Sanger, "Outline of Address at Kiwanis Club, Beacon, July 1925." Sanger/Library of Congress microfilm, LOC 130:25, 1-2.

VII

The Causes of
Race Superiority

1901

Dr. Edward A. Ross

Prominent Sociologist

For a case like this I can find no words so apt as "race suicide." There is no bloodshed, no violence, no assault of the race that waxes upon the race that wanes. The higher race quietly and unmurmuringly eliminates itself rather than endure individually the bitter competition it has failed to ward off from itself by collective action.

EDITOR

Originally an address to the American Academy of Political and Social Sciences, this article is best known for the first use of a term, *race suicide,* that soon became the focus of heated debate. Earlier in his speech, Dr. Ross had described the reasons he believed some races were superior. His Darwinian beliefs then forced him to ask whether those traits would enable a race to survive under every possible condition. Could a situation arise, he asked, that would allow an inferior (assumed to be Asian) race to defeat a superior (American) race? His answer reverberated through political debates for a generation and its effects are still felt today.

In her second autobiography, Sanger mentions reading a Ross article on, "the decline of the birth rate among the upper and educated classes and the increase among the unfit, the consequences of which were sure to be race suicide." In 1934 she took a tour of the Soviet Union along with Ross, whom she described as having an "impressive" personality as a "Nordic giant, six feet four."[1]

Edward A. Ross, "The Causes of Race Superiority." *Annals of the American Academy of Political and Social Science* 18 (1901), 67–89. Only the last portion is included.

—§§§—

1. Margaret Sanger, *Margaret Sanger, An Autobiography* (New York: W.W. Norton, 1938), 94, 434. Sanger claimed the article was in *Atlantic Monthly.* Although Ross had a number of articles in the magazine, I have been unable to find one with that theme. Perhaps Sanger confused her source and actually read a reprint of this article or one like it.

One question remains. Is the Superior Race as we have portrayed it, able to survive all competitions and expand under all circumstances? There is, I am convinced, one respect in which [the] very foresight and will power that mark the higher race dig a pit beneath its feet.

In the presence of the plenty produced by its triumphant energy the superior race forms what the economists call "a Standard of Comfort," and refuses to multiply save upon this plane. With his native ambition stimulated by the opportunity to rise and his natural foresight reinforced by education, the American, for example, overrules his strongest instincts and refrains from marrying or from increasing his family until he can realize his subjective standard of comfort or decency. The power to form and cling to such a standard is not only one of the noblest triumphs of reason over passion, but is, in sooth, the only sure hope for the elevation of the mass of men from the abyss of want and struggle. The progress of invention held out such a hope but it has proven a mockery. Steam and machinery, it is true, ease for a little the strain of population on resources; but if the birth-rate starts forward and the slack is soon taken up by the increase of mouths, the final result is simply more people living on the old plane. The rosy glow thrown upon the future by progress in the industrial arts proves but a false dawn unless the common people acquire new wants and raise the plane upon which they multiply.

Now this rising standard, which alone can pilot us toward the Golden Age, is a fatal weakness when a race comes to compete industrially with a capable race that multiplies on a lower plane. Suppose, for example, Asiatics flock to this country and, enjoying equal opportunities under our laws, learn our methods and compete actively with Americans. They may be able to produce and therefore earn in the ordinary occupations, say three-fourths as much as Americans; but if their standard of life is only half as high, the Asiatic will marry before the American feels able to marry. The Asiatic will rear two children while his competitor feels able to rear but one. The Asiatic will increase his children to six under conditions that will not encourage the American to raise more than four. Both, perhaps, are forward-looking and influenced by the worldly prospects of their children; but where the Oriental is satisfied with the outlook[,] the American, who expects to school his children longer and place them better, shakes his head.

Now, to such a competition there are three possible results. First, the American, becoming discouraged, may relinquish his exacting standard of decency and begin to multiply as freely as the Asiatic. This, however, is likely only to occur among the more reckless and worthless elements of our population. Second, the Asiatic may catch up our wants as well as our arts, and acquire the higher standard and lower rate of increase of the American. This is just what contact and education are doing for the French Canadians in New England, for the immigrants in the West, and for the negro in some parts of the South; but the members of a great culture race like the Chinese show no disposition, even when scattered sparsely among us, to assimilate to us or to adopt our standards. Not until their self-complacency has been undermined at home and an extensive intellectual ferment has taken place in China itself will the Chinese become assimilable elements. Thirdly, the standards may remain distinct, the rates of increase unequal, and the silent replacement of Americans by Asiatics go on unopposed until the latter monopolize all industrial occupations, and Americans shrink to a superior caste able perhaps by virtue of its genius, its organization, and its vantage of position to retain for a while its hold on government, education, finance, and the direction of industry, but hopelessly beatened and displaced as a race. In other words, the American farm hand, mechanic and operative might wither away before the heavy influx of a prolific race from the Orient, just as in classic times the Latin husbandman vanished before the endless stream of slaves poured into Italy by her triumphant generals.

For a case like this I can find no words so apt as "race suicide." There is no bloodshed, no violence, no assault of the race that waxes upon the race that wanes. The higher race quietly and unmurmuringly eliminates itself rather than endure individually the bitter competition it has failed to ward off from itself by collective action. The working classes gradually delay marriage and restrict the size of the family as the opportunities hitherto reserved for their children are eagerly snapped up by the numerous progeny of the foreigner. The prudent, self-respecting natives first cease to expand, and then, as the struggle for existence grows sterner and the outlook for their children darker, they fail even to recruit their own numbers. It is probably the visible narrowing of the circle of opportunity through the infiltration of Irish and French Canadians that has brought so low the native birth-rate in New England.

However this may be, it is certain that if we venture to apply to the American people of to-day the series of tests of superiority I have set forth to you at such length, the result is most gratifying to our pride. **It is true that our average of energy and character is lowered by the presence in the South of several millions of an inferior race. It is true that the last twenty years have diluted us with masses of fecund but beaten humanity from the hovels of far Lombardy and Galicia. It is true that our free land is gone and our opportunities will henceforth attract immigrants chiefly from the humbler strata of East European peoples.** Yet, while there are here problems that only high statesmanship can solve, I believe there is at the present moment no people in the world that is, man for man, equal to the Americans in capacity and efficiency. We stand now at the moment when the gradual westward migration has done its work. The tonic selections of the frontier have brought us as far as they can bring us. The testing individualizing struggle with the wilderness has developed in us what it would of body, brain and character.

Moreover, free institutions and universal education have keyed to the highest tension the ambitions of the American. He has been chiefly farmer and is only beginning to expose himself to the deteriorating influences of city and factory. He is now probably at the climax of his energy and everything promises that in the centuries to come he is destined to play a brilliant and leading role on the stage of history.

—§§§—

Perpetuating Mediocrity

Strongly attracted as I am by the hopeful and noble views that have been expressed, I cannot but feel that Dr. [D. Collin] Wells's is right. The theory that races are virtually equal in capacity leads to such monumental follies as lining the valleys of the South with the bones of half a million picked whites in order to improve the condition of four million unpicked blacks. I see no reason why races may not differ as much in moral and intellectual traits as obviously they do in bodily traits.... Consider the higher education and employment of women. A class of girls finishing a high school or normal are examined. Those that win high marks receive first-class certificates, get well placed, and are quite likely not to marry. Those with low marks find the extra-matrimonial path barred, and so nearly all marry and perpetuate their mediocrity. Is not this something to think about?[2]

—PROF. EDWARD A. ROSS, UNIV. OF WISCONSIN, 1907

Blind Breeders

In the masses of the Orient, which steam has made next-door neighbors of ours, the family customs and the status of women are such that the shortage, overcrowding, and economic stress have no appreciable effect in checking the flow of babies. With these folk economic necessity does not prompt to birth control.... Once a people *adapts* its production of children to the economic prospect, the free inflow of blindly fecund immigrants has a most calamitous effect upon its self-perpetuation.... For this behavior the writer coined twenty years ago the phase "race suicide," which unfortunately has come to be applied to every form of prudence in the matter of family.... During the two or three centuries that will be required for the practice of adaptive fecundity to become general among mankind, unhindered immigration, by favoring the blind breeders, would enable the stupid and inert peoples to poach on the preserves of the bright and aspiring peoples.[3]

—PROF. EDWARD A ROSS, 1921

Gradually Extending the Scope of Sterilization

One of these experts, E. A. Ross, professor of sociology at the University of Wisconsin and a staunch Progressive, asserted that the current of favorable opinion on the sterilization of the unfit had become very strong in recent years among sociologists, philanthropists, charity workers and penologists. With characteristic tough-mindedness, Ross wrote that "For my own part, I am entirely in favor of it. The objections to it are essentially sentimental, and will not bear inspection. Sterilization is not nearly so terrible as hanging a man, and the chances of sterilizing the fit are not nearly so great, as are the chances of hanging the innocent. In introducing the policy, the wedge should have a very thin end indeed. Sterilization should at first be applied only to extreme cases, where the commitments and the record pile up an overwhelming case. As the public becomes accustomed to it, and it is seen to be salutary and humane, it will be possible gradually to extend its scope until it fills its legitimate sphere of application.[4]

—RUDOLF J. VECOLI, *WISCONSIN MAGAZINE OF HISTORY*

Preaching the Gospel

Philanthropy and sectarian propaganda cite the golden rule and the Biblical command to preach the Gospel, forgetting that, among races as well as among individuals, the law of self-preservation antedates even the behest to love one's neighbor.[5]

—M. J. DEE, CHINESE IMMIGRATION, 1878

2. Edward A. Ross in a "Social Darwinism" discussion in *American Journal of Sociology* 12 (Mar. 1907), 715. 'High marks' girls are discussed in chapters XV and XVI. Much of today's feminist contempt for 'homemaking' mothers was born in this era and builds on elitist ideas such as these.

3. Edward Alsworth Ross, "The Menace of Migrating Peoples," *Century Magazine* 102 (May 1921), 132, 134. Today, a similar attitude underlies the zeal many industrialized countries have for funding 'family planning' programs in Asia and Africa— and for pressuring them to legalize abortion.

4. Rudolph J. Vecoli, "Sterilization: A Progressive Measure?" *Wisconsin Magazine of History* 43 (Spring 1960), 196. Quoting the Milwaukee *Sentinel* for Dec. 23, 1906. Notice how East saw the public as something to be manipulated with Fabian-like guile. "Sentimental" is how Ross and his colleagues typically described the beliefs of devout Catholics, Jews and Protestants. The difference between hanging and sterilizing, however, is not merely sentimental. Those East would sterilize have committed no crime and are being punished merely because they might do something (have children) that East and his colleagues assume as *their* right. East thus wants an end to any pretense of "equal justice under law." Fortunately, the "sentimental" public had a better understanding of law and never adopted his progressive point of view, requiring of his modern counterparts to abandon sterilization and turn to abortion legalization. The Supreme Court's role in legalizing sterilization and its religious opposition will be taken up in Chap. XXIII, "The Religious Are Astir."

5. M. J. Dee, "Chinese Immigration," *North American Review* 126 (May/June 1878), 508. Dee was attacking devout Christians who supported Chinese immigration as an aid to evangelism, ignoring what the author saw as the demands of racial "self-preservation," which he later links to "the natural law of evolution." This illustrates quite well how historic Christianity led to broad racial acceptance in an era when such attitudes were rare. In contrast, evolutionary thought led Ross, Dee and numerous others to regard Asians as biological foes.

VIII

Alarmed about the Future

1895–1919

Theodore Roosevelt

More than perhaps any other President, Theodore Roosevelt loved to live at the center of controversy. He did what he believed right, whatever the consequences. To give but one example, in 1901 he created a media fire storm by inviting the nation's most prominent black leader, Booker T. Washington, to dine at the White House. Meeting Washington in some public capacity might have been tolerable. But having him for dinner created an impression of social equality that all too many white Americans found upsetting.

In much the same fashion, taking the bull by the horns, Roosevelt made the race suicide issue his own. He spoke so often and so directly on the subject that he was able to give it his own much more tolerant meaning. When Edward Ross had written of race suicide (in the previous chapter), it had a heavy racist flavor—particularly against Asians—and offered no solution for the endangered race. In Roosevelt's hands, however, the term became broad and nationalistic rather than narrow and snobbish. Even more important, Roosevelt offered answers to the problem that his opponents found all too clear. Since Roosevelt's critics often twisted his words, it is necessary to go back to what he was saying even before Ross published his ground-breaking article.

One of Roosevelt's early comments came during the summer of 1895 in the *North American Review,* a paper published by and for the nation's New England elite. Reviewing a book that he disliked, he noted:

> To increase greatly a race must be prolific, and there is no curse so great as the curse of barrenness, whether for a nation or an individual. When a people gets to the position even now occupied by the mass of the French and by sections of the New Englanders, where the death rate surpasses the birth rate, then that race is not only fated for extinction but it deserves extinction. When the capacity and desire for fatherhood and motherhood is lost the race goes down, and should go down; and we

need to have the plainest kind of speaking addressed to those individuals who fear to bring children into the world.[1]

A year and a half later, Roosevelt reviewed a book more to his liking, one that described how civilizations grow and decay. Adding his own views to those of the author, Roosevelt saw in the more civilized nations of his day "a certain softness of fibre." One characteristic of that softness particularly bothered him:

> Most ominous of all, there has become evident, during the last two generations, a very pronounced tendency among the most highly civilized races, and among the most highly civilized portions of all races, to lose the power of multiplying, and even to decrease; so much so as to make the fears of the disciples of Malthus a century ago seem rather absurd to the dweller in France or New England.[2]

After the turn of the century and with the publicity that surrounded East's article about "race suicide," Roosevelt became increasingly blunt about what he considered the nation's most pressing problem. In the fall of 1902, he wrote to a woman in Philadelphia:

> Of course no one quality makes a good citizen, and no one quality will save a nation. But there are certain great qualities for the lack of which no amount of intellectual brilliancy or of material prosperity or of easiness of life can atone, and the lack of which shows decadence and corruption in the nation, just as much as if they were produced by selfishness and coldness and ease-loving laziness among comparatively poor people as if they are produced by vicious and frivolous luxury in the rich. If the men of the nation are not anxious to work in many different ways, with all their might and strength, and ready and able to fight at need, and anx-

---

1. T. Roosevelt, "Kidd's *Social Evolution," North American Review* 161 (July 1895), 97.
2. T. Roosevelt, "The Law of Civilization and Decay," *Forum* (Jan. 1897), 579.

ious to be fathers of families, and if the women do not recognize that the greatest thing for any woman is to be a good wife and mother, why, that nation has cause to be alarmed about its future.[3]

In public, Roosevelt was equally to the point. In March of 1905 he gave a speech to the National Congress of Mothers expressing sympathy for those who "through no fault of their own" could not have children. But he went on to state that "the man or woman" who simply avoids having children "merits contempt as hearty as any visited on the soldier who runs away in battle."[4]

Roosevelt's message did not soften over time. In a 1913 magazine article he blasted those so wealthy they were "in no danger of the poorhouse" but who nevertheless preferred "automobiles and lapdogs" to children and put "vapid excitement above the performance of the highest duty and the attainment of the highest excitement."[5]

Unable to refute his charges of decadence and selfishness, Roosevelt critics focused on misrepresenting what he said. Contrary to those who laid all the blame on the new roles for women, Roosevelt noted:

So I do not believe that, in itself, the growth of independence among women has anything to do with the trouble. By law and custom the Frenchwoman stands towards the man in a wholly subordinate and inferior position compared with the American woman, and yet it is in France that the evil has had its worst development.[6]

Nor was Roosevelt, as his opponents claimed, intent on having babies at any price. "Criminals," he said, and "shiftless and worthless people" should not "marry and have families which they are unable to bring up properly." "Reckless marriages" and couples who "thoughtlessly have multitudes of children who they are unable to bring up properly" also incurred his wrath as did "the man who forces upon an unfit wife excessive and unlimited childbearing."[7]

Before the race suicide controversy heated up, the debate about declining birthrates was relatively low key and confined to a few, almost all of whom were unwilling to take steps that some might find painful. But after

Roosevelt took the issue up, it became hotly debated, particularly among affluent New Englanders proud of their careful cataloged descent from the region's Puritan founders. Roosevelt, whose own roots were Old Dutch, did not hesitate to attack them:

We have heard much of the New England conscience—the Puritan conscience. It is lamentable to see this Puritan conscience, the New England conscience, so atrophied, so diseased and warped, the unpardonable crime against the race is the crime of race suicide.[8]

Of course, a genuine "Puritan conscience" had nothing to do with the early twentieth century obsession with national power. For Christians (Puritan or otherwise), children were a gift from God and uniquely valuable whatever their race because, of all the things a man or woman could do, only a child was eternal. Children were thus valuable in themselves, not for what they did or did not do for a nation. That attitude wasn't absent from Roosevelt's thinking as a father, but it played only a minor role in his political rhetoric. Like many in his day, Roosevelt's basic ethical framework was Victorian rather than Christian. Duty to one's country, race and family had replaced obedience to God. Fortunately, Roosevelt's sense of duty was not the narrow, 'my country right or wrong' variety. He genuinely believed in moral virtues and believed that those who displayed those virtues deserved to be rewarded while those who violated them deserved a dismal fate. That was why he could say:

The New England of the future will belong, and ought to belong, to the descendants of the immigrants of yesterday and to-day, because the descendants of the Puritans "have lacked the courage to live," have lacked the conscience which ought to make men and women fulfil the primary law of their being.[9]

Roosevelt's willingness to extend an open hand to new immigrants won their respect and support. This was most apparent in the Presidential campaign of 1912 when the fiercely independent Roosevelt ran against both his own Republican party and his usual foes in the Democratic party. As historian John Higham noted: "On the Democratic side Woodrow Wilson labored throughout the campaign under the embarrassing handicap of having to repudiate over and over again the contemptuous phrases he had written about southern and eastern European immigrants in his *History of the American People* a decade before." As a result, "Roosevelt captured the imagination and the loyalty of a large proportion of southern and eastern European votes. In three out of four New York City districts that gave Roosevelt a plurality,

3. T. Roosevelt, *Addresses and Presidential Messages, 1902–1904* (New York, 1904), 266. This Oct. 18, 1902 letter was to a Mrs. Bessie Van Vorst.

4. T. Roosevelt, *Presidential Addresses and State Papers, April 7, 1904 to May 9, 1905*, (New York, 1910), 238.

5. T. Roosevelt, "A Premium on Race Suicide," *Outlook* (Sept. 27, 1913), 164.

6. T. Roosevelt, "Race Decadence," *Outlook* (Apr. 8, 1911), 768.

7. T. Roosevelt, "A Premium on Race Suicide," *Outlook* (Sept. 27, 1913), 164.

8. T. Roosevelt, "Twisted Eugenics," *Outlook* (Jan. 3, 1914), 32.

9. T. Roosevelt, "Twisted Eugenics," *Outlook* (Jan. 3, 1914), 32.

Slavs and Russian Jews constituted the great majority of the electorate."[10]

Woodrow Wilson on Immigration

The census of 1890 showed the population of the country increased to 62,622,250, an addition of 12,466,467 within the decade. Immigrants poured steadily in as before, but with an alteration of stock which students of affairs marked with uneasiness. Throughout the century men of the sturdy stocks of the North of Europe had made up the main strain of foreign blood which was every year added to the vital working force of the country, or else men of the Latin-Gallic stocks of France and northern Italy; but now there came multitudes of men of the lower class from the south of Italy and men of the meaner sort out of Hungary and Poland, men out of the ranks where there was neither skill nor energy nor any initiative of quick intelligence; and they came in numbers which increased from year to year, as if the countries of the south of Europe were disburdening themselves of the more sordid and hapless elements of the population, the men whose standards of life and of work were such as the American workman had never dreamed of hitherto.[11] —WOODROW WILSON, 1902

To better understand the era, it helps to look at what well-known writer of the day was saying. A later generation would have said that Henry Adams—a descendant of two U.S. Presidents—spent much of his life trying to 'find himself.' Adams put it differently. As his autobiography explained, his life was a series of experiences intended to provide for *The Education of Henry Adams.*

Adams felt as strongly as any member of New England's old moneyed class the pessimism that dominated his generation and, like many of them, he confused their decline with the decline of the nation as a whole. Like his brother, Brooks Adams (another historian), he believed that democracy in the United States was doomed to decay and collapse. In 1910 he wrote a book predicting that the world would end in 1921. Speaking of the race suicide controversy and even exaggerating it to the point that the existence of the entire human race seemed at stake, in 1905 Henry Adams wrote:

> No honest historian can take part with—or against—the forces he has to study. To him even the extinction of the human race should be merely a fact to be grouped with other vital statistics. No doubt every one in society

discussed the subject, impelled by President Roosevelt if by nothing else, and the surface current of social opinion seemed set as strongly in one direction as the silent undercurrent of social action ran in the other; but the truth lay somewhere unconscious in the woman's breast.[12]

In a single sentence, Adams had summarized the situation as it existed in his day. As much as it might wish otherwise, social opinion could not deny the logic of Roosevelt's arguments. As a result, fashionable society was torn by two opposing currents. The surface current demanded that they forsake their easy decadence and at least have enough children to replace themselves. That was why Roosevelt could openly demand larger families, while his critics often wrote anonymously.[13] But underneath that current was another favoring few or no children.

In the first decade of the twentieth century, it was uncertain which current would dominate. The final answer lay, as Adams pointed out, "somewhere unconscious in the woman's breast." For scientifically inclined men, the race suicide debate (with its evolutionary ramifications) was an abstraction, dealing with what the human race would be far in the future. For pleasure-oriented men, its impact was limited. More children would have little impact on their careers but would reduce their after-hour pleasures. For those who, like Henry Adams, had a pessimistic historical perspective, it was yet another illustration of how civilizations decline and fall, something to be accepted whether one liked it or not. Even the men who opposed small families stood on shaky ground. Their enthusiasm for large families—and Roosevelt genuinely loved his children—was often attacked by feminists because men as wealthy as they could have it all. They could combine fatherhood with a successful career *and* a lively life outside the home. Perhaps that was why Roosevelt did not equate the sacrifices of a father with those of a mother, choosing instead to compare motherhood to military service.

For society and career women, however, the race suicide issue was of critical importance, for it was they who would bear the brunt of the cost of childbearing in lost social pleasures and mislaid careers. The attitude of these

10. John Higham, *Strangers in the Land* (New Brunswick: Rutgers University Press, 1988), 190.

11. Woodrow Wilson, *A History of the American People* (New York:1902), V: 212–13.

12. Henry Adams, *The Education of Henry Adams,* (Boston: 1918), 447.

13. Commenting on a similarly anonymous article by a "A Childless Wife," the feminist historian, Linda Gordon, noted: "Indeed, I have found no signed article that discussed the issue from a personal standpoint." Linda Gordon, *Woman's Body, Woman's Right* (New York: Penguin, 1976), 435, note 53. The next chapter provides an example of this sort of article.

women was not helped by two strange events that, according to Henry Adams, took place about 1903:

> An elderly man, trying only to learn the law of social inertia and the limits of social divergence, could not compel the Superintendent of the Census to ask every young woman whether she wanted children, and how many; he could not even require of an octogenarian Senate the passage of a law obliging every woman, married or not, to bear one baby—at the expense of the Treasury—before she was thirty years old, under penalty of solitary confinement for life; yet these were vital statistics in more senses than all that bore the name, and tended more directly to the foundation of a serious society in the future.[14]

This foolish and long forgotten attempt to legislate motherhood accomplished little. But the social climate that inspired it had a profound impact on feminism. As the feminist historian Linda Gordon noted: "The race suicide attacks led feminists to reject the cult of motherhood, which they had previously shared with more conventional women." As a result, what had been fairly broad movement to provide the vote for all (white) women began to narrow substantially. **As Gordon put it, "the race suicide movement was an additional factor identifying feminism almost exclusively with the aspirations of the more privileged women of the society."[15]** Like their male peers, these newly radicalized feminists resented social pressure to have larger families. The roots of the present-day feminist cries about 'forced motherhood' are rooted this era. The accompanying feminist

---

14. Henry Adams, *The Education of Henry Adams,* (Boston: 1918), 447. An extensive search through the *Congressional Record,* did not find evidence of this elderly man's attempt to legislate motherhood. His efforts probably never became a bill.

15. Linda Gordon, *Woman's Body, Woman's Right* (New York: Penguin, 1976), 142, 158.

criticism of male attitudes was unfair. In general, the men that they knew and married were as disinterested in large families as the feminists themselves. They simply paid a small cost when children did arrive.

As we saw with the East article, affluent professionals responded to accusations that they were having too few children for selfish reasons by appealing to what they called their 'standard of comfort.' More children, they said, would adversely affect the quality of their lives. Feminists responded with another 'quality' argument by insisting that their limited amount of childbearing be judged by the *quality* of their children rather than their *quantity.* Roosevelt, they said, was calling for more children with little concern for what those children would become. They, on the other hand, wanted "fewer but better children." The argument made excellent rhetoric, but it was not exactly true. Roosevelt had a great deal to say about quality. But when he called for quality he meant character traits such as responsibility, resourcefulness and courage, things virtually all American parents could pass on to their children. What the feminists meant by quality were cultural traits that were created by expensive amenities at home, that were taught in elite private schools, and that were ultimately stamped on young adults by Ivy League universities and elite women's colleges. Quality in that sense was expensive. It could only be afforded by a few and then only when families were kept small.

As a result, Roosevelt's warnings about race suicide and his calls for larger families were not well received by many members of his own social class. They would win him the undying enmity of powerful and proud elements of American society and enmity that is still reflected in the bias of much present-day scholarship. An example of their attitudes will be examined in the next chapter.

IX

'Race Suicide' and Common Sense

1903

Paterfamilias

Author well-to-do but anonymous

The young couple who get married in the city or the small village at this day have become accustomed to many things with which they are not willing to part. They have learned to dress well, to have expensive pleasures, the theatre, concerts. visits, and the like, which have been inspirations in their lives. They do not look forward to a life of self-sacrifice. . . . If one or two children are born, it is considered enough among those who are intelligent and even tolerably educated.

EDITOR

Theodore Roosevelt denounced the low birthrates of the nation's affluent New England elite in their own magazine, the *North American Review*. In 1903, his opponents used that same magazine to attack him. In this chapter, a critic—who preferred to remain anonymous—defended his way of life and that of his peers.

Perhaps the most revealing comment came when the author wrote: "If a time should come when we had to give up our present style of living (which, practically, means our friends, since in that event we would not and could not continue present relations with them), I would consider it, perhaps, the most serious day of my life." The circle of people in which he moved, he was admitting, was so self-centered that if he and his wife had a another child and could no long afford season tickets to the theater, "present relations" with their "friends" would cease. That and the general shallowness of his intellect illustrate why the country suffered little harm when those like him died out, to be replaced by Russian Jews, Italian Catholics, and subsequent waves of immigrants from Asia and Latin America.

Paterfamilias, "'Race Suicide' and Common Sense." *North American Review* 176 (June, 1903), 892–900. The magazine, now published at the University of Northern Iowa, has no record of the author's name.

—§§§—

I am going to express some convictions, based on experience, concerning the recent revival of interest in large families caused by the publication of a book by two women, with a preface by President Roosevelt, in which be issued his ukase against "race suicide." I have read the book very earnestly and confess to great disappointment. It is the well meant attempt of two women, born and reared in an atmosphere of wealth and luxury, to enter the domain of the wage-earner, with which, and its many and intricate problems they were unfamiliar, and, after a few days or weeks of observation and experience, express not only their ideas of certain great and fundamental problems, but, in addition, on the basis of slight and undigested data, to issue a document of extraordinary character in which the entire social and business organization of the country is attacked. I do not dispute the facts they allege. These could be duplicated a thousand times. But facts must be studied in relation to other facts. Deductions are drawn which to me are entirely inconclusive, and which betray ignorance concerning the fundamentals of social life and the history of its development. I have for many years been laboring privately and publicly in the interests of many kinds of social reform, and I find that our worst enemies are the emotional people who, in an earnest desire to help us, make statements which are either false or are based on information so slight as to be negligible. In any event, I cannot see how raising more children is a cure for the many undoubted existing evils, certainly not for those expressly stated in the book in question.

I should not, however, have paid much attention either to the book or to the prefatory letter of endorsement by the President, had it not been that almost daily of late there has been published a letter from the President to some parent of a large family, congratulating him on the number of his offspring, and giving expression to sentiments of one sort or another which, in their essence, amount to this: that the nearer Americans approach the physical status of rabbits the more patriotic they become. If their meaning is not misunderstood by the public, these letters indicate an ignorance of actual conditions in this country, which is all the more regrettable in the man who is the chief servant of the nation, and whose opinions have so much weight not only in legislation but in directing public sentiment.

The President's plain meaning is, that the larger the family the better, regardless of almost any other conditions. "This is the stuff that good Americans are made of," he says in a recent letter. In its last analysis, this means that women are to be judged by no other standard than the number of children they produce. The mother of twenty-four children is a high-priestess of the race: the mother of none is a cipher. Apparently, according to this doctrine, virginity is a crime; and, since reproduction is the sole aim, it does not appear that the marriage relation need be considered as absolutely necessary. I am aware that this is not what the President means, and that he would not stand for such a proposition a moment; but I claim that it is a possible deduction from his philosophy.

I was raised in an atmosphere where it was considered that the teachings of the ancient writers of the Bible are as binding in our day as in theirs, in certain respects. I remember that, although I was taught that every word in the Bible was written by the finger of God and should be implicitly obeyed, there were certain things which we constantly violated. For instance, we ate pork, which, I noticed, was expressly prohibited; but I was put off with the explanation that these things concerned the Jews only. I never found exactly, though I tried to find, which of the things enjoined in the Pentateuch were binding on the Jews and not on us, nor by what principle the differentiation was to be made.[1]

But I grew up believing, as did the great mass of the people of the country at that time, in certain selected texts and precepts, and among these the order to "multiply and replenish the earth" was believed and practised. There were large families in my day, and children were habitually referred to as "gifts from the Lord"; but I remember

---

1. Editor: Despite the high opinion this author has of his critical skills, his Biblical knowledge was limited. The applicability of Jewish dietary laws to Christians was a major issue in the book of Acts.

that the men did not seem to be particularly happy after three or four had appeared, and that the lives of the women, even those who were of education and refinement were often almost on a level with those of the slave.

I have not forgotten the day when there were women of culture and refinement who had ten children, who did most of the sewing and housework, and when, if there was more than a single servant in the family, it was a notable thing. I can remember that the lives of those women were lives of pain, anxiety and toil. I cannot remember in my youth a woman of thirty who was not accounted old, and I have verified this many times by looking over family albums. Women of thirty to-day whether married or single, are considered young, and there are plenty who at the age of forty-five have the bloom and beauty of youth. That was something unknown in my boyhood; and it is unknown in a great portion of this country to-day, more's the pity!

The problems that confront the married pair of to-day are essentially different from those of thirty years ago—not to say a century ago, when the ambition of most married people was said, to be to get "an acre of land and a baby a year." Cradles no longer are included in the equipment of the bride. The young couple who get married to-day must meet the problems that face themselves, and not those which met their ancestors whom they are urged to emulate. The social problem is the greatest. It is of no sort of use to deny that, rightly or wrongly, there is at present a scale of living adopted in all grades of society that is far more expensive than that which prevailed a generation ago. I do not refer so much to the rich or the well-to-do, but the grade of society where the man of very limited means has occupied and expects to occupy a position of comfort and enjoyment. Much of the increase is due to modern inventions, and to the relative cheapness of what were once esteemed luxuries but are now looked on as merely the common comforts. Partly, the result is due to the fact that woman has become "emancipated," and, instead of being solely and only a "breeder of sinners," has launched out into many vocations and has become a wage-earner. The woman who can earn money can spend it, That is a proposition so self-evident that I do not care to enlarge on it, especially to married men. It is true that, in many instances, the money thus earned is devoted to the most laudable purposes, such as the support of dependent relatives; but, in the majority of cases, it is spent on the women or girls themselves, and it is spent principally for personal adornment. This is not in my opinion a crime. In an age when the love for the beautiful is growing, when the public taste for the best things is being rapidly developed, it is not at all to the discredit of any person to wish to be well-clothed and to make a good appearance. In fact, this is the natural condition which long had general acceptation. It was repressed, so far as Anglo-Saxons are concerned, to a very great extent, by the Puritan domination which was so long exercised all over this country, and from which we are just now becoming emancipated.

I am glad the emancipation has come. I can remember, when my mother did not have, on an average, one new dress a year, and when a really nice one was supposed to last for ten. She had been reared in a home of comfort, but she married a clergyman of great spiritual qualities and little earning power, and she was offered up as a constant sacrifice on the altar of family development. I do not say that she regretted having a large family. She would not willingly have spared one of her loved ones; but I do know that some of them were not wanted at the time they came, and that twelve years of constant child-bearing reduced her to the physical wreck which she has remained for thirty years. Yet she was looked upon in her younger days as the typical wife and mother. I can testify that she was so in all the virtues; but that she suffered untold agonies, and does to this day, for the sake of bringing a large brood into the world, is undoubted.

The young couple who get married in the city or the small village at this day have become accustomed to many things with which they are not willing to part. They have learned to dress well, to have expensive pleasures, the theatre, concerts. visits, and the like, which have been inspirations in their lives. They do not look forward to a life of self-sacrifice. They want to retain these things. They have had a little home fitted up, and they do not want to give it up; and as usually the husband has all he can do to support two there is little anxiety to increase the number. If one or two children are born, it is considered enough among those who are intelligent and even tolerably educated. There is no room for more; because, in the first place, there is no money and because the wife does not want to care for more. If she has a single servant, she finds that her whole time must be taken up with the children; and if she is to have a large brood, she will either have to give up all expectation of living in the social atmosphere of her friends or the family will be plunged into debt. The result is, that families are small and are growing smaller. The wives are no longer pack-mules, but are getting some of the comforts of life. Why shouldn't they?

This is not the time or place to go into a broad discussion of the function of the sexual relation which is the basis of society. That has been set forth at great length by biologists, and receives more attention now from sociologists than at any other time. If the relations between the sexes were absolutely unrestrained, we should have a much larger number of children born than at present, though fewer would probably survive. If the sexual relations between husbands and wives were unrestrained, the same would be true in only less measure. We all know that as a matter of fact such is not the case. Is this wrong?

The President says it is, and constantly impresses his views on the public. There have been a few voices raised in approbation, but not one among them is a woman's. On the contrary, many protests have been made, and notably by the sex which is urged to bear all the burdens of over-population.

We may as well discuss this proposition from a common sense point of view. It is well known from vital statistics that the greatest mortality occurs among infants less than five years old. This is due to several causes—to diseases peculiar to infants, to prenatal influences, to lack of proper care and nourishment consequent upon poverty; but the fact is that in any large family there are almost always a number of deaths before the children reach maturity. It may be said, therefore, to be mathematically certain that in any large family there are some babies born only to die very soon. That is not an encouraging thought to any parent. On the other hand, it is true to a mathematical demonstration that where an income is fixed and in the great majority of cases in this country the income seldom increases, the whole must be divided among the greater number to the loss of those who were present before the new children came. It used to be said that it did not cost anything to raise a baby, but that on the contrary it was an investment. Such a proposition can no longer be maintained. Every baby costs a great deal of money. If the father is in any way able, he gets a good physician and a competent nurse—a trained nurse if possible; while all sorts of sanitary and other preparations must be made and maintained which involve expense. **Each baby cramps a little all that have come before it, with the result that the mother and father are soon obliged to sacrifice themselves almost entirely on the family altar. They must give up their comforts and pleasures; the mother must give up often even the necessities of life and take up its worst burdens in order that the children shall not suffer.** A death in the family is a double calamity, since the extortionate cost of modern burial is one of the crying evils, but one which cannot be ignored.

It makes me sick to look at friends of mine who ten years ago were young and happy, and are now prematurely old and wan and sad. The young fellow who used to have the elastic step and the bright laugh, is now gaunt and dyspeptic, and has populistic views of life. His wife who was such a pretty girl, whom we all liked so well, who played and sang so nicely, and was the charm of any social gathering, now looks like a little old hen. Her face is careworn, her look is haunted; she betrays every evidence of being drained mentally, physically and spiritually, to minister to four or five youngsters who must have "the best" of things, and who are lucky to get enough to make a decent appearance.

I presume that I am as fond a father as ever lived. I have four children; and if any of them were not welcome when they came, not one of them would be spared on any account. It happens that we are able to care for four, not quite in the style in which two could have been maintained, but to all intents and purposes quite well enough for them, and sufficiently well for us to maintain our social position, which is very dear to us, though to some such a statement may seem folly. **If a time should come when we had to give up our present style of living (which, practically, means our friends, since in that event we would not and could not continue present relations with them), I would consider it, perhaps, the most serious day of my life. So far as can be judged at present, the only thing that might threaten such an event would be the appearance say of a couple of more children.** I presume there are those who will think that this is an ignoble statement; but it is not only true, but it is true of about every family of which I have any personal acquaintance except in those rather numerous instances where there are no children at all. Nothing is sadder to me than a large family except one with no children at all. I am not in favor of race suicide, but I claim that the man who raises two, three or four children is doing all that ought to be expected of him, and probably in most cases a little more.

Why?

Because I foresee that I what has taken place industrially in the last thirty years or less is going to continue increasingly. The race for existence is going to be harder and the difficulties in the way are going to become much greater. As the great industrial and mercantile businesses of the country are constantly accumulating in the hands of a few corporations, it seems likely that less and less will a young man have a chance in life in a business of his own. If he is to be anything more than a hewer of wood and a drawer of water, it must needs be that he become fitted for the race in the best manner possible. Perhaps his best chance will be with the great corporations where only experts are wanted in the paying positions. It is even now a difficult question for the man with a fairly good income—say five thousand dollars in the cities and two thousand in the villages—to provide for a family of four children and give them the social status, intellectual atmosphere, and educational advantages which shall fit them for the swift race now in progress; and there is every reason to believe that the race is going to be harder in the future. If this is so, it simply means that bringing more children into the world than we can properly care for means death for some and a state of social degeneracy for the rest; or, at best, careers in which there will be nothing but a constant struggle, with the chances very much against them.

In point of fact, I have yet to see any reason in the world for a man bringing into the world a larger number of children than he is able to care for. On the contrary, there is every reason against this course. I am aware that there are many persons in the country who think that the sexual relation is a function designed solely for the propagation of the human race, and that nothing whatever should be allowed to interfere with this manifest purpose.

I deny this.

I deny it on the ground that it is a mere assumption, for which there has never been adduced the least proof. I deny it on the ground that it is contrary to human experience. I deny it on the ground that, although the marriage relation is designed partly for the propagation of the race, such is not its chief function, since the same result can be attained without marriage, and originally was so attained. **I hold that marriage is mainly for the highest good of the two individuals concerned, and that the rearing of children is only incidental and to be considered only as it adds to their happiness.** I deny that marriage is solely an institution for the promotion of self-sacrifice and misery and the propagation of children. If so, it is a failure. It is an institution to make all happy, and not to make slaves of parents at the very outset of maturity. My observation and experience have been that in ninety-nine cases out of a hundred, in large families there has been an immense amount of suffering and privation, and that the mother has usually had to bear the greater portion of it. And the worst of it is the fact that the large family has so many drawbacks, which are freely avowed by every member of it, does not prevent each member of that same family from getting married under circumstances which usually indicate an exact reproduction of the ills of which they have so long complained.

But people will say: Look at France!

Well, look at France! I have not only looked at her from a theoretical point of view, but have travelled over her soil pretty thoroughly.

It seems to me that the French are about the happiest people I know, and I do not refer to Paris, but to the other cities, the villages and the country. It seems to me that the French are the most frugal and comfortable people I know, and they just barely succeed in reproducing the race without any increase at all. I do not see why the Frenchman should be contrasted with the rabbit, to the discredit of the former. I have never noticed in history that large families and intellectual and moral development seemed to go together. Until some better example than France can be brought along, I shall feel confirmed in my views.

The last word I have to say is the most important. I am against large families principally on account of the women, who are compelled to bear most of the burdens of life, and who are asked to give up all the comforts which they crave and which in some measure they are beginning to enjoy, and to which they are justly entitled. I consider it brutal to reiterate constantly that childbearing is woman's function. I consider it no less than brutal to ask a woman to relegate herself to the position of a brood-mare not for the personal happiness of either man or wife, but simply that the aggregate number of human beings in the world may be increased. **I do not think that a large population in and of itself is a great blessing. In all things in the world I am concerned more with quality than quantity. It is certain that, if the President were to have his way and we were to have as many children in each family as he seems to think desirable, and they could be brought up to maturity, the time would soon come when they would scarcely have standing room.** The country could not support them.

In fact, we are getting quite as many people now as we need, unless we are going to be a military nation. I do not like to compare the President's expressions in his letters with the brutal sayings of Napoleon about the necessity of Frenchwomen breeding soldiers; but there is altogether too much of a resemblance to suit me. I have for the President the greatest respect and have always supported him politically, and I cannot believe that he wants to see the population of this nation grow simply because it will give us military strength. The fact is that we need better citizens, not more of them; and until there has been some way provided by which every child born into this world has as good a chance as it ought to have in the race for success, I shall continue to hold to the opinion that the fewer there are in the family the better. President Roosevelt has a large family, but he has always had abundant means to care for them. If he could know the sufferings of poor women, I do not believe he would encourage poor men to increase their families. I do not believe one woman has been convinced by what he has said on this subject. I believe in that married life where there is happiness for all, and I have little faith in the theory that if a man marries early, works and worries himself to death he may thus obtain a better position hereafter. I am certain that we ought to treat our wives better than we do. Most of us are moral cowards, who make our wives suffer and then blame it on the Lord, who, I believe, will resent such conduct. I have said some plain things because they need to be said. I cannot agree with the President, whose philosophy, if it seems brighter, is yet in truth responsible for a large part of the misery there is in the world.

—§§§—

X

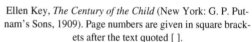

The Century of the Child

1909

Ellen Key

Famous Swedish Feminist

While earlier days regarded man as a fixed phenomenon, in his physical and psychical relations, with qualities that might be perfected but could not be transformed, it is now known that he can re-create himself. Instead of a fallen man, we see an incomplete man, out of whom, by infinite modifications in an infinite space of time, a new being can come into existence.

EDITOR

Displaying the same cultural imperialism they now denounce, in the early years of the twentieth century, liberal Protestants claimed that it would become the "Christian Century." In this controversial book Ellen Key (1849–1926) offered a feminist alternative. She saw a new religion arising, one that would worship the "holiness of generation" and create a "new" and "higher" race by allowing scientific experts to decide who has children. Sanger was well aware of Ellen Key and mentioned her fellow feminist a number of times in her 1938 autobiography. Her 1914 magazine, *Woman Rebel,* Sanger said, meant that she "corresponded with the leading Feminists of Europe—Ellen Key, then at the height of her fame. . ." At a population conference Sanger helped organize in 1927 Geneva, she described a group of women physicians this way: "They had a more Feminist point of view than ours in the United States; Ellen Key's liberal influence had seeped through from Scandinavia." And during the 1930s Sanger passed through Scandinavia and was disappointed to find that the great Key's influence was waning. Feminists had been rendered complacent by success and, "since population was not a problem in Scandinavia, they were interested chiefly in eugenics." Key's most lasting influence on Scandinavian feminism had proved to be its nasty zeal to keep other women from having "weak offspring."[1]

1. Margaret Sanger, *Margaret Sanger, An Autobiography* (New York: W. W. Norton, 1938), 111, 387, 435.

Ellen Key, *The Century of the Child* (New York: G. P. Putnam's Sons, 1909). Page numbers are given in square brackets after the text quoted [ ].

—§§§—

Filled with sad memories or eager hopes, people waited for the turn of the century, and as the clock struck twelve, felt innumerable undefined forebodings. They felt that the new century would certainly give them only one thing, peace. They felt that those who are labouring to-day would witness no new development in that process of change to which they had consciously or unconsciously contributed their quota.

The events at the turn of the century caused the new century to be represented as a small naked child, descending upon the earth, but drawing himself back in terror at the sight of a world bristling with weapons, a world in which for the opening century there was not an inch of free ground to set one's foot upon. Many people thought over the significance of this picture; they thought how in economic and in actual warfare all the lower passions of man were still aroused; how despite all the tremendous development of civilisation in the century just passed, man had not yet succeeded in giving to the struggle for existence nobler forms. Certainly to the question why this still is so, very different answers were given. Some contented themselves with declaring, after consideration, that things must remain just as they are, since human nature remains the same; that hunger, the propagation of the race, the desire for gold and power, will always control the course of the world. Others again were convinced that if the teaching which has tried in vain for nineteen hundred years to transform the course of the world could one day become a living reality in the souls of men, swords would be turned into pruning hooks.

My conviction is just the opposite. It is that nothing will be different in the mass except in so far as human nature itself is transformed, and that this transformation will take place, not when the whole of humanity becomes Christian, but when the whole of humanity awakens to the consciousness of the "holiness of generation." This consciousness will make the central work of society the new race, its origin, its management, and its education; about these all morals, all laws, all social arrangements will be grouped. This will form the point of view from which all other questions will be judged, all other regulations made. Up to now we have only heard in academic speeches and in pedagogical essays that the training of youth is the highest function of a nation. In reality, in the family, in the school, and in the state, quite other standards are put in the foreground.

The new view of the "holiness of generation" will not be held by mankind until it has seriously abandoned the Christian point of view and taken the [evolutionary] view, born thousands of years ago, whose victory has been first foreshadowed in the century just completed.

The thought of development not only throws light on the course of the world that lies behind us, continued through millions of years, with its final and highest point in man; it throws light, too, on the way we have to travel over; it shows us that we physically and psychically are ever in the process of becoming. **While earlier days regarded** *man* **as a fixed phenomenon, in his physical and psychical relations, with qualities that might be perfected but could not be transformed, it is now known that he can re-create himself. Instead of a fallen man, we see an incomplete man, out of whom, by infinite modifications in an infinite space of time, a new being can come into existence.** Almost every day brings new information about hitherto unsuspected possibilities; tells us of power extended physically or psychically. We hear of a closer reciprocal action between the external and internal world; of the mastery over disease; of the prolongation of life and youth; of increased insight into the laws of physical and psychical origins. People even speak of giving incurable blind men a new kind of capacity of sight, of being able to call back to life the dead; this and much else which it must be allowed still belongs simply to the region of hypothesis, to what psychical and physical investigators reckon among possibilities. But there are enough great results analysed already

to show that the transformations made by man before he became a human being are far from being the last word of his genesis. He who declares to-day that human nature always remains the same, that is, remains just as it did in those petty thousands of years in which our race became conscious of itself, shows in making this statement that he stands on the same level of reflection as an ichthyosaurus of the Jura period, that apparently had not even an intimation of man as a possibility of the future.

But he who knows that man has become what he now is under constant transformations, recognises the possibility of so influencing his future development that a higher type of man will be produced. The human will is found to be a decisive factor in the production of the higher types in the world of animal and plant life. With what concerns our own race, the improvement of the type of man, the ennobling of the human race, the accidental still prevails in both exalted and lower forms. But civilisation should make man conscious of an end and responsible in all these spheres where up to the present he has acted only by impulse, without responsibility. In no respect has culture remained more backward than in those things which are decisive for the formation of a new and higher race of mankind. [1-5]

Inferior Parents

All that the intelligence and genius of men and women can do for eugenics and the care of infants, for education and schools, is of small consequence so long as it is lavished on a human material constantly shrinking in value because produced by physically and psychically inferior parents, while those who have the making of good parents cannot afford, or have not the will, to supply children to the race.[2]

—ELLEN KEY, 1913

—§§§—

A Danish writer has shown how the Mosaic Seventh Commandment sinks back into nothing, as soon as one sees that marriage is only an accidental social form for the living together of two people, while the ethically decisive factor is the way they live together. In morality there is taking place a general displacement from objective laws of direction and compulsion to the subjective basis from which actions proceed. Ethics become an ethic of character, a matter dealing with the constitution of the temperament. We demand, we forgive, or we judge according to the inner constitution of the individual; we do not readily call an action immoral

2. Ellen Key, "Education for Motherhood, II" *Atlantic Monthly* 112 (Aug. 1913), 191–92.

which only in an external point of view does not harmonise with the law or is opposed to the law. In each particular case we decide according to the inner circumstances of the individual. Applying this point of view to marriage, we find in the first place that this form offers no guarantee that the proper disposition towards the relation of the two sexes is present. This can exist as well outside of as within marriage. Many noble and earnest human beings prefer for their relation the freer form as the more moral one. But as the result of this, the significance of the Seventh Commandment is altered, that states explicitly that every relationship of sex outside of marriage is immoral. People have commenced already to experiment with unions outside of marriage. People are looking for new forms for the common life between man and woman. The whole problem is being made the subject of debate. [6-7]

New Morality
Havelock Ellis, Edward Carpenter, and Ellen Key, three major spokespeople for the "New Morality," all considered sexual liberation to be primarily dependent on women's sexual liberation, which in turn required women's independence and opportunity to seek full, creative lives.[3]

—LINDA GORDON, *WOMAN'S BODY, WOMAN'S RIGHT*

—§§§—

The new ethic will call no other common living of man and woman immoral, except that which gives occasion to a weak offspring, and produces bad conditions for the development of the offspring.[4] The Ten Commandments on this subject will not be prescribed by the founders of religion, but by scientists. [13-14]

—§§§—

In Francis Galton's celebrated work, *Hereditary Genius,* almost all has been said that is required to-day from the point of view of the improvement of the race. Galton, as early as the seventies, opposed Darwin's view that acquired characteristics were inherited. In this respect he had a fellow-champion in the German Weismann, who on his side was opposed, among others, by the English Darwinian Romanes.

---

3. Linda Gordon, *Woman's Body, Woman's Right* (New York: Penguin, 1976), 187. There is a grimly pragmatic reason for this link. In a 'liberated' society, older men are likely to abandon aging wives for younger women, forcing former wives to fend for themselves.

4. Editor: Sanger hinted at a similar idea in Chap. 11, when she complains that, "Children born out of wedlock are deemed "illegitimate"—even healthy children."

Galton invented from a Greek word a name for the science of the amelioration of the race, Eugenics. He showed that civilised man, so far as care for the amelioration of the race is concerned, stands on a much lower plane than savages, not to speak of Sparta which did not allow the weak, the too young, and the too old to marry, and where national pride in a pure race, a strong offspring, was so great that individuals were sacrificed to the attainment of this end. Galton, like Darwin, Spencer, A. R. Wallace, and others, has brought out the fact that the law of natural selection, which in the rest of nature has secured the survival of the fittest, is not applicable to human society, where economic motives lead to unsuitable marriages, made possible by wealth. Poverty hinders suitable marriages. Besides the development of sympathy has come into the field as a factor which disturbs natural selection. The sympathy of love, chooses according to motives that certainly tend to the happiness of the individual, but this does not mean that they guarantee the improvement of the race. And while other writers hope for a voluntary abstinence from marriage in those cases where an inferior offspring is to be expected, Galton, on the other hand, is in favour of very strict rules to hinder inferior specimens of humanity from transmitting their vices or diseases, their intellectual or physical weaknesses. Just because Galton does not believe in the inheritance of acquired characteristics, selection has the greatest significance for him.

On the other side, he advocates using all means to encourage such marriages, where the family on both sides gives promise of distinguished offspring. For him, as later for Nietzsche, the purpose of married life is the production of strong, able personalities.

Heroic Nietzsche
The heroic attitude toward and in life, which the ancient world and Nietzsche in the modern world represent, will again become the ideal of happiness which guides the leaders of the race.[5]

—ELLEN KEY, 1913

Galton makes it plain that civilised man, by his sympathy with weak, inefficient individuals, has helped to continue their existence. This tendency on its own side has lessened the possibility of the efficient individuals to continue the species. Wallace, too, and several others, have on different occasions declared that men in relation

---

5. Ellen Key, "Education for Motherhood, II" *Atlantic Monthly* 112 (Aug. 1913), 192. She wanted genetically "good parents" to abandon their self-centered lifestyles and, as Nietzschean heroes, build a superior race.

THE PIVOT OF CIVILIZATION IN HISTORICAL PERSPECTIVE

to this question must have harder hearts, if the human race is not to become inferior. The moral, social, and sympathetic factors, they say, which in humanity work against the law of the survival of the fittest, and have made it possible for the lower type to continue and to multiply in excess, must give way to new points of view where certain moral and social questions are concerned. So the natural law will be supported by altruism, instead of as now being opposed by this sentiment. [19–22]

—§§§—

I will mention now from literary sources, some of Nietzsche's work on this subject. Although this author did not base his ideas of the "superman" directly on Darwin's theories, yet they are, as Brandes has lately shown, the great consequences of Darwinism, that Darwin himself did not see. **In no contemporary was there a stronger conviction than in Nietzsche that man as he now is, is only a bridge, only a transition between the animal and the "superman." In connection with this, Nietzsche looked upon the obligations of man for the amelioration of the race as seriously as Galton, but he expressed his principles with the power of poetic and prophetic expression, not with scientific proof.** [25–26]

—§§§—

What here must be first considered is the thought constantly being brought out by Darwinian writers, that the natural sciences, in which must now be numbered psychology, should be the basis of juristic science as well as of pedagogy. Man must come to learn the laws of natural selection and act in the spirit of these laws. Man must arrange the punishments of society in the service of development; they must be protective measures for natural selection. **In the first place this must be secured by hindering the criminal type from perpetuating itself. The characteristics of this type can only be determined by specialists. But the criminal must be prevented from handing on his characteristics to his posterity.**

So the human race will be gradually free from atavisms which reproduce lower and preceding stages of development. This is the first condition of that evolution by which kind will be able to let the ape and tiger die. Then comes the requirement that those inherited physical or psychical diseases shall not transmit them to all offspring. [46]

—§§§—

A young man, himself a physician, thought he was healthy when he married. He discovered his mistake and found himself confronting the choice of wronging his wife or separating from her. As they were deeply in love, the only possible way was separation. He chose death which he inflicted on himself in such a way that his wife thought it was caused by accident.

Another man acted in the same way after he had been married several years and had three children; he found out that he was his wife's half-brother.

But these incidents as the one before mentioned, where women are concerned, are notoriously only isolated examples. It will require the development of several generations before it will be the woman's instinct, an irresistibly mastering instinct, to allow no physically or psychically degenerated or perverted man to become the father of her children. The instinct of the man is far stronger in this direction, but it is dulled too by an antiquated legal conception, according to which the woman must subject herself a duty to requirements against which her who being revolts. In this respect a woman has only one duty, an unmistakable one, against which every transgression is a sin, namely that the new being to which she gives life, must be born in love and purity, in health and beauty, in full mutual harmony, in a complete common will, in a complete common happiness. Until women see this as a duty, the earth will continue to be peopled by beings, who in a moment of their existence have been robbed of the best pre-conditions of their life's happiness and their life's efficiency. [50–51]

—§§§—

Even the advocates of women's rights must allow that the limit of their claims to right is to be found where the right of another begins. They cannot suppose that the individual right of the woman to control her life should go so far that the woman could take a piece of a neighbour's property to lay out a garden, or use for an industrial scheme a part of the water supply belonging to some one else.

Can they not see that woman's individual freedom is limited by the rights of another, by the rights of the potential child? The potential child has its own property rights, its own vital power. This property, the woman has not the right to encroach upon in advance.[6] [75–76]

—§§§—

---

6. Editor: Taken literally, Key was denying that women have a right to abortion. But Key may have been thinking abstractly of an as-yet unconceived "potential child" whose genetic endowment must be the best possible.

XI

The Heredity of Richard Roe

1911

David Starr Jordan

President of Stanford University

If Richard Roe by chance is a defective, unable by heredity to rise to the level of helpfulness and happiness, it is not a wholesome act to help him to the responsibilities of parenthood. It is a wise charity to make him as comfortable as may be with the assurance that he shall be the last of his line.

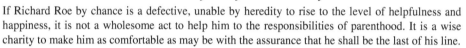

EDITOR

In the early decades of the twentieth century David Starr Jordan (1851–1931), President of what is today Stanford University, was a well-known supporter of eugenics. This chapter contains excerpts from a book he wrote to popularize those ideas. It is important to remember that in eugenic circles Jordan was a considered a moderate and in the next chapter the *New York Times* attacks him that attitude. His eugenics seems to have been much more restrained than most of his colleagues.

Notice, however, that the limits he placed on the eugenic agenda apply only to what is done to the "best of men and of women." Such people, he said, should not have *their* "love and initiative" crippled by being forced into a controlled breeding program that, by denying the importance of love in mating, might breed those

traits out. But his reservations *would not* apply to those whose hereditary traits are fated for extinction. Those people could be encouraged to engage in promiscuity and dependence as long as society could be sure they have few or no children.

Note also in the second paragraph quoted, that Jordan suggested eugenics could be applied to the *"bête noir"* or lit. a 'black beast,' meaning a person or thing that is strongly detested or avoided. That and the reference that follows to "Sambo"—a slur word for black men—hints that eugenists and birth controllers might someday set their sights on the nation's black population.

Never one to follow a fad, in the February 1922 issue of Sanger's *Birth Control Review,* Jordan professed skepticism about how successful birth control would be among the poor for, "Those classes who suffer most from congestion are the ones such information and arguments do not reach." In closing he revealed what may have been the most important reason for declining birthrates among the more affluent, one that had little to do with the cause Sanger was promoting. "A large factor" in that change, he said, was "the acquisition of separate apartments for the mother of the family."

David Starr Jordan, *The Heredity of Richard Roe: A Discussion of the Principles of Eugenics* (Boston: American Unitarian Assn., 1911). Page numbers are given in square brackets after the text quoted [ ]. Eugenics' claim to be scientific attracted religious liberals. Both this book and an earlier one by Jordan, *The Blood of the Nation: A Study of the Decay of Races through the Survival of the Unfit* (1902), were published by the American Unitarian Association.

—§§§—

When Richard Roe was born, "the gate of gifts was closed" to him. It was in fact closed long before that, at the moment of the blending of the two germ cells (ovum and sperm-cell) from the mingling of which his own personality arose. In the instant of conception, the gifts of life are granted. Nothing more comes of itself. Henceforth he must expect nothing new and must devote himself to the development of the heritage he has received from his father and mother. . . .

. . . . So far as methods and principles are concerned, Richard Roe may be your lapdog or your favorite horse— or even your *bête noir,* if you cherish beasts of that color.

Any beast will do. . . . with Sambo or Caesar the case would be the same. Let Richard Roe stand at present for the lay figure of heredity—or, if it seems best to you to humanize this discussion, let him be a *man*. [1, 3]

—§§§—

"This three or four per cent of our population [says Charles Davenport[1]] is a fearful drag on our civilization. Shall we as intelligent people, proud of our control of nature in other respects, do nothing but vote more taxes or be satisfied with the great gifts and bequests that philanthropists have made for the support of the delinquent, defective and dependent classes? Shall we not rather take the steps that scientific study dictates as necessary to dry up the springs that feed the torrent of defective and degenerate proplasm? . . .

. . . . A new plague that rendered four per cent of our population, chiefly at the most productive age, not only incompetent, but a burden costing 100 million dollars yearly to support would instantly attract universal attention, and millions would be forthcoming for its study as they have been for the study of cancer. But we have become so used to crime, disease and degeneracy that we take them as necessary evils. That they were, in the world's ignorance, is granted. That they must remain so is denied."

If Richard Roe by chance is a defective, unable by heredity to rise to the level of helpfulness and happiness, it is not a wholesome act to help him to the responsibilities of parenthood. It is a wise charity to make him as comfortable as may be with the assurance that he shall be the last of his line. [80–82]

Eugenics Creed

Davenport was not only the scientific spokesman of the American eugenics movement but, also, its spiritual head. It was in 1916 . . . that Davenport composed his credo of eugenics. It was unveiled in an address— "Eugenics as a Religion"—delivered at the ceremonies marking the fiftieth anniversary of the Battle Creek (Michigan) Sanitarium. . . .

In setting the stage for the first reading of the Eugenics Creed, Davenport explained:

1. Charles B. Davenport (1866–1944) was a leading eugenist. He taught zoology at Harvard (1892–99), was curator at the University of Chicago's zoological museum (1901-04), directed the genetics program at the Carnegie-funded Station for Experimental Evolution at Cold Spring Harbor (1904–34), and ran the Eugenics Record Office (1910-34). He also pioneered the use of statistics in genetic research.

"Eugenics has to do with racial development. It accepts the fact of differences in people—physical differences, mental differences, differences in emotional control. It is based on the principle that nothing can take the place of innate qualities. While it recognizes the value of culture it insists that culture of a trait is futile, where the germs [genes] are absent.[2]

ALLAN CHASE, *THE LEGACY OF MALTHUS*

—§§§—

As the destruction of the unadapted is the chief element of race progress, so is the survival of the weak the chief element in race decline. Race-decadence occurs when the strong are withdrawn without posterity, when weakness mates with weakness, when incentives to individual action are taken away, without reduction in security of life, and when the unfit are sheltered from the consequences of their folly, weakness or perversity. The increased effectiveness of altruism which goes with race progress furnishes a shelter under which race decay goes on. The growth of wisdom makes folly safe. At the same time the growth of wisdom works the death of fools when they are brought into life-and-death competition with those stronger and wiser. [89]

—§§§—

In one way or another, in time, most of the incapables are eliminated by the process of natural selection. But not all of them. Our social system is bound too closely. Hereditary incapacity of the few has been in all ages a burden on the men who could take care of themselves. With higher civilization and an increasing recognition of the value of mutual help it is becoming more and more possible for those to live who do not help. The descendants of these increase in number with the others. They are protected by the others. Thus the future of hereditary weakness is a growing problem in our social organization. [101–02]

—§§§—

It is evident that the human race is quite as plastic as the horse or sheep, and that if mating could be carried toward definite ends, even for a few generations, there might be startling results. But there seems to be no possibility that any group of scientific men could ever be called on to exercise such control. Moreover, those best worth while would never submit to it. **The best of men and of women will always choose their mates for themselves. The artificial breeding of the superman, if such a thing can be conceived as a practical matter for the state to undertake, would defeat its own ends. It**

2. Allan Chase, *The Legacy of Malthus* (Urbana: Univ. of Illinois Press, 1980), 161–62.

would breed out of existence the two most important factors the race has won, so far as mating is concerned. These are love and initiative. The superman produced by artificial eugenics would not take his fate into his own hands, and his descendants would not know the meaning of love.

The practice of Eugenics, has then, its limitations, and the Richard Roe of the future will be a chip of the same block as the Richard Roe of the past. [153–54]

—§§§—

3. David Starr Jordan, *The Blood of the Nation* (Boston: American Unitarian Assn., 1902), 25. In this book Jordan focused on the impact of war where, he claimed, the best die while the worst live on to father children.

Birth Control and Racial Betterment

By Margaret Sanger

The Eugenic Value of Birth Control Propaganda

By Margaret Sanger

[*The following brief statement of the dependence of any sound and effective program of Eugenics upon Birth Control, in view of the Second International Congress of Eugenics, recently held in New York at the Museum of Natural History, assumes a peculiar timeliness.*]

XII

How Bright a Torch

1912

New York Times

EDITOR

The year 1912 was a high point for eugenic propaganda in the United States. (It also was the year that Margaret Sanger, then living in New York City, became heavily politicized.) Leading the march into this brave new world of scientifically controlled human breeding was *The New York Times,* as eager then as now to tell its readers how to think. Liberal clergy also took up the cause. The *Times* article that follows described Episcopalian clergy proud of taking the "advanced position" on this issue—an expression often used by liberals of the day to describe themselves.

Note how the *Times* used expressions such as "how bright a torch" to inform its readers that the eugenic cause was an enlightened one, a "new science" that was being carefully developed by "great authorities" and "if we are patient, they may be able to tell us all how the race can be made healthy, happy, and wise."

A word of warning. While the first article reflects what the *Times* undoubtedly thought eugenists were saying, it is not a very accurate statement of what they were saying. For that reason, this text leaves out passages where the *Times* writer was particularly confused or inaccurate.[1] Serious eugenists were usually more precise about marriage restrictions than the Very Reverend Sumner's muddled, "have neither an incurable nor a communicable disease." If that were the case, weddings would be canceled if either party developed the sniffles.

Finally, note the parallel the article draws between the obsession the European nobility once had with "good blood," and that eugenists had about good heredity. Elitism dies hard. When it could no longer use tradition to defend itself, it turned to science. Science has proved all too willing to cooperate.

Bishops Approve Plan to Apply Eugenics to Marriage

After Fifty Years the Theories of Sir Francis Galton May Be Put into Practical Use by Chicago's Protestant Episcopal Clergy

New York Times, Dec. 21, 1912, 12.

Half a century ago, or fifty-three years, to be quite accurate, a British scientist of an original turn of mind by [the] name of Francis Galton published a work on "Heredity in Genius"[2] which received favorable and even flattering mention. He himself came of the Darwin family, which has given so many great names to science, but he probably did not suspect how bright a torch he had lighted. Interest in the questions to which he, first of all, aroused the modern world, has grown so that Legislatures more and more frequently pass laws regulating marriage. Books on the subject are constantly being published. The climax came this week when the Dean of the Protestant Episcopal Cathedral in Chicago announced that his Bishop approved a plan by which no marriage would be celebrated in the Cathedral unless the contracting parties could supply a "clean bill of health" from a physician.

The Very Rev. Walter Taylor Sumner, who promulgated the decree, says that hereafter the Cathedral of St. Peter and St. Paul will take an advanced position. "Beginning with Easter," he announces, "no persons will be married at the cathedral unless they present a certificate of health from a reputable physician to the effect that they are normal physically and mentally and have neither an incurable nor a communicable disease."

Health in Marriage

The "health in marriage" law of 1935 specified that before a couple could receive a marriage license they

---

1. For an accurate portrayal of eugenics, see the articles written by prominent eugenists in the appendices to the Inkling edition of G. K. Chesterton's *Eugenics and Other Evils.*

2. Editor: This apparently refers to Galton's 1869 *Hereditary Genius,* published 43 years earlier. Galton's first writing on the topic came in 1865 when he published two articles on "Hereditary Talent in Character" in *Macmillan's Magazine.*

had to present a certificate from a physician stating that they had passed a genetic health exam and were fit to marry.[3]

—HUGH G. GALLAGHER, *BY TRUST BETRAYED*

He had no sooner said this than a chorus of approbation arose. Clergymen, physicians, social workers, applauded, and the rest of the world, knowing little about it, admired and agreed. Sir Francis Galton, could he return to the world he left only two years ago, would find that the light he lighted in his youth had grown into a great flame.

Galton put, or at least began the work of putting on a basis the question of family resemblance about which people have always had innumerable ideas, correct and incorrect, and he created what is practically a new science. Like all new sciences, eugenics is a great deal talked about and proportionally misunderstood. The great authorities themselves are quite humble about what has so far been done. They are not far enough along to lay down many set rules, and they need the help of medicine, psychology, sociology, and any number of other sciences, but they are getting along, and in the course of time, if we are patient, they may be able to tell us all how the race can be made healthy, happy, and wise.

Birth Forbidden by Law

In the absence of suitable conscientiousness on the part of parents the State should intervene and give licenses to marry only to those who are healthy and fit to be fathers and mothers. The State has a right to place restrictions on marriage for the welfare of fellow citizens. Inveterate paupers, hopeless drunkards, incorrigible paupers, insane and idiotic people, and such as are afflicted with consumption and other diseases likely to injure the next generation should be denied the privilege of wedlock. A birth forbidden by law should be construed as a criminal offense, and the parents should be punished by fine or imprisonment. Science and not caprice should be the arbiter of life, and domestic sentiment in some cases must be sacrificed in behalf of the general good.[4]

—REV. JOHN J. SOUDDER, 1903

3. Hugh Gregory Gallagher, *By Trust Betrayed* (New York: Henry Holt, 1990), 192. The reference is to Nazi Germany.
4. "Rights of the Unborn," *New York Times* (Feb. 23, 1903), 7. Rev. Soudder was pastor of the First Congregational Church, Jersey City, NY. It is revealing that liberal denominations whose clergy once wanted to outlaw marriage and criminalize births for the sake of "the unborn" now support legalized abortion and claim to defend "reproductive choice."

Sir Francis Galton divided the classes of society into the desirable, the passable, and the undesirable. The majority of us are among the passable, who form the great mass of humanity; the desirables and the undesirables are quite small in comparison. The object of eugenics is, naturally, to show how the class of undesirables comes into existence and how it may be prevented; also how the desirables may be increased and bit by bit leaven the great lump of the passables.

Desirables cannot be exclusively claimed by any class or race; they may be rich, they may be poor, they may be our next door neighbors, or they may come from the ends of the earth. To recognize them is a difficult task. To tell the undesirables is easier, but not nearly so easy as it looks.

Hence comes in the question of environment. Does a man inherit his criminal tendencies or his poor health from the parents—in which case he would not be a fit father—or does he come by them from evil surroundings—in which his children will be as good as other people's?

All these are questions which the students of eugenics are dealing with, and since the workers are not yet many and the task is enormous the world must wait a while for them to speak on many points. Some things, however, they have found out and can tell us with assurance.

In the middle of the last century Gregor Mendel by dint of staying in a monastery and cultivating a little garden while other scientists were rushing over the earth after discoveries, found the great law, which is generally called by his name. He had no credit for it in his life time, but as he had simple taste his gardening pleased him, doubtless, quite as much as fame would have done, if not more. He found his law by crossing peas and noting the results.

Mendel crossed high peas with dwarf peas, and followed the history of their progeny. He found that the pea children inclined more to follow the tall and normal parent than the deformed one. After many experiments he was able to say that the proportion was about that of three to one; that is, three pea plants would be tall to one that was short. Having discovered this he wrote a pamphlet about it, which nobody read, worked a little more in his garden, and soon afterward died unsuspecting the fame that awaited him.

It happened, curiously, that Galton and Mendel were born in the same year—1822. Not only that but the little pamphlet was written about the time of Galton's "Heredity in Genius." It was Galton who rescued the monk's work from oblivion and made him the patron saint of workers in eugenics, for indeed it is on Mendel's law that an enormous part of the structure rests.

What Mendel did with peas has been done over and over again with animals, and the result is the same. Mate a pure black guinea pig with a pure white guinea pig and three out of four of the progeny will be black. In all cross mixtures the law has been tested.

It sounds very simple, but it is not really. For the great truth that eugenics teach is not that we inherit characteristics from our fathers and our mothers, but that we inherit their tendencies to certain characteristics. The black guinea pig is black, but if it has a white parent it has a tendency toward whiteness, inherited from that parent, and though it does not show that tendency it transmits it, along with other tendencies, to its children, and they may show it. Similarly the white guinea pig transmits the tendency toward blackness. The result is soon an astonishing mixture, by selection, the original types may be again created.

It will be the business of the science of eugenics to bring order into all these matters as soon as possible. It will find out what qualities are the result of certain combinations, and it will try to educate public opinion to the point of setting before young people the ideal of marrying "well" in the true sense. Sir Francis Galton said that he hoped some day a family of "good blood," in the sense in which the term is used in eugenics, would have the same sense of shame in an alliance with a house of "bad blood" as the Austrian nobility feel now when one of their number marries some one whose escutcheon has fewer than sixteen quarterings.

No scientist pretends that the world is yet near this consummation, for science itself is only feeling its way. But it can say one or two things with great emphasis and they are the things, perhaps, that the Chicago clergymen had in mind when they made their pronouncement.

First of all, it gives the cheering news that nature is all right if given half a chance. She tends to make us normal. If a parent with an hereditary taint, which is not shown, but is none the less there, because hidden, marries a person perfectly sound, without this tendency to hereditary weakness, there is a fine chance that the children of the union will be quite without the taint, and their children after them, if they marry normal persons, until it quite disappears. Just as the beans of Mendel struggle to be back to the normal condition of height, so we struggle back to the proper standard.

The second fact is that qualities which are altogether lacking cannot be transmitted. This seems a sufficiently obvious statement, but it has meant a vast deal of scientific research. . . .

In regard to blue eyes, this discovery has no tremendous importance, since few of us would care to see the world populated exclusively by persons of blue or brown eyes, but it is of immense value when it is applied to other subjects. When it comes to the feeble-minded, this law points the way for social reform.

No feeble-minded pair can possibly have normal children, for they cannot transmit what they have not. If one parent is normal there is always a chance, but if the two are feeble-minded it is utterly impossible, and there is at once a basis for practical work by reformers; since that particular question is not complicated by debatable matters, such as the influence of environment, and so forth.

Eugenics say, in short, that so far as feeble mindedness goes, it could all be stamped out very easily. Normal persons practically never have feebleminded children, while two feebleminded persons invariably will have abnormal children and between the two are the many who have a hereditary taint but who tend, through marriage with the sound, to have perfect children. . . .

Innumerable lists have been complied [compiled] with the end to show in just what proportion desirable characteristics are inherited. Although nothing like definite results have been reached as yet, many interesting things have been discovered. Dr. Charles Davenport, Director of the Carnegie Institution's station of experimental evolution at Cold Stream, L.I. is the greatest authority in America on such matters, and he has collected in his book, *Heredity in Relation to Eugenics,* many of the facts that have already been arrived at.

Musical and artistic ability he finds to be clearly inherited. The Bach family comprised twenty eminent musicians and forty others less eminent, and there is a pedigree of the painter Vecellio prepared by Galton, which shows six distinguished painters in three generations. The same is true of literary talent.

Indeed, genius developed so early, is clearly a thing inborn that it is quite obviously an inherited quality, only here again scientists are confronted with the peculiar question whether genius is a positive or a negative characteristic. Has a genius a quality over and above that of ordinary men, as we poetically say, or does it only mean that he lacks a controlling factor which makes the rest of us stop at placid mediocrity? That is not yet known, and it is sufficiently obvious that we are a long way from knowing how to produce to order, from suitable marriages, men and women who will paint great pictures or write great books and great operas.

On the other hand, there is disease. How far can that be eliminated by proper marriages? Here, of course, the controversy with the believers in environment begins vehemently unless both sides make concessions. There is first the physician, who talks about germs, and the student of social questions, who talks about proper living conditions, and he would be a daring scientist who in the name of eugenics would read them both out of court.

The scientist does claim, however, that a tendency to succumb to certain germs runs in certain families. The germs are with us all and did we all fail to resist, there would be and end of the world shortly, but some of us fail to resist the germs of tuberculosis and others of us go unharmed among them, and the eugenists will say that the "tendency to resist" is inherited.

Defects like weakness of the head and of the nervous system are being studied and tabulated to see what part heredity play, while, of course, charts have been made for such troubles as color blindness, short sightedness and so forth, but there is not as yet a great amount of data.

It has been settled, then, that nature is kind, much more often than she is cruel, and with a little encouragement she would do better things for us than she has done yet. It is only a fair chance that she asks, not even that, according to the law of Mendel, and she will make us happier than we ever have been. This question is how is she going to be given that chance?

By legislation? Scientists smile at most of the statutes so proudly passed by Legislatures in the alleged interest of the race. Except that two idiotic persons will invariably have idiotic children, there is not law that can be generally applied. Most scientists look forward to the education of public opinion and the resulting change that will come even over love's young dream.

Brothers and sisters do not fall in love with each other. The idea is shocking to us, but there is certainly nothing inherently immoral in it. Indeed, contrary opinion might be very early maintained to some one who had then been brought up in ignorance of our prejudices. We are shocked because we know that marriage of a brother and sister means physical degeneration. Scientists say—and it sounds rational—that if we were properly trained we would not desire to marry persons whom we should not marry. We would be revolted at the idea, and this is a better way to keep people apart than legislate.[5]

There remains, always, the problem of degeneracy in secluded rural communities where intermarriage has long been going on. There is no chance, is such spots, for edu-cation because the mental ability is below the line of education. That question the scientist would turn over to social workers and the Legislatures, for science itself has already spoken her word on the subject.

—§§§—

EDITOR

In the last chapter, we read what David Starr Jordan wrote in 1911. In the following two articles, we discover what the *New York Times* said about him the next year. Both the news story and the editorial two days later raise questions about whether the *Times* staff had actually read Jordan's brief book. His address to eugenists and the San Francisco interview that followed said little that wasn't in it. *The Times,* however, wasn't reacting to what Jordan was actually saying. They were reacting to his implication that eugenics could go astray. Nothing, they seemed to suggest, can go wrong with a cause we have taken under our wing. (For a modern parallel, imagine a well-respected scientist of today voicing concern over legalized abortion.)

If a Catholic archbishop or a fundamentalist preacher voiced the same concerns as Jordan, the *Times* would have sneered in contempt. Such people, the paper would tell us, "know little" about the subject. But this criticism came from within the ranks of the enlightened. Jordan was not only a "well-informed scientist," he was the author of a popular book on eugenics. His criticism, if such it was, could not be permitted to stand unchallenged. The *Times,* donning its robes as the enforcer of enlightened thought, served warning on Jordan. They professed themselves "both surprised and grieved" by what he is reported to have said. They are willing to let it pass, however, if only he will claim "that he was misquoted in his 'authorized statement.'"

Two things are clear. First, the *Times* would not permit the slightest shadow of wrongdoing to be placed on eugenists—their motives were above reproach and their methods always reasonable. Second, the *Times* seemed to know little about the eugenics it praised so lavishly. It claims that only the "stupid" accuse eugenics of "apply-

---

5. Editor: Modern research suggest that a disinterest in marrying those we grow up with is instinctive rather than taught. Efforts to train people to think eugenically would need to be *more* coercive than simple bans on marriage for a few. It would require not only the silencing of religious critics, but of all the authors, poets and song writers who extol the joys of romantic love. The more practical eugenists recognized this and wanted legal restrictions on marriage and the forced institutionalization or sterilization of those who weren't likely to regard the lack of a marriage license as a hindrance to childbearing.

ing to humanity the rules of the stock farm." In actual fact, from Francis Galton on, eugenists had pointed to thoroughbred horses and domesticated dogs as examples of just what eugenics could do if given a chance. And the *Times* soothing description of the eugenic agenda was silly almost beyond belief—"to add, one after another, a few more classes to those whose unfortunate members nobody now thinks of marrying because nobody wants to." Did the *Times* really think that the marital preferences of an entire nation would march in lockstep to its editorial page? And what would keep those 'unfortunates' from marrying one another or from having children outside marriage? The eugenic agenda always bore within it the ugly seeds of coercion.

What the *Times* referred to as his "strange passage" was Jordan's criticism of those who advocated "Burbanking the human race." But, alas, the famous plant biologist, Luther Burbank, does seem to have been quoted making rather chilling remarks. In a 1925 article in *Collier's*, Margaret Sanger quoted (with favor) a Burbank assertion that, "America . . . is like a garden in which the gardener pays no attention to the weeds. Our criminals are our weeds, and weeds breed fast and are intensely hardy. Stop permitting criminals and weaklings to reproduce. All over the country to-day we have enormous insane asylums and similar institutions where we nourish the unfit and criminal instead of exterminating them. Nature eliminates the weeds, but we turn them into parasites and allow them to reproduce."[6] As we will see, he wasn't the only one saying such things.

—§§§—

Can't "Burbank" the Race
Prof. Jordan Says Personal Preference Will Always Stand In Way

New York Times (Sept. 1, 1912), 1.

SAN FRANCISCO, Aug. 31—In an authorized interview here to-day President David Starr Jordan of Leland Stanford University expanded his recent address in Salt Lake on the possibilities of eugenics, or "Burbanking the human race."

"I used the phrase 'Burbanking the race,'" he said to-day, "to show that although systematic scientific selection of mates could be made to produce great physical strength, beauty, endurance, and even mental power, those very persons who would be thus effectively mated would never submit to State dictation.

6. Margaret Sanger, "Is Race Suicide Probable?" *Collier's* (Aug. 15, 1925), 25. The article is published here as Chap. XXXI.

"If they would, they must in time eliminate the most vital elements in human evolution—love and initiative. Love is the best basis for marriage, and love is a very real and noble thing, in spite of the baseness of many of its imitations.

"The value of eugenic study is in the diffusion of sound ideas of life and parenthood. Government can do something by refusing parenthood to those who cannot care for themselves because of feeble-mindedness, disease, and vice, but legislation must be undertaken very cautiously, giving the individual the benefit of all doubt."

—§§§—

Eugenists Are Not Burbanks

New York Times, September 3, 1912, 10.

As Dr. David Starr Jordan, the President of Leland Stanford University, has written a really excellent presentation, in popular form, of eugenic facts, theories, and expectations—it is called *The Heredity of Richard Roe* and is well worth anybody's reading—one cannot help being both surprised and grieved to learn that he has addressed to the eugenists a grave warning against trying to "Burbank the human race."

Such advice as that is familiar enough, since it comes every day from people who know little about Mr. Burbank's work and nothing at all about eugenics. As Dr. Jordan is a well-informed scientist, with a knowledge of both, one is almost forced to the conclusion that he was misquoted in the "authorized statement" containing this strange passage, the natural assumption being, of course, that as he knows better he couldn't have said it. Be that as it may, and whether he said it or not, as a matter of plain, easily ascertainable fact, no eugenist worthy of the name dreams of applying to the human race any methods of selection even remotely resembling those of the so-called "plant-wizard."

Mr. Burbank raises seedlings by the hundreds of thousands, picks out two or three or a dozen as promising to grow into what he desires, and ruthlessly kills all the others. In other words, he simply hastens the blind, slow plan of Nature to eliminate the unfit and save the fit. The eugenist follows, or would follow, a path quite different. His ideal, perhaps, is some day by taking thought to mate good with good and so to produce better, but his present purpose and hope is only to extend, little by little, that avoidance of the obviously injudicious which already exists and is everywhere practiced. He believes as strongly as anyone else in letting personal preference determine who shall marry: his aim is to make the preference and enlightened one—to add, one after another, a few more classes to those whose unfortunate members nobody now thinks of marrying because nobody wants to.

This is not "Burbanking the human race," nor is it "applying to humanity the rules of the stock farm," which is the other common—and stupid—accusation against the eugenists.

—§§§—

Editor: Lest readers not know where to send their money, *The Times* thoughtfully included with the letter below the full mailing address of this British eugenics society. (The author, Leonard Darwin, was Charles Darwin's grandson.) Note the author's vague remark about the 'unfit' being institutionalized "to prevent them from breeding." In practice that meant incarceration in unisex institutions from puberty until about age 45 for women and perhaps age 65 for men. It's difficult to imagine how people so treated would not feel that they were being unfairly "punished for a crime." In their zeal for this fashionable new science, both *The Times* and Major Darwin seem oblivious to the brutal implications of what they advocate. Most probably, they simply did not care. They were superior; this wasn't going to be done to them.

Babies of the Future

Major Leonard Darwin Tells True Purposes of Eugenics

New York Times, Dec. 21, 1912, 12.

Eugenics Education Society of Great Britain,
6 York Buildings, Adelphi, London, Dec. 11, 1912.

To the Editor of *The New York Times*:

As there appears to be a good deal of doubt on both sides of the Atlantic with regard to the objects and methods of eugenic societies, perhaps you will be good enough to give me an opportunity of stating briefly what they should be in our opinion.

The main aim of the eugenist is to be sure the interests of the unborn of the future always being held in view in connection with all our social customs and all our legislation. For the sake of our fellow-creatures of to-day and to-morrow, every effort should without doubt be made to improve the environment of mankind by rational methods. But, as regards the more distant future, we can now practically only beneficially affect the great stream of humanity through the agency of heredity. We desire therefore greatly to increase the sense of responsibility in connection with all matters pertaining to human parenthood, to spread abroad a knowledge of the laws of hered-

ity as far as now known, and to encourage further research in that domain of science.

With regard to this last point, about which there is little controversy, scientific investigation must remain to a great extent in the hands of such bodies as the Carnegie Institute of Washington, which is pouring forth such a volume of admirable work. Eugenic societies may perhaps play a useful part in collecting material, such as carefully compiled human pedigrees, and in impressing on the public the scientific value of such information when accurately rendered. By means of such co-operation between the general public and the expert investigator progress may be greatly facilitated.

As to our other aims, they will become more definite as our knowledge increases. We can, however, positively affirm that we do not advocate any interference whatever with the free selection of normal mates in marriage. But we firmly believe that, if the moral sense of the nation could be aroused to the importance of the eugenic problem, great benefits would result. These advantages, we hold, would arise because the fit, if suitably mated, would recognize more clearly than they do at present the moral evil of avoiding the duties of parenthood; whilst if not already mated, they would more often refuse to mate with the unfit. Again, as regards the unfit in body, they would more often refrain from marriage for fear of passing on their defects to future generations.

Hence we regard the educational campaign which we are carrying on as being of the greatest practical importance. There will no doubt always remain a class quite outside the pale of all moral influence, and of these there will be a small proportion who, if they become parents, are certain to pass on some grievous mental or bodily defect to a considerable proportion of their progeny. Here and here only must the law step in. As to whether surgical sterilization should ever be enforced on such persons we still have an open mind, but certainly not til further information on this subject is available. **Unquestionably these unfortunates must be treated with all practical consideration, and must be made to feel that they are not being punished for a crime, yet sufficient control must be maintained over them in institutions or elsewhere to prevent them from breeding.**

Finally, we advocate economic forces being brought to bear in certain directions; as for instance, in making taxation, and also the pay of employees in all public services, vary somewhat with the size of the family to be maintained, and in administering the poor law so as not to encourage reproduction on the part of degenerate paupers.

These are, in brief, the aims of our societies, for which we appeal for widespread sympathy.

Leonard Darwin, President

—§§§—

EDITOR

The Times occasionally allowed critics of eugenics to have their say. Note, however, that the paper's editors could not let this well-reasoned criticism pass without a rebuttal. Their reply came the very next day. This "youngest of the sciences" was already that important to them.

History has not been kind to *The Times*. The author of this letter got it exactly right. Eugenists did send out researchers indoctrinated with the bizarre conviction that they could spot the feebleminded three generations back based on little more than family gossip. (The next chapter is an example of such research.) Today their work gets mentioned only to be ridiculed. Ironically, some of these researchers may have been graduates of the same exclusive women's colleges whose failure to become mothers is described in Chapter XV and XVI.

Even more laughable were the illusions *The Times* at least *seemed* to harbor about eugenists. Bans on marriage along with forced institutionalization and sterilization—common elements in the eugenic agenda—are hardly "purely voluntary on the 'material's' part." And anyone who read eugenic writings from that era knew that they used terms such as 'fit' and 'unfit' often and aggressively. Did *The Times* know what it was saying was wrong? At some level it undoubtedly did. The real eugenic agenda was not that hard to discover. But in all probability the editors of *The Times* weren't thinking in terms of truth and falsity. They were thinking in terms "our sort of people" and "not our sort of people." Eugenists were *their* sort of people and hence their critics must be stupid or worse. That attitude remains common.

Weakness of Eugenics
Many Great Men Have Had Defective Heredity

New York Times, Dec. 26, 1912, 8.

To the Editor of *The New York Times:*

After reading Major Leonard Darwin's recent letter to *The Times* and the illuminating comment upon it in "Topics of the Times," it still seemed as if there were two difficulties with the eugenist programme that were not made clear. We are all agreed that the fit should inherit the earth, but just who are the fit? A perfect man is almost as rare biologically as a perfect day meteorologically.

Nearly all have some weakness or defect which may be handed down to coming generations, and few great men have been free from infirmities of body or mind that were their unfortunate inheritance.

Keats and Cecil Rhodes were pretty diverse sort of men, each entitled to be called great, yet both were tubercular; Peter the Great deserved the title, yet he was epileptic, and the close relation between great creative imaginations and mental instability is well known.[7] Were the ancestries of such men studied, examples of marked defects of one sort or another would probably be found to be quite common, yet a notable result seems to have been the issue. Take Lord Bacon, for instance. Here was a surpassingly brilliant intellect united to such a degree of moral obliquity that had he lived to-day in a humble station he would probably have been classed as a moral imbecile.

To judge human character is one of the most difficult of arts, and yet the theory of eugenics is largely based upon a study of human heredity. Now just what does this amount to? A young person with much scientific information but with little first-hand knowledge of life interrogates people without scientific habits of observations regarding the physical and mental status of members of their own and other families who have been dead, in many cases, so many years that the information comes at second or third hand. Pride, envy, jealousy, ignorance, all the weaknesses of human nature combine to minimize the value of such testimony.

E. C., New York, Dec. 24, 1912

—§§§—

Topics of the Times
Answering a Critic of Eugenics

New York Times, Dec. 27, 1912, 8.

Two objections to the eugenist programme, or rather two arguments against its practicality, were presented yesterday by one of our correspondents. There is difficulty, he said, even when all the facts are known, in deciding who is and who is not "fit" to survive, and to "hand on the torch" and the information on which are based the decisions made is for the most part obtained at second—or third, or fourth—hand from people whose judgment of

---

7. Editor: In this era, both epilepsy and a tendency to get tuberculosis were thought to a great extent to be inherited. Since both diseases were also much more costly to treat then than now, there was a great zeal to purge society of their victims. The social costs of social ills were never far from the minds of eugenists and their supporters. Ironically, Sanger herself was troubled by tuberculosis during pregnancy and for years after.

their relatives and ancestors is neither scientific nor disinterested and therefore untrustworthy.

That these criticisms have some weight need not be denied, but they amount to a little more than reassertion of human fallibility. **Eugenics is among the youngest of the sciences, and its practitioners have no illusions as to the extent of their present knowledge or the degree to which it can be made the basis of positive action.** Hence is it, doubtless, that they are among the most modest and cautious of reformers, and what distinguishes them especially from other reformers is the fact that they do not ask Legislatures to enforce their ideas on other people. Instead they distinctly say, over and over again, that their only desire or expectation is to extend such knowledge of heredity as can be obtained, and so, slowly, to change for the better and safer those human inclination which must always be, as they have always been, determinative of human descent.

This constitutes a great difference between the eugenist and the stock breeder. The latter uses his "material" arbitrarily, sacrificing what he pleases to gain what he wants; the former aims at progress from within and purely voluntary on the "material's" part.

As for the terms "fit" and "unfit," the eugenist fully realizes that they are vague and unsatisfactory, and uses them as little as possible.

Our correspondent was mistaken in assuming that the existence of a "close relation between great creative imagination and mental instability is well known." It is not know well—or at all. A few geniuses have been—or become—obviously "defective," but what multitudes have been or become defective without showing a hint of genius! The conclusion that defectiveness has nothing to do with genius contradicts an old belief, dear to the heart of mediocrity, but that is hardly sufficient for rejecting the conclusion. And there is no reason for doing so.

—§§§—

Editor: Some two decades later, Sanger seems to have assumed the *New York Times* continued to hold similar to those we have published here. In 1933 she wrote the newspaper's editor on the stationary of the National Committee on Federal Legislation for Birth Control. Some were arguing that the widespread adoption of birth control would result in an aging population and a stagnant economy. Sanger disagreed and quoted Professor Henry Pratt Fairchild, a well-known population expert. "A stationary population," Fairchild had written, "would permit a rational study of the standard of living, and a deliberate planning and social engineering for the achievement of the highest possible standard."[8] As you might suspect, social engineering meant that a few experts would determine who has children much as an engineer decides on the location of the steel and concrete in a dam.

8. Margaret Sanger to *New York Times* (May 8, 1933). Sanger/Smith microfilm, S07:0869.

BABES OF THE FUTURE

Major Leonard Darwin Tells True Purposes of Eugenics

XIII

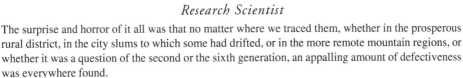

Kallikak Family

1912

Henry H. Goddard

Research Scientist

The surprise and horror of it all was that no matter where we traced them, whether in the prosperous rural district, in the city slums to which some had drifted, or in the more remote mountain regions, or whether it was a question of the second or the sixth generation, an appalling amount of defectiveness was everywhere found.

EDITOR

No book on Margaret Sanger would be complete without an illustration of the once well-respected scientific research that buttressed the fears she and her supporters had about rapidly multiplying horde of 'feeble-minded.' In the eighth chapter of *The Pivot of Civilization,* Sanger referred to that research this way: "Eugenics is chiefly valuable in its negative aspects. It is 'negative Eugenics' that has studied the histories of such families as the Jukeses and the Kallikaks, that has pointed out the network of imbecility and feeble-mindedness that has been sedulously spread through all strata of society."

The story behind this chapter is a depressing one. Early in the twentieth century, scientists wanting to build successful careers could do so by 'discovering' families—typically in isolated rural communities—where generation after generation of failure was thought to prove that such traits were inherited. Through an attractive young girl brought to his Training School, Goddard thought he had discovered just such a family and he intended to make the most of it.

Henry H. Goddard, *The Kallikak Family: A Study in the Heredity of Feeble-Mindedness* (New York: Macmillan, 1912). Page numbers are given in square brackets after the text quoted [ ].

On September 15, 1906, the Training School for Backward and Feeble-minded Children at Vineland, New Jersey, opened a laboratory and a Department of Research for the study of feeble-mindedness. . . .

As soon as possible after the beginning of this work, a definite start was made toward determining the cause of feeble-mindedness. After some preliminary work, it was concluded that the only way to get the information needed was by sending trained workers to the homes of the children, to learn by careful and wise questioning the facts that could be obtained. It was a great surprise to us to discover so much mental defect in the families of so many of these children. The results of the study of more than 300 families will soon be published, showing that about 65 per cent of these children have the hereditary taint.

The present study of the Kallikak family is a genuine story of real people. The name is, of course, fictitious, as are all of the names throughout the story. The results here presented come after two years of constant work, investigating the conditions of this family. [vii–viii]

—§§§—

Influence of the Kallikak Study

Although there were many studies of family degeneracy . . . the most powerful and influential was reported in 1912 by Henry Goddard in his book *The Kallikak Family.*[1]

—J. DAVID SMITH, *MINDS MADE FEEBLE,* 1985

One bright October day, fourteen years ago, there came to the Training School at Vineland, a little eight-year-old girl. She had been born in an almshouse. Her mother had afterwards married, not the father of this child, but the prospective father of another child, and later had divorced him and married another man, who was also the father of some of her children. She had been led to do this through the efforts of well-meaning people

1. J. David Smith, *Minds Made Feeble: The Myth and Legacy of the Kallikaks* (Rockville: Aspen Systems, 1985), 3.

who felt that it was a great misfortune for a child to be born into the world illegitimately. From their standpoint the argument was good, because the mother with four or five younger children was unable to provide adequately for this little girl, whom both husbands refused to support.

On the plea that the child did not get along well at school and might possibly be feeble-minded, she gained admission to the Training School, there to begin a career which has been interesting and valuable to the Institution, and which has led to an investigation that cannot fail to prove of great social import. [1–2]

—§§§—

The reader will see that Deborah's teachers have worked with her faithfully and carefully, hoping for progress, even seeing it where at a later date it became evident that no real advance had been made. Note the oft-repeated "She could if she would," or "If she would only pay attention," and similar expressions, which show the unwillingness of the teachers to admit even to themselves that she is really feeble-minded. In the earliest records it was noted that Deborah was not fond of music, while in later reports it is shown to be her one great accomplishment. To-day she is a woman of twenty-two. The consensus of opinion of those who have known her for the last fourteen years in the Institution is as follows:

> She is cheerful, inclined to be quarrelsome, very active and restless, very affectionate, willing, and tries; is quick and excitable, fairly good-tempered. Learns a new occupation quickly, but requires a half hour or twenty-four repetitions to learn four lines. Retains well what she has once learned. Needs close supervision. Is bold towards strangers, kind towards animals. Can run an electric sewing machine, cook, and do practically everything about the house. [7]

Editor: At the front of Goddard's book there is a photograph of an attractive 22-year-old Deborah reading a book. Later there is one of her with a dog taken at 17. Her teachers' assessments were probably accurate. She was a ordinary young woman with more than enough ability to make it on her own. In fact, the description that Goddard gave (above) is one that millions of parents might give of their own teenage daughters. God-

dard had to twist facts to make Deborah into a danger to society. In other pictures in his book, he does far worse. He crudely altered photographs of her relatives to make them look mentally deranged. The use of both types of photographs wasn't accidental. One of eugenics' primary messages was that many of the "feeble-minded" were indistinguishable—except by experts—from ordinary citizens. Perhaps the real crime in Deborah's case was that she was institutionalized at all and, as much of the rest of the book unwittingly illustrated, exploited to provide the school with a talented but unpaid worker.

This is a typical illustration of the mentality of a high-grade feeble-minded person, the moron, the delinquent, the kind of girl or woman that fills our reformatories. They are wayward, they get into all sorts of trouble and difficulties, sexually and otherwise, and yet we have been accustomed to account for their defects on the basis of viciousness, environment, or ignorance.

It is also the history of the same type of girl in the public school. Rather good-looking, bright in appearance, with many attractive ways, the teacher clings to the hope, indeed insists, that such a girl will come out all right. Our work with Deborah convinces us that such hopes are delusions.

Here is a child who has been most carefully guarded. She has been persistently trained since she was eight years old, and yet nothing has been accomplished in the direction of higher intelligence or general education. **To-day if this young woman were to leave the Institution, she would at once become a prey to the designs of evil men or evil women and would lead a life that would be vicious, immoral, and criminal, though because of her mentality she herself would not be responsible.** There is nothing that she might not be led into, because she has no power of control, and all her instincts and appetites are in the direction that would lead to vice.

We may now repeat the ever insistent question, and this time we indeed have good hope of answering it. The question is, "How do we account for this kind of individual?" The answer is in a word "Heredity,"—bad stock. We must recognize that the human family shows varying stocks or strains that are as marked and that breed as true as anything in plant or animal life.

Formerly such a statement would have been a guess, an hypothesis. We submit in the following pages what seems to us conclusive evidence of its truth. [11–12]

—§§§—

The Vineland Training School has for two years employed field workers.[2] These are women highly trained, of broad human experience, and interested in social problems. As a result of weeks of residence at the Training School, they become acquainted with the condition of the feeble-minded. They study all the grades, note their peculiarities, and acquaint themselves with the methods of testing and recognizing them. They then go out with an introduction from the Superintendent to the homes of the children and there ask that all the facts which are available may be furnished, in order that we can know more about the child and be better able to care for him and more wisely train him.

Sometimes all necessary information is obtained from the one central source, but more often, especially where the parents are themselves defective, many visits to other homes must be made. Parents often send the field worker to visit near and distant relatives as well as neighbors, employers, teachers, physicians, ministers, overseers of the poor, almshouse directors, etc. These must be interviewed and all the information thus obtained must be weighed and much of it verified by repeated visits to the same locality before an accurate chart of the particular child's heredity can be made.

In determining the mental condition of people in the earlier generations (that is, as to whether they were feeble-minded or not), one proceeds in the same way as one does to determine the character of a Washington or a Lincoln or any other man of the past. Recourse is had to original documents whenever possible. In the case of defectives, of course, there are not many original documents. [13–14]

—§§§—

In Deborah's case, the woman first visited was the one who interested herself in the child and its mother when the latter had just given birth to her baby in the almshouse. From this woman was learned the subsequent history of Deborah's mother as given in the first part of this description. But references, supplied by her, soon led to further discoveries. The present family was found living within twenty miles of what was afterwards learned to be its ancestral home and in a region that was neither the slums of a city nor the wild desolation of the extreme rural community, but rather in the midst of a populous farming country, one of the best districts in the State. Thorough and carefully conducted investigations in the small town and among the farmers of this region showed that the family had always been notorious for the number of defectives and delinquents it had produced; and this notoriety made it possible to trace them back for no less than six generations.

It was determined to make a survey of the entire family and to discover the condition, as far as possible, of every person in each generation.

The surprise and horror of it all was that no matter where we traced them, whether in the prosperous rural district, in the city slums to which some had drifted, or in the more remote mountain regions, or whether it was a question of the second or the sixth generation, an appalling amount of defectiveness was everywhere found. [15–16]

The Kallikak Family on Broadway

Goddard's book on the Kallikak family was received with acclaim by the public and by much of the scientific community. It went through several editions. Overtures were made to Goddard concerning the possibility of a Broadway production based on the book.[3]

—J. DAVID SMITH, *MINDS MADE FEEBLE*, 1985

—§§§—

The great-great-grandfather of Deborah was Martin Kallikak. That we knew. We had also traced the good family, before alluded to, back to an ancestor belonging to an older generation than this Martin Kallikak, but bearing the same name. He was the father of a large family. . . .

When Martin Sr., of the good family, was a boy of fifteen, his father died, leaving him without parental care or oversight. Just before attaining his majority, the young man joined one of the numerous military companies that were formed to protect the country at the beginning of the Revolution. At one of the taverns frequented by the militia he met a feeble-minded girl by whom he became the father of a feeble-minded son. This child was given, by its mother, the name of the father in full, and thus has been handed down to posterity the father's name and the mother's mental capacity. This illegitimate boy was Martin Kallikak Jr., the great-great-grandfather of our Deborah, and from him have come four hundred and eighty

---

2. According to J. David Smith in *Minds Made Feeble*, Deborah's field worker was Elizabeth Kite, someone with no formal training in social science (p. 4–5).

3. J. David Smith, *Minds Made Feeble*, 5. Broadway then, much like Hollywood now, could fixate on the most tasteless themes.

descendants. One hundred and forty-three of these, we have conclusive proof, were or are feeble-minded, while only forty-six have been found normal. The rest are unknown or doubtful. [17–18]

—§§§—

This is the ghastly story of the descendants of Martin Kallikak Sr., from the nameless feeble-minded girl.

Although Martin himself paid no further attention to the girl nor her child, society has had to pay the heavy price of all the evil he engendered.

Martin Sr., on leaving the Revolutionary Army, straightened up and married a respectable girl of good family, and through that union has come another line of descendants of radically different character. These now number four hundred and ninety-six in direct descent. All of them are normal people. Three men only have been found among them who were somewhat degenerate, but they were not defective. Two of these were alcoholic, and the other sexually loose.

All of the legitimate children of Martin Sr. married into the best families in their state, the descendants of colonial governors, signers of the Declaration of Independence, soldiers and even the founders of a great university. Indeed, in this family and its collateral branches, we find nothing but good representative citizenship. There are doctors, lawyers, judges, educators, traders, landholders, in short, respectable citizens, men and women prominent in every phase of social life. They have scattered over the United States and are prominent in their communities wherever they have gone. [29–30]

—§§§—

Fortunately for the cause of science, the Kallikak family, in the persons of Martin Kallikak Jr. and his descendants, are not open to this argument. **They were feeble-minded, and no amount of education or good environment can change a feeble-minded individual into a normal one, any more than it can change a red-haired stock into a black-haired stock.** The striking fact of the enormous proportion of feeble-minded individuals in the descendants of Martin Kallikak Jr. and the total absence of such in the descendants of his half brothers and sisters is conclusive on this point. Clearly it was not environment that has made that good family. They made their environment; and their own good blood, with the good blood in the families into which they married, told. [53]

—§§§—

The reader must remember that the type of feeble-mindedness of which we are speaking is the one to which Deborah belongs, that is, to the high grade, or moron. All the facts go to show that this type of people makes up a large percentage of our criminals. We may argue *a priori* that such would be the case. Here we have a group who, when children in school, cannot learn the things that are given them to learn, because through their mental defect, they are incapable of mastering abstractions. They never learn to read sufficiently well to make reading pleasurable or of practical use to them. The same is true of number work. Under our compulsory school system and our present courses of study, we compel these children to go to school, and attempt to teach them the three R's, and even higher subjects. Thus they worry along through a few grades until they are fourteen years old and then leave school, not having learned anything of value or that can help them to make even a meager living in the world. They are then turned out inevitably dependent upon others. A few have relatives who take care of them, see that they learn to do something which perhaps will help in their support, and then these relatives supplement this with enough to insure them a living.

A great majority, however, having no such interested or capable relatives, become at once a direct burden upon society. These divide according to temperament into two groups. Those who are phlegmatic, sluggish, indolent, simply lie down and would starve to death, if some one did not help them. When they come to the attention of our charitable organizations, they are picked up and sent to the almshouse, if they cannot be made to work. The other type is of the nervous, excitable, irritable kind who try to make a living, and not being able to do it by a fair day's work and honest wages, attempt to succeed through dishonest methods. "Fraud is the force of weak natures." These become the criminal type. The kind of criminality into which they fall seems to depend largely upon their environment. [54–55]

—§§§—

Although the foregoing facts, figures, and charts show conclusively the difference between good heredity and bad and the result of introducing mental deficiency into the family blood, yet because it is so difficult actually to appreciate the situation, because facts and figures do not have flesh and blood reality in them, we give in this chapter a few cases, graphically written up by our field worker, to show the differences in the types of people on the two sides of the family. These are only a few of the many, but are fairly typical of the condition of things that was found throughout the investigation. On the bad side we have the type of family which the social worker meets continually and which makes most of our social problems. A study of it will help to account for the conviction we have that no amount of work in the slums or removing the slums from our cities will ever be successful until we take care of those who make the slums what they are. Unless the two lines of work go on together, either one is bound to be futile in itself. If all of the slum districts of our cities were removed to-morrow and model tenements built in their places, we would still have slums in a week's time, because we have these mentally defective people who can never be taught to live otherwise than as they have been living. Not until we take care of this class and see to it that their lives are guided by intelligent people, shall we remove these sores from our social life.

There are Kallikak families all about us. They are multiplying at twice the rate of the general population, and not until we recognize this fact, and work on this basis, will we begin to solve these social problems. [70–71]

—§§§—

We have come to the point where we no longer leave babies or little children to die uncared for in our streets, but who has yet thought of caring intelligently for the vastly more pathetic child-man or child-woman, who through matured sex powers, which they do not understand, fill our land with its overflowing measure of misery and crime? Such thoughts as these filled the mind of the field worker on the ride home. [92–92]

—§§§—

But even so the real problem will not be solved. Had Martin Kallikak remained in the paths of virtue, there still remained the nameless feeble-minded girl, and there were other people, other young men, perhaps not of as good a family as Martin, perhaps feeble-minded like herself, capable of the same act and without Martin's respectability, so that the race would have come down even worse if possible than it was, because of having a worse father.

Others will look at the chart and say, "The difficulty began with the nameless feeble-minded girl; had she been taken care of, all of this trouble would have been avoided." This is largely true. Although feeble-mindedness came into this family from other sources in two generations at least, yet nevertheless these sources were other feeble-minded persons. When we conclude that had the nameless girl been segregated in an institution, this defective family would not have existed, we of course do not mean that one single act of precaution, in that case, would have solved the problem, but we mean that all such cases, male and female, must be taken care of, before their propagation will cease. The instant we grasp this thought, we realize that we are facing a problem that presents two great difficulties; in the first place the difficulty of knowing who are the feeble-minded people; and, secondly, the difficulty of taking care of them when they are known.

A large proportion of those who are considered feeble-minded in this study are persons who would not be recognized as such by the untrained observer. They are not the imbeciles nor idiots who plainly show in their countenances the extent of their mental defect. They are people whom the community has tolerated and helped to support, at the same time that it has deplored their vices and their inefficiency. They are people who have won the pity rather than the blame of their neighbors, but no one has seemed to suspect the real cause of their delinquencies, which careful psychological tests have now determined to be feeble-mindedness. [103–05]

—§§§—

The other method proposed of solving the problem is to take away from these people the power of procreation. The earlier method proposed was unsexing, asexualization, as it is sometimes called, or the removing, from the male and female, the necessary organs for procreation. The operation in the female is that of ovariectomy and in the male of castration.

There are two great practical difficulties in the way of carrying out this method on any large scale. The first is the strong opposition to this practice on the part of the public generally. It is regarded as mutilation of the human body and as such is opposed vigorously by many people. And while there is no rational basis for this, nevertheless we have, as practical reformers, to recognize the fact that the average man acts not upon reason, but upon sentiment and feeling; and as long as human sentiment and feeling are opposed to this practice, no amount of reasoning will avail. It may be shown over and over again that many a woman has had the operation of ovariectomy performed in order to improve her physical condition, and that it is just as important to improve the moral condition as the physical. Nevertheless, the argument does not convince, and there remains the opposition as stated.

In recent years surgeons have discovered another method which has many advantages. This is also sometimes incorrectly referred to as asexualization. It is more properly spoken of as sterilization, the distinction being that it does not have any effect on the sex qualities of the man or woman, but does artificially take away the power of procreation by rendering the person sterile. The operation itself is almost as simple in males as having a tooth pulled. In females it is not much more serious. The results are generally permanent and sure. Objection is urged that we do not know the consequences of this action upon the physical, mental, and moral nature of the individual. The claim is made that it is good in all of these. But it must be confessed that we are as yet ignorant of actual facts. It has been tried in many cases; no bad results have been reported, while many good results have been claimed.

A more serious objection to this last method comes from a consideration of the social consequences. What will be the effect upon the community in the spread of debauchery and disease through having within it a group of people who are thus free to gratify their instincts without fear of consequences in the form of children? The indications are that here also the evil consequences are more imaginary than real, since the feeble-minded seldom exercise restraint in any case. [106–08]

—§§§—

In 1866 an Austrian monk by the name of Gregor Mendel discovered and published a law of inheritance in certain plants, which, after lying practically unknown for nearly forty years, was rediscovered in 1900 and since then has been tested with regard to a great many plants and animals.

Mendel found that there were certain peculiarities in plants which he termed "unit characters" that were transmitted from parent to offspring in a definite way. . . .

This law has been found to hold true for many unit characters in many plants and animals. Since study in human heredity has been taken up, it has been a natural question, Does this same law apply to human beings? . . .

Our own studies lead us to believe that it also applies in the case of feeble-mindedness, but this will be taken up in a later work to which we have already referred. We do not know that feeble-mindedness is a "unit character." Indeed, there are many reasons for thinking that it cannot be. But assuming for the sake of simplifying our illustration that it is a "unit character," then we have something like the following conditions.

If two feeble-minded people marry, then we have the same unit character in both, and all of the offspring will be feeble-minded; and if these offspring select feeble-minded mates, then the same thing will continue. But what will happen if a feeble-minded person takes a normal mate? If feeble-mindedness is recessive (due to the absence of something that would make for normality), we would expect in the first generation from such a union all normal children, and if these children marry persons like themselves, i.e. the offspring of one normal and one defective parent, then the offspring would be normal and defective in the ratio of three to one. Of the normal children, one third would breed true and we would have a normal line of descent. [109–12]

—§§§—

From all of this the one caution follows. At best, sterilization is not likely to be a final solution of this problem. We may, and indeed I believe must, use it as a help, as something that will contribute toward the solution, until we can get segregation thoroughly established. But in using it, we must realize that the first necessity is the careful study of the whole subject, to the end that we may know more both about the laws of inheritance and the ultimate effect of the operation. [115–16]

—§§§—

XIV

The Village of a Thousand Souls

1913

Arnold L. Gesell

Child Development Clinic, Yale University

The banks of the racial river of life should be beautified and ennobled by all that the willing hands of man can rear and contrive; but those benefactors who labor now through science and wise legislation to purify the very springs of the dying and living stream will be thrice blessed by the generations unborn.

EDITOR

Eugenics never had a following among the great mass of Americans. But for a time it was fashionable among the nation's "chattering classes." As one of the nation's premier child psychologists, Arnold Gesell of Yale's medical school was drawn into the cause at the height of its popularity. In this article he took a eugenic-inspired look at a "real village located in a prosperous farming district in the Middle West." Others scientists targeted Kallikak-like abnormalities. Gesell chose to look at the normal. If problems could be found among the 1,000 residents of a successful farming community, then the nation's "racial river of life" was polluted at its source. That was exactly what Dr. Gesell found.

Arnold L. Gesell, "The Village of a Thousand Souls" *American Magazine* LXXVI (Oct. 1913), 11–15. Page numbers are given in square brackets after the text quoted [ ].

—§§§—

We do not know to what extent similar surveys would reveal village conditions which we have discovered, though we have our opinion. Meanwhile, we would like to arouse in the reader's mind the question: Is the village we show better; or is it worse? Is it possible to improve the human stock that lives in villages?

I once talked with a farmer who came to this village. We were discussing the inspection of cattle by state paid inspectors. He said he surely favored such inspection: "I want to see the bad stock cleaned out of the valley." He valued well-bred cattle. It is interesting to note in this connection that state aid and inspection can improve the breed of domestic animals. **Breeding, whether of plants or animals, is an art based on a science, the science of heredity. Eugenics is the science of the improvement of the human race by better breeding.**

For thirty-three years parents have lived and brought forth children in The Village of a Thousand Souls. At one end of the village lived a saloon keeper who is serving a life sentence for having taken a life. "His children are not quite right." I believe he is the only inhabitant of the village who ever committed manslaughter, though he had some neighbors who lived on the border of the law. In fact, there were several shiftless, ne'er-do-well families in this neighborhood, who were apparently not equal to successful life either on the farm or in the town. They undoubtedly represented a "border-line" stock in whom the social traits and physical energy necessary for even village civilization were somewhat deficient. Villages do not have slums, but they have the human material which in the city gravitates to the slums, if indeed it does not help to create the slums. Poverty may breed social incompetence, but the reverse is also true. The slum may be a symptom as well as a cause. The "slumlike" village hovel in a land of plenty proves it.

Not far from the "criminal" lived a curious, old, bristly-bearded character, unkempt and dilapidated. He had no other companion than a cat or two. Perhaps he was the crooked man who bought a crooked cat and lived in a crooked house. He had a mentality little above his contemporary, Simple Simon. We believe the latter fact explains his poverty, his "shiftlessness," his dilapidated estate. Feeble-mindedness is at the basis of a good fraction of economic failure and economic incompetence.

Economic incompetence often goes by the name of laziness, thriftlessness, shiftlessness. In every village we find some of this "worthless sort," and they usually get scant sympathy, and still scanter interpretation. Be careful of your own diagnosis of these cases, reader, or you may make the mistake of the ignorant parent who actually beats a feebleminded child, thinking the child *will* not obey, when as a pure matter of fact the child *can* not obey. There may be a kind of laziness which will respond to moral suasion; but there is another, important kind which is due to incurable deficiency of will. Feeble-mindedness is a blight which not only affects the intellect, but may also weaken the instincts which are at the basis, alike, of play, work, and thrift.[11]

—§§§—

And so we might continue our journey through the village, going from house to house as the local assessor does on his yearly rounds, but not to appraise the material goods and lands; rather to evaluate the grade and quality of the human "stock" which has found its family life and shelter in these two hundred homes. Every house has a human story or, we may say, a story of the human natures which have been associated with it—strong natures, happy natures, feeble, dejected, distraught, vacillating, composed, simple, ambitious natures. . . .

—§§§—

What is feeble-mindedness? Medically, feeble-mindedness is a permanent, early arrest of the development of the nervous system, particularly of the brain, cortex, or "gray matter." Pedagogically, feeble-minded persons are those who cannot be taught to read, write, or cipher, with any marked advantage to themselves or society. Psychologically, feeble-mindedness is a condition of permanent, incurable mental retardation limiting the individual to an intelligence less than that of a normal, thirteen-year-old child. Sociologically, feeble-mindedness is a condition of relative mental incompetence, dating from birth or infancy, which makes it impossible for the individual to get along in the world on equal terms with his normal fellows. . . .

It is interesting that only one or two of all these and other feeble-minded inhabitants were ever sent to an institution. The reasons are plain. In many cases the feeble-mindedness is not recognized or understood. The family realize that the boy is "slow," and wish that people would not tease him so much. "But he will get along all right," the parents say; and this prediction is partially justified. In a village, particularly a rural village, where gardens, barns and domestic animals are common the conditions of live are primitive. They may not be too severely complex for even the feeble-minded boy, who learns how to tend stable, is happy in a simple routine of chores, and masters a simple occupation like sawing wood. . . .

Putting it briefly, you may get a combination of circumstances in a village which are equivalent to the custodial supervision of a good institution for the feeble-minded. . . . The trouble is, some day, a "harmless" fellow who has been sawing wood in the village goes out into the country and marries and has children. . . . About 80 per cent of all cases of feeble-mindedness are due to neuropathic heredity. . . . and the feeble-minded have much larger families than normally prudent parents.

In an industrial city (the village under discussion has practically no manufacturing) the struggle for existence is more complex and feeble-mindedness comes to clearer expression. Turn one of these harmless feeble-minded villagers into such a city (where he cannot saw wood, where his relatives cannot look after him), and he easily drifts into unemployment, thieving, vagrancy, or the like. Hence the apparently larger number of feeble-minded in the city; and in this age all cities. A large amount of feeble-mindedness is masked in our villages because the conditions of life are simple and humane enough to maintain and protect the feeble-minded. We may rejoice that it is so; but we must recognize the very narrow factor of safety so far as the race is concerned. [12]

—§§§—

its inhabitants. He quoted a remark in which Karl Pearson noted that historically humanity has depended on "exceptional men" to rise out of the "commonplace" rather than imitate a good stock breeder, "selecting and isolating a [superior] stock" from "the mediocre element" until it is established. As harshly as eugenists were in dealing with the 'feeble-minded,' they never seemed to develop an urge to impose such measures on their own ranks. Segregating the 'unfit' in institutions for most of their lives was fine—when an unenlightened public could be made to see the wisdom of the idea, but their *own* freedom must not be hindered in any way. That was Gesell's next point.

No sane eugenist would, of course, attempt to apply the methods of cattle breeding in order to hasten the improvement of village or urban populations; and the premature eugenist will not have the opportunity to do so. There is not even much likelihood that The Village of a Thousand Souls will soon establish a eugenic bureau and issue eugenic certificates to those who desire to publish their bans; but there is a real possibility that the State will soon make a systematic attempt to secure a registration of the unfit and prevent the mating of the unfit. Only the rankest pessimists and believers in noninterference will condone the increase of feeble-mindedness and insanity which is occurring everywhere in the villages of the land. **We need not wait for the perfection of the infant science of eugenics before proceeding upon a course of supervision and segregation which will prevent the horrible renewal of this defective protoplasm that is contaminating the stream of village life.** . . .

A good high school principal can by his influence elevate the tone of the whole town; but no principal or teacher can by patient work after school save, restore, or make over a feeble-minded scholar. A philanthropist by founding a library or clubhouse may add greatly to the happiness of this village. No one who has lived long in one village has failed to notice the strong environmental influences both of educational institutions and inspiring individuals. Yet heredity remains the greater half.

The banks of the racial river of life should be beautified and ennobled by all that the willing hands of man can rear and contrive; but those benefactors who labor now through science and wise legislation to purify the very springs of the dying and living stream will be thrice blessed by the generations unborn.

—§§§—

EDITOR

Arnold Gesell would play only a minor role in promoting eugenics. However, his son, Gerhard Gesell would play a major role in a similar movement 56 years later. As a judge in the U.S. District Court for the District of Columbia, in November of 1969 Gerhard Gesell became a key player in abortion legalization.

U.S. v. Vuitch pooled the cases of two individuals who had separately challenged the district's law restricting abortions to the "preservation of the mother's life or health." Milan Vuitch was a physician and Shirley Boyd was a nurse's aide. Gesell did refuse to accept that weakest of all legal arguments, a claim that the law was vague and should be overturned. But as the son of a physician, he did rule in the physician's favor, essentially letting doctors (but not nurse's aides) decide the meaning of "health."

Revealingly, Judge Gesell found one of Boyd's claims intriguing: "that the statute discriminates against the poor and in its present operation denies medical help in city hospitals but is more liberally applied in some private hospitals." With one eye undoubtedly fixed on the high birthrate of the city's poor black population, he wrote: "National and local policy provides free medical care for the poor. It is legally proper and indeed imperative that uniform medical abortion services be provided for all segments of the population, the poor as well as the rich. Principles of equal protection under our Constitution require that policies in our public hospitals be liberalized immediately."

What the father had sought—a way to eugenically beautify the "banks of the racial river of life"—the son believed he had found. But there were to be no blessings for "generations unborn." Unborn children now received all the eugenic wrath once reserved for the 'unfit' and the 'defective.'[1]

---

1. Editor: Interestingly, in 1974 Judge Gerhard Gesell issued a ruling in *Relf v. Weinberger* against the use of coercion in federally funded sterilization programs. There the judge noted (very revealingly) that "the dividing line between family planning and eugenics is murky." Not so murky, however, that the much greater efficiency of abortion—legalized nationally the previous year—is not extremely obvious. The eugenic value of perhaps 30,000 sterilizations a year, not all of them coerced, pales in comparison to that of 1.5 million abortions a year.

XV

Education and Race Suicide

Women's Colleges Have Heavy Responsibility for Disappearance of Old American Stock in the United States— Reforms That Are Needed

1915

Robert J. Sprague

Massachusetts Agricultural College, Amherst

If we have forces which are drawing off the best blood of the American stock and sinking it in a dry desert of sterile intellectuality and paralytic culture, let us know the facts, and let these magnificent colleges face them and the race responsibilities involved, because without any doubt, all of our great educational institutions can and will become powerful agencies for race survival rather than race suicide when their wealth and influence become applied along the right lines.

Editor: When they weren't blaming Polish Jews and Italian Catholics for their low birthrates, the New England elite often linked the problem to the growth of higher education for women. That gave feminists a legitimate reason to loath race suicide arguments. This chapter gives extracts from a much quoted 1915 article.

Robert J. Sprague, "Education and Race Suicide"
Journal of Heredity 6 (Apr. 1915), 158–62.

—§§§—

During the twenty-five years from 1887–1911 the deaths among the native born population of Massachusetts exceeded the births among the native born parents by an aggregate of 269,918. During the same period the total births in families having foreign born parents exceeded the total of deaths by 526,987. . . .

I have no desire to hold up Massachusetts as a horrible example of a State committing race suicide. Conditions may be just as bad in other industrial and commercial populations, but unfortunately other States have not been wise enough to collect adequate data on these points, whereas the Bay State has led off for many years with a most efficient and commendable system of vital statistics.

If this apparent deficit of native births and the surplus of foreign births are true to the facts, and if they should be maintained for a number of generations, the writing on the wall is clear, and he who runs may read the fate of the Anglo-Saxon stock in every activity of Massachusetts life; and if the conditions in this Commonwealth are typical of American industrial populations generally, then it is a National as well as a local problem that faces us. . . .

The Women's Colleges

The classical college education for women without any doubt develops a high type of character and independence in the graduates as individuals, and such a training might be desirable for all girls that can afford it, if certain vital interests of the race and its future were taken into account. The standards of the home, school and office are all elevated when college graduates enter them, but how about the vital future of the race?

Is the women's college as now conducted a force which acts for or against the survival of the race which patronizes it? Whatever intellectual and moral superiority a race may have, it needs also a certain amount of reproductive impulse in order to remain on the earth. No culture, art, science, or morality can save it unless it produces about three matured children per married, child-bearing couple, and any race which does not do this is doomed to extinction. **If we have forces which are** drawing off the best blood of the American stock and sinking it in a dry desert of sterile intellectuality and paralytic culture, let us know the facts, and let these magnificent colleges face them and the race responsibilities involved, because without any doubt, all of our great educational institutions can and will become powerful agencies for race survival rather than race suicide when their wealth and influence become applied along the right lines. The work to be done is not a criticism and reform of the colleges alone, but a change in the ideals and race feelings of the types of people that are represented in these institutions.

Reliable statistics can be obtained from only a few of the institutions granting college degrees to women. Those mentioned below have collected data concerning their alumnae and have made them accessible for the purposes of this paper. . . .

Mt. Holyoke College

Editor: The data showed the percentage of the graduates who never marry more than tripling from 14.6 per cent in the period 1842–49 to an astonishing 50 per cent for 1890–92. That led Professor Hewes, who compiled the data, to estimate that less than 42 percent of the college's current graduates would marry. In addition, the number of children per graduate had declined almost 250 per cent, from 2.37 children for 1842–49 graduates to a mere 0.95 children for 1890–92.

Bryn Mawr College

From 1888 to 1900 Bryn Mawr graduated 376 alumnae and up to January 1, 1913, 165 or 43.9 per cent of these had married. Up to that date these alumnae had given birth to 138 children, or an average of .84 child per married alumnae, or .37 of a child per graduate in all classes up to 1900. Only 32.8 per cent of all graduates up to January 1, 1913 had married up to that date.

Vassar College

Editor: Vassar's data concealed the extent of change over time by lumping all graduates from 1867 to 1900 together. In spite of this, the statistics were dismal. Only 49 per cent of the graduates had married and the average number of children per graduate was 0.8, less than a third the replacement rate. For Sanger's 1926 remarks to Vassar students, see the end of this chapter.

Wellesley College

Editor: Wellesley is covered in the next chapter, but in this article, only 31 per cent for those graduating between 1890 and 1912 were married at the time of the survey and they had only 0.39 children per graduate.

A Few Pertinent Points

The space given to this paper is not sufficient for much discussion of the causes and remedies for the situation present by these statistics, and it might not be well to enter into that anyway; but I will mention a few points that seem important. . . .

2. **More strong men are needed on the staff of public schools and women's colleges, and in all of these institutions more married instructors of both sexes are desirable. The catalogue of one of the colleges referred to above shows 114 professors and instructors, of whom 100 are women, of whom only two have ever married.** Is it to be expected that the curriculum created by such a staff would idealize and prepare for the family and home life as the greatest work of the world and the highest goal of woman, and teach race survival as a patriotic duty? Or, would it be expected that these bachelor staffs would glorify the independent vocation and life for women and create employment bureaus to enable their graduates to get into the offices, schools and other lucrative jobs? The latter seems to be what occurs. . . .

4. **Women college graduates are not greatly sought after as mates, to share in the work of getting a living and founding a family, because they are not prepared psychologically and technically for the jobs of cooking, sanitation, nursing, and child rearing, and are not seeking that mode of life except under specially selected conditions.** They have culture and intelligence and demand high standards in husbands and homes, but they are not prizes in the matter of efficiency in domestic life. The principles of supply and demand are effective in this as in other things. If college women could combine their culture with domestic ideals and efficiency there would be a higher demand for them as helpmates and mothers of the new generation. The American people as a whole have idealized individual independence in both men and women, instead of the family which must be the fundamental basis of race survival, and as long as we maintain that attitude our race suicide statistics will be portentous.

—§§§—

A Message to Vassar College

The question of race betterment is one of immediate concern, and I am glad to say that the United States Government has already taken certain steps to control the quality of our population through the drastic immigration laws. . . .

But while we close our gates to the so-called "undesirables" from other countries, we make no attempt to discourage or cut down the rapid multiplication of the unfit and undesirable at home.

In fact through our archaic and inhuman laws against Birth Control information the breeding of defectives and insane becomes a necessity.

These types are being multiplied with breakneck rapidity and increasing far out of proportion to the normal and intelligent classes. . . . Year by year their numbers are increasing. Huge sums—yes, vast fortunes—are expended on these, while the normal parents and their children are compelled to shift for themselves and compete with each other. . . .

Our statistics tell us that the birth rate of the college men and women is lower than it should be. . . . There are some who deplore this condition and would remedy it by abusive epithets hurled at this conscientious group of decent and responsible citizens, who would rather have only the number of children they can decently rear, than to enter a cradle competition with the less responsible.

There is only one reply to a request for a higher birth rate among the intelligent, and that is to ask the government to *first* take off the burdens of the insane and feebleminded from your backs. Sterilization for these is the remedy.[1]

—MARGARET SANGER, VASSAR COLLEGE, AUG. 5, 1926

1. Margaret Sanger, "The Function of Sterilization," *Birth Control Review* (Oct. 1926), 299. Little should be read into her use of "so-called" before "undesirables." Sanger traveled widely and knew people in almost every country who shared her elitist point of view. She disliked the way the law indiscriminately lumped such people with the much larger number of 'undesirables' having the same 'country of origin.'

XVI

Wellesley's Birth-Rate

1915

Roswell H. Johnson & Bertha Stutzmann

University of Pittsburgh

Now, these select women, who should be having at least the 3.7 children each . . . are only giving to the race .83 of a child each. Their reproductivity is only 22 1/4% of being adequate merely for replacement.

EDITOR

In this chapter the marriage rate and number of surviving children of graduates at a particular women's college are examined in great detail. The statistics were undeniably dismal. Among the more talented students, the birthrate was less than one-fourth that required merely to replace their numbers.

In response, the authors suggested major changes in how women were educated. Some feminists would appreciate: more opportunity for women to study at elite universities such as Harvard and Columbia and relaxed rules about socializing with men. But others undoubtedly infuriated them: encouraging the teaching of "education for domestic efficiency" and (as described in the previous chapter) a reduction in the number of never-married female faculty at women's colleges. From a eugenic perspective, it is difficult to argue with data showing that, of 100 women teaching at one woman's college, only two had ever married. But feminists were unlikely to agree that these schools needed "more strong men" on the faculty.

Roswell H. Johnson & Bertha Stutzmann, "Wellesley's Birth-Rate" *The Journal of Heredity* (June 1915), 250–53.

—§§§—

No question is of greater importance to eugenics than that of the birth-rate among the eugenically superior parts of the population. The junior author has therefore been investigating the reproductivity of Wellesley College graduates; some of her data were presented by the senior author in his address on Marriage Selection before the Race Betterment Conference at Battle Creek, Michigan.[1]

This investigation has now been completed and the results are summed up in the following table:

Wellesley College Status in fall of 1912	Graduates	All Students
Per cent married (graduated 1879–1988)	55%	60%
Per cent married in: 10 years from graduation	35%	37%
20 years from graduation	48%	49%
Number of children (mothers graduated 1870–1888): Per student	.86	.97
Per wife	1.56	1.62

From a racial standpoint, the significant marriage rate of any group of women is the percentage that have married before the end of the child-bearing period. Classes graduating later than 1888 are therefore not included in the first case, in which the status is of reports in the fall of 1912. In compiling this data deceased members and a few lost from record are of course omitted.

It is desirable to find any change that may be taking place in the marriage or birth rates, so we have calculated the rate at the end of ten and twenty years after graduation for each class. The twenty-year period so nearly covers the effective fertile years of a woman's life that it is more significant than the unlimited rate of the 79–80 classes. The result destroys the defense put forward by certain apologists for separate colleges, *viz.*; that the earlier college women were more professionally inclined, that their marriage rate was abnormally low for this rea-

1. *Journal of Heredity,* V. 3, pp. 101–110, March 1914.

son, and that with the more varied classes of later years, the marriage rate must have risen. Let us hope there has been a change for the better in the uncharted last ten years: but there is nothing in the steady decline of the previous years to give any confident basis for such a hope.

In the address referred to above, statistics were given showing a lower rate of reproductivity[2] of the honor girls (Phi Beta Kappa) resulting principally from a lower marriage rate. In order to test this further, we give the results of an investigation of the honor girls before Phi Beta Kappa was established at Wellesley. These honors consisted of Durant and Wellesley scholarships, which carry no stipend and are therefore awarded by the faculty solely for excellence in studies. The previous findings in regard to Phi Beta Kappa girls are confirmed by this newer study, as follows:

Wellesley College: Graduates of 01, 02, 03, 04, Status of Fall of 1912	All	Durant or Wellesley Scholars
Per cent married	44	35
Number of children: Per graduate	.37	.20
Per wife	.87	.57

The extraordinary inadequacy of the reproductivity of these college graduates can hardly be taken too seriously. These women are in general, and from a eugenic point of view, clearly of superior quality for

(a) They have survived the weeding-out process of grammar school and high school.

(b) They have survived the repeated elimination by examination in college.

(c) They represent the number left, after those with lower mental abilities have grown tired of the mental strain and dropped out.

(d) Some have forced their way to college against obstacles, because seeking its mental activities, [was] congenial to their natures.

(e) Some have gone to college because their excellence has been discovered by teachers or others who have strongly urged it.

All these attributes cannot be wholly mere acquisitions, but must be in some degree inherent. Futhermore, these girls are not only superior in themselves, but are ordinarily from superior parents, because

(a) Their parents have in most cases cooperated by desiring this mental training for their daughters.

(b) The parents have in most cases had sufficient economic efficiency to be able to afford a college course for their daughters.

Now, these select women, who should be having at least the 3.7 children each, which Sprague[3] calculates as necessary to maintain a stationary population, are only giving to the race .83 of a child each. Their reproductivity is only 22 1/4% of being adequate merely for replacement.

There are at least three causes for this abnormally low birth-rate, *viz.*:

(1) Lack of coeducation.

(2) The failure of their education to make them desirous of having homes of their own and efficient in these homes.

(3) Excessive limitations of the students' opportunity for social life.

Sprague expresses a doubt whether any adequate data in regard to the influence of coeducation on the marriage and birth rates has yet been collected. But we see no reason for rejecting the results of Miss Shinn's investigation (*Century Magazine,* October 1895), desirable as further studies may be. She found that nearly 50% of the coeducational women married before the age of 30, but only 40% of the women from separate colleges. If one thinks this difference small, let him remember that even 1%, carried over a long period of time, would produce a great effect in a cumulative process such as evolution.

Furthermore co-education produces a larger percentage of marriages with college men.

Separate colleges for women, in the United States, are from the viewpoint of the eugenist an historical blunder. They arose because (1) women were debarred from the eastern men's colleges—a most unfortunate circumstance, (2) because the mental capacity of women was at that time all to frequently considered to be too inferior for college training. It was, therefore, a natural result that colleges for women should be established. But, unfortunately, to correct the current depreciation of woman's mentality, it was thought necessary to give her the same curriculum as that used by men.

The results of this experiment, however, have been utterly inconclusive because no direct comparison of the men and women was possible. It was in the coeducational colleges that the test was conducted under satisfactory

2. The word *reproductivity* is used as a convenient term to give the net result as expressed in number of children per total number of women married or unmarried.

3. Sprague, Robert J. "Education and Race Suicide." *Journal of Heredity* (Organ of the American Genetic Association) Vol. VI No. 4 pp. 158–162. Washington, D.C. April 1915.

conditions. Today it is well known that the women capture more than their proportion in the honors and average higher in their marks. Is there any real reason, then, for these eastern, separate women's colleges to continue along the same old lines, with the unsatisfactory results that see have seen?

The stubborn resistance of these colleges to the introduction of education for domestic efficiency, especially in the care of the infant, has been amazing. They are thereby neglecting one of the most important factors in a woman's sound education.

May it not be that this ill-adjusted education is partly responsible for the fact that Cantell finds in American men of science at the time of his inquiry that those having college graduates as wives had 2.02 children each, while those with wives of partial college training had 2.21 children and those with wives of no college education 2.35 children?

The very proper preference in many intelligent men for girls trained to be efficient wives and mothers is one of the causes of the low marriage rate and late time of marriage of the graduates of women's colleges. The trained girl can and will marry a man with an income too restricted for the support of an inefficient wife.

Rules in force at various women's colleges, which lead to social limitations, not to say asceticism, throws up barriers to the social opportunities of the students. And this during the critical years of maximum attractiveness when, as we have elsewhere shown, so many of the non-collegiate girls are marrying or making acquaintances leading to marriage. To take a specific instance, at Wellesley no young man are allowed to call on a student during her one free day, Sunday.

Since then, the separation of sexes in different colleges, and the failure to teach girls domestic science, are contrary to the interests of society and the race, should we not urge:

(1) Parents to send their daughters to coeducational universities, or at least to semi-coeducational ones such as Harvard and Columbia, where they will have some opportunity to meet superior young men.

(2) The state or private benefactor to provide all-men's colleges with closely affiliated women's colleges, and to provide all women's colleges with strong departments for the teaching of domestic science in the broadest sense of the term. In case of refusal of the institution to accept such provisions, discrimination in the distribution of funds might well be made in favor of the more soundly organized institutions.[4]

—§§§—

If the Feminist Ideal Be Realised

We have to face the practical certainty that the gradual throwing open of trades and professions to women will involve the payment of large salaries to the more capable, and that this will place a premium, in women, upon celibacy or childlessness.

In any case there seems to be no other prospect, if the full feminist ideal be realised, than the entire extinction of British or American intelligence within the next two or three generations. The fate which, according to Bateson, overtook ancient Greece will be ours; only in our case it seems likely that it will be, if possible, more complete.[5]

—S. H. HALFORD, 1917

---

4. Editor: The original article included a chart showing marriage rates and number of children.

5. S. H. Halford, "Dysgenic Tendencies of Birth-Control, and the Feminist Movement" *Population and Birth Control,* Eden Paul, ed. (New York: Critic and Guide, 1917), 232–33. Editor: Note how he equates professional employment outside the home with "intelligence" and the "feminist ideal" with the collapse of our civilization. Feminists who agreed with the first (and almost all did) had trouble denying the second.

XVII

Birth-Rate in Harvard and Yale Graduates

1916

John C. Phillips

In his Report for 1901–02, President Eliot summarized the classes 1872-77 as to their surviving children, and found that the birth-rate of Harvard graduates was extremely low. He stated that these sample classes had failed to reproduce themselves by 28 per cent, and that obviously the entering classes of Harvard can be recruited from the sons of Harvard graduates in only a small degree.

EDITOR

Though the statistics for elite men's colleges were not quite as dismal as those for women's colleges, readers should not be under the impression that elite men were spared eugenics-inspired looks at *their* marriage and birth rates. Here is an article that created quite a stir when it first appeared.

John C. Phillips, "A Study of the Birth-Rate in Harvard and Yale Graduates." *Harvard Graduates Magazine* 25 (Sept. 1916), 25–34. Page numbers are given in square brackets after the text quoted [ ].

—§§§—

No one of thoughtful tendencies can fail to view with alarm the lowered birth-rate of Americans, and the spread of a standard of living among the upper and middle classes which is based on comfort and luxury rather than on education and culture.

New England was the first part of this country to feel the modern trend, and that this trend has been influenced by the crowding in of a large foreign industrial population seems likely. Walker, Fairchild, and others have found in the immigration since 1850 a sufficient cause for the falling birth-rate among native Americans.[1] It is said that the native laborer, in order to maintain his standard of living in competition with cheaper foreign labor, has

---

1. Editor: Francis A. Walker's 1891 "Immigration and Degradation" is reprinted as Chapter III. Fairchild is probably Henry Pratt Fairchild, author of *Immigration: A World Movement and Its American Significance* (1913).

had to decrease the size of his family. But the decreasing families are seen in all classes, and the causes are undoubtedly complex and not fully understood; moreover, the phenomenon is almost world-wide. **In a letter to me, former [Harvard] President Eliot analyzed one of these causes as a "preference on the part of both men and women for freedom from care and responsibility, and for passing pleasures rather than solid satisfactions."** Certainly there is no single causative agent to account for the remarkable changes in birth-rate since the middle of the last century. The psychologist must help out the sociologist in the study of the subtler influences at work among us.

My attention was called to college birth-rate by reading the various papers in the *Journal of Heredity* on "Race Suicide," and the birth-rate of the graduates of women's colleges. There did not seem to be any data of the same sort for the larger men's colleges, and I was particularly interested to see whether the rate had changed in recent years. The only available source from which to extract this information for Harvard University was the Class Reports. Harvard and Yale are here considered in the same way. In the case of Harvard the reports became fairly trustworthy for the Class of 1853, and for Yale they were usable back to the Class of 1850. I did not attempt to record births later than the Class of 1890, for the twenty-five year Report of this Class was just published at the time this work was done (summer of 1915), and earlier Class Reports are of little interest where the total number of children is sought for. [25–26]

—§§§—

Consideration of Tables

It is scarcely necessary to call attention to these two tables; the falling birth-rate is shown in all four columns where children are considered. Roughly, the number of children born per capita per married graduate has fallen from about 3.25 in the first decade to 2.50 in the last decade. The per cent of graduates marrying has remained about the same for forty years, and is a trifle higher for Yale; but the low figure, 68 per cent for the first decade of Harvard, is probably due to faulty records, and must not be taken as significant.

The next most interesting figure is the "Children Surviving per Capita per Graduate." This has fallen from over 2.50 to about 1.9. The per cent of childless marriages increased very markedly during the first two decades and held nearly level for the last two decades. For the last decade at Yale it has even dropped slightly, an encouraging sign. It is worthy of note that the number of children born to Yale graduates is almost constantly a trifle higher than that for Harvard, while the number of childless marriages is slightly less.

Consideration of Birth-Curves

The two curves show the same condition of affairs; a sharp drop during the first decades and a "flattening" tendency during the last two decades. This tendency for the curves to flatten is the one encouraging thing brought out by this investigation. The uncharted last sixteen years will be of great interest, and it is fair to assume that this period will show a relative, if not in absolute, improvement in birth-rate over the period 1881-90. The great irregularity in the curves for the earlier years is caused by the smaller number of graduates in each Class, increasing the probable error.

General Considerations

In his Report for 1901–02, President Eliot summarized the classes 1872-77 as to their surviving children, and found that the birth-rate of Harvard graduates was extremely low. He stated that these sample classes had failed to reproduce themselves by 28 per cent, and that obviously the entering classes of Harvard can be recruited from the sons of Harvard graduates in only a small degree.

In a letter to me dated June 8, 1918, Dr. Eliot noted a number of causes to which be attributed this "disastrous state of things." He also says that he is "inclined to believe that there has, within recent years, been an improvement as to the number of children in Harvard families," but adds that he has "no proof of it." My tables show that Dr. Eliot's surmise is right at least in a relative

sense, and there is ground for hope that it will soon be true in an absolute sense.

Dr. Davenport[2] says that Harvard does not reproduce itself and that at the present rate 1000 graduates of today will have only 50 descendants 200 years hence. This statement is apparently based on Dr. Eliot's figures and is a little hard to account for, because in the forty-year period considered here (or strictly thirty-six years), 5618 Harvard graduates had 8224 surviving children, not counting a few other children that do not appear because their fathers' records are not complete. If we reckon three generations to a century, and if we use the present ratio of graduates to children (8224 children divided by 5618 graduates), we get 1.46 children of surviving age for each graduate. Carry out this simple calculation for six generations (200 years), and consider the male line only, and we have our 5618 graduates leaving 852 sons. We should, of course, allow for the mortality of children that died after the last Class Report, an unknown quantity for us.

Dr. Davenport's calculation gives us 50 sons at the end of 200 years for 1000 graduates. On the same basis our 5618 graduates should give us 280 sons; but instead we get 852. We have, of course, entirely omitted the female line, which may produce as many Harvard men as the male line, and also we have not figured on a possible further falling of the birth rate. This survey gives a gloomy enough picture, but it is not quite so gloomy as Dr. Davenport would have us believe.

Sprague[3] calculated that among American stock of the East the families must average 3.7 children "for every mother who demonstrates any ability to bear offspring." According to him every married woman bearing children must bring three to a marriageable age. He says that 15 per cent of the stock be studied (New England) did not marry, or married too late, and that 20 per cent of marriages produced no children. We have seen that 22 to 25 per cent of Harvard and Yale graduates never marry, and that 19 to 23 per cent of marriages are infertile; therefore, on Sprague's basis every married graduate having children must average a little more than three surviving children to perpetuate the stock.

Another way of looking at the question is as follows: Allowing for 25 per cent who never marry and 21 per cent who contract childless marriages, we have left 54 per cent of fathers to supply the succeeding generation. Therefore 46 per cent of children should be added to the two surviving children that each graduate must leave to

---

2. *Heredity and Eugenics*, p. 309.

3. *Journal of Heredity* (April 1915), p. 159. Editor: Entitled "Education and Race Suicide."

fill the place of himself and his wife. This gives us 2.92 surviving children for each father in order barely to continue the race. This function our Harvard graduates fail to perform by 1.2 children each.

In the *Harvard Graduates' Magazine* for June, 1907, Mr. Keene shows that the death-rate of Harvard men has declined at a very satisfactory rate ever since the founding of the College, but we may well ask how much longer this state of affairs can continue. We know, for instance, that recent vital statistics begin to show an increasing death-rate among men about 45 years of age, and if this continues it will tend to counteract the effect of lowering infant mortality.

It is not my purpose here to suggest reforms or to analyze causes. I think every one in every walk of life will agree that the college graduate should at least perpetuate himself. Many of us disagree as to the eugenic ideal, for there is no single ideal possible, but all must admit that college men are at least fair samples of American manhood. The causes of the great decline in birth-rate are almost world-wide, and they concern the economist, the psychologist, and the physician. **Reform must come from within, not from without, and it will be brought about by a sterner sense of duty and a realization that the vain stampede after pleasure for pleasure's sake is leading us only to restlessness and discontent.**

Before concluding it will be well to compare the results of this study with the only investigation which gives us any real light upon the birth-rate of the old American stock. I refer to the *Report of the Immigration Commission,* vol. 28. Here are a few of the facts touching on birth-rate of Americans.

Among American women under 45 years of age who had been married 10 to 19 years, 13.1 per cent were sterile (childless): in Rhode Island, 17.5 to 19.4 per cent; in rural Minnesota, 5.1 per cent; and in the city of Minneapolis, 12.7 per cent.

Considering the number of children among this category of married American women, we find the table on page 34 based on nearly 16,000 individuals from various sample districts.

According to the *Report of the Immigration Commission* native American stock cannot be holding its own in the East or in the cities of the Middle West. In the rural districts of the Middle West the women have just one more child each than in the urban districts, and this rural stock may be said to be a little more than holding its own. The birth-rate in the South is supposed to be much higher.

In Massachusetts the State Report, *Births, Deaths, and Marriages,* for the 25 years ending 1911 shows us that the deaths among the native-born population exceeded the births among the native-born by nearly 270,000. During the same period the total births in families having foreign-born parents exceeded the total deaths by nearly 527,000. Comment is unnecessary.

The birth-rate of college women is quite the most pathetic spectacle of all. Johnson and Stutzmann[4] showed that for Wellesley College, period 1879-88, only about half the graduates married and that the mothers had only 1.56 children each. Per graduate there was but .86 of a child each. Among the honor girls (Durant and Wellesley scholarships) those that married had about half this number of children, or just about half a child each!

It is the writer's hope that these pages may fall among some readers who will take serious thought of the lesson they teach. Each generation has new duties and new distractions, but amidst the whirl of modernism let us not forget the oldest duty of all, that of the fathers and mothers of America in their care for the future of their country and the ideals of their race.

—§§§—

---

4. *Journal of Heredity* (1915), 250. Editor: Reprinted here as Chapter XV.

XVIII

Eugenics and Other Evils

1922

G. K. Chesterton

British Catholic Writer

So at least it seemed, doubtless in a great degree subconsciously, to the man who had wagered all his wealth on the usefulness of the poor to the rich and the dependence of the rich on the poor. The time came at last when the rather reckless breeding in the abyss below ceased to be a supply, and began to be something like a wastage; ceased to be something like keeping foxhounds, and began alarmingly to resemble a necessity of shooting foxes.

EDITOR

Some historians have misunderstood the early history of the birth control movement. Because the early Sanger (pre-1920s) was obviously a radical feminist and a fire-breathing socialist, they conclude that she must have changed when her movement began to draw support from the more well-to-do segments of society. In the next six chapters we will explore that misconception, illustrating the actual situation by giving the contemporary views of socialists, humanists, liberals, feminists, judges, and the mainstream press.

Because they differed on economics, some historians assume capitalists and socialists did not agree about the top-down control over who can have children—that Rockefeller and Lenin had nothing in common. Nothing could be further from the truth. Their differences were significant, but they centered not on any basic agenda but on when and how it was implemented. Worried about social unrest, capitalists wanted the birthrate of the under-class to be cut *immediately* but fussed that, if birth control knowledge was made too easily available, the 'better' sort of workers might not have enough children for indus-trial needs. Socialist intellectuals, on the other hand, often wanted to *defer* action until they were in power. Too early a revelation of their contempt for ordinary working people would make that task much harder. Once they were in control, however, the wishes of workers would not matter, particularly if, as many hoped, socialism had the entire world in its grasp. Then there would be no place for would-be parents to flee.

Liberals, obsessed with controlling people by manipulat-ing their environment, fretted when the rationale for lim-iting births became too obviously hereditarian. Though they clearly believed that some social groups were more valuable than others, they did not want those attitudes to become too obvious. They preferred to work by stealth, using free-speech and personal choice arguments to con-ceal their essential agreement with coercive, hereditarian eugenics. Because Sanger often used free speech argu-ments and blurred the distinction between heredity and environment, liberals could praise her for 'bravery' and a 'pioneering spirit.' They turned a blind eye to her more open expressions of bigotry because they shared many of those sentiments (see Chapter XXI).

Some of the ugliest rhetoric came from prominent femi-nists such as Martin (Chapter IV), Gilman (Chapter XXII), Stopes,[1] and Sanger herself. From the feminist perspective, their fear and anger were justified. However, it was not until the Great Depression that a consensus developed across all these groups that the problems cre-ated by the higher birthrate of socially troublesome groups had to dealt with almost exclusively by restricting births among the 'unfit' rather than by raising them among the 'fit.' Until then, feminists had to live in fear that their own peers would force them out of active social lives and careers and into childbearing—fears they con-cealed behind rhetoric about a "Catholic hierarchy" that had no conceivable reason for wanting to force unbeliev-

---

1. For Marie Stopes's bigotries see Appendices G–I in the Inkling edition of Chesterton's *Eugenics and Other Evils.*

ing and often ill-tempered social radicals into motherhood. In this arena, emotions ran so high that arguments often turned irrational.

There were also scientific humanists such as William Robinson (Chapter XX) and Lothrop Stoddard (Chapter XXVII). (In 1926, Stoddard published a book entitled *Scientific Humanism.*) Though often poor organizers, they were influential through their writings, showing—as many have observed—their love for humanity in the abstract along with their loathing for real people.

In this chapter, we look at the capitalist perspective. Unfortunately, the sort of capitalist who supported eugenics and birth control seems to have written little for public consumption. They expressed their opinions with their money and let others persuade. As a result, we break with our usual pattern and look at them from the viewpoint of one of their more vocal critics, the talented writer and journalist, G. K. Chesterton.

In its October, 1922 issue, *Birth Control News,* a British magazine owned by Marie Stopes's Society for Constructive Birth Control and Racial Progress, published a review of G. K. Chesterton's *Eugenics and Other Evils.* "His tendency is reactionary," it told readers, "and as he succeeds in making most people laugh, his influence in the wrong direction is considerable." In this chapter, extracted from that book, Chesterton explained why wealthy capitalists (he mentioned John Rockefeller Sr.) often supported eugenics. Read with care, his argument also explains why their support, given through giant, tax-exempt foundations, would shift to birth control and later to its close cousins, population control and legalized abortion. Be advised, this chapter is a delight. Unlike his grim-faced foes, Chesterton knew how to handle a serious topic humourously.

G. K. Chesterton, *Eugenics and Other Evils,* Michael W. Perry, ed. (Seattle: Inkling Books, 1922, 2000). Page numbers are given in square brackets after the text quoted [ ].

—§§§—

He does not live in a dark lonely tower by the sea, from which are heard the screams of vivisected men and women. On the contrary, he lives in Mayfair. He does not wear great goblin spectacles that magnify his eyes to moons or diminish his neighbours to beetles. When he is more dignified he wears a single eyeglass; when more intelligent, a wink. He is not indeed wholly without interest in heredity and Eugenical biology; but his studies and experiments in this science have specialised almost exclusively in *equus celer,* the rapid or running horse. He is not a doctor; though he employs doctors to work up a

case for Eugenics, just as he employs doctors to correct the errors of his dinner. He is not a lawyer, though unfortunately often a magistrate. He is not an author or a journalist; though he not infrequently owns a newspaper. He is not a soldier, though he may have a commission in the yeomanry; nor is he generally a gentleman, though often a nobleman. His wealth now commonly comes from a large staff of employed persons who scurry about in big buildings while he is playing golf. But he very often laid the foundations of his fortune in a very curious and poetical way, the nature of which I have never fully understood. It consisted in his walking about the street without a hat and going up to another man and saying, "Suppose I have two hundred whales out of the North Sea." To which the other man replied, "And let us imagine that I am in possession of two thousand elephants' tusks." They then exchange, and the first man goes up to a third man and says, "Supposing me to have lately come into the possession of two thousand elephants' tusks, would you, etc.? If you play this game well, you become very rich; if you play it badly you have to kill yourself or try your luck at the Bar. The man I am speaking about must have played it well, or at any rate successfully. [79–80]

—§§§—

To-day the rich man knows in his heart that he is a cancer and not an organ of the State. He differs from all other thieves or parasites for this reason: that the brigand who takes by force wishes his victims to be rich. But he who wins by a one-sided contract actually wishes them to be poor. Rob Roy in a cavern, hearing a company approaching, will hope (or if in a pious mood, pray) that they may come laden with gold or goods. But Mr. Rockefeller, in his factory, knows that if those who pass are laden with goods they will pass on. He will therefore (if in a pious mood) pray that they may be destitute, and so be forced to work his factory for him for a starvation wage. It is said (and also, I believe, disputed) that Blücher riding through the richer parts of London exclaimed, "What a city to sack!" But Blücher was a soldier if he was a bandit. The true sweater feels quite otherwise. It is when he drives through the poorest parts of London that he finds the streets paved with gold, being paved with prostrate servants; it is when he sees the grey lean leagues of Bow and Poplar that his soul is uplifted and he knows he is secure. This is not rhetoric, but economics.

I repeat that up to a point the profiteer was innocent because he was ignorant; he had been lured on by easy and accommodating events. He was innocent as the new Thane of Glamis was innocent, as the new Thane of Cawdor was innocent; but the King—The modern manufacturer, like Macbeth, decided to march on, under the mute menace of the heavens. He knew that the spoil of the poor was in his houses; but he could not, after careful calculation, think of any way in which they could get it out of his houses without being arrested for housebreaking. He faced the future with a face flinty with pride and impenitence. This period can be dated practically by the period when the old and genuine Protestant religion of England began to fail; and the average business man began to be agnostic, not so much because he did not know where he was, as because he wanted to forget. Many of the rich took to scepticism exactly as the poor took to drink; because it was a way out. But in any case, the man who had made a mistake not only refused to unmake it, but decided to go on making it. But in this he made yet another most amusing mistake, which was the beginning of all Eugenics. [84–85]

Editor: Among the capitalists who began to fear the consequences of their deeds, none was better known John Rockefeller Sr., once considered the "most hated man in America." His son, John Rockefeller Jr., would be given the enviable task of giving away much of the vast wealth his father had taken. Sanger would have contact with the family both professionally—the son founded the Bureau of Social Hygiene—and personally. (Her papers at Smith College contain some 200 letters between Sanger and the Rockefeller family or a family organization.) In a trial during the early 1920s, she faced a hostile attorney who attempted to tar her with the brush of political radicalism. "Do you know Emma Goldman?" he asked, looking at the judge. "Yes," Sanger replied, "but I also know Mrs. Andrew Carnegie and Mr. John D. Rockefeller Jr. My social relations are with people of varying ideas and opinions." The relationship that she and others in her movement would have with the Rockefeller family would prove long and enduring. In 1970, *Ramparts* magazine published an article on, "Why the Population Bomb is a Rockefeller Baby?"[2] Chesterton tells us why.

—§§§—

. . . . He (or the most intelligent section of him) had by now realised his position, and knew in his heart it was a false position. He thought a margin of men out of work

2. Margaret Sanger, *Margaret Sanger, An Autobiography* (New York: W. W. Norton, 1938), 78, 315. Steve Weissman, "Why the Population Bomb is a Rockefeller Baby," *Ramparts* (May 1970), 42–47. "Social hygiene" dealt with health issues such as sexually transmitted diseases. Sanger criticized it in *Pivot* at the start of Chap. 5.

was good for his business; he could no longer really think it was good for his country. He could no longer be the old "hardheaded" man who simply did not understand things; he could only be the hard-hearted man who faced them. But he still marched on; he was sure he had made no mistake.

However, he had made a mistake—as definite as a mistake in multiplication. It may be summarised thus: that the same inequality and insecurity that makes cheap labour may make bad labour, and at last no labour at all. It was as if a man who wanted something from an enemy, should at last reduce the enemy to come knocking at his door in the despair of winter, should keep him waiting in the snow to sharpen the bargain; and then come out to find the man dead upon the doorstep.

He had discovered the divine boomerang; his sin had found him out. The experiment of Individualism[3]**—the keeping of the worker half in and half out of work—was far too ingenious not to contain a flaw.** It was too delicate a balance to work entirely with the strength of the starved and the vigilance of the benighted. It was too desperate a course to rely wholly on desperation. And as time went on the terrible truth slowly declared itself; the degraded class was really degenerating. It was right and proper enough to use a man as a tool; but the tool, ceaselessly used, was being used up. It was quite reasonable and respectable, of course, to fling a man away like a tool; but when it was flung away in the rain the tool rusted. But the comparison to a tool was insufficient for an awful reason that had already begun to dawn upon the master's mind. If you pick up a hammer, you do not find a whole family of nails clinging to it. If you fling away a chisel by the roadside, it does not litter and leave a lot of little chisels. **But the meanest of the**

3. "Individualism" was a political philosophy that was closely linked to Social Darwinism. The government, it claimed, should not intervene in social conflicts such as those between employers and employees or between large businesses and small. Doing so would interfere with the natural, evolutionary struggle and result in inefficiency and coddling of the incompetent. It is usually contrasted to socialism, which wants to manage practically every conflict in the name of 'equality.' In practice, however, the advocates of both often accept the same evolutionary worldview and, with that, the urge to control birthrates. Like Malthusianism before it, Individualism advocated standing aside and letting the 'unfit' die. By the late 19th century, however, it was obvious that technique was not working. As a result, socialism's scheme for using the power of the state to control childbearing became appealing even to non-socialists. For an example, see Sidney's Webb's conversation with Dr. Saleeby in Chapter VI.

tools, Man, had still this strange privilege which God had given him, doubtless by mistake. Despite all improvements in machinery, the most important part of the machinery (the fittings technically described in the trade as "hands") were apparently growing worse. The firm was not only encumbered with one useless servant, but he immediately turned himself into five useless servants. "The poor should not be emancipated," the old reactionaries used to say, "until they are fit for freedom." But if this downrush went on, it looked as if the poor would not stand high enough to be fit for slavery.

Immigrants as Tools

In this sense it is fair to say that the blood now being injected into the veins of our people is "sub-common." Observe immigrants not as they come travel-wan up the gang-plank, nor as they come toil-begrimed from the pit's mouth or the mill gate, but in their gatherings, washed, combed, and in their Sunday best. You are struck by the fact that from ten to twenty per cent are histute, low-browed, big-faced persons of obviously low mentality. Not that they suggest evil. They simply look out of place in black clothes and stiff collar, since they clearly belong in skins, in wattled huts at the close of the Great Ice Age. These oxlike men are descendants of those *who always stayed behind.* Those in whom the soul burns with the dull, smoky flame of the pine-knot stuck to the soil, and are now thick in the sluiceways of immigration. Those in whom it burns with a clear, luminous flame have been attracted to the cities of the home land and, having prospects, have no motive to submit themselves to the hardships of the steerage. . . .

Our captains of industry give a crowbar to the immigrant . . . make a dividend out of him, and imagine that is the end of the matter. They overlook that this man will beget children in his image—two or three times as many as the American—and that these children will in turn beget children. **They chuckle at having opened an inexhaustible store of cheap tools and, lo! the American people is being altered for all time by these tools.** Once before, captains of industry took a hand in making this people. Colonial planters imported Africans to hoe in the sun, to "develop" the tobacco, indigo and rice plantations. Then, as now, business-minded men met with contempt the protests of a few idealists against their way of "building up the country."

Without likening immigrants to negroes, one may point out how the latter-day employer resembles the old-time

planter in his blindness to the effects of his labor policy upon the blood of the nation.[4]

—EDWARD A. ROSS, UNIVERSITY OF WISCONSIN, 1913

So at least it seemed, doubtless in a great degree subconsciously, to the man who had wagered all his wealth on the usefulness of the poor to the rich and the dependence of the rich on the poor. **The time came at last when the rather reckless breeding in the abyss below ceased to be a supply, and began to be something like a wastage; ceased to be something like keeping foxhounds, and began alarmingly to resemble a necessity of shooting foxes.** The situation was aggravated by the fact that these sexual pleasures were often the only ones the very poor could obtain, and were, therefore, disproportionately pursued, and by the fact that their conditions were often such that prenatal nourishment and such things were utterly abnormal. The consequences began to appear. To a much less extent than the Eugenists assert, but still to a notable extent, in a much looser sense than the Eugenists assume, but still in some sort of sense, the types that were inadequate or incalculable or uncontrollable began to increase. Under the hedges of the country, on the seats of the parks, loafing under the bridges or leaning over the Embankment, began to appear a new race of men—men who are certainly not mad, whom we shall gain no scientific light by calling feeble-minded, but who are, in varying individual degrees, dazed or drinksodden, or lazy or tricky or tired in body and spirit. In a far less degree than the teetotallers tell us, but still in a large degree, the traffic in gin and bad beer (itself a capitalist enterprise) fostered the evil, though it had not begun it. Men who had no human bond with the instructed man, men who seemed to him monsters and creatures without mind, became an eyesore in the market-place and a terror on the empty roads. The rich were afraid.

Moreover, as I have hinted before, the act of keeping the destitute out of public life, and crushing them under confused laws, had an effect on their intelligences which paralyses them even as a proletariat. Modern people talk of "Reason versus Authority"; but authority itself involves reason, or its orders would not even be understood. If you say to your valet, "Look after the buttons on my waistcoat," he may do it, even if you throw a boot at his head. But if you say to him, "Look after the buttons on my top-hat," he will not do it, though you empty a boot-shop over him. If you say to a schoolboy, "Write out that Ode of Horace from memory in the original Latin,"

---

4. Edward A. Ross, *The Old World in the New* (New York: Century, 1913, 1914), 285–87. Notice that for Ross, "negroes" ranked even lowered than "Ice Age" and "oxlike" immigrants.

he may do it without a flogging. If you say, "Write out that Ode of Horace in the original German," he will not do it with a thousand floggings. If you will not learn logic, he certainly will not learn Latin. And the ludicrous laws to which the needy are subject (such as that which punishes the homeless for not going home) have really, I think, a great deal to do with a certain increase in their sheepishness and short-wittedness, and, therefore, in their industrial inefficiency. By one of the monstrosities of the feeble-minded theory, a man actually acquitted by judge and jury could *then* be examined by doctors as to the state of his mind—presumably in order to discover by what diseased eccentricity he had refrained from the crime. In other words, when the police cannot jail a man who is innocent of doing something, they jail him for being too innocent to do anything. I do not suppose the man is an idiot at all, but I can believe he feels more like one after the legal process than before. Thus all the factors—the bodily exhaustion, the harassing fear of hunger, the reckless refuge in sexuality, and the black botheration of bad laws—combined to make the employee more unemployable.

Now, it is very important to understand here that there were two courses of action still open to the disappointed capitalist confronted by the new peril of this real or alleged decay. First, he might have reversed his machine, so to speak, and started unwinding the long rope of dependence by which he had originally dragged the proletarian to his feet. In other words, he might have seen that the workmen had more money, more leisure, more luxuries, more status in the community, and then trusted to the normal instincts of reasonably happy human beings to produce a generation better born, bred and cared for than these tortured types that were less and less use to him. It might still not be too late to rebuild the human house upon such an architectural plan that poverty might fly out of the window, with the reasonable prospect of love coming in at the door. In short, he might have let the English poor, the mass of whom were not weak-minded, though more of them were growing weaker, a reasonable chance, in the form of more money, of achieving their eugenical resurrection themselves. It has never been shown, and it cannot be shown, that the method would have failed. But it can be shown, and it must be closely and clearly noted, that the method had very strict limitations from the employers' own point of view. If they made the worker too comfortable, he would not work to increase another's comforts; if they made him too independent, he would not work like a dependent. If, for instance, his wages were so good that he could save out

of them, he might cease to be a wage-earner. If his house or garden were his own, he might stand an economic siege in it. **The whole capitalist experiment had been built on his dependence; but now it was getting out of hand, not in the direction of freedom, but of frank helplessness. One might say that his dependence had got independent of control.**

But there was another way. And towards this the employer's ideas began, first darkly and unconsciously, but now more and more clearly, to drift. Giving property, giving leisure, giving status costs money. But there is one human force that costs nothing. As it does not cost the beggar a penny to indulge, so it would not cost the employer a penny to employ. He could not alter or improve the tables or the chairs on the cheap. **But there were two pieces of furniture (labelled respectively "the husband" and "the wife") whose relations were much cheaper. He could alter the *marriage* in the house in such a way as to promise himself the largest possible number of the kind of children he did want, with the smallest possible number of the kind he did not. He could divert the force of sex from producing vagabonds.** And he could harness to his high engines unbought the red unbroken river of the blood of a man in his youth, as he has already harnessed to them all the wild waste rivers of the world. [88–91]

—§§§—

Now, if any ask whether it be imaginable that an ordinary man of the wealthier type should analyse the problem or conceive the plan, the inhumanly farseeing plan, as I have set it forth, the answer is: "Certainly not." Many rich employers are too generous to do such a thing; many are too stupid to know what they are doing. The eugenical opportunity I have described is but an ultimate analysis of a whole drift of thoughts in the type of man who does not analyse his thoughts. He sees a slouching tramp, with a sick wife and a string of rickety children, and honestly wonders what he can do with them. But prosperity does not favour self-examination; and he does not even ask himself whether he means "How can I help them?" or "How can I use them?"—what he can still do for them, or what they could still do for him. Probably he sincerely means both, but the latter much more than the former; he laments the breaking of the tools of Mammon much more than the breaking of the images of God. It would be almost impossible to grope in the limbo of what he does think; but we can assert that there is one thing he doesn't think. He doesn't think, "This man might be as jolly as I am, if he need not come to me for work or wages."

That this is so, that at root the Eugenist is the Employer, there are multitudinous proofs on every side, but they are of necessity miscellaneous, and in many cases negative. The most enormous is in a sense the most negative: that no one seems able to imagine capitalist industrialism being sacrificed to any other object. By a curious recurrent slip in the mind, as irritating as a catch in a clock, people miss the main thing and concentrate on the mean thing. "Modern conditions" are treated as fixed, though the very word "modern" implies that they are fugitive. "Old ideas" are treated as impossible, though their very antiquity often proves their permanence. Some years ago some ladies petitioned that the platforms of our big railway stations should be raised, as it was more convenient for the hobble skirt. It never occurred to them to change to a sensible skirt. Still less did it occur to them that, compared with all the female fashions that have fluttered about on it, by this time St. Pancras is as historic as St. Peter's.

I could fill this book with examples of the universal, unconscious assumption that life and sex must live by the laws of "business" or industrialism, and not vice versa; examples from all the magazines, novels, and newspapers. In order to make it brief and typical, I take one case of a more or less Eugenist sort from a paper that lies open in front of me—a paper that still bears on its forehead the boast of being peculiarly an organ of democracy in revolt. To this a man writes to say that the spread of destitution will never be stopped until we have educated the lower classes in the methods by which the upper classes prevent procreation. The man had the horrible playfulness to sign his letter "Hopeful." Well, there are certainly many methods by which people in the upper classes prevent procreation; one of them is what used to be called "platonic friendship," till they found another name for it at the Old Bailey. I do not suppose the hopeful gentleman hopes for this; but some of us find the abortion he does hope for almost as abominable. That, however, is not the curious point. The curious point is that the hopeful one concludes by saying, "When people have large families and small wages, not only is there a high infantile death-rate, but often those who do live to grow up are stunted and weakened by having had to share the family income for a time with those who died early. There would be less unhappiness if there were no unwanted children." **You will observe that he tacitly takes it for granted that the small wages and the income, desperately shared, are the fixed points, like day and night, the conditions of human life. Compared with them marriage and maternity are luxuries, things to be modi-**

fied to suit the wage-market. There are unwanted children; but unwanted by whom? This man does not really mean that the parents do not want to have them. He means that the employers do not want to pay them properly. Doubtless, if you said to him directly, "Are you in favour of low wages?" he would say, "No." But I am not, in this chapter, talking about the effect on such modern minds of a cross-examination to which they do not subject themselves. I am talking about the way their minds work, the instinctive trick and turn of their thoughts, the things they assume before argument, and the way they faintly feel that the world is going. And, frankly, the turn of their mind is to tell the child he is not wanted, as the turn of my mind is to tell the profiteer he is not wanted. Motherhood, they feel, and a full childhood, and the beauty of brothers and sisters, are good things in their way, but not so good as a bad wage. About the mutilation of womanhood, and the massacre of men unborn, he signs himself "Hopeful." He is hopeful of female indignity, hopeful of human annihilation. But about improving the small bad wage he signs himself "Hopeless." [92–94]

—§§§—

A third proof is the strange new disposition to regard the poor as a _race;_ as if they were a colony of Japs or Chinese coolies. It can be most clearly seen by comparing it with the old, more individual, charitable, and (as the Eugenists might say) sentimental view of poverty. In Goldsmith or Dickens or Hood there is a basic idea that the particular poor person ought not to be so poor: it is some accident or some wrong. Oliver Twist or Tiny Tim are fairy princes waiting for their fairy godmother. They are held as slaves, but rather as the hero and heroine of a Spanish or Italian romance were held as slaves by the Moors. The modern poor are getting to be regarded as slaves in the separate and sweeping sense of the negroes in the plantations. The bondage of the white hero to the black master was regarded as abnormal; the bondage of the black to the white master as normal. The Eugenist, for all I know, would regard the mere existence of Tiny Tim as a sufficient reason for massacring the whole family of Cratchit; but, as a matter of fact, we have here a very good instance of how much more practically true to life is sentiment than cynicism. The poor are not a race or even a type. It is senseless to talk about breeding them; for they are not a breed. They are, in cold fact, what Dickens describes: "a dustbin of individual accidents," of damaged dignity, and often of damaged gentility. The class very largely consists of perfectly promising children, lost like Oliver Twist, or crippled like Tiny Tim. It contains very valuable things, like most dustbins. But the

Eugenist delusion of the barbaric breed in the abyss affects even those more gracious philanthropists who almost certainly do want to assist the destitute and not merely to exploit them. It seems to affect not only their minds, but their very eyesight. Thus, for instance, Mrs. Alec Tweedie almost scornfully asks, "When we go through the slums, do we see beautiful children?" The answer is, "Yes, very often indeed." I have seen children in the slums quite pretty enough to be Little Nell or the outcast whom Hood called "young and so fair." Nor has the beauty anything necessarily to do with health; there are beautiful healthy children, beautiful dying children, ugly dying children, ugly uproarious children in Petticoat Lane or Park Lane. There are people of every physical and mental type, of every sort of health and breeding, in a single back street. They have nothing in common but the wrong we do them. [96–97]

—§§§—

There is one strong, startling, outstanding thing about Eugenics, and that is its meanness, Wealth, and the social science supported by wealth, had tried an inhuman experiment. The experiment had entirely failed. They sought to make wealth accumulate—and they made men decay. Then, instead of confessing the error, and trying to restore the wealth, or attempting to repair the decay, they are trying to cover their first cruel experiment with a more cruel experiment. They put a poisonous plaster on a poisoned wound. Vilest of all, they actually quote the bewilderment produced among the poor by their first blunder as a reason for allowing them to blunder again. They are apparently ready to arrest all the opponents of their system as mad, merely because the system was maddening. Suppose a captain had collected volunteers in a hot, waste country by the assurance that he could lead them to water, and knew where to meet the rest of his regiment. Suppose he led them wrong, to a place where the regiment could not be for days, and there was no water. And suppose sunstroke struck them down on the sand man after man, and they kicked and danced and raved. And, when at last the regiment came, suppose the captain successfully concealed his mistake, because all his men had suffered too much from it to testify to its ever having occurred. What would you think of the gallant captain? It is pretty much what I think of this particular captain of industry.

Of course, nobody supposes that all Capitalists, or most Capitalists, are conscious of any such intellectual trick. Most of them are as much bewildered as the battered proletariat; but there are some who are less well-meaning and more mean. And these are leading **their more generous colleagues towards the fulfilment of this ungenerous evasion, if not towards the comprehension of it.** Now a ruler of the Capitalist civilisation, who has come to consider the idea of ultimately herding and breeding the workers like cattle, has certain contemporary problems to review. He has to consider what forces still exist in the modern world for the frustration of his design. The first question is how much remains of the old ideal of individual liberty. The second question is how far the modern mind is committed to such egalitarian ideas as may be implied in Socialism. The third is whether there is any power of resistance in the tradition of the populace itself. These three questions for the future I shall consider in their order in the final chapters that follow. It is enough to say here that I think the progress of these ideals has broken down at the precise point where they will fail to prevent the experiment. Briefly, the progress will have deprived the Capitalist of his old Individualist scruples, without committing him to his new Collectivist obligations. He is in a very perilous position; for he has ceased to be a Liberal without becoming a Socialist, and the bridge by which he was crossing has broken above an abyss of Anarchy. [98–99]

—§§§—

Socialism is one of the simplest ideas in the world. It has always puzzled me how there came to be so much bewilderment and misunderstanding and miserable mutual slander about it. At one time I agreed with Socialism, because it was simple. Now I disagree with Socialism, because it is too simple. . . . Friends and foes alike talked as if it involved a sort of faith in ideal human nature; why I could never imagine. The Socialist system, in a more special sense than any other, is founded not on optimism but on original sin. It proposes that the State, as the conscience of the community, should possess all primary forms of property; and that obviously on the ground that men cannot be trusted to own or barter or combine or compete without injury to themselves. Just as a State might own all the guns lest people should shoot each other, so this State would own all the gold and land lest they should cheat or rackrent or exploit each other. It seems extraordinarily simple and even obvious; and so it is. It is too obvious to be true. But while it is obvious, it seems almost incredible that anybody ever thought it optimistic.

. . . . I only remark in passing that it is vain for the more vulgar sort of Capitalist, sneering at ideals, to say to me that in order to have Socialism "You must alter human nature." I answer "Yes. You must alter it for the worse. . . ."

The clouds were considerably cleared away from the meaning of Socialism by the Fabians of the 'nineties; by Mr. Bernard Shaw, a sort of anti-romantic Quixote, who charged chivalry as chivalry charged windmills, with Sidney Webb for his Sancho Panza. . . .[5]

It may be said of Socialism, therefore, very briefly, that its friends recommended it as increasing equality, while its foes resisted it as decreasing liberty. On the one hand it was said that the State could provide homes and meals for all; on the other it was answered that this could only be done by State officials who would inspect houses and regulate meals. The compromise eventually made was one of the most interesting and even curious cases in history. It was decided to do everything that had ever been denounced in Socialism, and nothing that had ever been desired in it. Since it was supposed to gain equality at the sacrifice of liberty, we proceeded to prove that it was possible to sacrifice liberty without gaining equality. Indeed, there was not the faintest attempt to gain equality, least of all economic equality. But there was a very spirited and vigorous effort to eliminate liberty, by means of an entirely new crop of crude regulations and interferences. . . .

In short, people decided that it was impossible to achieve any of the good of Socialism, but they comforted themselves by achieving all the bad. All that official discipline, about which the Socialists themselves were in doubt or at least on the defensive, was taken over bodily by the Capitalists. They have now added all the bureaucratic tyrannies of a Socialist state to the old plutocratic tyrannies of a Capitalist State. For the vital point is that it did not in the smallest degree diminish the inequalities of a Capitalist State. It simply destroyed such individual liberties as remained among its victims. It did not enable any man to build a better house; it only limited the houses he might live in— or how he might manage to live there; forbidding him to keep pigs or poultry or to sell beer or cider. It did not even add anything to a man's wages; it only took away something from a man's wages and locked it up, whether he liked it or not, in a sort of money-box which was regarded as a medicine-chest. It does not send food into the house to feed the children; it only sends an inspector into the house to punish the parents for having no food to feed them. It does not see that they have got a fire; it only punishes them for not having a fireguard. It does not even occur to it to provide the fireguard.

. . . . The purely negative stage of interference, at which we have stuck for the present, is in itself quite

5. Shaw and Webb are covered in Chap. VI.

favourable to all these eugenical experiments. The capitalist whose half-conscious thought and course of action I have simplified into a story in the preceding chapters, finds this insufficient solution quite sufficient for his purposes. What he has felt for a long time is that he must check or improve the reckless and random breeding of the submerged race, which is at once outstripping his requirements and failing to fulfil his needs. Now the anomalous situation has already accustomed him to stopping things. The first interferences with sex need only be negative; and there are already negative interferences without number. **So that the study of this stage of Socialism brings us to the same conclusion as that of the ideal of liberty as formally professed by Liberalism. The ideal of liberty is lost, and the ideal of Socialism is changed, till it is a mere excuse for the oppression of the poor.** . . .

Finally one thing may be added which is at least clear. Whether or no the organisation of industry will issue positively in a eugenical reconstruction of the family, it has already issued negatively, as in the negations already noted, in a partial destruction of it. It took the form of a propaganda of popular divorce, calculated at least to accustom the masses to a new notion of the shifting and re-grouping of families. I do not discuss the question of divorce here, as I have done elsewhere, in its intrinsic character; I merely note it as one of these negative reforms which have been substituted for positive economic equality. It was preached with a weird hilarity, as if the suicide of love were something not only humane but happy. But it need not be explained, and certainly it need not be denied, that the harassed poor of a diseased industrialism were indeed maintaining marriage under every disadvantage, and often found individual relief in divorce. Industrialism does produce many unhappy marriages, for the same reason that it produces so many unhappy men. But all the reforms were directed to rescuing the industrialism rather than the happiness. Poor couples were to be divorced because they were already divided. **Through all this modern muddle there runs the curious principle of sacrificing the ancient uses of things because they do not fit in with the modern abuses.** When the tares are found in the wheat, the greatest promptitude and practicality is always shown in burning the wheat and gathering the tares into the barn. And since the serpent coiled about the chalice had dropped his poison in the wine of Cana, analysts were instantly active in the effort to preserve the poison and to pour away the wine. [107–112]

—§§§—

XIX

Eugenics, Birth-Control, and Socialism

1917

Eden Paul

Socialist Editor and Writer

Unless the socialist is a eugenist as well, the socialist state will speedily perish from racial degradation.

EDITOR

In Chapter I we quoted from Eden Paul's correspondence with Margaret Sanger. In this chapter we illustrate how Eden Paul linked birth control to eugenics and socialism. As Chesterton noted in the previous chapter, some of the viler sort of capitalists felt eugenics was necessary *in the present* to correct the problems created by exploiting the poor and rendering them dependent. Socialism faced similar problems, but its problems existed *in the future* and were born of its oft-repeated claim to provide for all equally, whatever their ability. Under capitalism, socialists could be relatively indifferent to eugenics. But once a socialist state began to be established, the fact that all would be provided for created serious problems for socialists who took their evolution seriously.

Sanger understood this. After her 1934 visit to the Soviet Union, she warned that the nation wasn't taking the future seriously enough: "Unless she [the U.S.S.R.] looked ahead and educated her people in the problems which arose out of population, within two generations she would find herself with the same differential birth rate then existing in England and the United States. . . . which even the greatest effort of the Soviet dictatorship running at top speed could not pull up and out of their evolutionary environment."[1]

Eden Paul, "Eugenics, Birth-Control, and Socialism." In *Population and Birth Control,* Eden and Cedar Paul, ed. (New York: Critic and Guide, 1917), 121–46. Page numbers are given in square brackets after the text quoted [ ]. The

---

1. Sanger, *An Autobiography*, 450–51.

publisher of Critic and Guide was William Robinson, a humanist who is the author of the next chapter.

—§§§—

Socialists advocate a scheme of social reconstruction wherein, by communal ownership, under democratic control, of the means of production, distribution, and exchange, there will be provided a secure and adequate livelihood for all who are willing and able to make, in return, a fair contribution to the common good. From every competent adult, this return will be demanded in the form of manual labour, poietic and executive mental work, supervision, or service. To women, the choice will be open of employment in any of these four fields on the same or on similar terms with men; in addition, the socialist community will accept the fulfilment (under certain conditions) of woman's specialised sexual function in the bearing of children as a complete discharge of her social duties; and thus will be secured the economic independence of woman, recognised ever more widely as one of the first prerequisites of further social and moral advance. **It is unnecessary to consider here the numerous difficulties, recognised by every socialist, in the way of socialist reorganisation, or to consider the general question of its practicability.** One of the most serious of these difficulties, and one upon which especial stress is always laid by the opponents of socialism, is that of ensuring from the individual an adequate return in the matter of social service without subjecting him to a tyranny as grinding as that of capitalism—perhaps even a worse tyranny, for the coercion, we are told, will be overt instead of latent. Suffice it to say that it is a reasoned socialist belief, in view of the remarkable plasticity of the qualities summed up in the expression "human nature," that, as the transition to socialism is effected, as the disappearance of economic individualism removes the present conflict between theoretical and practical morality, and as the inculcation of a social instinct in our schools no longer tends, in proportion to the educator's ability, to unfit the pupil for a reasonable measure of success in life, the number of competent adults who will endeavour to evade the performance of their due share of social labour will become an ever-diminishing quantity. But persons who desire, like those who live upon dividends under capitalism, to exist as parasites on the community, together with the thieves and homicides, the directly predatory and violent types, will, be they many or be they few, constitute an anti-social residuum, the criminals of the socialist state. What is to be done with them? **How are we to deal also with those who, because they are ill, insane, or feeble-minded, are unable to make an adequate contribution to the common good? On humanist principles they will be entitled (as they are to-day) to a share of the communal product. But, as today, they will receive that share on conditions, and in the writer's view the conditions will be largely determined by eugenist considerations.** [121–23]

—§§§—

Editor: Odd as it may seem, the political left often looks at society from the same perspective as the upper class. Here a socialist equates female fitness with the few privileged women in her day who were able to get a professional education. Hers was an strange subculture, one where women were pressured to marry the nation's few rich but possibly genetically inferior monopoly capitalists—not a situation most women face.

A third great cause of racial degeneration is the working of our marriage system in modern capitalist society (the fault lies, be it noted, with capitalism more than with marriage). The anti-selective influence of marriage under capitalism is one of the principal themes of *The Sexual Crisis,* the translation of a German work by Grete Meisel-Hess. This writer's views may be summarised as follows. The general result of the existing "sexual order," that is to say, of our marriage customs as they work under the capitalist system, is, she declares, that the ablest and most energetic women, unwilling, on the one hand, to accept the economic dependence on man involved in marriage, and competent, on the other, to earn their own livelihood, are, by our industrial and social system, condemned to celibacy. **From this point of view, marriage selects the less fit women to be the mothers of the new genera-**

tion. The same system selects as fathers of the coming race, not the ablest, the strongest, the handsomest men, or those who excel in moral cultivation—but those who are "fittest" because they have been successful competitors (or because their forebears have been successful competitors) in the arena of economic individualism. She goes on to speak of the prevalence of various forms of physical and moral degeneracy, and declares that in her opinion these wide-spread manifestations are the inevitable outcome of the cessation of sexual selection, of the fact that it is to-day impossible for a woman to choose freely from among those who seek her favour the mate who appears to her the most desirable. The selective process whereby the less fit males will be excluded from parenthood can, she considers, be reestablished in no other way than by rendering women economically independent. She urges this elementary demand of the woman's movement from the joint outlook of socialism and of eugenics. [129–30]

—§§§—

. . . In this essay, the need for a vast transformation in the social environment is taken for granted, and the writer's aim is to show that to improve the conditions of life will not suffice, but that we must also improve the conditions of being born—that, important as eugenics is under capitalism, it will become even more essential under socialism. The socialist tendency is to overrate the importance of environment, great as this undoubtedly is. Nor has the error been confined to the socialist camp, for, as Karl Pearson writes, the nation has for years been backing the wrong horse, "putting its money on 'Environment' when 'Heredity' wins in a canter."[2] The impatience of the socialist and even of the social reformer with eugenist proposals has this justification, that many evils thoughtlessly attributed to inferiority of stock are unquestionably the outcome of a faulty environment. Until all are given a fair chance in life, there must be numerous cases in which, with our present knowledge, we cannot distinguish between the effects of environment and the results of heredity. Even to-day, however, we can wisely and humanely apply restrictive eugenist practice in the case of the feeble-minded and perhaps in that of the habitual (instinctive) criminal. But how much more feasible and necessary will such practice become when through the perfectionment of social environment under socialism the effects of bad inheritance have become the

---

2. Editor: This Karl Pearson quote apparently comes from Havelock Ellis, *Studies in the Psychology of Sex,* vol. 6 (Philadelphia: Davis, 1910), 618. Ellis, once considered an expert on human sexuality, was an early mentor to Sanger and provided her with the preface to her first major book, *Woman and the New Race.*

sole factor in producing inefficient and anti-social members of the community. **A socialist commonwealth indiscreet enough to allot to all defectives a share of the communal product without imposing any restrictions on their right to perpetuate their kind would deserve all the evil that would ensue.** [134–35]

—§§§—

Editor: Eden Paul then described the socialist agenda as clearly as it could be safely stated. Left unsaid was what he meant by adopting an agenda of "suitably qualified permission" rather than "irksome" prohibition. Non-parenthood among the unwanted, he did tell us, was to be made "bright and comfortable," while parenthood was to be accompanied with "hardship and discomfort." Numerous ways of achieving that come to mind. A compliant mass media could portray parenthood in a bad light and encourage child-free promiscuity. Divorce could be made easy, making parenthood risky. Schools in certain neighborhoods could be kept poor and crime rampant—making parenting grim and unrewarding. Most important of all, public schools could be structured to deny parents the satisfaction of rearing a child as they see fit—the very technique the feminist Over Mothers of Gilman's *Herland* used (see Chapter XXII) and disturbingly similar to modern "It takes a village to rear a child" agendas. It is an illusion to believe that socialists care about the poor and unfortunate. For many, life in Paul's socialist state would be worse than under the most rabidly individualistic forms of Capitalism.

The eugenist conclusion is irresistible. Imagine the social environment perfected as socialists believe it can be perfected, so that, apart from inborn deficiencies, every one has a fair chance in life, then, if the state provides an adequate subsistence for all alike, inefficients as well as efficients, making no attempt to limit the right to procreate of members of the former category, racial degeneration from the excessive multiplication of the unfit will be a more pressing danger than it is even today. Whether under socialism there will be wages at all must be left for the future to decide; the coming social order may devise some other means for the distribution of the communal product. **But putting the matter in the terminology of the existing economic system, my contention is that the socialist state will have to make ability to earn the minimum wage a precondition of the right to become a parent.** All human beings born into the socialist state will be entitled, on humanist principles, to a fair share of the communal wealth. It may well be, as Bernard Shaw contends, that the only criterion of

fairness in this matter will be equality of shares. But from all competent adults the state will demand a return in the form of manual labour, poietic and executive manual work, supervision, or service; and those who are incompetent, or unwilling, to make an adequate return will receive their share on conditions. **In accordance with restrictive eugenist principles, a national minimum of social efficiency will be the indispensable prerequisite to the right to parenthood.** This notion has been expounded with characteristic brilliancy by H. G. Wells in *A Modern Utopia*.[3] "The state," he writes, "is justified in saying, before you may add children to the community for the community to educate and in part to support, you must be above a certain minimum of personal efficiency, and this you must show by holding a position of solvency and independence in the world; you must be above a certain age, and a certain minimum of physical development, and free of any transmissible disease. You must not be a criminal, unless you have expiated your offence. Failing these simple qualifications, if you and some person conspire and add to the population of the state, we will, for the sake of humanity, take over the innocent victim of your passions, but we shall insist that you are under a debt to the state of a peculiarly urgent sort, and one you will certainly pay, even if it is necessary to use restraint to get the payment out of you; it is a debt that has in the last resort your liberty as a security;[4] and, moreover, if this thing happens a second time, or if it is disease or imbecility you have multiplied, we will take an absolutely effectual guarantee that neither you nor your partner offend again in this matter. 'Harsh,' you say, and 'Poor Humanity!' You have the gentler alternative to study in your terrestrial slums and asylums. It may be urged that to permit conspicuously inferior people to have one or two children in this way would be to fail to attain the desired end, but, indeed, this is not so. **A suitably qualified permission, as every statesman knows, may produce the desired social effects without producing the irksome pressure of a direct prohibition.** Amidst bright and comfortable circumstances, and with an easy practicable alternative, people will exercise foresight and restraint to escape even the possibilities of hardship and discomfort; and free life in Utopia is to be well worth this trouble even for inferior people."

3. Editor: H. G. Wells, *A Modern Utopia* (1905), 182–3. Wells, do not forget, wrote the introduction to the Sanger portion of this book. For more about what socialists intended to do, see Chap. 5 and 6.

4. In other words, socialism will take an idea that capitalism abandoned as excessively cruel, the debtor's prison, and use it against those who only crime is parenthood.

Thus the policy of the national minimum is common ground to socialism and to eugenics. The socialist maintains the right of every member of the community to the minimum essentials for a decent life. The eugenist makes the same demand because, until that demand is satisfied, restrictive eugenist practise gropes vainly in the dark. But, the minimum once granted, the right to live once secured, the eugenist insists that ability to earn the minimum wage, can alone give the additional and more momentous right to become a parent. **Unless the socialist is a eugenist as well, the socialist state will speedily perish from racial degradation.**[5] [137–39]

Editor: Eden Paul then turned to technology. At this time birth control methods were primarily barrier-type methods requiring some skill and motivation to use. Except for the radical European left, eugenists, feminists and others denounced abortion as an "evil" and claimed, at least publicly, to oppose its legalization. That left only two effective ways to coerce birth control: sterilization and single-sex institutionalization. Note that forced sterilization and confinement (almost for life) were not to be considered "punishment." George Orwell would blast this sort of convoluted reasoning in his anti-utopian novel, *1984*.

—§§§—

Operative sterilisation is already practical politics, though in England solely as a matter of recommendation. Modern surgery provides a simple operation, practically devoid of risk, by which, without mutilation, sterilisation can be secured with no loss of any of the distinctive powers and attribute of sex other than that of the capacity for parenthood. [142–43]

—§§§—

Finally, as regards directly anti-social types, it must be remembered that under socialism there will *ex hypothesi*

5. Editor: Stated bluntly, socialism gives everyone the "right" to a decent living and demands in exchange the power to decide who is a parent. But socialism's 'gift' is something most adults in most societies earn for themselves. Having given nothing, what right does it have to become a birth dictator?

be no criminals produced by faulty environment; there will be none but instinctive or "born" criminals—precisely the kind that tend to leave criminal or otherwise defective offspring.[6] The community will have to segregate these for its own comfort and well-being: and, unless the sexes are to be separated, it will have to sterilise them as well. But it will not inflict punishment, for the socialist state will have completely freed itself from the ideas of retributive and deterrent "justice," together with other obsolete superstitions. . . .

I accept, unhesitatingly, this solution of the problem of how to deal with the instinctively anti-social types. **We must protect ourselves from their activities, not merely as noxious members of their own generation, but as possible begetters of anti-social stocks which would injure generations to come. If it reject the lethal chamber, what other alternative can the socialist state devise? But what applies to the habitual criminal, applies no less to the other defective and anti-social types of which mention has been made in this paper. Neither the environmental nor the selective factor, working in isolation, is competent to effect a lasting amelioration of the human lot. Socialism and eugenics must go hand in hand.** [144–46]

—§§§—

Waiting for Power

I had previously cast my lot with the women of the Socialist movement. . . . Their answer to the misery of women and the ignorance of contraceptive knowledge was like that of the Feminists: "Wait until we get the vote to put *us* into power!"[7]

—MARGARET SANGER, *MY FIGHT FOR BIRTH CONTROL*

---

6. Editor: This is nonsense. Some people will want a standard of living that is higher than socialism is willing to provide. By working harder or smarter, capitalism offers them a way to do that which is legal and socially useful. Socialism creates an environment that forces them to become criminals.

7. Margaret Sanger, *My Fight for Birth Control* (Farrar & Rinehart: New York, 1931), 61. Sanger was referring to the years 1913–14.

XX

Who Are The Unfit?

1917

William J. Robinson, M.D.

New York City Humanist, Physician, Author and Publisher

And I will say here, in passing, that personally I would be in favor of the sterilization, preferably by castration, of all brutal criminals, such as pimps, burglars, gunmen, etc., and this entirely independently of the question whether their criminality is transmissible to their offspring or not.

EDITOR

In early November of 1922, Edward M. East of Harvard's Bussey Institute for Research in Applied Biology wrote a letter to Margaret Sanger. He had just finished reading *The Pivot of Civilization* and praised it lavishly. "I am really surprised," he wrote, "that the subject could be treated in such an interesting style without losing dignity and intellectual quality. It will take its place with the essays of Havelock Ellis and Dean Inge[1] as a classic. . . . I agree on the whole with your strictures on eugenics, though I think the birth control work is in itself such a eugenic measure as Galton would approve."

But in the next paragraph East's comments turned nasty and even anti-Semitic. "There ought to be more literature of this sort," he continued. "Frankly I am disgusted with such things as the Robinson books. He has a certain facility with the few, but his ignorance is so colossal, and his monumental Jewish egotism sticks out in every line. I think he does more harm than good."[2]

Sanger responded a few days later, thanking him for his "kind letter" and, with uncharacteristic modesty, referred to *Pivot* as a "serious, dry book about civilization." Sanger went on to agree with his assessment of Robinson and to get in an attack on her English competitor, Marie Stopes. "I agree with you perfectly about Dr. Robinson's books," she replied. "I have never been able to recommend them fully and wholly, and the same egotism seems

to have spread [illegible] Dr. Marie Stopes's books, which to me is very sad, because she has a great literary ability. The movement of birth control—both here and in England, is in danger of being swamped through such egotism."[3] (Those who knew Sanger well would have found her criticism of egotism in others amusing. She hated to see anyone get the fame she felt she deserved.)

Readers shouldn't assume that Robinson differed that much from East and Sanger simply because they considered him ignorant and egotistical. Much of what he believed, they believed, and much of what he wanted to do, they wanted to do. They simply saw his blunt style as counterproductive. The fact that he was Jewish also illustrates that the difference between birth controllers and their foes was not racial or ethnic. A Jew whose family had immigrated to America two generations earlier might dislike the new waves of poor Polish and Russian Jews as strongly as any New England blue blood.

This chapter quotes from Robinson's introduction to explain why he believed as he did. It then quotes all of his Chapter 11, "Who Are the Unfit?" to provide some meaning for that often abused word. Like Lothrop Stoddard (Chapter XXVII), Robinson considered himself a scientific humanist and his opinions should not be taken with that as a source and *not* as reflective of other Jews—particularly not Jews whose religious views were similar to those of conservative Catholics and Protestants. Last of all, note that his eugenic agenda is in the end independent of heredity. Misbehave for whatever reason, he says, and we will sterilize you or even castrate you.

---

1. William Ralph Inge was a prominent liberal English clergyman and eugenist. In the June 1921 issue of *Birth Control Review,* Sanger would praise him in an editorial entitled, "A Great Churchman on Birth Control."

2. Edward M. East to Margaret Sanger, Nov. 4, 1922. Sanger/ Smith microfilm, S02:0196–97.

3. Margaret Sanger to Edward M. East, Nov. 9, 1922. Sanger/ Smith microfilm, S02:0198.

William J. Robinson, *Eugenics, Marriage and Birth Control* (New York: Critic and Guide, 1917), 7–8, 108–13. Page numbers are in square brackets after the text quoted [ ].

—§§§—

My religion is the Religion of Humanity. The ultimate aim of all activity should be the happiness of the human race. This is the only criterion which should be applied to every man's life work. I recognize no other standard. Whatever contributes to the happiness and welfare of the human race, and of its individual members, is right and moral; whatever contributes to its unhappiness and suffering is wrong and immoral. This is my only religion, my only morality. I recognize no other and I cannot see how any rational thinker can recognize any other standard or guide.

I have nothing in common with the theologian who tells us that we have to work for the glory of God and who tries to reconcile us to our present-day sufferings with promises of a future heaven, who tries to quench our hunger in this world with the hope of an everlasting banquet in the next, And I have just as little in common with the narrow, selfish individualist, who thinks that his little ego is the whole world, that he is the supreme law, that his little pleasures must not be interfered with even if the entire human race went to perdition, who has no regard for the rights or sufferings of others, and who justifies his pernicious activity or lack of activity by high-sounding phrases, by the plea of being a superman. The superman is very often a superdevil, or a disgustingly selfish prig, or a good-for-nothing lazy vagabond, who believes that the world *owes* him a living, and a luxurious living at that, no matter whether he does anything for the world or not.[4] [7–8]

—§§§—

One of the objections raised to eugenics by its opponents is that there is no criterion by which we can determine as to who is fit and who is unfit. They are afraid that in our anxiety to eliminate the unfit we might condemn to segregation or sterilization many people who are fit. Who is great enough, they say, to determine the fitness or unfitness of any individual in the human race, and who will determine the fitness or unfitness of the examiners themselves?

There are a great number of people in this world, who, because there are certain borderline cases on which decision is difficult would discredit any movement which attempts to deal with cases on which decision is not difficult. There are certain microscopic organisms about

which it is impossible to decide whether they belong to the vegetable or animal kingdom. This does not mean that there is any difficulty in differentiating between a cow and a potato. Because there are a few moments at dusk when it is difficult to say whether it is day or night it does not mean that we have any difficulty to decide between 11 A.M. and 11 P.M. And because there are a few cases on the borderline about which there may exist some difficulty in deciding whether they are normal or abnormal it does not mean that there would be any difficulty in deciding the classification of a gibbering idiot, of a patient with dementia precox or with general paresis, of a feebleminded moron, of an imbecile cretin, of a confirmed brutal criminal, or of an incurable epileptic. To avoid any possible injustice or error the eugenists would deal only with cases about which no doubt could be possible. All borderline or questionable cases would be left alone, and there is not the slightest danger that anybody would be unjustly segregated or sterilized. The safeguards of individual liberty are too strong, in Anglo-Saxon countries particularly, for any one to fear any such danger.

As to the objection that sterilization is a cruel and unusual punishment and that we have "no right" to interfere with the "most sacred" of human functions, the function of reproduction, I will merely say that to me this objection is puerile and silly. The criminal seldom objects to being deprived of the function of reproduction, while the feebleminded and the insane have no rights whatever in the matter. Being incapable of discharging any of the functions of social beings, society need not ask them their permission for certain procedures which it considers necessary for its welfare. We have no right to make the insane suffer, but we certainly have a right to prevent them from reproducing.

As to the criminal, society does deprive him of his liberty, incarcerates him—so why has it not the right to deprive him of a function the exercise of which is apt to be very injurious to the race? **And I will say here, in passing, that personally I would be in favor of the sterilization, preferably by castration, of all brutal criminals, such as pimps, burglars, gunmen, etc., and this *entirely independently* of the question whether their criminality is transmissible to their offspring or not.** For, assuming even that criminal traits, like those of the burglar, rowdy, pimp, etc., are not transmissible, their environment certainly is, and we cannot think of the offspring of criminals growing up other than criminal; not on account of heredity necessarily, but on account of the horrible environment.

---

4. Editor: This particular "superman" is much like the Nietzschean "Super Rebel" discussed near the end of Chap. I.

Society cannot prevent the birth of all the unfit and degenerates, but it certainly has the right to prevent the birth of as many as it can. The sentimental objection that the criminal is not responsible for what he is, and therefore we have no right to do to him this or that, is also worthless. The tiger is not responsible for what he is and still society would not permit any savage beast roaming about undisturbed in its midst merely because nature created him so, and when it comes to distinctly and unquestionably anti-social acts, a human being has no more rights than an animal. We pity the paranoiac, we pity the insane, we pity the degenerate, but none the less we have not only the right but it is our duty to prevent the paranoiac, the insane, and the degenerate from reproducing their kind, from polluting the racial stock, and from being a social and economic burden to the sane, the normal and the healthy.

A minor objection to sterilization may be referred to here. The opponents of sterilization of criminals and the feebleminded say that this measure would prove a menace to the community in the following way; with their sexual libido and power unimpaired, and knowing that they are free from the danger of impregnating and becoming impregnated, they would give themselves up to unrestrained licentious debauchery, and would thus become great sources of venereal infection.

To this I will say that criminals, degenerates and the feebleminded do not refrain now from sexual indulgence thru fear of impregnation or thru any other considerations. [108–13]

The Forgotten Dr. Robinson

To the Editors of *The Nation:*

Sir: I wish to file a protest against your omission of Dr. William J. Robinson from among the contributors to the birth control number of *The Nation.* For over a quarter of a century, when no one had ever heard of Margaret Sanger, when the subject of birth control was still taboo to Drs. Pusey, Lake, and Knopf, Dr. Robinson agitated for birth control among physicians in his *Critic and Guide,* books, lectures, and so on. It was Dr. Robinson who converted the late Dr. Abraham Jacoby, former president of the American Medical Association to the movement.[5]

—M. E. KOHN, M.D., DETROIT, 1932

5. M. E. Kohn, "Correspondence" *Nation* 134 (Feb. 17, 1932), 195. Chapter XXI has an extract from the "birth control number" arranged by Sanger. The author was right. Dr. Robinson is a better candidate for "birth control pioneer" than Sanger.

EDITOR
We now turn to a touchy and difficult subject—Sanger's attitude toward Jews. Remember, however, that any negative attitudes that she displayed toward Jews in general were predominately cultural and social rather than based on race and biology. To a great extent, they parallel her anti-Catholicism and reflect the attitude of the affluent and progressive circles in which she moved. Her first husband was Jewish and, though she treated him badly in the last years of their marriage, her motives do not appear to have been anti-Semitic. She simply wanted to be promiscuous and he objected.

We will take up her remarks about Jews chronologically. The first comes from her son, Grant, on board a vessel bound for Havana from Kingston, Jamaica the day after Christmas, 1927. I could not locate any reply from Sanger criticizing him for his attitude. That is hardly surprising, since he would have known if she disliked such remarks.

Less Obnoxious

The Jews aboard are gradually becoming less obnoxious, at last. About 1/2 the passengers are Hebrews.[6]

A Tribal Devil Called Jah

Editor: In the spring of 1929, Herbert Sturges, an occasional correspondent of Sanger's, wrote her the following letter. His remarks about the Bible did not mean he had much regard for it, merely that he played the two biblical testaments against another to confuse the ill-informed. His anti-Semitic idea was an ancient heresy. In 144 A.D. the church excommunicated Marcion for claiming the God of the Old Testament was evil. His odd reference to Sanger in the third person may be because he was also writing her two sons.

To Mrs. Sanger I had written I believe rather cautiously, suggesting that Birth Control would have to be linked up with Eugenics in order to be a real benefit to the world. I think her reply helped me to understand it better then. . . .

I remember very well that some time, probably in Paris, Mrs. Sanger told me that she was first of all a feminist. How often I have said that of her to others She would not take a stand solely on the Labor problem at all. . . . Her stand was for women, and she has certainly

6. Grant Sanger to Margaret Sanger, Dec. 26, 1927 Sanger/Smith microfilm S04:0202. The remark may seem odd since Grant was half-Jewish. But he may not have know that. Sanger said very little about her first husband being Jewish.

made good in that great cause! I need hardly add that men and children are necessarily benefitted by the things which help to emancipate women from their bondage. (I often quote Gen. 3:16 as the terrible antithesis to John 3:16, and tell people not to accept as Christian the curse pronounced by a despotic tribal devil, call Jah.)[7]

Jewish, Catholic and Protestant Conspiracy

Editor: The next letter is less revealing of Sanger than of some of her more conspiracy-minded supporters. It does suggest, however, that the nasty attitudes that Sanger had toward her Catholic opponents probably carried over to the Jews and Protestants who also opposed her. The author seems to be a friend who was helping her son, Stuart, then going through a difficult time. Mr. Slee was Sanger's second husband, a wealthy retired businessman who suffered financial setbacks during the Depression.

Yours of the 4th was eagerly awaited because we are ever anxious to hear about Stuart and his whereabouts. But aside from that every time you write to us it is a great help to you and your work. With every letter from you some imps who are active against you and your work come along and th[r]ough them I can trace and get hold of the more powerful ones who set them going. So it was today I was able to make quite a big haul. The most powerful (tho there are still more powerful ones than these) were Jews, 200 of them, and each of them had set to work against you and B. Control at least 10,000 during the past 4 years, that is over 2 millions. Their main work was to deprive you of income, of money to carry on the work and to live, prevent people from contributing. Also prevented Mr. Slee from financial gain and caused him loss. These 200 will now gather in their hordes (Christians, both Catholics & Protestants, and Jews) as fast as they are able to find them. Hence you may now expect that money will come in more freely, in spite of all depression and hard times.

As to Stuart, there is a quandary. As you say, you cannot let him starve. On the other hand, as long as he is being supplied with money he will spend and indulge and drift. I got hold of a gang since your letter came, also Jews? who said they were with him in San Antonio, inducing him to drink & women.[8]

7. Herbert A. Sturges to Margaret Sanger *et al,* (Mar. 30, 1929), Sanger/Smith microfilm, S04:1022. Sturges was at Lombard College.

8. Otto Werner to Margaret Sanger, Jan. 8, 1932, Sanger/Smith microfilm, S06:0677.

Rabbis Steeped in Superstition

Editor: In 1934, Sanger's secretary, Florence Rose, received a letter from a birth control supporter who had heard her (Rose) speak at an "orthodox rabbis' convention in Washington." This woman's suggestion for dealing with a "people steeped in superstition" was to work with a few willing women and one compliant rabbi to convert the others. B.C. is birth control and M.S. is Margaret Sanger. "Doesn't want any children" seems to have been how this writer distorted Sanger all-too-real agenda to reduce the birthrates of poor Jewish immigrants. The "material about abortions" would be literature presenting birth control as a way to prevent the 'evil of abortion.' The time for abortion legalization had not arrived.

I think it would be a wonderful "Ad" for B.C. if a letter from Rabbi Friedman could be read before this orthodox group of people steeped in superstition re B.C. . . . Mrs. S[o]ltman said that half these people are prejudiced against M.S. because they think she doesn't want any children in the world—and the Jewish people are very strong for propagating the race—that is, the really orthodox ones. Every little bit helps so let us try. Send her material about abortions—She is willing to educate herself on this subject, and is one of those slavers for causes, so that whatever time you spend sending her material is going to be fruitful.[9]

Jewish Bankers

Editor: Always eager for a chance to promote herself, in a 1939 speech draft on "Hitler and War," Sanger claimed to have been an opponent of Nazism "before Hitler came to power in Germany." In reality, she seems to have done little more than lend her name to the Anti-Nazi Committee, a fashionable cause. But what is disturbing was her vision of a Jewish conspiracy so powerful that it controlled England's press.

By every means this committee tried to arouse the interests of England's Prime Minister and Press, to combat the advance of Nazism. They refused to print the warnings or to listen to the facts given until the Jewish bankers in Europe began to realize that Natzism [Nazism] was a twin sister to Communism as far as private property was concerned.[10]

9. Henriette Posner to Florence Rose, November 1934, Sanger/Smith microfilm, S09:0360.

10. Margaret Sanger, speech draft: "Hitler and War," Sanger/Smith microfilm, S72:0122.

The speech as a whole reveals a Sanger who is so isolationist that she lumped the leaders of England and France with Hitler and Mussolini as "War Lords." Some of her pacifism was undoubtedly personal. She had two sons whose lives would be interrupted by war.

Among her papers is a copy of an address given by Charles Lindbergh in New York on April 23, 1941 and published by the America First Committee. From her handwritten annotations, it is obvious that she agreed with the aviator's belief that the United States should stay out of the European war. Her remarks included: "This is the whole story." "I agree with this absolutely." "here herr:" and "It sounds sense to me."[11] Attitudes like that were common before Pearl Harbor and certainly do not mean that Sanger liked Hitler or agreed with what he was doing. She did not and, like many in her social class, she particularly deplored his persecution of artists. She merely felt that the U.S. was unprepared and too far away to be of use in a European war. In a letter to a friend, Sanger said that she only wanted to know the truth and "Lindbergh represents the kind of courage I respect."[12]

Eugenics and Reformed Judaism

Editor: The effort that birth controllers made to conceal their anti-Semitic attitudes seems to have been successful. What follows are remarks by a well-known reformed rabbi, Stephen S. Wise.

One thing I mean to say this afternoon, I can say in just one word. I believe in the teachings and I believe in the practice of Birth Control, I am not a fanatical believer—that the Messianic reign will dawn when Birth Control is universally accepted. I ought to make that reservation . . . because, frankly, I think of Birth Control as an item, an important item, but just an item in the eugenic program. I think it is supremely important as an item in the eugenic program, and the eugenic program is not Messianic. It again is an item, a very important item in a still larger program, and that larger program for me means this: The translation of the ideals of human justice

11. C. Lindbergh, *Address,* Sanger/Smith microfilm C17:0642f.

12. Margaret Sanger to Juliet Barrett Rublee, June 8, 1941, Sanger/Smith microfilm, C07:0245.

and human decency and human brotherliness in the life of the world. That is all. But without a eugenic program we shall not have a beginning, let alone the end of the realization of the social programs of which we are dreaming, and Birth Control, I repeat, is the fundamental, primary element or item in the eugenic program.[13]

During the 1930s and 40s Rabbi Stephen Wise was the nation's most prominent Jewish leader. While feminists and socialists tended to have the most brutal eugenic agendas, most liberal clergy of various faiths spoke so blandly that readers might wonder if they were even listening to what was being said. One reason for their restraint is probably reflected by Rabbi Wise's remarks about neither birth control nor eugenics being the "Messianic reign." Even the most liberal of clergy wanted religion to play some role in the ideal world to come, so talk of science and technology left them flat.

On the other hand, it is difficult to understand how Rabbi Wise managed to link eugenics to "human brotherliness." At its very heart, eugenics teaches that there are certain sorts of people who should be purged from society. You can argue that once those "undesirables" are eliminated, the rest of us might get along better. But is such conditional acceptance really "brotherliness?" Would it stop with the insane and feebleminded—then targeted for sterilization? Nazism started by sterilizing those same two groups (1933) and quickly progressed to eugenic abortion (1935), euthanasia (1939), and racial genocide (1941). If we accept the principle that society is better off without some people, exactly where do we draw the line? Though well-intentioned, Rabbi Wise seems to have lacked sufficient skepticism to examine what he undoubtedly regarded as merely another fashionable and progressive cause needing endorsement.

13. Rabbi Stephen S. Wise, "The Synagogue and Birth Control," *Birth Control Review* (Oct. 1926), 302. The quote is from an address to the Sixth International Neo-Malthusian and Birth Control Conference in New York City in late March, 1925. Notice how closely he linked birth control with eugenics. All too many critical studies of eugenics ignore this important link. Today, overt eugenics has become unfashionable and can be criticized at will. But Sanger's movement has remained fashionable and criticism of it remains risky.

XXI

Fill the World with Horror

1915–16

New Republic

If the quality of human births and the nurture of children is the supreme concern of the race, then a refusal to discuss the question of a controlled family is equivalent to asserting that intelligence should not govern the central issues of life.

EDITOR

No study of Margaret Sanger would be complete without a look at her many liberal supporters and why they considered her so "brave." In this chapter we examine what *The New Republic,* a well-respected liberal "journal of opinion" had to say about Sanger and her movement during its early years. The next chapter includes quotes from another prominent liberal magazine, *Nation.*

Sanger clearly appreciated the magazine's support. In a May 1929 letter to Havelock Ellis, she enclosed two articles from the most recent issue, one a Catholic's defense of his church's stance, the other the magazine's response. Mr. Ward, the magazine said, had done the best he could with the facts, but was obviously "under the influence of a profound emotional bias which is beyond the reach of reason." The magazine went on to brand both the Catholic position and similar ones held by "some Protestant churches" as "obscurantism." It denounced Catholicism for "having its views embodied in legislation which applies to all citizens." (Following this bizarre reasoning, one person in the entire nation could derail the entire liberal agenda.) Sanger's description of this ugly bit of intolerance was, "Very good too."[1]

The reasoning in the first article quoted below is equally odd. If, as the magazine claimed, all but a "few intelligent people" agreed with Sanger's point of view and if birth control arguments were shared by almost all "reasoning people," what need was there for Sanger to display courage? After all, she wasn't an elected official in desperate

need of the blue-collar Catholic vote. Adored by wealthy females (who could nag well-connected husbands), she need not fear more than a token sentence for her rare but much trumpeted episodes of lawbreaking.[2]

The answer lies in the contrast between liberalism's professed and true agendas. Liberals profess tolerance and claim concern for the poor and unfortunate. In practice, they often seem more interested in getting rid of poverty than in helping the poor. You see that attitude in the second paragraph of the first article, where "poor" is equated with "the diseased, the weak-minded, the incompetent" who fill the world a "horror" that includes "the multiplication of the unfit, the production of a horde of unwanted souls." What liberals wanted was "a morality which is the making of a finer race. Fewer children and better ones is the only policy a modern state can afford." That is *not* a philosophy that fits with leaving parenthood to parents. Remember too, that this is early liberalism. The growth of the welfare state under Franklin Roosevelt gave liberalism the same incentive to squelch "the multiplication of the unfit" that socialists had.

Although this view was widely shared among intellectuals, it was not popular among ordinary citizens whose support liberals needed to carry out their broader social agenda. Sanger's "courage" lay in the zeal with which she thrust one of liberalism's many agendas—controlling

---

1. Margaret Sanger to Havelock Ellis (May 30, 1929), Sanger/Smith microfilm, S05:0105. The articles were Patrick J. Ward, "The Catholics and Birth Control" and "In Reply to Mr. Ward" in *New Republic* (May 29, 1929), 35–38 and 32–33.

2. Sanger's wealthy female supporters demonstrate that upper-class status isn't linked to a first-class intellect. Often, the very women who felt poor mothers were 'unfit' to rear their own children, wanted those same women to care for their children. Behind their support for Sanger lay a desire to solve the "servant problem" by keeping poor women childless, so they would work for a pittance. The South displayed a similar attitude toward its black nannies.

who had children—to the forefront. It was a risky step, and for that cautious liberals praised her. There is a hint of that in the April 17, 1915 article (quoted below) where the magazine noted that a "serious discussion of sex cast suspicion over all other ideas" and talks vaguely about the "quality of human births" and the need for a "controlled family." Groups who did not rank among those the *New Republic* considered of high quality had good reason to fear Sanger's new movement and her liberal allies.

The Control of Births I

"The Control of Births," *New Republic*
(Mar. 6, 1915), 116–17.

Few intelligent people would still maintain that it is better to have been born an imbecile than not to have been born at all. . . . Yet this hideous doctrine is to-day an American policy enforced whenever possible by long imprisonment. The time is at hand when men and women must denounce it as a conspiracy by the superstitious against the race, when public opinion must compel the amendment of laws which make it a criminal offense to teach people how to control their fertility. . . .

But what so many of the well-to-do and the educated practice, the poor are prevented from learning. The law in effect insists that where conditions are worst, breeding shall be most unregulated, that those who can care for children least shall stagger under a succession of pregnancies, that the race shall be replenished by ignorance and accident, that the diseased, the weak-minded, the incompetent shall by law be compelled to fill the world with horror. Men and women pay for it. They pay for it by a high infant mortality, that monument of tragic waste. They pay for it by the multiplication of the unfit, the production of a horde of unwanted souls. They pay for it in the health of women, the neglect of children, and the fierce burden of destitution. They pay for it in late marriages and their complement of prostitution and disease, in the widespread practice of abortion, in illegitimate births, in desertions and adulteries. There is not one of these miseries which cannot be largely reduced by the extension to all classes of inventions already the property of the educated. . . .

Among reasoning people the argument from superstition is no longer heard, and the supposed injury to health is urged less and less. The ground of the discussion to-day is moral. It is said that if sexual intercourse is severed from childbearing, a great increase of promiscuity will result. . . . The use of contraceptives would undoubtedly diminish the real evils of illegitimacy and abortion. . . .

. . . . It should not be necessary for brave women like Mrs. Sanger to risk their liberty. . . .

It has been claimed that the knowledge of how to limit births is the most immediate practical step that can be taken to increase human happiness. The relief it would bring to the poor is literally incalculable. The assistance it would lend all effort to end destitution and fight poverty is enormous. And to the mind of man it would mean a release from terror, and the adoption openly and frankly of the civilized creed that man must make himself the master of his fate; instead of natural selection and accident, human selection and reason; instead of a morality which is fear of punishment, a morality which is the making of a finer race. Fewer children and better ones is the only policy a modern state can afford. . . .

Editor: Critics of birth control often blamed promiscuous males for the ills that birth control was to correct. Since birth control did nothing about that problem—and even made life easier for such males—they quite reasonably suggested that it might worsen social ills.

Against "The Control of Births"
A.B.L, Montclair, NJ

A. B. L. "Against 'The Control of Births,'"
New Republic (Mar. 20, 1915), 184.

Sir: Your argument for the control of births commands respect, as do most of your opinions, through its evident integrity of motive and the courageous sincere effort at some human solution of human problems that dignifies it. . . .

Among the people from whom *The New Republic* would lift the burden of unwanted and unfit children, the men are for the most part responsible for conditions unspeakable. They are unawakened, uncontrolled, animal. *The New Republic* remedy leaves them no less animal. It is by arguments such as this for control of births, that marriage—in a growing proportion of the community—has been degraded from the highest of human relations to a condition of legalized vice.

Editor: Like Sanger, liberals often concealed their real agenda in vagueness. "Intelligence" here really means that the 'intelligent' will do the controlling.

The Control of Births II

"The Control of Births," *New Republic*
(Apr. 17, 1915), 273–75.

One fact is clear from the response to an editorial in *The New Republic* in the issue of March sixth on the control of births: the subject is one which large numbers of men and women all over the country are ready to discuss. If we were at liberty to name some of the people who have approved the position there taken, no doubt would exist in anyone's mind that there is to educated people nothing strange and nothing outlandish in the propaganda. There have been arguments, of course, and a great deal of objection, but what is really important is that there has been very little objection to arguing the question. When men and women are willing to reason, the first taboo is shattered.

It would be folly, however, to underestimate the opposition. There were a few people so angered that they could not find words to express themselves. They referred us to the Bible, and more than one of them cancelled his subscription. . . .

Some of our friends thought that we were compromising anything we might say about social problems. They reminded us that the serious discussion of sex cast suspicion over all other ideas. . . . To all this friendly advice the answer is very simple. The population question is a social question of the first magnitude, and there can be no enlightened approach to economic problems which shirks a study of the human family. If the family is the foundation of the state, then ignorance, accident, and misery cannot be permitted to eat into the foundation of the family. **If the quality of human births and the nurture of children is the supreme concern of the race, then a refusal to discuss the question of a controlled family is equivalent to asserting that intelligence should not govern the central issues of life**. . . .

Editor: The next article is much like that in Chapter IX. But in this case, the author wanted the situation changed. But notice that he was *not* calling on the rich to help all parents, merely the superior sort like himself.

An Open Letter to the Rich
by John Lincoln

John Lincoln, "An Open Letter to the Rich,"
New Republic (Dec. 11, 1915), 139–41.

This letter deals with the most important matter in the world, I warn you not to throw it away unread. Your mail, your answer, is crowded every day with letters from unknown correspondents. Long experience has taught you that it is best to ignore them. It saves your time. Often it saves your feelings. Who am I to demand an exception to your rule? Let me begin by telling you who I am not.

I am not a man who holds that your class is in conspiracy against the rest of the race. I do not believe that you

are bent on the one end of becoming masters, nor that you take satisfaction in beholding the rest of the community your slaves. A few of you do, perhaps, but a few of the rest of us do things just as bad. On the whole you are much like men and women the world over: pretty kindhearted, pretty thoughtless, pretty selfish, pretty wellmeaning. But in your place I should have acted much as you have: a chastening reflection. I write, then, not to rebuke or castigate you. I write to warn you and set you thinking. And now let me tell you who I am.

I am a teacher in a small city in the West. I am married to the best woman in the world. We have two children, a boy and a girl, fast growing-up. We "own" a small house, heavily mortgaged. I think I may, without vanity, call myself an effective teacher. Not exceptionally so, perhaps, but well above the average. Needless to say, I should not mention this were it not an essential link in what I have to say.

My salary is, as teachers' salaries go, a fair one. But it has already practically reached the limit which I can expect to receive. There is no disguising the fact that we have to watch our expenses pretty closely, though we have thus far prevented disproportionate concern over bank accounts or undue apprehension for the future from diverting us from the worth-while things of life. Not that I never reflect on the arrangement of things whereby you have three motor-cars while I have none. But that aspect of the case never troubles me for long. The things that do hit a bit harder are our inability to travel, to indulge in an occasional dissipation in music or drama, to squander a little on dressing up the children, or to pay a competent instructor to find out just how much there is in certain artistic tendencies in our little girl. But there are compensations even in these privations. For when my wife and I do go to the theatre we are as happy as a pair of children on a picnic. And if we ever get a few days away from home just by ourselves, we are positively as romantic as if we were on our honeymoon.

But by this time you are asking what I am driving at and what in the world all this has to do with you. I will tell you—and in very few words.

I want more children, and I cannot afford to have them. And you, though you do not know it, are to blame. There is my case in a nutshell.

I wonder whether you know what it is to want more children. There was a time a few years ago when I used to come home at night and stumble on something soft on the stairway in the dark. "That infernal dog again," I would say, and turning on the light, would pick up a bit of stuffed brown felt with sprawling legs, dilapidated ears, and button eyes—eyes with the oddest expression in the world.

Well, my children are outgrowing the stage of toy dogs, and I do not like to contemplate that fact. I do not love them less as they grow older, but I want some more of them in the smaller sizes. I want a little fellow small enough to sit on my shoulder and pull my hair. I want to steal into an upper room in the dark, and going over in one corner grope around in a crib for a little fist into which to thrust my finger. I want a little lady at the breakfast table who when I feel a bit blue will suddenly out with a remark that would put to shame Aristophanes, Mark Twain, and Mr. Dooley rolled in one. I call these perfectly manly and reasonable desires. What is more, my wife wants the same things—and many others. And finally, our two children need younger brothers and sisters, for I have come to believe that the only way to bring up two children right is to make them a small minority in the household.

"Well," you say, "if you want more children, why don't you have them?" If you were really candid with yourself you would admit that is a superfluous, not to say a stupid question. **How can a sane man, who is now just living within his income, talk about increasing his family when his salary is being lowered every year? Yes, being lowered; not in dollars and cents, to be sure, but in butter, milk, and eggs.** The trouble is that to you the high cost of living is a mere abstraction. You have never realized it vividly and concretely, for the simple reason that it is years since you have looked at your own grocery bill. And the grocery bill is only the beginning of the difficulty. There is the problem of household help. My wife has brought up two children past babyhood and has done the work practically alone, but there are limits to her strength. There is the matter of insurance. A woman in this very neighborhood, left with five children all under nine and not a cent, brought that home forcibly to me only last month. There are doctors' bill—unavoidable with children in the house, however healthy. There is the fact that one more child, probably two, at any rate, would mean that my present house would be too small. There is the tremendous fact that children as they grow older grow costlier. And in that connection there is the question of provision for their later education. Why! if I were not afraid of trying your patience, I could go on specifying things which in the aggregate sometimes make it seem as if our whole social and economic fabric were deliberately devised to penalize the people who have children.

Perhaps your comment at this point is that I insist on too high a standard of living. I do not think that remark comes with good taste from you, but if you wish to know, it is true—I do refuse to have more children at the price of lowering the standard of our living, and I refuse, not for my own sake, or even for my wife's, but for the sake of the children we already have.

And so the upshot of it all is that I shall probably never have more children. It will be a disappointment, but we human beings are born to encounter disappointment. If the matter ended there, I should not be writing you this letter. But the matter does not end there.

I ask you to take a glance at my two children. To begin with they are both good-looking—if you can't see it, I have their grandmothers' word for it. Their health is excellent. They are both, in the opinion of several teachers, above the average intellectually, the girl especially being quick as a flash. They are as full of explosive force as a cannon is of powder, and they are sufficiently stubborn to show that they have wills of their own. **It is a fair presumption, I believe, that if I had more children they would share some of these same characteristics— at any rate, their blood would go back through all four of their grandparents to stock that was in this country, in New England, before the year 1675: along two of those lines to the Mayflower. In the light of these facts, is it overbold to declare that the nation needs those children?**

But I am not willing to rest my contention on my own case. Let me rest it on the case of my neighbor Jones. Even if I have not been stating my own case correctly, I have at least been stating his. The country could use thousands of men such as Jones's two little boys will, unless I miss my guess, grow up to be. In fact the country has simply got to have them. But Jones, in spite of the fact that there are few abler or harder-working men in our city, is in an economic box much like my own. I doubt if he ever has more children either.

And what, you ask, have you to do with my financial difficulties and Jones's? Everything, my friend, everything; and you know it.

I hear you muttering something under your breath to the effect that if Jones and I want more children we can get busy and earn enough to support them. But the fact that you only mutter it under your breath proves that in your heart you know it is a lie. No, it's altogether too late in the world's history to perpetrate that hoary jest that men's incomes are proportionate to their ability and enterprise.

With that point settled, the facts of the situation are perfectly plain. The nation must have more of the right kind of babies. There are plenty of the right kind of parents who want the babies. There is plenty of wealth to support the babies. And the conclusion is: more of that wealth must be put into those parents' hands.

In other words, this problem is here, regardless of how big your income is or where it comes from. It has got to be settled, regardless, possibly, of how small your income becomes or where it goes to. The incomes must be arranged to suit the babies, not the babies to suit the incomes. **Do not construe this, I beg of you, as a call for a higher birthrate. On the contrary, it may mean a lower birthrate. It is merely a demand for a higher birthrate among the Joneses, a demand, in other words, for a higher rate of better births.**[3]

This problem of arranging the incomes to suit the babies is, I willingly grant, quite the reverse of simple, but it is the most urgent problem that the nation, that humanity, now faces. You can help toward its solution in just one way: by standing up openly against the present method of distribution of wealth and in favor of a method that will eradicate at least the grosser features of its injustice.

How is it to be done, you ask? A tremendously important question, but not the one that you and I are now discussing. Where there's a will there's a way. It is not with the way but with the will, your will, that I am now concerned. Which means I must make you see certain things. First I must make you see, not vaguely but as vividly as if they were right before you, the children that might be but are not now alive to-day: their bright faces, their happy voices, the rush and the glow of the life they enjoy and radiate.

Then I must make you realize that when, as last year, you made that cross at the top of a certain column of your ballot; when, as last month, you made that liberal subscription to the building fund of your club; when, as last week, you assented to your wife's social program for the winter; when, as to-day and yesterday and the day before, you encouraged, however unconsciously, someone around you to imitate the paltry desires, to indulge the foolish whims, to intrench the false standards which your excessive income calls into being—you denied by every

---

3. Editor: The total birthrate would only be lower if, along with financial incentives for his sort to have more children, some nasty disincentives were placed in the path of other potential parents: poor schools, crime-ridden neighborhoods, a sense of powerlessness as parents, a culture separating sex from parenthood, and the like.

one of those acts, existence to a child. And when, as you have long been doing, you go further and help turn the stream of capital into channels that lead to the means of gratifying those tastes, you deny existence to whole families of children. No cold figures in your bank account are facts more certain.

Because you have not understood these things, I have written, as I promised, in a spirit, not of anger but of warning. I have faith that you will hear and act. But if, having heard, you do not act, I shall put in more terrible and vivid imagery the true relation which you will then bear to the little hands that are knocking, the little voices that are calling, at the door of existence. I shall speak in another temper. I shall not mince my terms. I shall cast in your face the word that from the beginning has been allotted to the deliberate destroyer of life.

Editor: As a "journal of opinion," *The New Republic* sometimes printed articles it disagreed with. The next article is one of those. Note the arguments this writer felt would and would not move the liberals with whom he disagreed. In his love of Felicia despite the burden she brought, he feared they would only see a "faded argument" that is nothing "nothing but thinly disguised theology." He knew they preferred the grim but respectably scientific Malthus. Even more revealing, the key argument *against* birth control he felt they would find persuasive was a Darwinian one. Liberals, he recognized, wanted birth control to get rid of the 'unfit.' But what, he asks them, if it proves more effective at getting rid of the 'fit.' Only coercion could redress that imbalance. This article is a masterpiece.

Freedom That Kills
by Caspar Lang

Caspar Lang, "Freedom that Kills,"
New Republic (May 27, 1916), 85–87.

Reactionary, thus you will describe me. I do not like the movement for birth control. It is with reluctance I confess it, because *The New Republic,* for which I wait impatiently out here on the prairie, to shape my thought on war and public policy and what else is big and baffling, does not share my aversion. Thought should be wholly free, I admit. Speech should be as free. Action, so far as it is at all possible, should be free too. I might quibble, to be sure, over the difference between freedom of individual thought, speech, action and the freedom of organized schools of doctrine, systematic propaganda. They are really different, you know. They are not to be defended in identical terms. But this is not the kernel of my dissent. Since I became alive to my ineradicable antipathy to the agitation for placing the key to life in human control, I have found many solid psychological and sociological reasons in support of my position. Aha, you say, this reactionary set out with a bias. So indeed I did, and so did you and all the rest. One has been biased by the teachings of the Church, another by those of Dr. Malthus. One has seared upon his imagination the utter wreck of values created by the death of an only child; another has been revolted by the fathomless misery of the reeking tenement, bursting with anemic, unkempt children. One has a sense of a world exuberant with life: another, of a world growing colder, harder, declining toward universal death. As we live, so we must be biased on life and its renewal through birth. We can not escape prejudice, and the only possibility of a meeting of minds lies in frank confession of the source of the prejudice. What is yours? Mine, in a word, is Felicia. Wee daughter of light, swift and sure of desire, uncertain of steps, fourth to take her place in the highest chair at my table. And mine is an income class in which the Zweikinder [two-child] system is rapidly acquiring the force of Mosaic law.

Felicia, fountain of bubbling laughter, you were a sad indiscretion, in the secret thought of my friends, effusively felicitating. Felicia, compact of sunshine and spring flowers, you are an omen of black disaster, in the thought of some of my friends (very deep, they) who hold every birth to be a murder, murder of another child starved for want of such a bit of bread as you eat. We might debate this question, you and I: should you have been at all? Wiser man than I have debated this delicate question with women less wise than you, for as yet you have hardly any words of your own to stop your pretty ears with vanity.

You have placed a barrier across the path of us, your parents, toward our chosen careers—you and the other three blonde heads rising stepwise into the future. A career, you ask, what is that? It is a glittering formula, a potent abracadabra, that men do not doubt in these days when they doubt truth and life and God. It is to do, not the work that lies next, but the work that lies farthest, veiled in the horizon's blue mist. It is to be admired by those who do not understand, esteemed by those who do not weigh. It is to gain contact with wise and brilliant and powerful persons whose wisdom and brilliancy and power are not, alas, contagious. It is like the fruit that grows on Christmas trees; look upon it and you are soon tired; touch it, and it breaks and cuts your fingers. And my parents would have preferred this pretty hollow thing

to me? Not to a smile of yours, or a cry of your deepest woe, sweet as the sobbing of doves. Not now when we know you, Felicia. But we did not know you always, and the propagandists of birth control would have placed at our discretion to deny you life, unseen, unheard, unknown. Monstrous, isn't it?

What kind of faded argument is this that is being foisted upon me, demands the reader, outraged. It is nothing but thinly disguised theology; its sociology and economics are pre-Malthusian. It premises a household well above the breadline, but the case that concerns us is the household where the fourth child quarrels with the third for its rightful share of milk and both snatch at the bread in the thin fingers of the second and first. The argument premises wide prairies where food is cheap and wholesome, where green hills and meadows invite even the poorest child to play, and sweet smelling haylofts to sleep. We are concerned with the slum, where the sun is an infrequent and disdainful visitor, where the cramped tenements offer little air and bad, where the food is dear and its quality not specified. In short, you are generalizing from the obsolescent simplicity of your prairie cottage to the infinite complexities of an urban society.

I seem to stand convicted. Here, on my prairie no child has ever gone to bed hungry. Here men do not hunt despairingly for work; rather, they are disposed to run away from it, regarding it as the curse of Adam. And if your movement for birth control can make over the industrial centers, destroy the slum, place the urban working class on a secure and comfortable plane of living, I will gladly sink my prejudices in the matter. But can it? Misery is just as deep in infertile Paris as in Berlin, mother of multitudinous sons. Look behind the semblance of prosperity of the prudent French peasantry; you will find that fair fields and sad hearts go very well together. You are requiring of birth control a remedy for the consequences of the inadequate education and lack of initiative of the workers, the inefficiency and short-sightedness of employers, the chaotic distributive system of society at large. But these evils afflict a sparse population as well as one that is dense. The working household with many children is wretched. Only when the working household with few or none at all is far from humanly comfortable. And what guaranty have you that if the working-class as a whole voluntarily lightened their family burdens, wages would not be readjusted accordingly? The childless female factory towns do not live in exemplary comfort. Wages there are made to fit the childless state.

You who now urge birth control are ardent social reformers. Do you realize that you are taking a leaf out of the political manual of anti-reformers of a hundred years ago? They, too, insisted that the poverty of the working class was due to their excessive fertility. "Serves them right; let them learn prudence." Malthusianism was a lightning rod, to sink into the ground the thunderbolts of social justice. The birth-control movement is Malthusianism in modern guise. It will yet be appropriated by your enemies.

But the question, you say, involves something more fundamental than economic consequences nobody understands well enough to dogmatize about. It involves essential human liberties. We are seeking to place each person's destinies in his own control. One is adverse to parenthood; let him not be constrained to it through ignorance. Another wishes many offspring; let him be free, in Heaven's name. No, that is just what he cannot be. Discretion, in the long run and for the mass, means conformity, social constraint. Free the priest from his cassock; he will be constrained to follow the fashions. Free the youth from his vows of total abstinence; he will be constrained to drink. Subject the creation of new life to the canons of free reason, it will be community reason, not individual, that will eventually dominate. Have I not indicated how many friends in their secret thought voted non-existence, retrospectively, to Felicia, joy of my life? We are not here dealing with matter of brute fact and abstract number, but with life and its values, in an instable, swelling, shrinking stream, readily thrown into deep shadow or brightly illuminated by the general approval or disapproval. **Let me shut you in a cell with my friend X, materialist, rationalist; in a week you would become profoundly skeptical of the value of your own life. But the value of new life is of all values the one most easily killed. You would establish freedom? Your freedom may easily become the most brutal of tyrannies, reaching into the very soul and choking it to the relinquishment of purposes the tenderest and most wholesome in the world.**

Let us return to sociology. You are proponents of quality of life versus quantity, you say. What kind of population would develop under the selective influence of the social forces you set in motion? Suppose that we consider first the more comfortable, property-owning class. To be sure, your propaganda is not directed toward these, but social propaganda can not be counted on to keep the direction you intend to give it. As likely as not, it blows back, like the fumes from German gas bombs. Well, in the property-owning class rational birth control is sure to merge itself with the institution of property itself. The property builder cannot look with equanimity upon the infinite subdivision of his possessions. A son to inherit the estate, a daughter to be adequately dowered, this is the rule that has prevailed and, in reason, is bound to prevail. You cannot take chances with your one son, inheritor of your lands and goods; you will not send him forth upon adventures; you will see that the chief adventure of his life, mating, is governed by the rules of your prudence. You will take no chances with your daughter's fate; you will choose wisely for her with an eye especially to property. It is a safe, solid system. But life is unsafe, unstable. Infallibly it rejects in the end a class exposed to this system. Such a class cannot possibly be self-perpetuating. And if it is true that in the secular progress of society it is the better stock into whose hands property drifts, the selective process in so far makes for qualitative deterioration.

Well, let the property-owning stocks die out, you say. As good stocks will come up from the working classes now held under. Such to be sure has been past experience. But you are proposing to introduce a selective process among these classes. Now, will your kind of birth control select out specially for suppression the Simple Simons, the Peeping Toms, the Dumme Lisas? Oh, no, indeed. As a chemical stain permeates a bacteriological culture, infallibly selecting certain specific bacteria to encarnadine and kill, so would the influence of your propaganda permeate the working class, selecting out for suppression the more sensitive, intelligent, responsible. Better these stocks should die, you say, than that the present relentless strife for bread should continue. Let us reflect upon the point.

The strength of an army consists chiefly in its officers, especially in its subordinate officers. The most consummate generalship is vain unless the general can find to his hand abundant material for his staff, for the colonelcies and captaincies, and most of all for the posts of sergeant and corporal. Given a fully manned organization of command and Simple Simon and his tribe will fight effectively in the ranks. Extirpate the lower grades in the hierarchy in which the organization is visibly embodied, and all the greatest general can do is to lead his Simple Simons to precipitate and disastrous flight. It is not otherwise with our industrial armies. Their efficiency depends upon their organization, and the organization in the concrete is the body of men officering industry. We could multiply our productive power twofold, threefold, or more if our industry were sufficiently well officered. Give us our needed officers, well born, well trained, and we will make the world yield its fruits in abundance for its children, though they swarm multitudinously over its surface. Weed out the officers, and the mass must shrink down through starvation to something like the sparse groups of prowling wrenches, without joy, without vision but with unbreakable endurance that represented human life in time of barbarism. Our industrial officers of the future can not come from the propertied classes or from the class embodying industrial leadership to-day. These classes already enjoy your freedom and are on the road to extinction. Leadership in the mass must come, if at all, from the better working stocks. And these are the stocks most likely to succumb to the prudence that sterilizes, the freedom that kills. Excellent are your intentions, O self-selected guardians of the gates of life.

Editor: The liberals at the *New Republic* had nasty things to say about the opponents of birth control, often blaming them for social ills over which they had no control. But the magazine was revealingly silent about the slanders Sanger and her colleagues directed at the 'unfitness' of millions of parents. Remember, at this time Sanger was not dusty history, she was a current event. The old articles by her and others that are republished in this book were common knowledge among the well-read. Liberals knew what she was doing and for that they called her "courageous."

The Other Side of Birth Control

"The Other Side of Birth Control,"
New Republic (Mar. 24, 1917), 216–17.

Two weeks ago the New York legislature held public hearings on a bill to permit doctors and trained nurses to give information on birth control. "Even seasoned legislators," it is reported, were "outraged" by the plainspoken language of some of its women advocates. . . .

Blessed be the pure in spirit who inhabit our legislatures and who have the morals of the commonwealth in their keeping. Argument by imputation of corrupt motives is a sorry business in a day when scientific facts are available. . . .

And now that the heinous bill has been quashed, the defenders of public virtue and anointed vicars of God will feel free to turn to the constructive side of their program. . . . Their work is laid out for them in the report on maternal mortality just published by the Children's Bureau of Washington.

More than fifteen thousand American women die annually in childbirth from diseases "proved over forty years ago to be almost entirely preventable. In the registration area, which includes about two-thirds of our population, "for every 154 babies born alive, one woman loses her life. . . ."

And yet the courageous minority who attempt to dispel this fatalistic ignorance are denounced as enemies of God and one with the traffickers in commercialized vice. But surely if it is a mortal sin to give to the generality of women the facts about rational birth control, which are freely imparted to-day by all physicians with well paid practices, it can hardly be held a crime to make child-bearing safe and protect the newborn from the penalties of ignorance. . . .

Outside of hospitals, deaths from childbirth are still piously referred to as "acts of God." Puerperal septicemia is not a reportable disease even in the registration area. It is a thing which physicians are expected to pass over in mystical silence. And as a result of this pseudo-religious obscurantism, the death-rate among the poor is, of course, much higher than among the well-to-do. It is always the poor whom we sacrifice to our taboos. . . .

Would it be a crime against humanity to spread the economic and medical information for lack of which these children die? A devout clergyman once told us that he had no time for a campaign of education against infant mortality because he was too busy preparing the souls of dead children for the blessed ascension. Is this the other side of the propaganda for birth control?

—§§§—

Children of God

Some few years ago a man who had dedicated his life to bettering social conditions vehemently announced his bitterness toward eugenic ideas somewhat as follows: "Heredity! Heredity! The word has rung in my ears until I am sick of it. There is just one heredity in this world of ours—we are the children of God." The audience showed their approval of this burst of emotion by prolonged applause. The press gave the incident extended and appreciative notice.[4]

—EDWARD EAST, HARVARD, 1923

---

4. Edward M. East, *Mankind at the Crossroads* (New York: Charles Scribner's Sons, 1923), 284. East, as you might expect, deplored such ideas, especially when they drew the applause of the scientifically unenlightened masses. On the other had, mere assertions like this did little to counter the rational and scientific arguments of birth controllers and their allies.

XXII

From Herland to Ourland

1890–1932

Charlotte Perkins Gilman

Feminist Writer and Sociologist

We are mortified at our moronic average, alarmed at the increasing numbers of those far below it. Further, we find that the unfitter they are, the more lavishly they fulfil what some religionists assure us is the divine commandment—to increase and multiply and replenish the earth.

Editor: In this chapter we look at Charlotte Perkins Gilman, perhaps the leading feminist intellectual in the United States during the late nineteenth to early twentieth century. In some ways Gilman and Sanger were much alike. Both built upon the ideas of Malthus and Darwin a belief in the necessity of curtailing the birthrates of inferior groups through birth control and sterilization. There was nothing unusual about that. As we have seen, those ideas were almost universally accepted in the socialist, liberal and feminist circles in which both moved and were, in fact, a point of pride for such people—beliefs that set them off from the untutored masses. We begin with a revealing excerpt from a poem Gilman wrote during her first marriage, one in which she expressed optimism about how easily human nature could be altered.

Similar Case—1890

Excerpted from: Charlotte Perkins Stetson [Gilman], "Similar Case." In "The Editors' Table, *New England Magazine* 3 (Sept. 1890), 134–35.

There was once a Neolithic Man, an enterprising wight,
Who made his simple implements unusually bright.
Unusually clever he, unusually brave,
And he sketched delightful mammoths on the borders of his cave.
To his Neolithic neighbors, who were startled and surprised,
Said he: "My friends, in the course of time, we shall be civilized!"

. . . .

Then they all rose up in fury against their boastful friend;

For prehistoric patience comes quickly to an end.
Said one: "This is chimerical! Utopian! Absurd!"
Said another: "What a stupid life! Too dull, upon my word."
Cried all: "Before such things can come, you idiotic child,
You must alter Human Nature!" and they all sat back and smiled.
Thought they: "An answer to the last will be hard to find!"
It was a clinching argument—to the Neolithic Mind!"

The Economic Basis—1898

Editor: Gilman's reputation as a sociologist was built on her controversial views on the economic role of women. In this early article, she attacks women who remain at home, rearing their own children, as a "sluggish mass of primitive prejudice" and the chief foe of "social progress." Career women, Gilman believed, would be content to let the State rear their children as it saw fit. Note that she assumed one of the chief duties of women was to build up a superior race—an idea Nazism would later adopt and feminists now claim to have never supported. Later we find that meant some women would be denied not only mothering, but motherhood itself, the sort of the agenda Margaret Sanger would adopt a quarter century later. Sanger was hardly the pioneer she is made out to be.

Charlotte Perkins Stetson [Gilman] "The Economic Basis of the Woman Question," *Woman's Journal* (Oct. 1, 1898), 313–14.

The question before women is how best to do their duty upon earth. To define individual duty is difficult; but the collective duty of a class or sex is clear. It is the duty of women to develop and improve themselves; to bring children into the world who are superior to their parents; and to forward the progress of the race. . . .

The progressive changes and social evolution accomplish wonders in those fields of life open to their influence; but the motionless, sheltered, inner places [of the home] remain unchanged among us, like the frozen mastodons, confronting us with their complacent presence, an immense anachronism. . . .

Against all this so visible a trend of change rises the great cry of frightened motherhood; the protest that women must stay alone at home and do their housework because only so can they do their duty by their children.

How do we know this? How do we know that the care of children by the individual mother in the personally conducted home is the best thing for the world? . . .

Moreover, while women are content with their economic position of house-servant, this cannot be bettered. Only an independent motherhood, working wisely in well-organized businesses, will grow to see that the care of children is a profession in itself—the noblest and most important of all human work, and not to be lightly undertaken and bungling struggle through by every female who can bear young. . . .

. . . . **And with all the negative moral superiority of women, there is nothing more absolutely in the way of social progress to-day than the huge, blind, sluggish mass of primitive prejudice embodied in the economically dependent woman.**

Woman of the Future

The woman of the future will have nothing to do with the house except to let herself out of it with a key in the morning and into it at night. . . . Leaving out the small but growing fraction of women who are working in the industrial world, as men do, nine-tenths of the women of the world are working in exactly the same way the antediluvian squaw did.[1]

—CHARLOTTE PERKINS GILMAN, 1903

A Suggestion on the Negro Problem—1908

Editor: Perhaps the clearest description of how far Gilman would go to solve social ills lies in her answer to the "Negro problem." Here something disturbingly like the Nazi slave labor program was called, "not enslave-

ment but enlistment." Most blacks (the "whole body"), although guilty of no crime, were to be placed in something disturbingly like a chain gang on rails and some were to be confined for all their reproductive lives in sexually segregated institutions. Statements such as these have nothing to harm Gilman's reputation as a feminist intellectual.

Charlotte Perkins Gilman, "A Suggestion on the Negro Problem," *American Journal of Sociology* 14 (July 1908), 78–85.

Admitting that in a certain number of cases the negro has developed an ability to enter upon our plane of business life, and further admitting, most cheerfully, that this proves the ultimate capacity of the race to do so; there remains the practical problem of how to accelerate the process.

We have to consider the unavoidable presence of a large body of aliens, of a race widely dissimilar and in many respects inferior, whose present status is to us a social injury. . . .

The problem—the question of conduct—the pressing practical issue—is: What can we do to promote the development of the backward race so that it may become an advantageous element in the community? This is not a question of "equality" in any sense. Society is an organic relation, it is not composed of constituents all alike and equally developed, but most diverse and unequal. It is quite possible to have in a society members far inferior to other members, but yet essential to the life of the whole. . . .

He is here: we can't get rid of him; it is all our fault; he does not suit us as he is; what can we do to improve him?

At last the suggestion: Let each sovereign state carefully organize in every county and township an enlisted body of all negroes below a certain grade of citizenship. Those above it—the decent, self-supporting, progressive negroes—for no problem and call for nothing but congratulation. **But the whole body of negroes who do not progress, who are not self-supporting, who are degenerating into an increasing percentage of social burdens or actual criminals, should be taken hold of by the state.**

The proposed organization is not enslavement, but enlistment. The new army should have its uniforms, its decorations, its titles, its careful system of grading, its music and banners and impressive ceremonies. It is no dishonor but an honorable employment from the first, and the rapid means of advancement. Men, women, and children, all should belong to it—all, that is, below the grade of efficiency which needs no care. For the children—this

1. "Women and Work," *New York Tribune* (Feb. 26, 1903), 7.

is the vital base of the matter—a system of education, the best we have, should guarantee the fullest development possible to each; from the carefully appointed nursery and kindergarten up to the trade school fitting the boy or girl for life; or, if special capacity be shown, for higher education. . . .

All these are but the internal functions of the new body; its direct service to society would be in meeting the crying need of the whole South for better roads, harbors, river banks, and the general development of the country. **Construction trains, carrying bands of the new workman, officers, and men, with their families, with work for the women and teaching for the children, would carry the laborer along the roads he made, and improve the country at tremendous speed.** . . .

. . . . As fast as any individuals proved themselves capable of working on their own initiative they would be graduated with honor. This institution should be compulsory[2] at the bottom, perfectly free at the top. . . .

What this amounts to is simply state organization of the negro, under conditions wholly to his advantage, and therefore, to ours. Some persons, hasty in speech, will now be asking, "Who is to pay for all this?" To which the answer is "The same who paid for all the comforts and luxuries of the South in earlier years [under slavery]—the working negro. . . .

A certain percentage of degenerates and criminals would have to be segregated and cared for as they are now, only far more wisely. But the saving to the state in cutting off the supply of these degenerates would go far to establish the economy of the proposition.[3]

Herland—1915

EDITOR

Perhaps still angry about not getting flowers for Valentine's Day, in early March of 1914, Gilman launched a nasty attack on Cupid, the mythical "fat baby with a bow and arrow" at New York City's Hotel Astoria. A reporter for the *New York Times* noted both her feminist theme

2. Editor: Would any state-run labor camp, once established, willingly discharge its best workers while retaining the lazy and incompetent? Not likely. Notice that Gilman expects the "working Negro" to pay for his own enslavement.

3. Editor: A much cheaper alternative to institutionalization, surgical sterilization, was only beginning to attract attention. Indiana had legalized it in 1907 (perhaps due to the influence of one physician). In 1909 it became legal in California, Connecticut and Washington. States with reputations for being 'progressive' were early adopters of forced sterilization. Despite their large black populations, less 'enlightened' states in the Deep South resisted the longest. The next chapter explains why.

("the uplift of woman from her present state of subjection to man") and the great wealth of her audience ("200 expensively gown examples of present-day subjection"). The half-dozen men present, the *Times* told readers, kept quiet lest "a single spark" trigger a revolution.

Cupid's fault, it seemed, was that he was male and selected marriage partners by male rules. "Man, dominant, selected woman for her sex attraction; and woman, deep in the mire of subjection, accepted." Gilman had an alternative called "Mother Love." When woman recognized her "real duty . . . then we can free the world of its ills." Though not completely clear in the *Times* story, Mother Love had to do with breeding a race free of social problems. Women, she assumed, wanted that, while all men wanted was a pretty face.

Opened up for questions, the subject turned to eugenics. Revealingly, the only point on which all present agreed, Gilman told her audience of well-to-do women, was "what she termed 'negative eugenics,' or the movement to prevent the entering into the world of unfit persons. The protest even against this [elsewhere], she said, was so great that one begun to believe that there were many people who could not supply the medical certificates which proposed legislation demanded."[4]

The situation is clear. In early 1914, the stage was set for Sanger's soon-to-be movement to take birth control to the poor. Almost without exception, wealthy women (at least in New York City) were eager to see "unfit persons" (meaning poor immigrant mothers and their native-born counterparts) pressured to have few or no children. Even the ugly rhetoric that would become a trademark of the birth control movement was already in place. The opponents of negative eugenics were so stupid, Gilman claimed, that the state should bar them from marrying or having children. This was the revealing beginning of a movement that would later call itself "pro-choice."

The next year Gilman transferred her ideas about motherhood to a utopian novel, *Herland,* which she serialized in a magazine she published (ironically, with financial assistance from her second husband). It describes a remote nation (perhaps in the Andes) where a combination of war, disaster and revolution had left its population entirely female and isolated on a remote mountain plateau. Miraculously, one woman acquired the ability to produce babies—all girls—without the bother of men. That trait was passed on to her daughters, and it was from her that, some 2,000 years later, the entire population of

4. "Cupid is Scorned by Mrs. C. P. Gilman" *New York Times* (Mar. 5, 1914), 8. She will repeat her attack on religious conservatives later in this chapter.

Herland traced its descent. (The dating is important, since it allows Gilman to exclude Jewish or Christian ideas from her utopia. Later, we discover the importance of that.) Hearing rumors from natives, three men fly onto the plateau. One of them, Van (a sociologist), became the story's narrator. It is he who describes the idyllic life there.

In 1979 feminists were elated to rediscover this little-known novel, fussing only that, in her endeavor to give her women what was then the most fashionable of all racial endowments, Gilman had traced their roots to Aryans. But, as we will see, her utopia had a far darker side, one centered on a chilling vision of motherhood. Her name for it was Maternal Pantheism. A more apt name would be a Dictatorship by Domineering Over Mothers. These feminists on steroids did not look kindly on young women who rebelled against their matriarchy or who had a less than ideal genetic endowment. The former were denied any influence on their child's rearing. The latter weren't even permitted to have children at all. Gilman brushed past that bit of nastiness with a passing comment about little period of "negative eugenics."

Keep in mind as you read what follows that many in the today's media find as little to criticize in the novel as their counterparts did 65 years earlier when Gilman spoke on the eugenic schemes on which it was based. A modern *New York Times* reviewer, for instance, praised the tale, asking that "the goddess smile on those who have rescued the book from long oblivion."[5] Little, it seems, has changed from then to now.

Charlotte Perkins Gilman, "Herland." In *Forerunner* 6 (Jan.–Dec. 1915). Reprinted in: *Herland*, Ann J. Lane, ed. (New York: Pantheon, 1979). Quotes from 1915 original.

—§§§—

As to geography—at about the time of the Christian era this land had a free passage to the sea. I'm not saying where, for good reasons. But there was a fairly easy pass through that wall of mountains behind us, and there is no doubt in my mind that these people were of Aryan stock, and were once in contact with the best civilization of the old world.

—*Forerunner* (May 1915), 125–26.

—§§§—

Here at last was Motherhood, and though it was not for all of them personally, it might—if the power was inherited—found here a new race.

—*Forerunner* (May 1915), 127.

—§§§—

5. Louise Bernikow, "Women Sans Men." *New York Times Book Review* (Apr. 8, 1979), 29.

The power of mother-love, that maternal instinct we so highly laud, was theirs of course, raised to its highest power; and a sister-love which, even while recognizing the actual relationship, we found it hard to credit.

—*Forerunner* (May 1915), 128.

—§§§—

The religion they had to begin with was much like that of old Greece—a number of gods and goddesses; but they lost all interest in deities of war and plunder, and gradually centered on their Mother Goddess altogether. Then, as they grew more intelligent, this had turned into a sort of Maternal Pantheism.

—*Forerunner* (May 1915), 129.

Editor: Though cut off from the rest of the world, Gilman's new mothers were sufficiently 'advanced' in their thinking to have discovered the scientific 'truths' of Malthus (population) and Darwin (breeding). Note the contrast Gilman drew between traditional mothers, having no interest in "common needs," and the utopia's new mothers, who were no less than "Conscious Makers of People." The latter phrase is odd since, despite all the talk about motherhood, at no point in the novel does she present a believable description of a child. Hers was a world of womanly philosophers living lives untroubled by dirty diapers, runny noses, and scrapped knees, yet talking incessantly about motherhood. Weird, to say the least.

—§§§—

Then came the filling up of the place. When a population multiplies by five every thirty years it soon reaches the limits of a country, especially a small one like this. They very soon eliminated all the grazing cattle—sheep were the last to go, I believe. Also they worked out a system of intensive agriculture surpassing anything I ever heard of, with the very forests all reset with fruit or nut-bearing trees.

Do what they would, however, there soon came a time when they were confronted with the problem of "the pressure of population" in an acute form. There was really crowding, and with it, unavoidably, a decline in standards.

And how did these women meet it?

Not by a "struggle for existence" which would result in an everlasting writhing mass of underbred people trying to get ahead of one another—some few on top, temporarily, many constantly crushed out underneath, a hopeless substratum of paupers and degenerates, and no serenity or peace for anyone, no possibility for really noble qualities among the people at large.

Neither did they start off in predatory excursions to get more land from somebody else, or to get more food from somebody else, to maintain their struggling mass.

Not at all. They sat down in council together and thought it out. Very clear, strong thinkers they were. They said: "With our best endeavors this country will support about so many people, with the standard of peace, comfort, health, beauty, and progress we demand. Very well. That is all the people we will make."

There you have it. You see, they were Mothers, not in our sense of helpless involuntary fecundity, forced to fill and overfill the land, every land, and then see their children suffer, sin, and die, fighting horribly with one another; but in the sense of Conscious Makers of People. Mother-love with them was not a brute passion, a mere "instinct," a wholly personal feeling; it was—A Religion.

It included that limitless feeling of sisterhood, that wide unity in service which was so difficult for us to grasp. And it was National, Racial, Human—oh, I don't know how to say it.

We are used to seeing what we call "a mother" completely wrapped up in her own pink bundle of fascinating babyhood, and taking but the faintest theoretic interest in anybody else's bundle, to say nothing of the common needs of *all* the bundles. But these women were working all together at the grandest of tasks—they were Making People—and they made them well.

There followed a period of "negative eugenics" which must have been an appalling sacrifice. We are commonly willing to "lay down our lives" for our country, but they had to forego motherhood for their country—and it was precisely the hardest thing for them to do.

When I got this far in my reading I went to Somel for more light. We were as friendly by that time as I had ever been in my life with any woman. A mighty comfortable soul she was, giving one the nice smooth mother-feeling a man likes in a woman, and yet giving also the clear intelligence and dependableness I used to assume to be masculine qualities. We had talked volumes already.

"See here," said I. "Here was this dreadful period when they got far too thick, and decided to limit the population. We have a lot to talk about that among us, but your position is so different that I'd like to know a little more about it.

"I understand that you make Motherhood the highest social service—a sacrament, really; that it is only undertaken once, by the majority of the population; that those held unfit are not allowed even that; and that to be encouraged to bear more than one child

is the very highest reward and honor in the power of the State."

(She interpolated here that the nearest approach to an aristocracy they had was to come of a line of "Over Mothers"—those who had been so honored.)

Editor: Gilman then made remarks that modern feminists must find embarrassing. In this feminist utopia, it seems, abortion was a deed so terrible it can only be blamed upon that most terrible of creatures—men.

"But what I do not understand, naturally, is how you prevent it. I gathered that each woman had five. You have no tyrannical husbands to hold in check—and you surely do not destroy the unborn—"

The look of ghastly horror she gave I shall never forget. She started from her chair, pale, her eyes blazing.

"Destroy the unborn—!" she said in a hard whisper. "Do men do that in your country?"

"Men!" I began to answer, rather hotly, and then saw the gulf before me. None of us wanted these women to think that *our* women, of whom we boasted so proudly, were in any way inferior to them. I am ashamed to say that I equivocated. I told her about Malthus and his fears. I told her of certain criminal types of women—perverts, or crazy, who had been known to commit infanticide. I told her, truly enough, that there was much in our land which was open to criticism, but that I hated to dwell on our defects until they understood us and our conditions better.

And, making a wide detour, I scrambled back to my question of how they limited the population.

As for Somel, she seems sorry, a little ashamed even, of her too clearly express amazement. As I look back now, knowing them better, I am more and more amazed as I appreciate the exquisite courtesy with which they had received over and over again statements and admissions on our part which must have revolted them to the soul.

She explained to me, with sweet seriousness, that as I had supposed, at first each woman bore five children; and that, in their eager desire to build up a nation, they had gone on in that way for a few centuries, till they were confronted with the absolute need of a limit. This fact was equally plain to all—all were equally interested.

They were now as anxious to check their wonderful power as they had been to develop it; and for some generations gave the matter their most earnest thought and study.

"We were living on rations before we worked it out," she said. "But we did work it out. You see, before a child comes to one of us there is a period of utter exaltation— the whole being is uplifted and filled with a concentrated desire for that child. We learned to look forward to that period with the greatest caution. Often our young women, those to whom motherhood had not yet come, would voluntarily defer it. When that deep inner demand for a child began to be felt she would deliberately engage in the most active work, physical and mental; and even more important, would solace her longing by the direct care and service of the babies we already had."

She paused. Her wise sweet face grew deeply, reverently tender.

"We soon grew to see that mother-love has more than one channel of expression. I think the reason our children are so—so fully loved, by all of us, is that we never—any of us—have enough of our own."

This seemed to me infinitely pathetic, and I said so. "We have much that is bitter and hard in our life at home," I told her, "but this seems to me piteous beyond words—a whole nation of starving mothers!"

But she smiled her deep contented smile, and said I quite misunderstood.

"We each go without a certain range of personal joy," she said, "but remember—we each have a million children to love and serve—*our* children."

It was beyond me. To hear a lot of women talk about "our children"! But I suppose that is the way the ants and bees would talk—do talk, maybe.

—*Forerunner* (June 1915), 153–54.

Editor: It is easy to suspect that ants and bees would adapt more easily to Gilman's utopia than real women. Recall, however, the poem that began this chapter—the one about a clever Neolithic man who believed it *was* possible to "alter Human Nature." Gilman now described how she felt that altering could be done. Note that she wanted to breed out the very same traits of initiative and individualized love that David Starr Jordan (Chapter XII) was so intent on preserving.[6]

—§§§—

Somel set her chin upon her hand, her elbow on the low wall beside her, and looked off over the fair land.

"Of course we have faults—all of us," she said. "In one way you might say that we have more than we used to—that is, our standard of perfection seems to get farther and farther away. But we are not discouraged, because our records do show gain—considerable gain.

"When we began even with the start of one particularly noble mother—we inherited the characteristics of a

6. David Starr Jordan knew Gilman and helped her build contacts within the male world of sociology. See the 1997 reprint of *With Her in Ourland* edited by Mary Jo Deegan, p. 13.

long race record behind her. And they cropped out from time to time—alarmingly. But it is—yes, quite six hundred years since we have had what you call a 'criminal.'

"We have, of course, made it our first business to train out, to breed out, when possible, the lowest types."

"Breed out?" I asked. "How could you—with parthenogenesis?"

"If the girl showing the bad qualities had still the power to appreciate social duty, we appealed to her, by that, to renounce motherhood. Some of the few worst types were, fortunately, unable to reproduce. But if the fault was in a disproportionate egotism—then the girl was sure she had the right to have children, even that hers would be better than others."

"I can see that," I said, "And then she would be likely to rear them in the same spirit."

"That we never allowed," answered Somel quietly.

"Allowed?" I queried. "Allowed a mother to rear her own children?"

"Certainly not," said Somel, "unless she was fit for that supreme task."

This was rather a blow to my previous convictions.

"But I thought motherhood was for each of you—"

"Motherhood—yes, that is, maternity, to bear a child. But education is our highest art, only allowed to our highest artists."

"Education?" I was puzzled again. "I don't mean education. I mean by motherhood not only child-bearing, but the care of babies."

"The care of babies involves education, and is entrusted only to the most fit," she repeated.

"Then you separate mother and child!" I cried in cold horror, something of Terry's feeling creeping over me, that there must be something wrong among these many virtues.

"Not usually," she patiently explained. "You see, almost every woman values her maternity above everything else, Each girl holds it close and dear, an exquisite joy, a crowning honor, the most intimate, most personal, most precious thing. That is the child-rearing has come to be with us a culture so profoundly studied, practised with such subtlety and skill, that the more we love our children the less we are willing to trust that process to unskilled hands—even our own."

"But a mother's love "I ventured.

She studied my face, trying to work out a means of clear explanation.

"You told us about your dentists," she said, at length, "those quaintly specialized persons who spend their lives filling little holes in other persons' teeth—even in children's teeth sometimes."

"Yes?" I said, not getting her drift.

"Does mother-love urge mothers—with you—to fill their own children's teeth? Or to wish to?"

"Why no—of course not," I protested. "But that is a highly specialized craft. Surely the care of babies is open to any woman—any mother!"

"We do not think so," she gently replied. "Those of us who are the most highly competent fulfill that office; and a majority of our girls eagerly try for it—I assure you we have the very best."

"But the poor mother—bereaved of her baby—"

"Oh no!" she earnestly assured me. "Not in the least bereaved. It is her baby still—it is with her—she has not lost it. But she is not the only one to care for it. There are others whom she knows to be wiser. She knows it because she has studied as they did, practised as they did, and honors their real superiority. For the child's sake, she is glad to have for it this highest care."

I was unconvinced. Besides, this was only hearsay; I had yet to see the motherhood of Herland.

—*Forerunner* (July 1915), 186–87.

Motherhood as Superstition

The child's need of the mother and the mother's need of the child is a prejudice which must vanish with all other superstitions from lower stages of culture, if the mothers are to be coequal with men, community members capable of work, and if the children are to be well reared for the social vocations which must soon determine the trend of all our lives.[7]

—ELLEN KEY DESCRIBING GILMAN'S PHILOSOPHY, 1913

Editor: Gilman had already made it clear that she would not allow mere biological mothers to interfere with her scheme to alter human nature. She now turns her wrath on fathers whose role is often less nurturing and more that of authority. She attacks the father's role by criticizing the idea of God as a father. In *With Her in Ourland*," her attack on the fatherly "Hebrew God" will turn virulently anti-Semitic.

"You have no theory of eternal punishment then, I take it?" Ellador laughed. Her eyes were as bright as stars, and there were tears in them, too. She was so sorry for me.

---

7. Ellen Key, "Education for Motherhood I," *Atlantic Monthly* 112 (Aug. 1913), 49. Key rejected that point of view, calling it "Spartan."

"How could we?" she asked, fairly enough. "We have no punishments in life, you see, so we don't imagine them after death."

"Have you *no* punishments? Neither for children nor criminals—such mild criminals as you have?" I urged.

"Do you punish a person for a broken leg or a fever? We have preventive measures, and cures; sometimes we have to 'send the patient to bed,' as it were; but that's not a punishment—it's only part of the treatment," she explained.

Then studying my point of view more closely, she added: "You see, we recognize, in our human motherhood, a great tender limitless uplifting force—patience and wisdom and all subtlety of delicate method. We credit God—our idea of God—with all that and more. Our mothers are not angry with us—why should God be?"

"Does God mean a person to you?"

This she thought over a little. "Why—in trying to get close to it in our minds we personify the idea, naturally; but we certainly do not assume a Big Woman somewhere, who is God. What we call God is a Pervading Power, you know, an Indwelling Spirit, something inside of us that we want more of. Is your God a Big Man?" she asked innocently. . . .

I explained that the God of the Christian world was really the ancient Hebrew God, and that we had simply taken over the patriarchal idea—that ancient one which quite inevitably clothed its thought of God with the attributes of the patriarchal ruler, the grandfather." [112–13]

—*Forerunner* (Oct. 1915), 266–67.

Assisted Evolution—1916

Editor: In her magazine, Gilman placed the following article just before the first installment in a new series of stories called *With Her in Ourland*. It aptly summarized the main message of both that series and *Herland*—that the scientific control of human breeding could rapidly create a superior race. As we saw in Chapter XII, the *New York Times* had claimed that, "no eugenist worthy of the name" wanted methods "even remotely resembling" those of Luther Burbank. Here, Gilman advocates precisely that.

Charlotte Perkins Gilman, "Assisted Evolution."
Forerunner 8 (Jan. 1916), 5.

It took Mother Nature long, long ages to make a tree with small, bitter nuts. It has only taken us a few centuries to make from that tree almond and apricot, peach and nectarine.

It took Mother Nature long, long ages to make the common bramble with its soft, black berries. Mr. Burbank, in part of one lifetime, has given us the rich blended Logan Berry—and scores of new varieties.

It has taken Mother Nature long, long ages to turn fierce greedy hairy ape-like beasts into such people as we are. It will take us but two or three close-linked generations to make human beings far more superior to us than we are to the apes.

With Her in Ourland—1916

Editor: In the sequel to *Herland* that Gilman published throughout 1916, Van, the sociologist, marries Ellador, a Herlander, and the two travel the world, visiting a Europe at war, the mysterious Orient, and Van's own United States. Again the story is narrated by Van, but this time we see how a Herlander sees our world. (Note the debt of gratitude Gilman pays to Winwood Reade's long-lived book, quoted in Chapter I.)

Charlotte Perkins Gilman, "With Her in Ourland."
In *Forerunner* 7 (Jan.–Dec. 1916). Reprinted in: *With Her in Ourland*, Mary Jo Degan, ed. (Westport: Greenwood, 1997). Quotes are from the 1916 original.

The rapid grasp she [Ellador] made in the whole framework of our history would have astonished anyone not acquainted with Herland brains and Herland methods of education. It did astonish the young historian. She by no means set herself to learn all that he wanted to teach her; on the contrary, she continually checked the flow of information, receiving only what she wanted to know.

A very few good books on world evolution—geological, botanical, zoological, and ethnic, gave her the background she needed, and such a marvel of condensation as Winwood's Reade's *Martyrdom of Man* supplied the outline of history. [78]

—*Forerunner* (Feb. 1916), 42.

Editor: Utopian stories lose realism when readers ask, "But, as nice as this sounds, would all my friends want to live there?" Since the answer is typically "No," the author is forced to create some scheme to rid a round-holed world of square-pegged people. In *Herland*, Gilman described how women were coerced into conformity by the population crisis that threatened their cliff-rimmed world. When her Ellador visited America, it was obvious that a country so rich in land and resources faced no such crisis. Gilman had to adopt a different approach to create a "like-minded" nation. What follows is ugly. Immigrants not fitting into her plans—particularly the "poor and oppressed of all nations"—

are to be kept out. Here we see that her definition of 'democracy' meant 'rule by those who agree with me.' It is easy to see in that simply an 'old stock' New Englander lamenting that her sort not longer ran the country. But something more was involved. Gilman was a radical feminist not a backward-looking sentimentalist. According to her ideology, poor and often exploited immigrant women should have been her allies. But they weren't. Many were very conservative on issues such as home life and children. These women had immigrated to America for what it was, not what Gilman and those like her wanted to make of it. That made them her enemies, hence the anger she directs at them and her chilling unwillingness to let them be part of what she deceptively calls "democracy."

—§§§—

"Do you think we're too big?" I asked. "Too much country to be handled properly?"

"Oh, *no!*" she answered promptly. "Not too big in land. That would have been like the long lean lines of youth, the far-reaching bones of a country gradually rounding out and filling in as you grow. But you couldn't wait to grow, you just—swelled."

"What on earth do you mean, Ellador?"

"You have stuffed yourself with the most ill-assorted and unassimilable mass of human material that ever was held together by artificial means," she answered remorselessly. "You go to England, and the people are English. Only three per cent of aliens even in London, I understand. And in France the people are French—bless them! And in Italy, Italian. But here—it's no wonder I was discouraged at first. It has taken a lot of study and hard thinking, to see a way out at all. But I do see it. It was simply awful when I begun.

"Just look! Here you were, a little band of really promising people, of different nations, yet of the same general stock, and *like-minded*—that was the main thing. The real union is the union of idea; without that—no nation. You made settlements, you grew strong and bold, you shook off the old government, you set up a new flag, and then —!"

"Then," said I proudly, "we opened our arms to all the world, if that is what you are finding fault with. We welcomed other people to our big new country—'the poor and oppressed of all nations!'" I quoted solemnly.

"That's what I mean by saying you were ignorant of sociology," was her cheerful reply. "It never occurred to you that the poor and oppressed were not necessarily good stuff for a democracy." [118]

—*Forerunner* (June 1916), 153–54.

Race Mixing

We used fondly to take for granted that the incoming millions loved the country as we did, and felt eager to join it. Some of them do. Enormous numbers do not. It is quite true that we ourselves are a mixed race—as are all races today—and that we were once immigrants. All Americans have come from somewhere else. But all persons who come from somewhere else are not therefore Americans. The American blend is from a few closely connected races. . . .

Since *genus homo* is one species, it is physically possible for all races to interbreed, but not therefore desirable. Some combine well, making a good blend, some do not. We are perfectly familiar in this country with the various blends of black and white, and the wisest of both races prefer the pure stock.

The Eurasian mixture is generally considered unfortunate by most observers. Of European races, some seem to mate with better results than others. . . .

It is an entire mistake to suppose that the well-ordered World Federation to which we look forward requires the wiping out of national entity, or the physical compounding of racial stocks.[8]

—CHARLOTTE PERKINS GILMAN, 1923

The Menace of the Migrating

To-day every people desires to be a *nation,* that is, a *spiritual unit.* In the Roman Empire this ideal played no part, and there resulted an amazing hodgepodge of population. We moderns are afraid of such collections of human odds and ends as came to people Roman Africa or Syria or the valley of the Nile, because we realize that always such muddled mixing begets absolutist government. Dreading a government not subject to the collective will of the governed, we wish a people to be like-minded enough to develop a common opinion upon political questions. . . . Any prosperous country which leaves its doors ajar will presently find itself not the home of a nation, but a polyglot boarding house.[9]

—PROF. EDWARD A. ROSS, SOCIOLOGIST, 1921

8. Charlotte Perkins Gilman, "Is American Too Hospitable?" *Forum* 70 (Oct. 1923), 1984–85. Restrictions on race mixing was once openly regarded as quite scientific.

9. Edward Alsworth Ross, "The Menace of Migrating Peoples," *Century Magazine* 102 (May 1921), 131. The Ross quoted here (and in Chap. VII) was a close personal friend of Gilman and it was to him that she wrote of her plans to commit suicide just before her 1935 death. (See Mary Jo Deegan's edition of *With Her in Ourland,* p. 13.)

Editor: In addition to excluding newcomers, Gilman's agenda led her to deny the usefulness of many of those who had been here for many generations. In her mind, they were the "coal dust and plain dirt" corrupting the "good metal" that she and those like her wanted to create. This is political correctness with a vengeance.

—§§§—

She saw that I was about to defend our foreign born, and went on: "I do not mean the immigrants solely. There are Bostonians of Beacon Hill who belong in London; there are New Yorkers of five generations who belong in Paris; there are vast multitudes who belong in Berlin, in Dublin, in Jerusalem; and there are plenty of native Sons and Daughters of the Revolution who are aristocrats, plutocrats, anything but democrats."

"Why of course there are! We believe in having all kinds—there's room for everybody—this is the 'melting pot' you know."

"And do you thin that you can put a little of everything into a melting-pot and produce a good metal? Well fused and flawless? Gold, silver, copper and iron, lead, radium, pipe clay, coal dust and plain dirt?"[10]

—*Forerunner* (June 1916), 43–44.

Editor: Gilman then unleashed another blast at mothers who insist on rearing their own children, particularly in religion. "Socialization of home industry" meant that the State would take over much of the mother's role, preparing meals, cleaning homes, and training children to think as it wanted "from infancy." "Home-bound" mothers threaten that agenda because they have a narrower focus than women caught up in careers. Gilman may have been influenced in this by John Dewey, whose *Democracy and Education* came out the same year as this series. She and Dewey knew each other through Chicago's Hull House.

10. The idea of national uniformity was a popular, nineteenth-century liberal idea that historians term *cultural nationalism*—an idea that bore dreadful fruit in Germany. There it was used to drive 'divisive' religion from public life, leaving a moral and spiritual vacuum that Nazism exploited. Of course, if a group *wanted* to enlarge the power of the central government and weaken public opinion, turning a nation into warring factions with tension-creating rhetoric about multiculturalism and diversity would provide a good rationale. Even though the artificially isolated groups agreed about such things as parental control of education, they would be kept too distrustful of one another to counter moves by the modern day equivalents of Gilman. It's an ancient trick called "divide and conquer."

"It has this to do with it," she answered slowly and sadly. "Your children grow up in the charge of home-bound mothers who recognize no interest, ambition, or duty outside the home—except to get to heaven if they can. **These home-bound women are man-suckers; all they get he must give them, and they want a great deal. . . .**"

"What do you want *done?*" I asked, after awhile.

"Definite training in democratic thought, feeling and action, from infancy. An economic administration of common resources under which the home would cease to be a burden and become an *unconscious* source of happiness and comfort. And, of course, the socialization of home industry.

—*Forerunner* (July 1916), 185.

—§§§—

Editor: Before Nazism drove 'respectable' anti-Semitism underground, much of the hostility toward a biblical worldview and religious 'chosenness' was directed at its original source, the Jews, rather than at the 'Catholic hierarchy' or Protestant 'fundamentalists.' This was especially true in Germany, where Gilman's Ellador got her "latest study and criticism" of the Bible. Here she offers a disturbing solution to the "Jewish race question." Jewish parents who taught their children their ancient faith were engaging, she said, in the "evil of filling up new minds with old foolishness." That, she believed, should not be permitted. Notice how many of the arguments she uses her are now directed by liberals at conservative Christians.

I ducked this large proposition, and asked her if she had an answer to the Jewish race question as simple as that of the negro.

"What's the question," she countered.

"I suppose there's more than one question involved," I answered slowly, "but mine would be: why don't people like Jews?" . . . .

"I soon discovered that the very general dislike to this one people is not due to the religious difference between them and Christians; it was quite as general and strong, apparently, in very ancient times."

". . . . Here's one of them. The Jews are the only surviving modern people that have ever tried to preserve the extremely primitive custom of endogenous marriage. Everywhere else, the exogenous habit proved itself best and was generally accepted. **This people is the only one which has always assumed itself to be superior to every other people and tried to prevent intermarriage with them. . . .**"

"I have two other suggestions, one sociologic, one psychic. **The first is this. In the successive steps of social evolution, the Jewish people seem not to have passed the tribal stage. They never made a real nation. Apparently they can't. . . .**"

"But, Ellador, do not the modern Jews make good citizens in whatever country they are in?"

"They do, in large measure, wherever they are allowed," she agreed; "and both this difference and the old marriage difference would long ago have been outgrown but for the last one—the psychic one. . . ."

"Oh dear me, Van, they're only one people. I get so interested in the world at large that I forget them. Well, what the Jews did was to make their patriomania into a religion."

I did not get that and said so.

"It was poorly put," she admitted. "They couldn't be patriomaniacs without a fatherland, could they? But it was the same feeling at a lower stage, applied only to the race. They thought they were 'the chosen people'—of God."

"Didn't other races think the same thing? Don't they yet?" I urged.

"Oh in a way, they do—some of them. Especially since the Jews made a Bible of it. You see, Van, the combination was peculiar. The special talent of this race is in literary expression. Other races had their sorrows but could not utter them. Carthage had no Jeremiah; nor has Armenia. . . ."

"Why Ellador, don't you call their religion anything? Haven't they lifted the world with great religious concepts?"

She smiled at me, that gentle warm, steady smile of hers. "Forgive an outsider, please. I know that the Christian religion rests on the Jewish books, and that it is hard indeed to see around early teachings. But I have read your Bible carefully, and some little of the latest study and criticism upon it. I think the Christian races have helped the Jews to overestimate their religion."

"You've never said much about our various religions, my fair foreigner, What do you really think about them?"

This she pondered carefully.

"It's a large subject to try to comment on in a few words, but I can say this—they are certainly improving."

I had to laugh. This was such faint praise for our highest institution.

"How do you measure them, O casual observer?"

"By their effect upon the people, of course. Naturally, each set of believers holds its own to be the All True, and as naturally that is impossible. But there is enough truth and enough good will in your religions if you would only use them, instead of just believing them."

"And do you not think, especially considering the time of its development, that the Jewish concept of one God, the Jewish ethical ideal, was a long step upward?"

"It was a step, certainly, but, Van, they did not think their God was the only one. He was just Theirs. A private tribal God, openly described as being jealous of the others. And as to their ethics and the behavior of the people—you have only to read their own books to see how bad it was. Van, no religion can be truly good where the initial doctrines are false, or even partly false. That utterly derogatory concept of a God who could curse all humanity because of one man's doing what he knew he would, a God so petty as to pick out one small people for no better reason than that they gave him some recognition, and to set his face against all the rest of his equally descended 'children'—can't you see how unethical, how morally degrading, such a religion must be?"

"It was surely better than others at the time," I insisted.

"That may be, but the others of that period have mercifully perished. They weren't so literary. **Don't you see, by means of their tremendous art this people have immortalized their race egotism**[11] **and their whole record of religious aspirations, mistakes and failures, in literature. That is what has given them their lasting place in the world. But the effect of this primitive religion, immortalized by art, and thrust upon the world so long, has been far from good.** It has well-nigh killed Christianity, from its cradle. It has been the foundation of most of those hideous old wars and persecutions. With quotations from that Hebrew 'voice of God' the most awful deeds have been committed and sanctioned. I consider it in many ways a most evil religion."

"But we have, as you say, accepted it; so it does not account for the general dislike for which you were offering explanations."

"The last explanation was the psychic one," she went on. "What impresses me here is this: The psychic attitude of this people presents to all the other inhabitants of the world a spirit of concentrated pride. It rests first on the tribal animus, with that old endogenous marriage custom; and then on this tremendous literary-religious structure. One might imagine generations of Egyptians making their chief education a study of the pyramids, sphinxes and so on, or generations of Greeks bringing up their children in the ceaseless contemplation of the Acropolis, or

the works of their dramatists; but with the Jews, as a matter of fact, we do see, century after century of education in their ancient language, in their ancient books, and everlasting study and discussion of what remote dead men[12] have written. This has given a peculiar intensity to the Jewish character—a sort of psychic inbreeding; they have a condensed spirit, more and more so as time passes, and it becomes increasingly inimical to the diffused spirit of modem races. . . ."

I was silent a bit. Her suggestions were certainly novel, and in no way resembled what I had heard before, either for or against this "peculiar people."

"What's the answer?" I said at last. "Is it hopeless?"

"Certainly not. Aren't they born babies, with dear little, clean, free minds? Just as soon as people recognize the evil of filling up new minds with old foolishness, they can make over any race on earth."

"That won't change 'race characteristics,' will it?"

"No, not the physical ones," she answered. **"Intermarriage will do that."**

"It looks to me as though your answer to the Jewish question was—leave off being Jews. Is that it?"

"In a measure it is," she said slowly. "They are world-people and can enrich the world with their splendid traits. They will keep, of course, their high race qualities, their special talents and virtues, by a chosen, not an enforced, selection. **Some of the noblest people are Jews, some of the nicest. That can't be denied. But this long-nursed bunch of ancient mistakes—it is high time they dropped it. What is the use of artificially maintaining characteristics which the whole world dislikes,**[13] **and then complaining of race prejudice?** Of course, there is race prejudice, a cultural one; and all the rest of you will have to bring up your children without that. It is only the matter of a few generations at most."

This was a part of the spirit of Herland to which I was slow in becoming accustomed. Their homogeneous, well-ordered life extended its social consciousness freely, ahead as well as backwards; their past history was common knowledge, and their future development even more commonly discussed. They planned centuries ahead and accomplished what they planned. When I thought of their making over the entire language in the interests of childhood, of their vast field of cultural literature, of such material achievements as their replanting all their forests, **I began to see that the greatness of a country is not to**

---

11. Editor: Recall that in a 1922 letter to Margaret Sanger, Edward East would write about William Robinson's "monumental Jewish egotism" (Chap. XX).

12. Editor: This is similar to modern feminism's attacks on books by "dead white men."

13. Editor: Not the whole world, but certainly the progressive circles in which Gilman ran.

be measured by linear space, in extent of land, nor arithmetically by numbers of people, nor shallowly by the achievements of the present and a few left-overs, but by the scope of its predetermined social advance.

As this perception grew within me, it brought first a sense of shame for all the rest of the world, and even more intensely for my own country, which had such incomparable advantages. But after a little, instead of shame, which is utter waste, I began to see life as I never had before: as a great open field of Work, in which we were quite free to do as we would. We have always looked at it as a hopeless tangle of individual lives, short, aimless threads, as blindly mixed as the grass stems in a haystack. But collectively, as nations, taking sufficient time, there was nothing we could not do. I told her of my new vision, and she was dumbly happy—just held my hand, her eyes shining.

"That's how to stand the misery and failure, isn't it?" I said. "That's how not to be discouraged at the awfulness of things; and the reason you take up these separate 'questions' so lightly is that none of them mean much alone. The important thing is to get people to think and act together."

"There's nothing on earth to hinder them, Van, dear, except what's in their heads. And they can stop putting it in, in the babies, I mean, and can put it out of their own, at least enough to get to work. They are beginning, you know."

She spoke most encouragingly, most approvingly, of the special efforts we were making in small groups or as individuals to socialize various industries and functions, but with far more fervor of the great "movements."

"The biggest of all, and closest related, are your women's movement and labor movement. Both seem to be swiftly growing stronger. **The most inclusive forward-looking system is Socialism, of course. What a splendid vision of immediate possibilities that is.**[14] I can not accustom myself to your not seeing it at once. Of course, the reason is plain: your minds are full of your ancient mistakes, too; not so much racial and religious, as in beliefs of economic absurdities. It is so funny!"

—Forerunner (Oct. 1916), 264–68.

Editor: Next the "Jewish religion" was blamed for a "contemptible lie" and "unspeakable injustice." Today, to keep from exposing the nasty, anti-Semitic roots that

lie behind such claims, feminists direct their hostility at the more conservative branches of Christianity.

". . . . And then, as if that was not enough—really, my dear, I'm not joking, I'm ashamed, as if I'd done it myself—we, in our superior freedom, in our monopoly of education, with the law in our hands, both to make and to execute, with every conceivable advantage—we have blamed women for the sins of the world!"

She interrupted here, eagerly—"Not *all* of you, Van dear! That was only a sort of legend with some people. **It was only in the Jewish religion you think so much of that the contemptible lie was actually stated as a holy truth—and even God made to establish that unspeakable injustice."**

—Forerunner (Nov. 1916), 292.

—§§§—

And I thought of her sisters, that fair land of full grown women, all of whom, with room for wide personal distinction, were beautiful and strong. There were differences enough. A group of thoroughbred race horses might vary widely in color, size, shape, markings and individual expression; yet all be fine horses. There would be no need of scrubs and cripples to make variety.[15] And I looked again out of our window, at the city street, with its dim dirtiness, its brutal noise, and the unsatisfied, unsatisfying people going so hurriedly about after their food, crowding, pushing, hurrying like hungry rats; the sordid eagerness of the men, the shallow folly of the women. And all at once there swept over me a great wave of homesickness for Herland.

—Forerunner (Nov. 1916), 293–94.

—§§§—

"I am getting rather discouraged, if you are not, Ellador. As compared with a rational country like yours, this is rather a mess. And it looks so hopeless. I suppose it will take a thousand years to catch up."

"You could do it in three generations." She calmly replied.

"Three generations! That's barely a century."

"I know it. The whole outside part of it you could do inside twenty years; it is the people who will take three generations to remake. You could improve this stock, say 5 per cent in one, 15 in two and 80 per cent in three. Perhaps faster."

"Aren't you rather sanguine, my dear girl?"

"I don't think so," she answered gravely. "People are not *bad* now; they are only weighed down with all this falsehood and foolishness in their heads. There is always

14. Editor: Here Gilman linked her cultural anti-Semitism to feminism and socialism. The connection is apt. Among its "ancient mistakes," the Jewish religion believes in parental rights, male leadership, and free enterprise, all ideas Gilman loathed.

15. Editor: To do this, her society must kill babies born with disabilities. Hints of that come in the next article.

the big lifting force of life to push you on as fast as you will let it. There is the wide surrounding help of conditions, such conditions as you even now know how to arrange. **And there is the power of education—which you have hardly tried. With these all together and with proper care in breeding you could fill the world with glorious people—soon. Oh, I wish you'd do it. I *wish* you'd do it.**

—*Forerunner* (Nov. 1916), 296–97.

—§§§—

Sexual Reform

After about 1910, a radical shift in sexual attitudes occurred among leading intellectuals and reformers, who were greatly influenced by European sexual theorists. Although there were American traditions of sex radicalism, they were rather unsystematic. . . . The Europeans, by contrast, offered more empirical, "scientific" investigations of sexual behavior through psychology and anthropology. Or, like Edward Carpenter and Ellen Key, they continued in the old, utopian style but had powerful social movements behind them (such as Fabian socialism and feminism), unlike the tiny sectarian groups of the American sex reformers.[16]

—LINDA GORDON, WOMAN'S BODY, WOMAN'S RIGHT

The Sanctity of Human Life

Charlotte Perkins Gilman, "The Sanctity of Human Life,"
Forerunner (May 1916), 128–29.

Editor: Note her "while it is going on" remark. Without a perspective that people are eternal, Gilman and those like her can only value people by appearance, intelligence and productivity. Those without value by such standards can and should be eliminated.

There has been a great deal of talk about the case of the poor malformed baby, doomed to crippled and distorted idiocy, who was wisely allowed to die by both doctors and mother.

George MacDonald once brought into one of his novels a pair of dwarfs, brother and sister, quite pitifully deformed, but of a high and noble spirit. They were instrumental in "saving the soul" of the hero, or heroine, or somebody, if I remember aright, and the purpose of the author was to show that we have no right to condemn human creatures because of physical limitations.[17]

---

16. Linda Gordon, *Woman's Body, Woman's Right* (New York: Penguin, 1976), 186.

17. Editor: I have been told the novel is *Thomas Wingfold* (1876). As you might expect, MacDonald was a Christian writer.

But how about mental limitations? How about idiots? They are no good to themselves or to anybody else, and they are, on the contrary, an injury.

Many speak of the ennobling effect of caring for the helpless. But is it ennobling? Are the guards and warders of the prisons, the "keepers" of the insane, those who manage orphan asylums and the like, noted for their tender sympathy? On the contrary the daily contact with persons who are absolutely dependent, who make a good deal of trouble, who may be dangerous, or who are positively repellent, has a coarsening and hardening effect.

We talk about "the sanctity of human life," and we are right. Human life is sacred, far too sacred to be allowed to fall into hideous degeneracy. If we had a proper regard for human life we should take instant measures to check the supply of feeble-minded and defective persons, and further measures to prevent the reproduction of such unfortunates. . . .

Human life is sacred *while it is going on.* It is not merely a matter of filling the world with people—any kind of people; or of keeping alive every wretched little monstrosity; it is a theory which calls for better living—for everybody.

Back of Birth Control

EDITOR

Though Gilman agreed with Sanger and her feminist allies on the need for "proper care in breeding" to create a world filled "with glorious people," she disliked the sexual mysticism they used to cloak their promiscuity. Gilman had rejected the religion of her Puritan ancestors, but she retained parts of their ethical code, giving it a new, biological twist. She might say nasty things about mothers who stayed at home, fixing cookies and rearing children, but she was a strong believer not just in monogamy but in the need for sexual restraint *within* marriage. (Ellador and Van travel the world and return to Herland before they consummated their marriage.) That clashed with the birth control movement's hidden sexual agenda. The conflict came out in the March 1922 issue of *Birth Control Review* when Sanger permitted Gilman to publish an article entitled "Back of Birth Control."

Perhaps to make her magazine widely read, Sanger did not insist that every article keep with her own beliefs. She allowed eugenists, for instance, to argue the case for positive eugenics, though few things outraged her as much as the suggestion that *her* sort of people should be forced to have more children. Eugenists, after all, were allies and had to be humored. But it is clear that in her article Gilman crossed into areas Sanger absolutely would not tolerate. Sanger published the article—she could hardly turn down someone as well-known as Gilman—but she was clearly displeased with its content. Immediately after it came one with the subtitle, "A Reply to 'Back of Birth Control'" and the next month saw yet another subtitled, "Being a Reply to 'Back of Birth Control' by Charlotte Perkins Gilman."[18] The two 'replies' are summed up by a nasty remark in the first claiming that in Gilman, "the imperious tormenting inhibitions of the Puritan break through the intellectual independence of the Radical feminist." Only in May did Sanger allow Gilman to respond with a brief, "In Rejoiner."

In what follows, we give Gilman's point of view. Revealingly, her nasty remark about savage "plantation negroes" triggered no outrage from her feminist critics. On that all agreed. In fact, the first reply opened with an muddled argument that can best be summarized as: let the "unbridled" have their pleasures as long as we keep them from becoming parents. That would become the birth controllers ultimate agenda—so separate sex from parenthood that they could keep those they dislike sexually active but virtually childless. Understand that and you understand much of today's sexual politics.[19]

Charlotte Perkins Gilman, "Back of Birth Control"
Birth Control Review 6 (Mar. 1922), 31–33.

All these claims made by the courageous advocates of Birth Control are true, important, and pressing. Why then does so visibly good a measure lack general support? . . . .

There are two good reasons. The first and most conspicuous is this: Among the many evils which beset the world none is more injurious than that sum of vice and disease, shame, crime and common unhappiness, which springs from excessive sex-indulgence. In marriage or

---

18. F. W. Stella Browne, "Birth Control and Sex Psychology" in March, p. 33–34, Grace Potter, "The Purpose of Mating" in April, p. 63 and "In Rejoinder" in May, p. 86.

19. Editor: This oft-concealed agenda surfaced at the close of Brown's article in the remark: "Let us, in the words of Havelock Ellis: 'prepare the way by undermining and destroying those degrading traditional conceptions which have persisted so long that they are instilled into us almost from birth, to work like a virus in the heart and to become almost a disease of the soul.'" Expressed bluntly, traditional sexual morality is a "disease" that must be destroyed by not allowing its adherents to pass its "virus" on to their children. That agenda underlies much of modern, secular sex education. Whatever its advocates may claim, that is *not* a tolerant, diverse, pluralistic society. For certain groups, it is intended to be a prelude to genocide.

out, this unbridled indulgence works harm to our species, a harm so conspicuous that nothing but long submission and utter ignorance can account for our indifference.

In our day the after-affects of the war, and the morbid doctrine of Freud as to the bad results of "suppressed desires" have accentuated what was always an evil, and made this human disorder not only more common but offensively conspicuous. It is oddly amusing to see people who have flatly repudiated their old religious faith, instantly give the same blind acceptance to any new theory they happen to pick up. Has no one had the mental agility to try the test of comparison on this suppressed desire bugaboo? How about the people who never do suppress their desires? Are they so much better off? The plantation negroes, and their savage prototypes do very little suppressing. . . .

. . . .There are in the movement men and women of the highest moral character . . . and there are others, too many others, who advocate and sometimes practice a degree of sex-indulgence which is the more unbridled for the guarantee of "safety": this not meaning safety from any ulterior punishment, civil, social or eternal, for they think what they do is right and proper—but safety from responsibility. . . .

Back of this is the other reason, deeper, stronger far to the serious student of social evolution.

Of all the errors incident to the development of human consciousness in a race of animals, none has had wider ill effects than our misuse of the sex function. . . .

Very early in our unwritten history, man's ingenious effort to give himself pleasure, enforced upon an economically subject woman, soon resulted in a world cult of indulgence of which Freud and his followers furnish a lingering echo. No man thought of suppressing his desires if he had the ability to gratify them, either in his household in peace, or anybody's household in war. . . .

The monogamy natural to our race, as to so many other animals, has had a hard time developing under this handicap. . . .

To those who see our sex difficulties in this light it seems a poor thing at best to be agitating for Birth Control. We need a much more radical control than that. . . .

. . . . What we need is recognition of what ails us, and a gradual increase of rational restraint until we are again in the healthy condition of our "lower" brethren [mammals], whose desires only appear at the right period of fulfilment, and do not trouble them at all in the rest of the time.

—§§§—

Vanguard, Rear-Guard, and Mud-Guard

Editor: With that attitude, Gilman found the Roaring Twenties' promiscuity and its self-centered use of birth control repulsive. Four months after her *Birth Control Review* article, she published this one.

Charlotte Perkins Gilman, "Vanguard, Rear-Guard, and Mud-Guard." *Century Magazine* 104 (July 1922), 348–53.

Time was when age meant dignity, authority and power, while youth was helpless slavery. The child was the property of the father. . . .

All this overwhelming of children by their domineering fathers is due to the anomalous position of the human male as owner and master of his female and, as a matter of course, her progeny.

The mother is nature's chief agent in that race-improvement business, and she, unless a diseased or criminal type, does not maltreat her child. That is, not intentionally. But she has done her share in the benevolent despotism of the family, an affectionate tyranny often harder to escape than a harsh one. . . .

Throughout virtually all our historic period, and even back of it, as far as we can tell, we find age dominant, an immovable rear-guard, doing its venerable best to keep mankind hitched to the starting post.

But now the scene changes—changes beyond recognition. . . .

Youth, fearless and hopeful, each generation more fully charged with the social spirit, more justly impatient with the repeated follies of the past, pushes on as the vanguard of that long, slow, advancing column; at least it should. . . .

Gay and proud and impudent, they have escaped from authority and duty and decorum, and, like Humpty Dumpty, have had a great fall. . . .

What does glaringly distinguish this period, among those who consider themselves most "advanced" and superciliously condemn the nineteenth century, is an unchecked indulgence in appetite and impulse; a coarseness and looseness in speech, dress, manner, and habit of life; and a wholesale resistance to any restraint more worthy of a fractious young mule than a reasonable being. . . .

. . . . The young people of to-day know more, much more, than the old people of past ages, and that is why there is so little excuse for their behavior. They repudiate age as being conservative, as maintaining the past, and they themselves, in their wildest flights toward what they

consider freedom, have merely reverted to the behavior of ten thousand years ago. . . .

The greatest single perception that ever came to the human mind is that of evolution. Many thinkers worked it out, but no one name is more closely associated with it than that of Darwin. If we called it the Darwinian age instead of the Victorian, we should show more intelligence.

No single century has meant so much to the world. Its main glory is in the freeing of the human mind from the immovable clamps of religious doctrine and legend by which it had been fettered for many changeless years. . . .

. . . . **By a strong, well-informed, rigidly selective motherhood the young women of to-day could cleanse the human race of its worst inheritance by a discriminating refusal of unfit fathers. Instead of which their concern seems to be chiefly in mastering birth-control and acquiring "experience."**

With a proud ambition to improve our stock, we might see these "free" young women grow straight and strong, with trained, active bodies and well filled, well used minds. What we do see is the "débutante slouch," white-washed noses and painted lips, plucked eyebrows obscured by hats worn like the caricatures of an old clothes man, and legs whose scanty shelter is a skirt having almost the frankness of the ballet without its freedom of movement. . . .

As women their dress, their facial decoration, their behavior, show no hope of better motherhood, which is what they are women for. As human beings, companions and equals of men—

By all means let us throw off the arbitrary shackles of that lagging rear-guard which has so long and so successfully kept the world back. . . .

But this acceptance of foolish fashions, this adoption of old vices as modern advances, this "protest" which has no more direction than the bounce of a ball, the infantile delight of an ill trained child in doing what he has been told not to do—all these promise nothing for our future.

Perhaps they will learn presently that there is no date to the laws of nature, and that youth as youth is not in itself a guaranty of anything except the exceeding importance of its own impressions. **Then we may hope to cut loose from that rear-guard forever, to have a vanguard that will move ahead instead of reel around in one place, and to erect a mud-guard, strong, effective, permanent, against the ancient weaknesses of an undeveloped race.**

—§§§—

Birth Control, Religion, and the Unfit

Editor: In early December of 1931, Margaret Sanger wrote Gilman a letter: "A wonderful offer has just been made to me by Mr. Oswald Garrison Villard to devote a special issue of *The Nation* to the subject of Birth Control."[20] She went on the ask if Gilman might be able be able to "contribute a short article." Gilman did and extracts from that article follow.

Charlotte Perkins Gilman, "Birth Control, Religion, and the Unfit." *Nation* 134 (Jan. 27, 1932), 108–09. In a 1936 letter Sanger received from the magazine, it proclaimed itself, "America's Foremost Liberal Weekly Since 1865."

Earnest persons, studying social difficulties, find them gravely complicated by "the unfit." . . . .

We are mortified at our moronic average, alarmed at the increasing numbers of those far below it. Further, we find that the unfitter they are, the more lavishly they fulfil what some religionists assure us is the divine commandment—to increase and multiply and replenish the earth. Confronted with this difficulty, we propose to check the undesirable increase by the simple device of sterilizing the unfit. Unfortunately, when urging the necessary legislation on the subject, we meet not only religious objections, but those of the unfit who are voters.

On further thought, seeking to antedate the disadvantageous reproduction, we seize on the benefits of birth control, a practice which does not interfere with the pleasures of the unfit but saves society from the reduplication.[21] Again we are met by the indifference of the unfit as voters, and mere ignorance and stupidity are likewise often backed by the enormous power of religion.

Every religion believes itself to be the Truth, and warmly desires to increase its membership, not intelligence and ability being requisite, but numbers. On no account does it wish to check the increase of constituents, and low mentality among converts offers no obstacle. What terrors has our moronic level, the average intelligence of twelve-year-olds, to those who believe that of such is the kingdom of heaven?

Thus we find individual fundamentalists[22] strongly opposed to any prudential checks to the increase of population, and in particular the immense authority of the hierarchy of the Roman Catholic church forbidding as a sin the use of contraceptives. Members of this faith not only are forbidden to practice birth control themselves, or even to study the facts and figures as to its social necessity, but they are urged to prevent other people from studying the question.

—§§§—

Like the Rest of the Left

Like the rest of the Left, the feminist birth controllers tended to accept racist and ethnocentric attitudes. Like most middle-class reformers, the feminists also had a reserve of anti-working-class attitudes. . . . Many feminists had been active in the temperance movement and saw immigrants and working-class men as drunken undesirables. Anti-Catholicism in particular, stimulated by Catholic opposition to prohibition and women's rights, had been an undercurrent in the women's rights movement for decades. Southern feminists used the fear of the black vote as an argument for female suffrage, and were supported by the national woman-suffrage organizations in doing so.[23]

—Linda Gordon, *Woman's Body, Woman's Right*

---

20. Margaret Sanger to Charlotte Gilman (Dec. 8, 1931). Sanger/Smith microfilm, C05:0302.

21. Editor: What Gilman says here can't be repeated often enough, Liberals and feminists supported brutal schemes of reproductive coercion, while their foes on the 'religious right' stood almost alone in opposing it. Note again that the "pleasures of the unfit" are *not* to be interfered with, just their childbearing. However Gilman may have disagreed with liberals and younger feminists about sex, on this topic they all agreed.

22. This would include public figures such as William Jennings Bryan and Billy Sunday. At that time fundamentalism was loosing the battle for control of some of the nation's major denominations, so, unlike Catholicism it could not speak with an institutional voice.

23. Linda Gordon, *Woman's Body, Woman's Right* (New York: Penguin, 1976), 281. A feminist herself, Gordon attempted to argue that "the birth controllers' conversion to eugenics" necessarily involved a "desertion of feminism" (p. 284). As readers have seen in the articles by Victoria Woodhull Martin (Chap. IV), Ellen Key (Chap. X), Gilman (here), and Sanger herself, that was quite untrue. Affluent, well-educated women with social or career aspirations and no interest in rearing large families, had excellent reasons *as feminists* for forcing down the birthrates of more prolific but less fortunate women. As 'intelligent' and 'enlightened' supporters of 'progressive' causes, they had reasons galore for keeping conservative religious women from passing their 'reactionary' beliefs on to their children. Blasts at "the hierarchy of the Roman Catholic Church and "individual fundamentalists" were a smoke screen to conceal the hatred—wrong but certainly rational—that these feminists had for millions of women.

XXIII

The Religious Are Astir

1913–27

Oliver Wendell Holmes Jr.

U.S. Supreme Court Justice

It is better for all the world, if instead of waiting to execute degenerate offspring for crime, or to let them starve for their imbecility, society can prevent those who are manifestly unfit from continuing their kind. The principle that sustains compulsory vaccination is broad enough to cover cutting the Fallopian tubes.

EDITOR

On that February day in 1913, the *New York Times* was filled with news of a world that was changing all too rapidly. In Mexico, after only six days of fighting, a rebellion appeared ready to topple the government. In the nation's capital, President Taft, a Republican, fulfilled a campaign promise by vetoing an immigration restriction bill requiring literacy, complaining about how unevenly it would be applied. In Europe during that last full year of peace before the war, royalty was struggling to keep up with the times. England's King George had visited an airplane exhibition in London and professed an interest in taking an airplane flight, "but not yet."

Even the well-endowed world of the nation's elite universities were feeling the winds of change. The day before—Valentine's Day—a Suffrage Army marched into Princeton, weary and footsore, singing "Tramp, tramp, the girls are marching" to the glee of Princeton University's male students. That same day and in the same town the Secret Service doubled to four men the guard that watched over Princeton President Woodrow Wilson, a Democrat who was to become the nation's President in a little over two weeks. Finally, that Saturday evening, the all-male members of the New York City's Harvard Law School Association braved the cold and blustery weather to hear one of their most famous graduates speak.

Oliver Wendell Holmes Jr.'s career was long and distinguished. Wounded three times in the Civil War and appointed to the U.S. Supreme Court in 1902 by Theodore Roosevelt, he would retire from the Court at the age of 90 the year before Franklin Roosevelt became President. No other Supreme Court Justice has served to such a great age.

Known as the "Great Dissenter" for his sometimes eloquent dissents to the Court majority, Holmes was skeptical (some would say cynical) of those who believed that beneath the law lay ultimate principles on which humans could rely for all time. He reflected that attitude at the start of his speech, but also unwittingly revealed that he did attach an ultimate value to his own opinions. When ordinary citizens criticized a person of his importance, he believed that their motivation was mere "hatred and distrust" and that their words had no more than a "germ of inarticulate truth." He cites the working poor who thought it unfair that a few should have so much while many went without. The rich, Holmes believed, withdraw little from society's wealth as the prize of their success. No doubt his well-heeled audience liked that remark.

Near the end of his speech, Holmes turned to his vision for the future. It was a theme we see repeated often in this book. In fitting with the Malthus and Darwin, he saw world's resources threatened and its races at war. But his thought remained optimistic. We are, he told his audience, to be assured by the thought that science would reduce our numbers and breed us to "greatness and splendor." Fourteen years later he would get an opportunity to enshrine that sort of scientifically controlled breeding into the law of the land. Here are extracts from that 1913 speech when, as he put it, he read his "sympathies . . . prematurely into the law."

Law and the Court

Oliver Wendell Holmes, *The Occasional Speeches of Justice Oliver Wendell Holmes,* Mark DeWolfe Howe, ed. (Cambridge, Harvard University Press, 1961), 168–73.

Speech at a Dinner of the Harvard Law School Association of New York on February 15, 1913

Mr. Chairman and Gentlemen: Vanity is the most philosophical of those feelings that we are taught to despise. For vanity recognizes that if a man is in a minority of one we lock him up, and therefore longs for an assurance from others that one's work has not been in vain. . . .

But let me turn to more palpable realities—to that other visible Court to which for ten now accomplished years it has been my opportunity to belong. We are very quiet there, but it is the quiet of a storm center, as we all know. Science has taught the world skepticism and has made it legitimate to put everything to the test of proof. Many beautiful and noble reverences are impaired, but in these days no one can complain if any institution, system, or belief is called on to justify its continuance in life. Of course we are not excepted and have not escaped. . . . I get letters, not always anonymous, intimating that we are corrupt. Well, gentlemen, I admit that it makes my heart ache. It is very painful, when one spends all the energies of one's soul in trying to do good work, with no thought but that of solving a problem according to the rules by which one is bound, to know that many see sinister motives and would be glad of evidence that one was consciously bad. But we must take such things philosophically and try to see what we can learn from hatred and distrust and whether behind them there may not be some germ of inarticulate truth. . . . Most men think dramatically, not quantitatively, a fact that the rich would be wise to remember more than they do. We are apt to contrast the palace with the hovel, the dinner at Sherry's with the working man's pail, and never ask how much or realize how little is withdrawn to make the prizes of success (subordinate prizes—since the only prize much cared for by the powerful is power. The prize of the general is not a bigger tent, but command.) . . . .

. . . . It is a misfortune if a judge reads his conscious or unconscious sympathy with one side or the other prematurely into the law, and forgets that what seems to him to be first principles are believed by half his fellow men to be wrong. . . .

If I am right it will be a slow business for our people to reach rational views, assuming that we are allowed to work peaceably to that end. But as I grow older I grow calm. If I feel what are perhaps an old man's apprehensions, that competition from new races will cut deeper than working man's disputes and will test whether we can hang together and can fight; if I fear that we are running through the world's resources at a pace that we cannot keep; I do not lose my hopes. I do not pin my dreams for the future to my country or even to my race. **I think it probable that civilization somehow will last as long as I care to look ahead—perhaps with smaller numbers, but perhaps also bred to greatness and splendor by science. I think it not improbable that man, like the grub that prepares a chamber for the winged thing it never has seen but is to be—that man may have cosmic destinies that he does not understand.** And so beyond the vision of battling races and an impoverished earth I catch a fleeting glimpse of peace. . . .

Holmes to Laski, July 17, 1925

Editor: From the serenity of his summer home, in the summer of 1925 Holmes wrote Harold J. Laski, a prominent British socialist. (The pamphlet he found unrealistically "in the air" was probably Fabian Tract #216, *Socialism and Freedom.*) Note how this Supreme Court justice reduced people to mere "products" of propagation, a term better fitted for farm animals, and that he felt our society should not be keeping the 'unfit' alive. He found socialism even more disappointing because he felt it would be even more systematic at keeping the unfit alive than capitalism. He apparently had not read what socialists were actually saying on that topic. (See Chapter XIX.)

Dear Laski, Your letter (6th) came with the book and the pamphlet. I shall begin the book in a day or two—the pamphlet seems to me to be somewhat in the air—to exaggerate the evils peculiar to capitalism—and to take a good deal for granted as to socialism. One can change institutions by a fiat but populations only by slow degrees and as I don't believe in millennia and still less in the possibility of attaining one by tinkering with property while propagation is free and we do all we can to keep the products, however bad, alive, I listen with some skepticism to plans for fundamental amelioration. I should expect more from a systematic prevention of the survival of the unfit. . . .[1]

Holmes to Laski, July 23, 1925

Editor: In his next letter, Holmes found fault with the socialism and future world government in Laski's *A*

---

1. *Holmes–Laski Letters,* Mark DeWolfe Howe, ed., (Cambridge: Harvard University Press: 1953), vol. 1, 761.

Grammar of Politics. Though he believed that Laski thought "more nobly of man" as a child in need of "papa Laski's" regulation than Holmes did seeing them as rapidly multiplying Malthusian flies, neither man attached genuine value to people. Without inherent worth, the only rights people have "are what they are willing to fight for." Might makes right. Soon, the world would see exactly where that led.

.... I like very much your realization of the dependence of a large part of what you would like to see upon a world movement. Being old, I don't expect to see it. As you will have expected, I don't sympathize very greatly with your dream. You think more nobly of man than I do—and of course, you may be right. But I look at man through Malthus's glasses—as like flies—here swept away by a pestilence—there multiplying unduly and paying for it. . . . I think I perceive at critical moments a tacit assumption that papa Laski, or those who think like him, are to regulate paternally the popular desires. . . . and I can see no justification in a government's undertaking to rectify social desires—except on an aristocratic assumption that you know what is good for them better than they—(which no doubt you do). . . . I have always said that the rights of a given crowd are what they will fight for.[2]

Laski to Holmes, July 28, 1925

Editor: Laski now responded to Holmes's first letter, contrasting his optimism with Holmes pessimism and agreeing on the need for population control. Laski's claims about the voluntary nature of birth control shouldn't be taken seriously. The real power of birth control as a tool lies in the fact that some can use against others. (That is why limiting its use was a "betrayal of the future.") As we will see later, both Holmes and Laski have targets in mind.

A brief but charming letter from you tells me that my book arrived safely; you know how eager I shall be to hear of your opinion. Agreement I don't expect, for I have convictions built on faith while you (forgive me!) have doubts built on fears. . . . The one thing I grant you freely is the urgent need of controlling population. But that, I think, is a two-fold problem. First it is a matter of gaining a permanently higher standard of living. For statistically it is clear that a certain level of comfort brings with it voluntary limitation of offspring, as Webb showed years ago in his comparison of birth-rates among different sections of the working-class.[3] But there cannot be a

2. *Holmes–Laski Letters,* vol. 1, 762.

higher standard without greater productivity, and there cannot be greater productivity until we enlist new motives to effort from workers. Hence my second assumption that a change in social direction is essential. And thirdly, there must be unfettered distribution of knowledge about birth-control. I believe this is increasingly important. **The power voluntarily and with prevision to restrict numbers seems to me the greatest weapon placed in the hands of man since the discovery of fire. To prevent its use on what are either sentimental or theological (perhaps they're the same) grounds seems to me as near a betrayal of the future as one can easily conceive.** I believe Holmes J. (whom you may know) pointed to the same thing in his speech of 1913 to the Harvard Law Review [sic] Association.[4] But, of course, if people like [William Jennings] Bryan are going at all seriously to effect the mind of Anglo-Saxon peoples, the outlook is a very dismal one. What upset me in the Tennessee [Scopes' Monkey] trial was not the conviction, but the methods of the defense. Why it was even necessary to adduce testimony to suggest that science and the bible square, I do not know. I think the job of people who are fighting ignorance is not to submit to the basis of its prejudices. However, it may be that I misunderstand the nature of the advocate's task.[5]

Holmes to Laski, August 7, 1925

Editor: Though they disagreed about economics, the two agreed on the need for population control and, as Holmes pointed out in the next letter, that led all too logically to the necessity for global population control, so one group's 'birth dearth' did not create the sort of immigration that replaced New England Yankees with the Irish. (A *rar avis* is a rare bird or unusual person. A simoon is a hot, dry wind out of the Asian or African deserts. Readers can decide if Holmes's allusion was deliberately racial.)

.... I am glad we agree about population—but there as elsewhere you need world control. If France doesn't produce Frenchmen people of some other nation come in to fill the lower places—and you have new troubles. I remember how I used to envy London when I saw Englishmen in the poor streets and not a different race.

3. Editor: This refers to Webb's "The Decline in the Birth-Rate" discussed in Chap. VI.

4. Editor: Laski meant the "Law and the Court" speech quoted at the start of this chapter.

5. *Holmes–Laski Letters,* vol. 1, 770–71. Bryan, a well-known politician and fundamentalist speaker, warned of the moral dangers of a Darwinian worldview.

And I can remember the time when it was mentioned in a certain block in Broad Street (Boston) there were Irish—supposed to be a bad lot, the rest of the population was Yankee. Now an old Yankee like me is a *rar avis*—except in some country regions. The Catholic Church here, which I once contributed to for the servants, is now the dominant one and the old Baptist Church barely keeps alive with contributions from the summer people—I bow my head and feel not the simoon pass. Must stop.[6]

Holmes to Laski, April 25, 1927

Editor: We now move forward to the spring of 1927 and a case called *Buck v. Bell* in which the Supreme Court was asked to rule on the constitutionally of a Virginia law legalizing the forced sterilization of residents of state institutions. Notice that protests against the law came from the state's more conservative Protestants and not from feminists or liberals. Those who consult an old calendar will discover that Holmes got the case on Saturday evening, wrote his decision on Sunday and was gloating about it to Laski on Monday. He obviously saw no reason to agonize over what he was doing. Why should he? His mind had been made up at least as far back as 1913.

. . . . I have done nothing but law—my opinion for this morning is held up by McReynolds for a dissent. That which was given to me Saturday evening and was written yesterday concerned the constitutionality of an act for sterilizing feeble-minded people, with due precaution—as to which my lad tells me the religious are astir, I have just sent what I think to the printer.[7]

Holmes to Laski, April 29, 1927

Editor: Holmes seemed more interested in being allowed his "own style" in writing an opinion than in what that opinion meant for others not as important as he. Note again his low opinion of humanity—a mere cog in the machinery of the cosmos—very Darwinian.

. . . . Apart from events all my ideas are in the law. I have had some rather interesting cases—the present one, as I believe I mentioned, on the Constitutionality of a Virginia act for the sterilization of imbeciles, which I believe is a burning theme. In most cases the difficulty is rather with the writing than with the thinking. To put the case well and from time to time to hint at a vista is the job. I am amused (between ourselves) at some of the rhetorical changes suggested, when I purposely used short and

rather brutal words for an antithesis, polysyllables that made them mad. I am pretty accommodating in cutting out even thought that I think important, but a man must be allowed his own style. . . .[8]

How solemnly men have taken themselves. Theology has helped it. If there is to be the revival that you for France and Wallas for America predict, I hope that a corner-stone will be that speculatively man is interesting only as part of the cosmos, and that he cannot assume that he is specially needed as its confidential friend. The time for departure to Court has come and I must say *adieu pro tem.*

Laski to Holmes, May 7, 1927

Editor: Laski shares Holmes's indifference to young Carrie Buck as anything except the butt of a crude joke. He is also woefully ignorant of the case. As Holmes noted in his opinion, Carrie already had a child.

Life here is rapid because of this Trade Union Bill. . . . The problems are less interesting than settling whether a feeble-minded Virginia is to remain virgin, but, as Carlyle said, they make "bonny fechtin'." . . .

My love to you both. Get that stomach better, please. Sterilise *all* the unfit, among whom I include *all* fundamentalists.[9]

Religious Objections

Despite the direct influence of big business on eugenics, the cause carried with it some of its historic aura of radicalism for many years. . . . But the eugenists' appearance of being progressive reformers was based primarily on their use of apocalyptic warnings. . . . Many conservative and religious people objected equally to this tone, to syphilis tests, and to more coercive programs such as compulsory sterilization of the insane; and this opposition tended to rally progressives to the eugenics camp.[10]

—LINDA GORDON, 1976

EDITOR

In their correspondence, Holmes kept returning to *Buck v. Bell* to gloat yet again. "Real reform" below probably meant an array of measures in addition to sterilization—birth control, sexually segregated institutionalization and, in today's context, legalized abortion. In perhaps the

6. *Holmes–Laski Letters*, vol. 1, 773.
7. *Holmes–Laski Letters*, vol. 2, 937–38.

8. *Holmes–Laski Letters*, vol. 2, 938–39.
9. *Holmes–Laski Letters*, vol. 2, 940–41.
10. Linda Gordon, *Woman's Body, Woman's Right* (New York: Penguin, 1976), 276. Notice that coercion did not bother the progressives.

most bizarre twist in legal history, when Justice Harry Blackmun wrote *Roe v. Wade*, the decision legalizing abortion, he referred with favor to *Buck v. Bell*. That itself is not surprising since, as Blackmun noted at the beginning of his opinion, "population growth, pollution, poverty, and racial overtones" all impacted on abortion legalization. Historically, that meant that abortion was to play the same role as previous measures in limiting the birthrate of the 'unfit.'

But Blackmun, at least on the surface, attempted to twist *Buck v. Bell* into a strange limitation to abortion-on-demand. Because Carrie Buck couldn't keep the state of Virginia from sterilizing her, an abortion-minded woman couldn't keep a state from banning some abortions, perhaps late in pregnancy. Since the Court majority—including Blackmun—have since been shrill in attacking state laws attempting to limit late abortions, it seems unlikely that Blackmun really intended for *Buck v. Bell* to limit a woman's right to abortion. Instead, it could have been a subtle hint that the state had a right to *impose* abortion on women in cases like Carrie Buck's. The continuing abortion controversy has kept that from happening for much the same reason that the furor that Catholics, fundamentalists and some religious Jews generated kept forced sterilization from being as widely used as its supporters had hoped.

Holmes to Laski, May 12, 1927

. . . . I wrote and delivered a decision upholding the constitutionality of a state law for sterilizing imbeciles the other day—and felt that I was getting near to the first principle of real reform. I say merely getting near. I don't mean that the surgeon's knife is the ultimate symbol.[11]

Holmes to Laski, July 23, 1927

Cranks as usual do not fail. One letter yesterday told me that I was a monster and might expect the judgment of God for a decision that a law allowing the sterilization of imbeciles was constitutional and for the part that I had taken in other cases that were dragging the country down.[12]

If I Were Dictator—Laski to Liberals

Harold J. Laski, "If I Were Dictator"
Nation 134 (Jan. 6, 1932), 15–16.

6. I should like, further, to see the rapid erosion of organized religions. The accusation that they are the

---

11. *Holmes–Laski Letters*, vol. 2, 942.
12. *Holmes–Laski Letters*, vol. 2, 965.

---

opium of the people seems to me the more justified, the more completely their history and consequences are understood. They make men satisfied with, or complacent about, the injustice of the present social order by the prospect they offer, without a tithe of serious evidence, of a future state of blessedness.[13] They perpetuate all over the world obsolete systems of morality and sex relations. . . .

7. I desire, also, to see the practice of birth control—perhaps the greatest discovery since the invention of fire—made freely available to all social classes. It is the main avenue to the emancipation of women. . . . I know few things so intolerable as the fact that divine revelation should be claimed for the obsolete habits of an Eastern nomadic tribe and their consequent imposition upon a society which might otherwise open a highroad to freedom.[14] Birth control alone makes possible the conquest by society of heredity degeneracy. If Roman Catholics and others find its methods offensive, no one asks that they should practice them. But they ought not to make their private view of moral truth the measure of permissible social practice.[15]

EDITOR

Much as in Britain a generation earlier, during early decades of the twentieth century the meaning of liberal changed from referring to a defender of limited government to an advocate of ever-expanding government. This infuriated the old liberal in the crusty H. L. Mencken, and he said so in a revealing 1930 magazine article. In his

---

13. Editor: Readers need not take Laski's remarks about religion as honest. As we have already seen, the two writers real complaint was that other-worldly religions such as fundamentalism and Catholicism were *not* "complacent." They got "astir" and made trouble for a "present social order" that wanted to dictate sterilization. Laski knew that. His world socialist state (Steps 1 and 4 in his future dictatorship) would have benefited from that complacency *if* it existed—and yet he wanted to see religion erode away. It had to disappear so men like Laski could exercise a god-like rule over the rest of humanity. Science offered no threat to Laske's agenda. Historic Christianity did.

14. Editor: Did the same man who wanted Carrie Buck and millions of fundamentalist women forcibly sterilized really want women emancipated? Of course not. Emancipation here has a special meaning. They were to be free of "obsolete systems of morality and sex relations" (dependent, in part, on the risk of pregnancy), so the more "bonny fetchin" among them could be sexually exploited and discarded by Laski-like males. In similar fashion, promiscuous feminists—at least while still young—could exploit their sexuality for career advancement. Notice how easily Laski slipped from religious anti-Semitism into anti-Catholicism. The two are much the same.

The Pivot of Civilization in Historical Perspective

youth, Mencken noted, he had been taught that "the very aim of the Constitution was to keep lawmakers from running amok" and that the "highest duty of the Supreme Court" was "to safeguard it against their forays," however noble sounding. But Justice Holmes, he lamented, thinks otherwise. "He held, it would seem, that violating the Bill of Rights is a rare and difficult business, possible only by summoning up deliberate malice, and that it is the chief business of the Supreme Court to keep the Constitution loose and elastic, so that blasting holes through it may not be too onerous." It was Holmes' "loose and elastic" view of the Constitution, Mencken said, that endeared Holmes with the new liberals: "Bear this doctrine in mind," Mencken wrote, "and you will have an adequate explanation, on the one hand, of those forward looking opinions which console the Liberals—for example . . . the Virginia case upholding the sterilization of imbeciles—and the reactionary opinions which they politely overlook."[16]

With his observation in mind we present the relevant portions of Holmes' "forward looking" opinion in the critical Supreme Court decision that legalized the ultimate in reproductive unfreedom—forced sterilization. Equally revealing, the one dissent to the Court's eight-to-one majority was Pierce Butler, "remembered today, by legal scholars, as one of the most reactionary judges to ever be on the Supreme Court."[17] Only reactionaries, it seems, wanted men and women to decide for themselves whether to have children. Liberals, feminists and socialists regarded it as yet another area for the government to control, directly or indirectly, openly or covertly.

Buck v. Bell, 274 U.S. 200 (1927)

Argued April 22, 1927. Decided May 2, 1927.
Mr. Justice Holmes delivered the opinion of the Court.

This is a writ of error to review a judgment of the Supreme Court of Appeals of the State of Virginia, affirming a judgment of the Circuit Court of Amherst County, by which the defendant in error, the superintendent of the State Colony for Epileptics and Feeble Minded, was ordered to perform the operation of salpingectomy upon Carrie Buck, the plaintiff in error, for the purpose of making her sterile. . . .

Carrie Buck is a feeble-minded white woman who was committed to the State Colony above mentioned in due form. She is the daughter of a feeble-minded mother in the same institution, and the mother of an illegitimate feeble-minded child. She was eighteen years old at the time of the trial of her case in the Circuit Court in the latter part of 1924. An Act of Virginia approved March 20, 1924 (Laws 1924, c. 394) recites that the health of the patient and the welfare of society may be promoted in certain cases by the sterilization of mental defectives, under careful safeguard, etc.; that the sterilization may be effected in males by vasectomy and in females by salpingectomy, without serious pain or substantial danger to life; that the Commonwealth is supporting in various institutions many defective persons who if now discharged would become [274 U.S. 200, 206] a menace but if incapable of procreating might be discharged with safety and become self-supporting with benefit to themselves and to society; and that experience has shown that heredity plays an important part in the transmission of insanity, imbecility, etc. . . .

The attack is not upon the procedure but upon the substantive law. It seems to be contended that in no circumstances could such an order be justified. It certainly is contended that the order cannot be justified upon the existing grounds. The judgment finds the facts that have been recited and that Carrie Buck 'is the probable potential parent of socially inadequate offspring, likewise afflicted, that she may be sexually sterilized without detriment to her general health and that her welfare and that of society will be promoted by her sterilization,' and thereupon makes the order. In view of the general declarations of the Legislature and the specific findings of the Court obviously we cannot say as matter of law that the grounds do not exist, and if they exist they justify the result. **We have seen more than once that the public welfare may call upon the best citizens for their lives. It would be strange if it could not call upon those who already sap the strength of the State for these lesser sacrifices, often not felt to be such by those concerned, in order to prevent our being swamped with incompetence. It is better for all the world, if instead of waiting to execute degenerate offspring for crime, or to let them starve for their imbecility, society can prevent**

15. Editor: "Heredity degeneracy" refers to negative eugenics. Again, Laski had no intention of leaving Catholics alone. Biological "degeneracy" is as common among them as among any other group. If they took his advice and 'privatized' their faith—losing political skills—they would soon become targets of legally coerced restrictions on births. Recall that *Buck v. Bell*, which Laski found delightful, had no religious exemption.

16. H. L. Mencken, *The Vintage Mencken*, Alistair Cooke, ed. (New York: Vintage Books, 1917–55), 190–91. Original was in *American Mercury*, May 1930 and May 1932.

17. Allan Chase, *The Legacy of Malthus* (Urbana: University of Illinois Press, 1980), 317.

those who are manifestly unfit from continuing their kind. The principle that sustains compulsory vaccination is broad enough to cover cutting the Fallopian tubes. *Jacobson v. Massachusetts,* 197 U.S. 11, 25 S. Ct. 358, 3 Ann. Cas. 765. **Three generations of imbeciles are enough.** [274 U.S. 200, 208] But, it is said, however it might be if this reasoning were applied generally, it fails when it is confined to the small number who are in the institutions named and is not applied to the multitudes outside. It is the usual last resort of constitutional arguments to point out shortcomings of this sort. But the answer is that the law does all that is needed when it does all that it can, indicates a policy, applies it to all within the lines, and seeks to bring within the lines all similarly situated so far and so fast as its means allow. Of course so far as the operations enable those who otherwise must be kept confined to be returned to the world, and thus open the asylum to others, the equality aimed at will be more nearly reached.

Judgment affirmed. Mr. Justice Butler dissents.

—§§§—

EDITOR

There was no justification for Holmes's remark about "three generations of imbeciles." The IQ test that gave Carrie a mental age of nine years and her mother Emma one of seven years and eleven months was culturally biased. Years later, when interest in Carrie's case resurfaced, visitors to her home found she read newspapers daily and "mental health professionals who examined her in later life" reported that "she was neither mentally ill nor retarded."

Even more impressive was a school report card from 1931, which revealed that Vivian, the third generation, had average grades in school and was bright enough to make the honor roll in reading. Even more disturbing, we now know that Carrie was actually sent to the state mental institution to cover up a pregnancy resulting from being raped by a relative of her foster parents.

As we have seen, prominent feminists enthusiastically supported Carrie's sterilization (Chapters IV, XV, and XXII). In a 1984 magazine article, Harvard professor Stephen Jay Gould noted that opposition to the sterilization came from "conservative Virginia Christians."[18] These were the "religious" that Holmes found "astir."

18. Stephen Jay Gould, "Carrie Buck's Daughter" *Natural History* 93 (July 1984), 14–18. Vivian died in 1932 of an ordinary childhood illness, while her mother lived until 1983.

Sterilization of the Unfit
A Contribution to the First American Birth Control Conference
By Norman Haire, M.B., Ch.M.
London, England

Harmonious Movements

At times I find a tendency to confound Birth Control with sterilization and custodial care. Birth Control is a measure requiring intelligent understanding of reproduction by the responsible classes in society. The reproduction of irresponsible classes must be regulated by society itself, and among the methods that have been favored are sterilization and permanent custodial care. . . .

Under Negative Eugenics we shall include among the racially less desirable only those who possess sufficient intellect and control to render them responsible individuals. The irresponsible, it is obvious, must be excluded from our consideration, and their reproduction subjected to social control.[19]

—HARRIETTE M. DILLA, *BIRTH CONTROL REVIEW,* 1922

Encyclical on Sterilization

Magistrates have no direct power over the bodies of their subjects. Therefore, when no crime has taken place, they can never directly harm or tamper with the integrity of the body, either for reasons of eugenics or any other reason.[20] —POPE PIUS XI

19. Harriette M. Dilla, "The Social Significance of Birth Control" *Birth Control Review* 6 (Mar. 1922), 34. In other words, if you are among the "racially less desirable" but use birth control successfully, we will leave you alone. But if you don't use it successfully, we will label you "irresponsible" and use "sterilization and permanent custodial care" to make sure you don't have children. Seen that way, the three techniques complement one another. Dilla's remarks are from the First American Birth Control Conference in 1921.

20. "Full Text of Pope Pius' Encyclical on Marriage, Divorce and Birth Control," *New York Times* (Jan. 9, 1931), 15. Note that it was a Catholic Pope who proclaimed that the State had no authority over the body's reproductive powers. The *Times* own pages prove quite conclusively that today's "pro-choice" groups were not only on the wrong side of this important issue, they organized led the debate on that side and engaged in the merciless slander of their religious opponents. It was they who fed the hysteria that led to the sterilization of tens of thousands of unwilling men and women.

XXIV

Japanese "Picture Brides" Become Frights

1919

Literary Digest

We are threatened with an overproduction of Japanese children. First come the men, then the picture brides, then the families. If California is to be preserved for the next generation as a "white man's country" there must be some movement started that will restrict the Japanese birth-rate in California.

EDITOR

Those who feared the higher birthrates of immigrants from southern and eastern Europe were careful *not* to make their attitudes widely known, particularly in the press. The reason was simple. Those they hoped to target with birth control were closely tied to ethnic and religious groups (Catholics and Jews) that were here in sufficient numbers to exert considerable political power—particularly in large, eastern cities. There exists one particularly disturbing illustration of that deception.

In a 1913 book highly critical of immigration, Edward Ross, a professor at the University of Wisconsin (and the anti-Asian author of Chap. VII), described how the Roman politician Cicero lowered his voice when he spoke of the Jews, "for, as he explains to the judges, there are persons who might excite against him this numerous, clannish and powerful element. With much greater reason," Ross went on, "might an American lower his voice to-day in discussing two million Hebrew immigrants united by a strong race consciousness and already ably represented at every level of wealth, power, and influence in the United States." Ross then described what he called, "the endeavor of the Jews to control the immigration policy of the United States."[1] With her eyes on Catholics and perhaps fundamentalists, Sanger hinted at the same problem when she lamented that in our democracy the "moron's vote" was as good as that of the "genius."

1. Edward A. Ross, *The Old World in the New* (New York: Century, 1913, 1914), 143–44. Sanger's remark is quoted in full near the end of this chapter.

On the west coast, the situation was different. Restrictions on immigration from China and Japan had been imposed early enough that neither group formed a significant voting block. This meant that national publications as well as major west-coast newspapers (quoted here) could discuss—with almost complete freedom—what to do about the "yellow peril" on our shores. As a result, papers such as the *Los Angeles Times* and the *Sacramento Bee* were unusually candid and offer a window into the minds of their eastern colleagues. Note that the statistics they used were grossly distorted—for each Caucasian women having a child, there wasn't a Japanese woman having "several hundred" babies. Much the same thing happened with the "population explosion" hysteria in the late 1960s and for much the same reason.

"Japanese 'Picture Brides' Become Frights in California," *Literary Digest* (August 9, 1919), 53-54.

—§§§—

Little ladies from Japan—toylike, delicate little ladies such as inspire some of our most popular magazine poets and light-opera librettists—are developing into perfect frights out in California. At least they are frightening a good many Californians, who suspect them of engineering a kind of "inside" Japanese invasion of the State. For the little Japanese lady is about the most sturdy opponent of race suicide on the globe, even exceeding the German Frau, who is her nearest rival, and our Far-Western Japanese population is growing several hundred times as fast, proportionately, as the native American. **A new baby arrives in the Japanese home as regularly and as often as the springtime, and is just as welcome to its proud**

parents.[2] Since the old adage that "the hand that rocks the cradle is the hand that rules the world" is quite as true in California as elsewhere, local editors and statesmen are predicting that it will not be long before the Pacific coast is ruled by Japanese, thanks to the cradle-filling proclivities of the Japanese "picture brides."

They are called "picture brides" because they are picked out by their future husbands from a bunch of pictures, which the Jap bride-merchant carries around him as samples of his stock of available wives back in Japan. The Jap immigrant invests in a wife, on the strength of the picture, the merchant sends for her, and then the trouble, or domestic felicity, depending on the point of view, begins. By the terms of our "gentlemen's agreement" with Japan this traffic in brides has been much reduced, but the brides already landed are showing motherly inclinations which one Coast editor describes as "appalling." "We did not reclaim the valleys of California to make a Japanese colony," protests the *Zanjero* (El Centro, California), the *Sacramento Bee* speaks of the "menace of the problem" supplied by dutiful Japanese wives, and the *Los Angeles Times* takes up the whole situation in this fashion:

> During the last ten years there has been an increase in the number of children born of Japanese parentage in California of a little more than 3,000 per cent. During the last four years there has been a decrease in the number of children of Caucasian parentage of about 8 per cent. Those who are interested in figuring out mathematical progression will find it interesting to compute the number of years that would elapse were these converging ratios to be maintained until the population of Japanese descent in this State would outnumber and outvote all the rest. It is no false alarm.
>
> At the time when the first anti-Japanese bills were introduced in the State legislature, a little more than ten years ago, there were but 246 children born in California of Japanese parents in twelve months. During the last twelve months the number of Japanese births increased to 4,920. In one northern California county 176 children were born of Japanese parents and but eighty-six white children.
>
> Bringing the comparison closer home, the county health records show that during the last month one-

---

2. Editor: Note that the fact that these children are wanted by "proud parents" was treated negatively. Rhetoric about children being "unwanted" by their parents was a scam. The real issue was that they were not wanted by birth controllers. Notice on the next page where the *Los Angeles Times* draws a parallel between the nation's "growing colored population" and that of Japanese-Americans. Blacks, isolated in the rural South, were not a major target at this time, but they had not been forgotten.

third of the children born in Los Angeles county outside the incorporated cities were of Japanese descent. **The problem of our increasing colored population sinks into insignificance before the one involving the increase in the number of Californians of Japanese stock. During the last year the ratio of Japanese to colored births was more than ten to one.**

It is instructive to note that during the ten years prior to the agitation of the anti-Japanese land bills the average number of Japanese children born in California was less than one hundred a year. No one who considers that jump from one hundred a year to five thousand a year can believe that the "gentlemen's agreement" by which the Japanese Government was to restrict rigorously Japanese emigration to this country is serving the purpose for which it was intended.

There may have been a time when an anti-Japanese land bill would have limited Japanese immigration. But such a law would be impotent now to keep native Japanese from possessing themselves of the choicest agricultural and horticultural land in California. For there are now more than 30,000 children in the State of Japanese parentage, native-born; they possess all the rights of leasing and ownership held by white children born here.

It is not necessary for a Japanese to incorporate some kind of holding company to own or lease land in the State. All that he has to do is to purchase or lease as the guardian of one of these thousands of American-born Japanese children. The Japanese picture brides have done their work too well for any such restrictive legislation to drive the Japanese from the agricultural and horticultural districts of the State.

There is no necessity for this country to exercise itself over a rumored or threatened Japanese invasion. If the campaign was to be waged on this coast the Japanese would not be especially formidable antagonists. The birth statistics seem to prove that the danger is not from the Japanese soldiers, but from the picture brides. The fruitfulness of those brides is almost uncanny.

There would be another side to the problem if the Japanese and American stocks intermingled, altho whether a tendency in this direction would simplify matters or start an entirely new series of troubles none of the current commentators attempt to say. *The Times* contents itself with noting facts based on statistics:

> A perusal of the birth statistics of the State during recent years proves that intermarriage and intermating between Japanese and white populations in California is almost unknown, We have received millions of immigrants from European countries during recent years and assimilated them as fast as they came. But to assimilate the Japanese immigrants is impossible.

Apparently nature never intended the Caucasian and the Japanese peoples to interbreed.

Most of the Japanese who come to California seek to secure a start in fruit-growing or vegetable-growing. They are frugal farmers and they prefer leasing land and raising their own crops to working for wages. This condition accounts for the rapid increase in the Japanese population in the agricultural districts. The Japanese hold tens of thousands of acres of California land under lease, generally appearing as guardians for American-born Japanese. They thus become *de-facto* owners; and it is a matter of indisputable record that they are in possession of much of the best farming land in the Santa Clara, Sacramento, and San Joaquin valleys.

Here is a Japanese problem of sufficient gravity to merit serious consideration. We are threatened with an overproduction of Japanese children. First come the men, then the picture brides, then the families. If California is to be preserved for the next generation as a "white man's country" there must be some movement started that will restrict the Japanese birth-rate in California. When a condition is reached in which two children of Japanese parentage are born in some districts for every white child it is time something else was done than making speeches about it in the American Senate.

That "gentlemen's agreement" concerning Japanese immigration is beginning to assume the appearance of a celebrated "scrap of paper" that was responsible for bringing both Great Britain and America into the world-war. The situation has passed from the land-leasing stage to something more vital.

If the same present birth-ratio were maintained for the next ten years there would be 150,000 children of Japanese descent born in California in 1929 and but 40,000 white children. And in 1949 the majority of the population of California would be Japanese, ruling the State.

In a later editorial *The Times* touches on some political and sociological aspects of the case, quoting an authority whose views are enough to make any true-blue opponent of race-suicide perfectly wild:

Now comes Dr. Millard, British health officer, with the theory that Pan-Germanism and Japanese aggression are the result of the prolific breeding-proclivities of the German and Japanese women. He avers that there is a direct relation between a growing birth-rate and the nationalistic tendency toward territorial expansion. He is convinced that systematic birth control is the surest method of insuring the future peace of the world. Many theories have been advanced concerning the cause of the world-war, but few of the theorists have

been so ungallant as to blame the fruitful mothers for the sins of their offspring.

The *New York Evening Post,* which attains a calm and detached view, no doubt, by considering the matter from the distance of some three or four thousand miles, refuses to get excited over the dangers of any Japanese invasion through the air-lanes reported to be frequented by the well-known stork. Says *The Post* with some asperity:

Senator Phelan[3] furnishes the appalling information that in the last decade Japanese births in California have increased 3,000 per cent, and that the State is to be classified with Hawaii as "a tributary colony to Japan." The white race is being steadily driven out by yellow hordes. But let us catch at what straws of hope we can. In the whole United States in 1910 there were but 5,581 married Japanese women. The total number of American-born Japanese children in the whole country in 1910 could have been only a few thousand at most. In 1910 there were some 15,000 married Japanese men, about 10,000 of whom were entitled to bring in their wives. Japanese children might increase thirty-fold without making them more than a drop in the general population increase. And California had in 1910 only four-seventh of our whole Japanese population. Senator Phelan wisely dealt in no figures but percentages. Otherwise we should find a great State of nearly 3,000,000 whites being inundated by a few thousand Japanese children.

Forced Migration

The greatest forced migration in American history was getting under way today.

Along the entire Pacific Coast, and from the southern half of Arizona, some 120,000 enemy aliens and American-born Japanese were moving, or preparing to move,

---

3. Editor: James Duval Phelan (1861–1930) was mayor of San Francisco (1897–1903) and U. S. Senator (1914–20). The April 11, 1942 issue of the *San Francisco News* called "prophetic" Phelan's testimony in a classified 1924 Senate report. Phelan had said: "If there is any trouble in the Pacific, we would not only have to meet a frontal attack, but a rear attack. The 110,000 Japanese living in the Hawaiian Islands are, many of them, veterans of the [Russo-Japanese] war, great fighting men, and they could range up behind our guns where we are spending millions of dollars for fortifications and rout our gunners because we cannot maintain a garrison to meet a hostile attack of overwhelming numbers from the rear. And nobody believes for a moment that the Japanese are loyal to the American Flag." Released by Congress during the anti-Japanese hysteria after Pearl Harbor, advocates of internment claimed that the report was "suppressed" to avoid embarrassing the "Republican administrations of 1924-32 which failed to heed" its warnings. We now know the warnings were bogus and bigoted.

to areas in which the threat of possible espionage, sabotage or fifth column activities would be minimized.

None of the Japanese had actual orders to get out of the coastal military area designated yesterday by Lieut. Gen. John L. DeWitt, Western defense and Fourth Army commander, but all had his warning that eventually they must go.[4]

—SAN FRANCISCO NEWS, 1942

EDITOR

As you might expect, a debate this fierce would not easily die down. In April of 1925 *Literary Digest* would take up the issue of relative birthrates up yet again. But this time much had changed. Some five years earlier the *Los Angeles Times* had noted, "If California is to be preserved for the next generation as a 'white man's country' there must be some movement started that will restrict the Japanese birth-rate in California."

To the delight of that sort of mind, just such a movement now existed—Margaret Sanger's pioneering American Birth Control League. An international conference it was holding in New York City was drawing the praise of the Eastern press. The conference had an important historical context. Just the year before and a bit more crudely than the "gentlemen's agreement with Japan, a radical reform of our laws had drastically curtailed immigration from Europe. But, as with the Japanese 'picture brides' on the West coast, the law was doing nothing to squelch the birthrates of "undesirable aliens" who were already here. That deficiency would be the source of Sanger's anger quoted below. The Japanese were not forgotten at the conference. The full article quotes Harold Cox, editor of the *Edinburgh Review,* lamenting a population in Japan that was "rapidly increasing." These remarks demonstrate that at least some in the mainstream press were aware of the real agenda of the birth control movement and wholeheartedly agreed with it. (The Edward Alsworth Ross mentioned below is the same Dr. Ross who coined the term "race suicide" in Chapter VII.)

Are There Too Many of Us? (1925)

"Are There Two Many of Us?"
Literary Digest (April 11, 1925), 10–11.

Fewer children and better is the ideal that was advocated at the Sixth International Neo-Malthusian and Birth Control Conference, held a few days ago in New York,

4. "Japanese on West Coast Face Wholesale Uprooting," *San Francisco News* (Mar. 4, 1942). Source: Museum of San Francisco online.

and widely reported and discussed by the newspapers, many of which note with interest the change in public sentiment toward the organization and its campaign. As one paper remarks, "birth control is moving out of the range of angry thinking, raids and jails," and the *New York World* fearlessly terms this "a mark of progress"— indeed, uses that very phase in the headline of an editorial beginning,

> Turn back to 1917. All through that year the press carried reports having to do with birth control, and all that news was news of violent argument, of law courts and of jails: Mrs. Sanger choosing to go to prison, the hunger-strike of Mrs. Byrne [Sanger's sister], stories of forcible feeding denied and reaffirmed, Cannon Chase maintaining that birth control was an affront to God, Mrs. Sanger fighting to keep the police from taking her fingerprints, Billy Sunday mauling the subject in his tabernacle on Washington Heights; the whole question fought over, quarreled over, torn over, against a background of sensationalism.

Four years later, opposition to the movement was still dramatic, and *The World* goes on to remind us that, "in 1921 came the raid of a police force into a meeting in the Town Hall: more arrests, more violence, some clubbings, more charges and denials and fierce accusations, followed by lawsuits for false arrest." The editorial continues:

> Four years more, and in 1925 an international birth control conference opens quietly at the Hotel McAlpin. It is attended by social workers and medical men from this country, from England, from Austria, India, China and a dozen other countries. On the register of its delegates, not all advocates of birth control but all ready to discuss the question on its merits, are such distinguished scientists and scholars as Alice Hamilton, Raymond Pearl, Alonzo Taylor, Edward Alsworth Ross, Dr. E. V. McCollum of Johns Hopkins, Owen R. Lovejoy, Rabbi Stephen S. Wise, Ellsworth Huntington of Yale University, Irving Fisher, Dr. A. A. Brill, John Hayes Holmes, and Dr. Cary M. Thomas, President Emeritus of Bryn Mawr.

In her speech of welcome to the delegates, Mrs. Sanger is reported to have said:

> **While the United States shuts her gates to foreigners, no attempt whatever is made to discourage the rapid multiplication of undesirable aliens—and natives—within our own borders.** On the contrary, the Government of the United States deliberately encourages and even makes necessary by its laws the breeding, with a breakneck rapidity, of idiots, defectives, diseased, feeble-minded and criminal classes.

Billions of dollars are expended by our State and Federal Governments and by private charities and philanthropies for the care, the maintenance, and the perpetuation of these classes. Year by year their numbers are mounting. Year by year more money is expended. The American public is heavily taxed to maintained and increasing race of morons which threatens the very foundations of our civilization. More than one-quarter of the total incomes of our States is spent upon the maintenance of asylums, prisons and other institutions for the care of the defective, the diseased and the delinquent.

Do not conclude, however, that all our feeble-minded and mentally defective are segregated in institutions. This as a free country, a democratic country, a country of universal suffrage. **We can all vote, even the mentally arrested. And so it is no surprise to find the moron's vote as good as that of the genius. The outlook is not a cheerful one.**[5]

Editor: Remarks like these did not diminish by one iota the enthusiastic support that liberals gave Sanger's movement. Her critics were of a different sort, one now referred to as the "religious right." Billy Sunday, a well-known baseball player turned fundamentalist preacher, was mentioned above and Catholics will be quoted below. Continuing the work of his father (who died in 1919), Colonel Theodore Roosevelt Jr. was also an active critic.

One evening while the Convention was in session, Col. Theodore Roosevelt spoke at the Madison Avenue Methodist Church, where, as *The Times* relates, he "sharply assailed birth control advocates," and—

> denounced them as "hog selfish and bad citizens," referring especially to young married people who, after their first baby, agreed that they could not afford, for various reasons, to have any more.
>
> "What they really mean, if they are honest," said Colonel Roosevelt, "is that they don't want another child because they want an automobile and luxurious living."

In the Buffalo *Express,* Mrs. Sanger and her adherents are merely "weak-minded," but *America,* a Catholic weekly published in New York, finds them at once weak-minded and immoral, and declares:

> Birth control is wrong, not because the Church declares it to be sinful, but because it is a violation of the natural law. To non-Catholics who ask whether the Catholic Church may not change her uncompromising attitude in this matter at some future time, the answer must be that the Catholic Church can not dispense with or change the natural law. Some acts are 'wrong' merely because they are forbidden; others are forbidden because they are wrong in themselves and to this second class birth control belongs. It is 'wrong' just as lying is wrong and murder is wrong.

—§§§—

Woodrow Wilson on Asian Immigration

In the following year [1888] an act was passed which excluded Chinese immigrants from the United States.... The law which excluded Chinese immigrants had been passed at the urgent solicitation of the men of the Pacific coast. Chinese laborers had poured in there, first by the hundreds, then by the thousands, finally by hundreds of thousands, until the labor situation of the whole coast had become one almost of revolution. Caucasian laborers could not compete with the Chinese, could not live upon a handful of rice and work for a pittance, and found themselves being steadily crowded out from occupation after occupation by the thrifty, skilful Orientals, who, with their yellow skin and strange debasing habits of life, seemed to them hardly fellow men at all, but evil spirits, rather. For years together the laborers of the coast and those who wished to aid them had demanded of Congress the exclusion of the Chinese. Failing of aid from that quarter, riot had become their almost habitual means of agitation and self-defense—riot which sometimes went to the awful length of wholesale slaughter in wanton attacks upon the Chinese quarters of the towns. San Francisco had found the matter a veritable menace to government itself. Congress had passed an exclusion bill in 1879, but Mr. [President Rutherford] Hayes had vetoed it. Negotiation with China had been tried, but she had refused to agree to the exclusion of her people by her own act and consent; and an end was at last made of the matter by the Act of 1888.[6]

—WOODROW WILSON, 1902

5. Editor: This quote is virtually identical to that in the official conference proceedings, published as: Margaret Sanger, ed. *International Aspects of Birth Control* (New York: American Birth Control League, 1925), 5.

6. Woodrow Wilson, *A History of the American People* (New York:1902), 184–86. Wilson's remarks reflect the prejudices of the time. The Chinese (and Japanese) did not work for "a pittance" and were quite skilled at getting full-market price for their labor. In addition, as noted earlier, Japanese immigrants were particularly eager to own their own farms.

XXV

Birth Control— From the Positive Side

1917

Theodore Roosevelt

President of the United States

> But if, in a community of a thousand men and a thousand women, a large proportion of them remain unmarried, and if of the marriages so many are sterile or with only one or two children, that the population is decreasing, then there is something radically wrong with the people of that community as a whole.

Editor: In this chapter, the former President Theodore Roosevelt continued his attack on race suicide by taking on the birth control movement in a fashionable New York magazine. The next chapter has Sanger's reply.

Theodore Roosevelt, "Birth Control—From the Positive Side" *Metropolitan Magazine* (Oct. 1917), 5, 67, 69–70.

—§§§—

Reforms are excellent, but if there is nobody to reform their value becomes somewhat problematical. In order to make a man into it better citizen we must first have the man. In order that there shall be a "fuller and better expressed life for the average woman," that average woman must be in actual existence. And the first necessity in "bringing up the child right" is to produce the child.

Stated in the abstract, these propositions are of bromidic triteness. But an astonishingly large number of persons, including a lamentably large number who call themselves social reformers, either are, or act as if they were, utterly blind to them when they try to deal with life in the concrete. This is true of every group of persons who treat Bernard Shaw seriously as a social reformer. It is true of every group of reformers who discuss the home and the school, but regard it as indelicate to lay stress on the fact that neither is worth discussing unless there are children in sufficient numbers to make the home and the school worth perpetuating. It is true of all blatant sham reformers who in the name of a new morality, preach the

old, old vice and self-indulgence which rotted out first the moral fiber and then even the external greatness of Greece and Rome. It is true of the possibly well-meaning but certainly silly persons who fail to see that we merely enunciate a perfectly plain mathematical truth when we say that the race will die out unless the average family contains at least three children, and therefore that less than this number always means that, whether because of their fault or their misfortune the parents are bearing less than their share of the common burdens, and are rendering less than their due proportion of patriotic service to the nation.

There has recently been published a "Study of the Birth Rate in Harvard and Yale Graduates," by John C. Phillips, of Boston.[1] It should be circulated as a tract among all those most foolish of all foolish people, the half-baked educated people who advocate a profoundly immoral attitude toward life in the name of "reform" through "birth control." These people see that in the "submerged tenth" of society, and even among all the very poor, excessive child bearing is a grave evil which crushes the woman, turning her into a broken-spirited, over-worked, slatternly drudge; and which therefore crushes the family also, making it difficult for the children, on the average, to rise above a very low level. They do not see that it is the directly reverse danger against which we have to guard as soon as we rise above the class

1. Editor: Chap. XVII, "Birth-Rate in Harvard and Yale Graduates."

of the very poor, of those whose livelihood is so precarious that they are always on the brink of the gulf of disaster. As soon as we get above this lowest class the real danger in American families, whether of mechanics, farmers, railroad workers, railroad presidents, deep-sea fishermen, bankers, teachers or lawyers, is not lest they have too many children, but lest they have too few. Yet it is precisely these people who are really influenced by the "birth control" propaganda. **What this nation vitally needs is not the negative preaching of birth control to the submerged tenth, and the tenth immediately adjoining, but the positive preaching of birth encouragement to the eight-tenths who make up the capable, self-respecting American stock which we wish to see perpetuate itself.**

Mr. Phillips studies the birth rate for the two colleges in question by decades from 1850 to 1890. The figures for both colleges are substantially similar, Yale making a trifle better showing. They prove conclusively that for over fifty years the men who have been graduated from Harvard and Yale have left behind them a number of sons inferior to their own number—that is, to the number of fathers—and that, therefore, this college stock, which in point of worthy achievement is certainly among the thoroughly good stocks of the country, is tending to die out; and they show that this tendency has hitherto been slightly accentuated with each decade.

For the decade ending in 1870, for example, the showing was a trifle better than in 1880; and in 1890 there was a further, although a slighter, drop; 1890 was taken as the last year, because the number of children born to graduates after they have been graduated for a quarter of a century is too few materially to affect the average.

On the average, during the thirty years, the graduate who married did so after he had left college eight years. About 78 per cent married, roughly four-fifths. But over 20 per cent of the marriages were childless. This leaves only three-fifths of the men of the class who contracted fertile marriages, and who, therefore, if their stock were to progress, had to make good the shortcomings of their fellows. The average number of children per capita per married graduate was about 2.3, and shrank decade by decade. Taking the entire number of graduates the average number of children surviving was 1.55 per capita (of whom, of course, on the average half are daughters). This means roughly, that in these thirty classes of Harvard and Yale, graduates, representing, of course, a high average of the energy, ambition and cultivation, and a reasonably high average of the wealth of the land, every four fathers left behind them three sons. If this ratio continues it will

mean that 140 years hence—a period as long as that which divides us from the Declaration of Independence—the average college graduates of to-day will be represented in their descendants by only three-tenths of their present number.

This would be bad enough if the disease were confined to college graduates. But, as Mr. Phillips shows in the brief summaries at the end of his article, it is merely representative of what is taking place among native-born Americans generally.

The most pitiable showing is made by the graduates of the women's colleges. So far, among the older classes of the older among these colleges, the average girl is represented in the next generation by only 0.86 of a child. This means, that for every five possible mothers there were two daughters. Do these colleges teach "domestic science," and if so, *what* is it that they teach? There is something radically wrong with the home training and the school training that produce such results. To say this, is not in the least to join with the ignorant and foolish man who denounces higher education for woman; he is usually himself a striking illustration of the need of wiser education for men. But it most certainly is a recognition of the fact, not that there should be any abandonment of, nor indeed any failure to enlarge, the scheme of higher education for women, but that for women as for men this higher education should keep a firm grip on the true perspective of life, and should refuse to sacrifice the great essentials of existence to even the easiest and pleasantest nonessentials.

The trouble in our national life, however, is far more deep-seated than anything affecting only the most highly educated classes. The same drift is visible among our people generally; most so in the East, and in the cities and big towns of the West. In Massachusetts for the twenty-five years ending in 1911, the deaths among the native-born population exceeded the births by 270,000, whereas during the same period the births in families with foreign-born parents exceeded the deaths by nearly 530,000. If this process continues the work of perfecting the boasted common school and college system for Massachusetts native Americans will prove about as useful as the labor of those worthy missionaries who on different occasions have translated the Bible into the tongues of savage races who thereupon died out.

In the West the native stock—and I use the term with elasticity to include all children of mothers and fathers who were born on this side of the water—is only just about holding its own. It is a little less than holding its own in the cities, a little more than doing so in the country districts. In the cities of Minneapolis and Cleveland, for example, such families average less than three children. In the country districts of Minnesota and Ohio they average about one child more a family, which in this case marks just the difference between increase and decrease. In the South the native white stock is still increasing, although with diminishing rapidity.

The figures given for the Harvard and Yale graduates show that, taking into account the number of children that die before growing up, the number of adults that do not marry and the number of marriages where for physical and natural reasons—that is, reasons presumably implying no moral blame in the parents—there are no children or only one or two children, it is necessary that the family physically be able to produce children shall average over three or the race will slowly decrease in numbers. When the health conditions become such that child mortality is reduced still lower than at present, and when marriages become more universal, and the having and rearing of a sufficient number of children is recognized for both man and woman as the highest duty and the greatest and most extraordinary pleasure of life, then an average family of three children may mean a slow increase. Under any circumstances an average of one or two children means rapid race suicide, and therefore profound moral delinquency in those wilfully responsible for it. But this is not all! At present whoever has only three children must be understood to represent a slight drag on the forward movement of the nation, a slight falling below the average necessary standard in the performance of the indispensable duty without which there will in the end be no nation; the duty, failure to perform which means that all talk of eugenics and social reform and moral uplift and self-development represents mere empty threshing of the air, as pointless as similar talk by a suicide.

Apparently some persons regard it as a satisfactory answer to point out that some worthless or hopelessly poverty-stricken families would benefit themselves and the country by having fewer children. I heartily agree to this, and will support any measures to make this agreement effective by limiting the production of the unfit, after we have first taken effective measures to promote the production of the fit. Doubtless there are communities which it would be to the interest of the world to have die out. But these are not the communities reached by the "birth-control" propagandists—even by that rather small proportion of these propagandists who are neither decadent nor immoral. I hold that the average American is a decent, self-respecting man, with large capacities for good service to him-

self, his country and the world if a right appeal can be made to him and the right response evoked. Therefore, I hold that it is not best that he and his kind should perish from the earth. Except in a small number of cases, the State can exercise little active control against the perpetuation of the unfit.[2] Therefore, the real and great service must be rendered by those who help put an aroused and effective public opinion on the side of the perpetuation of the stocks from which it is particularly important that the future citizenship of the nation should be drawn.

Really intelligent eugenists understand and insist on these facts. The *Journal of Heredity* for July, 1917, contains one article showing the evil which has come from permitting the unrestricted breeding of a feebleminded, utterly shiftless and worthless family in Ohio; and another, and even more important article showing that the idea that, in a normal and healthy community, large families are an evil is false and dangerous in the highest degree. The writer says: "Large families in the slums may be considered undesirable; unregulated [excessive] child-bearing for any woman may be considered undesirable; but this [is untrue as to] large families separated from the influence of poverty. It is doubtless true that in the Hull House district, where many children have feeble and unintelligent parents and lack the necessities of life, a large family means weakness. But the reverse is true in normally sound stocks, in sections of population which have average intelligence, physique and prosperity." The writer shows that in such normal stocks the health of the mother is best, and the infant mortality lowest, in families with at least six children. He shows that in superior parts of the population large families are desirable from the point of view of the parents, the children and the world, alike; but that "in eugenically inferior parts of the population the smaller the family the better for all concerned."

At different times in different nations the needs and the duties differ widely. Professor Ross has shown that China has suffered immeasurably because of the reckless overbreeding of its people. France is now in hazard of her national existence because of exactly the opposite cause. A century ago France was as populous as Germany. Her soil is fertile, her natural advantages great. But France's population remained nearly stationary while Germany's population increased, until the two countries stand nearly as five to three. The increase in Germany's population was accompanied by such industrial and social development as also to mean a marked increase in social and

---

2. Editor: Although supportive of eugenics, Roosevelt didn't have the same view of government as many on the left. His State would exercise "little active control" over parenthood.

national efficiency. In consequence, all of France's heroic gallantry and self-devotion and her utmost self-sacrifice have been needed in order to enable her, with the help of potent allies, even to hold back a foe whom once she was able to meet single-handed.

In instancing France I merely take what the best and most patriotic Frenchmen say. A French newspaper before me says: "In 1850 the population of France surpassed that of Germany. When this war broke out it had become inferior by 27 millions. It was this fact to which the war was really due. If the Germans had had before them 60 millions of French instead of 39 they would have hesitated long. The cause of the war was that we had not furnished to France enough children. . . . If the French birth rate continues to diminish we shall some day face a new war of conquest waged against us. It is a question of life or death which confronts France. She must live! But in order to live she must face the implacable realities of existence. The national conscience should insist that our legislators put the matter of the repopulation of France in the first place." The lesson applies as much to the United States. If our birth rate continues to diminish we shall by the end of this century be impotent in the face of powers like Germany, Russia or Japan; we shall have been passed by the great states of South America.

In a small group there may be good and sufficient explanations why the individual men and women have remained unmarried; and the fact that those that marry have no children, or only one or two children, may be cause only for sincere and respectful sympathy. But if, in a community of a thousand men and a thousand women, a large proportion of them remain unmarried, and if of the marriages so many are sterile or with only one or two children, that the population is decreasing, then there is something radically wrong with the people of that community as a whole. The evil may be partly physical, partly due to the strange troubles which accompany an over-strained intensity of life. But even in this case the root trouble is probably moral; and in all probability the whole trouble is moral, and is due to a complex tissue of causation in which coldness, love of ease, striving after social position, fear of pain, dislike of hard work and sheer inability to get life values in their proper perspective all play a part.

The fundamental instincts are not only the basic but also the loftiest instincts in human nature. The qualities that make men and women eager lovers, faithful, duty-performing, hard-working husbands and wives, and wise and devoted fathers and mothers stand at the foundations of all possible social welfare, and also represent the lofti-

est heights of human happiness and usefulness. No other form of personal success and happiness or of individual service to the state compares with that which is represented by the love of the one man for the one woman, their joint work as home-maker and home-keeper, and their ability to bring up the children that are theirs.

Among human beings, as among all other living creatures, if the best specimens do not, and the poorer specimens do, propagate, the type will go down. If Americans of the old stock lead lives of celibate selfishness (whether profligate or merely frivolous or objectless, matters little), or if the married are afflicted by that base fear of living which, whether for the sake of themselves or of their children, forbids them to have more than one or two children, disaster awaits the nation. It is not well for a nation to import its art and its literature; but it is fatal for a nation to import its babies. And it is utterly futile to make believe that fussy activity for somebody else's babies atones for failure of personal parenthood.

The remedy? There are many remedies, all of them partial. The state can do something, as the state is now doing in France. Legislation must be for the average, for the common good. Therefore legislation should at once abandon the noxious sentimentality of thinking that in America at this time the "only son" is entitled to preferential consideration, either for the sake of himself or of his mother. The preference, as regards all obligations to the state, should be given to the family having the third and fourth children. In all public offices in every grade the lowest salaries should be paid the man or woman with no children, or only one or two children, and a marked discrimination made in favor of the man or woman with a family of *over* three children. In taxation, the rate should be immensely heavier on the childless and on the families with one or two children, while an equally heavy discrimination should lie in favor of the family with *over* three children. This should apply to the income tax and inheritance tax, and as far as possible to other taxes. I speak, as usual, of the average, not the exception. Only the father and mother of over three children have done their full duty by the state; and the state should emphasize this fact. No reduction should be made in a man's taxes merely because he is married. But he should be exempted on an additional $500 of income for each of his first two children, and on an additional $1000 of income for every subsequent child—for we wish to put especial emphasis on the vital need of having the third, and the fourth and the fifth children. The men and women with small or reasonable incomes are the ones who should be encouraged to have children; they do not represent a class which will be tempted by such exemption to thriftlessness or extravagances. I do not believe that there should be any income exemption whatever for the unmarried man or the childless married couple; let all the exemptions be for the married couples of moderate means who have children.

An aroused and enlightened public opinion can do infinitely more. There must be a sterner sense of duty and a clearer vision of the perspectives among which duty must work. That standard of living is poor, whether for mechanic or bank president, which is based on ease, comfort, luxury and social ambition rather than on education, culture and wide ability to shift for oneself. The oldest duty of all is that owed by the fathers and mothers of Americans to care for the future of their country and the ideals of their race. I would be the first to admit that no universal rule can be laid down, applicable to all people under all conditions. But let our people study, not only books on sociology, but also stories like Kathleen Norris's *Mother,* Cornelia Comer's *Preliminaries,* and Dorothy Canfield's *Hillsboro People.*[3] These books are wholesome reading for man and for woman—and they have the additional merit of being interesting.

The serious student can turn to one of the best books recently written by an American scientific man: *Heredity and Environment,* by Professor Edwin G. Conklin, of Princeton. Let him look at pages 434–5, 450–455, and 498–507. I wish these pages could be circulated as a teacher's leaflet in all our schools and universities, in all the editorial rooms of our magazines and newspapers—especially in those whose editors pose as reformers and advocate every form of quack remedy from pacifism to birth control. Says Mr. Conklin (I condense): "The cause for alarm is the declining birth rate in the best elements of a population, while it continues to increase among the poorer elements. The descendants of the Puritans and the Cavaliers, who have raised the cry for 'fewer and better children,' are already disappearing, and in a few centuries, at most, will have given place to more fertile races of mankind . . . if we had fewer luxuries we could have, and could afford to have, more children. . . . We need not 'fewer and better children' but more children of the better sort and fewer of the worse variety. **There is great enthusiasm today on the part of many childless reformers for negative eugenical measures.** [They forget that] sterility is too easily acquired; what is not so easily brought about is the fertility of the better lines. . . . The chief motive for limiting the size of families is personal

comfort and pleasure rather than the welfare of the race. It is more important for the welfare of the race that children with good inheritance [in mind, body and will] should be brought into the world than that parents should live easy lives and have no more children than they can conveniently rear amid all the comforts of a luxury-loving age. . . . Race preservation, not self-preservation, is the first law of nature. Among the higher organisms, the strongest of all the instincts are those connected with reproduction. The struggle to be free is part of a great evolutionary movement, but the freedom must be a sane one, which neither injures others nor eliminates posterity. [Any movement which] demands freedom from marriage and reproduction is suicidal."

In any discussion such as this, where it is necessary to deal in sweeping manner with great truths, the statements made must be accepted as referring to the general and the average conditions. It is not possible at every point to qualify them so as to allow for exceptions. In this case, it is, in my judgment, vital to establish the principles above laid down as generally applicable, and to insist that no country is healthy, indeed, that any country is sick nigh to death, where these principles are not in general lived up to. But, of course, there are exceptions. There are a few—a very few—good men and women who, when unmarried, can do such admirable work that the question of marriage is negligible so far as they are concerned. There are men and women who remain unmarried for good and sufficient reasons, even although they never do great work in the outside world. Then, among married couples who are childless or have only one or two children, there are plenty to whom this is a dreadful grief and who are morally in no way to blame. For these men and women I have the same respectful sympathy that I have for a gallant man, of soldier stock, who, because of physical trouble for which he is in no way responsible, is denied the chance to serve his country under arms when that country's need is sore. **There is no more fearless and danger-defying heroism than that shown by some women of the true heroic type, in walking through the valley of the shadow to bring into life the babies they love; and there is no punishment too heavy for the man who does not revere and serve such a woman as he reveres and serves nothing else that is human.** And it may be his highest duty if the danger is too great to see that she does not face it. I know one girl who has just for the second time eagerly faced motherhood; and to bring the second baby to join her first she had to show a splendid courage which (and I speak accurately) ranges her beside any of the men who in their ragged blue and buff and

3. Editor: Kathleen T. Norris, *Mother* (1911); Cornelia A. P. Comer, *The Preliminaries and Other Stories* (1912); and Dorothy Canfield, *Hillsboro People,* 1915.

their gaping shoes followed Washington, or any gaunt Confederate who charged with Pickett, or any of the sailormen who held the sinking launch steady while Cushing torpedoed the Albemarle—courage which ranges her beside her husband and brothers who have crossed the sea to face the German and Turkish armies.

It would be wicked, without due thought, to expose woman or man, girl or young man, to the possible stroke of fate; but we revere them all alike, precisely because they face the stroke of fate, high-hearted, if the need warrants it. Only those who are not afraid to die are fit to live!

—§§§—

EDITOR

President Theodore Roosevelt not only lived the courage he wrote about, he accomplished that most difficult of all tasks, he passed it on to his children.

As a 57-year-old combat general, his son, Theodore Roosevelt Jr. was the oldest soldier to land with first wave on D-Day. General Omar Bradley later said that the bravest thing he had seen in his entire military career was the courage Roosevelt displayed that day leading his men under fire. In the push inland from Normandy, he drove himself relentlessly. Less than six weeks later, he was dead of a heart attack. Fighting in North Africa, Sicily and France, he earned every combat medal awarded to a soldier, including the Congressional Medal of Honor.

Unfortunately, few Americans learned of his sacrifice. In response to a mysterious request from U.S. intelligence, the British banned his name and that of his son, Quentin, from all press reports. Theodore was aware of the blackout and suspected the source was his kinsman, President Franklin Roosevelt, whose own sons were doing virtually nothing for the war effort.

In his *The Roosevelts,* Peter Collier summarized the difference between the two families when he noted that Theodore's children, were "obsessed with living up to their heritage. The FDR children had no such tradition to follow in making their way to self-definition. Their parents' example suggest that life was a matter of every man and woman for him—and herself—a scramble to satisfy personal needs and appetites."[4]

The contrast between those two branches of the Roosevelt family aptly illustrates the difference between Theodore Roosevelt's own strong sense of responsibility and Sanger's self-centered "scramble to satisfy personal needs and appetites."

---

4. Peter Collier, *The Roosevelts* (New York: Simon & Schuster, 1994), 361. The description of the son's heroism begins on page 418.

Birth Control—From the Positive Side
By Theodore Roosevelt

REFORMS are excellent, but if there is nobody to reform their value becomes somewhat problematical. In order to make a man into a better citizen we must first have the man. In order that there shall be a "fuller and better expressed life for the average woman," that average woman must be in actual existence. And the first necessity in "bringing up the child right" is to produce the child.

Stated in the abstract, these propositions are of bromidic triteness. But an astonishingly large number of persons, including a lamentably large number who call themselves social reformers, either are, or act as if

For the decade ending in 1870, for example, the showing was a trifle better than in 1880; and in 1890 there was a further, although a slighter, drop; 1890 was taken as the last year, because the number of children born to graduates after they have been graduated for a quarter of a century is too few materially to affect the average.

On the average, during the thirty years, the graduate who married did so after he had left college eight years. About 78 per cent married, roughly four-fifths. But over 20 per cent of the marriages were childless. This leaves only three-fifths of the men of the class who contracted fertile marriages, and who, therefore, if their stock were to progress, had to make good the shortcomings of their fellows. The average number of children per capita per married graduate was about 2.3, and shrank decade by decade. Taking the entire number of graduates the average number of children surviving was 1.55 per capita (of whom, of course, on the average half are daughters). This means, roughly, that in these thirty classes of Harvard and Yale graduates, representing, of course, a high average of the energy, ambition and cultivation, and a reasonably high average of the wealth of the land, every four fathers left behind them three sons. If this ratio continues it will mean that 140 years hence—a period as long as that which divides us from the Declaration of Independence—the average college

XXVI

An Answer to Mr. Roosevelt

1917

Margaret Sanger

President, American Birth Control League

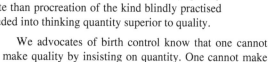

The best thing that the modern American college does for young men or young women is to make of them highly sensitized individuals, keenly aware of their responsibility to society. They quickly perceive that they have other duties toward the State than procreation of the kind blindly practised by the immigrant from Europe. They cannot be deluded into thinking quantity superior to quality.

Margaret Sanger, "An Answer to Mr. Roosevelt." *Birth Control Review* (Dec. 1917), 13–14. An interlibrary search did not locate this article in the December issue of *Metropolitan Magazine* as claimed. But Ellen Chesler, *Woman of Valor* (p. 508) says it appeared on page 66.

—§§§—

(In the October issue of the *Metropolitan Magazine* appeared an article by former-President Roosevelt, entitled "Birth Control—From the Positive Side." It revealed a desire to arrive at the same results of race betterment which we advocate. It swept aside, however, not only the principle of voluntary motherhood, but the existing racial and class conditions[1] which must be taken into consideration if the desired end is to be attained. The following is Margaret Sanger's reply, which appears in the December number of the *Metropolitan*.—Ed.)

The trouble with nearly all writers who oppose birth control is that they consider only proximate instead of ultimate effects. They want large numbers of high quality citizens. Therefore, they contend, let the existing high quality citizens have more children. They assume that families now living in comfortable circumstances will be able to maintain their standards, no matter how many additional children are born. In other words, they expect quality to take care of itself.

We advocates of birth control know that one cannot make quality by insisting on quantity. One cannot make better people simply by having more people.

Mr. Roosevelt says that in order to make a man into a better citizen, we must first have the man. The right environment in which to receive and develop the man is of greater importance. Society, as at present constituted, does not provide the means of rearing unrestricted hordes of human beings into intelligent citizenship. Therefore, birth control has become necessary as a check upon the blind working of ignorance and poverty.

When considering the problems of the class known as the "submerged tenth," even the most conservative are willing to admit its need of birth control. But it is an error to suppose that the proportion of families sunk in destitution constitutes only one-tenth of the population. Figures are available to prove that it is closer to three-tenths, or well over one quarter.[2] The census of 1910 shows that 10.7 per cent of married women in the United States went to work outside their homes to help keep their families together. There, without looking farther, is a submerged tenth among women alone. There is little doubt that the proportion of wage-earning mothers has greatly increased since 1910, and it is equally beyond question that an enormous number of poverty-stricken women are prevented by their excessive family burdens from seeking to earn money outside the home.

They who ban the open and legal dissemination of birth control practically say—Let the slums spawn if

---

1. Editor: Sanger's "voluntary motherhood" was one-sided. It meant that poor women must not to be deprived of birth control. But she also supported what might be called "involuntary non-motherhood." The "existing racial and class conditions" remark hints at coercion, as does the article itself.

2. Editor: Roosevelt distinguished poverty from actual parental inability. Sanger did not.

they must; the prime aim is to goad the upper classes into greater fertility. Both effects are deplorable. There is no greater national waste than the spawning of the slums, with its resultant high maternal and infant mortality rates, child labor and prostitution. As for increasing the fertility of the upper classes, it is certain that the majority of such parents even now have as many children as any rational eugenist could ask them to do, were he in possession of all the facts of each case—health, income, educational needs and provision for the future, etc. Admitting that they give birth to fewer children, the fact is that they bring, relatively, to maturity almost as many as the poor succeed in doing. The following figures prepared by the French authority, Dr. J. Bertillon,[3] demonstrate this point.

For the whole of France 86.6 per cent of the children of rich parents reach twenty years of age, and only 48.6 per cent of the children of poor parents. The figures for Paris give a fertility rate of about 100 births per 1,000 poor mothers, and of about 50 per 1,000 rich mothers. Combining these with the former figures, it appears that for each 1,000 rich mothers there would be 43.3 children surviving to twenty years annually, and for each 1,000 poor mothers only 48.6 children. In France, as elsewhere, the poor mother is handicapped in rearing her surviving offspring. This results in a percentage of unfitness, and the contribution of the high birth rate classes to the adult effective population is consequently no higher proportionately than that of the low birth rate classes.

The world over, the intelligent parents of three children or less have been, and are, the upholders of national standards. This is particularly true of America.

By regarding the bringing of a child into the world as a great social responsibility, the modern American woman shows a fine sense of morality. Since the State does not compel marriage, but leaves it to individual choice, she does not see why motherhood, which is a much more serious problem, should be enforced.

The American woman of today is physically and nervously unable to compete with her grandmother in the matter of bearing unlimited offspring. In Colonial times, the environment was favorable and women specialized on reproduction with eminent success. The prospective mothers of this generation are compelled to divide their creative energies between child bearing and social and economic complexities. It has been estimated that last year seven and a half million women were engaged in industry in the United States, the majority of them in nerve-racking trades. Ten hours a day at a sewing machine or a telephone switchboard are not conducive to either a physical or mental receptiveness to maternity.

It is a very common fallacy that the decadence of Greece and Rome was due to the artificial limitation of offspring. It is surprising to find a historian like Mr. Roosevelt repeating the error. During the periods he refers to, birth control was, indeed, practised, and as a result some of the greatest poets, thinkers and geniuses, generally, of that, or any other age, were developed. Birth control was one of the few serious moral forces at work tending to preserve the integrity of the State. But, in Rome especially, it was not quite effective enough to combat the soft luxury and vice which had come as an aftermath of an orgy of conquest.

The falling birth rate of college graduates, as demonstrated by the statistics gathered in Harvard and Yale by John C. Phillips,[4] should not be considered alarming. **The best thing that the modern American college does for young men or young women is to make of them highly sensitized individuals, keenly aware of their responsibility to society. They quickly perceive that they have other duties toward the State than procreation of the kind blindly practised by the immigrant from Europe. They cannot be deluded into thinking quantity superior to quality.** But they can be trusted not to suffer extinction. The operation of natural law will prevent the ratio of reproduction from remorselessly falling to zero. In this, as in all other population phenomena, a new level of fertility is being sought—that is all.

Copyrighted by the Chicago "Tribune."

MAKING A BAD SITUATION WORSE.

---

3. Editor: Jacque Bertillon (1851–1919), author of *La dépopulation de la France* (1911).

4. Editor: Included in this book as Chap. XVII.

In many other isolated groups, the same process can be observed today. The editor of *The Journal of Heredity* has found that out of 1,512 families of Methodist ministers in America, the average number of children is now only 3.12. The birth rate in the English Society of Friends has fallen from 20 per 1,000 in 1876 to less than 8 per 1,000 in 1915. Or, to take an illustration from an entire racial group, statistics show that the size of Jewish families in Europe has been rapidly decreasing since 1876. They contain now only two to four children, with a growing tendency to restrict the number to two, whilst only twenty years ago they had four to six.

But it is well to emphasize that we advocates of birth control are not so much disturbed by the stationary birth rate of the thinking classes, as by the reckless propagation of the ignorant. We consider that the falling birth rate is a worldwide movement of civilization.

Mr. Roosevelt quotes approvingly the statement of a French newspaper that the present war was really due to the increasing birth rate of Germany and the falling birth rate of France. Had Germany had to face 60,000,000 Frenchmen, instead of 39,000,000, this authority holds, the war would not have taken place. In my opinion, two overpopulated nations would have fought even more readily and long before. The war was due to the overpopulation of Germany and Russia, not to France's stationary population. But once put to the ordeal, the French soldiers, sturdy and highly individualistic because they came from small families, proved at the Battle of the Marne and Verdun the efficacy of birth control, by defeating an enemy mechanically much more formidable than themselves.

On the other hand, the same Germany who had failed against France easily routed the hordes of Russian soldiers, who owed their numbers to an unlimited system of reckless propagation. Germany's birth rate is falling.

In 1860 it was 37.9 per thousand inhabitants and in 1912 only 29.1. It is common knowledge that the economists of Europe do not hope for universal peace until the birth rate of Russia also begins to decline.

The intelligent class, with its acceptance of birth control, holds the same position in American society that France does among the nations of the world.

It is an error to suppose that woman avoids motherhood because she is afraid to die. Rather does she fear to live. She fears a life of poverty and drudgery, weighed down by the horror of unwanted pregnancy and tortured by the inability to rear decently the children she has already brought into the world.

—§§§—

Editorial Comment

Editor: The verbal duel between President Roosevelt and Sanger continued into 1918. One issue of *Birth Control Review* contained the following remarks about the President. Notice that Sanger chose to mail these mothers an issue of her magazine rather than personally bring them a much-needed quart of milk—even as a rather tasteless 'photo opportunity.'

"Editorial Comment," *Birth Control Review* (Feb.–Mar. 1918), 16.

Colonel Roosevelt's race suicide rant was bad enough in times of peace. With the poor paying war prices for the bare necessities of life, it becomes intolerable. But there does not seem to be any way of restraining the self-appointed godfather of the American people. His latest ebullition has been to tour the East Side of New York City and congratulate half-starved mothers of large families on their patriotism, while expressing concern at their inability to buy Grade B milk at 15 cents a quart. The accuracy of newspaper accounts is open to doubt, but a report from the *New York Evening Mail,* which we have before us, rings true to the Rooseveltian psychology. An Italian household of father, mother, and ten children is described as being "a family after the Colonel's own prescription, comfortably fixed with a total income of $27 a week." Twenty-seven dollars for 12 persons. The mockery of it! Of an Irish mother, whose husband had been out of work, but who had recently given birth to her fifth child, Roosevelt burst out with: "Straight United States and no whining! That's the stuff!" This in spite of the fact that the woman had told him that one of her children had been sent to the country, a victim of malnutrition. However, we are doing our little best to counteract the effects of the Ex-President's frivolous and dangerous optimism. He may be interested to know that we have sent a copy of *The Birth Control Review* to every family reported to have been visited by him.

—§§§—

XXVII

Revolt Against Civilization

1922

Lothrop Stoddard

Scientific Humanist

Unfortunately for the race, it was the latter alternative which prevailed. Instead of spreading contraceptive knowledge among the masses and thus mitigating as far as possible the evils of a racially destructive differential birth-rate, society succeeded in keeping the masses in ignorance and high fecundity, whereas it emphatically did not succeed in keeping contraceptive knowledge from the more intelligent, who increasingly practised birth control and diminished their contributions to the population.

EDITOR

In 1921, Margaret Sanger would hold the First American Birth Control Conference in New York City. The conference was to close on Sunday evening, November 13, with a public meeting at Town Hall on "Birth Control, Is It Moral?" At that time birth control proponents denied that making birth control widely available would increase teenage promiscuity with as much zeal as they now promote it *because* of such promiscuity. Fearing corruption of the city's youth, Catholic leaders in New York City pressured the police to block access to the meeting. As a result, when Sanger arrived hundreds of people were standing outside the hall, unable to enter. Watching for a break in police vigilance, Sanger managed to slip into the auditorium. At that point, we take up the narrative from her second autobiography.

"I fairly flew up the aisle but halted in front of the footlights; they were as high as my head and another blue uniform was obstructing the steps leading to the stage.

Suddenly Lothrop Stoddard, the author, tall and strong, seized me and literally tossed me up to the platform. A messenger boy was aimlessly grasping flowers which were to be presented after my speech. Stoddard grabbed them briskly, handed them to me, and shouted, 'Here's Mrs. Sanger!'"[1]

As a board member of Sanger's American Birth Control League, Lothrop Stoddard's presence there was hardly a surprise. Nor should we be surprised to find numerous similarities between his claim that birth control was needed to protect civilization from civilization-destroying "Underman" and Sanger's claim that it would protect civilization from the "feeble-minded." After all, Stod-

---

1. Margaret Sanger, *Margaret Sanger, An Autobiography* (New York: W. W. Norton, 1938), 302. (Stoddard also spoke at the conference, Sanger, *My Fight*, 213.) The graphic of the ABCL board of directors (above) comes from the April 1922 issue of *Birth Control Review*.

dard's book came out the same year as Sanger's and the two were friends. In many ways, the two books can be read side by side. Their goals were similar, but Sanger focused on domestic issues, while Stoddard provided a global perspective.[2]

In this chapter we let Stoddard explain, in his own words, how the more advanced societies should deal with the 'threat' posed by prolific but inferior races. Stoddard's book also illustrates how the results of IQ tests that had been given to recent immigrants and to millions of World War I Army recruits were seen in 1922. When Sanger, Gilman and others denounce feeble-mindedness, the well-publicized results of these tests provided scientific justification. Today, they are known to be culturally biased and their value nearly worthless. They certainly did not measure innate intelligence.

Lothrop Stoddard, *The Revolt Against Civilization: The Menace of the Underman* (New York: Charles Scribner's Sons, 1922). Page numbers are given in square brackets after the text quoted [ ].

—§§§—

Indeed, even the first light burdens [of civilization] had in some cases proved too heavy to be borne. Not all the branches of the human species attained the threshold of civilization. Some, indeed, never reached even the limits of savagery. Existing survivals of low-type savage man, such as the Bushmen of South Africa and the Australian "Blackfellows," have vegetated for countless ages in primeval squalor and seem incapable of rising even to the level of barbarism, much less to that of civilization. **It is fortunate for the future of mankind that most of these survivals from the remote past are to-day on the verge of extinction.**[3] Their persistence and possible incorporation into higher stocks would produce the most depressive and retrogressive results.

Much more serious is the problem presented by those far more numerous stocks which, while transcending the plane of mere savagery, have stopped at some level of barbarism. Not only have these stocks never originated a civilization themselves, but they also seem constitutionally incapable of assimilating the civilization of others. Deceptive veneers of civilization may be acquired, but

---

2. Editor: In modern terminology, Sanger's stress was on "family planning" while Stoddard's was on "population control."

3. Editor: In Darwinian/progressive terms this was exactly what should happen. H. G. Wells had toyed with the idea of token 'diversity' and a multi-racial ruling "samurai," but the use of such tricks to conceal a selective birthrate-limiting agenda was not yet widely accepted.

reversion to congenital barbarism ultimately takes place. **To such barbarian stocks belong many of the peoples of Asia, the American Indians, and the African negroes. These congenital barbarians have always been dangerous foes of progress.** Many a promising civilization has been ravaged and ruined by barbarians without the wit to rebuild what they had destroyed. Today, the progress of science may have freed our own civilization from the peril of armed conquest by barbarian hordes; nevertheless, these peoples still threaten us with the subtler menace of "pacific penetration." Usually highly prolific, often endowed with extraordinary physical vigor, and able to migrate easily, owing to modern facilities of transportation, the more backward peoples of the earth tend increasingly to seek the centres of civilization, attracted thither by the high wages and easier living conditions which there prevail. The influx of such lower elements into civilized societies is an unmitigated disaster. It upsets living standards, socially sterilizes the higher native stocks, and if (as usually happens in the long run) interbreeding occurs, the racial foundations of civilization are undermined, and the mongrelized population, unable to bear the burden, sinks to a lower plane. [4–6]

Stoddard's Ability

One of the ablest writers among the exponents of the doctrine that there is a very real danger of the colored races supplanting the white race is Lothrop Stoddard.[4]
—EDWARD A. EAST, HARVARD UNIVERSITY

—§§§—

The ruin of civilizations was variously ascribed to luxury, vice, town life, irreligion, and much more besides. Yet all these theories somehow failed to satisfy. They might be shown to have been contributing causes in particular cases, but they could not account universally for the phenomena of declining civilization.

Within the past two decades, however, the rapid progress of biological knowledge has thrown a flood of light on this vexed question, and has enabled us to frame a theory so in accordance with known facts that it seems to offer substantially the correct answer.[5]

And this answer is that, in the last analysis, civilization always depends upon the qualities of the people who are the bearers of it. All these vast accumulations of instru-

---

4. Edward M. East, *Mankind at the Crossroads* (New York: Charles Scribner's Sons, 1923), 111. He was referring to Stoddard's "stirring book *The Rising Tide of Color*" published in 1920 and favorably reviewed by Havelock Ellis in *Birth Control Review* (Oct. 1920).

ments and ideas, massed and welded into marvellous structures rising harmoniously in glittering majesty, rest upon living foundations—upon the men and women who create and sustain them. So long as those men and women are able to support it, the structure rises, broad-based and serene; but let the living foundations prove unequal to their task, and the mightiest civilization sags, cracks, and at last crashes down into chaotic ruin.

Civilization thus depends absolutely upon the *quality* of its human supporters. Mere numbers mean nothing. The most brilliant civilization the world has ever seen arose in Athens—a tiny community where the number of freemen (*i. e.,* genuine Athenians) numbered perhaps 50,000 all told. We therefore see that, for civilization to arise at all, a superior human stock is first necessary; while to perfect, or even to maintain that civilization, the human stock must be kept superior. And these are requirements more exacting than might be imagined. Surveying human history, we find that superior stocks are the exception rather than the rule. We have already seen how many races of men have never risen above the planes of savagery or barbarism, while relatively few races have shown the ability to create high and enduring civilizations.

Furthermore, even inside the superior racial groups there exists a similar differentiation. When we speak of a "superior race"[6] we do not imply that all the members of that race stand on the same lofty plane. Of course, the average level runs higher than do the averages of less favored races. But besides this statistical consideration there is the even more important fact that within the higher group itself there exist a relatively large number of very superior individuals, characterized by unusual energy, ability, talent, or genius. It is this elite which leavens the group and initiates progress. Here, again, we see the supreme importance of quality. In no human society has the percentage of really superior individuals ever been large—in fact, their percentage has been always statistically negligible. Their influence, however, has been incalculable. Athens was not made up

---

5. Editor: Stoddard meant the theory that acquired traits are not passed on to offspring (as Darwin assumed), so the primary mechanism of evolutionary progress is genetic. This meant that barbaric races *cannot* be improved by contact with a civilized one, particularly when that civilization allows both fit and unfit to survive. August Weissmann (1834–1914) played a critical role in developing the idea in his *The Germ Plasm: A Theory of Heredity* (1893) and *The Evolution Theory* (1904).

6. Editor: Note the parallel in terminology ("superior race") and content, to Edward Ross's 1903 "The Causes of Race Superiority" (Chap. VII).

of Platos or Xenophons: it had its quota of dullards, knaves, and fools—as is vividly shown in the immortal satires of Aristophanes. Yet the dynamic power of its elite made Athens the glory of the world, and only when the Athenian stock ceased to produce superiors did Athens sink into insignificance.

Thus we see that civilization depends absolutely upon quality, while quality, in turn, depends upon inheritance. Environment may bring out all there is in a man, but heredity predetermines what there is to bring. We now begin to see the fallacy of such fatalistic notions as "The Law of Civilization and Decay." Civilizations, unlike living organisms, have no appointed cycle of life and death. Given a high-type stock producing an adequate quota of superior individuals, and a civilization might be immortal. [9–11]

—§§§—

Let us see how this comes about.

Consider, first, man's condition before the advent of civilization. Far, far back in its life history the human species underwent a profound differentiation. **Fossil bones tens of thousands of years old, show mankind already divided into distinct races differing markedly not merely in bodily structure but also in brain capacity, and hence in intelligence.** This differentiation probably began early and proceeded rapidly, since biology teaches us that species are plastic when new, gradually losing this plasticity as they "set" with time and development.

However, at whatever rate it proceeded, differentiation went on for untold ages, operating not only between separate races but also within the various stocks, so that each stock came to consist of many "strains" varying considerably from one another in both physical and mental capacity.

Now the fate of these strains depended, not upon chance, but upon the very practical question whether or not they could survive. And since man was then living in the "state of nature," qualities like strength, intelligence, and vigor were absolutely necessary for life, while weakness, dulness, and degeneracy spelled speedy death. Accordingly, individuals endowed with the former qualities survived and bred freely, whereas those handicapped by the latter qualities perished oftener and left fewer offspring. **Thus, age after age, nature imposed upon man her individually stern but racially beneficent will; eliminating the weak, and preserving and multiplying the strong.** Surely, it is the most striking proof of human differentiation that races should display such inequalities after undergoing so long a selective process so much the same.

However, differentiated mankind remained, and at last the more gifted races began to create civilizations. Now civilization wrought profound changes, the most important of which was a modification of the process of selection for survival. So long as man was a savage, or even a barbarian, nature continued to select virtually unhindered according to her immemorial plan—that of eliminating the weak and preserving the strong. **But civilization meant a change from a "natural" to a more or less artificial, man-made environment, in which natural selection was increasingly modified by "social" selection.** And social selection altered survival values all along the line. In the first place, it enabled many weak, stupid, and degenerate persons to live and beget children who would have certainly perished in the state of nature, or even on the savage and barbarian planes. Upon the strong the effect of social selection was more subtle but equally important. The strong individual survived even better than before—but he tended to have fewer children.

The reason for this lessened fecundity of the superior was that civilization opened up to them a whole new range of opportunities and responsibilities. Under primitive conditions, opportunities for self-expression were few and simple, the most prized being desirable mates and sturdy offspring. Among savages and barbarians the choicest women and many children are the acknowledged perquisites of the successful, and the successful are those men endowed with qualities like strength, vigor, and resourceful intelligence, which are not only essential for continued survival under primitive conditions, but which are equally essential for the upbuilding and maintenance of civilization. In short, when a people enters the stage of civilization it is in the pink of condition, because natural selection has for ages been multiplying superior strains and eliminating inferiors.

Such was the high biological level of the selected stocks which attained the plane of civilization. But, as time passed, the situation altered. The successful superiors who stood in the vanguard of progress were alike allured and constrained by a host of novel influences. **Power, wealth, luxury, leisure, art, science, learning, government—these and many other matters increasingly complicated life. And, good or bad, temptations or responsibilities, they all had this in common: that they tended to divert human energy from racial ends to individual and social ends.**

Now this diverted energy flowed mainly from the superior strains in the population. Upon the successful

superior, civilization laid both her highest gifts and her heaviest burdens. The effect upon the individual was, of course, striking. Powerfully stimulated, he put forth his inherited energies. Glowing with the fire of achievement, he advanced both himself and his civilization. But, in this very fire, he was apt to be racially consumed. Absorbed in personal and social matters, racial matters were neglected. Late marriage, fewer children, and celibacy combined to thin the ranks of the successful, diminish the number of superior strains, and thus gradually impoverish the race.

Meanwhile, as the numbers of the superior diminished, the numbers of the inferior increased. No longer ruthlessly weeded by natural selection, the inferior survived and multiplied.

Here, then, was what had come to pass: instead of dying off at the base and growing at the top, civilized society was dying at the top and spreading out below. The result of this dual process was, of course, as disastrous as it was inevitable. Drained of its superiors, and saturated with dullards and degenerates, the stock could no longer support its civilization. And, the upper layers of the human foundation having withered away, the civilization either sank to a lower level or collapsed in utter ruin. The stock had regressed, "gone back," and the civilization went back too. [16–19]

—§§§—

Let us now pass to America. The United States offers a more instructive field, because, with its more fluid social structure and its heterogeneous racial make-up, the correlations between intelligence, social or economic status, and racial origin can be studied simultaneously.

Before discussing these American experiments, let us recall certain facts. For a long time past American biologists and sociologists have been coming more and more to the following conclusions: (1) That the old "Native American" stock, favorably selected as it was from the races of northern Europe, is the most superior element in the American population; (2) that subsequent immigrants from northern Europe, though coming from substantially the same racial stocks, were less favorably selected and average somewhat less superior; (3) that the more recent immigrants from southern and eastern Europe average decidedly inferior to the north European elements; (4) that the negroes are inferior to all other elements. Now let us see how psychological tests have confirmed these biological and sociological conclusions.

One of the most recent of these experiments[7] was that conducted upon several hundred school children in the primary grades. The children were classified in two ways: according to racial origin, and according to economic-social status of parents. The racial classifications were: (a) children of American-born white parents; (b) children of Italian immigrants (mostly south Italians); (c) colored (negroes and mulattoes). The economic-social classifications of parents were: (1) professional; (2) semi-professional and higher business; (3) skilled labor; (4) semi-skilled and unskilled labor. The "I. Q." (intelligence quotient) of each category was then obtained, the object being to discover what correlations (if any) existed between racial origin, economic-social status, and intelligence. Here are the results:

Americans of social status (1) I. Q. = 125

Americans of social status (2) I. Q. = 118

Americans of social status (3) I. Q. = 107

Americans of social status (4) I. Q. = 92

All Americans grouped together I. Q. = 106

Italians I. Q. = 84

Colored I. Q. = 83

A similar experiment made on children in New York City public schools by the well-known authority, Professor S. M. Terman,[8] yields strikingly similar results. In this case the children were graded simply according to racial origin of parents, the classifications being: (1) Parents native-born white Americans; (2) parents north European immigrants; (3) parents Italian immigrants; (4) parents Portuguese immigrants. Here are the results:

American I. Q. = 106

North European I. Q. = 105

Italian I. Q. = 84

Portuguese I. Q. = 84

Note how the respective I. Q.'s of both the American and the Italian groups are identical in both experiments, although the children examined were, of course, not the same. . . .

Finally, let us note, in passing, some of the numerous researches which have been made on the intelligence of colored school children. Space forbids our going into this point. Suffice it to say that the results accord with what has been previously stated, namely: that **the intelligence of the colored population averages distinctly lower than the intelligence of native American whites, and somewhat lower than the intelligence of our least promising east and south European elements.**

So much for experiments upon children. Now let us consider similar psychological investigations of the intelligence of adults. Fortunately, we possess a great mass of valuable data from the mammoth investigations conducted by the United States army authorities upon more than 1,700,000 officers and men during the late war.[9] These investigations were planned and directed by a board of eminent psychologists. It is interesting to note that they were inspired, not by abstract scientific motives, but by motives of practical efficiency. . . .

So much for the aims behind the tests. Now for the tests themselves. As already stated, they were administered to more than 1,700,000 officers and men. Great care was taken to eliminate the disturbing influence of environmental factors like lack of education and ignorance of the English language. Separate tests were devised, and the close correlations obtained showed that inborn intelligence had been successfully segregated. Besides general intelligence gradings, special studies according to army rank, civilian occupation, racial origin, etc., were made on large groups consisting of "samples" taken at many points from the general mass.

The following is the system of general grading employed to indicate the degree of individual intelligence:

A = very superior intelligence; B = superior intelligence; C+ = high average intelligence; C = average intelligence; C– = low average intelligence; D = inferior intelligence; D– = very inferior intelligence; E = "unteachable men," rejected at once or after a short time.

Let us now see how the 1,700,000 men examined graded according to intelligence, and what *mental* age these classifications implied:

Grade	Percentage	Mental Age
A	4 1/2	18-19 (+)
B	9	16–17
C+	16 1/2	15
C	25	13–14
C–	20	12
D	15	11
D–	10	10

7. This experiment, conducted by Miss A. H. Harlitt of Bryn Mawr College, is quoted by McDougall [*Is America Safe for Democracy*] (p. 63–64), he having obtained the data directly from Miss Arlitt in advance of her own publication. The experiment seems to have been conducted in the year 1920.

8. L. M. Terman, *Intelligence of School Children*, p. 56 (New York, 1919).

9. Editor: For a full report on the U.S. Army intelligence tests see: *Memoirs of the National Academy of Sciences*, vol. XV, edited by then Major R. M. Yerkes. For an abridged version see Yerkes and Yoakum, *Army Mental Tests* (New York, 1920).

This table is assuredly depressing. Probably never before has the relative scarcity of high intelligence been so vividly demonstrated. **It strikingly reinforces what biologists and sociologists have long been telling us: that the number of really superior persons is small, and that the great majority of even the most civilized populations are of mediocre or low intelligence— which, be it remembered, neither education nor any other environmental agency can ever raise.** Think of this table's social significance! Assuming that these 1,700,000 men are a fair sample of the entire population of approximately 100,000,000 (and there is every reason to believe that it is a fair sample), this means that the average mental age of Americans is only about fourteen; that forty-five millions, or nearly one-half of the whole population, will never develop mental capacity beyond the stage represented by a normal twelve-year-old child; that only thirteen and one-half millions will ever show superior intelligence, and that only four and one-half millions can be considered "talented."

Still more alarming is the prospect for the future. The overwhelming weight of evidence (as we shall later show) indicates that the A and B elements in America are barely reproducing themselves, while the other elements are increasing at rates proportionate to their decreasing intellectual capacity: in other words, that intelligence is today being steadily *bred out* of the American population.

So much for the general results of the American army tests. Now let us consider some of the special classifications, notably those relating to the correlation of intelligence with army rank, civilian occupation, and racial origin. . . .

Finally, as to the correlation between intelligence and racial origin: two separate researches were made. The first of these was a comparison between white and colored drafted men; the other was a double grading of drafted men of foreign birth. . . .

	A	B	C+	C	C–	D	D–	E
White-Draft	2.0	4.8	9.7	20	22	30	8	2
Colored-Draft	.8	1.0	1.9	6	15	37	30	7
Officers	55	29	12	4	0	0	0	0

The above table needs no comment: it speaks for itself.

Now as to the second study concerning the correlation between intelligence and racial origin: the grading of foreign-born drafted men. This investigation, as already stated, was dual: the men were graded both up and down the scale; *i.e.,* both according to superiority and inferiority of intelligence. In the following tables "superiority" means A and B grades combined, while "inferiority" means D and E grades combined.

Table I. Percentage of Inferiority

Country of Birth	Percentage	Country of Birth	Percentage
England	8.7	Norway	25.6
Holland	9.2	Austria	37.5
Denmark	13.4	Ireland	39.4
Scotland	13.6	Turkey	42.0
Germany	15.0	Greece	43.6
Sweden	19.4	Russia	60.4
Canada	19.5	Italy	63.4
Belgium	24.0	Poland	69.9

Table II. Percentage of Superiority

Country of Birth	Percentage	Country of Birth	Percentage
England	19.7	Ireland	4.1
Scotland	13.0	Turkey	3.4
Holland	10.7	Austria	3.4
Canada	10.5	Russia	2.7
Germany	8.3	Greece	2.1
Denmark	5.4	Italy	.8
Sweden	4.3	Belgium	.8
Norway	4.1	Poland	.5

These tables are very interesting. Note how constant are the positions of national groups in both tables. Also, note how surely a high percentage of superiority connotes as low percentage of inferiority—and *vice versa.* Of course, these tables refer merely to the intelligence of foreign-born groups *in America;* they many not be particularly good criteria for the entire home populations of the countries mentioned. But they *do* give us a good indication of the sort of people America is getting by immigration from those countries, and they indicate clearly the intelligence levels of various foreign-born groups in America. And, once more we see a confirmation of those biological, sociological and psychological researches which we have previously mentioned; viz., that the intelligence level of the racial elements which American received from northern Europe is far above that of the south and east European elements. [62–72]

—§§§—

The unprecedented rapidity of our racial impoverishment seems due, as already stated, to many causes, some old and others new. We have seen that the stressful complexity of high civilizations has always tended to eliminate superior stocks by diverting their energy from racial ends to individual or social ends, the effects showing in an increase of celibacy, late marriage, and few children. Most of the phenomena underlying these racially destructive phenomena can be grouped under two heads: the high cost of living and the cost of high living. Behind those two general phrases stand a multitude of special factors, such as rising prices, higher standards, desire for luxury, social emulation, inefficient government, high taxation, and (last but not least) the pressure of ever-multiplying masses of low-grade, incompetent humanity, acting like sand in the social gears and consuming an ever-larger portion of the national wealth and energy for their charitable relief, doctoring, educating, policing, etc.

Now all these varied factors, whatever their nature, have this in common: they tend to make children more and more of a burden for the superior individual, however necessary such children may be for civilization and the race. The fact is that, under present conditions, comparatively few people of the right sort can afford to raise large families of well-born, well-cared-for, and well-educated children. This is the basic reason for that sharp drop in the birth-rates of the upper and middle classes of all civilized lands which has occurred during the past half century. Of course, the drop has been hastened by the simultaneous discovery of various methods for preventing conception which are collectively termed "birth control." However, it was not so much the new methods as the insistent economic and social pressure to employ them which accounts for the rapidity in the fecundal decline. Under the conditions of modern life a pronounced decline in the birth-rate was inevitable. To cite only one of several reasons, the progress of medical science had greatly reduced the death-rate and had thus made possible an enormous *net* increase of population. To have maintained an unchecked birth-rate would have meant for the Western nations congested masses of humanity like those of Asia, dwelling on a low level of poverty.

To escape this fate, the more intelligent and far-sighted elements in every civilized land began quickly to avail themselves of the new contraceptive methods and to limit the size of their families in this manner. That raised a great public outcry (largely on religious grounds), and in most countries[10] the imparting of contraceptive knowledge was legally prohibited. Such action was extremely stupid—and very disastrous. To far-sighted communities it should have been evident that with the appearance of new social factors like lowered death-rates, higher living costs, and rising standards, a lower birth-rate was simply inevitable; that civilized peoples could not, and would not, go on breeding like animals, as they had done in the old days of cheap living and low standards, when a high birth-rate was offset by the unchecked ravages of death.

But, a reduced birth-rate being inevitable, the only questions which remained were: How, and by whom, should it be reduced? Should it be by the traditional methods of celibacy (tempered by illicit sex-relations and prostitution), deferred marriage, infanticide, and abortion; or should it be by the new contraceptive methods? Again: Should all sections of the population lower their birth-rates, or should only the more intelligent classes? Unfortunately for the race, it was the latter alternative which prevailed. Instead of spreading contraceptive knowledge among the masses and thus mitigating as far as possible the evils of a racially destructive differential birth-rate, society succeeded in keeping the masses in ignorance and high fecundity, whereas it emphatically did not succeed in keeping contraceptive knowledge from the more intelligent, who increasingly practised birth control—and diminished their contributions to the population.

Here, then, was a great *potential* instrument of race betterment perverted into an agent of race decadence. With blind insistence upon mere numbers and an utter disregard of quality, society deliberately fostered the inferior elements at the expense of the superiors. The results are such as we have already examined in our study of the differential birth-rates of to-day. [117–120]

10. In a few enlightened communities, notably Australia, Holland, and New Zealand, contraceptive methods were welcomed and birth-control knowledge is freely imparted to all classes. The social and racial results have been excellent, particularly in minimizing differential birth-rates and thus averting sudden group shifts in the population.

The Birth Control Review

Population Problems in Asia

By Lothrop Stoddard
(Contributed to the First American Birth Control Conference)

XXVIII

Little Angels in the Flesh

1921

Archbishop Patrick Hayes versus Margaret Sanger

The Christ-Child did not stay His own entrance into this mortal life because His mother was poor, roofless and without provision for the morrow. He knew that the Heavenly Father who cared for the lilies of the fields and the birds of the air loved the children of men more than these.

—ARCHBISHOP PATRICK HAYES

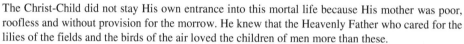

EDITOR

Many Sanger supporters—feminist, liberal, socialist or simply wealthy—had no problem with her enlightened, scientifically inspired bigotry. But as the most visible representative of 'unwanted' immigrants from southern Europe, the leadership of the Catholic church certainly did. Sanger was quite aware of this, noting in her second autobiography that, "it had been apparent that in the United States the Catholic hierarchy and officialdom was going to be the principal enemies of birth control."[1] What follows is the full text of a clash between New York City's Archbishop and Sanger as it appeared in the pages of the *New York Times* during Christmas of 1921.

Readers may wonder why the Archbishop did not attack Sanger's bigotry more aggressively, choosing instead to focus on the long-ago and far-from-home birth of a poor Jewish child as well as the births of severely deformed children. One reason is that it typically takes two or three generations before an immigrant group begins to feel enough at home in America to defend its right to speak out politically. Sanger was an exception to this pattern, an example of those who escape from a disliked group by adopting the attitudes of its enemies. Though her father was an Irish immigrant and her mother born into Catholicism, Sanger had so internalized the views of the nation's 'old stock' elite and modern liberals, that she did not hesitate to tell Catholics to shut up. The result was the grossest of hypocrisies. Sanger was delighted that liberal

1. Margaret Sanger, *Margaret Sanger, An Autobiography* (New York: W.W. Norton, 1938), 411.

Protestants, Unitarians, and newspapers such as the *New York Times* supported negative eugenic measures that included laws *requiring* the forced sterilization of anyone regarded as 'feebleminded'—including Catholics. But Catholics, Sanger claimed, had no right to oppose such laws. It was the foulest of double standards.

In addition, we should remember that well-regarded science and much of the establishment press of that day supported what Sanger said about the dangers of rapidly breeding immigrants and the feebleminded. The Archbishop may have read the *New York Times* daily and labored under the mistaken impression that he needed to take what it said seriously (Chapter XII). To his credit, however, he was willing to attack the dangerously slippery slope behind liberalism's better "not to have been born at all" arguments (Chapter XXI).

Though the Archbishop's remarks were intended for the Church faithful, it is somewhat unfortunate that he chose to speak in terms that, to non-Catholics, must have sounded like little more than religious platitudes. Talk of the "lilies of the field and the birds of the air" had its place, but those words did nothing to alter the high maternal and infant mortality in lower Manhattan. He also played into Sanger's hand by turning attention to extreme cases, those who "may appear to human eyes hideous, misshapen, a blot on civilized society." Sanger's target was far broader than a few severely disabled babies.

His failings became Sanger's opportunity, allowing her to use dismal maternal and infant mortality statistics to promote her agenda—even though logic would suggest that if you want to get rid of 'unfit' the death of a poor mother or her newborn baby is just as effective as birth control. Note from Sanger's remarks that at this time her movement considered it useful to regard abortion as "taking life." When circumstances changed, that deception would be cast aside.

There was a powerful literary model that the archbishop could have followed. In his classic, *A Christmas Carol,* Charles Dickens made a much more appealing case that the disabled and poor have as much right to be here as their more 'well born' counterparts. He did it by making such people attractive and their lives full of love and meaning.

—§§§—

Archbishop Hayes on Birth Control
Pastoral to "The Faithful" Calls Murder Horrible, but Terms Prevention Satanic.

Inveighs Against Divorce

And Condemns "the Freer and More Indulgent Conduct, More Particularly" Among Women.

"Archbishop Hayes on Birth Control,"
New York Times (Dec. 18, 1921), 16.

"In the name of the Babe of Bethlehem," Archbishop Patrick J. Hayes yesterday issued a Christmas pastoral to "the faithful" which will be read at all masses today in all of the more than three hundred churches of the Archdiocese of New York.

The pastoral is especially a protest against birth control. His former denunciation was against public discussion of birth control and arguments against it from the scientific and legal standpoint. The pastoral to be read today condemns birth control itself from the religious and moral standpoint.

Archbishop Hayes likewise denounces divorce and "the freer and more indulgent conduct, more particularly amongst the younger members of the female sex." The Archbishop commands his "faithful" to keep from their homes any literature on birth control as they would an evil spirit.

A second reason for the episcopal pastoral at this time was that Dec. 14 was the fiftieth anniversary of the proclamation by the Vatican of St. Joseph as "Patron of the Universal Church."

"The Christ-Child did not stay His own entrance into this mortal life because His mother was poor, roofless and without provision for the morrow," wrote Archbishop Hayes. "He knew that the Heavenly Father who cared for the lilies of the fields and the birds of the air loved the children of men more than these."

Calls Birth Control Satanic

"Children troop down from Heaven because God wills it. He alone has the right to stay their coming, while He blesses at will some homes with many, others with but a few or with none at all. They come in one way ordained by His wisdom. Woe to those who degrade, pervert, or do violence to the law of nature as fixed by the eternal decree of God Himself! Even though some little angels in the flesh, through the moral, mental or physical deformity of parents may appear to human eyes hideous, misshapen, a blot on civilized society, we must not lose sight of this Christian thought that under and within such visible malformation there lives an immortal soul to be saved and glorified for all eternity among the blessed of heaven.

"Heinous is the sin committed against the creative Act of God, who through the marriage contract invites man and woman to co-operate with him in the propagation of the human family. To take life after its inception is a horrible crime; but to prevent human life that the Creator is about to bring into being is satanic. In that first instance, the body is killed, while the soul lives on, in the latter not only a body but an immortal soul is denied existence in time and in eternity. It has been reserved to our day to see advocated shamelessly the legalizing of such a diabolical thing.

An "Unclean Abomination," He Says.

"In the name of the Babe of Bethlehem, whose law you Christian fathers and mothers love and obey, stop your ears to that pagan philosophy, worthy of a Herod, which ignoring revelation and even human wisdom sets itself above the law and the prophets of the old and the new dispensation of which the Christ Child is the beginning, the bond and the end. Keep far from the sanctuary of your Christian homes, as you would an evil spirit, the literature of this unclean abomination. Sin not against child who, after all, are the noblest stimulus and protection to marital affection, fidelity and continency.

"Another Christian reason the world needs to learn is God's law against divorce. Disastrous beyond possibility of description to society is the condition when women measure their lives, not by the number of their offspring but by the number of their husbands. Let us thank our Heavenly Father for the valiant women we all know— and their ideals of wifehood and motherhood carry on heroically the honor of the family. Neither height, nor depth, nor sorrow, nor pain, nor sin of husband nor ingratitude of children, nor privation, nor loss, nor opportunity of comfort, nor lure of pleasure can tempt such noble women to shirk their duty or break up their home.

—§§§—

Difficulties with Large Families

The Church recognizes the great difficulty experienced by parents in raising a large family, owing to conditions of society which man has made for himself by neglecting God's laws, but consider that this fact should be met by less capitalistic control of the labor market, higher wages, better housing, etc., and the stand of the Catholic Church is that the Birth Control League is endeavoring to correct a great evil by advocating another error.[2]

—P. J. WARD, CATHOLIC WELFARE COUNCIL, 1925

Mrs. Sanger Replies to Archbishop Hayes
Pastoral Letter Shows Church Clearly Understands Birth Control, She Says.

"Mrs. Sanger Replies to Archbishop Hayes,"
New York Times (Dec. 20, 1921), 20.

Mrs. Margaret Sanger, Chairman of the First American Birth Control Conference, yesterday replied to the statements regarding birth control in the Christmas pastoral letter of Archbishop Patrick J. Hayes.

"I am glad to learn from Archbishop Hayes's Christmas pastoral that the Church has a clear understanding of birth control, separating it definitely from taking life," says Mrs. Sanger in a statement. "Many people have been of the opinion that the Church confused the two ideas. From Archbishop Hayes's statement we at last realize that there is a perfect understanding by the Church of Rome of what the birth control movement stands for. For this I am grateful.

"I do not care to answer the Archbishop's theological statement concerning the will of the Almighty. His arguments are purely those based on assumption. He knows no more about the fact of the immortality of the soul than the rest of us human beings. What he believes concerning the soul after life is based on theory, and he has a perfect right to that belief; but we who are trying to better

2. Anne Kennedy, "Report of an Interview with Mr. P. J. Ward of the National Catholic Welfare Council, Washington, D.C." (Mar. 2, 1925), Sanger/Smith microfilm, S61:0197. Controversy resulted from this interview about whether Mr. Ward was empowered to speak for the Catholic Church and was quoted accurately. (This portion, however, does appear to reflect the stance of the Catholic Church.) It is possible that Sanger's organization was trying to set the Council up to say something that could be taken out of context and used to discredit it.

humanity fundamentally believe that a healthy, happy human race is more in keeping with the laws of God than disease, misery and poverty perpetuating themselves generation after generation.

"There is no objection to the Catholic Church inculcating its doctrines to its own people, but when it attempts to make these ideas legislative acts and enforce its opinions and code of morals upon the Protestant members of this country, then I do consider its attempt an interference with the principles of this democracy, and I have a right to protest."

—§§§—

Editor: Two months after their newspaper debate, Sanger published a reply. It included the following series of questions. There is little doubt that the Archbishop's reply would have been an unmistakable: "Yes, all children born under every sort of circumstance, however horrible, are to be regarded as gifts from God and never as 'imps fished up from perdition.' It is our responsibility to see that they have lives filled with love, lives that are infinitely better than 'non-existence.'" That was the great moral divide separating the evolutionary world view of Sanger and her colleagues and the Archbishop's Christian one. God doesn't blame children for the circumstances of their birth and isn't intent on exterminating all less-than-perfect people from the world. If that were the case, we would all be in trouble.

In the Name of the Babe of Bethlehem

Ralcy Husted Bell, "In the Name of the Babe of Bethlehem," *Birth Control Review* (Feb. 1922), 16–17.

"Children troop down from heaven," is a perfectly good religious phrase, and like all such phrases, perfectly meaningless; but as a poetic expression it is not bad; for the begetting of a babe should occur only during a heavenly state of mind in which both parties equally participate. Therefore, children conceived in this happy state may be said, poetically, to "troop down from heaven." But how about the children conceived in the Hell of brutality and hatred, of want and woe, of disease and crime? Are they also "little angels?" Are the children begotten in beastly passion by drunken fathers, and conceived by helpless, loathing mothers to be truthfully or even metaphorically described as little angels trooping down from Heaven? It seems rather more fitting to think of them as little imps fished up from perdition. Surely babes born of ignorance and debauchery, of disease and crime—children conceived in rape, terror, and imbecility—can not be regarded as having issued from Heaven, wherever Heaven is or whatever it may be. Would not the non-existence of such beings be better, all 'round, than their existence?

—§§§—

EDITOR

As you might expect, Sanger did not forget this debate. An expression that the Archbishop used, "Children Troop Down from Heaven," became the title for Chapter 3 of this book and her account of the clash found its way into Chapter 9.

In the latter she calls his Christmas Pastoral an example of just how "extreme" the Catholic point of view was, blaming it for "making this world a vale of tears." At that time, however, there was no way to spot "hideous" and "misshapen" children in the womb (much less before conception), so her argument made sense only if she thought that such children should be killed at birth and their mothers conditioned to regard such killing without sorrow. Fortunately for such babies, she did not seem self-critical enough to think that idea through. In all probability she was simply doing what she often did, indulging in self-righteous hatred—in this case against both Catholics and disabled children.

Sanger went on to claim that all "noble minds" recognized the Archbishop's Christian orthodoxy as a "menace to civilization." Her point of view, Sanger said, placed her among those who want to "better the conditions of this world." It also placed her and those "noble minds" in some rather nasty company.

Lives Devoid of Value

Whatever proportions these crimes finally assumed, it became evident to all who investigated them that they had started from small beginnings. The beginnings at first were merely a subtle shift in emphasis in the basic attitude of physicians. It started with the acceptance of the attitude, basic to the euthanasia movement, that there is such a thing as a life not worthy to be lived. This attitude in its early stages concerned itself merely with the severely and chronically sick. Gradually the sphere of those to be included in this category was enlarged to encompass the socially unproductive, the ideologically unwanted, the racially unwanted and finally all non-Germans. But it is important to realize that the infinitely small wedged-in lever from which this entire trend of mind received its impetus was the attitude toward the nonrehabilitable sick.[3]

—Dr. Leo Alexander, *New England Journal of Med.*

3. Leo Alexander, "Medical Science Under Dictatorship" *The New England Journal of Medicine* 241 (July 14, 1949), 44. Dr. Alexander, a Vienna-trained psychiatrist, was the medical consultant at the Nuremberg Trials. Readers may recall that we encountered these same "better not to live" arguments in the liberal *New Republic* editorials supporting birth control (Chap. XXI). These attitudes toward the less-than-perfect are apparently very deep-seated. Early calls for abortion legalization began with a 1962 case involving a woman, Sherri Finkbine, who had taken thalidomide, a drug that could cause birth defects.

Birth Control Review

UNPROFITABLE CHILDREN

Are these Bodies Fit Temples for Immortal Souls?

> *Every year millions of dollars are collected in taxes and spent on the maintenance of the defective, the feeble-minded, the insane and the criminals. This means that every man who is able to earn his own living has not merely to support himself and his family, but also to help to carry these expensive members of society. Every year the burden grows heavier, and yet most of it is easily avoidable. Mothers do not want to bear children who are bound to grow up to join the ranks of the dependent and unfit. The mothers are begging to be allowed to save society these huge expenditures, and yet the law and our inherited prejudices foolishly forbid them the knowledge of Birth Control which would speedily cut down the numbers of those who are now filling our hospitals, asylums and reformatories.*

XXIX

The Pivot of Civilization Reviewed

1923

Samuel J. Holmes

Zoology Professor, University of California, Berkeley

Mrs. Sanger makes no plea for an increased birthrate among the better stocks, although there is much evidence to show that these are in serious danger of extinction. She is so obsessed by the notion of birth control as a remedy for racial and social ills that the idea that any class should have more children is apparently not entertained.

Editor: No republication of Sanger's book would be complete without an illustration of how the original book was reviewed, in this case by a friendly but somewhat skeptical eugenist. This article reflects some of the doubts eugenists had about how successful Sanger's agenda would be in achieving a goal both so desperately wanted, a reduction in the birthrate of the 'unfit.'

"Book Reviews," *Eugenics Review* 15 (1923), 415–18. Holmes taught at the University of California, Berkeley. His books include: *The Trend of the Race* (1921), *Studies in Evolution and Eugenics (circa* 1923), *A Bibliography of Eugenics* (1924), *The Eugenic Predicament* (1933), and *The Negro's Struggle for Survival* (1937).

—§§§—

Mrs. Margaret Sanger has written a new book, *The Pivot of Civilization,* which is highly commended in the introduction contributed by H. G. Wells. Those familiar with Mrs. Sanger's writings will probably surmise that the pivot of civilization is birth control. On this the fate of civilization hinges. Mr. Wells tells us in the introduction that birth control is a *sine qua non* of world peace as well as of making the world a fit place in which to live. He warns the old civilization that "we cannot go on giving you health, freedom, enlargement, limitless wealth, if all our gifts to you are to be swamped by an indiscriminate torrent of progeny. We want fewer and better children who can be reared up to their full possibilities in unencumbered homes and we cannot make the social life and the world peace we are determined to make, with the ill-bred, ill-trained swarms of inferior citizens that you inflict upon us."

But we must not tarry with Mr. Wells. *The Pivot of Civilization* is a plea for birth control as a remedy both for social evils and the biological degeneracy of the race. Unlike many social reformers, Mrs. Sanger is not blind to the great differences in hereditary endowments among human beings and the profound bearing of these differences on our social and economic problems. She dwells upon the portentous "fertility of the feeble-minded," and the folly of a charity that results only in the increase of incapables and the imposition of increased burdens upon the normal elements of the community. Laws restricting marriage, it is pointed out, are powerless to correct these evils, for the feeble-minded and the degenerate would pay little attention to such well-meaning legislation. **On the other hand, "the programme of segregation and sterilization must be faced immediately. Every feeble-minded girl or woman of the hereditary type, especially of the moron class, should be segregated during the reproductive period."** Like Prof. Bateson,[1] however, Mrs. Sanger would "hesitate to proscribe the criminal," because crime is by no means a reliable index of bad heredity.

"Eugenics," the author tells us, "is chiefly valuable in its negative aspects." Birth control extended throughout all ranks of society would do much to reduce the fecun-

---

1. Editor: William Bateson, author of *Common Sense in Racial Problems,* is mentioned in Chap. 8 of *Pivot.*

dity of the dull and borderline cases which form no small part of our population, besides affording a great relief from the physical drag of frequent pregnancies and the burdens of large families. **The reviewer is in hearty accord with most of what Mrs. Sanger says on the evils of the present differential birth rate and the necessity of curtailing the propagation of undesirable breeds of humanity. The treatment of what is called positive or constructive eugenics is far less satisfactory.** If this subject "fails to awaken any permanent interest" more's the pity. It is something of a surprise to meet the statement that "constructive Eugenics aims to arouse the enthusiasm or the interest of the world fifteen or twenty generations in the future." Thus interpreted, it is not remarkable that it fails to arouse any enthusiasm in Mrs. Sanger. Racially, it is admitted the world is out of joint. But the eugenists, Mrs. Sanger thinks, will accomplish little by appealing to religion or a racial conscience in order to restore the balance. "The appeal to enter again into competitive child-bearing, for the benefit of the nation or the race or any other abstraction will fall on deaf ears."

Eugenists in general are, I believe, quite acutely conscious of the difficulties of positive eugenics, and are by no means suffering from the limitations of outlook of which they are accused. Prof. Karl Pearson would doubtless be amused by being told that he and his school "ignore or at least fail to record" the chief cause of the differential birth rate. "The scientific Eugenists," Mrs. Sanger tells us, "fail to recognize that this restraint of fecundity is due to a deliberate foresight, and is a conscious effort to elevate standards of living for the family and the children of the more responsible—and possibly more selfish—sections of the community." One is left in doubt as to what, according to Mrs. Sanger, the scientific eugenists really do think is the cause of this restraint of fecundity. If they are accused of making a futile appeal to the better stocks to "enter again into competitive child-bearing for the benefit of the nation or race," they must surely regard undue family restriction as resting on a voluntary basis or else they stultify their own advice. As a matter of fact, the scientific eugenists, far from ignoring the causes to which the author refers, have repeatedly dwelt upon them at length, as is shown, for instance, by Miss Elderton's[2] intimate study of the decline in the birth-rate in the north of England which was issued from Prof. Pearson's own laboratory.

2. Editor: Probably Ethel M. Elderton, author of *Report on the English Birthrate* (1914).

In her treatment of positive eugenics, Mrs. Sanger seems to be handicapped by a sort of blind spot in her vision of the subject. She may justly criticize many eugenists for their failure to advocate birth control for those classes whose multiplication it would be most desirable to curtail. But it is far more important to rescue our best inheritance from extinction than it is to apply birth control methods in the lower levels of humanity. **Mrs. Sanger makes no plea for an increased birthrate among the better stocks, although there is much evidence to show that these are in serious danger of extinction. She is so obsessed by the notion of birth control as a remedy for racial and social ills that the idea that any class should have more children is apparently not entertained.** Whatever may be said of its future possibilities, it must be admitted that, thus far, birth control is largely responsible for our present dysgenic situation. If one remedy for the present evils of birth control is more birth control, the remedy is quite inadequate if this practice is so overdone among the better stocks that it is causing their actual disappearance.

Readers of Mrs. Sanger's book will not find anything to disabuse their minds of the idea that such extreme birth restriction is quite justifiable. When we hear educated women glibly remark that "two children are quite enough," and exclaim over four children as a "large family," it indicates that they possess only the shallowest notions in regard to the most important function of their sex. And yet those who talk in this way are not stupid—at least not all of them—else we should be quite content to see their breed become extinct; they are simply incredibly ignorant and unreflecting in regard to the perpetuation of life. That our racial inheritance will deteriorate unless people of good hereditary qualities have at least the minimum of three or four children needed to keep up the stock is a proposition seemingly too obvious to require stating, nevertheless, it is something that needs to be said. It is something which probably most people do not know. It should have been said in Mrs. Sanger's book. The race cannot be regenerated by restriction alone. And to preach restriction without emphasizing the dangers of too much restriction is to incur a risk of doing more harm than good.

Birth control is a biological innovation of great moment in the history of the race. Man has evolved without it, although at the cost of much suffering and sacrifice of life. Its unwise employment for a few generations would have a disastrous effect upon our racial inheritance which it has taken untold ages to create. If so powerful an instrument for good or for ill is placed in the hands of human beings, they should know how to use it wisely. The birth control movement would gain greatly in usefulness and moral force if it laid greater stress upon the responsibility of those who take into their own hands the regulation of the birth supply. **There are multitudes of people of good inheritance whose financial circumstances would permit them to rear fair-sized families, but who are suffering their lines to become extinct through ignorance of one of the most important of all duties.** If no constructive eugenic scheme can succeed in getting more progeny out of the dwindling families of our intellectual and successful classes, we are indeed in a bad way.

There is no use in trying to force humanity into reckless, indiscriminate breeding, with all its attendant ills of war, misery and a high death rate, whatever may be said for these scourges from the standpoint of natural selection. Birth control has come to stay. Preaching and legislation are powerless to prevent it, and attempts to put it under the ban are productive only of harm. The advocates of birth control are doing a good work in their efforts to abolish our fanatical legislation against the dissemination of knowledge of the means of contraception. They are making a useful plea for a wider knowledge of sex, and a recognition of the importance of a normal sex life for both men and women. They are doing humanity a service in extending the benefits of birth control to the over-burdened mothers among the toiling masses. But their remedy is very far from a panacea for social ills, and, while our racial ills would be reduced by extending the practice throughout all ranks of society, our racial inheritance is bound to deteriorate unless the fecundity of superior types can somehow be increased.

There is no need of a "cradle competition." With birth control carried out most where it would do the most good, the race would still increase in numbers without burdening the capables with more than three or four children per family.[3] **Birth control can be and should be made a potent adjunct to eugenics, however far from being so it may be now.**

Notwithstanding the limitations of its counsel, Mrs. Sanger's book will prove of value in breaking down prejudice and in directing attention to problems of vital importance. It is written in an interesting and spirited manner; it manifests a broad humanitarian outlook; and in general, it is tempered with common sense.

—§§§—

Italians as Low-Grade

For the June General Meeting, the Society [for Constructive Birth Control and Racial Progress] had the pleasure of hearing a lecture by Dr. C. W. Saleeby . . . on "Birth Control and Eugenics—My Hopes and Fears."

He drew attention to the steady decline of the percentage of Anglo-Saxon stock in the United States, and the grave figures discussed in MacDougal's [McDougall's] little book, *National Welfare and National Decay*. . . .

At the same time in the States, certain low-grade races such, for instance, as the Southern Italians, have an extremely high birth-rate, which the lecturer maintained, formed too high a proportion of the American population.[4]

—BIRTH CONTROL NEWS, LONDON, 1922

3. Editor: It is doubtful that "capables" who believe that two children are enough liked these remarks about four children not being burdensome. Sanger herself had two sons and a daughter, but the daughter died young. Particularly in her second marriage, she had more than enough money to send her sons to boarding schools and employ servants for housework, making motherhood more a leisure-time activity than the great burden that she claimed it was for superior sorts of people such as herself.

4. "Dr. Saleeby's Lecture," *Birth Control News*, 1, No. 3 (July 1922), 2. Reprinted in: G. K. Chesterton, *Eugenics and Other Evils*, (Seattle: Inkling Books, 2000), 156. *Birth Control News* was published by Marie Stopes and was the British equivalent of Sanger's *Birth Control Review*.

XXX

Has America Too Many Children?

1925

Louis I. Dublin, Ph. D.

Statistician, Metropolitan Life Insurance

What is the usual effect on the spiritual life of those who through continued control keep their families down to next to nothing? This is probably the most serious single consequence of the current fashion, for the sterility of the body often leads to the even more serious sterility of the soul. A family without children to live for and to work for is tragic. This misfortune is courted by those who practice birth control.

Editor: In the 1920s, the federal government collected far less data about its citizens than it does today. As a result, large insurance companies were often the best source of information about population trends. In this article, an expert at one of those companies gave his opinion about population trends for a popular magazine. Sanger responds in the next chapter.

Louis I. Dublin, "Has American Too Many Children?" *Collier's* (April 25, 1925), 23.

—§§§—

Birth-control propaganda to date has emphasized almost altogether the necessity for population reduction as though there could be no doubt of overpopulation in the United States. I am willing enough to admit when I go home by subway that there are too many people in the world, and I have often felt that way with reference to the congested areas of our large cities. These undoubtedly represent ineffective community organization. On the other hand, we have a problem of underpopulation in our open rural areas. But neither picture alone justifies a snap judgment on the present status of our population.

A sound population analysis is called for which would attempt to relate our present population structure to the natural resources of the country and the efficiency with which we utilize our resources. These are highly technical matters which cannot be decided out of hand, not even by generous and high-minded people. If there ever was a question which called for expert handling, it is this one.

The impression in some places that our numbers are increasing too rapidly might perhaps follow from a cursory examination of the population figures of the country, but not from a more intensive study of the facts. It is true that past decades have shown large increases, but we must not forget that this growth, certainly in recent years, has been mainly the result of immigration and the relatively high fertility of the newcomers. It is only in the southern states and in the rural communities that the native population has much more than maintained itself in late years.

Now that immigration has been almost completely cut off as a source of population increase,[1] we must look to the fertility of the groups within the country and learn what the conditions of natural increase are among them. After careful study of the situation, I have become convinced that we are, in fact, rapidly approaching the condition of a stationary population. Our study shows that the accepted rates of natural increase in the United States are spurious and misleading.

If the age distribution of our population were the result of a prolonged continuation of our present rate of procreation, unaffected by padding from immigration, we

1. Editor: Dublin was referring to the strict 1924 immigration law, which set ample quotas for northern Europeans, who did not want to come here, and small quotas for those in eastern and southern Europe who did. The restriction on Jewish immigration from eastern Europe would bear particularly bitter fruit since it fed European anti-Semitism and gave Jews no place to flee as Nazism grew in power and influence.

should find that the ratio would fall from 23 per 1,000, which it is approximately to-day, to well below 20; and the corresponding death rate would increase from a little over 12 per 1,000, the present figure, to well over 15. These two corrections reduce the rate of natural increase from over 1 per cent per annum to only one half of 1 per cent. Our birth rate, moreover, is falling rapidly. It has declined more than 30 per cent in the last thirty years and the end is not yet. Even at its present level and with our current death rate, it will take more than 120 years to double our numbers. These figures agree with the estimates of Professor Pearl,[2] who on biological assumptions forecasts a population of less than two hundred millions in 2040.

It is not true that we are multiplying too rapidly and that we must resort to a nation-wide policy of birth reduction to keep our population within reasonable bounds. The real danger, if there is one, lies rather in the change in our internal composition which will follow a too rapidly declining birth rate and our approach to a stationary population. There is always grave danger, in such a shift, of weakening the social organization by increasing the proportion of defective and dependent stock. For it is

always the least desirable parents who are the last to curtail their fecundity. We likewise unduly increase the percentage of old people, whose support falls, more or less, upon the young, who, therefore, face the prospect in coming years of carrying greater burdens. Reduce the proportion of our young people, as we shall by curtailing birth rates, and at once the whole spirit of our intellectual and economic life will be modified.

Gynecologists and obstetricians of the highest standing have been very suspicious of some of the contraceptive devices in use and have traced serious affections [infections] back to them. I know nothing so tragic as the case of young people who avoid children in the first years of their married life only to find later that they cannot have them when they want them. The number of childless marriages is rapidly increasing to the point of becoming a serious problem, and there is evidence that contraceptive practices by young people may have a good deal to do with it. What is the usual effect on the spiritual life of those who through continued control keep their families down to next to nothing? This is probably the most serious single consequence of the current fashion, for the sterility of the body often leads to the even more serious sterility of the soul. A family without children to live for and to work for is tragic. This misfortune is courted by those who practice birth control.

—§§§—

---

2. Editor: Raymond Pearl (1879–1940) was the author of books such as: *The Biology of Population Control* (1925) and *The Present Status of Eugenics* (1928).

XXXI

Is Race Suicide Probable?

1925

Margaret Sanger

President, American Birth Control League

We have not chosen this Sisyphean task; it has been forced on us because we have left the production of American children to chance, instead of bringing this most important of all human functions within the sphere of choice.

EDITOR

A little more than three months after Dublin's article, *Collier's* published Sanger's response. As you might expect, her handling of population data was less professional than Dublin's. The high growth rate of the previous five years reflected the birthrate of recent immigrants, something would come down as a result of the strict immigration law that had taken effect the previous year. Sanger should have know that.

This article is particularly good at providing a window into what Sanger meant by various terms. She moved so easily from debating the country's rate of growth to hammering away at the costs of caring for the "incurably defective" that it is easy to suspect that her *quantity* arguments were merely a cover for *quality* arguments. She wrote about having too many people when her real objection centered on the sort of people they were.

Even more revealing was her claim that "we have left the production of American children to *chance,* instead of bringing this most important of all human functions within the sphere of *choice.*" She immediately followed that with a chilling quote from Luther Burbank, in which the world famous plant biologist was said to call for the nation to "stop permitting criminals and weaklings to reproduce." *Chance,* in Sanger's mind, meant the "haphazard, traditional, happy-go-lucky methods in producing the Americans of to-morrow—the *laisser-faire* policy," which had created, she believed, so many problems. (*Laisser faire,* from the French "to let do" means that the government does not interfere in an individual's behavior—that was what Sanger *opposed.*) When Sanger used the word "choice," she did not mean a choice made by each and every mother. She meant policies by which a few chose scientifically the childbearing of the many, typically concealing the coercion involved behind vague terms like "intelligent." Fabians first exposed her to this idea in 1913 Glasgow (and describe how it can be applied in Chapters V and VI). Though the idea was one that liberals and socialists were likely to find most congenial, in this article, Sanger attempted to link it to good business practices by pointing out how a good businessman manages his "overhead" and a "breeder of livestock" his cattle. For Sanger, people are a manufactured commodity whose quality and quantity are subject to the control of others. Her use of this argument suggests she believed most businessmen had not yet adopted her ideas.

Today we hear little of such arguments, but that isn't because they are no longer believed. Sanger's feminist and liberal successors have discovered that such arguments, while highly persuasive to themselves, do not win over a broader population that ranges from small businessmen to carpenters and housewives. To be effective, the arguments require an almost religious faith in evolution and an elitist attitude that the incompetent many exist to be manipulated by the few in the name of progress.

With that, we turn to the article that expresses, perhaps better than any other, what Sanger intended to do. Remember that she wrote this for *Collier's,* a general circulation magazine with a large and educated readership. There has never been any excuse for not knowing what her ideology and agenda.

Margaret Sanger, "Is Race Suicide Probable?"
Collier's (August 15, 1925), 25.

—§§§—
Mrs. Margaret Sanger here presents the positive argument on birth control. In the issue of April 25th Dr. Louis I. Dublin, took the other side. —[Collier's] Editor.

The people of the United States have been warned against the menace of birth control. If they exercise intelligent self-discipline, it is said, Americans may bring this country to destruction through depopulation. The fear that the present rate of increase in the population of the United States may be decreased and that our population may indeed be brought to a standstill through the practice of birth control is hardly substantiated by the last estimate of the Bureau of the Census. Within the last five years there has been an increase in our native population of approximately 6,000,000, or 1,200,000 a year.[1]

We are a nation of business men and women. We believe in efficiency, accuracy, and sound economic policy. If this is so, it strikes me that it is high time that not only American science but American business as well should begin to analyze the cost to the community of the haphazard, traditional, happy-go-lucky methods in producing the Americans of to-morrow—the *laissez-faire* policy approved by those who forget that the Biblical injunction "be fruitful and multiply" was given to Noah immediately after the Flood, when, according to the Biblical narrative, the entire population of the globe was eight.

It has been conservatively estimated that no less than one quarter of the gross incomes of our states is expended upon the upkeep of asylums for the feeble-minded and insane, the mentally defective, the criminal, the congenitally defective, the delinquent and the dependent. We are spending, billions, literally billions, keeping alive thousands who never, in all human compassion, should have been brought into this world. We are spending more in maintaining morons than in developing the inherent talents of gifted children. We are coddling the incurably defective and neglecting potential geniuses.

We have not chosen this Sisyphean task; it has been forced on us because we have left the production of American children to chance, instead of bringing

this most important of all human functions within the sphere of choice.

Until the leaders of American business decide to cooperate in this analysis of our biological and racial problems we shall be at a loss to answer such critics as Luther Burbank, to whom American civilization is deeply indebted. In a recent interview he is quoted as asserting:

America . . . is like a garden in which the gardener pays no attention to the weeds. Our criminals are our weeds, and weeds breed fast and are intensely hardy. They must be eliminated. Stop permitting criminals and weaklings to reproduce. **All over the country to-day we have enormous insane asylums and similar institutions where we nourish the unfit and criminal instead of exterminating them.** Nature eliminates the weeds, but we turn them into parasites and allow them to reproduce.[2]

Could any business maintain itself with the burden of such an "overhead"? Could any breeder of live stock conduct his enterprise on such a basis? I do not think so.

It is one of the bad habits of us Americans to estimate everything by magnitude, in terms of millions and billions. But in the matter of increasing population we must hesitate before throwing bouquets at ourselves. I am not a calamity howler, and I think my vision of the future of America is as cheerful as anyone's. But let me conclude with the emphatic statement of my conviction that mere increase in population has nothing to do with progress, nor can a decreasing birth rate by any stretch of the imagination be interpreted as an omen of national calamity.

The State v. Laissez Faire

The real and significant distinction is not that between "State interference" and "laissez faire," but between intelligent and scientific, i.e. systematic and far-sighted State-action on the one side and that peddling kind of playing at an occasional and condescending providence in small matters, which is often much worse than doing nothing at all.[3]

—DAVID G. RITCHIE, 1901

---

1. Editor: Dublin was highly critical of Sanger's use of population data. See: Louis I. Dublin, "The Fallacious Propaganda for Birth Control, *Atlantic Monthly* (Feb. 1926), 186–94.

2. Editor: I was unable to locate the source of this quote and remarks I did locate were more moderate. Perhaps this interview, if true, came on a day when he was in a bad mood.

3. David G. Ritchie, *Darwinism and Politics* (New York, 1901), 18.

THE PIVOT OF CIVILIZATION

By Margaret Sanger

WHAT THE PRESS IS SAYING:

"To read 'The Pivot of Civilization' is to bring the blush of shame to every sane-minded woman's face, shame because she has not given her help to Margaret Sanger in her noble crusade against the injustice done her own sex. Almost alone, Mrs. Sanger has fought the evil of enforced motherhood. But unjust opposition and cruel persecution have only strengthened her in her purpose and now she has gathered around her many of the greatest minds of the day . . . This is not a long book considering the enormous subject it so ably deals with; the style of writing is vivid, the facts horrifying—were it not that Mrs. Sanger has a solution of the problem."—MAUD DAVIS WALKER in *The New York Call.*

"She sees in voluntary motherhood the only way in which a better civilization can be started, and to the reader she gives most vividly her reasons for this belief." —*Bookman.*

"Mrs. Sanger's book is a clear and impressive statement of the case for Birth Control."—*N. Y. Herald.*

"Mrs. Sanger does not reveal herself as a professional feminist carried away by the emotional thrill of reform, but as a practical seer, unhampered by any sentimental glamour."—NALBRO BARTLY in *Philadelphia Ledger.*

"'The Pivot of Civilization' is an intelligent, courageous expression uttered with the breadth of the modern spirit and on the plane of a rational understanding of the complexity of social problems."—HARRY L. LURIE in Detroit *Free Press.*

"Steel-cold in its assembly and analysis of the facts accenting the discords in modern life, yet white-hot in its conviction that a new answer must be had for our social riddle, Mrs. Sanger's book is perhaps the most important, because the most challenging of the year.

"Mrs. Sanger is wholly convincing as to the urgent need of Birth Control, especially as to its greater promise than the program of the eugenists for the improvement of the race. . . . To whatever extent one agrees or disagrees, this is one of the books that should be read."—*Coast Artillery Journal.*

"A stimulating, moving, and genuinely valuable study of Birth Control viewed from the standpoint of its effect upon the race at large and upon the current confusion. Mrs. Sanger has done much and is doing much to make it clear that life can be better if women are more free and children are less cheap than they now are."—*N. Y. Nation.*

"Mrs. Sanger's book deserves a wide reading because it sets forth sanely and dispassionately a cause that has been much misunderstood, much of the misunderstanding being due to intentional misrepresentation."—Boston *Herald.*

Introduction
H. G. Wells

Birth control, Mrs. Sanger claims, and claims rightly, to be a question of fundamental importance at the present time. I do not know how far one is justified in calling it the pivot or the corner-stone of a progressive civilization.[1] These terms involve a criticism of metaphors that may take us far away from the question in hand. Birth Control is no new thing in human experience, and it has been practised in societies of the most various types and fortunes. But there can be little doubt that at the present time it is a test issue between two widely different interpretations of the word civilization, and of what is good in life and conduct. The way in which men and women range themselves in this controversy is more simply and directly indicative of their general intellectual quality than any other single indication. I do not wish to imply by this that the people who oppose are more or less intellectual than the people who advocate Birth Control, but only that they have fundamentally contrasted general ideas— that, mentally, they are *different*. Very simple, very complex, very dull and very brilliant persons may be found in either camp, but all those in either camp have certain attitudes in common which they share with one another, and do not share with those in the other camp.

There have been many definitions of civilization. Civilization is a complexity of countless aspects, and may be validly defined in a great number of relationships. A reader of James Harvey Robinson's *Mind in the Making*[2]

will find it very reasonable to define a civilization as a system of society-making ideas at issue with reality. Just so far as the system of ideas meets the needs and conditions of survival or is able to adapt itself to the needs and conditions of survival of the society it dominates, so far will that society continue and prosper. We are beginning to realize that in the past and under different conditions from our own, societies have existed with systems of ideas and with methods of thought very widely contrasting with what we should consider right and sane to-day. The extraordinary neolithic civilizations of the American continent that flourished before the coming of the Europeans, seem to have got along with concepts that involved pedantries and cruelties and a kind of systematic unreason, which find their closest parallels to-day in the art and writings of certain types of lunatic. There are collections of drawings from English and American asylums extraordinarily parallel in their spirit and quality with the Maya inscriptions of Central America. Yet these neolithic American societies got along for hundreds and perhaps thousands of years. they respected seed-time and harvest, they bred and they maintained a grotesque and terrible order. And they produced quite beautiful works of art. Yet their surplus of population was disposed of by an organization of sacrificial slaughter unparalleled in the records of mankind. Many of the institutions that seemed most normal and respectable to them, filled the invading Europeans with perplexity and horror.[3]

When we realize clearly this possibility of civilizations being based on very different sets of moral ideas and upon different intellectual methods, we are better able to appreciate the profound significance of the schism in our modern community, which gives us side by side,

---

1. Editor: As we saw in Chap. 5, Wells thought economically and politically. For him, socialism and a world state must come first. Only after they were established could serious attention be directed at using birth control to refine the human race. In contrast, Sanger thought sexually. She believed birth control could create a "race of thoroughbreds," who would establish an "earthly paradise." She blamed this disagreement on differences between men and women. Men, she said, recognized that wars and similar crimes were driven by *hunger*. But they failed to see the problems that resulted from uncontrolled *sex* and its inevitable product, large numbers of low quality children. In practice, both groups faced difficulties that required them to work together.

2. Editor: *The Mind in the Making: The Relation of Intelligence to Social Reform* (1921).

3. Editor: Are bloody human sacrifices really "respectable" or are they something that *ought* to fill us with "horror" wherever we are born? Clearly, the distinction between these two civilizations is not about small matters.

honest and intelligent people who regard Birth Control as something essentially sweet, sane, clean, desirable and necessary, and others equally honest and with as good a claim to intelligence who regard it as not merely unreasonable and unwholesome, but as intolerable and abominable. We are living not in a simple and complete civilization, but in a conflict of at least two civilizations, based on entirely different fundamental ideas, pursuing different methods and with different aims and ends.

I will call one of these civilizations our Traditional or Authoritative Civilization. It rests upon the thing that is, and upon the thing that has been. It insists upon respect for custom and usage; it discourages criticism and enquiry. It is very ancient and conservative, or, going beyond conservation, it is reactionary. The vehement hostility of many Catholic priests and prelates towards new views of human origins, and new views of moral questions, has led many careless thinkers to identify this old traditional civilization with Christianity, but that identification ignores the strongly revolutionary and initiatory spirit that has always animated Christianity, and is untrue even to the realities of orthodox Catholic teaching. The vituperation of individual Catholics must not be confused with the deliberate doctrines of the Church which have, on the whole, been conspicuously cautious and balanced and sane in these matters. The ideas and practices of the Old Civilization are older and more widespread than and not identifiable with either Christian or Catholic culture, and it will be a great misfortune if the issues between the Old Civilization and the New are allowed to slip into the deep ruts of religious controversies that are only accidentally and intermittently parallel.[4]

Contrasted with the ancient civilization, with the Traditional disposition, which accepts institutions and moral values as though they were a part of nature, we have what I may call—with an evident bias in its favour—the civilization of enquiry, of experimental knowledge, Creative and Progressive Civilization. The first great outbreak of the spirit of this civilization was in republican Greece; the martyrdom of Socrates, the fearless Utopianism of Plato, the ambitious encyclopaedism of Aristotle, mark the dawn of a new courage and a new wilfulness in human affairs. The fear of set limitations, of punitive and restrictive laws imposed by Fate upon human life was visibly fading in human minds. These names mark the first clear realization that to a large extent, and possibly to an illim-itable extent, man's moral and social life and his general destiny could be seized upon and controlled by man. But—he must have knowledge. Said the Ancient Civilization—and it says it still through a multitude of vigorous voices and harsh repressive acts: "Let man learn his duty and obey." Says the New Civilization, with ever-increasing confidence: "Let man know, and trust him."

For long ages, the Old Civilization kept the New subordinate, apologetic and ineffective, but for the last two centuries, the New has fought its way to a position of contentious equality. The two go on side by side, jostling upon a thousand issues. The world changes, the conditions of life change rapidly, through that development of organized science which is the natural method of the New Civilization. The old tradition demands that national loyalties and ancient belligerence should continue. The new has produced means of communication that break down the pens and separations of human life upon which nationalist emotion depends. The old tradition insists upon its ancient blood-letting of war; the new knowledge carries that war to undreamt of levels of destruction. The ancient system needed an unrestricted breeding to meet the normal waste of life through war, pestilence, and a multitude of hitherto unpreventable diseases. The new knowledge sweeps away the venerable checks of pestilence and disease, and confronts us with the congestions and explosive dangers of an over-populated world.[5] The old tradition demands a special prolific class doomed to labor and subservience; the new points to mechanism and to scientific organization as a means of escape from this immemorial subjugation. Upon every main issue in life, there is this quarrel between the method of submission and the method of knowledge. More and more do men of science and intelligent people generally realize the hopelessness of pouring new wine into old bottles. More and more clearly do they grasp the significance of the Great Teacher's parable.

The New Civilization is saying to the Old now: "We cannot go on making power for you to spend upon international conflict. You must stop waving flags and bandying insults. You must organize the Peace of the World; you must subdue yourselves to the Federation of all mankind. And we cannot go on giving you health, freedom, enlargement, limitless wealth, if all our gifts to you are to

---

4. Editor: Wells' hope (feigned or real) that historic Christianity would come to terms with his New Civilization have so far proved unfounded. Perhaps he realized that and simply wanted to draw off the poorly informed and less-committed.

5. Editor: Despite Wells' deceptive names, his new civilization had to be very authoritarian. If births were left unregulated, the economic success of the New Civilization would create increasing numbers (Malthus) of inferior people (Darwin). In what follows, Wells slid lightly over what he knew the New Civilization really meant: a world dictatorship, the systematic elimination of 'inferiors,' and the silencing of dissent.

be swamped by an indiscriminate torrent of progeny. **We want fewer and better children who can be reared up to their full possibilities in unencumbered homes, and we cannot make the social life and the world-peace we are determined to make, with the ill-bred, ill-trained swarms[6] of inferior citizens that you inflict upon us.**" And there at the passionate and crucial question, this essential and fundamental question, whether procreation is still to be a superstitious and often disastrous mystery, undertaken in fear and ignorance, reluctantly and under the sway of blind desires, or whether it is to become a deliberate creative act, the two civilizations join issue now. It is a conflict from which it is almost impossible to abstain. Our acts, our way of living, our social tolerance, our very silences will count in this crucial decision between the old and the new.

In a plain and lucid style without any emotional appeals, Mrs. Margaret Sanger sets out the case of the new order against the old. There have been several able books published recently upon the question of Birth Control, from the point of view of a woman's personal life, and from the point of view of married happiness, but I do not think there has been any book as yet, popularly accessible, which presents this matter from the point of view of the public good, and as a necessary step to the further improvement of human life as a whole. I am inclined to think that there has hitherto been rather too much personal emotion spent upon this business and far too little attention given to its broader aspects. Mrs. Sanger with her extraordinary breadth of outlook and the real scientific quality of her mind, has now redressed the balance. She has lifted this question from out of the warm atmosphere of troubled domesticity in which it has hitherto been discussed, to its proper level of a predominantly important human affair.

—H. G. WELLS, EASTON GLEBE

DUNMOW, ESSEX, ENGLAND

—§§§—

How Pivot Was Written

The movement was older in England and had already established its dignity there. Consequently, the presence at the [First National Birth Control] Conference of such an outstanding Englishman as Harold Cox was certain to carry weight. To persuade him to take the sea voyage I sailed for Europe. When I arrived in London I found him unwell, and his doctors at first refused him permission to travel. Under the circumstances it was very fine of him to promise to come. . . .

My object in England having been attained, I went on to Switzerland with a definite aim; I had formed a habit in my nursing days, when I was waiting in the night to give medicine or treatment to a patient, of occupying the time putting down experiences and thoughts that came to me. The same habit continued. After lectures, while I was still sizzling with excitement, I often relieved the tenseness by writing down answers to questions I feared I had not covered adequately. Before I knew it I had material gathered for a book, and even some chapters in rough draft. They needed pulling together and polishing off and I went to bed in Montreux for a month to do this. I had regarded *Woman and the New Race* as my heart book; this, *The Pivot of Civilization,* was to be my head book. I brought it back with me to the United States and Wells, who was reporting the Washington Disarmament Conference for the New York *World,* wrote an introduction.[7]

—MARGARET SANGER, 1938

6. Editor: "Ill-bred" refers to heredity and "ill-trained" to environment. Like Sanger, Wells cared little for fine distinctions between the two. In everyday life, parents provide both and that justifies all the brutal impositions that the New Civilization's ruling elite chooses to impose on them.

7. Margaret Sanger, *Margaret Sanger, An Autobiography* (New York: W. W. Norton, 1938), 299. (Also see her *My Fight for Birth Control,* p. 17.) Robert Parker helped to edit *Pivot* and became Sanger's ghostwriter. Sanger was in Switzerland for treatment at a TB sanitarium, and a pocket of the infection was later found beneath her tonsils. She explained her head/heart conflict in her 1938 biography (p. 25), when she described a time as a girl when she almost stole money from a woman's purse, only to be prevented by events she did not control. "Following this experience," she wrote, "which might have been called a spiritual awakening, I began to connect my desires with reasoning about consequences. This was difficult, because my feelings were strong and urgent. I realized I was made up of two Me's—one the thinking Me, the other, willful and emotional, which sometimes exercised too great a power; there was danger in her leadership and I set myself the task of uniting the two by putting myself through ordeals of various sorts to strengthen the head Me." This book, she was saying, is one dominated by "reasoning about [the] consequences" to civilization if certain birthrates are not curtailed. Sanger used this head/heart contrast often, most notably in Chap. 5 of this book.

1

A New Truth Emerges

Be not ashamed, women, your privilege encloses the rest, and is the exit of the rest,
You are the gates of the body, and you are the gates of the soul.—WALT WHITMAN

This book aims to be neither the first word on the tangled problems of human society to-day, nor the last. My aim has been to emphasize, by the use of concrete and challenging examples and neglected facts, the need of a new approach to individual and social problems. Its central challenge is that civilization, in any true sense of the word, is based upon the control and guidance of the great natural instinct of Sex. Mastery of this force is possible only through the instrument of Birth Control.

It may be objected that in the following pages I have rushed in where academic scholars have feared to tread, and that as an active propagandist I am lacking in the scholarship and documentary preparation to undertake such a stupendous task. My only defense is that, from my point of view at least, too many are already studying and investigating social problems from without, with a sort of Olympian detachment. And on the other hand, too few of those who are engaged in this endless war for human betterment have found the time to give to the world those truths not always hidden but practically unquarried, which may be secured only after years of active service.

Of late, we have been treated to accounts written by well-meaning ladies and gentlemen who have assumed clever disguises and have gone out to work—for a week or a month—among the proletariat. But can we thus learn anything new of the fundamental problems of working men, working women, working children? Something, perhaps, but not those great central problems of Hunger and Sex. We have been told that only those who themselves have suffered the pangs of starvation can truly understand Hunger. You might come into the closest contact with a starving man; yet, if you were yourself well-fed, no amount of sympathy could give you actual insight into the psychology of his suffering. This suggests an objective and a subjective approach to all social problems. Whatever the weakness of the subjective (or, if you prefer, the feminine) approach, it has at least the virtue that its conclusions are tested by experience. Observation of facts about you, intimate subjective reaction to such facts, generate in your mind certain fundamental convictions—truths you can ignore no more than you can ignore such truths as come as the fruit of bitter but valuable personal experience.

Regarding myself, I may say that my experience in the course of the past twelve or fifteen years has been of a type to force upon me certain convictions that demand expression. For years I had believed that the solution of all our troubles was to be found in well-defined programs of political and legislative action. At first, I concentrated my whole attention upon these, only to discover that politicians and law-makers are just as confused and as much at a loss in solving fundamental problems as anyone else. And I am speaking here not so much of the corrupt and ignorant politician as of those idealists and reformers who think that by the ballot society may be led to an earthly paradise. They may honestly desire and intend to do great things. They may positively glow—before election—with enthusiasm at the prospect they imagine political victory may open to them. Time after time, I was struck by the change in their attitude after the briefest enjoyment of this illusory power. Men are elected during some wave of reform, let us say, elected to legislate into practical working existence some great ideal. They want to do big things; but a short time in office is enough to show the political idealist that he can accomplish nothing, that his reform must be debased and dragged into the dust, so that even if it becomes enacted, it may be not merely of no benefit, but a positive evil. It is scarcely necessary to emphasize this point. It is an accepted commonplace of American politics. So much of life, so large a part of all our social problems, moreover, remains untouched by political and legislative action. This is an old truth too often ignored by those who plan political campaigns upon the most superficial knowledge of human nature.

My own eyes were opened to the limitations of political action when, as an organizer for a political group in New York, I attended by chance a meeting of women laundry-workers who were on strike. We believed we could help these women with a legislative measure and asked their support. "Oh! that stuff!" exclaimed one of these women. "Don't you know that we women might be dead and buried if we waited for politicians and lawmakers to right our wrongs?" This set me to thinking—not merely of the immediate problem—but to asking myself how much any male politician could understand of the wrongs inflicted upon poor working women.

I threw the weight of my study and activity into the economic and industrial struggle. Here I discovered men and women fired with the glorious vision of a new world, of a proletarian world emancipated, a Utopian world—it glowed in romantic colors for the majority of those with whom I came in closest contact. The next step, the immediate step, was another matter, less romantic and too often less encouraging. In their ardor, some of the labor leaders of that period almost convinced us that the millennium was just around the corner. Those were the pre-war days of dramatic strikes. But even when most under the spell of the new vision, the sight of the overburdened wives of the strikers, with their puny babies and their broods of under-fed children, made us stop and think of a neglected factor in the march toward our earthly paradise. It was well enough to ask the poor men workers to carry on the battle against economic injustice. But what results could be expected when they were forced in addition to carry the burden of their ever-growing families? This question loomed large to those of us who came into intimate contact with the women and children. We saw that in the final analysis the real burden of economic and industrial warfare was thrust upon the frail, all-too-frail shoulders of the children, the very babies—the coming generation. In their wan faces, in their undernourished bodies, would be indelibly written the bitter defeat of their parents.

The eloquence of those who led the underpaid and half-starved workers could no longer, for me, at least, ring with conviction. Something more than the purely economic interpretation was involved.[1] The bitter struggle for bread, for a home and material comfort, was but one phase of the problem. There was another phase, perhaps even more fundamental, that had been absolutely neglected by the adherents of the new dogmas. That other

phase was the driving power of instinct, a power uncontrolled and unnoticed. The great fundamental instinct of sex was expressing itself in these ever-growing broods, in the prosperity of the slum midwife and her colleague the slum undertaker. In spite of all my sympathy with the dream of liberated Labor, I was driven to ask whether this urging power of sex, this deep instinct, was not at least partially responsible, along with industrial injustice, for the widespread misery of the world.

To find an answer to this problem which at that point in my experience I could not solve, I determined to study conditions in Europe. Perhaps there I might discover a new approach, a great illumination. Just before the outbreak of the war, I visited France, Spain, Germany and Great Britain. Everywhere I found the same dogmas and prejudices among labor leaders, the same intense but limited vision, the same insistence upon the purely economic phases of human nature, the same belief that if the problem of hunger were solved, the question of the women and children would take care of itself. In this attitude I discovered, then, what seemed to me to be purely masculine reasoning; and because it was purely masculine, it could at best be but half true. Feminine insight must be brought to bear on all questions; and here, it struck me, the fallacy of the masculine, the all-too-masculine, was brutally exposed.[2] I was encouraged and strengthened in this attitude by the support of certain leaders who had studied human nature and who had reached the same conclusion: that civilization could not solve the problem of Hunger until it recognized the titanic strength of the sexual instinct. In Spain, I found that Lorenzo Portet, who was carrying on the work of the martyred Francisco Ferrer, had reached this same conclusion. In Italy, Enrico Malatesta, the valiant leader who was after the war to play so dramatic a role, was likewise combating the cur-

1. Editor: This was one of the few places where Sanger admitted that poor pay had something to do with social problems and she quickly dismissed that as a "purely economic interpretation." Beneath her abstractions, she blamed slum dwellers for the world's misery.

2. Editor: As we saw in this book's "historical perspective," there was nothing particularly "feminine" about Sanger's point of view. Both men and women held ideas much like hers long before she became politically active. These ideas were simply the theories of Malthus and Darwin applied rather unfeelingly to human society. Her reasoning was "feminine" only if feminine thinking means an ability to claim to hold two morally contradictory views at the same time—birth control *for* the poor and birth control *to get rid of* the poor. Many men shared that dubious ability. But as a woman, Sanger could more plausibly lie and claim concern for poor women.

rent dogma of the orthodox Socialists. In Berlin, Rudolph Rocker was engaged in the thankless task of puncturing the articles of faith of the orthodox Marxian religion.[3] It is quite needless to add that these men who had probed beneath the surface of the problem and had diagnosed so much more completely the complex malady of contemporary society were intensely disliked by the superficial theorists of the neo-Marxian School.

The gospel of Marx had, however, been too long and too thoroughly inculcated into the minds of millions of workers in Europe, to be discarded. It is a flattering doctrine, since it teaches the laborer that all the fault is with someone else, that he is the victim of circumstances, and not even a partner in the creation of his own and his children's misery. Not without significance was the additional discovery that I made. I found that the Marxian influence tended to lead workers to believe that, irrespective of the health of the poor mothers, the earning capacity of the wage-earning fathers, or the upbringing of the children, increase of the proletarian family was a benefit, not a detriment to the revolutionary movement. The greater the number of hungry mouths, the emptier the stomachs, the more quickly would the "Class War" be precipitated. The greater the increase in population among the proletariat, the greater the incentive to revolution. This may not be sound Marxian theory; but it is the manner in which it is popularly accepted. It is the popular belief, wherever the Marxian influence is strong. This I found especially in England and Scotland. In speaking to groups of dock-workers on strike in Glasgow, and before the communist and co-operative guilds throughout England, I discovered a prevailing opposition to the recognition of sex as a factor in the perpetuation of poverty. The leaders and theorists were immovable in their opposition. But when once I succeeded in breaking through the surface opposition of the rank and file of the workers, I found that they were willing to recognize the power of this neglected factor in their lives.

So central, so fundamental in the life of every man and woman is this problem that they need be taught no elaborate or imposing theory to explain their troubles. To approach their problems by the avenue of sex and reproduction is to reveal at once their fundamental relations to the whole economic and biological structure of society. Their interest is immediately and completely awakened. But always, as I soon discovered, the ideas and habits of thought of these submerged masses have been formed

through the Press, the Church, through political institutions, all of which had built up a conspiracy of silence around a subject that is of no less vital importance than that of Hunger. A great wall separates the masses from those imperative truths that must be known and flung wide if civilization is to be saved. As currently constituted, Church, Press, Education seem to-day organized to exploit the ignorance and the prejudices of the masses, rather than to light their way to self-salvation.

Such was the situation in 1914, when I returned to America, determined, since the exclusively masculine point of view had dominated too long, that the other half of the truth should be made known. The Birth Control movement was launched because it was in this form that the whole relation of woman and child—eternal emblem of the future of society—could be more effectively dramatized.  The amazing growth of this movement dates from the moment when in my home a small group organized the first Birth Control League. Since then we have been criticized for our choice of the term "Birth Control" to express the idea of modern scientific contraception.[4] I have yet to hear any criticism of this term that is not based upon some false and hypocritical sense of modesty, or that does not arise out of a semi-prurient misunderstanding of its aim. On the other hand: nothing better expresses the idea of purposive, responsible, and self-directed guidance of the reproductive powers.

Those critics who condemn Birth Control as a negative, destructive idea, concerned only with self-gratification, might profitably open the nearest dictionary for a definition of "control." There they would discover that the verb "control" means to exercise a directing, guiding, or restraining influence;—to direct, to regulate, to counteract. Control is guidance, direction, foresight. it implies intelligence, forethought and responsibility. They will find in the Standard Dictionary a quotation from Lecky[5] to the effect that, "The greatest of all evils in politics is power without control." In what phase of life is not "power without control" an evil? Birth Control, therefore,

---

3. Editor: In an age when European travel was only for the rich, Sanger's international name dropping must have impressed America-bound readers.

4. Editor: The term "birth control was actually coined by a journalist named Otto Bobsein but first used publicly by Sanger.

5. Editor: This is probably William E. H. Lecky (1838–1903), a historian and the author of many books including *History of European Morals from Augustus to Charlemange* (1900).

THE BIRTH CONTROL REVIEW

Dedicated to the Principle of Intelligent and Voluntary Motherhood

| Volume One | FEBRUARY 1917 | Number One |

means not merely the limitation of births, but the application of intelligent guidance over the reproductive power. It means the substitution of reason and intelligence for the blind play of instinct.[6]

The term "Birth Control" had the immense practical advantage of compressing into two short words the answer to the inarticulate demands of millions of men and women in all countries. At the time this slogan was formulated, I had not yet come to the complete realization of the great truth that had been thus crystallized. It was the response to the overwhelming, heart-breaking appeals that came by every mail for aid and advice, which revealed a great truth that lay dormant, a truth that seemed to spring into full vitality almost over night—that could never again be crushed to earth!

Nor could I then have realized the number and the power of the enemies who were to be aroused into activity by this idea. So completely was I dominated by this conviction of the efficacy of "control," that I could not until later realize the extent of the sacrifices that were to be exacted of me and of those who supported my campaign. The very idea of Birth Control resurrected the spirit of the witch-hunters of Salem. Could they have usurped the power, they would have burned us at the stake. Lacking that power, they used the weapon of suppression, and invoked medieval statutes to send us to jail. These tactics had an effect the very opposite to that intended. They demonstrated the vitality of the idea of Birth Control, and acted as counter-irritant on the actively intelligent sections of the American community. Nor was the interest aroused confined merely to America. The neo-Malthusian[7] movement in Great Britain with its history of undaunted bravery, came to our support; and I had the comfort of knowing that the finest minds of England

did not hesitate a moment in the expression of their sympathy and support.

In America, on the other hand, I found from the beginning until very recently that the so-called intellectuals exhibited a curious and almost inexplicable reticence in supporting Birth Control.[8] They even hesitated to voice any public protest against the campaign to crush us which was inaugurated and sustained by the most reactionary and sinister forces in American life.[9] It was not inertia or any lack of interest on the part of the masses that stood in our way. It was the indifference of the intellectual leaders.

Writers, teachers, ministers, editors, who form a class dictating, if not creating, public opinion, are, in this country, singularly inhibited or unconscious of their true function in the community. One of their first duties, it is certain, should be to champion the constitutional right of free speech and free press, to welcome any idea that tends to awaken the critical attention of the great American public. But those who reveal themselves as fully cognizant of this public duty are in the minority, and must possess more than average courage to survive the enmity such an attitude provokes.

One of the chief aims of the present volume is to stimulate American intellectuals to abandon the mental habits which prevent them from seeing human nature as a whole, instead of as something that can be pigeonholed into various compartments or classes. Birth Control affords an approach to the study of humanity because it cuts through the limitations of current methods. It is economic, biological, psychological and spiritual in its aspects. It awakens the vision of mankind moving and changing, of humanity growing and developing, coming

---

6. Editor: The term leaves unsaid who does the controlling. Obviously, for birth control to be "intelligent" those doing it must be "intelligent," something not true of the "feeble-minded." Sanger's shrewder supporters knew to read between the lines.

7. Editor: Malthus and the movement he spawned, political economy, felt population could only be limited by sexual restraint or death, not the primitive birth control technology of his day. Neo-Malthusians arose with improvements in that technology and believed birth control could solve the population problem.

8. Editor: As we've seen, this reticence was anything but indifference. There was a confusion over whether to push for increased birthrates among the "fit" or lower birthrates among "unfit." The law is a blunt instrument. Ending bans on birth control would make it easier for both the "fit" and "unfit" to have smaller families. The long and vocal debate centered on which would be most affected. From her other remarks, we know that Sanger understood this. Here she is simply trying to promote herself as a 'courageous pioneer.'

9. Editor: The reactionary forces were: 1. Catholicism, 2. Theodore Roosevelt, 3. Fundamentalism, and 4. Anthony Comstock (U. S. Post Office). "Sinister" hardly describes such people and opposing them took no courage. Sanger simply did not take kindly to those who refused to praise her.

to fruition, of a race creative, flowering into beautiful expression through talent and genius.[10]

As a social program, Birth Control is not merely concerned with population questions. In this respect, it is a distinct step in advance of earlier Malthusian doctrines, which concerned themselves chiefly with economics and population.[11] Birth Control concerns itself with the spirit no less than the body. It looks for the liberation of the spirit of woman and through woman of the child. To-day motherhood is wasted, penalized, tortured. Children brought into the world by unwilling mother suffer an initial handicap that cannot be measured by cold statistics. Their lives are blighted from the start. To substantiate this fact, I have chosen to present the conclusions of reports on Child Labor and records of defect and delinquency published by organizations with no bias in favor of Birth Control. The evidence is before us. It crowds in upon us from all sides. But prior to this new approach, no attempt had been made to correlate the effects of the blind and irresponsible play of the sexual instinct with its deep-rooted causes.

The duty of the educator and the intellectual creator of public opinion is, in this connection, of the greatest importance. For centuries official moralists, priests, clergymen and teachers, statesmen and politicians have preached the doctrine of glorious and divine fertility. To-day, we are confronted with the world-wide spectacle of the realization of this doctrine. It is not without significance that the moron and the imbecile set the pace in living up to this teaching, and that the intellectuals, the educators, the archbishops, bishops, priests, who are most insistent on it, are the staunchest adherents in their own lives of celibacy and non-fertility. It is time to point out to the champions of unceasing and indiscriminate fertility the results of their teaching.

One of the greatest difficulties in giving to the public a book of this type is the impossibility of keeping pace with the events and changes of a movement that is now, throughout the world, striking root and growing. The changed attitude of the American Press indicates that enlightened public opinion no longer tolerates a policy of silence upon a question of the most vital importance. Almost simultaneously in England and America, two incidents have broken through the prejudice and the

guarded silence of centuries. At the church Congress in Birmingham, October 12, 1921, Lord Dawson, the king's physician, in criticizing the report of the Lambeth Conference concerning Birth Control, delivered an address defending this practice. Of such bravery and eloquence that it could not be ignored, this address electrified the entire British public. It aroused a storm of abuse, and yet succeeded, as no propaganda could, in mobilizing the forces of progress and intelligence in the support of the cause.

Just one month later, the First American Birth Control Conference culminated in a significant and dramatic incident. At the close of the conference a mass meeting was scheduled in the Town Hall, New York City, to discuss the morality of Birth Control.[12] Mr. Harold Cox, editor of the *Edinburgh Review,* who had come to New York to attend the conference, was to lead the discussion. It seemed only natural for us to call together scientists, educators, members of the medical profession, and theologians of all denominations, to ask their opinion upon this uncertain and important phase of the controversy. Letters were sent to eminent men and women in different parts of the world. In this letter we asked the following questions:—

1. Is over-population a menace to the peace of the world?
2. Would the legal dissemination of scientific Birth Control information, through the medium of clinics by the medical profession, be the most logical method of checking the problem of over-population?
3. Would knowledge of Birth Control change the moral attitude of men and women toward the marriage bond, or lower the moral standards of the youth of the country?
4. Do you believe that knowledge which enables parents to limit their families will make for human happiness, and raise the moral, social and intellectual standards of population?

We sent this questionnaire not only to those who we thought might agree with us, but we sent it also to our known opponents.

When I arrived at the Town Hall the entrance was guarded by policemen. They told me there would be no meeting. Before my arrival executives had been greeted by Monsignor Dineen, secretary of Archbishop Hayes, of the Roman Catholic archdiocese, who informed them that the meeting would be prohibited on the ground that it was contrary to public morals. The police had closed the doors. When they opened them to permit the exit of the

---

10. Editor: In other words, Sanger hoped this book would convince waffling intellectuals to support her agenda.
11. Editor: Sanger claimed that Neo-Malthusians focused on the problems created by excessive *quantity* rather than a decline in the *quality* of those born. That she intended to change. She got more specific in the pages that follow.

---

12. Editor: This Catholic-led disruption is discussed in the introduction to Chap. XXVII.

The World

FRIDAY, OCTOBER 15, 1920

N.Y. WOMEN'S CLUBS COME OUT IN FAVOR OF BIRTH CONTROL

large audience which had gathered, Mr. Cox and I entered. I attempted to exercise my constitutional right of free speech, but was prohibited and arrested. Miss Mary Winsor, who protested against this unwarranted arrest, was likewise dragged off to the police station. The case was dismissed the following morning. The ecclesiastic instigators of the affair were conspicuous by their absence from the police court. But the incident was enough to expose the opponents of Birth Control and the extreme methods they used to combat our progress. The case was too flagrant, too gross an affront, to pass unnoticed by the newspapers. The progress of our movement was indicated in the changed attitude of the American Press, which had perceived the danger to the public of the unlawful tactics used by the enemies of Birth Control in preventing open discussion of a vital question.[13]

No social idea has inspired its advocates with more bravery, tenacity, and courage than Birth Control. From the early days of Francis Place and Richard Carlile, to those of the Drysdales and Edward Tru[e]love, of Bradlaugh and Mrs. Annie Besant,[14] its advocates have faced imprisonment and ostracism. In the whole history of the English movement, there has been no more courageous figure than that of the venerable Alice Drysdale Vickery,

the undaunted torch-bearer who has bridged the silence of forty-four years—since the Bradlaugh-Besant trial. She stands head and shoulders above the professional feminists. Serenely has she withstood jeers and jests. Today, she continues to point out to the younger generation which is devoted to newer palliatives the fundamental relation between Sex and Hunger.

The First American Birth Control Conference, held at the same time as the Washington Conference for the Limitation of Armaments, marks a turning-point in our approach to social problems. The Conference made evident the fact that in every field of scientific and social endeavor the most penetrating thinkers are now turning to the consideration of our problem as a fundamental necessity to American civilization. They are coming to see that a *qualitative* factor as opposed to a *quantitative* one is of primary importance in dealing with the great masses of humanity.

Certain fundamental convictions should be made clear here. The program for Birth. Control is not a charity. It is not aiming to interfere in the private lives of poor people, to tell them how many children they should have, nor to sit in judgment upon their fitness to become parents.[15] It aims, rather, to awaken responsibility, to answer the demand for a scientific means by which and through which each human life may be self-directed and self-controlled. The exponent of Birth Control, in short, is convinced that social regeneration, no less than individual regeneration, must come from within. Every potential parent, and especially every potential mother, must be brought to an acute realization of the primary and individual responsibility of bringing children into this world. Not until the parents of this world are given control over their reproductive faculties will it be possible to improve the quality of the generations of the future, or even to maintain civilization at its present level. Only when given intelligent mastery of the procreative powers can the great mass of humanity be aroused to a realization of responsibility of parenthood. We have come to the conclusion, based on widespread investigation and experi-

---

13. Editor: It would be more accurate to say that the press and liberals who were uneasy about being *openly* connected with Sanger's anti-immigrant, anti-poor stance were delighted to take it on as a free-speech issue. That provided cover.

14. Editor: Francis Place and Richard Carlile were radical 19th century reformers. Charles Bradlaugh and Anne Besant were prosecuted (but only mildly punished) in 1876–77 England for publishing Charles Knowlton's early birth control tract, *The Fruits of Philosophy*. In 1878, Edward Truelove was unsuccessfully prosecuted in an English court for publishing Robert Dale Owen's 1833 pamphlet on birth control. In the quaint English fashion, the Drysdale family made Neo-Malthusianism its personal cause and included Alice Drysdale Vickery, to whom Sanger dedicated *The Pivot of Civilization.*

15. Editor: Given the great wealth of cases where Sanger said otherwise, this disclaimer shouldn't be taken seriously. The best that can be made of it, without turning it into an outright lie, is that Sanger heavily qualifies her non-interference with a requirement that the poor come to think as she thinks—hence her remarks about "acute realization," "aroused to a realization," and "education for parenthood." Think like her, and you can do as you please (meaning as she pleases). Think otherwise and things get nasty. Because they deny any role for 'faith,' secular ideologies leave little room for those who disagree—as little as a mathematician might give to someone claiming that 2+2=5.

ence, that education for parenthood must be based upon the needs and demands of the people themselves. An idealistic code of sexual ethics, imposed from above, a set of rules devised by high-minded theorists who fail to take into account the living conditions and desires of the masses, can never be of the slightest value in effecting change in the customs of the people. Systems so imposed in the past have revealed their woeful inability to prevent the sexual and racial chaos into which the world has drifted.[16]

The universal demand for practical education in Birth Control is one of the most hopeful signs that the masses themselves to-day possess the divine spark of regeneration. It remains for the courageous and the enlightened to answer this demand, to kindle the spark, to direct a thorough education in sex hygiene based upon this intense interest.

Birth Control is thus the entering wedge for the educator. In answering the needs of these thousands upon thousands of submerged mothers, it is possible to use their interest as the foundation for education in prophylaxis, hygiene and infant welfare. The potential mother can then be shown that maternity need not be slavery but may be the most effective avenue to self-development and self-realization. Upon this basis only may we improve the quality of the race.

How Civilizations Decline and Fall

Every human being, and therefore every community of human beings, every populace, inherits from its ancestry a stock of innate qualities which enable it to enjoy, to sustain, to promote, a civilization of a certain degree of complexity. As civilization advances, it makes greater and greater demands on these qualities, requires their exercise and development in ever fuller degree; until it approaches a point at which its complexity outruns the possibilities of the innate qualities. At the same time it tends positively to impair those qualities; so that, as the demands increase, the latent reserves of human quality are diminished. Therefore a time comes when the supply no longer equals the demand; that

moment is the culminating point of that civilization and of that people, the turning-point of the curve from which the downward plunge begins.[17]

—WILLIAM McDOUGALL, HARVARD

The lack of balance between the birth-rate of the "unfit" and the "fit," admittedly the greatest present menace to the civilization, can never be rectified by the inauguration of a cradle competition between these two classes. The example of the inferior classes, the fertility of the feeble-minded, the mentally defective, the poverty-stricken, should not be held up for emulation to the mentally and physically fit, and therefore less fertile, parents of the educated and well-to-do classes.[18] On the contrary, the most urgent problem to-day is how to limit and discourage the over-fertility of the mentally and physically defective. Possibly drastic and Spartan methods[19] may be forced upon American society if it continues complacently to encourage the chance and chaotic breeding that has resulted from our stupid, cruel sentimentalism.

To effect the salvation of the generations of the future—nay, of the generations of to-day—our greatest need, first of all, is the ability to face the situation without flinching; to cooperate in the formation of a code of sexual ethics based upon a thorough biological and psychological understanding of human nature; and then to answer the questions and the needs of the people with all the intelligence and honesty at our command. If we can summon the bravery to do this, we shall best be serving the pivotal interests of civilization.

To conclude this introduction: my initiation, as I have confessed, was primarily an emotional one. My interest in Birth Control was awakened by experience. Research and investigation have followed. Our effort has been to raise our program from the plane of the emotional to the plane of the scientific. Any social progress, it is my belief, must purge itself of sentimentalism and pass through the crucible of science. We are willing to submit Birth Control to this test. It is part of the purpose of this book to appeal to the scientist for aid, to arouse that interest which will result in widespread research and investigation. I believe that my personal experience with this

---

16. Editor: Sanger was referring to those who simply told the poor to avoid children by avoiding sex. She wanted something more practical. In the end, her agenda boiled down to an attempt to use birth control technology as the "entering wedge" to import into the culture of the poor the same attitudes that were reducing elite birthrates: the separation of sex from reproduction and a mindset that children interfere with "self-realization." Unfortunately, the first increases promiscuity, while the second leads to the neglect and abuse of children who are born. It seems likely that the two attitudes create more problems than they solve.

17. William McDougall, *Is America Safe for Democracy?* (New York: Charles Scribner's Sons, 1921), 17. Replace McDougall's "turning-point" with "pivot" and you have Sanger's main point, that without birth control applied as she describes, our civilization will plunge downward into oblivion.

18. Editor: Notice how quickly Sanger discarded her promise not "sit in judgment" on poor parents.

19. Editor: The ancient Greeks in Sparta killed defective babies.

idea must be that of the race at large. We must temper our emotion and enthusiasm with the impersonal determination of science. We must unite in the task of creating an instrument of steel, strong but supple, if we are to triumph finally in the war for human emancipation.[20]

—§§§—

Supernatural Implantation

For the plain man, and law and medicine also, accepted the traditional assumption that our mental powers are the expression of a supernatural principle, the soul,

miraculously implanted in each one of us at birth; and, while they recognized great differences in bodily endowment, they ignored comparable differences of mental endowment, with certain exceptions.[21]

—WILLIAM McDOUGALL, HARVARD

20. Editor: "Emancipation" here has a special meaning. Individual couples are *not* to be free to have children as they desire. Instead, an abstraction, humanity, is to be freed from two other abstractions threatening our civilization: overpopulation and the multiplication of the 'unfit.' In the language of Winwood Reade, the "martyrdom of man" to nature's cruel laws will come to an end through scientifically applied birth control.

21. William McDougall, *Is America Safe for Democracy?* (New York: Charles Scribner's Sons, 1921), 39. The exceptions were idiocy, madness and genius. McDougall also noted that medicine and law were beginning to differ with the "plain man" on this point. To improve his debating position, he exaggerated the 'plain man's' viewpoint. Ordinary people (i.e. those who are not Harvard professors) recognized as a matter of course that people vary greatly in abilities. But, reflecting their Judeo-Christian heritage (Sanger's "sentimentalism"), they believed that there was a God-given specialness of about being human that far outweighs those differences and gave value to each and every human being.

IS IT FAIR?

26 Families—80 Children—3 Rooms to a Family

Morris in the New York Mail
1 Family—2 Children—35 Rooms

2

Conscripted Motherhood

Their poor, old ravaged and stiffened faces, their poor, old bodies dried up with ceaseless toil, their patient souls made me weep. They are our conscripts. They are the venerable ones whom we should reverence. All the mystery of womanhood seems incarnated in their ugly being—the Mothers! the Mothers! Ye are all one! —From the *Letters of William James*

Motherhood, which is not only the oldest but the most important profession in the world, has received few of the benefits of civilization. It is a curious fact that a civilization devoted to mother-worship, that publicly professes a worship of mother and child, should close its eyes to the appalling waste of human life and human energy resulting from those dire consequences of leaving the whole problem of child-bearing to chance and blind instinct. It would be untrue to say that among the civilized nations of the world to-day, the profession of motherhood remains in a barbarous state. The bitter truth is that motherhood, among the larger part of our population, does not rise to the level of the barbarous or the primitive. Conditions of life among the primitive tribes were rude enough and severe enough to prevent the unhealthy growth of sentimentality, and to discourage the irresponsible production of defective children. Moreover, there is ample evidence to indicate that even among the most primitive peoples the function of maternity was recognized as of primary and central importance to the community.[1]

If we define civilization as increased and increasing responsibility based on vision and foresight, it becomes painfully evident that the profession of motherhood as practised to-day is in no sense civilized. Educated people derive their ideas of maternity for the most part, either from the experience of their own set, or from visits to impressive hospitals where women of the upper classes receive the advantages of modern science and modern nursing. From these charming pictures they derive their complacent views of the beauty of motherhood and their confidence for the future of the race. The other side of the picture is revealed only to the trained investigator, to the patient and impartial observer who visits not merely one or two "homes of the poor," but makes detailed studies of

---

1. Editor: Though Sanger seemed to be directing her attack at our society's "profession of motherhood," her real target is not hard to discern. By engaging in the "irresponsible production of defective children" under barbaric conditions, poor mothers were not showing proper "vision and foresight." Simply bringing them birth control technology may seem non-coercive, but what if they continue their barbaric behavior?

town after town, obtains the history of each mother, and finally correlates and analyzes this evidence. Upon such a basis are we able to draw conclusions concerning this strange business of bringing children into the world.[2]

Every year I receive thousands of letters from women in all parts of America, desperate appeals to aid them to extricate themselves from the trap of compulsory maternity. Lest I be accused of bias and exaggeration in drawing my conclusions from these painful human documents, I prefer to present a number of typical cases recorded in the reports of the United States Government, and in the evidence of trained and impartial investigators of social agencies more generally opposed to the doctrine of Birth Control than biased in favor of it.

A perusal of the reports on infant mortality in widely varying industrial centers of the United States, published during the past decade by the Children's Bureau of the United States Department of Labor, forces us to a realization of the immediate need of detailed statistics concerning the practice and results of uncontrolled breeding. Some such effort as this has been made by the Galton Laboratory of National Eugenics in Great Britain. The Children's Bureau reports only incidentally present this impressive evidence. They fail to coordinate it. While there is always the danger of drawing giant conclusions from pigmy premises, here is overwhelming evidence concerning irresponsible parenthood that is ignored by governmental and social agencies.

I have chosen a small number of typical cases from these reports. Though drawn from widely varying sources, they all emphasize the greatest crime of modern civilization—that of permitting motherhood to be left to blind chance, and to be mainly a function of the most abysmally ignorant and irresponsible classes of the community.[3]

Here is a fairly typical case from Johnstown, Pennsylvania. A woman of thirty-eight years had undergone thirteen pregnancies in seventeen years. Of eleven live births and two premature stillbirths, only two children were alive at the time of the government agent's visit. The second to eighth, the eleventh and the thirteenth had died of bowel trouble, at ages ranging from three weeks to four months. The only cause of these deaths the mother could give was that "food did not agree with them." She confessed quite frankly that she believed in feeding babies, and gave them everything anybody told her to give them. She began to give them at the age of one month, bread, potatoes, egg, crackers, etc. For the last baby that died, this mother had bought a goat and gave its milk to the baby; the goat got sick, but the mother continued to give her baby its milk until the goat went dry. Moreover, she directed the feeding of her daughter's baby until it died at the age of three months. "On account of the many children she had had, the neighbors consider her an authority on baby care."

Motherhood as a Luxury

The curious point is that the hopeful one concludes by saying, "When people have large families and small wages, not only is there a high infantile death-rate, but often those who do live to grow up are stunted and weakened by having had to share the family income for a time with those who died early. There would be less unhappiness if there were no unwanted children." You will observe that he tacitly takes it for granted that the small wages and the income, desperately shared, are the fixed points, like day and night, the conditions of human life. Compared with them marriage and maternity are luxuries, things to be modified to suit the wage-market.[4]

—G. K. CHESTERTON, *EUGENICS AND OTHER EVILS*

Lest this case be considered too tragically ridiculous to be accepted as typical, the reader may verify it with an almost interminable list of similar cases.[5] Parental irresponsibility is significantly illustrated in another case:

---

2. Editor: Sanger's arguments appealed to women like herself, women who provide for their children materially but who, because of a career or busy social life, neglect them emotionally. Sanger attached no value to the love a poor mother may bestow on her children. For her, such pregnancies are almost always "compulsory" and the children "unwanted." Throughout this book, readers should remember that the "product" of this "irresponsible parenthood" was a generation that did have a difficult time growing up during the 1920s and 1930s, as Sanger went to great pains to portray as darkly as possible. But they also served the nation quite nobly in World War II and, after the war, many took advantage of the GI Bill to get a college education and provide their children with a better childhood than their own. There was no reason for Sanger's doom and gloom.

3. Editor: Ponder a moment whether the hard-working mothers that Sanger described in this chapter deserved to be branded as "irresponsible."

4. G. K. Chesterton, *Eugenics and Other Evils,* Michael W. Perry, ed. (Seattle: Inkling Books, 2000), 93-94. When Sanger wrote *The Pivot of Civilization,* few women in American had better access to the more affluent classes (especially women). Yet she never seemed to find an occasion to tell employers to give ill-paid fathers better pay. Nor did she ask her adoring female fans to pay their maids and nannies decently. Catholic leaders might campaign for a 'living wage,' but not Sanger. For her marriage and maternity must yield to the greed of the better classes. That is undoubtedly why she was so popular with them.

A mother who had four live births and two stillbirths in twelve years lost all of her babies during their first year. She was so anxious that at least one child should live that she consulted a physician concerning the care of the last one.[6] "Upon his advice," to quote the government report, "she gave up her twenty boarders immediately after the child's birth, and devoted all her time to it. Thinks she did not stop her hard work soon enough; says she has always worked too hard, keeping boarders in this country, and cutting wood and carrying it and water on her back in the old country. Also says the carrying of water and cases of beer in this country is a great strain on her." But the illuminating point in this case is that the father was furious because all the babies died. To show his disrespect for the wife who could only give birth to babies that died, he wore a red necktie to the funeral of the last. Yet this woman, the government agent reports, would follow and profit by any instruction that might be given her.

It is true that the cases reported from Johnstown, Pennsylvania, do not represent completely "Americanized" families. This lack does not prevent them, however, by their unceasing fertility from producing the Americans of to-morrow. Of the more immediate conditions surrounding child-birth, we are presented with this evidence, given by one woman concerning the birth of her last child:

On five o'clock on Wednesday evening she went to her sister's house to return a washboard, after finishing a day's washing. The baby was born while she was there. Her sister was too young to aid her in any way. She was not accustomed to a midwife, she confessed. She cut the cord herself, washed the new-born baby at her sister's house, walked home, cooked supper for her boarders, and went to bed by eight o'clock. The next day she got up and ironed. This tired her out, she said, so she stayed in bed for two whole days. She milked cows the day after the birth of the baby and sold the milk as well. Later in the week, when she became tired, she hired someone to do that portion of her work. This woman, we are further informed, kept cows, chickens, and lodgers, and earned additional money by doing laundry and charwork. At times her husband deserted her. His earnings amounted to

$1.70 a day, while a fifteen-year-old son earned $1.10 in a coal mine.

One searches in vain for some picture of sacred motherhood, as depicted in popular plays and motion pictures, something more normal and encouraging. Then one comes to the bitter realization that these, in very truth, are the "normal" cases, not the exceptions. The exceptions are apt to indicate, instead, the close relationship of this irresponsible and chance parenthood to the great social problems of feeble-mindedness, crime and syphilis.

Nor is this type of motherhood confined to newly arrived immigrant mothers, as a government report from Akron, Ohio, sufficiently indicates. In this city, the government agents discovered that more than five hundred mothers were ignorant of the accepted principles of infant feeding, or, if familiar with them, did not practise them. "This ignorance or indifference was not confined to foreign-born mothers. . . . A native mother reported that she gave her two-weeks-old baby ice cream, and that before his sixth month, he was sitting at the table 'eating everything.'" This was in a town in which there were comparatively few cases of extreme poverty.

The degradation of motherhood, the damnation of the next generation before it is born, is exposed in all its catastrophic misery, in the reports of the National Consumers' League. In her report of living conditions among night-working mothers in thirty-nine textile mills in Rhode Island, based on exhaustive studies, Mrs. Florence Kelley[7] describes the "normal" life of these women:

When the worker, cruelly tired from ten hours' work, comes home in the early morning, she usually scrambles together breakfast for the family. Eating little or nothing herself, and that hastily, she tumbles into bed—not the immaculate bed in an airy bed-room with dark shades, but one still warm from its night occupants, in a stuffy little bed-room, darkened imperfectly if at all. After sleeping exhaustedly for an hour perhaps she bestirs herself to get the children off to school, or care for insistent little ones, too young to appreciate that mother is tired out and must sleep. Perhaps later in the forenoon, she again drops into a fitful sleep, or she may have to wait until after dinner. There is the midday meal to get, and, if her husband cannot come home, his dinner-pail to pack with a hot lunch to be sent or carried to him. If he is not at home, the lunch is rather a makeshift. The midday meal is scarcely over before supper

5. U. S. Department of Labor: Children's Bureau. Infant Mortality Series, No. 3, pp. 81, 82, 83, 84.

6. Editor: Notice how desperately this woman wanted her children to live and how much she was willing to do to protect them. Yet for Sanger she remained an example of "parental irresponsibility."

7. Editor: Florence Kelley (1859–1932) was the author of *Women in Industry* (1916) and *Wage-earning Women in War Time: The Textile Industry* (1919). For Sanger these horror stories were *not* a springboard from which to call for better pay or shorter working hours.

must be thought of. This has to be eaten hurriedly before the family are ready, for the mother must be in the mill at work, by 6, 6:30 or 7 P.M. . . .Many women in their inadequate English, summed up their daily routine by, "Oh, me all time tired. *Too much work, too much baby, too little sleep!*"

Only sixteen of the 166 married women were without children; thirty-two had three or more; twenty had children on year old or under. There were 160 children under school-age, below six years, and 246 of school age.[8]

"A woman in ordinary circumstances," adds this impartial investigator, "with a husband and three children, if she does her own work, feels that her hands are full. How these mill-workers, many of them frail-looking, and many with confessedly poor health, can ever do two jobs is a mystery, when they are seen in their homes dragging about, pale, hollow-eyed and listless, often needlessly sharp and impatient with the children. These children are not only not mothered, never cherished, they are nagged and buffeted. The mothers are not superwomen, and like all human beings, they have a certain amount of strength and when that breaks, their nerves suffer."

We are presented with a vivid picture of one of these slave-mothers: a woman of thirty-eight who looks at least fifty with her worn, furrowed face. Asked why she had been working at night for the past two years, she pointed to a six-months old baby she was carrying, to the five small children swarming about her, and answered laconically, "Too much children!" She volunteered the information that there had been two more who had died. When asked why they had died, the poor mother shrugged her shoulders listlessly, and replied, "Don't know." In addition to bearing and rearing these children, her work would sap the vitality of any ordinary person. "She got home soon after four in the morning, cooked breakfast for the family and ate hastily herself. At 4:30 she was in bed, staying there until eight. But part of that time was disturbed for the children were noisy and the apartment was a tiny, dingy place in a basement. At eight she started the three oldest boys to school, and cleaned up the débris of breakfast and of supper the night before. At twelve she

8. Editor: Sad as they were, the cases that Sanger described were not typical. Only 19 percent of these mothers had three or more children and the families averaged a modest 2.4 children each. In all probability these women already had access to some form of birth control. They simply didn't have what Sanger's social class often had—separate bedrooms for husband and wife— and thought the lower birthrates of the rich were due to some secret technique known only to them.

carried a hot lunch to her husband and had dinner ready for the three school children. In the afternoon, there were again dishes and cooking, and caring for three babies aged five, three years, and six months. At five, supper was ready for the family. The mother ate by herself and was off to work at 5:45."

Another of the night-working mothers was a frail looking Frenchwoman of twenty-seven years, with a husband and five children ranging from eight years to fourteen months. Three other children had died. When visited, she was doing a huge washing. She was forced into night work to meet the expenses of the family. She estimated that she succeeded in getting five hours' sleep during the day. "I take my baby to bed with me, but he cries, and my little four-year-old boy cries, too, and comes in to make me get up, so you can't call that a very good sleep."

The problem among unmarried women or those without family is not the same, this investigator points out. "They sleep longer by day than they normally would by night." We are also informed that pregnant women work at night in the mills, sometimes up to the very hour of delivery. "It's queer," exclaimed a woman supervisor of one of the Rhode Island mills, "but some women, both on the day and the night shift, will stick to their work right up to the last minute, and will use every means to deceive you about their condition. I go around and talk to them, but make little impression. We have had several narrow escapes. . . . A Polish mother with five children had worked in a mill by day or by night, ever since her marriage, stopping only to have her babies. One little girl had died several years ago, and the youngest child, says Mrs. Kelley, did not look promising. It had none of the charm of babyhood; its body and clothing were filthy; and its lower lip and chin covered with repulsive black sores.

It should be remembered that the Consumers' League, which publishes these reports on women in industry, is not advocating Birth Control education, but is aiming "to awaken responsibility for conditions under which goods are produced, and through investigation, education and legislation, to mobilize public opinion in behalf of enlightened standards for workers and honest products for all." Nevertheless, in Miss Agnes de Lima's report of conditions in Passaic, New Jersey, we find the same tale of penalized, prostrate motherhood, bearing the crushing burden of economic injustice and cruelty; the same blind but overpowering instincts of love and hunger driving young women into the factories to work, night in and night out, to support their procession of uncared for and undernourished babies. It is the married women with young children who work on the inferno-like shifts. They are driven to it by the low wages of their husbands. They choose night work in order to be with their children in the daytime. They are afraid of the neglect and ill-treatment the children might receive at the hands of paid caretakers. Thus they condemn themselves to eighteen or twenty hours of daily toil. Surely no mother with three, four, five or six children can secure much rest by day.

"Take almost any house"—we read in the report of conditions in New Jersey—"knock at almost any door and you will find a weary, tousled woman, half-dressed, doing her housework, or trying to snatch an hour or two of sleep after her long night of work in the mill. . . . The facts are there for any one to see; the hopeless and exhausted woman, her cluttered three or four rooms, the swarm of sickly and neglected children."

These women claimed that night work was unavoidable, as their husbands received so little pay. This in spite of all our vaunted "high wages." Only three women were found who went into the drudgery of night work without being obliged to do so. Two had no children, and their husbands' earnings were sufficient for their needs. One of these was saving for a trip to Europe, and chose the night shift because she found it less strenuous than the day. Only four of the hundred women reported upon were unmarried, and ninety-two of the married women had children. Of the four childless married women, one had lost two children, and another was recovering from a recent miscarriage. There were five widows. The average number of children was three in a family. Thirty-nine of the mothers had four or more. Three of them had six children, and six of them had seven children apiece. These women ranged between the ages of twenty-five and forty, and more than half the children were less than seven years of age. Most of them had babies of one, two and three years of age.

At the risk of repetition, we quote one of the typical cases reported by Miss De Lima with features practically identical with the individual cases reported from Rhode Island. It is of a mother who comes home from work at 5:30 every morning, falls on the bed from exhaustion, arises again at eight or nine o'clock to see that the older children are sent off to school. A son of five, like the rest of the children, is on a diet of coffee—milk costs too much. After the children have left for school, the over-worked mother again tries to sleep, though the small son bothers her a great deal. Besides, she must clean the house, wash, iron, mend, sew and prepare the midday meal. She tries to snatch a little sleep in the afternoon, but explains: "When you got big family, all time work.

Night-time in mill drag so long, so long; day-time in home go so quick." By five, this mother must get the family's supper ready, and dress for the night's work, which begins at seven. The investigator further reports: "The next day was a holiday, and for a diversion, Mrs. N. thought she would go up to the cemetery: 'I got some children up there,' she explained, 'and same time I get some air. No, I don't go nowheres, just to the mill and then home.'"

Here again, as in all reports on women in industry, we find the prevalence of pregnant women working on night-shifts, often to the very day of their delivery. "Oh, yes, plenty women, big bellies, work in the night time," one of the toiling mothers volunteered. "Shame they go, but what can do?" The abuse was general. Many mothers confessed that owing to poverty they themselves worked up to the last week or even day before the birth of their children. Births were even reported in one of the mills during the night shift. A foreman told of permitting a night-working woman to leave at 6:30 one morning, and of the birth of her baby at 7:30. Several women told of leaving the day-shift because of pregnancy and of securing places on the nightshift where their condition was less conspicuous, and the bosses more tolerant. One mother defended her right to stay at work, says the report, claiming that as long as she could do her work, it was nobody's business. In a doorway sat a sickly and bloodless woman in an advanced stage of pregnancy. Her first baby had died of general debility. She had worked at night in the mill until the very day of its birth. This time the boss had told her she could stay if she wished, but reminded her of what had happened last time. So she had stopped work, as the baby was expected any day.

Again and again we read the same story, which varied only in detail: the mother in the three back rooms; the sagging porch overflowing with pale and sickly children; the over-worked mother of seven, still nursing her youngest, who is two or three months old. Worn and haggard, with a skeleton-like child pulling at her breast, the women tries to make the investigator understand. The grandmother helps to interpret. "She never sleeps," explains the old woman, "how can she with so many children?" She works up to the last moment before her baby comes, and returns to work as soon as they are four weeks old.

Another apartment in the same house; another of those night-working mothers, who had just stopped because she is pregnant. The boss had kindly given her permission to stay on, but she found the reaching on the heavy spinning machines too hard. Three children, ranging in age from five to twelve years, are all sickly and forlorn and must be cared for. There is a tubercular husband, who is unable to work steadily, and is able to bring in only $12 a week. Two of the babies had died, one because the mother had returned to work too soon after its birth and had lost her milk. She had fed him tea and bread, "so he died."

The most heartrending feature of it all—in these homes of the mothers who work at night—is the expression in the faces of the children; children of chance, dressed in rags, undernourished, underclothed, all predisposed to the ravages of chronic and epidemic disease.

The reports on infant mortality published under the direction of the Children's Bureau substantiate for the United States of America the findings of the Galton Laboratory for Great Britain, showing that an abnormally high rate of fertility is usually associated with poverty, filth, disease, feeblemindedness and a high infant mortality rate. It is a commonplace truism that a high birth-rate is accompanied by a high infant-mortality rate. No longer is it necessary to dissociate cause and effect, to try to determine whether the high birth rate is the cause of the high infant mortality rate. It is sufficient to know that they are organically correlated along with other anti-social factors detrimental to individual, national and racial welfare. The figures presented by Hibbs[9] likewise reveal a much higher infant mortality rate for the later born children of large families.

The statistics which show that the greatest number of children are born to parents whose earnings are the lowest,[10] that the direst poverty is associated with uncontrolled fecundity emphasize the character of the parenthood we are depending upon to create the race of the future.

A distinguished American opponent of Birth Control some years ago spoke of the "racial" value of this high infant mortality rate among the "unfit." He forgot, however, that the survival-rate of the children born of these overworked and fatigued mothers may nevertheless be large enough, aided and abetted by philanthropies and charities, to form the greater part of the population of tomorrow. As Dr. Karl Pearson has stated: "Degenerate stocks under present social conditions are not short-lived; they live to have more than the normal size of family."

Reports of charitable organizations; the famous "one hundred neediest cases" presented every year by the *New York Times* to arouse the sentimental generosity of its readers; statistics of public and private hospitals, charities and corrections; analyses of pauperism in town and country—all tell the same tale of uncontrolled and irresponsible fecundity. The facts, the figures, the appalling truth are there for all to read. It is only in the remedy proposed, the effective solution, that investigators and students of the problem disagree.

Confronted with the "startling and disgraceful" conditions of affairs indicated by the fact that a quarter of a million babies die every year in the United States before they are one year old, and that no less than 23,000 women die in childbirth, a large number of experts and enthusiasts have placed their hopes in maternity-benefit measures.

Such measures sharply illustrate the superficial and fragmentary manner in which the whole problem of motherhood is studied to-day. It seeks a *laisser faire* policy of parenthood or marriage,[11] with an indiscriminating paternalism concerning maternity. It is as though the Government were to say: "Increase and multiply; we shall assume the responsibility of keeping your babies alive." Even granting that the administration of these measures might be made effective and effectual, which is more than doubtful, we see that they are based upon a complete ignorance or disregard of the most important fact in the situation—that of indiscriminate and irresponsible fecundity. They tacitly assume that all parenthood is desirable, that all children should be born, and that infant mortality can be controlled by external aid. In the great world-problem of creating the men and women of tomorrow, it is not merely a question of sustaining the lives of all children, irrespective of their hereditary and physical qualities, to the point where they, in turn, may reproduce their kind. Advocates of Birth Control offer and accept no such superficial solution. This philosophy is based upon a clearer vision and a more profound comprehension of human life. Of immediate relief for the crushed and enslaved motherhood of the world through State aid, no better criticism has been made than that of Havelock Ellis:

> To the theoretical philanthropist, eager to reform the world on paper, nothing seems simpler than to cure the present evils of child-rearing by setting up State nurseries which are at once to relieve mothers of everything connected with the men of the future beyond the plea-

---

9. Henry H. Hibbs, Jr. *Infant Mortality: Its Relation to Social and Industrial Conditions,* p. 39. Russell Sage Foundation, New York, 1916. Editor: With her 'shotgun' approach to social problems, Sanger had little interest in separating cause from effect.

10. Cf. U. S. Department of Labor. Children's Bureau: Infant Mortality Series, No. 11. p. 36.

---

11. Editor: We discovered what Sanger meant by *laisser faire* in Chap. XXXI.

sure—if such it happens to be—of conceiving them, and the trouble of bearing them, and at the same time to rear them up independently of the home, in a wholesome, economical and scientific manner. Nothing seems simpler, but from the fundamental psychological point of view nothing is falser.... A State which admits that the individuals composing it are incompetent to perform their most sacred and intimate functions, and takes it upon itself to perform them itself instead, attempts a task that would be undesirable, even if it were possible of achievement."[12]

It may be replied that maternity benefit measures aim merely to aid mothers more adequately to fulfil their biological and social functions. But from the point of view of Birth Control, that will never be possible until the crushing exigencies of overcrowding are removed—overcrowding of pregnancies as well as of homes. As long as the mother remains the passive victim of blind instinct, instead of the conscious, responsible instrument of the life-force, controlling and directing its expression, there can be no solution to the intricate and complex problems that confront the whole world to-day. This is, of course, impossible as long as women are driven into the factories, on night as well as day shifts, as long as children and girls and young women are driven into industries to labor that is physically deteriorating as a preparation for the supreme function of maternity.

The philosophy of Birth Control insists that motherhood, no less than any other human function, must undergo scientific study, must be voluntarily directed and controlled with intelligence and foresight. As long as we countenance what H. G. Wells has well termed "the monstrous absurdity of women discharging their supreme social function, bearing and rearing children, in their spare time, as it were, while they 'earn their living' by contributing some half-mechanical element to some trivial industrial product" any attempt to furnish "maternal education" is bound to fall on stony ground. Children

brought into the world as the chance consequences of the blind play of uncontrolled instinct, become likewise the helpless victims of their environment. It is because children are cheaply conceived that the infant mortality rate is high. But the greatest evil, perhaps the greatest crime, of our so-called civilization of to-day, is not to be gauged by the infant-mortality rate. In truth, unfortunate babies who depart during their first twelve months are more fortunate in many respects than those who survive to undergo punishment for their parents' cruel ignorance and complacent fecundity. If motherhood is wasted under the present regime of "glorious fertility," childhood is not merely wasted, but actually destroyed. Let us look at this matter from the point of view of the children who survive.

—§§§—

Early in Childhood
Very early in my childhood I associated poverty, toil, unemployment, drunkenness, cruelty, quarreling, fighting, debts, jails with large families.

The people who lived on the hilltops owned their own homes, had few children, dressed them well, and kept their houses and their yards clean and tidy. Mothers of the hills played croquet and tennis with their husbands in the evening. They walked hand in hand with their children through the streets to shop for suitable clothing. They were young looking mothers with pretty, clean dresses, and they smelled of perfume. I often watched them at play as I looked through the gates in passing.[13]

—MARGARET SANGER, MY FIGHT FOR BIRTH CONTROL, 1931

---

12. Havelock Ellis, *Sex in Relation to Society*, p. 31. Editor: Note the conflict between what Ellis says here and what others on the left (such as Gilman) were saying about the necessity for the State to take over more parenting roles. One way to resolve the conflict would be to keep the "incompetent" from having children, while providing state subsidized child care for 'fit' mothers, married or not. Typically, this could be done by providing government subsidies for more expensive sorts of child care but not for the more informal sorts used by ordinary people.

13. Margaret Sanger, *My Fight for Birth Control* (Farrar & Rinehart: New York, 1931), 5. Sanger's childhood was spent in Corning, New York in a family that was neither poor nor rich. However, their income was uncertain due to the eccentricities of her father, a maker of tombstones, whose strident anti-Catholicism did not endear him to potential customers among the community's prolific Irish Catholics. The psychologically inclined may see in this reasons why Sanger feared the multiplying masses beneath. But it doesn't explain why so many others, born into security and wealth, held those same fears. At most, childhood emotions can cause us to choose ideas that resolve those fears. But it is usually best to focus on those ideas, whether for good or evil. That's what this book does.

3

"Children Troop Down From Heaven"

Failure of emotional, sentimental and so-called idealistic efforts, based on hysterical enthusiasm, to improve social conditions, is nowhere better exemplified than in the undervaluation of child-life. A few years ago, the scandal of children under fourteen working in cotton mills was exposed. There was muckraking and agitation. A wave of moral indignation swept over America. There arose a loud cry for immediate action. Then, having more or less successfully settled this particular matter, the American people heaved a sigh of relief, settled back, and complacently congratulated itself that the problem of child labor had been settled once and for all.[1]

Conditions are worse to-day than before. Not only is there child labor in practically every State in the Union, but we are now forced to realize the evils that result from child labor, of child laborers now grown into manhood and womanhood. But we wish here to point out a neglected aspect of this problem. Child labor shows us how cheaply we value childhood. And moreover, it shows us that cheap childhood is the inevitable result of chance parenthood. Child labor is organically bound up with the problem of uncontrolled breeding and the large family.

The selective draft of 1917—which was designed to choose for military service only those fulfilling definite requirements of physical and mental fitness—showed some of the results of child labor. It established the fact that the majority of American children never got beyond the sixth grade, because they were forced to leave school at that time. Our overadvertised compulsory education does not compel—and does not educate. The selective-

draft,[2] it is our duty to emphasize this fact, revealed that 38 per cent of the young men (more than a million) were rejected because of physical ill-health and defects. And 25 per cent were illiterate.

These young men were the children of yesterday. Authorities tell us that 75 per cent of the school-children are defective. This means that no less than fifteen million schoolchildren, out of 22,000,000 in the United States, are physically or mentally below par.

This is the soil in which all sorts of serious evils strike root. It is a truism that children are the chief asset of a nation. Yet while the United States government allotted 92.8 per cent of its appropriations for 1920 toward war expenses, three per cent to public works, 3.2 per cent to "primary governmental functions," no more than one per cent is appropriated to education, research and development.[3] Of this one per cent, only a small proportion is devoted to public health. The conservation of childhood is a minor consideration. While three cents is spent for the more or less doubtful protection of women and children, fifty cents is given to the Bureau of Animal Industry, for the protection of domestic animals. In 1919, the State of Kansas appropriated $25,000 to protect the health of pigs, and $4,000 to protect the health of children. In four years our Federal Government appropriated—roughly speaking—$81,000,000 for the improvement of rivers; $13,000,000 for forest conservation; $8,000,000 for the experimental plant industry; $7,000,000 for the experimental animal industry; $4,000,000 to combat the foot and mouth disease; and less than half a million for the protection of child life.

Competent authorities tell us that no less than 75 per cent of American children leave school between the ages

---

1. Editor: Look for *any* place in this chapter where Sanger called for better wages for poorly paid fathers and migrant workers, so their children need not work. In places, it is true, she did seem to lament that so little money is spent on public health and education for poor children. But, in the end, her solution came down to pressuring the poor to end their "uncontrolled breeding," so that same public money went further.

2. Editor: Sanger's birth control colleague Lothrop Stoddard described the WWI IQ tests of draftees in Chap. XXVII.

3. Editor: Sanger's statistics are distorted. Educated is funded at the state and local level. Despite what she claimed, this was an era when high school attendance increased.

of fourteen and sixteen to go to work. This number is increasing. According to the recently published report on *The Administration of the First Child Labor Law,* in five states in which it was necessary for the Children's Bureau to handle directly the working certificates of children, one-fifth of the 25,000 children who applied for certificates left school when they were in the fourth grade; nearly a tenth of them had never attended school at all or had not gone beyond the first grade; and only one-twenty-fifth had gone as far as the eighth grade. But their educational equipment was even more limited than the grade they attended would indicate. Of the children applying to go to work 1,803 had not advanced further than the first grade even when they had gone to school at all; 3,379 could not even sign their own names legibly, and nearly 2,000 of them could not write at all. The report brings automatically into view the vicious circle of child-labor, illiteracy, bodily and mental defect, poverty and delinquency. And like all reports on child labor, the large family and reckless breeding looms large in the background as one of the chief factors in the problem.

Despite all our boasting of the American public school, of the equal opportunity afforded to every child in America, we have the shortest school-term, and the shortest school-day of any of the civilized countries. In the United States of America, there are 106 illiterates to every thousand people. In England there are 58 per thousand, Sweden and Norway have one per thousand.

The United States is the most illiterate country in the world—that is, of the so-called civilized countries. Of the 5,000,000 illiterates in the United States, 58 per cent are white and 28 per cent native whites. Illiteracy not only is the index of inequality of opportunity. It speaks as well a lack of consideration for the children. It means either that children have been forced out of school to go to work, or that they are mentally and physically defective.[4]

One is tempted to ask why a society, which has failed so lamentably to protect the already existing child life upon which its very perpetuation depends, takes upon itself the reckless encouragement of indiscriminate procreation. The United States Government has recently inaugurated a policy of restricting immigration from foreign countries.[5] Until it is able to protect childhood from criminal exploitation, until it has made possible a reasonable hope of life, liberty and growth for American chil-

dren, it should likewise recognize the wisdom of voluntary restriction in the production of children.

Reports on child labor published by the National Child Labor Committee only incidentally reveal the correlation of this evil with that of large families. Yet this is evident throughout. The investigators are more bent upon regarding child labor as a cause of illiteracy.

But it is no less a consequence of irresponsibility in breeding. A sinister aspect of this is revealed by Theresa Wolfson's study of child-labor in the beet-fields of Michigan.[6] As one weeder put it: "Poor man make no money, make plenty children—plenty children good for sugar-beet business." Further illuminating details are given by Miss Wolfson:

> Why did they come to the beet-fields? Most frequently families with large numbers of children said that they felt that the city was no place to raise children—things too expensive and children ran wild—in the country all the children could work." Living conditions are abominable and unspeakably wretched. An old woodshed, a long-abandoned barn, and occasionally a tottering, ramshackle farmer's house are the common types. "One family of eleven, the youngest child two years, the oldest sixteen years, lived in an old country store which had but one window; the wind and rain came through the holes in the walls, the ceiling was very low and the smoke from the stove filled the room. Here the family ate, slept, cooked and washed.
>
> In Tuscola County a family of six was found living in a one-room shack with no windows. Light and ventilation was secured through the open doors. Little Charles, eight years of age, was left at home to take care of Dan, Annie and Pete, whose ages were five years, four years, and three months, respectively. In addition, he cooked the noonday meal and brought it to his parents in the field. The filth and choking odors of the shack made it almost unbearable, yet the baby was sleeping in a heap of rags piled up in a corner.

Social philosophers of a certain school advocate the return to the land—it is only in the overcrowded city, they claim, that the evils resulting from the large family are possible. There is, according to this philosophy, no overcrowding, no over-population in the country, where in the open air and sunlight every child has an opportunity for health and growth. This idyllic conception of American country life does not correspond with the picture presented by this investigator, who points out:

> To promote the physical and mental development of the child, we forbid his employment in factories, shops

---

4. I am indebted to the National Child Labor Committee for these statistics, as well as for many of the facts that follow.

5. Editor: Before the 1924 immigration law based on country of origin, there were increasingly strict laws based on health standards and literacy.

6. "People Who Go to Beets" Pamphlet No. 299, National Child Labor Committee.

and stores. On the other hand, we are prone to believe that the right kind of farm-work is healthful and the best thing for children. But for a child to crawl along the ground, weeding beets in the hot sun for fourteen hours a day—the average workday—is far from being the best thing. The law of compensation is bound to work in some way, and the immediate result of this agricultural work is interference with school attendance.

How closely related this form of child-slavery is to the over-large family, is definitely illustrated: "In the one hundred and thirty-three families visited, there were six hundred children. A conversation held with a "Rooshian-German' woman is indicative of the size of most of the families:

"How many children have you?" inquired the investigator.

"Eight—Julius, und Rose, und Martha, dey is mine; Gottlieb und Philip, und Frieda, dey is my husband's;—und Otto und Charlie—dey are ours."

William and 'Tonio

When a more developed element is obliged to compete on the same economic plane with a less-developed element, the standards of cleanliness or decency or education cherished by the advanced element act on it like a slow poison. William does not leave as many children as 'Tonio, because he will not huddle his family into one room, eat macaroni off a bare board, work his wife barefoot in the field, and keep his children weeding onions instead of at school.[7]

—EDWARD ROSS, UNIVERSITY OF WISCONSIN

Families with ten and twelve children were frequently found, while those of six and eight children are the general rule. The advantage of a large family in the beet fields is that it does the most work. In the one hundred thirty-three families interviewed, there were one hundred eighty-six children under the age of six years, ranging from eight weeks up; thirty-six children between the ages of six and eight, approximately twenty-five of whom had never been to school, and eleven over sixteen years of age who had never been to school. One ten-year-old boy had never been to school because he was a mental defective; one child of nine was practically blinded by cataracts. This child was found groping his way down the beet-rows pulling out weeds and feeling for the beet-plants—in the glare of the sun he had lost all sense of light and dark. Of the three hundred and forty children who were

not going or had never gone to school, only four had reached the point of graduation, and only one had gone to high school. These large families migrated to the beet-fields in early spring. Seventy-two per cent of them are retarded. When we realize that feeble-mindedness is arrested development and retardation, we see that these "beet children" are artificially retarded in their growth, and that the tendency is to reduce their intelligence to the level of the congenital imbecile.

Nor must it be concluded that these large "beet" families are always the "ignorant foreigner" so despised by our respectable press. The following case throws some light on this matter, reported in the same pamphlet: "An American family, considered a prize by the agent because of the fact that there were nine children, turned out to be a 'flunk.' They could not work in the beet-fields, they ran up a bill at the country-store, and one day the father and the eldest son, a boy of nineteen, were seen running through the railroad station to catch an out-going train. The grocer thought they were 'jumping' their bill. He telephoned ahead to the sheriff of the next town. They were taken off the train by the sheriff and given the option of going back to the farm or staying in jail. They preferred to stay in jail, and remained there for two weeks. Meanwhile, the mother and her eight children, ranging in ages form seventeen years to nine months, had to manage the best way they could. At the end of two weeks, father and son were set free. . . . During all of this period the farmers of the community sent in provisions to keep the wife and children from starving." Does this case not sum up in a nutshell the typical American intelligence confronted with the problem of the too-large family—industrial slavery tempered with sentimentality!

Let us turn to a young, possibly a more progressive state. Consider the case of "California, the Golden" as it is named by Emma Duke, in her study of child-labor in the Imperial Valley, "as fertile as the Valley of the Nile."[8] Here, cotton is king, and rich ranchers, absentee landlords and others exploit it. Less than ten years ago ranchers would bring in hordes of laboring families, but refuse to assume any responsibility in housing them, merely permitting them to sleep on the grounds of the ranch. Conditions have been somewhat improved, but, sometimes, we read, "a one roomed straw house with an area of fifteen by twenty feet will serve as a home for an entire family, which not only cooks but sleeps in the same room." Here, as in Michigan among the beets, children are "thick as bees." All kinds of children pick, Miss Duke reports,

---

7. Edward A. Ross, *The Old World in the New* (New York: Century, 1913, 1914), 303. A none-too-subtle attack on Italians.

8. "California the Golden," by Emma Duke. Reprinted from *The American Child*, Vol. II, No. 3. November 1920.

"even those as young as three years! Five-year-old children pick steadily all day. . . . Many white American children are among them—pure American stock, who have gradually moved from the Carolinas, Tennessee, and other southern states to Arkansas, Texas, Oklahoma, Arizona, and on into the Imperial Valley." Some of these children, it seems, wanted to attend school, but their fathers did not want to work; so the children were forced to become bread-winners. One man whose children were working with him in the fields said, "Please, lady, don't send them to school; let them pick a while longer. I ain't got my new auto paid for yet." The native white American mother of children working in the fields proudly remarked: "No; they ain't never been to school, nor me nor their poppy, nor their granddads and grandmoms. We've always been pickers!"—and she spat her tobacco over the field in expert fashion.[9]

"In the Valley one hears from townspeople," writes the investigator, "that pickers make ten dollars a day, working the whole family. With that qualification, the statement is ambiguous. One Mexican in the Imperial Valley was the father of thirty-three children—'about thirteen or fourteen living,' he said. If they all worked at cotton-picking, they would doubtless altogether make more than ten dollars a day."

One of the child laborers revealed the economic advantage—to the parents—in numerous progeny: "Us kids most always drag from forty to fifty pounds of cotton before we take it to be weighed. Three of us pick. I'm twelve years old and my bag is twelve feet long. I can drag nearly a hundred pounds. My sister is ten years old, and her bag is eight feet long. My little brother is seven and his bag is five feet long."

Evidence abounds in the publications of the National Child Labor Committee of this type of fecund parenthood.[10] It is not merely a question of the large family versus the small family. Even comparatively small families among migratory workers of this sort have been large families. The high infant mortality rate has carried off the weaker children. Those who survive are merely those who have been strong enough to survive the most unfavorable living conditions. No; it is a situation not unique, nor even unusual in human history, of greed and stupidity

and cupidity encouraging the procreative instinct toward the manufacture of slaves. We hear these days of the selfishness and the degradation of healthy and well-educated women who refuse motherhood; but we hear little of the more sinister selfishness of men and women who bring babies into the world to become child-slaves of the kind described in these reports of child labor.

The history of child labor in the English factories in the nineteenth century throws a suggestive light on this situation. These child-workers were really called into being by the industrial situation. The population grew, as Dean Inge has described it, like crops in a newly irrigated desert. During the nineteenth century, the numbers were nearly quadrupled. "Let those who think that the population of a country can be increased at will, consider whether it is likely that any physical, moral, or psychological change came over the nation co-incidentally with the inventions of the spinning jenny and the steam engine. It is too obvious for dispute that it was the possession of capital wanting employment, and of natural advantages for using it, that called those multitudes of human beings into existence, to eat the food which they paid for by their labor."[11]

But when child labor in the factories became such a scandal and such a disgrace that child-labor was finally forbidden by laws that possessed the advantage over our own that they were enforced, the proletariat ceased to supply children. Almost by magic the birth rate among the workers declined. Since children were no longer of economic value to the factories, they were evidently a drug in the home. This movement, it should not be forgotten however, was coincident with the agitation and education in Birth Control stimulated by the Besant-Bradlaugh trial.

Large families among migratory agricultural laborers in our own country are likewise brought into existence in response to an industrial demand. **The enforcement of the child labor laws and the extension of their restrictions are therefore an urgent necessity, not so much, as some of our child-labor authorities believe, to enable these children to go to school, as to prevent the recruiting of our next generation from the least intelligent and most unskilled classes in the community.**[12] As long as we officially encourage and countenance the production of large families, the evils of child labor will confront us. On the other hand, the prohibition of child

---

9. Editor: In the previous chapter, parents were branded 'irresponsible' despite the long hours they worked. Here they are portrayed selfishly exploiting their children. Obviously, Sanger did not intend for us to sympathize with these people.

10. *Child Welfare in Oklahoma; Child Welfare in Alabama; Child Welfare in North Carolina; Child Welfare in Kentucky; Child Welfare in Tennessee.* Also *Children in Agriculture,* by Ruth McIntire, and other studies.

11. W. R. Inge: *Outspoken Essays:* p. 92.

12. Editor: This was Sanger's primary motivation for ending child labor.

labor may help, as in the case of English factories, in the decline of the birth rate.

Uncontrolled breeding and child labor go hand in hand. And to-day when we are confronted with the evils of the latter, in the form of widespread illiteracy and defect, we should seek causes more deeply rooted than the enslavement of children. The cost to society is incalculable, as the National Child Labor Committee points out. "It is not only through the lowered power, the stunting and the moral degeneration of its individual members, but in actual expense, through the necessary provision for the human junk, created by premature employment, in poor-houses, hospitals, police and courts, jails and by charitable organizations."

To-day we are paying for the folly of the over-production—and its consequences in permanent injury to plastic childhood—of yesterday. To-morrow, we shall be forced to pay for our ruthless disregard of our surplus children of to-day. The child-laborer of one or two decades ago has become the shifting laborer of to-day, stunted, underfed, illiterate, unskilled, unorganized and unorganizable. "He is the last person to be hired and the first to be fired." Boys and girls under fourteen years of age are no longer permitted to work in factories, mills, canneries and establishments whose products are to be shipped out of the particular state, and children under sixteen can no longer work in mines and quarries. But this affects only one quarter of our army of child labor—work in local industries, stores, and farms, homework in dark and unsanitary tenements is still permitted. Children work in "homes" on artificial flowers, finishing shoddy garments, sewing their very life's blood and that of the race into tawdry clothes and gewgaws that are the most unanswerable comments upon our vaunted "civilization." And to-day, we must not forget, the child-laborer of yesterday is becoming the father or the mother of the child laborer of to-morrow.

"Any nation that works its women is damned," once wrote Woods Hutchinson.[13] The nation that works its children, one is tempted to add, is committing suicide. Loud-mouthed defenders of American democracy pay no attention to the strange fact that, although "the average education among all American adults is only the sixth grade," every one of these adults has an equal power at the polls. The American nation, with all its worship of efficiency and thrift, complacently forgets that "every child defective in body, education or character is a charge upon the community," as Herbert Hoover declared in an address before the American Child Hygiene Association (October, 1920): "The nation as a whole," he added, "has the obligation of such measures toward its children. . .as will yield to them an equal opportunity at their start in life. If we could grapple with the whole child situation for one generation, our public health, our economic efficiency, the moral character, sanity and stability of our people would advance three generations in one."

The great irrefutable fact that is ignored or neglected is that the American nation officially places a low value upon the lives of its children. The brutal truth is that *children are cheap.* When over-production in this field is curtailed by voluntary restriction, when the birth rate among the working classes takes a sharp decline, the value of children will rise. Then only will the infant mortality rate decline, and child labor vanish.

Investigations of child labor emphasize its evils by pointing out that these children are kept out of school, and that they miss the advantages of American public school education. They express the current confidence in compulsory education and the magical benefits to be derived from the public school. But we need to qualify our faith in education, and particularly our faith in the American public school. Educators are just beginning to wake up to the dangers inherent in the attempt to teach the brightest child and the mentally defective child at the same time. They are beginning to test the possibilities of a "vertical" classification as well as a "horizontal" one. That is, each class must be divided into what are termed Gifted, Bright, Average, Dull, Normal, and Defective.[14] In the past the helter-skelter crowding and over-crowding together of all classes of children of approximately the same age, produced only a dull leveling to mediocrity.[15]

An investigation of forty schools in New York City, typical of hundreds of others, reveals deplorable conditions of overcrowding and lack of sanitation.[16] The worst conditions are to be found in locations the most densely populated. Thus of Public School No. 51, located almost in the center of the notorious "Hell's Kitchen" section, we read: "The play space which is provided is a mockery of the worst kind. The basement play-room is dark, damp, poorly lighted, poorly ventilated, foul smelling, unclean, and wholly unfit for children for purposes of play. The drainpipes from the roof have decayed to such a degree that in some instances as little as a quarter of the pipe

13. Editor: The source may be *That "Biological Argument"* (circa 1914). Gilman linked working women to progress. Sanger believed work indicated desperate finances.

14. Editor: "Normal" should probably read "Subnormal."

15. Cf. Tredgold: "Inheritance and Educability." *Eugenics Review,* Vol. XIII, No. 1, pp. 839 *et seq.*

16. Cf. *New York Times,* June 4, 1921.

remains. On rainy days, water enters the class-rooms, hall-ways, corridors, and is thrown against windows because the pipes have rotted away. The narrow stair-ways and halls are similar to those of jails and dungeons of a century ago. The class-rooms are poorly lighted, inadequately equipped, and in some cases so small that the desks of pupils and teachers occupy almost all of the floor-space."

Another school, located a short distance from Fifth Avenue, the "wealthiest street in the world," is described as an "old shell of a structure, erected decades ago as a modern school building. Nearly two thousand children are crowded into class-rooms having a total seating capacity of scarcely one thousand. Narrow doorways, intricate hallways and antiquated stairways, dark and pre-cipitous, keep ever alive the danger of disaster from fire or panic. Only the eternal vigilance of exceptional super-vision has served to lessen the fear of such a catastrophe. Artificial light is necessary, even on the brightest days, in many of the class-rooms. In most of the class-rooms, it is always necessary when the sky is slightly overcast." There is no ventilating system.

In the crowded East Side section conditions are reported to be no better. The Public Education Associa-tion's report on Public School No. 130 points out that the site at the corner of Hester and Baxter Streets was pur-chased by the city years ago as a school site, but that there has been so much "tweedledeeing and tweedleduming" that the new building which is to replace the old, has not even yet been planned! Meanwhile, year after year, thou-sands of children are compelled to study daily in dark and dingy class-rooms. "Artificial light is continually neces-sary," declares the report. "The ventilation is extremely poor. The fire hazard is naturally great. There are no rest-rooms whatever for the teachers." Other schools in the neighborhood reveal conditions even worse. In two of them, for example; "In accordance with the requirements of the syllabus in hygiene in the schools, the vision of the children is regularly tested. In a recent test of this charac-ter, it was found in Public School 108, the rate of defec-tive vision in the various grades ranged from 50 to 64 per cent! In Public School 106, the rate ranged from 43 to 94 per cent!"

The conditions, we are assured, are no exceptions to the rule of public schools in New York, where the fatal effects of overcrowding in education may be observed in their most sinister but significant aspects.

The forgotten fact in this case is that efforts for univer-sal and compulsory education cannot keep pace with the overproduction of children. Even at the best, leaving out of consideration the public school system as the inevita-ble prey and plundering-ground of the cheap politician and job-hunter, present methods of wholesale and syndi-cated "education" are not suited to compete with the unceasing, unthinking, untiring procreative powers of our swarming, spawning populations.

Into such schools as described in the recent reports of the Public Education Association, no intelligent parent would dare send his child. They are not merely fire-traps and culture-grounds of infection, but of moral and intel-lectual contamination as well. More and more are public schools in America becoming institutions for subjecting children to a narrow and reactionary orthodoxy, aiming to crush out all signs of individuality, and to turn out boys and girls compressed into a standardized pattern, with ready-made ideas on politics, religion, morality, and eco-nomics. True education cannot grow out of such compul-sory herding of children in filthy fire-traps.

Character, ability, and reasoning power are not to be developed in this fashion. **Indeed, it is to be doubted whether even a completely successful educational sys-tem could offset the evils of indiscriminate breeding and compensate for the misfortune of being a super-fluous child.** In recognizing the great need of education, we have failed to recognize the greater need of inborn health and character. "If it were necessary to choose between the task of getting children educated and getting them well born and healthy," writes Havelock Ellis, "it would be better to abandon education. There have been many great peoples who never dreamed of national sys-tems of education; there have been no great peoples with-out the art of producing healthy and vigorous children. The matter becomes of peculiar importance in great industrial states, like England, the United States and Ger-many, because in such states, a tacit conspiracy tends to grow up to subordinate national ends to individual ends, and practically to work for the deterioration of the race."[17]

Much less can education solve the great problem of child labor. Rather, under the conditions prevailing in modern society, child labor and the failure of the public schools to educate are both indices of a more deeply rooted evil. Both bespeak *the undervaluation of the child*. This undervaluation, this cheapening of child life, is to speak crudely but frankly the direct result of overproduc-tion. "Restriction of output" is an immediate necessity if we wish to regain control of the real values, so that unim-peded, unhindered, and without danger of inner corrup-tion, humanity may protect its own health and powers.

---

17. *Studies in the Psychology of Sex,* Vol. VI, p. 20.

4

The Fertility of the Feeble-Minded

What vesture have you woven for my year?
O Man and Woman who have fashioned it
Together, is it fine and clean and strong,
Made in such reverence of holy joy,
Of such unsullied substance, that your hearts
Leap with glad awe to see it clothing me,
The glory of whose nakedness you know?
—"The Song of the Unborn," Amelia Josephine Burr

There is but one practical and feasible program in handling the great problem of the feeble-minded. That is, as the best authorities are agreed, to prevent the birth of those who would transmit imbecility to their descendants. Feeble-mindedness as investigations and statistics from every country indicate, is invariably associated with an abnormally high rate of fertility. Modern conditions of civilization, as we are continually being reminded, furnish the most favorable breeding-ground for the mental defective, the moron, the imbecile. "We protect the members of a weak strain," says Davenport, "up to the period of reproduction, and then let them free upon the community, and encourage them to leave a large progeny of 'feeble-minded': which in turn, protected from mortality and carefully nurtured up to the reproductive period, are again set free to reproduce, and so the stupid work goes on of preserving and increasing our socially unfit strains."

The philosophy of Birth Control points out that as long as civilized communities encourage unrestrained fecundity in the "normal" members of the population—always of course under the cloak of decency and morality—and penalize every attempt to introduce the principle of discrimination and responsibility in parenthood, they will be faced with the ever-increasing problem of feeble-mindedness, that fertile parent of degeneracy, crime, and pauperism.[1] Small as the percentage of the imbecile and half-witted may seem in comparison with the normal members of the community, it should always be remembered that feeble-mindedness is not an unrelated expression of modern civilization. Its roots strike deep into the

social fabric. Modern studies indicate that insanity, epilepsy, criminality, prostitution, pauperism, and mental defect, are all organically bound up together and that the least intelligent and the thoroughly degenerate classes in every community are the most prolific. Feeble-mindedness in one generation becomes pauperism or insanity in the next. There is every indication that feeble-mindedness in its protean forms is on the increase, that it has leaped the barriers, and that there is truly, as some of the scientific eugenists have pointed out, a feeble-minded peril to future generations—unless the feeble-minded are prevented from reproducing their kind. To meet this emergency is the immediate and peremptory duty of every State and of all communities.

The curious situation has come about that while our statesmen are busy upon their propaganda of "repopulation," and are encouraging the production of large families, they are ignoring the exigent problem of the elimination of the feeble-minded. In this, however, the politicians are at one with the traditions of a civilization which, with its charities and philanthropies, has propped up the defective and degenerate and relieved them of the burdens borne by the healthy sections of the community,

---

1. Editor: Sanger believed the feeble-minded often appeared "normal" and, apart from their large families, could only be detected by scientists. If we wait until the next generation when their taint will be obvious, she warned, it will be too late. In a disturbing prelude to Nazi anti-Semitic propaganda, she called them a "menace," compared them to insect pests and diseases and suggested legal action to restrict their birthrate.

thus enabling them more easily and more numerously to propagate their kind. "With the very highest motives," declares Dr. Walter E. Fernald,[2] "modern philanthropic efforts often tend to foster and increase the growth of defect in the community.... The only feeble-minded persons who now receive any official consideration are those who have already become dependent or delinquent, many of whom have already become parents. We lock the barn-door after the horse is stolen. **We now have state commissions for controlling the gipsy-moth and the boll weevil, the foot-and-mouth disease, and for protecting the shell-fish and wild game, but we have no commission which even attempts to modify or to control the vast moral and economic forces represented by the feeble-minded persons at large in the community.**"

How the feeble-minded and their always numerous progeny run the gamut of police, alms-houses, courts, penal institutions, "charities and corrections," tramp shelters, lying-in hospitals, and relief afforded by privately endowed religious and social agencies, is shown in any number of reports and studies of family histories. We find cases of feeble-mindedness and mental defect in the reports on infant mortality referred to in a previous chapter, as well as in other reports published by the United States government. Here is a typical case showing the astonishing ability to "increase and multiply," organically bound up with delinquency and defect of various types:

The parents of a feeble-minded girl, twenty years of age, who was committed to the Kansas State Industrial Farm on a vagrancy charge, lived in a thickly populated Negro district which was reported by the police to be the headquarters for the criminal element of the surrounding State.... The mother married at fourteen, and her first child was born at fifteen. In rapid succession she gave birth to sixteen live-born children and had one miscarriage. The first child, a girl, married but separated from her husband.... The fourth, fifth and sixth, all girls, died in infancy or early childhood. The seventh, a girl, remarried after the death of her husband, from whom she had been separated. The eighth, a boy who early in life began to exhibit criminal tendencies, was in prison for highway robbery and burglary. The ninth, a girl, normal mentally, was in quarantine at the Kansas State Industrial Farm at the time this study was made; she had lived with a man as his common-law wife, and had also been arrested several times for soliciting. The tenth, a boy, was involved in several delinquencies when young and was sent to the detention-

house but did not remain there long. The eleventh, a boy... at the age of seventeen was sentenced to the penitentiary for twenty years on a charge of first-degree robbery; after serving a portion of his time, he was paroled, and later was shot and killed in a fight. The twelfth, a boy, was at fifteen years of age implicated in a murder and sent to the industrial school, but escaped from there on a bicycle which he had stolen; at eighteen, he was shot and killed by a woman. The thirteenth child, feeble-minded, is the girl of the study. The fourteenth, a boy was considered by police to be the best member of the family; his mother reported him to be much slower mentally than his sister just mentioned; he had been arrested several times. Once, he was held in the detention-home and once sent to the State Industrial school; at other times, he was placed on probation. The fifteenth, a girl sixteen years old, has for a long time had a bad reputation. Subsequent to the commitment of her sister to the Kansas State Industrial Farm, she was arrested on a charge of vagrancy, found to be syphilitic, and quarantined in a state other than Kansas. At the time of her arrest, she stated that prostitution was her occupation. The last child was a boy of thirteen years whose history was not secured....[3]

The notorious fecundity of feeble-minded women is emphasized in studies and investigations of the problem, coming from all countries. "The feeble-minded woman is twice as prolific as the normal one." Sir James Crichton-Browne[4] speaks of the great numbers of feeble-minded girls, wholly unfit to become mothers, who return to the work-house year after year to bear children, "many of whom happily die, but some of whom survive to recruit our idiot establishments and to repeat their mothers' performances." Tredgold[5] points out that the number of children born to the feeble-minded is abnormally high. Feeble-minded women "constitute a permanent menace to the race and one which becomes serious at a time when the decline of the birth-rate is ...unmistakable." Dr. Tredgold points out that "the average number of children born in a family is four, whereas in these degenerate families, we find an average of 7.3 to each. Out of this total only a little more than *one-third*—456 out of a total of

3. United States Public Health Service: *Psychiatric Studies of Delinquents*. Reprint No. 598: pp.64–65. Editor: This particular 'feeble-minded' family was the subject of an official U. S. government report. It was not just individual scientists spreading the alarm.

4. Editor: Sir James Crichton-Browne (1840–1938). The quote may be from one of several books he wrote offering anecdotes about his work as a physician.

5. Editor: Alfred F. Tredgold (1870–1956) was the author of *The Problem of Degeneracy* (*circa* 1917).

2. Editor: The quote may be from his *The Burden of Feeble-mindedness* (*circa* 1918).

1,269 children—can be considered profitable members of the community, and that, be it remembered, at the parents' valuation.

Another significant point is the number of mentally defective children who survive. "Out of the total number of 526 mentally affected persons in the 150 families, there are 245 in the present generation—an unusually large survival."[6]

Speaking for Bradford, England, Dr. Helen U. Campbell[7] touches another significant and interesting point usually neglected by the advocates of mothers' pensions, milk-stations, and maternity-education programs.

"We are also confronted with the problem of the actually mentally deficient, of the more or less feeble-minded, and the deranged, epileptic . . . or otherwise mentally abnormal mother," writes this authority. "The 'bad mothering' of these cases is quite unimprovable at an infant welfare center, and a very definite if not relatively very large percentage of our infants are suffering severely as a result of dependence upon such 'mothering.'"[8]

Thus we are brought face to face with another problem of infant mortality. Are we to check the infant mortality rate among the feeble-minded and aid the unfortunate offspring to grow up, a menace to the civilized community even when not actually certifiable as mentally defective or not obviously imbecile?[9]

Other figures and studies indicate the close relationship between feeble-mindedness and the spread of venereal scourges. We are informed that in Michigan, 75 per cent of the prostitute class is infected with some form of venereal disease, and that 75 per cent of the infected are mentally defective—morons, imbeciles, or "border-line" cases most dangerous to the community at large. At least 25 per cent of the inmates of our prisons, according to Dr. Fernald, are mentally defective and belong either to the feeble-minded or to the defective-delinquent class. Nearly 50 per cent of the girls sent to reformatories are

---

6. *The Problem of the Feeble-minded: An Abstract of the Report of the Royal Commission on the Cure and Control of the Feeble-Minded,* London: P. S. King & Son.

7. Editor: This is probably the Helen Campbell (1839–1918) who wrote: *Unto the Third and Fourth Generation, A Study* (1880); *Prisoners of Poverty: Women Wage-Workers, Their Trades and Lives* (1887); and *Women Wage-Earners* (1893).

8. *Feeble-Minded in Ontario: Fourteenth Report for the year ending October 31st, 1919.* Editor: This appears to be an annual report by the Ontario Provincial Secretary.

9. Editor: Here Sanger brought up a grisly solution advocated by Social Darwinians: reduce social services and return society to a 'state of nature' where the 'unfit' die off.

mental defectives. To-day, society treats feeble-minded or "defective delinquent" men or women as "criminals," sentences them to prison or reformatory for a "term," and then releases them at the expiration of their sentences. They are usually at liberty just long enough to reproduce their kind, and then they return again and again to prison. The truth of this statement is evident from the extremely large proportion in institutions of neglected and dependent children, who are the feeble-minded offspring of such feeble-minded parents.

Confronted with these shocking truths about the menace of feeble-mindedness to the race, a menace acute because of the unceasing and unrestrained fertility of such defectives, we are apt to become the victims of a "wild panic for instant action." There is no occasion for hysterical, ill-considered action, specialists tell us. They direct our attention to another phase of the problem, that of the so-called "good feeble-minded." We are informed that imbecility, in itself, is not synonymous with badness. If it is fostered in a "suitable environment," it may express itself in terms of good citizenship and useful occupation. It may thus be transmuted into a docile, tractable, and peaceable element of the community. The moron and the feeble-minded, thus protected, so we are assured, may even marry some brighter member of the community, and thus lessen the chances of procreating another generation of imbeciles. We read further that some of our doctors believe that "in our social scale, there is a place for the good feeble-minded."

In such a reckless and thoughtless differentiation between the "bad" and the "good" feeble-minded, we find new evidence of the conventional middle-class bias that also finds expression among some of the eugenists. We do not object to feeble-mindedness simply because it leads to immorality and criminality; nor can we approve of it when it expresses itself in docility, submissiveness and obedience. We object because both are burdens and dangers to the intelligence of the community. As a matter of fact, there is sufficient evidence to lead us to believe that the so-called "borderline cases" are a greater menace than the out-and-out "defective delinquents" who can be supervised, controlled and prevented from procreating their kind. The advent of the Binet-Simon and similar psychological tests indicates that the mental defective who is glib and plausible, bright looking and attractive, but with a mental vision of seven, eight or nine years, may not merely lower the whole level of intelligence in a school or in a society, but may be encouraged by church and state to increase and multiply until he dominates and gives the prevailing "color"—culturally speaking—to an entire community.[10]

Goddard and Immigrants

The results of the Binet testing of the immigrant samples [by Goddard] is incredible in more ways than one. . . . over 83 percent of all the Jews tested were feebleminded, as were 80 percent of the Hungarians, 79 percent of the Italians, and 87 percent of the Russians.[11]
—J. DAVID SMITH, *MINDS MADE FEEBLE*, 1985

The presence in the public schools of the mentally defective children of men and women who should never have been parents is a problem that is becoming more and more difficult, and is one of the chief reasons for lower educational standards. As one of the greatest living authorities on the subject, Dr. A. Tredgold,[12] has pointed out,[13] this has created a destructive conflict of purpose. "In the case of children with a low intellectual capacity, much of the education at present provided is for all practical purposes a complete waste of time, money and patience. . . . On the other hand, for children of high intellectual capacity, our present system does not go far enough. I believe that much innate potentiality remains undeveloped, even amongst the working classes, owing to the absence of opportunity for higher education, to the disadvantage of the nation. In consequence of these fundamental differences, the catchword 'equality of opportunity' is meaningless and mere claptrap in the absence of any equality to respond to such opportunity. What is wanted is not equality of opportunity, but education adapted to individual potentiality; and if the time and money now spent in the fruitless attempt to make silk-purses out of sows' ears, were devoted to the higher edu-

cation of children of good natural capacity, it would contribute enormously to national efficiency."[14]

In a much more complex manner than has been recognized even by students of this problem, the destiny and the progress of civilization and of human expression has been hindered and held back by this burden of the imbecile and the moron. While we may admire the patience and the deep human sympathy with which the great specialists in feeble-mindedness have expressed the hope of drying up the sources of this evil or of rendering it harmless, we should not permit sympathy or sentimentality to blind us to the fact that health and vitality and human growth likewise need cultivation. "A *laisser faire* policy," writes one investigator, "simply allows the social sore to spread. And a quasi *laisser faire* policy wherein we allow the defective to commit crime and then interfere and imprison him, wherein we grant the defective the personal liberty to do as he pleases, until he pleases to descend to a plane of living below the animal level, and try to care for a few of his descendants who are so helpless that they can no longer exercise that personal liberty to do as they please,"—such a policy increases and multiplies the dangers of the over-fertile feeble-minded.[15]

The Mental Survey of the State of Oregon recently published by the United States Health Service,[16] sets an excellent example and should be followed by every state in the Union and every civilized country as well. It is greatly to the credit of the Western State that it is one of the first officially to recognize the primary importance of this problem and to realize that facts, no matter how fatal to self-satisfaction, must be faced. This survey, authorized by the state legislature, and carried out by the University of Oregon, in collaboration with Dr. C. L. Carlisle of the Public Health service, aided by a large number of volunteers, shows that only a small percentage of mental defectives and morons are in the care of institutions. The rest are widely scattered and their condition unknown or

---

10. Editor: In this paragraph Sanger revealed the broad reach of her agenda. She claimed that the most dangerous threat does not lie with the few who are well below average in intelligence and inclined to social vices, but with the many who are a little below average. It is they whose high birthrates drag down humanity's average intelligence. There may be racial overtones to Sanger's mention of "color," since African-Americans typically scored low on the IQ tests in which she placed so much trust.

11. J. David Smith, *Minds Made Feeble,* 119–20. The reference is to a 1917 Goddard article, "Mental Tests and the Immigrant" in the *Journal of Delinquency,* p. 252. Goddard admitted that his workers deliberately excluded obviously intelligent people from their testing. That was done, he claimed, to correct for the fact that immigration officials had already excluded those who were "obviously feebleminded."

12. Editor: Probably Dr. Alfred F. Tredgold (1870–1952), author of *Mental Deficiency* (1922).

13. *Eugenics Review,* Vol. XIII, p. 339 *et seq.*

14. Editor: In the late nineteenth century, "efficiency" became a explanation for why some races created nations that were more successful than others. Thus, inefficient groups within a society held it back and, if allowed to multiply, threatened its survival.

15. *Dwellers in the Vale of Siddem: A True Story of the Social Aspects of Feeble-mindedness.* By A[rthur]. C. Rogers and Maud A. Merrill: Boston (1919). Editor: Merrill worked on IQ testing with Lewis Terman.

16. Editor: This may be *Preliminary Statistical Report of the Oregon State Survey of Mental Defect, Delinquency, and Dependency* by Chester Lee Carlisle (b. 1876), published in 1922 by the USGPO. Carlisle also wrote *The Problem of the Mental Defective and the Delinquent* (1918) for the NY State Board of Social Welfare.

neglected. They are docile and submissive. They do not attract attention to themselves as do the criminal delinquents and the insane. **Nevertheless, it is estimated that they number no less than 75,000 men, women, and children, out of a total population of 783,000, or about ten per cent. Oregon, it is thought, is no exception to other states. Yet under our present conditions, these people are actually encouraged to increase and multiply and replenish the earth.**

Concerning the importance of the Oregon survey, we may quote Surgeon General H. [S.] Cumming:[17] "the prevention and correction of mental defectives is one of the great public health problems of to-day. It enters into many phases of our work and its influence continually crops up unexpectedly. For instance, work of the Public Health Service in connection with juvenile courts shows that a marked proportion of juvenile delinquency is traceable to some degree of mental deficiency in the offender. For years Public Health officials have concerned themselves only with the disorders of physical health; but now they are realizing the significance of mental health also. The work in Oregon constitutes the first state-wide survey which even begins to disclose the enormous drain on a state, caused by mental defects. One of the objects of the work was to obtain for the people of Oregon an idea of the problem that confronted them and the heavy annual loss, both economic and industrial, that it entailed. Another was to enable the legislators to devise a program that would stop much of the loss, restore to health and bring to lives of industrial usefulness, many of those now down and out, and above all, to save hundreds of children from growing up to lives of misery."

It will be interesting to see how many of our State Legislatures have the intelligence and the courage to follow in the footsteps of Oregon in this respect. Nothing could more effectually stimulate discussion, and awaken intelligence as to the extravagance and cost to the community of our present codes of traditional morality.[18] But we should make sure in all such surveys, that mental defect is not concealed even in such dignified bodies as state legislatures and among those leaders who are urging men and women to reckless and irresponsible procreation.

I have touched upon these various aspects of the complex problem of the feeble-minded, and the menace of the moron to human society, not merely for the purpose of reiterating that it is one of the greatest and most difficult social problems of modern times, demanding an immediate, stern and definite policy, but because it illustrates the actual harvest of reliance upon traditional morality, upon the biblical injunction to increase and multiply, a policy still taught by politician, priest and militarist. Motherhood has been held universally sacred; yet, as Bouchacourt[19] pointed out, "to-day, the dregs of the human species, the blind, the deaf-mute, the degenerate, the nervous, the vicious, the idiotic, the imbecile, the cretins and the epileptics—are better protected than pregnant women." The syphilitic, the irresponsible, the feeble-minded are encouraged to breed unhindered, while all the powerful forces of tradition, of custom, or prejudice, have bolstered up the desperate effort to block the inevitable influence of true civilization in spreading the principles of independence, self-reliance, discrimination and foresight upon which the great practice of intelligent parenthood is based.

To-day we are confronted by the results of this official policy. There is no escaping it; there is no explaining it away. Surely it is an amazing and discouraging phenomenon that the very governments that have seen fit to interfere in practically every phase of the normal citizen's life, dare not attempt to restrain, either by force or persuasion, the moron and the imbecile from producing his large family of feeble-minded offspring.

In my own experience, I recall vividly the case of a feeble-minded girl who every year, for a long period, received the expert attention of a great specialist in one of the best-known maternity hospitals of New York City. The great obstetrician, for the benefit of interns and medical students, performed each year a Caesarian operation upon this unfortunate creature to bring into the world her defective, and, in one case at least, her syphilitic, infant. "Nelly" was then sent to a special room and placed under the care of a day nurse and a night nurse, with extra and special nourishment provided. Each year she returned to the hospital. Such cases are not exceptions; any experienced doctor or nurse can recount similar stories. In the interest of medical science this practice may be justified.

17. Editor: Hugh Smith Cumming (1869–1948) was U. S. Surgeon General from 1920–36. In 1925, he set up a program to inspect potential immigrants in their country of origin to spot those whose immigration was barred. The infamous Tuskegee Syphilis Experiment also began under him. It followed untreated syphilis in African-Americans and did not tell clients that treatment was available. The experiment was not halted until 1973. For details, see *Bad Blood* by James H. Jones.

18. Editor: Note the contrast Sanger drew between the legislature in what was considered a progressive state and "our present codes of traditional morality."

19. Editor: I could not locate this reference. One slight possibility is Leon Bouchacourt, a French-speaking physician (b. 1865) who wrote *De l'Exploration des Organes Internes* (1898).

I am not criticising it from that point of view. I realize as well as the most conservative moralist[20] that humanity requires that healthy members of the race should make certain sacrifices to preserve from death those unfortunates who are born with hereditary taints. But there is a point at which philanthropy may become positively dysgenic, when charity is converted into injustice to the self-supporting citizen, into positive injury to the future of the race. Such a point, it seems obvious, is reached when the incurably defective are permitted to procreate and thus increase their numbers.

The problem of the dependent, delinquent and defective elements in modern society, we must repeat, cannot be minimized because of their alleged small numerical proportion to the rest of the population. The proportion seems small only because we accustom ourselves to the habit of looking upon feeble-mindedness as a separate and distinct calamity to the race, as a chance phenomenon unrelated to the sexual and biological customs not only condoned but even encouraged by our so-called civilization. The actual dangers can only be fully realized when we have acquired definite information concerning the financial and cultural cost of these classes to the community, when we become fully cognizant of the burden of the imbecile upon the whole human race; when we see the funds that should be available for human development, for scientific, artistic and philosophic research, being diverted annually, by hundreds of millions of dollars, to the care and segregation of men, women, and children who never should have been born. The advocate of Birth Control realizes as well as all intelligent thinkers the dangers of interfering with personal liberty. Our whole philosophy is, in fact, based upon the fundamental assumption that man is a self-conscious, self-governing creature, that he should not be treated as a domestic animal; that he must be left free, at least within certain wide limits, to follow his own wishes in the matter of mating and in the procreation of children. Nor do we believe that the community could or should send to the lethal chamber the defective progeny resulting from irresponsible and unintelligent breeding.

But modern society, which has respected the personal liberty of the individual only in regard to the unrestricted and irresponsible bringing into the world of filth and poverty an overcrowding procession of infants foredoomed to death or hereditable disease, is now confronted with the problem of protecting itself and its future generations against the inevitable consequences of this long-practised policy of *laisser-faire*.

The emergency problem of segregation and sterilization must be faced immediately. Every feeble-minded girl or woman of the hereditary type, especially of the moron class, should be segregated during the reproductive period.[21] Otherwise, she is almost certain to bear imbecile children, who in turn are just as certain to breed other defectives. The male defectives are no less dangerous. Segregation carried out for one or two generations would give us only partial control of the problem. **Moreover, when we realize that each feeble-minded person is a potential source of an endless progeny of defect, we prefer the policy of immediate sterilization, of making sure that parenthood is absolutely prohibited to the feeble-minded.**

This, I say, is an emergency measure. But how are we to prevent the repetition in the future of a new harvest of imbecility, the recurrence of new generations of morons and defectives, as the logical and inevitable consequence of the universal application of the traditional and widely approved command to increase and multiply?

At the present moment, we are offered three distinct and more or less mutually exclusive policies by which civilization may hope to protect itself and the generations of the future from the allied dangers of imbecility, defect and delinquency. No one can understand the necessity for Birth Control education without a complete comprehension of the dangers, the inadequacies, or the limitations of the present attempts at control, or the proposed programs for social reconstruction and racial regeneration. It is, therefore, necessary to interpret and criticize the three programs offered to meet our emergency. These may be briefly summarized as follows:

(1) **Philanthropy and Charity:** This is the present and traditional method of meeting the problems of human defect and dependence, of poverty and delinquency. It is emotional, altruistic, at best ameliorative, aiming to meet the individual situation as it arises and presents itself. Its effect in practise is seldom, if ever, truly preventive. Concerned with symptoms, with the allaying of acute and catastrophic miseries, it cannot, if it would, strike at the

---

20. Editor: Two paragraphs back, Sanger saw her foes among those who believed in "traditional morality" and the Bible. Here Sanger saw the "conservative moralist" resisting her agenda on compassionate grounds. Sanger assumed she had the support of liberals, socialists, the more radical feminists, and others with an expansionist view of government.

21. Editor: Note how quickly she discarded her offer of freedom within "wide limits." Two paragraphs back she attacked the high costs of institutional segregation, as a result her ultimate solution is large scale sterilization.

radical causes of social misery. At its worst, it is sentimental and paternalistic.

(2) Marxian Socialism: This may be considered typical of many widely varying schemes of more or less revolutionary social reconstruction, emphasizing the primary importance of environment, education, equal opportunity, and health, in the elimination of the conditions (i. e. capitalistic control of industry) which have resulted in biological chaos and human waste. I shall attempt to show that the Marxian doctrine is both too limited, too superficial and too fragmentary in its basic analysis of human nature and in its program of revolutionary reconstruction.

(3) Eugenics: Eugenics seems to me to be valuable in its critical and diagnostic aspects, in emphasizing the danger of irresponsible and uncontrolled fertility of the "unfit" and the feeble-minded establishing a progressive unbalance in human society and lowering the birth-rate among the "fit." But in its so-called "constructive" aspect, in seeking to reestablish the dominance of healthy strain over the unhealthy, by urging an increased birth-rate among the fit, the Eugenists really offer nothing more farsighted than a "cradle competition" between the fit and the unfit. They suggest in very truth, that all intelligent and respectable parents should take as their example in this grave matter of child-bearing the most irresponsible elements in the community.[22]

---

22. Editor: Sanger's only major disagreement with eugenists was that they wanted to pressure the 'fit' (such as herself) to have more children. She had no problem with their demands that childbearing among the 'unfit' be halted.

—§§§—

Tossing Out the Nuisance!

Mother's eleven children were all ten-pounders and more when born. I used to hear her say with pride: "Not one of them born with a blotch, mark or blemish." We had heard about new-born babies in the neighborhood being "born sick." I had horrible visions of little bodies with sores covering their scrawny frames, and was convinced that this was possible when I saw a sickly baby in the arms of a terrified woman whose drunken husband had thrown the wailing, naked infant into the snow. The child evidently had eczema, and whined night and day. The father was one of those ugly taciturn men who became frenzied at the realization of his wife's pregnancies. She had had ten children, five of them living, and this eleventh was too much for the father's nerves.

I remember having keen sympathy with that man! I could picture him returning home after a hard day's work to a household shrieking with the cries of that suffering baby. They were all baffled at any effort to cure it or to stop its noise. Desperate for want of sleep and quiet, his nerves overcame him, and out the door into the snow the nuisance went![23]

—MARGARET SANGER, *MY FIGHT FOR BIRTH CONTROL,*
1931

---

23. Margaret Sanger, *My Fight for Birth Control* (Farrar & Rinehart: New York, 1931), 12–13. The fact that her sympathies lay with the ill-tempered father rather than his unfortunate child illustrates how she often regarded children as little more than a "nuisance."

"Weeds" by Richard Connell

EDITOR

The same year that Sanger authored *The Pivot of Civilization,* she also published the following short story in her magazine, *Birth Control Review*. It has been added to this new edition of *Pivot* because, as fiction, it exposes the prejudices of Sanger and many of her supporters far more vividly than their more veiled factual statements.

The story is set on a state-run poor farm in New Jersey. Note the number of parallels the writer draws between the people at the farm and animals. Old Man Eggers has fingers "like a crab's legs," their conversation resembles "the buzzing of flies," a beard gives an old man "a simian aspect," and a new-born baby cries "as if someone had trod on the tail of a cat."

In this story, a wide variety of once scientifically impeccable bigotries are blurred together. The conversation is intended to convey an impression of feeble-mindedness. Bit by bit, the little group is linked to other inferior groups and races. Those in a mental asylum are joined to backwoods "piners," babies born with odd-shaped heads, black people, Wops (Polish), Chinks (Asians) and the Irish. True, the inmates themselves do display some prejudice, but far too little from the author's perspective, definitely not enough to prevent breeding across racial lines. Such people, Sanger was telling us, are good targets for birth control. The story leaves uncertain just what the Chairman wanted done with Nettie, perhaps sterilization or placement in a sexually segregated state institution. But he (and by extension Sanger's readers) were clearly not happy to discover what the farm's dull-witted but somewhat religious superintendent had done.

Richard Connell, "Weeds." *Birth Control Review*
(March & April 1922), 38–39, 61–62.

—§§§—

The paupers huddled around the fire in the drafty kitchen, trying to keep warm. Old Man Eggers, from time to time, stirred the smouldering drift-wood with a cane held in fingers gnarled by rheumatism until they looked like a crab's legs.

A raw wind, so salt and moist one might have gargled with it, swept from the sea across the dank, rotting sedge-marsh and soughed through the joints of the loose-knit old farm house that served to shelter the destitute of the town—a rich town in one of the great Eastern states. It was a brutal fall night in the year of 1921.

The dozen inmates—old men and old women—were engaged in a desultory conversation; their voices were like the buzzing of flies. But there was an air of expectancy in all the drabness of their tone. Occasionally an old woman would go and stand near door that opened off the kitchen; she'd listen there, her hand cupped to her ear, and then return, muttering, to her place near the fire. The others would search her face for news.

"The last one came at three o'clock in the morning," said Mrs. Purley, from a toothless mouth. "I helped." Mrs. Purley was the aristocracy of the poor farm; she was the widow of a once prosperous barber.

"A boy wasn't it?" asked Old Man Eggers, stirring the smoking fire, till his eyes smarted.

"It was not," replied Mrs. Purley.

"Ah, a girl then?" said Old Man Eggers, nodding sagely. "Drat this wet wood."

"A *little* girl," confirmed Mrs. Purley, emphasizing the adjective as if new-born children were, as a general rule, enormous.

A very old man, bent and bleary, with a fringe of white beard that gave him a simian aspect, who had been drowsing in a corner, suddenly remarked, in a high, faltering voice:

"I dug nigh onto twenty thousand claims in the summer of ninety-one."

"Drat you and your clams," cried Old Man Eggers, turning on the speaker with an impotent viciousness. "We don't care how many clams you dug, you old fool."

"I did though," said the clam-digger, mildly, and lapsed into somnolence again.

An old woman returned from listening at the door.

"She's a-groaning and a-moaning'" she reported.

"Ah" exclaimed Mrs. Purley, brightening perceptibly, "she's beginnin'. We'll hear some fine moanin' and groanin' before she's through." . . . .

"Where's the little girl now?" asked a thin, tride, middle-aged woman, on the outer rim of the circle about the reluctant fire. She was, plainly, a newcomer.

"'Sylum" answered Mrs. Purley, briefly, as one who does not wish to encourage familiarity. She had her dignity to preserve; the woman was just a common 'piner,' and not the social equal of the widow of a barber. A 'piner' is a dweller in the squalid settlements among the scrub pines, a descendant, if local history is correct, from the pirates who once ravaged the coast. The stock is enfeebled and decadent from generations of inbreeding.

"'Sylum?" quavered the piner. "Sylum? Why?"

"Buggy?" the piner's tone was puzzled. "But she was only a baby?"

"You should have saw her head," retorted Mrs. Purley, with finality.

"Hey, you! Can't you realise that we need quality, not quantity?"

"Why? Was they anything wrong with it." The piner was fascinated by the thought.

"Was they?" Mrs. Purley lowered her voice. "It was shaped just like a peanut!"

"And it wasn't no bigger than a potato," collaborated Old Man Eggers, pottering with the fire.

The lean piner woman nodded comprehendingly.

"How many did ya have," asked the fat man. A spurt of flickering light from the fire made him seem to leer.

"Eleven, or maybe it was twelve. I disremember," the woman answered."

"All livin'?" asked the fat man.

All dead, 'ceptin' Luke," she replied, dully.

"Where's Luke," he inquired.

"'Sylum," she replied, in her colorless voice. The moan of a human being, now faint, now louder, came from behind the door. . . .

"It won't be long now," said Mrs. Purley, with the air of an expert. "She's a quick one, Nettie is."

A fat man sniggered and spat into the flames.

"I wonder if it'll be black," he said.

"You'd better not let Clem Skiff hear you say that," said Old Man Eggers. "It's his'n."

"So he says," growled the fat man. "But what about them Wops that was makin' a road here last Spring?'

"Well, what of it," demanded Mrs. Purley, testily. "Wops ain't black, are they?"

"No," said the fat man, as if making a concession, "they ain't. But Wops is Chinks. Maybe it will be yella."

"Wops ain't Chinks," put in the lean piner woman, shrilly.

Mrs. Purley made the newcomer quail before her glance, as she pronounced her judgment.

"Wops *is* Chinks. I guess I know. When Mr. P. was head barber to the American House in Paterson, he had two Wops workin' for him and they was both Chinks. Yes, it may turn out to be yella."

"The last boy was black, just the same," said the fat man, argumentatively. "Black as soot."

"What become of him?" asked the Piner woman, without interest.

"'Sylum," answered Mrs. Purley.

"Head shaped like a peanut?" asked the piner woman.

"Naw," answered Old Man Eggers. "It come to a point."

There was silence again, and a clock ticked noisily.

"Nettie said that her pa had a head like that," observed Mrs. Purley. "It must run in the family."

"Her pa and ma livin'?" asked the lean woman.

"Her pa is. Her ma die, havin' her ninth."

"Why don't her pa take care of her?" asked the piner woman.

"Huh," grunted Mrs. Purley, "she had to take care of him. He's a Moran."

"He's a what?"

"A Moran. So Doctor Roach said, anyhow. Irish, I suppose," said Mrs. Purley.

"Where is he," asked the piner woman.

"'Sylum," answered Mrs. Purley, drawing her shawl more tightly around her bony shoulders.

The fat man broke another lull in the conversation by throwing out a question.

"How old would ya say Nettie is, now," he asked replenishing his quid.

"Well," said Mrs. Purley, judiciously, "she looks to be all of thirty-six. But let's see now. She come her six years ago, and she was only a slip of a girl then. Four months after she come she had her first, a boy. I helped. She told me then she was twenty. So now she must be around twenty-six, I guess." . . .

Old Man Eggers jabbed at the fire.

"I wonder what's keepin' Clem Skiff," he said. "He went out to fetch some fire-wood half an hour ago."

"Clem ain't very quick," remarked Mrs. Purley.

"He's quick enough at some things," sniggered the fat man, missing the fire-place by an inch.

"He's got the mind of a child," said Mrs. Purley, ignoring the fat man's remark. "Dr. Roach made him play with blocks, one day, and I heard him say, 'Why his brain is only seven years old.'"

"He must be all of thirty, though," put in Old Man Eggers. . . .

Sounds of pain from the next room grew loud. The women made clucking noises of sympathy.

"Clem Skiff don't seem to show much interest," remarked one of the women, a faded creature in dingy black.

"Oh, this ain't the first time for Clem," said the fat man, with a sound approaching a titter. "He's always been quite a hand with the ladies."

"I told Nettie to watch out," said Mrs. Purley, virtuously. "But she didn't pay no heed."

The faded woman in black sniffed.

"Sinfully hussy," she snapped. "Ain't got no more morals than a mud-turtle. The Heavenly Redeemer will punish her."

The other women said, "Hush;" the cries of the woman beyond the door grew louder still.

"Perhaps it'll be a Chink, after all," observed the fat man, hopefully.

They listened in silence to the woman's screams of anguish. The wind rattled the old farm house. Then there was a new sound, as if some one had trod on the tail of a cat.

The door opened. A messy man, a doctor gone to seed, appeared.

"I don't suppose there's such a thing as a swig of brandy in the house," he said over his shoulder to a thin, washed-out man behind him.

The washed-out man was Caleb Frear, the superintendent of the poor farm.

"Nary a swig," replied Caleb Frear, loudly, so that all might hear. Then he whispered something to the doctor, who grinned knowingly, and they started to pass through the kitchen on their way to the superintendent's "office."

But as they passed, Old Man Eggers caught the doctor by the sleeve.

"What is it?" he asked. The old men and women craned their necks to hear.

"It's a child!" replied the doctor, who had a local reputation as a wit.

"Is it a Chink," asked the fat man anxiously.

"No, it's white all right," said the doctor.

"Girl?"

"Nope."

"Boy?"

"What else could it be?"

The lean piner woman plucked at the doctor's arm.

"How is its head," she asked, a sudden excitement in her voice.

"It's just the shape of a peanut," replied the doctor, cheerfully.

Mixing Races

If dogs are left to themselves, in some canine "asylum" or "melting pot," they are cheerfully promiscuous, but do not produce a super-dog. On the contrary they tend to revert to the "yallar dog," the jackal type so far behind them.[24]

—CHARLOTTE PERKINS GILMAN, 1923

—II—

The chairman of the State Board for the Guardianship of Orphans, in his office in the capital of the state, received, the following day, a report of the birth at the poor farm. The Board would, of course, be responsible for the child.

With pursed lips he glanced over the official communication from Superintendent Caleb Frear, and ran over the records in the case.

"Nettie Pinkney," the letter ran, "aged 26 years, a mentally defective pauper, gave birth to a boy, November 29, 1920. Father is believed to be one Clem Skiff, a moron, also an inmate of this institution. Dr. C. B. Roach reports that the formation of the child's head is abnormal."

The Chairman sighed as he put down the paper.

"Her fourth in six years," he remarked to Gaines, his assistant. "All of them hopeless imbeciles. And one of them a black. What a record!"

He was a new Chairman, with a zeal for his work, and the affair plainly shocked him.

"Gaines," he said, decisively, to his assistant, "we'll have to take a run down there and put a stop to this sort of thing. Unless we do something about it, that Pinkney woman will people the state with idiots. She's had four already, and she's only twenty-six. Four more charges for the state. Just think, from the financial side alone, what that will mean. Why, we'll have another Jukes family on our hands."

"Shall I notify the Superintendent you are coming?" asked Gaines.

"Yes," said the Chairman, "I think you'd better. Tell him we'll be down Wednesday. Make the letter good and hot so it will scare him a bit. Of course, we can't do much about the case now; the thing's happened. But we can try to prevent it from happening again."

Weeds in the Garden

It is also a mistake to think that social evolution requires the even march of all races to the same

24. Charlotte Perkins Gilman, "Is American Too Hospitable?" *Forum* 70 (Oct. 1923), 1986. She refers to mixing human races.

goal. . . . Evolution selects, and social evolution follows the same law. If you are trying to improve corn you do not wait to bring all the weeds in the garden to the corn level before going on.[25]

—CHARLOTTE PERKINS GILMAN, 1923

—III—

Caleb Frear received the Chairman's letter the next day, and adjusting his spectacles to his thin, red nose, he turned up the kerosene lamp on his office, and spelled out the document. Caleb Frear was superintendant of the poor farm because he was the brother-in-law of a minor local politician. His policy in public office was to avoid "trouble," and here was trouble, through no fault of his. How could he exercise control over that Pinkney woman's morals? They grieved him, of course, for he was a religious man and each day at the poor farm opened and closed with prayers. But he couldn't quite see how he could be held responsible. Still, there was the Chairman's letter, plain as day. So Caleb Frear locked up the inmates in the old farm house, and strolled over to town to consult his political brother-in-law, who would be sure to suggest a solution; he was very adept at fixing things.

When the Chairman and his assistant arrived at the poor farm, which was situated on a bleak road near the sea because the county had secured that property when its owner failed to pay the taxes on it, they found Caleb Frear, in his ceremonial collar and tie, waiting for them, with a bland smile.

"Ah, gentlemen, and how are you," he exclaimed, warmly shaking their hands.

"We have come—" began the Chairman in a tone calculated to impress the Superintendent with the seriousness of the situation.

"Yes, yes, of course," interrupted Frear, "and I'm sorry. Because, gentlemen, you have had this long, cold trip for nothing."

"For nothing?" the Chairman raised his eye-brows.

"Why, yes," said the Superintendent. "You come about the—er—goings-on of that Pinkney girl, didn't you?"

"Yes," said the Chairman, sternly. "We did." We came to see to it that—"

"Well," said the Superintendent, rubbing his hands, "it's all fixed up!"

He spoke with the serenity of one who is conscious of a good deed well done.

"All—fixed—up?" the Chairman repeated the words slowly with knitted brow. "I don't understand."

"Yep," said the Superintendent, with a calm smile, "it can't never happen again!"

"Can't happen again?" the Chairman was alarmed. "Good Heavens, man, what have you done?"

"Y'see gentlemen," said the Superintendent with an air of extreme benevolence, "y'ah know I'm a moral man. The goings-on of that there Pinkney woman grieved me."

He struck a righteous attitude and went on.

"What she done was contrary to the Laws of Man," he said dramatically. "They was contrary to the Laws of Nature. And to the Laws of God. So, I've made it impossible for her to have any more illegitimate children!"

"What did you do?" demanded the Chairman.

"Well," said the Superintendent proudly, "I called in a minister and had him marry them. Now they can have all the kids they're a mind to."

—§§§—

Breeding Like Weeds

Here then is my plan. Free women from compulsory or accidental maternity. Free men from undesired paternity. Teach them the truth and science of parenthood. . . . By the establishment of clinics or bureaus in which men and women will be taught the science of parenthood and the science of breeding. In brief, by the universal establishment of Birth Control clinics where contraception will be taught in a clean, scientific manner, and out of which all potential parents will be shown why children should be brought into the world by choice and not by chance.

The value of child life will thus be greatly enhanced. Each one will be valued and loved and give a chance to develop his full potentialities. And with the development of this constructive program, less and less money would be diverted to purely ameliorated efforts to succor the dependent and the delinquent—since these classes would be decreasing in number instead of breeding like weeds.[26]

—MARGARET SANGER, "WE MUST BREED A RACE OF THOROUGHBREDS," 1929

---

25. Charlotte Perkins Gilman, "Is American Too Hospitable?" *Forum* 70 (Oct. 1923), 1985–86.

26. Margaret Sanger, "We Must Breed a Race of Thoroughbreds." Attached to a letter to C. Harold Smith of the *New York Evening World* (May 7, 1929). Quote from a draft in which all this text was crossed out. A handwritten note on the letter says, "Notpub." Sanger/Library of Congress, LOC131:122.

5

The Cruelty of Charity

"Fostering the good-for-nothing at the expense of the good is an extreme cruelty. It is a deliberate storing up of miseries for future generations. There is no greater curse to posterity than that of bequeathing them an increasing population of imbeciles." —HERBERT SPENCER

The last century has witnessed the rise and development of philanthropy and organized charity.[1] Coincident with the all-conquering power of machinery and capitalistic control, with the unprecedented growth of great cities and industrial centers, and the creation of great proletarian populations, modern civilization has been confronted, to a degree hitherto unknown in human history, with the complex problem of sustaining human life in surroundings and under conditions flagrantly dysgenic.

The program, as I believe all competent authorities in contemporary philanthropy and organized charity would agree, has been altered in aim and purpose. It was first the outgrowth of humanitarian and altruistic idealism, perhaps not devoid of a strain of sentimentalism, of an idealism that was aroused by a desperate picture of human misery intensified by the industrial revolution. It has developed in later years into a program not so much aiming to succor the unfortunate victims of circumstances, as to effect what we may term social sanitation. Primarily, it is a program of self-protection. Contemporary philanthropy, I believe, recognizes that extreme poverty and overcrowded slums are veritable breeding-grounds of epidemics, disease, delinquency and dependency. Its aim, therefore, is to prevent the individual family from sinking to that abject condition in which it will become a much heavier burden upon society.[2]

There is no need here to criticize the obvious limitations of organized charities in meeting the desperate problem of destitution. We are all familiar with these criticisms: the common indictment of "inefficiency" so often brought against public and privately endowed agencies. The charges include the high cost of administration; the pauperization of deserving poor, and the encouragement and fostering of the "undeserving"; the progressive destruction of self-respect and self-reliance by the paternalistic interference of social agencies; the impossibility of keeping pace with the ever-increasing multiplication of factors and influences responsible for the perpetuation of human misery; the misdirection and misappropriation of endowments; the absence of inter-organization and coordination of the various agencies of church, state, and privately endowed institutions; the "crimes of charity" that are occasionally exposed in newspaper scandals. These and similar strictures we may ignore as irrelevant to our present purpose, as inevitable but not incurable faults that have been and are being eliminated in the slow but certain growth of a beneficent power in modern civilization. In reply to such criticisms, the protagonist of modern philanthropy might justly point to the honest and sincere workers and disinterested scientists it has mobilized, to the self-sacrificing and hard-working executives who have awakened public attention to the evils of poverty and the menace to the race engendered by misery and filth.

Even if we accept organized charity at its own valuation, and grant that it does the best it can, it is exposed to a more profound criticism. It reveals a fundamental and irremediable defect. Its very success, its very efficiency, its very necessity to the social order, are themselves the most unanswerable indictment. Organized charity itself is the symptom of a malignant social disease.

---

1. Editor: Along with his socialist newspapers and free-thinking books, Sanger's father liked Herbert Spencer, who, Sanger said, "was modern for that time." But as Spenser's Social Darwinism went out of fashion, Sanger came to consider the British philosopher "old fogyish" (See her 1938 autobiography, pp. 44, 103). In the preceding chapter, however, Sanger had hinted at using Social Darwinian solutions to eliminate the 'unfit.'
2. Editor: Sanger was referring to the social hygiene movement.

Drawn by Cornelia Barns

THE NEW VOTER AT WORK

Those vast, complex, interrelated organizations aiming to control and to diminish the spread of misery and destitution and all the menacing evils that spring out of this sinisterly fertile soil, are the surest sign that our civilization has bred, is breeding and is perpetuating constantly increasing numbers of defectives, delinquents and dependents. My criticism, therefore, is not directed at the "failure" of philanthropy, but rather at its success.

These dangers inherent in the very idea of humanitarianism and altruism, dangers which have to-day produced their full harvest of human waste, of inequality and inefficiency, were fully recognized in the last century at the moment when such ideas were first put into practice. Readers of Huxley's attack on the Salvation Army[3] will

_____

3. Editor: This refers to a series of letters that Thomas H. Huxley, England's most celebrated agnostic, wrote to *The Times* of London in 1890 and 1891 and later published in *Collected Essays,* IX. Sanger may be recalling Huxley's description of Salvation Army belief: "That the only adequate means to such reformation of the individual man is the adoption of that form of somewhat corybantic Christianity of which the soldiers of the Salvation Army are the militant missionaries. This implies the belief that the excitement of the religious emotions (largely by processes described by their employers as 'rousing' and 'convivial') is a desirable and trustworthy method of permanently amending the conduct of mankind." Huxley claimed history was "wholly adverse" to the idea.

recall his penetrating and stimulating condemnation of the debauch of sentimentalism which expressed itself in so uncontrolled a fashion in the Victorian era. One of the most penetrating of American thinkers, Henry James, Sr., sixty or seventy years ago wrote:

I have been so long accustomed to see the most arrant deviltry transact itself in the name of benevolence, that the moment I hear a profession of good will from almost any quarter, I instinctively look around for a constable or place my hand within reach of a bell-rope.[4] My ideal of human intercourse would be a state of things in which no man will ever stand in need of any other man's help, but will derive all his satisfaction from the great social tides which own no individual names. I am sure no man can be put in a position of dependence upon another, without the other's very soon becoming—if he accepts the duties of the relation—utterly degraded out of his just human proportions. No man can play the Deity to his fellow man with impunity—I mean, spiritual impunity, of course. For see: if I am at all satisfied with that relation, if it contents me to be in a position of generosity towards others, I must be remarkably indifferent at bottom to the gross social inequality which permits that position, and, instead of resenting the enforced humiliation of my fellow man to myself in the interests of humanity, I acquiesce in it for the sake of the profit it yields to my own self-complacency. I do hope the reign of benevolence is over; until that event occurs, I am sure the reign of God will be impossible.

To-day, we may measure the evil effects of "benevolence" of this type, not merely upon those who have indulged in it, but upon the community at large. These effects have been reduced to statistics and we cannot, if we would, escape their significance. Look, for instance (since they are close at hand, and fairly representative of conditions elsewhere) at the total annual expenditures of public and private "charities and corrections" for the State of New York. For the year ending June 30, 1919, the expenditures of public institutions and agencies amounted to $33,936,205.88. The expenditures of privately supported and endowed institutions for the same year, amount to $58,100,530.98. This makes a total, for public and private charities and corrections of

_____

4. Editor: James' remark illustrates the mindset of many who supported Sanger. Without questioning their right to do so, they see society as something that *they* control, with a "constable" always on call and a "bell-rope" to summon a servant always within reach. Deciding who will have children comes easily to such people. It is easy to suspect that his remarks about not want to humiliate with benevolence was simply a cover for a desire to rid the world of all who need assistance.

$92,036,736.86. A conservative estimate of the increase for the year (1920-1921) brings this figure approximately to one-hundred and twenty-five millions. These figures take on an eloquent significance if we compare them to the comparatively small amounts spent upon education, conservation of health and other constructive efforts. Thus, while the City of New York spent $7.35 per capita on public education in the year 1918, it spent on public charities no less than $2.66. Add to this last figure an even larger amount dispensed by private agencies, and we may derive some definite sense of the heavy burden of dependency, pauperism and delinquency upon the normal and healthy sections of the community.

Statistics now available also inform us that more than a million dollars are spent annually to support the public and private institutions in the state of New York for the segregation of the feeble-minded and the epileptic. A million and a half is spent for the up-keep of state prisons, those homes of the "defective delinquent." Insanity, which, we should remember, is to a great extent hereditary, annually drains from the state treasury no less than $11,985,695.55, and from private sources and endowments another twenty millions. When we learn further that the total number of inmates in public and private institutions in the State of New York—in alms-houses, reformatories, schools for the blind, deaf and mute, in insane asylums, in homes for the feeble-minded and epileptic—amounts practically to less than sixty-five thousand, an insignificant number compared to the total population, our eyes should be opened to the terrific cost to the community of this dead weight of human waste.

Like Rats from Holes

Early in the year 1912 I came to a sudden realization that my work as a nurse and my activities in social service were entirely palliative and consequently futile and useless to relieve the misery I saw all about me. . . .

Were it possible for me to depict the revolting conditions existing in the homes of some of the women I attended in that one year, one would find it hard to believe. There was at that time, and doubtless is still today, a sub-stratum of men and women whose lives are absolutely untouched by social agencies.

The way they live is almost beyond belief. They hate and fear any prying into their homes or into their lives. They resent being talked to. The women slink in and out of their homes on their way to market like rats from their holes. The men beat their wives sometimes black and blue, but no one interferes. The children are cuffed, kicked, and chased about, but woe to the child who dares to tell tales out of the home![5]

—MARGARET SANGER, *MY FIGHT FOR BIRTH CONTROL,*

The United States Public Health Survey of the State of Oregon, recently published, shows that even a young community, rich in natural resources, and unusually progressive in legislative measures, is no less subject to this burden. Out of a total population of 783,000 it is estimated that more than 75,000 men, women and children are dependents, feeble-minded, or delinquents. Thus about 10 per cent of the population is a constant drain on the finances, health, and future of that community. These figures represent a more definite and precise survey than the rough one indicated by the statistics of charities and correction for the State of New York. The figures yielded by this Oregon survey are also considerably lower than the average shown by the draft examination,[6] a fact which indicates that they are not higher than might be obtained from other States.

Organized charity is thus confronted with the problem of feeble-mindedness and mental defect. But just as the State has so far neglected the problem of mental defect until this takes the form of criminal delinquency, so the tendency of our philanthropic and charitable agencies has been to pay no attention to the problem until it has expressed itself in terms of pauperism and delinquency. Such "benevolence" is not merely ineffectual; it is positively injurious to the community and the future of the race.

But there is a special type of philanthropy or benevolence, now widely advertised and advocated, both as a federal program and as worthy of private endowment, which strikes me as being more insidiously injurious than any other. This concerns itself directly with the function of maternity, and aims to supply *gratis* medical and nursing facilities to slum mothers.[7] Such women are to be visited by nurses and to receive instruction in the "hygiene of pregnancy"; to be guided in making arrangements for confinements; to be invited to come to the doctor's clinics for examination and supervision. They are, we are informed, to "receive

5. Margaret Sanger, *My Fight for Birth Control* (Farrar & Rinehart: New York, 1931), 46–47. Sanger would often claim she left part-time nursing for birth control activism to help such women. It might be more accurate to say that her nursing led her to loathe them, and she got into birth control to get rid of such people one unborn child at a time. Viewed that way, the suspicions these people had were amply justified.

6. Editor: For how a colleague of Sanger's interpreted the Army IQ tests, see Chap. XXVII.

adequate care during pregnancy, at confinement, and for one month afterward." Thus are mothers and babies to be saved. "Childbearing is to be made safe." The work of the maternity centers in the various American cities in which they have already been established and in which they are supported by private contributions and endowment, it is hardly necessary to point out, is carried on among the poor and more docile sections of the city, among mothers least able, through poverty and ignorance, to afford the care and attention necessary for successful maternity. Now, as the findings of Tredgold and Karl Pearson and the British Eugenists so conclusively show, and as the infant mortality reports so thoroughly substantiate, a high rate of fecundity is always associated with the direst poverty, irresponsibility, mental defect, feeble-mindedness, and other transmissible taints. The effect of maternity endowments and maternity centers supported by private philanthropy would have, perhaps already have had, exactly the most dysgenic tendency. **The new government program would facilitate the function of maternity among the very classes in which the absolute necessity is to discourage it.**

Vision, Integrity and Valor

Mrs. Margaret Sanger, founder of the American Birth Control League, has been awarded the annual medal of the American Woman's Association, which cites her for the qualities of "vision, integrity and valor." Mrs. Sanger deserves this honor; she deserves more honors than a world against whose darkness of mind she has fought bravely and consistently for twenty years is every likely to give her.[8]

— *NEW YORK HERALD TRIBUNE,* 1931

Such "benevolence" is not merely superficial and near-sighted. It conceals a stupid cruelty, because it is not courageous enough to face unpleasant facts. Aside from the question of the unfitness of many women to become mothers, aside from the very definite deterioration in the human stock that such programs would inevitably hasten, we may question its value even to the normal though

unfortunate mother.[9] For it is never the intention of such philanthropy to give the poor over-burdened and often undernourished mother of the slum the opportunity to make the choice herself, to decide whether she wishes time after to time to bring children into the world. It merely says "Increase and multiply: We are prepared to help you do this." Whereas the great majority of mothers realize the grave responsibility they face in keeping alive and rearing the children they have already brought into the world, the maternity center would teach them how to have more. The poor woman is taught how to have her seventh child, when what she wants to know is how to avoid bringing into the world her eighth.

Such philanthropy, as Dean Inge has so unanswerably pointed out, is kind only to be cruel, and unwittingly promotes precisely the results most deprecated. It encourages the healthier and more normal sections of the world to shoulder the burden of unthinking and indiscriminate fecundity of others; which brings with it, as I think the reader must agree, a dead weight of human waste. Instead of decreasing and aiming to eliminate the stocks that are most detrimental to the future of the race and the world, it tends to render them to a menacing degree dominant.

On the other hand, the program is an indication of a suddenly awakened public recognition of the shocking conditions surrounding pregnancy, maternity, and infant welfare prevailing at the very heart of our boasted civilization. So terrible, so unbelievable, are these conditions of child-bearing, degraded far below the level of primitive and barbarian tribes, nay, even below the plane of brutes, that many high-minded people, confronted with

---

7. Editor: Sanger is probably referring to the 1921 Sheppard-Towner Act which provided federal funding for state-run maternal and infant-care clinics. Her hostility toward programs that assisted poor mothers should be kept in mind when reading her statistics and stories about the plight of poor mothers. Contrast that to the zeal she had for programs to give those same women birth control.

8. From the *New York Herald Tribune,* Nov. 13, 1931. Quoted in Ellen Chesler, *Woman of Valor* (New York: Simon & Schuster, 1992), 7. One wonders if anyone in the nation's news media ever read Sanger. If so, did they agree with her agenda?

9. Editor: Note that Sanger regarded "many mothers" as inherently unfit "to become mothers" at all, not simply that a lack of birth control knowledge was forcing them to have more children than their family's income could support. The argument that follows borders on the bizarre. A mother of seven certainly didn't need a maternity center to teach her "how to have more." She knew that quite well. But the center could help her keep the children she had from dying of preventable causes. Sanger, it seems, was angry that poor children existed at all and was happy to see them disappear by any means.

such revolting and disgraceful facts, lose that calmness of vision and impartiality of judgment so necessary in any serious consideration of this vital problem. Their "hearts" are touched; they become hysterical; they demand immediate action; and enthusiastically and generously they support the first superficial program that is advanced. Immediate action may sometimes be worse than no action at all. **The "warm heart" needs the balance of the cool head.**[10] **Much harm has been done in the world by those too-good-hearted folk who have always demanded that "something be done at once."**

They do not stop to consider that the very first thing to be done is to subject the whole situation to the deepest and most rigorous thinking. As the late Walter Bagehot wrote in a significant but too often forgotten passage:

> The most melancholy of human reflections, perhaps, is that on the whole it is a question whether the benevolence of mankind does more good or harm. Great good, no doubt, philanthropy does, but then it also does great evil. It augments so much vice, it multiplies so much suffering, it brings to life such great populations to suffer and to be vicious, that it is open to argument whether it be or be not an evil to the world, and this is entirely because excellent people fancy they can do much by rapid action, and that they will most benefit the world when they most relieve their own feelings; that as soon as an evil is seen, 'something' ought to be done to stay and prevent it. One may incline to hope that the balance of good over evil is in favor of benevolence; one can hardly bear to think that it is not so; but anyhow it is certain that there is a most heavy debt of evil, and that this burden might almost all have been spared us if philanthropists as well as others had not inherited from their barbarous forefathers a wild passion for instant action.

It is customary, I believe, to defend philanthropy and charity upon the basis of the sanctity of human life. Yet recent events in the world reveal a curious contradiction in this respect. Human life is held sacred, as a general Christian principle, until war is declared, when humanity indulges in a universal debauch of bloodshed and barbarism, inventing poison gases and every type of diabolic suggestion to facilitate killing and starvation. Blockades are enforced to weaken and starve civilian populations—women and children.[11] This accomplished, the pendulum of mob passion swings back to the opposite extreme, and the compensatory emotions express themselves in hysterical fashion. Philanthropy and charity are then unleashed. We begin to hold human life sacred again. We try to save the lives of the people we formerly sought to weaken by devastation, disease and starvation. We indulge in "drives," in campaigns of relief, in a general orgy of international charity.

We are thus witnessing to-day the inauguration of a vast system of international charity. As in our more limited communities and cities, where self-sustaining and self-reliant sections of the population are forced to shoulder the burden of the reckless and irresponsible, so in the great world community the more prosperous and incidentally less populous nations are asked to relieve and succor those countries which are either the victims of the widespread havoc of war, of militaristic statesmanship, or of the age-long tradition of reckless propagation and its consequent over-population.

The people of the United States have recently been called upon to exercise their traditional generosity not merely to aid the European Relief Council in its efforts to keep alive three million, five hundred thousand starving children in Central Europe, but in addition to contribute to that enormous fund to save the thirty million Chinese who find themselves at the verge of starvation, owing to one of those recurrent famines which strike often at that densely populated and inert country, where procreative recklessness is encouraged as a matter of duty. The results of this international charity have not justified the effort nor repaid the generosity to which it appealed. In the first place, no effort was made to prevent the recurrence of the disaster; in the second place, philanthropy of this type attempts to sweep back the tide of miseries created by unrestricted propagation, with the feeble broom of sentiment. As one of the most observant and impartial of authorities on the Far East, J. O. P. Bland,[12] has pointed out: "So long as China maintains a birth-rate that is estimated at fifty-five per thousand or more, the only possible alternative to these visitations would be emigration and this would have to be on such a scale as would speedily overrun and overfill the habitable globe. Neither humanitarian schemes, international charities nor philanthropies can prevent widespread disaster to a people

10. Editor: Sanger described this as her "head" book. Here she explains what head-centered thinking means.

11. Editor: Here Sanger equates those who start wars with those who opposed her. It seems unlikely, however, that the "Catholic hierarchy" she saw as her greatest foe had much to do with World War I. Sanger was simply smearing all those she disliked with a very broad brush. Nor was there inconsistency between the need to defeat the Germany and a willingness to supply starving German children with food after the war.

12. Editor: This was probably John Otway Percy Bland (1863–1945) author of numerous books on Asia including *Recent Events and Present Policies in China* (1912) and *China, Japan and Korea* (1921).

which habitually breeds up to and beyond the maximum limits of its food supply." Upon this point, it is interesting to add, Mr. Frank A. Vanderlip has likewise pointed out the inefficacy and misdirection of this type of international charity.[13]

Mr. Bland further points out:

> The problem presented is one with which neither humanitarian nor religious zeal can ever cope, so long as we fail to recognize and attack the fundamental cause of these calamities. As a matter of sober fact, the benevolent activities of our missionary societies to reduce the death-rate by the prevention of infanticide and the checking of disease, actually serve in the end to aggravate the pressure of population upon its food-supply and to increase the severity of the inevitably resultant catastrophe. What is needed for the prevention, or, at least, the mitigation of these scourges, is an organized educational propaganda, directed first against polygamy and the marriage of minors and the unfit, and, next, toward such a limitation of the birth-rate as shall approximate the standard of civilized countries.[14]
> **But so long as Bishops and well meaning philanthropists in England and America continue to praise and encourage 'the glorious fertility of the East' there can be but little hope of minimizing the penalties of the ruthless struggle for existence in China, and Nature's law will therefore continue to work out its own pitiless solution, weeding out every year millions of predestined weaklings.**

This rapid survey is enough, I hope, to indicate the manifold inadequacies inherent in present policies of philanthropy and charity. The most serious charge that can be brought against modern "benevolence" is that it encourages the perpetuation of defectives, delinquents and dependents. These are the most dangerous elements in the world community, the most devastating curse on human progress and expression. Philanthropy is a gesture characteristic of modern business lavishing upon the unfit the profits extorted from the community at large. Looked at impartially, this compensatory generosity is in its final effect probably more dangerous, more dysgenic, more blighting than the initial practice of profiteering and the social injustice which makes some too rich and others too poor.

—§§§—

13. *Birth Control Review.* Vol. V. No. 4, p. 7.

14. Editor: In other words, Westerners will dictate Chinese marriage customs, indoctrinate them in negative eugenists, and force their birthrate down to the level of France. Note how Bland shaped events in China into a Malthusian and Darwinian mold called "Nature's law."

The Cost to the State of the Socially Unfit

By Mary Winsor

A Paper Read at the Fifth International Birth Control Conference, London.

6

Neglected Factors of the World Problem

War has thrust upon us a new internationalism. To-day the world is united by starvation, disease and misery. We are enjoying the ironic internationalism of hatred. The victors are forced to shoulder the burden of the vanquished. International philanthropies and charities are organized. The great flux of immigration and emigration has recommenced. Prosperity is a myth; and the rich are called upon to support huge philanthropies, in the futile attempt to sweep back the tide of famine and misery. In the face of this new internationalism, this tangled unity of the world, all proposed political and economic programs reveal a woeful common bankruptcy. They are fragmentary and superficial. None of them go to the root of this unprecedented world problem. Politicians offer political solutions—like the League of Nations or the limitation of navies. Militarists offer new schemes of competitive armament. Marxians offer the Third Internationale and industrial revolution. Sentimentalists offer charity and philanthropy. Coordination or correlation is lacking. And matters go steadily from bad to worse.

The first essential in the solution of any problem is the recognition and statement of the factors involved. Now in this complex problem which to-day confronts us, no attempt has been made to state the primary factors. The statesman believes they are all political. Militarists believe they are all military and naval. Economists, including under the term the various schools for Socialists, believe they are industrial and financial. Churchmen look upon them as religious and ethical. What is lacking is the recognition of that fundamental factor which reflects and coordinates these essential but incomplete phases of the problem—the factor of reproduction. For in all problems affecting the welfare of a biological species, and particularly in all problems of human welfare, two fundamental forces work against each other. There is hunger as the driving force of all our economic, industrial

and commercial organizations; and there is the reproductive impulse in continual conflict with our economic, political settlements, race adjustments and the like. Official moralists, statesmen, politicians, philanthropists and economists display an astounding disregard of this second disorganizing factor. They treat the world of men as if it were purely a hunger world instead of a hunger-sex world. Yet there is no phase of human society, no question of politics, economics, or industry that is not tied up in almost equal measure with the expression of both of these primordial impulses. You cannot sweep back overpowering dynamic instincts by catchwords. You can neglect and thwart sex only at your peril. You cannot solve the problem of hunger and ignore the problem of sex. They are bound up together.

While the gravest attention is paid to the problem of hunger and food, that of sex is neglected. Politicians and scientists are ready and willing to speak of such things as a "high birth rate," infant mortality, the dangers of immigration or over-population. But with few exceptions they cannot bring themselves to speak of Birth Control. **Until they shall have broken through the traditional inhibitions concerning the discussion of sexual matters, until they recognize the force of the sexual instinct, and until they recognize Birth Control as the *pivotal factor* in the problem confronting the world to-day, our statesmen must continue to work in the dark.** Political palliatives will be mocked by actuality. Economic nostrums are blown willy-nilly in the unending battle of human instincts.

A brief survey of the past three or four centuries of Western civilization suggests the urgent need of a new science to help humanity in the struggle with the vast problem of to-day's disorder and danger. That problem, as we envisage it, is fundamentally a sexual problem. Ethical, political, and economic avenues of approach are

insufficient. We must create a new instrument, a new technique to make any adequate solution possible.

The history of the industrial revolution and the dominance of all-conquering machinery in Western civilization show the inadequacy of political and economic measures to meet the terrific rise in population. The advent of the factory system, due especially to the development of machinery at the beginning of the nineteenth century, upset all the grandiloquent theories of the previous era. To meet the new situation created by the industrial revolution arose the new science of "political economy,"[1] or economics. Old political methods proved inadequate to keep pace with the problem presented by the rapid rise of the new machine and industrial power. The machine era very shortly and decisively exploded the simple belief that "all men are born free and equal." Political power was superseded by economic and industrial power. To sustain their supremacy in the political field, governments and politicians allied themselves to the new

industrial oligarchy. Old political theories and practices were totally inadequate to control the new situation or to meet the complex problems that grew out of it.

Just as the eighteenth century saw the rise and proliferation of political theories, the nineteenth witnessed the creation and development of the science of economics, which aimed to perfect an instrument for the study and analysis of an industrial society, and to offer a technique for the solution of the multifold problems it presented. But at the present moment, as the outcome of the machine era and competitive populations, the world has been thrown into a new situation, the solution of which is impossible solely by political or economic weapons.

The industrial revolution and the development of machinery in Europe and America called into being a new type of working-class. Machines were at first termed "labor-saving devices." In reality, as we now know, mechanical inventions and discoveries created unprecedented and increasingly enormous demand for "labor." The omnipresent and still existing scandal of child labor is ample evidence of this. Machine production in its opening phases, demanded large, concentrated and exploitable populations. Large production and the huge development of international trade through improved methods of transport, made possible the maintenance upon a low level of existence of these rapidly increasing proletarian populations. With the rise and spread throughout Europe and America of machine production, it is now possible to correlate the expansion of the "proletariat." The working-classes bred almost automatically to meet the demand for machine-serving "hands."

The rise in population, the multiplication of proletarian populations as a first result of mechanical industry, the appearance of great centers of population, the so-called urban drift, and the evils of overcrowding still remain insufficiently studied and stated. **It is a significant though neglected fact that when, after long agitation in Great Britain, child labor was finally forbidden by law, the supply of children dropped appreciably. No longer of economic value in the factory, children were evidently a drug in the "home."** Yet it is doubly significant that from this moment British labor began the long unending task of self-organization.[2]

---

1. Editor: As mentioned earlier, political economy was an economic system built on Thomas Malthus and his theories about population and scarcity. Note her approval of it as a "science."

2. It may be well to note, in this connection, that the decline in the birth rate among the more intelligent classes of British labor followed upon the famous Bradlaugh-Besant trial of 1878, the outcome of the attempt of these two courageous Birth Control pioneers to circulate among the workers the work of an American physician, Dr. Knowlton's *The Fruits of Philosophy,* advocating Birth Control, and the widespread publicity resulting from this trial.

Nineteenth century economics had no method of studying the interrelation of the biological factors with the industrial. Overcrowding, overwork, the progressive destruction of responsibility by the machine discipline, as is now perfectly obvious, had the most disastrous consequences upon human character and human habits.[3] Paternalistic philanthropies and sentimental charities, which sprang up like mushrooms, only tended to increase the evils of indiscriminate breeding. From the physiological and psychological point of view, the factory system has been nothing less than catastrophic.

Dr. Austin Freeman has recently pointed out[4] some of the physiological, psychological, and racial effects of machinery upon the proletariat, the breeders of the world. Speaking for Great Britain, Dr. Freeman suggests that the omnipresence of machinery tends toward the production of large but inferior populations. Evidences of biological and racial degeneracy are apparent to this observer. **"Compared with the African negro," he writes, "the British sub-man is in several respects markedly inferior.[5] He tends to be dull; he is usually quite helpless and unhandy; he has, as a rule, no skill or knowledge of handicraft, or indeed knowledge of any kind.... Over-population is a phenomenon connected with the survival of the unfit, and it is mechanism which has created conditions favorable to the survival of the unfit and the elimination of the fit."[6]** The whole indictment against machinery is summarized by Dr. Freeman: "Mechanism by its reactions on man and his environment is antagonistic to human welfare. It has destroyed industry and replaced it by mere labor; it has degraded and vulgarized the works of man; it has destroyed social unity and replaced it by social disintegration and class antagonism to an extent which directly threatens civilization; it has injuriously affected the structural type of society by developing its organization at the expense of the individual; it has endowed the inferior man with political power which he employs to the common disadvantage by creating political institutions of a socially destructive type; and finally by its reactions on the activities of war it constitutes an agent for the wholesale physical destruction of man and his works and the extinction of human culture."

It is not necessary to be in absolute agreement with this diagnostician to realize the menace of machinery, which tends to emphasize quantity and mere number at the expense of quality and individuality. One thing is certain. If machinery is detrimental to biological fitness, the machine must be destroyed, as it was in Samuel Butler's *Erewhon*. But perhaps there is another way of mastering this problem.

Machines as Diseases

I also questioned them about the museum of old machines, and the cause of the apparent retrogression in all arts, sciences, and inventions. I learnt that about four hundred years previously, the state of mechanical knowledge was far beyond our own, and was advancing with prodigious rapidity, until one of the most learned professors of hypothetics wrote an extraordinary book (from which I propose to give extracts later on), proving that the machines were ultimately destined to supplant the race of man, and to become instinct with a vitality as different from, and superior to that of animals as animal to vegetable life. So convincing was his reasoning, or unreasoning, to this effect, that he carried the country with him and they made a clean sweep of all machinery that had not been in use for more than two hundred and seventy-one years (which period was arrived at after a series of compromises), and strictly forbade all further improvements and inventions under pain of being considered in the eye of the law to be labouring under typhus fever, which they regard as one of the worst of all crimes.[7]

—SAMUEL BUTLER, *EREWHON*

Altruism, humanitarianism and philanthropy have aided and abetted machinery in the destruction of responsibility and self-reliance among the least desirable elements of the proletariat. In contrast with the previous epoch of discovery of the New World, of exploration and

---

3. Cf. *The Creative Impulse in Industry,* by Helen Marot. *The Instinct of Workmanship,* by Thorstein Veblen.

4. *Social Decay and Regeneration.* By R. Austin Freeman. London, 1921.

5. Editor: Note how dreadful this "British sub-man" must be to be "markedly inferior" to the "African negro."

6. Editor: In the older, agricultural and craft-centered economy that prevailed until the mid-nineteenth century, he is saying, the 'fit' were rewarded and the 'unfit' brutally eliminated. A man too incompetent to farm or weave cloth soon found himself without shelter or food and starved, froze, or died of disease. In the new industrial economy, however, incompetence is no barrier to survival. The factories needed dull sub-men to work on their assembly lines. While the pay for such work may be low, it is enough to keep the 'sub-men' and their numerous brood alive. The old policy of simply letting births happen under the assumption that the wrong sort will die out—what Sanger termed a *laissez faire*—no longer worked. Short of reversing industrialization, which Sanger rejected in the next paragraph, there was only one solution.

7. Editor: The quote is from Chap. 9. A fear that machines are likely to "supplant the race of man" is also the theme of the popular movie "Terminator."

colonization, when a centrifugal influence was at work upon the populations of Europe, the advent of machinery has brought with it a counteracting centripetal effect. The result has been the accumulation of large urban populations, the increase of irresponsibility, and ever-widening margin of biological waste.

Just as eighteenth century politics and political theories were unable to keep pace with the economic and capitalistic aggressions of the nineteenth century, so also we find, if we look closely enough, that nineteenth century economics is inadequate to lead the world out of the catastrophic situation into which it has been thrown by the débâcle of the World War. Economists are coming to recognize that the purely economic interpretation of contemporary events is insufficient. Too long, as one of them has stated, orthodox economists have overlooked the important fact that "human life is dynamic, that change, movement, evolution, are its basic characteristics; that self-expression, and therefore freedom of choice and movement, are prerequisites to a satisfying human state."[8]

Economists themselves are breaking with the old "dismal science" of the Manchester school,[9] with its sterile study of "supply and demand," of prices and exchange, of wealth and labor. Like the Chicago Vice Commission, nineteenth-century economists (many of whom still survive into our own day) considered sex merely as something to be legislated out of existence. They had the idea that wealth consisted solely of material things used to promote the welfare of certain human beings. Their idea of capital was somewhat confused. They apparently decided that capital was merely that part of capital used to produce profit. Prices, exchanges, commercial statistics, and financial operations comprised the subject matter of these older economists. It would have been considered "unscientific" to take into account the human factors involved. They might study the wear-and-tear and depreciation of machinery: but the depreciation or destruction of the human race did not concern them. Under "wealth" they never included the vast, wasted treasury of human life and human expression.

Economists to-day are awake to the imperative duty of dealing with the whole of human nature, with the relation of men, women, and children to their environment—physical and psychic as well as social; of dealing with all those factors which contribute to human sustenance, happiness and welfare. The economist, at length, investigates human motives. Economics outgrows the outworn metaphysical preconceptions of nineteenth century theory. To-day we witness the creation of a new "welfare" or social economics, based on a fuller and more complete knowledge of the human race, upon a recognition of sex as well as of hunger; in brief, of physiological instincts and psychological demands. The newer economists are beginning to recognize that their science heretofore failed to take into account the most vital factors in modern industry—it failed to foresee the inevitable consequences of compulsory motherhood; the catastrophic effects of child labor upon racial health; the overwhelming importance of national vitality and well-being; the international ramifications of the population problem; the relation of indiscriminate breeding to feeble-mindedness, and industrial inefficiency. It speculated too little or not at all on human motives. Human nature riots through the traditional economic structure, as Carlton Parker pointed out, with ridicule and destruction; the old-fashioned economist looked on helpless and aghast.

Inevitably we are driven to the conclusion that the exclusively economic interpretation of contemporary history is inadequate to meet the present situation. In his suggestive book, *The Acquisitive Society,* R. H. Tawney, arrives at the conclusion that "obsession by economic issues is as local and transitory as it is repulsive and disturbing. To future generations it will appear as pitiable as the obsession of the seventeenth century by religious quarrels appears to-day; indeed, it is less rational, since the object with which it is concerned is less important. And it is a poison which inflames every wound and turns each trivial scratch into a malignant ulcer. Society will not solve the particular problems of industry until that poison is expelled, and it has learned to see industry in its proper perspective. *If it is to do that it must rearrange the scale of values.* It must regard economic interests as one element in life, not as the whole of life. . . ."[10]

In neglecting or minimizing the great factor of sex in human society, the Marxian doctrine reveals itself as no stronger than orthodox economics in guiding our way to a sound civilization. It works within the same intellectual limitations. Much as we are indebted to the Marxians for pointing out the injustice of modern industrialism, we should never close our eyes to the obvious limitations of their own "economic interpretation of history." While we must recognize the great historical value of Marx, it is now evident that his vision of the "class struggle," of the

------

8. Carlton H. Parker: *The Casual Laborer and Other Essays:* p. 30.

9. Editor: The Manchester school of economics stressed free trade and government non-interference or *laissez faire,* the very opposite of Marxism, which Sanger also criticized for being too narrow and economic.

10. R. H. Tawney. *The Acquisitive Society,* p. 184.

bitter irreconcilable warfare between the capitalist and working classes was based not upon historical analysis, but upon on unconscious dramatization of a superficial aspect of capitalistic régime.

In emphasizing the conflict between the classes, Marx failed to recognize the deeper unity of the proletariat and the capitalist. Nineteenth century capitalism had in reality engendered and cultivated the very type of working class best suited to its own purpose—an inert, docile, irresponsible and submissive class, progressively incapable of effective and aggressive organization. Like the economists of the Manchester school, Marx failed to recognize the interplay of human instincts in the world of industry. All the virtues were embodied in the beloved proletariat; all the villainies in the capitalists. The greatest asset of the capitalism of that age was, as a matter of fact, the uncontrolled breeding among the laboring classes. The intelligent and self-conscious section of the workers was forced to bear the burden of the unemployed and the poverty-stricken.

Marx was fully aware of the consequences of this condition of things, but shut his eyes tightly to the cause. He pointed out that capitalistic power was dependent upon "the reserve army of labor," surplus labor, and a wide margin of unemployment. He practically admitted that over-population was the inevitable soil of predatory capitalism. But he disregarded the most obvious consequence of that admission. It was all very dramatic and grandiloquent to tell the workingmen of the world to unite, that they had "nothing but their chains to lose and the world to gain." Cohesion of any sort, united and voluntary organization, as events have proved, is impossible in populations bereft of intelligence, self-discipline and even the material necessities of life, and cheated by their desires and ignorance into unrestrained and uncontrolled fertility.

In pointing out the limitations and fallacies of the orthodox Marxian opinion, my purpose is not to depreciate the efforts of the Socialists aiming to create a new society, but rather to emphasize what seems to me the greatest and most neglected truth of our day—**Unless sexual science is incorporated as an integral part of world-statesmanship and the pivotal importance of Birth Control is recognized in any program of reconstruction, all efforts to create a new world and a new civilization are foredoomed to failure.**

We can hope for no advance until we attain a new conception of sex, not as a merely propagative act, not merely as a biological necessity for the perpetuation of the race, but as a psychic and spiritual avenue of expression. It is the limited, inhibited conception of sex that

SELF-APPOINTED GUARDIAN OF THE PUBLIC MORALS

PURITY SLEUTH

vitiates so much of the thought and ideation of the Eugenists.

Like most of our social idealists, statesmen, politicians and economists, some of the Eugenists suffer intellectually from a restricted and inhibited understanding of the function of sex. This limited understanding, this narrowness of vision, which gives rise to most of the misconceptions and condemnations of the doctrine of Birth Control, is responsible for the failure of politicians and legislators to enact practical statutes or to remove traditional obscenities from the law books. The most encouraging sign at present is the recognition by modern psychology of the central importance of the sexual instinct in human society, and the rapid spread of this new concept among the more enlightened sections of the civilized communities. The new conception of sex has been well stated by one to whom the debt of contemporary civilization is well-nigh immeasurable. "Sexual activity," Havelock Ellis has written, "is not merely a baldly propagative act, nor, when propagation is put aside, is it merely the relief of distended vessels. It is something more even than the foundation of great social institutions. It is the function by which all the finer activities of the organism, physical and psychic, may be developed and satisfied."[11]

No less than seventy years ago, a profound but neglected thinker, George Drysdale, emphasized the necessity of a thorough understanding of man's sexual nature in approaching economic, political and social problems. "Before we can undertake the calm and impartial investigation of any social problem, we must first of all free ourselves from all those sexual prejudices which are so vehement and violent and which so completely distort our vision of the external world. Society as a whole

11. *Medical Review of Reviews*: Vol. XXVI, p. 116.

has yet to fight its way through an almost impenetrable forest of sexual taboos." Drysdale's words have lost none of their truth even to-day:

> There are few things from which humanity has suffered more than the degraded and irreverent feelings of mystery and shame that have been attached to the genital and excretory organs. The former have been regarded, like their corresponding mental passions, as something of a lower and baser nature, tending to degrade and carnalize man by their physical appetites. But we cannot take a debasing view of any part of our humanity without becoming degraded in our whole being.[12]

Drysdale moreover clearly recognized the social crime of entrusting to sexual barbarians the duty of legislating and enforcing laws detrimental to the welfare of all future generations. "They trust blindly to authority for the rules they blindly lay down," he wrote, "perfectly unaware of the awful and complicated nature of the subject they are dealing with so confidently and of the horrible evils their unconsidered statements are attended with. They themselves break through the most fundamentally important laws daily in utter unconsciousness of the misery they are causing to their fellows. . . ."

Psychologists to-day courageously emphasize the integral relationship of the expression of the sexual instinct with every phase of human activity. Until we recognize this central fact, we cannot understand the implications and the sinister significance of superficial attempts to apply rosewater remedies to social evils—by the enactment of restrictive and superficial legislation, by wholesale philanthropies and charities, by publicly burying our heads in the sands of sentimentality. Self-appointed censors, grossly immoral "moralists," makeshift legislators, all face a heavy responsibility for the miseries, diseases, and social evils they perpetuate or intensify by enforcing the primitive taboos of aboriginal customs, traditions, and outworn laws, which at every step hinder the education of the people in the scientific knowledge of their sexual nature. Puritanic and academic taboo of sex in education and religion is as disastrous to human welfare as prostitution or the venereal scourges. "We are compelled squarely to face the distorting influences of biologically aborted reformers as well as the wastefulness of seducers," Dr. Edward A. Kempf recently declared. "Man arose from the ape and inherited his passions, which he can only refine but dare not attempt to castrate unless he would destroy the fountains of energy that maintain civi-

lization and make life worth living and the world worth beautifying. . . . We do not have a problem that is to be solved by making repressive laws and executing them. Nothing will be more disastrous. Society must make life worth the living and the refining for the individual by conditioning him to love and to seek the love-object in a manner that reflects a constructive effect upon his fellowmen and by giving him suitable opportunities. The virility of the automatic apparatus is destroyed by excessive gormandizing or hunger, by excessive wealth or poverty, by excessive work or idleness, by sexual abuse or intolerant prudishness. **The noblest and most difficult art of all is the raising of human thoroughbreds.**"[13]

—§§§—

A Race of Thoroughbreds

Such a plan would automatically reduce the necessity for public charities. It would reduce the birthrate among the diseased, the sickly, the poverty stricken and anti-social classes of society, elements unable to provide for themselves and the burden of which we are all per force carrying. Unable to provide for themselves and their too numerous offspring they threaten to lower the biological and economic standards of their generation, these classes are now breeding much such uncontrolled fertility that they are a menace to the race. Unless their birthrate is controlled and unless new responsibility toward children and the future of the race is instilled in the minds of humanity at large, no scheme for public welfare can function efficiently.[14]

—MARGARET SANGER, "WE MUST BREED A RACE OF
THOROUGHBREDS," 1929

---

13. *Proceedings of the International Conference of Women Physicians.* Vol. IV, pp. 66–67. New York, 1920. Editor: Kempf was attempting to place himself midway between two exaggerated stereotypes. The inability of women's college graduates to marry and raise families he blasted as "the puritanical and academic castration of the sexual cravings in education" which led "to racial suicide, repressed hatred, and dementia praecox." That he contrasted with "the profligacy of prostitution and alcoholism" which leads to "degeneracy, crime and paresis [from syphilis]." His point was that, given the animal roots of our sex drives, improving human society requires a difficult balancing act. He was discussing our sexual culture rather than eugenics, but Sanger, revealing her own obsession, pushed his argument into the eugenic arena by using it to reinforce her earlier claim that "some of the Eugenists suffer intellectually from a restricted and inhibited understanding of the function of sex." Dr. Kempf was a physician at St. Elizabeth's Hospital in Washington, D.C. and author of *The Autonomic Functions of the Personality.*

---

12. *The Elements of Social Science:* London, 1854.

14. Margaret Sanger, "We Must Breed a Race of Thoroughbreds." Attached to a letter to C. Harold Smith of the *New York
Evening World* (May 7, 1929). In Sanger/Library of Congress,
LOC131:122. Her "plan" was for birth control clinics to be
linked to "all the social agencies" that work with mothers and
infants. The text is from a draft where what is quoted above was
crossed out and thus not in a later version, suggesting that
Sanger realized that her attitude toward "the diseased, the sickly, the poverty stricken and anti-social classes of society"
would not be appreciate by the general public still under the influence of religion and sentiment. A handwritten note on the
letter says, "Notpub." On a related theme, the November and
December of 1921 masthead of Sanger's *Birth Control Review*
displayed the slogan, "Birth Control: To create a race of thoroughbreds." That page from the December issue is reproduced
as the background for the cover of this book.

7

Is Revolution the Remedy?

Marxian Socialism, which seeks to solve the complex problem of human misery by economic and proletarian revolution, has manifested a new vitality. Every shade of Socialistic thought and philosophy acknowledges its indebtedness to the vision of Karl Marx and his conception of the class struggle. Yet the relation of Marxian Socialism to the philosophy of Birth Control, especially in the minds of most Socialists, remains hazy and confused. No thorough understanding of Birth Control, its aims and purposes, is possible until this confusion has been cleared away, and we come to a realization that Birth Control is not merely independent of, but even antagonistic to the Marxian dogma. In recent years many Socialists have embraced the doctrine of Birth Control, and have generously promised us that "under Socialism" voluntary motherhood will be adopted and popularized as part of a general educational system. We might more logically reply that no Socialism will ever be possible until the problem of responsible parenthood has been solved.[1]

Many Socialists to-day remain ignorant of the inherent conflict between the idea of Birth Control and the philosophy of Marx. The earlier Marxians, including Karl Marx himself, expressed the bitterest antagonism to Malthusian and neo-Malthusian theories. A remarkable feature of early Marxian propaganda has been the almost complete unanimity with which the implications of the Malthusian doctrine have been derided, denounced and repudiated. Any defense of the so-called "law of population" was enough to stamp one, in the eyes of the orthodox Marxians, as a "tool of the capitalistic class," seeking to dampen the ardor of those who expressed the belief that men might create a better world for themselves. Malthus, they claimed, was actuated by selfish class motives. He was not merely a hidebound aristocrat, but a pessimist who was trying to kill all hope of human progress. By

Marx, Engels, Bebel,[2] Karl Kautsky,[3] and all the celebrated leaders and interpreters of Marx's great "Bible of the working class," down to the martyred Rosa Luxemburg and Karl Liebknecht, Birth Control has been looked upon as a subtle, Machiavellian sophistry created for the purpose of placing the blame for human misery elsewhere than at the door of the capitalist class. Upon this point the orthodox Marxian mind has been universally and sternly uncompromising.

Marxian vituperation of Malthus and his followers is illuminating. It reveals not the weakness of the thinker attacked, but of the aggressor. **This is nowhere more evident than in Marx's _Capital_ itself. In that monumental effort, it is impossible to discover any adequate refutation or even calm discussion of the dangers of irresponsible parenthood and reckless breeding, any suspicion that this recklessness and irresponsibility is even remotely related to the miseries of the proletariat.** Poor Malthus is there relegated to the humble level of a footnote. "If the reader reminds me of Malthus, whose essay on Population appeared in 1798," Marx remarks somewhat tartly, "I remind him that this work in its first form is nothing more than a schoolboyish, superficial plagiary of De Foe, Sir James Steuart, Townsend, Franklin, Wallace, etc., and does not contain a single sentence thought out by himself. The great sensation this pamphlet caused was due solely to party interest. The French Revolution had passionate defenders in the United Kingdom.... _The Principles of Population_ was quoted with jubilation by the English oligarchy as the great destroyer of all hankerings after human development."[4]

---

1. Editor: Notice that socialism "promised . . . voluntary parenthood," but Sanger believed it must insist on "responsible parenthood." The two are very different.

2. Editor: August Bebel (1840–1913) helped found the German Social Democratic Party and was a popular politician for over 40 years.

3. Editor: Karl Kautsky (1854–1938) was a Marxist theorist and a leader in the German Social Democratic Party.

4. Marx: _Capital._ Vol. 1, p. 675.

The only attempt that Marx makes here toward answering the theory of Malthus is to declare that most of the population theory teachers were merely Protestant parsons—"Parson Wallace, Parson Townsend, Parson Malthus and his pupil the Arch-Parson Thomas Chalmers, to say nothing of the lesser reverend scribblers in this line." The great pioneer of "scientific" Socialism then proceeds to berate parsons as philosophers and economists, using this method of escape from the very pertinent question of surplus population and surplus proletariat in its relation to labor organization and unemployment. It is true that elsewhere[5] he goes so far as to admit that "even Malthus recognized over-population as a necessity of modern industry, though, after his narrow fashion, he explains it by the absolute over-growth of the laboring population, not by their becoming relatively supernumerary." A few pages later, however, Marx comes back again to the question of over-population, failing to realize that it is to the capitalists' advantage that the working classes are unceasingly prolific. "The folly is now patent," writes the unsuspecting Marx, "of the economic wisdom that preaches to the laborers the accommodation of their numbers to the requirements of capital. The mechanism of capitalist production and accumulation constantly affects this adjustment. The first work of this adaptation is the creation of a relatively surplus population or industrial reserve army. Its last work is the misery of constantly extending strata of the army of labor, and the dead weight of pauperism." A little later he ventures again in the direction of Malthusianism so far as to admit that "the accumulation of wealth at one pole is. . . at the same time the accumulation of misery, agony of toil, slavery, ignorance, brutality and mental degradation at the opposite pole." Nevertheless, there is no indication that Marx permitted himself to see that the proletariat accommodates its numbers to the "requirements of capital" precisely by breeding a large, docile, submissive and easily exploitable population.

Had the purpose of Marx been impartial and scientific, this trifling difference might easily have been overcome and the dangers of reckless breeding insisted upon. But beneath all this wordy pretension and economic jargon, we detect another aim. That is the unconscious dramatization of human society into the "class conflict." Nothing was overlooked that might sharpen and accentuate this "conflict." Marx depicted a great melodramatic conflict, in which all the virtues were embodied in the proletariat and all the villainies in the capitalist. In the end, as always in such dramas, virtue was to be rewarded and vil-

5. *Op. cit.* pp. 695, 707, 709.

lainy punished. The working class was the temporary victim of a subtle but thorough conspiracy of tyranny and repression. Capitalists, intellectuals and the *bourgeoisie* were all "in on" this diabolic conspiracy, all thoroughly familiar with the plot, which Marx was so sure he had uncovered. In the last act was to occur that catastrophic revolution, with the final transformation scene of the Socialist millennium. Presented in "scientific" phraseology, with all the authority of economic terms, *Capital* appeared at the psychological moment. The heaven of the traditional theology had been shattered by Darwinian science, and here, dressed up in all the authority of the new science, appeared a new theology, the promise of a new heaven, an earthly paradise, with an impressive scale of rewards for the faithful and ignominious punishments for the capitalists.

Critics have often been puzzled by the tremendous vitality of this work. Its predictions have never, despite the claims of the faithful, been fulfilled. Instead of diminishing, the spirit of nationalism has been intensified tenfold. In nearly every respect Marx's predictions concerning the evolution of historical and economic forces have been contradicted by events, culminating in the great war. Most of his followers, the "revolutionary" Socialists, were swept into the whirlpool of nationalistic militarism. Nevertheless, this "Bible of the working classes" still enjoys a tremendous authority as a scientific work. By some it is regarded as an economic treatise; by others as a philosophy of history; by others as a collection of sociological laws; and finally by others as a moral and political book of reference. Criticized, refuted, repudiated and demolished by specialists, it nevertheless exerts its influences and retains its mysterious vitality.

We must seek the explanation of this secret elsewhere. Modern psychology has taught us that human nature has a tendency to place the cause of its own deficiencies and weaknesses outside of itself, to attribute to some external agency, to some enemy or group of enemies, the blame for its own misery. In his great work Marx unconsciously strengthens and encourages this tendency. **The immediate effect of his teaching, vulgarized and popularized in a hundred different forms, is to relieve the proletariat of all responsibility for the effects of its reckless breeding, and even to encourage it in the perpetuation of misery.**

Happiness & Marriage

The mass of happiness among the common people cannot but be diminished when one of the strongest checks to idleness and dissipation is thus removed, and when men are thus allured to marry with little or no prospect of being able to maintain a family in independence.[6]

—THOMAS MALTHUS, 1798

The inherent truth in the Marxian teachings was, moreover, immediately subordinated to their emotional and religious appeal. A book that could so influence European thought could not be without merit. But in the process of becoming the "Bible of the working classes," *Capital* suffered the fate of all such "Bibles." The spirit of ecclesiastical dogmatism was transfused into the religion of revolutionary Socialism. This dogmatic religious quality has been noted by many of the most observant critics of Socialism. Marx was too readily accepted as the father of the church, and *Capital* as the sacred gospel of the social revolution. All questions of tactics, of propaganda, of class warfare, of political policy, were to be solved by apt quotations from the "good book." New thoughts, new schemes, new programs, based upon tested fact and experience, the outgrowth of newer discoveries concerning the nature of men, upon the recognition of the

mistakes of the master, could only be approved or admitted according as they could or could not be tested by some bit of text quoted from Marx. His followers assumed that Karl Marx had completed the philosophy of Socialism, and that the duty of the proletariat thenceforth was not to think for itself, but merely to mobilize itself under competent Marxian leaders for the realization of his ideas.

From the day of this apotheosis of Marx until our own, the "orthodox" Socialist of any shade is of the belief that the first essential for social salvation lies in unquestioning belief in the dogmas of Marx.

The curious and persistent antagonism to Birth Control that began with Marx and continues to our own day can be explained only as the utter refusal or inability to consider humanity in its physiological and psychological aspects—these aspects, apparently, having no place in the "economic interpretation of history." It has remained for George Bernard Shaw, a Socialist with a keener spiritual insight than the ordinary Marxist, to point out the disastrous consequences of rapid multiplication which are obvious to the small cultivator, the peasant proprietor, the lowest farmhand himself, but which seem to arouse the orthodox, intellectual Marxian to inordinate fury. "But indeed the more you degrade the workers," Shaw once wrote,[7] "robbing them of all artistic enjoyment, and all chance of respect and admiration from their fellows, the more you throw them back, reckless, upon the one pleasure and the one human tie left to them—the gratification of their instinct for producing fresh supplies of men. You will applaud this instinct as divine until at last the excessive supply becomes a nuisance: there comes a plague of men; and you suddenly discover that the instinct is diabolic, and set up a cry of 'over-population.' But your slaves are beyond caring for your cries: they breed like rabbits: and their poverty breeds filth, ugliness, dishonesty, disease, obscenity, drunkenness."

Lack of insight into fundamental truths of human nature is evident throughout the writings of the Marxians. The Marxian Socialists, according to Kautsky, defended women in industry: it was right for woman to work in factories in order to preserve her equality with man! Man must not support woman, declared the great French Socialist Guesde,[8] because that would make her the *proletaire* of man! Bebel, the great authority on woman,

---

6. Thomas Malthus, *A Essay on the Principle of Population,* Antony Flew, ed. (London: Penguin Books, 1970), 99.

7. *Fabian Essays in Socialism.* p. 21. Editor: G. K. Chesterton, an ideological foe of Shaw says much the same thing with much more kindness in Chap. XVIII.

8. Editor: Jules Guesde (1845–1922) was an early leader in the Marxist wing of the French labor movement.

famous for his erudition, having critically studied the problem of population, suggested as a remedy for too excessive fecundity the consumption of a certain lard soup reputed to have an "anti-generative" effect upon the agricultural population of Upper Bavaria! Such are the results of the literal and uncritical acceptance of Marx's static and mechanical conception of human society, a society perfectly automatic; in which competition is always operating at maximum efficiency; one vast and unending conspiracy against the blameless proletariat.

Population Law in the USSR

Knowledge of the laws of population for socialist society has been gleaned, as indeed has that relating to other laws of socialism—first from experience in the USSR and later from that of the other socialist countries. Detailed investigation and comprehension of the methodological guidelines found in the writings of Marx, Engels and Lenin have played a central role in the formulation and elaboration of these laws[9] . . .

—AN OUTLINE THEORY OF POPULATION, MOSCOW, 1980

This lack of insight of the orthodox Marxians, long represented by the German Social-Democrats, is nowhere better illustrated than in Dr. Robinson's account of a mass meeting of the Social-Democrat party to organize public opinion against the doctrine of Birth Control among the poor.[10] "Another meeting had taken place the week before, at which several eminent Socialist women, among them Rosa Luxemburg and Clara Zetkin, spoke very strongly against limitation of offspring among the poor—in fact the title of the discussion was *Gegen den Geburtstreik!* 'Against the birth strike!' The interest of the audience was intense. One could see that with them it was not merely a dialectic question, as it was with their leaders, but a matter of life and death. I came to attend a meeting *against* the limitation of offspring; it soon proved to be a meeting very decidedly *for* the limitation of offspring, for every speaker who spoke in favor of the artificial prevention of conception or undesired pregnancies, was greeted with vociferous, long-lasting applause; while those who tried to persuade the people that a limited number of children is not a proletarian weapon, and would not improve their lot, were so hissed that they had difficulty in going on. The speakers who were against the. . . idea soon felt that their audience was against

them. . . . Why was there such small attendance at the regular Socialistic meetings, while the meetings of this character were packed to suffocation? It did not apparently penetrate the leaders' heads that the reason was a simple one. Those meetings were evidently of no interest to them, while those which dealt with the limitation of offspring were of personal, vital, present interest. . . . What particularly amused me—and pained me—in the anti-limitationists was the ease and equanimity with which they advised the poor women to keep on bearing children. The woman herself was not taken into consideration, as if she was not a human being, but a machine. What are her sufferings, her labor pains, her inability to read, to attend meetings, to have a taste of life? What does she amount to? The proletariat needs fighters. Go on, females, and breed like animals. Maybe of the thousands you bear a few will become party members. . . ."

The militant organization of the Marxian Socialists suggests that their campaign must assume the tactics of militarism of the familiar type. As represented by militaristic governments, militarism like Socialism has always encouraged the proletariat to increase and multiply. Imperial Germany was the outstanding and awful example of this attitude. Before the war the fall in the birth-rate was viewed by the Junker party with the gravest misgivings. Bernhardi[11] and the protagonists of *Deutschland-über-Alles* condemned it in the strongest terms. The Marxians unconsciously repeat the words of the government representative, Krohne, who, in a debate on the subject in the Prussian Diet, February 1916, asserted: "Unfortunately this view has gained followers amongst the German women. . . . These women, in refusing to rear strong and able children to continue the race, drag into the dust that which is the highest end of women—motherhood. It is to be hoped that the willingness to bear sacrifices will lead to a change for the better. . . . We need an increase in human beings to guard against the attacks of envious neighbors as well as to fulfil our cultural mission. Our whole economic development depends on increase of our people." To-day we are fully aware of how imperial Germany fulfilled that cultural mission of hers; nor can we overlook the fact that the countries with a smaller

9. D. J. Valentey, ed. *An Outline Theory of Population* (Moscow: Progress Publishers, 1980), 166. In this book, written much later than Sanger's, more stress is placed on experience than on the writings of Marx.

10. *Uncontrolled Breeding,* by Adelyne More. p. 84.

11. Editor: Shortly before World War I, General Friedrich von Bernhardi (1849–1930), commander of the German Seventh Army Corps, wrote the influential *Germany and the Next War.* The book claimed war was a natural part of Darwinian evolution and that a nation must expand through conquest or die. Others, however, argued that war, because it killed the healthiest young men, was contrary to evolution, illustrating the strange diversity of ideas that find support in evolution's vague "survival of the fittest."

birth-rate survived the ordeal. Even from the traditional militaristic standpoint, strength does not reside in numbers, though the Caesars, the Napoleons and the Kaisers of the world have always believed that large exploitable populations were necessary for their own individual power. If Marxian dictatorship means the dictatorship of a small minority wielding power in the interest of the proletariat, a high-birth rate may be necessary, though we may here recall the answer of the lamented Dr. Alfred Fried to the German imperialists: "It is madness, the apotheosis of unreason, to wish to breed and care for human beings in order that in the flower of their youth they may be sent in millions to be slaughtered wholesale by machinery. We need no wholesale production of men, have no need of the 'fruitful fertility of women,' no need of wholesale wares, fattened and dressed for slaughter. What we do need is careful maintenance of those already born. If the bearing of children is a moral and religious duty, then it is a much higher duty to secure the sacredness and security of human life, so that children born and bred with trouble and sacrifice may not be offered up in the bloom of youth to a political dogma at the bidding of secret diplomacy."

Marxism has developed a patriotism of its own, if indeed it has not yet been completely crystallized into a religion. Like the "capitalistic" governments it so vehemently attacks, it demands self-sacrifice and even martyrdom from the faithful comrades. But since its strength depends to so great a degree upon "conversion," upon docile acceptance of the doctrines of the "Master" as interpreted by the popes and bishops of this new church, it fails to arouse the irreligious proletariat. The Marxian Socialist boasts of his understanding of "working class psychology" and criticizes the lack of this understanding on the part of all dissenters. But, as the Socialists' meetings against the "birth strike" indicate, the working class is not interested in such generalities as the Marxian "theory of value," the "iron law" of wages, "the value of commodities" and the rest of the hazy articles of faith. Marx inherited the rigid rationalistic psychology of the eighteenth century, and his followers, for the most part, have accepted his mechanical and superficial treatment of instinct.[12] Discontented workers may rally to Marxism because it places the blame for their misery outside of themselves and depicts their conditions as the result of a capitalistic conspiracy, thereby satisfying that innate tendency of every human being to shift the blame to some

living person outside himself, and because it strengthens his belief that his sufferings and difficulties may be overcome by the immediate amelioration of his economic environment. In this manner, psychologists tell us, neuroses and inner compulsions are fostered. No true solution is possible, to continue this analogy, until the worker is awakened to the realization that the roots of his malady lie deep in his own nature, his own organism, his own habits. To blame everything upon the capitalist and the environment produced by capitalism is to focus attention upon merely one of the elements of the problem. The Marxian too often forgets that before there was a capitalist there was exercised the unlimited reproductive activity of mankind, which produced the first overcrowding, the first want. This goaded humanity into its industrial frenzy, into warfare and theft and slavery. Capitalism has not created the lamentable state of affairs in which the world now finds itself. It has grown out of them, armed with the inevitable power to take advantage of our swarming, spawning millions. As that valiant thinker Monsieur G. Hardy has pointed out[13] the proletariat may be looked upon, not as the antagonist of capitalism, but as its accomplice. Labor surplus, or the "army of reserve" which as for decades and centuries furnished the industrial background of human misery, which so invariably defeats strikes and labor revolts, cannot honestly be blamed upon capitalism. It is, as M. Hardy points out, of *sexual* and proletarian origin. In bringing too many children into the world, in adding to the total of misery, in intensifying the evils of overcrowding, the proletariat itself increases the burden of organized labor; even of the Socialist and Syndicalist organizations themselves with a surplus of the docilely inefficient, with those great uneducable and unorganizable masses. With surprisingly few exceptions, Marxians of all countries have docilely followed their master in rejecting, with bitterness and vindictiveness that is difficult to explain, the principles and teachings of Birth Control.

Hunger alone is not responsible for the bitter struggle for existence we witness to-day in our over-advertised civilization. Sex, uncontrolled, misdirected, over-stimulated and misunderstood, has run riot at the instigation of priest, militarist and exploiter. **Uncontrolled sex has rendered the proletariat prostrate, the capitalist powerful. In this continuous, unceasing alliance of sexual instinct and hunger we find the reason for the decline of all the finer sentiments.** These instincts tear asunder the thin veils of culture and hypocrisy and expose to our gaze the dark sufferings of gaunt humanity. So have we

---

12. For a sympathetic treatment of modern psychological research as bearing on Communism, by two convinced Communists see *Creative Revolution* [1920], by Eden and Cedar Paul.

13. *Neo-Malthusianisme et Socialisme*, p. 22.

become familiar with the everyday spectacle of distorted bodies, of harsh and frightful diseases stalking abroad in the light of day; of misshapen heads and visages of moron and imbecile; of starving children in city streets and schools. This is the true soil of unspeakable crimes. Defect and delinquency join hands with disease, and accounts of inconceivable and revolting vices are dished up in the daily press. When the majority of men and women are driven by the grim lash of sex and hunger in the unending struggle to feed themselves and to carry the dead-weight of dead and dying progeny, when little children are forced into factories, streets, and shops, education—including even education in the Marxian dogmas—is quite impossible; and civilization is more completely threatened than it ever could be by pestilence or war.

But, it will be pointed out, the working class has advanced. Power has been acquired by labor unions and syndicates. In the beginning power was won by the principle of the restriction of numbers. The device of refusing to admit more than a fixed number of new members to the unions of the various trades has been justified as necessary for the upholding of the standard of wages and of working conditions. This has been the practice in precisely those unions which have been able through years of growth and development to attain tangible strength and power. Such a principle of restriction is necessary in the creation of a firmly and deeply rooted trunk or central organization furnishing a local center for more extended organization. It is upon this great principle of restricted number that the labor unions have generated and developed power. They have acquired this power without any religious emotionalism, without subscribing to metaphysical or economic theology. For the millennium and the earthly paradise to be enjoyed at some indefinitely future date, the union member substitutes the very real politics of organization with its resultant benefits. He increases his own independence and comfort and that of his family. He is immune to superstitious belief in and respect for the mysterious power of political or economic nostrums to reconstruct human society according to the Marxian formula.

In rejecting the Marxian hypothesis as superficial and fragmentary, we do so not because of its so-called revolutionary character, its threat to the existing order of things, but rather because of its superficial, emotional and religious character and its deleterious effect upon the life of reason. Like other schemes advanced by the alarmed and the indignant, it relies too much upon moral fervor and enthusiasm. To build any social program upon the shifting sands of sentiment and feeling, of indignation or enthusiasm, is a dangerous and foolish task. **On the other hand, we should not minimize the importance of the Socialist movement in so valiantly and so courageously battling against the stagnating complacency of our conservatives and reactionaries, under whose benign imbecility the defective and diseased elements of humanity are encouraged "full speed ahead" in their reckless and irresponsible swarming and spawning.** Nevertheless, as George Drysdale pointed out nearly seventy years ago:

> . . . If we ignore this and other sexual subjects, we may do whatever else we like: we may bully, we may bluster, we may rage, We may foam at the mouth; we may tear down Heaven with our prayers, we may exhaust ourselves with weeping over the sorrows of the poor; we may narcotize ourselves and others with the opiate of Christian resignation; we may dissolve the realities of human woe in a delusive mirage of poetry and ideal philosophy; we may lavish our substance in charity, and labor over possible or impossible Poor Laws; we may form wild dreams of Socialism, industrial regiments, universal brotherhood, red republics, or unexampled revolutions; we may strangle and murder each other, we may persecute and despise those whose sexual necessities force them to break through our unnatural moral codes; we may burn alive if we please the prostitutes and the adulterers; we may break our own and our neighbor's hearts against the adamantine laws that surround us, but not one step, not one shall we advance, till we acknowledge these laws, and adopt the only possible mode in which they can be obeyed.

These words were written in 1854. Recent events have accentuated their stinging truth.

—§§§—

8

Dangers of Cradle Competition

Eugenics has been defined as "the study of agencies under social control that may improve or impair the racial qualities of future generations, either mentally or physically." While there is no inherent conflict between Socialism and Eugenics, the latter is, broadly, the antithesis of the former. In its propaganda, Socialism emphasizes the evil effects of our industrial and economic system. It insists upon the necessity of satisfying material needs, upon sanitation, hygiene, and education to effect the transformation of society. The Socialist insists that healthy humanity is impossible without a radical improvement of the social—and therefore of the economic and industrial—environment. The Eugenist points out that heredity is the great determining factor in the lives of men and women. Eugenics is the attempt to solve the problem from the biological and evolutionary point of view. You may ring all the changes possible on "Nurture" or environment, the Eugenist may say to the Socialist, but comparatively little can be effected until you control biological and hereditary elements of the problem. Eugenics thus aims to seek out the root of our trouble, to study humanity as a kinetic, dynamic, evolutionary organism, shifting and changing with the successive generations, rising and falling, cleansing itself of inherent defects, or under adverse and dysgenic influences, sinking into degeneration and deterioration.

"Eugenics" was first defined by Sir Francis Galton in his "Human Faculty" in 1884, and was subsequently developed into a science and into an educational effort. Galton's ideal was the rational breeding of human beings. The aim of Eugenics, as defined by its founder, is to bring as many influences as can be reasonably employed, to cause the useful classes of the community to contribute *more* than their proportion to the next generation. Eugenics thus concerns itself with all influences that improve the inborn qualities of a race; also with those that develop them to the utmost advantage. It is, in short, the attempt to bring reason and intelligence to bear upon *heredity*.

But Galton, in spite of the immense value of this approach and his great stimulation to criticism, was completely unable to formulate a definite and practical working program. He hoped at length to introduce Eugenics "into the national conscience like a new religion. . . . I see no impossibility in Eugenics becoming a religious dogma among mankind, but its details must first be worked out sedulously in the study. Over-zeal leading to hasty action, would do harm by holding out expectations of a new golden age, which will certainly be falsified and cause the science to be discredited. The first and main point is to secure the general intellectual acceptance of Eugenics as a hopeful and most important study. Then, let its principles work into the heart of the nation, who will gradually give practical effect to them in ways that we may not wholly foresee."[1]

Galton formulated a general law of inheritance which declared that an individual receives one-half of his inheritance from his two parents, one-fourth from his four grandparents, one-eighth from his great-grandparents, one-sixteenth from his great-great grandparents, and so on by diminishing fractions to his primordial ancestors, the sum of all these fractions added together contributing to the whole of the inherited make-up. The trouble with this generalization, from the modern Mendelian point of view, is that it fails to define what "characters" one would get in the one-half that came from one's parents, or the one-fourth from one's grandparents. The whole of our inheritance is not composed of these indefinitely made up fractional parts. We are interested rather in those more

---

1. Galton. *Essays in Eugenics,* p. 43. Editor: To read what Galton and other eugenists were writing, see the appendices in the Inkling Books edition of G. K. Chesterton's *Eugenics and Other Evils.* At that time, the idea of eugenics as religion did not seem as far-fetched as it might today. But a rebellion against positive eugenics, and a heavy focus on negative eugenics would make it a disturbing sort of religion, one intent on making non-believers obey its principles rather than believers.

specific traits or characters, mental or physical, which, in the Mendelian view, are structural and functional units, making up a mosaic rather than a blend. The laws of heredity are concerned with the precise behavior, during a series of generations, of these specific unit characters. This behavior, as the study of Genetics shows, may be determined in lesser organisms by experiment. Once determined, they are subject to prophecy.

The problem of human heredity is now seen to be infinitely more complex than imagined by Galton and his followers, and the optimistic hope of elevating Eugenics to the level of a religion is a futile one. Most of the Eugenists, including Professor Karl Pearson and his colleagues of the Eugenics Laboratory of the University of London and of the biometric laboratory in University College, have retained the age-old point of view of "Nature vs. Nurture" and have attempted to show the predominating influence of Heredity *as opposed to* Environment. This may be true; but demonstrated and repeated in investigation after investigation, it nevertheless remains fruitless and unprofitable from the practical point of view.

We should not minimize the great outstanding service of Eugenics for critical and diagnostic investigations. It demonstrates, not in terms of glittering generalization but in statistical studies of investigations reduced to measurement and number, that uncontrolled fertility is universally correlated with disease, poverty, overcrowding and the transmission of hereditable taints. Professor Pearson and his associates show us that "if fertility be correlated with anti-social hereditary characters, a population will inevitably degenerate."

This degeneration has already begun. Eugenists demonstrate that two-thirds of our manhood of military age are physically too unfit to shoulder a rifle; that the feeble-minded, the syphilitic, the irresponsible and the defective breed unhindered; that women are driven into factories and shops on day-shift and night-shift; that children, frail carriers of the torch of life, are put to work at an early age; that society at large is breeding an ever-increasing army of under-sized, stunted and dehumanized slaves; that the vicious circle of mental and physical defect, delinquency and beggary is encouraged, by the unseeing and unthinking sentimentality of our age, to populate asylum, hospital and prison.

All these things the Eugenists sees and points out with a courage entirely admirable. But as a positive program of redemption, orthodox Eugenics can offer nothing more "constructive" than a renewed "cradle competition" between the "fit" and the "unfit." It sees that the most

responsible and most intelligent members of society are the less fertile; that the feeble-minded are the more fertile. Herein lies the unbalance, the great biological menace to the future of civilization. Are we heading to biological destruction, toward the gradual but certain attack upon the stocks of intelligence and racial health by the sinister forces of the hordes of irresponsibility and imbecility? This is not such a remote danger as the optimistic Eugenist might suppose. The mating of the moron with a person of sound stock may, as Dr. Tredgold points out, gradually disseminate this trait far and wide until it undermines the vigor and efficiency of an entire nation and an entire race. This is no idle fancy. We must take it into account if we wish to escape the fate that has befallen so many civilizations in the past.

"It is, indeed, more than likely that the presence of this impairment in a mitigated form is responsible for no little of the defective character, the diminution of mental and moral fiber at the present day," states Dr. Tredgold.[2] Such populations, this distinguished authority might have added, form the veritable "cultures" not only for contagious physical diseases but for mental instability and irresponsibility also. They are susceptible, exploitable, hysterical, non-resistant to external suggestion. Devoid of stamina, such folk become mere units in a mob. "The habit of crowd-making is daily becoming a more serious menace to civilization," writes Everett Dean Martin. "Our society is becoming a veritable babel of gibbering crowds."[3] It would be only the incorrigible optimist who refused to see the integral relation between this phenomenon and the indiscriminate breeding by which we recruit our large populations.

The danger of recruiting our numbers from the most "fertile stocks" is further emphasized when we recall that in a democracy like that of the United States every man and woman is permitted a vote in the government, and that it is the representatives of this grade of intelligence who may destroy our liberties, and who may thus be the most far-reaching peril to the future of civilization.

Woodrow Wilson on Immigrant Voters

The cities were filling up with foreigners of the sort the Know Nothings had feared; men who had left their homes dissatisfied not merely with the governments they had lived under but with society itself, and who had come to America to speak treasons elsewhere forbidden. For many a long year their incendiary talk had

---

2. *Eugenics Review,* Vol. XIII, p. 349.

3. Cf. Martin, *The Behavior of Crowds,* p. 6. Editor: Martin's degenerate "mob" resembles Hitler's "mass-animal" quoted in Chap. I.

fallen without effect upon the ears of workingmen in America, and politicians were wont to boast that men born in America and men trained in America's school of labor and politics would not listen to it. But the air of the industrial regions of the country had sensibly thickened with the vapors of unwholesome opinion in these last years of unlooked for concentration of capital and unparalleled growths of corporate power. They still showed themselves most in cities where discontented men and women out of the proletariat of European countries most congregated. . . . But the infection was spreading outside the cities, too. It began to be seen, when once the matter was laid bare, that men of American training, as well as foreigners, had begun to take the taint of anarchistic sentiment.[4]

—WOODROW WILSON, 1902

"It is a pathological worship of mere number," writes Alleyne Ireland, "which has inspired all the efforts—the primary, the direct election of Senators, the initiative, the recall and the referendum—to cure the evils of mob rule by increasing the size of the mob and extending its powers."[5]

Equality of political power has thus been bestowed upon the lowest elements of our population. We must not be surprised, therefore, at the spectacle of political scandal and graft, of the notorious and universally ridiculed low level of intelligence and flagrant stupidity exhibited by our legislative bodies. *The Congressional Record* mirrors our political imbecility.

All of these dangers and menaces are acutely realized by the Eugenists; it is to them that we are most indebted for the proof that reckless spawning carries with it the seeds of destruction. But whereas the Galtonians reveal themselves as unflinching in their investigation and in their exhibition of fact and diagnoses of symptoms, they do not on the other hand show much power in suggesting practical and feasible remedies.

On its scientific side, Eugenics suggests the reestablishment of the balance between the fertility of the "fit" and the "unfit." The birth-rate among the normal and healthier and finer stocks of humanity, is to be increased by awakening among the "fit" the realization of the dangers of a lessened birth-rate in proportion to the reckless breeding among the "unfit." By education, by persuasion, by appeals to racial ethics and religious motives, the ardent Eugenist hopes to increase

4. Woodrow Wilson, *A History of the American People* (New York, 1902), 186–87.
5. Cf. *Democracy and the Human Equation*. E. P. Dutton & Co., 1921.

the fertility of the "fit." Professor Pearson thinks that it is especially necessary to awaken the hardiest stocks to this duty. These stocks, he says, are to be found chiefly among the skilled artisan class, the intelligent working class. Here is a fine combination of health and hardy vigor, of sound body and sound mind.

Professor Pearson and his school of biometrics here ignore or at least fail to record one of those significant "correlations" which form the basis of his method. The publications of the Eugenics Laboratory all tend to show that a high rate of fertility is correlated with extreme poverty, recklessness, deficiency and delinquency; similarly, that among the more intelligent, this rate of fertility decreases. **But the scientific Eugenists fail to recognize that this restraint of fecundity is due to a deliberate foresight and is a conscious effort to elevate standards of living for the family and the children of the responsible—and possibly more selfish—sections of the community. The appeal to enter again into competitive child-bearing, for the benefit of the nation or the race, or any other abstraction, will fall on deaf ears.**

Pearson has done invaluable work in pointing out the fallacies and the false conclusions of the ordinary statisticians. But when he attempts to show by the methods of biometrics that not only the first child but also the second, are especially liable to suffer from transmissible pathological defects, such as insanity, criminality and tuberculosis, he fails to recognize that this tendency is counterbalanced by the high mortality rate among later children. If first and second children reveal a greater percentage of heritable defect, it is because the later born children are less liable to survive the conditions produced by a large family.

In passing, we should here recognize the difficulties presented by the idea of "fit" and "unfit." Who is to decide this question? **The grosser, the more obvious, the undeniably feeble-minded should, indeed, not only be discouraged but prevented from propagating their kind.** But among the writings of the representative Eugenists one cannot ignore the distinct middle-class bias that prevails. As that penetrating critic, F. W. Stella Browne, has said in another connection, "The Eugenics Education Society has among its numbers many most open-minded and truly progressive individuals but the official policy it has pursued for years has been inspired by class-bias and sex bias. The society laments with increasing vehemence the multiplication of the less fortunate classes at a more rapid rate than the possessors of leisure and opportunity. (I do not think it relevant here to discuss whether the innate superiority of endowment in the governing class really is so overwhelming as to justify the Eugenics Education Society's peculiar use of the terms 'fit' and 'unfit'!) Yet it has persistently refused to give any help toward extending the knowledge of contraceptives to the exploited classes. Similarly, though the *Eugenics Review*, the organ of the society, frequently laments the 'selfishness' of the refusal of maternity by healthy and educated women of the professional classes, I have yet to learn that it has made any official pronouncement on the English illegitimacy laws or any organized effort toward defending the unmarried mother."

This peculiarly Victorian reticence may be inherited from the founder of Eugenics. Galton declared that the "Bohemian" element in the Anglo-Saxon race is destined to perish, and "the sooner it goes, the happier for mankind." The trouble with any effort of trying to divide humanity into the "fit" and the "unfit," is that we do not want, as H. G. Wells recently pointed out,[6] to breed for uniformity but for variety. "We want statesmen and poets and musicians and philosophers and strong men and delicate men and brave men. The qualities of one would be the weaknesses of the other." We want, most of all, genius.

Proscription on Galtonian lines would tend to eliminate many of the great geniuses of the world who were not only "Bohemian," but actually and pathologically abnormal—men like Rousseau, Dostoevsky, Chopin, Poe, Schumann, Nietzsche, Comte, Guy de Maupassant—and how many others? But such considerations should not lead us into error of concluding that such men were geniuses merely because they were pathological specimens, and that the only way to produce a genius is to breed disease and defect. It only emphasizes the dangers of external standards of "fit" and "unfit."

These limitations are more strikingly shown in the types of so-called "eugenic" legislation passed or proposed by certain enthusiasts. Regulation, compulsion and prohibitions affected and enacted by political bodies are the surest methods of driving the whole problem underground. As Havelock Ellis has pointed out, the absurdity and even hopelessness of effecting Eugenic improvement by placing on the statute books prohibitions of legal matrimony to certain classes of people, reveal the weakness of those Eugenists who minimize or undervalue the importance of environment as a determining factor. They affirm that heredity is everything and environment nothing, yet forget that it is precisely those who are most universally subject to bad environment who procreate most copiously, most recklessly and most disastrously. Such

marriage laws are based for the most part on the infantile assumption that procreation is absolutely dependent upon the marriage ceremony, an assumption usually coupled with the complementary one that the only purpose in marriage is procreation. Yet it is a fact so obvious that it is hardly worth stating that the most fertile classes who indulge in the most dysgenic type of procreating—the feeble-minded—are almost totally unaffected by marriage laws and marriage-ceremonies.

As for the sterilization of habitual criminals, not merely must we know more of heredity and genetics in general, but also acquire more certainty of the justice of our laws and the honesty of their administration before we can make rulings of fitness or unfitness merely upon the basis of a respect for law. On this point the eminent William Bateson writes:[7] "Criminals are often feeble-minded, but as regards those that are not, the fact that a man is for the purposes of Society classified as a criminal, tells me little as to his value, still less as to the possible value of his offspring. It is a fault inherent in criminal jurisprudence, based on non-biological data, that the law must needs take the nature of the offenses rather than that of the offenders as the basis of classification. A change in the right direction has begun, but the problem is difficult and progress will be very slow.... We all know of persons convicted, perhaps even habitually, whom the world could ill spare. Therefore I hesitate to proscribe the criminal. Proscription... is a weapon with a very nasty recoil. Might not some with equal cogency proscribe army contractors and their accomplices, the newspaper patriots? The crimes of the prison population are petty offenses by comparison, and the significance we attach to them is a survival of other days. Felonies may be great events, locally, but they do not induce catastrophes. The proclivities of the war-makers are infinitely more dangerous than those of the aberrant beings whom from time to time the law may dub as criminal. Consistent and portentous selfishness, combined with dulness of imagination is probably just as transmissible as want of self-control, though destitute of the amiable qualities not rarely associated with the genetic composition of persons of unstable mind."

In this connection, we should note another type of "respectable" criminality noted by Havelock Ellis: "If those persons who raise the cry of 'race-suicide' in face of the decline of the birth-rate really had the knowledge and the intelligence to realize the manifold evils which

---

6. Cf. *The Salvaging of Civilization.*

7. *Common Sense in Racial Problems.* By W. Bateson, M.A.A., F.R.S.

they are invoking, they would deserve to be treated as criminals."[8]

Our debt to the science of Eugenics is great in that it directs our attention to the biological nature of humanity. Yet there is too great a tendency among the thinkers of this school, to restrict their ideas of sex to its expression as a purely procreative function. Compulsory legislation which would make the inevitably futile attempt to prohibit one of the most beneficent and necessary of human expressions, or regulate it into the channels of preconceived philosophies, would reduce us to the unpleasant days predicted by William Blake, when

> Priests in black gowns will be walking their rounds
> And binding with briars our joys and desires.

Eugenics is chiefly valuable in its negative aspects. It is "negative Eugenics" that has studied the histories of such families as the Jukeses and the Kallikaks,[9] that has pointed out the network of imbecility and feeble-mindedness that has been sedulously spread through all strata of society. On its so-called positive or constructive side, it fails to awaken any permanent interest. "Constructive" Eugenics aims to arouse the enthusiasm or the interest of the people in the welfare of the world fifteen or twenty generations in the future. On its negative side it shows us that we are paying for and even submitting to the dictates of an ever increasing, unceasingly spawning class of human beings who never should have been born at all— that the wealth of individuals and of states is being diverted from the development and the progress of human expression and civilization.

While it is necessary to point out the importance of "heredity" as a determining factor in human life, it is fatal to elevate it to the position of an absolute. As with environment, the concept of heredity derives its value and its meaning only in so far as it is embodied and made concrete in generations of living organisms. Environment and heredity are not antagonistic. Our problem is not that of "Nature vs. Nurture," but rather of Nature X Nurture, of heredity multiplied by environment, if we may express it thus. The Eugenist who overlooks the importance of environment as a determining factor in human life, is as short-sighted as the Socialist who neglects the biological nature of man. We cannot disentangle these two forces, except in theory. To the child in the womb, said Samuel Butler, the mother is "environment." She is, of course,

likewise "heredity." **The age-old discussion of "Nature vs. Nurture" has been threshed out time after time, usually fruitlessly, because of a failure to recognize the indivisibility of these biological factors. The opposition or antagonism between them is an artificial and academic one, having no basis in the living organism.**[10]

The great principle of Birth Control offers the means whereby the individual may adapt himself to and even control the forces of environment and heredity. Entirely apart from its Malthusian aspect or that of the population question, Birth Control must be recognized, as the Neo-Malthusians pointed out long ago, not "merely as the key of the social position," and the only possible and practical method of human generation, but as the very pivot of civilization. Birth Control which has been criticized as negative and destructive, is really the greatest and most truly eugenic method, and its adoption as part of the program of Eugenics would immediately give a concrete and realistic power to that science. As a matter of fact, Birth Control has been accepted by the most clear thinking and far seeing of the Eugenists themselves as the most constructive and necessary of the means to racial health.[11]

—§§§—

A Consequence of Feminism

Birth-control, as already pointed out, implies forethought; this indicates superior brains; and therefore we get the races with superior mentalities rapidly lowering their rate of reproduction, and, within these races, the most intelligent classes doing this at a much greater speed than the rest. Thus we see a vicious and essentially dysgenist process at work. The higher races are using the resources of scientific knowledge to reduce the death-rate of the inferior peoples and the birth-rate of the superior. . . .

We can get no comfort from realising that the whole course of what is called "feminine emancipation" intensifies these disastrous tendencies, that all influences making restriction of births greater in the circles in

---

8. Editor: In Chap. V we pointed out that H. G. Wells wanted Theodore Roosevelt treated as a criminal for his use of race suicide arguments. Neither Ellis nor Sanger seem to attach much importance to free speech.

9. Editor: For what was believed at that time about the Kallikaks, see Chap. XIII.

10. Editor: As before, Sanger stressed that distinctions which seem important in scientific circles matter little in real life. Parents provide their children with both heredity and environment. If either is flawed, their children menace our "racial health."

11. Among these are Dean W. R. Inge, Professor J. Arthur Thomson, Dr. Havelock Ellis, Professor William Bateson, Major Leonard Darwin and Miss Norah March. Editor: William Bateson (1861–1926) wrote *Biological Fact and the Structure of Society* (1912) and *Heredity* (1915). Norah Helena March was the author of *Toward Racial Health* (1915) and *Sex Knowledge* (1920).

which it should least operate are those receiving the approval of every "woman's advocate."[12]

—S. H. HALFORD, 1917

—§§§—

12. S. H. Halford, "Dysgenic Tendencies of Birth-Control, and the Feminist Movement" *Population and Birth Control*, Eden Paul, ed. (New York: Critic and Guide, 1917), 229.

9

A Moral Necessity

I went to the Garden of Love,
And saw what I never had seen;
A Chapel was built in the midst,
Where I used to play on the green.
And the gates of this Chapel were shut,
And "Thou shalt not" writ over the door;
So I turned to the Garden of Love
That so many sweet flowers bore.
And I saw it was filled with graves,
And tombstones where flowers should be;
And priests in black gowns were walking their rounds,
And binding with briars my joys and desires.
—WILLIAM BLAKE

Orthodox opposition to Birth Control is formulated in the official protest of the National Council of Catholic Women against the resolution passed by the New York State Federation of Women's Clubs which favored the removal of all obstacles to the spread of information regarding practical methods of Birth Control. The Catholic statement completely embodies traditional opposition to Birth Control. It affords a striking contrast by which we may clarify and justify the ethical necessity for this new instrument of civilization as the most effective basis for practical and scientific morality.

"The authorities at Rome have again and again declared that all positive methods of this nature are immoral and forbidden," states the National Council of Catholic Women. "There is no question of the lawfulness of birth restriction through abstinence from the relations which result in conception. The immorality of Birth Control as it is practised and commonly understood, consists in the evils of the particular method employed. These are all contrary to the moral law because they are unnatural, being a perversion of a natural function. Human faculties are used in such a way as to frustrate the natural end for which these faculties were created. This is always intrinsically wrong—as wrong as lying and blasphemy. No

supposed beneficial consequence can make good a practice which is, in itself, immoral. . . .

"The evil results of the practice of Birth Control are numerous. Attention will be called here to only three. The first is the degradation of the marital relation itself, since the husband and wife who indulge in any form of this practice come to have a lower idea of married life. They cannot help coming to regard each other to a great extent as mutual instruments of sensual gratification, rather than as cooperators with the Creating in bringing children into the world. This consideration may be subtle but it undoubtedly represents the facts.

"In the second place, the deliberate restriction of the family through these immoral practices deliberately weakens self-control and the capacity for self-denial, and increases the love of ease and luxury. The best indication of this is that the small family is much more prevalent in the classes that are comfortable and well-to-do than among those whose material advantages are moderate or small. The theory of the advocates of Birth Control is that those parents who are comfortably situated should have a large number of children (*sic!*) while the poor should restrict their offspring to a much smaller number. This theory does not work, for the reason that each married couple have their own idea of what constitutes unreasonable hardship in the matter of bearing and rearing children. A large proportion of the parents who are addicted to Birth Control practices are sufficiently provided with worldly goods to be free from apprehension on the economic side; nevertheless, they have small families because they are disinclined to undertake the other burdens involved in bringing up a more numerous family. A practice which tends to produce such exaggerated notions of what constitutes hardship, which leads men and women to cherish such a degree of ease, makes inevitably for inefficiency, a decline in the capacity to endure and to achieve, and for a general social decadence.

"Finally, Birth Control leads sooner or later to a decline in population...." (The case of France is instanced.) But it is essentially the moral question that alarms the Catholic women, for the statement concludes: "The further effect of such proposed legislation will inevitably be a lowering both of public and private morals. What the fathers of this country termed indecent and forbade the mails to carry, will, if such legislation is carried through, be legally decent. The purveyors of sexual license and immorality will have the opportunity to send almost anything they care to write through the mails on the plea that it is sex information. Not only the married but also the unmarried will be thus affected; the ideals of the young contaminated and lowered. The morals of the entire nation will suffer.

"The proper attitude of Catholics... is clear. They should watch and oppose all attempts in state legislatures and in Congress to repeal the laws which now prohibit the dissemination of information concerning Birth Control. Such information will be spread only too rapidly despite existing laws. To repeal these would greatly accelerate this deplorable movement.[1]"

Meeting Her Match

Above all, Sanger more than met her match in the powerful political opposition that was mounted against her by the American Catholic Church. For the first time in its history in this country, the church created a national mechanism for lobbying and for mobilizing its core constituency of faithful women. Sanger was identified as a dangerous subversive, intent on destroying the family and limiting the fertility of the very people she was trying to help.[2]

—ELLEN CHESLER, *WOMAN OF VALOR,* 1992

1. Quoted in the *National Catholic Welfare Council Bulletin:* Vol. II, No. 5. p. 21 (January, 1921). Editor: For a sympathetic, scholarly history of the development of Catholic doctrine about birth control, see John T. Noonan, *Contraception.*

The Catholic position has been stated in an even more extreme form by Archbishop Patrick J. Hayes of the archdiocese of New York.[3] In a "Christmas Pastoral" this dignitary even went to the extent of declaring that "even though some little angels in the flesh, through the physical or mental deformities of their parents, may appear to human eyes hideous, misshapen, a blot on civilized society, we must not lose sight of this Christian thought that under and within such visible malformation, lives an immortal soul to be saved and glorified for all eternity among the blessed in heaven."[4]

With the type of moral philosophy expressed in this utterance, we need not argue. It is based upon traditional ideas that have had the practical effect of making this world a vale of tears. Fortunately such words carry no weight with those who can bring free and keen as well as noble minds to the consideration of the matter. To them the idealism of such an utterance appears crude and cruel. The menace to civilization of such orthodoxy, if it be orthodoxy, lies in the fact that its powerful exponents may be for a time successful not merely in influencing the conduct of their adherents but in checking freedom of thought and discussion. To this, with all the vehemence of emphasis at our command, we object. From what Archbishop Hayes believes concerning the future blessedness in Heaven of the souls of those who are born into this world as hideous and misshapen beings he has a right to seek such consolation as may be obtained; but we who

2. Ellen Chesler, *Woman of Valor* (New York: Simon & Schuster, 1992), 15. It's difficult to know what to say about an author who writes a book of over 600 pages about Sanger and yet fails so utterly to explain what her subject's intentions were.

3. Editor: Often, when Sanger wanted to say something particularly vile, she muddled her words and slandered her opponents. In such cases, it helps to restate what she said in simple, concrete language. Society is menaced, she claimed, by extremists such as Catholics who believe we should love and care for children born with visible imperfections. Since birth control has no magical ability to target such children, Sanger doesn't tell us how she intends to prevent their birth. But that isn't her real concern. In Chap. 7 she tried to bring socialists to her point of view, and in Chap. 8 she turned to eugenists. As readers can see from editorials reprinted from the *New Republic* (Chap. XXI), this chapter (including its strident anti-Catholicism) was intended to appeal to liberals who regard such babies with "horror" and want to rid the world of them. (For that they would need not just birth control but also eugenic abortion and perhaps infanticide.) Liberals support for Sanger did not come in ignorance of her agenda or in spite of it. It came because of it.

4. Quoted in the daily press, Dec. 19, 1921. Editor: The published remarks of both are quoted in full in Chap. XXVIII, "Little Angels in the Flesh."

are trying to better the conditions of this world believe that a healthy, happy human race is more in keeping with the laws of God, than disease, misery and poverty perpetuating itself generation after generation. Furthermore, while conceding to Catholic or other churchmen full freedom to preach their own doctrines, whether of theology or morals, nevertheless when they attempt to carry these ideas into legislative acts and force their opinions and codes upon the non-Catholics, we consider such action an interference with the principles of democracy and we have a right to protest.[5]

A Leipzig Child

In particular, Hitler's attention had been focused upon the issue of mercy killing in the early part of 1939. He had received a petition from a Nazi Party member, a father asking that his handicapped daughter be killed. Hitler personally directed his escort physician (as Brandt was then) to investigate. Physician Brandt went to the child's home in Leipzig to assess the situation. He found, in his own words, "a child who was born blind, an idiot—at least it seemed to be an idiot—and it lacked one leg and part of one arm." . . . Brandt was directed by Hitler to inform the family physician to proceed with euthanasia. Hitler did not want the parents to feel guilt about this.[6]

—H. GREGORY GALLAGHER, *BY TRUST BETRAYED*

Religious propaganda against Birth Control is crammed with contradiction and fallacy. It refutes itself. Yet it brings the opposing views into vivid contrast. In stating these differences we should make clear that advocates of Birth Control are not seeking to attack the Catho-

lic church. We quarrel with that church, however, when it seeks to assume authority over non-Catholics and to dub their behavior immoral because they do not conform to the dictatorship of Rome. The question of bearing and rearing children we hold is the concern of the mother and the potential mother. If she delegates the responsibility, the ethical education, to an external authority, that is her affair. We object, however, to the State or the Church which appoints itself as arbiter and dictator in this sphere and attempts to force unwilling women into compulsory maternity.

When Catholics declare that "The authorities at Rome have again and again declared that all positive methods of this nature are immoral and forbidden," they do so upon the assumption that morality consists in conforming to laws laid down and enforced by external authority, in submission to decrees and dicta imposed from without. In this case, they decide in a wholesale manner the conduct of millions, demanding of them not the intelligent exercise of their own individual judgment and discrimination, but unquestioning submission and conformity to dogma. The Church thus takes the place of all-powerful parents, and demands of its children merely that they should obey.

---

5. Editor: If Sanger's point of view was applied consistently, no group could call for laws that applied to anyone outside its membership. Obviously, no society, democratic or otherwise, could function under such a rule. Keep in mind, however, that the real issue wasn't technology, but where that technology was applied. Sanger and her liberal allies saw society menaced by the births of imperfect children and believed birth control would eliminate them. Catholicism and its conservative Jewish and Protestant allies felt that such children should be valued and loved as they were, rather than branded "hideous" or a "horror" and targeted for elimination.

6. Hugh Gregory Gallagher, *By Trust Betrayed: Patients, Physicians and the License to Kill in the Third Reich* (New York: Henry Holt, 1990), 47. This was the first death in Germany's euthanasia program, a program that lay the groundwork for the Jewish genocide. Unlike Sanger, Catholic and Protestant leaders in Germany did not believe it was wrong to "force their opinions" on others. At some risk to their lives, they publicly protested, forcing Hitler to move the program underground and reduce its scope.

In my belief such a philosophy hampers the development of individual intelligence. Morality then becomes a more or less successful attempt to conform to a code, instead of an attempt to bring reason and intelligence to bear upon the solution of each individual human problem.

But, we read on, Birth Control methods are not merely contrary to "moral law," but forbidden because they are "unnatural," being "the perversion of a natural function." This, of course, is the weakest link in the whole chain. Yet "there is no question of the lawfulness of birth restriction through abstinence"—as though abstinence itself were not unnatural! For more than a thousand years the Church was occupied with the problem of imposing abstinence on its priesthood, its most educated and trained body of men, educated to look upon asceticism as the finest ideal; it took one thousand years to convince the Catholic priesthood that abstinence was "natural" or practicable.[7] Nevertheless, there is still this talk of abstinence, self-control, and self-denial, almost in the same breath with the condemnation of Birth Control as "unnatural."

If it is our duty to act as "cooperators with the Creator" to bring children into the world, it is difficult to say at what point our behavior is "unnatural." If it is immoral and "unnatural" to prevent an unwanted life from coming into existence, is it not immoral and "unnatural" to remain unmarried from the age of puberty? Such casuistry is unconvincing and feeble. We need only point out that rational intelligence is also a "natural" function, and that it is as imperative for us to use the faculties of judgment, criticism, discrimination of choice, selection and control, all the faculties of the intelligence, as it is to use those of reproduction. It is certainly dangerous "to frustrate the natural ends for which these faculties were created." This also, is always intrinsically wrong—as wrong as lying and blasphemy—and infinitely more devastating. Intelligence is as natural to us as any other faculty, and it is fatal to moral development and growth to refuse to use it and to delegate to others the solution of our individual problems. The evil will not be that one's conduct is divergent from current and conventional moral codes. There may be every outward evidence of conformity, but this agreement may be arrived at, by the restriction and suppression of subjective desires, and the more or less successful attempt at mere conformity. Such "morality" would conceal an inner conflict. The fruits of this conflict would be neurosis and hysteria on the one hand; or concealed gratification of suppressed desires on the other,

with a resultant hypocrisy and cant. True morality cannot be based on conformity. There must be no conflict between subjective desire and outward behavior.

To object to these traditional and churchly ideas does not by any means imply that the doctrine of Birth Control is anti-Christian. On the contrary, it may be profoundly in accordance with the Sermon on the Mount. One of the greatest living theologians and most penetrating students of the problems of civilization is of this opinion. In an address delivered before the Eugenics Education Society of London,[8] William Ralph Inge, the Very Reverend Dean of St. Paul's Cathedral, London, pointed out that the doctrine of Birth Control was to be interpreted as of the very essence of Christianity.

"We should be ready to give up all our theories," he asserted, "if science proved that we were on the wrong lines. And we can understand, though we profoundly disagree with, those who oppose us on the grounds of authority.... We know where we are with a man who says, 'Birth Control is forbidden by God; we prefer poverty, unemployment, war, the physical, intellectual and moral degeneration of the people, and a high death-rate to any interference with the universal command to be fruitful and multiply'; but we have no patience with those who say that we can have unrestricted and unregulated propagation without those consequences. It is a great part of our work to press home to the public mind the alternative that lies before us. Either rational selection must take the place of the natural selection which the modern State will not allow to act, or we must go on deteriorating. When we can convince the public of this, the opposition of organized religion will soon collapse or become ineffective." Dean Inge effectively answers those who have objected to the methods of Birth Control is [as] "immoral" and in contradiction and inimical to the teachings of Christ. Incidentally he claims that those who are not blinded by prejudices recognize that "Christianity aims at saving the soul—the personality, the nature, of man, not his body or his environment. According to Christianity, a man is saved, not by what he has, or knows, or does, but by what he is. It treats all the apparatus of life with a disdain as great as that of the biologist; so long as a man is inwardly healthy, it cares very little whether he is rich or poor, learned or simple, and even whether he is happy, or unhappy. It attaches no importance to quantitative measurements of any kind. The Christian does not gloat over favorable trade-statistics, nor congratulate himself on the disparity between the number of births and deaths. For him. . . the test of the

7. H. C. Lea: *History of Sacerdotal Celibacy* (Philadelphia, 1867).

8. *Eugenics Review,* January 1921.

welfare of a country is the quality of human beings whom it produces. Quality is everything, quantity is nothing. And besides this, the Christian conception of a kingdom of God upon the earth teaches us to turn our eyes to the future, and to think of the welfare of posterity as a thing which concerns us as much as that of our own generation. This welfare, as conceived by Christianity, is of course something different from external prosperity; it is to be the victory of intrinsic worth and healthiness over all the false ideals and deep-seated diseases which at present spoil civilization."

"It is not political religion with which I am concerned," Dean Inge explained, "but the convictions of really religious persons; and I do not think that we need despair of converting them to our views."

Dean Inge believes Birth Control is an essential part of Eugenics, and an essential part of Christian morality. **On this point he asserts: "We do wish to remind our orthodox and conservative friends that the Sermon on the Mount contains some admirably clear and unmistakable eugenic precepts.**[9] **'Do men gather grapes of thorns, or figs of thistles? A corrupt tree cannot bring forth good fruit, neither can a good tree bring forth evil fruit. Every tree which bringeth not forth good fruit is hewn down, and cast into the fire.'** We wish to apply these words not only to the actions of individuals, which spring from their characters, but to the character of individuals, which spring from their inherited qualities. This extension of the scope of the maxim seems to me quite legitimate.[10] Men do not gather grapes of thorns. As our proverb says, you cannot make a silk purse out of a sow's ear. If we believe this, and do not act upon it by trying to move public opinion towards giving social reform, education and religion a better material to work upon, we are sinning against the light, and not doing our best to bring in the Kingdom of God upon earth."

As long as sexual activity is regarded in a dualistic and contradictory light—in which it is revealed either as the

instrument by which men and women "cooperate with the Creator" to bring children into the world, on the one hand; and on the other, as the sinful instrument of self-gratification, lust and sensuality, there is bound to be an endless conflict in human conduct, producing ever increasing misery, pain and injustice. In crystallizing and codifying this contradiction, the Church not only solidified its own power over men but reduced women to the most abject and prostrate slavery. It was essentially a morality that would not "work." **The sex instinct in the human race is too strong to be bound by the dictates of any church.** The church's failure, its century after century of failure, is now evident on every side: for, having convinced men and women that only in its baldly propagative phase is sexual expression legitimate, the teachings of the Church have driven sex under-ground, into secret channels, strengthened the conspiracy of silence, concentrated men's thoughts upon the "lusts of the body," have sown, cultivated and reaped a crop of bodily and mental diseases, and developed a society congenitally and almost hopelessly unbalanced. How is any progress to be made, how is any human expression or education possible when women and men are taught to combat and resist their natural impulses and to despise their bodily functions?

Humanity, we are glad to realize, is rapidly freeing itself from this "morality" imposed upon it by its self-appointed and self-perpetuating masters. From a hundred different points the imposing edifice of this "morality" has been and is being attacked. Sincere and thoughtful defenders and exponents of the teachings of Christ now acknowledge the falsity of the traditional codes and their malignant influence upon the moral and physical well-being of humanity.[11]

Planned Parenthood and Promiscuity

When *Look* magazine, in its issue of April 1, 1947, published a sober, factual review of the clinical work of the Planned Parenthood Federation, the top-ranking layman of the Archdiocese of New York, under Cardinal Spellman, wrote a reply in the issue of May 6th in which he accused the planned-parenthood leaders of advocating "education in animal functions completely divorced from morality and ethics," and declared that such education meant training people "to be sexually

9. Editor: This illustrates yet again that opposition to eugenics and birth control came from the religious orthodox and politically conservative rather than liberals.

10. Editor: Inge's "extension of the scope" is implausible. In fact, Matthew 21:31 could be paraphrased, "I tell you the truth, the tax collectors and prostitutes will enter the kingdom of God ahead of Dean Inge of St. Paul's Cathedral in London." Jesus addressed his biting remarks to the proud eugenic elite of his day, "the chief priests and elders of the people." Paul said much the same thing in 1 Corinthians 1:26 when he told early believers that among them were "not many wise according to the flesh, not many mighty, not many noble." The Kingdom of God is not a stud farm for breeding supermen.

11. Editor: Here Sanger revealed that one of her targets was the "malignant influence" spread by the "traditional codes" of sexual behavior held by conservative Catholics, Jews and Protestants. Elsewhere, when Sanger denied that such was her agenda, she was simply lying. Most of the mainstream press never caught on to this chronic dishonesty—or didn't care.

promiscuous with least risk of pregnancy or venereal disease." "The planned parenthood program," he wrote, "assumes that the cure for beastliness is to teach juveniles how to get away with acting like beasts."[12]

PAUL BLANSHARD, 1949

Ecclesiastical opposition to Birth Control on the part of certain representatives of the Protestant churches, based usually on quotations from the Bible, is equally invalid, and for the same reason. The attitude of the more intelligent and enlightened clergy has been well and succinctly expressed by Dean Inge, who, referring to the ethics of Birth Control, writes: *"This is emphatically a matter in which every man and woman must judge for themselves, and must refrain from judging others."* We must not neglect the important fact that it is not merely in the practical results of such a decision, not in the small number of children, not even in the healthier and better cared for children, not in the possibility of elevating the living conditions of the individual family, that the ethical value of Birth Control alone lies. Precisely because the practice of Birth Control does demand the exercise of decision, the making of choice, the use of the reasoning powers, is it an instrument of moral education as well as of hygienic and racial advance. It awakens the attention of parents to their potential children. It forces upon the individual consciousness the question of the standards of living. In a profound manner it protects and reasserts the inalienable rights of the child-to-be.[13]

---

12. Paul Blanshard, *American Freedom and Catholic Power* (Boston: Beacon Press, 1949), 141-42. We now know Cardinal Spellman was right. Understanding the organization Sanger founded required no great intellect. All one had to do was read what Sanger wrote with some understanding. Unfortunately, that understanding seems to have been denied the respected liberal "clergymen and rabbis" that, Blanshard tells us, were "formally associated with the Planned Parenthood Federation." (Then again, maybe they knew but chose to deceive.) Blanshard was once an associate editor of *The Nation,* a liberal magazine whose pro-eugenic, anti-Catholic mindset we saw in Chap. XXII. Blanshard's book, venting his fury at the Catholic "hierarchy," was praised by educator John Dewey and honored by the American Library Association as one of "50 Books of the Year." The chapter this quote was taken from is entitled "Sex, Birth Control and Eugenics." The realities of Nazism had not yet driven eugenics underground. In 1949, it was still an openly liberal idea. Only reactionaries, the liberal Blanshard said, called it "most dangerous" (p. 148).

13. Editor: At this time, Sanger claimed to oppose abortion, hence she could write about the "inalienable rights of the child-to-be." But the child referred to here is no more than an abstraction, a tool of "hygienic and racial advance."

Psychology and the outlook of modern life are stressing the growth of independent responsibility and discrimination as the true basis of ethics. The old traditional morality, with its train of vice, disease, promiscuity and prostitution, is in reality dying out, killing itself off because it is too irresponsible and too dangerous to individual and social well-being. The transition from the old to the new, like all fundamental changes, is fraught with many dangers. But it is a revolution that cannot be stopped.

The smaller family, with its lower infant mortality rate, is, in more definite and concrete manner than many actions outwardly deemed "moral," the expression of moral judgment and responsibility. It is the assertion of a standard of living, inspired by the wish to obtain a fuller and more expressive life for the children than the parents have enjoyed. If the morality or immorality of any course of conduct is to be determined by the motives which inspire it, there is evidently at the present day no higher morality than the intelligent practice of Birth Control.

The immorality of many who practise Birth Control lies in not daring to preach what they practise. What is the secret of the hypocrisy of the well-to-do, who are willing to contribute generously to charities and philanthropies, who spend thousands annually in the upkeep and sustenance of the delinquent, the defective and the dependent; and yet join the conspiracy of silence that prevents the poorer classes from learning how to improve their conditions, and elevate their standards of living? It is as though they were to cry: "We'll give you anything except the thing you ask for—the means whereby you may become responsible and self-reliant in your own lives."

The brunt of this injustice falls on women, because the old traditional morality is the invention of men. "No religion, no physical or moral code," wrote the clear-sighted George Drysdale, "proposed by one sex for the other, can be really suitable. Each must work out its laws for itself in every department of life." In the moral code developed by the Church, women have been so degraded that they have been habituated to look upon themselves through the eyes of men. Very imperfectly have women developed their own self-consciousness, the realization of their tremendous and supreme position in civilization. Women can develop this power only in one way; by the exercise of responsibility, by the exercise of judgment, reason or discrimination. They need ask for no "rights." They need only assert power. Only by the exercise of self-guidance and intelligent self-direction can that inalienable, supreme, pivotal power be expressed. More than ever in history women need to realize that nothing can ever come to us from another. Everything we attain we must owe to ourselves. Our own spirit must vitalize it. Our own heart must feel it. For we are not passive machines. We are not to be lectured, guided and molded this way or that. We are alive and intelligent, we women, no less than men, and we must awaken to the essential realization that we are living beings, endowed with will, choice, comprehension, and that every step in life must be taken at our own initiative.

Moral and sexual balance in civilization will only be established by the assertion and expression of power on the part of women. This power will not be found in any futile seeking for economic independence or in the aping of men in industrial and business pursuits, nor by joining battle for the so-called "single standard." Woman's power can only be expressed and make itself felt when she refuses the task of bringing unwanted children into the world to be exploited in industry and slaughtered in wars. When we refuse to produce battalions of babies to be exploited; when we declare to the nation; "Show us that the best possible chance in life is given to every child now brought into the world, before you cry for more! At present our children are a glut on the market. You hold infant life cheap. Help us to make the world a fit place for children. When you have done this, we will bear you children—then we shall be true women." The new morality will express this power and responsibility on the part of women.

Women as Eugenic Enforcers

Ellis made his most important contribution to eugenic doctrine, at least from the standpoint of Margaret's interest, when he assigned women to act as its chief enforcers. Women are critical agents of civilization's progress, he argued, because as individuals they alone have the power to produce and nurture fewer, fitter babies, while, collectively, they can exercise the will to reduce substantially the pressure of population on the environment and the competition of labor in the marketplace. Increased sex expression and wider use of birth control were thus significant tools in the eugenic program, and accordingly, he condemned eugenicists who refused to endorse birth control because they wanted more children for the better classes.[14]

—ELLEN CHESLER, *WOMAN OF VALOR*

"With the realization of the moral responsibility of women," writes Havelock Ellis, "the natural relations of life spring back to their due biological adjustment. Motherhood is restored to its natural sacredness. It becomes the concern of the woman herself, and not of society nor any individual, to determine the conditions under which the child shall be conceived. . . ."

Moreover, woman shall further assert her power by refusing to remain the passive instrument of sensual self-gratification on the part of men. Birth Control, in philosophy and practice, is the destroyer of that dualism of the old sexual code. It denies that the sole purpose of sexual activity is procreation; it also denies that sex should be reduced to the level of sensual lust, or that woman should permit herself to be the instrument of its satisfaction. In increasing and differentiating her love demands, woman must elevate sex into another sphere, whereby it may subserve and enhance the possibility of individual and human expression. Man will gain in this no less than woman; for in the age-old enslavement of woman he has enslaved himself; and in the liberation of womankind, all of humanity will experience the joys of a new and fuller freedom.

On this great fundamental and pivotal point new light has been thrown by Lord Bertrand Dawson, the physician of the King of England. In the remarkable and epoch-making address at the Birmingham Church Congress (referred to in my introduction), he spoke of the supreme morality of the mutual and reciprocal joy in the most intimate relation between man and woman. Without this reciprocity there can be no civilization worthy of the name. Lord Dawson suggested that there should be added to the clauses of marriage in the Prayer Book "the complete realization of the love of this man and this woman one for another," and in support of his contention declared that sex love between husband and wife—apart from parenthood—was something to prize and cherish for its own sake. The Lambeth Conference, he remarked, "envisaged a love invertebrate and joyless," whereas, in his view, natural passion in wedlock was not a thing to be ashamed of or unduly repressed. The pronouncement of the Church of England, as set forth in Resolution 68 of the Lambeth Conference seems to imply condemnation of

---
14. Ellen Chesler, *Woman of Valor* (New York: Simon & Schuster, 1992), 123. On that same page Chesler claimed that "only the most conservative faction of the eugenics movement engaged in explicit racial stereotyping." Wells and Gilman as "conservative"? Hardly. Chesler is playing the nasty little game of labeling once progressive evils as conservative. Time and again, Sanger made clear that conservatives were her foes. In Chap. 7, for instance, she blasted the "stagnating complacency of our conservatives and reactionaries, under whose benign imbecility the defective and diseased elements of humanity are encouraged 'full speed ahead' in their reckless and irresponsible swarming and spawning." The socialist and feminist segments of eugenics had the most brutal agendas.

sex love as such, and to imply sanction of sex love only as a means to an end—namely, procreation. The Lambeth Resolution stated:

> In opposition to the teaching which under the name of science and religion encourages married people in the deliberate cultivation of sexual union as an end in itself, we steadfastly uphold what must always be regarded as the governing considerations of Christian marriage. One is the primary purpose for which marriage exists—namely, the continuation of the race through the gift and heritage of children; the other is the paramount importance in married life of deliberate and thoughtful self-control.

In answer to this point of view Lord Dawson asserted:

> Sex love has, apart from parenthood, a purport of its own. It is something to prize and to cherish for its own sake. It is an essential part of health and happiness in marriage. And now, if you will allow me, I will carry this argument a step further. If sexual union is a gift of God it is worth learning how to use it. Within its own sphere it should be cultivated so as to bring physical satisfaction to both, not merely to one. . . . The real problems before us are those of sex love and child love; and by sex love I mean that love which involves intercourse or the desire for such. It is necessary to my argument to emphasize that sex love is one of the dominating forces of the world. Not only does history show the destinies of nations and dynasties determined by its sway—but here in our every-day life we see its influence, direct or indirect, forceful and ubiquitous beyond aught else. Any statesmanlike view, therefore, will recognize that here we have an instinct so fundamental, so imperious, that its influence is a fact which has to be accepted; suppress it you cannot. You may guide it into healthy channels, but an outlet it will have, and if that outlet is inadequate and unduly obstructed irregular channels will be forced. . . .
>
> The attainment of mutual and reciprocal joy in their relations constitutes a firm bond between two people, and makes for durability of the marriage tie. Reciprocity in sex love is the physical counterpart of sympathy. More marriages fail from inadequate and clumsy sex love than from too much sex love. The lack of proper understanding is in no small measure responsible for the unfulfilment of connubial happiness, and every degree of discontent and unhappiness may, from this cause, occur, leading to rupture of the marriage bond itself. How often do medical men have to deal with these difficulties, and how fortunate if such difficulties are disclosed early enough in married life to be rectified. Otherwise how tragic may be their consequences, and many a case in the Divorce Court has thus had its origin. To the foregoing contentions, it might be objected, you are encouraging passion. My reply would be, passion is a worthy possession—most men, who are any good, are capable of passion. You all enjoy ardent and passionate love in art and literature. Why not give it a place in real life? Why some people look askance at passion is because they are confusing it with sensuality. Sex love without passion is a poor, lifeless thing. Sensuality, on the other hand, is on a level with gluttony—a physical excess—detached from sentiment, chivalry, or tenderness. It is just as important to give sex love its place as to avoid its over-emphasis. Its real and effective restraints are those imposed by a loving and sympathetic companionship, by the privileges of parenthood, the exacting claims of career and that civic sense which prompts men to do social service. Now that the revision of the Prayer Book is receiving consideration, I should like to suggest with great respect an addition made to the objects of marriage in the Marriage Service, in these terms, "The complete realization of the love of this man and this woman, the one for the other.

Turning to the specific problem of Birth Control, Lord Dawson declared, "that Birth Control is here to stay. It is an established fact, and for good or evil has to be accepted. Although the extent of its application can be and is being modified, no denunciations will abolish it. Despite the influence and condemnations of the Church, it has been practised in France for well over half a century, and in Belgium and other Roman Catholic countries is extending. And if the Roman Catholic Church, with its compact organization, its power of authority, and its disciplines, cannot check this procedure, it is not likely that Protestant Churches will be able to do so, for Protestant religions depend for their strength on the conviction and esteem they establish in the heads and hearts of their people. The reasons which lead parents to limit their offspring are sometimes selfish, but more often honorable and cogent."

A report of the Fabian Society[15] on the morality of Birth Control, based upon a census conducted under the chairmanship of Sidney Webb, concludes: "These facts—which we are bound to face whether we like them or not—will appear in different lights to different people. In some quarters it seems to be sufficient to dismiss them with moral indignation, real or simulated. Such a judgment appears both irrelevant and futile. . . . If a course of conduct is habitually and deliberately pursued by vast multitudes of otherwise well-conducted people, forming probably a majority of the whole educated class of the

---

15. Fabian Tract No. 131. Editor: Additional quotes from that tract are in Chap. VI.

nation, we must assume that it does not conflict with their actual code of morality. They may be intellectually mistaken, but they are not doing what they feel to be wrong."

The moral justification and ethical necessity of Birth Control need not be empirically based upon the mere approval of experience and custom. Its morality is more profound. Birth Control is an ethical necessity for humanity to-day because it places in our hands a new instrument of self-expression and self-realization. It gives us control over one of the primordial forces of nature, to which in the past the majority of mankind have been enslaved, and by which it has been cheapened and debased. It arouses us to the possibility of newer and greater freedom. It develops the power, the responsibility and intelligence to use this freedom in living a liberated and abundant life. It permits us to enjoy this liberty without danger of infringing upon the similar liberty of our fellow men, or of injuring and curtailing the freedom of the next generation. It shows us that we need not seek in the amassing of worldly wealth, not in the illusion of some extra-terrestrial Heaven or earthly Utopia of a remote future the road to human development. The Kingdom of Heaven is in a very definite sense within us. Not by leaving our body and our fundamental humanity behind us, not by aiming to be anything but what we are, shall we become ennobled or immortal. By knowing ourselves, by expressing ourselves, by realizing ourselves more completely than

has ever before been possible, not only shall we attain the kingdom ourselves but we shall hand on the torch of life undimmed to our children and the children of our children.

—§§§—

The Catholic Priest Was His Enemy

Father joined the Knights of Labor, and his anti-Catholic attitude did not make for his popularity in a community mainly Irish. About this time came Bob Ingersoll's ringing challenge to dogmas and creeds, and Father organized a meeting one Sunday afternoon for the orator. . . .

From that day on the Catholic priest was his enemy. No more angels to be carved out of stone or granite, if the priest had anything to say about it. We were known, from this time on, as children of the Devil, atheists and heretics. Catholic children called us names and made faces as they passed our house. The fight of the fathers extended to the younger generation.[16]

—MARGARET SANGER, *MY FIGHT FOR BIRTH CONTROL*

16. Margaret Sanger, *My Fight for Birth Control* (Farrar & Rinehart: New York, 1931), 7. Robert G. Ingersoll (1833–99) was a famous agnostic and a traveling speaker who earned as much as $3500 for a single night's oration. According to Sanger, her father did not care how clashes like this affected his wife, who had been raised Catholic.

10

Science the Ally

There is but one hope. Ignorance, poverty, and vice must stop populating the world. This cannot be done by moral suasion. This cannot be done by talk or example. This cannot be done by religion or by law, by priest or by hangman. This cannot be done by force, physical or moral. To accomplish this there is but one way. Science must make woman the owner, the mistress of herself. Science, the only possible savior of mankind, must put it in the power of woman to decide for herself whether she will or will not become a mother. —*Robert G. Ingersoll*

THE BIRTH CONTROL REVIEW

OFFICIAL ORGAN OF THE AMERICAN BIRTH CONTROL LEAGUE

MARGARET SANGER, Editor

VOL. V.   DECEMBER, 1921   No. 12

Birth Control: To create a race of thoroughbreds.

"Science is the great instrument of social change," wrote A. J. Balfour in 1908; "all the greater because its object is not change but knowledge, and its silent appropriation of this dominant function, amid the din of religious and political strife, is the most vital of all revolutions which have marked the development of modern civilization."[1] The Birth Control movement has allied itself with science, and no small part of its present propaganda is to awaken the interest of scientists to the pivotal importance to civilization of this instrument. Only with the aid of science is it possible to perfect a practical method that may be universally taught. As Dean Inge recently admitted: "We should be ready to give up all our theories if science proved that we were on the wrong lines."

One of the principal aims of the American Birth Control League has been to awaken the interest of scientific investigators and to point out the rich field for original research opened up by this problem. The correlation of reckless breeding with defective and delinquent strains has not, strangely enough, been subjected to close scientific scrutiny, nor has the present biological unbalance been traced to its root. This is a crying necessity of our day, and it cannot be accomplished without the aid of science.

Secondary only to the response of women themselves is the awakened interest of scientists, statisticians, and research workers in every field. If the clergy and the defenders of traditional morality have opposed the movement for Birth Control, the response of enlightened scientists and physicians has been one of the most encouraging aids in our battle.[2]

---

1. Editor: Balfour also pointed out the limitations of science in his *Theism and Humanism,* remarking in Chap. 4: "My main contention rests, not upon the difficulty of harmonising moral ends in a Godless universe, but upon the difficulty of maintaining moral values if moral origins are purely naturalistic." However, they may differ in details, most of those quoted in this book illustrate the difficulty of retaining "moral values" when the naturalistic principles of Malthus and Darwin dominate thought.

2. Editor: Most scientists and physicians stayed out of this debate, though neither profession as a whole had the courage to expose the rather obvious evil inherent in ranking people as fit and unfit. Note Sanger's use of "enlightened." Agree with her and you were "enlightened." Disagree and she said all sorts of nasty things about you.

Recent developments in the realm of science—in psychology, in physiology, in chemistry and physics—all tend to emphasize the immediate necessity for human control over the great forces of nature. The new ideas published by contemporary science are of the utmost fascination and illumination even to the layman. They perform the invaluable task of making us look at life in a new light, of searching close at hand for the solution to heretofore closed mysteries of life. In this brief chapter, I can touch these ideas only as they have proved valuable to me. Professor Soddy's *Science and Life*[3] is one of the most inspiring of recent publications in this field; for this great authority shows us how closely bound up is science with the whole of Society, how science must help to solve the great and disastrous unbalance in human society.

As an example: a whole literature has sprung into being around the glands, the most striking being *The Sex Complex* by Blair Bell.[4] This author advances the idea of the glandular system as an integral whole, the glands forming a unity which might be termed the generative system. Thus is reasserted the radical importance of sexual health to every individual. The whole tendency of modern physiology and psychology, in a word, seems gradually coming to the truth that seemed intuitively to be revealed to that great woman, Olive Schreiner, who, in *Woman and Labor*[5] wrote:

> . . . Noble is the function of physical reproduction of humanity by the union of man and woman. Rightly viewed, that union has in it latent, other and even higher forms of creative energy and life-dispensing power, and. . . its history on earth has only begun; as the first wild rose when it hung from its stem with its center of stamens and pistils and its single whorl of pale petals had only begun its course, and was destined, as the ages passed, to develop stamen upon stamen and petal upon petal, till it assumed a hundred forms of joy and beauty.

> And it would indeed almost seem, that, on the path toward the higher development of sexual life on earth, as man has so often had to lead in other paths, that here it is perhaps woman, by reason of those very sexual conditions which in the past have crushed and trammeled her, who is bound to lead the way and man to follow. So that it may be at last that sexual love—that tired angel who through the ages has presided over the

march of humanity, with distraught eyes, and feather-shafts broken and wings drabbled in the mires of lust and greed, and golden locks caked over with the dust of injustice and oppression—till those looking at him have sometimes cried in terror, 'He is the Evil and not the Good of life': and have sought if it were not possible, to exterminate him—shall yet, at last, bathed from the mire and dust of ages in the streams of friendship and freedom, leap upwards, with white wings spread, resplendent in the sunshine of a distant future—the essentially Good and Beautiful of human existence.

To-day science is verifying the truth of this inspiring vision. Certain fundamental truths concerning the basic facts of Nature and humanity especially impress us. A rapid survey may indicate the main features of this mysterious identity and antagonism.

Mankind has gone forward by the capture and control of the forces of Nature. This upward struggle began with the kindling of the first fire. The domestication of animal life marked another great step in the long ascent. The capture of the great physical forces, the discovery of coal and mineral oil, of gas, steam and electricity, and their adaptation to the everyday uses of mankind, wrought the greatest changes in the course of civilization. With the discovery of radium and radioactivity, with the recognition of the vast stores of physical energy concealed in the atom, humanity is now on the eve of a new conquest. But, on the other side, humanity has been compelled to combat continuously those great forces of Nature which have opposed it at every moment of this long indomitable march out of barbarism. Humanity has had to wage war against insects, germs, bacteria, which have spread disease and epidemics and devastation. Humanity has had to adapt itself to those natural forces it could not conquer but could only adroitly turn to its own ends. Nevertheless, all along the line, in colonization, in agriculture, in medicine and in industry, mankind has triumphed over Nature.

But lest the recognition of this victory lead us to self-satisfaction and complacency, we should never forget that this mastery consists to a great extent in a recognition of the power of those blind forces, and our adroit control over them. It has been truly said that we attain no power over Nature until we learn natural laws and conform and adapt ourselves to them.

The strength of the human race has been its ability not merely to subjugate the forces of Nature, but to adapt itself to those it could not conquer. And even this subjugation, science tells us, has not resulted from any attempt to suppress, prohibit, or eradicate these forces, but rather to transform blind and undirected energies to our own purposes.

---

3. Editor: Frederick Soddy (1877–1956) published *Science and Life* in 1920.
4. Editor: William Blair Bell (1871–1936) published *The Sex Complex* in 1916.
5. Editor: Olive Schreiner (1855–1920) published *Woman and Labor* in 1911.

These great natural forces, science now asserts, are not all external. They are surely concealed within the complex organism of the human being no less than outside of it. These inner forces are no less imperative, no less driving and compelling than the external forces of Nature. As the old conception of the antagonism between body and soul is broken down, as psychology becomes an ally of physiology and biology, and biology joins hands with physics and chemistry, we are taught to see that there is a mysterious unity between these inner and outer forces. They express themselves in accordance with the same structural, physical and chemical laws. The development of civilization in the subjective world, in the sphere of behavior, conduct and morality, has been precisely the gradual accumulation and popularization of methods which teach people how to direct, transform and transmute the driving power of the great natural forces.

Psychology is now recognizing the forces concealed in the human organism. In the long process of adaptation to social life, men have had to harness the wishes and desires born of these inner energies, the greatest and most imperative of which are Sex and Hunger. From the beginning of time, men have been driven by Hunger into a thousand activities. It is Hunger that has created "the struggle for existence." Hunger has spurred men to the discovery and invention of methods and ways of avoiding starvation, of storing and exchanging foods. It has developed primitive barter into our contemporary Wall Streets. It has developed thrift and economy—expedients whereby humanity avoids the lash of King Hunger. The true "economic interpretation of history" might be termed the History of Hunger.

But no less fundamental, no less imperative, no less ceaseless in its dynamic energy, has been the great force of Sex. We do not yet know the intricate but certainly organic relationship between these two forces. It is obvious that they oppose yet reinforce each other—driving, lashing, spurring mankind on to new conquests or to certain ruin. Perhaps Hunger and Sex are merely opposite poles of a single great life force. In the past we have made the mistake of separating them and attempting to study one of them without the other. Birth Control emphasizes the need of re-investigation and of knowledge of their integral relationship, and aims at the solution of the great problem of Hunger and Sex at one and the same time.

In the more recent past the effort has been made to control, civilize, and sublimate the great primordial natural force of sex, mainly by futile efforts at prohibition, suppression, restraint, and extirpation. Its revenge, as the psychoanalysts are showing us every day, has been great.

Insanity, hysteria, neuroses, morbid fears and compulsions, weaken and render useless and unhappy thousands of humans who are unconscious victims of the attempt to pit individual powers against this great natural force. In the solution of the problem of sex, we should bear in mind what the successful method of humanity has been in its conquest, or rather its control of the great physical and chemical forces of the external world. Like all other energy, that of sex is indestructible. By adaptation, control and conscious direction, we may transmute and sublimate it. Without irreparable injury to ourselves we cannot attempt to eradicate it or extirpate it.

The study of atomic energy, the discovery of radioactivity, and the recognition of potential and latent energies stored in inanimate matter, throw a brilliant illumination upon the whole problem of sex and the inner energies of mankind. Speaking of the discovery of radium, Professor Soddy writes: "Tracked to earth the clew to a great secret for which a thousand telescopes might have swept the sky forever and in vain, lay in a scrap of matter, dowered with something of the same inexhaustible radiance that hitherto has been the sole prerogative of the distant stars and sun." Radium, this distinguished authority tells us, has clothed with its own dignity the whole empire of common matter.

Much as the atomic theory, with its revelations of the vast treasure house of radiant energy that lies all about us, offers new hope in the material world, so the new psychology throws a new light upon human energies and possibilities of individual expression. Social reformers, like those scientists of a bygone era who were sweeping the skies with their telescopes, have likewise been seeking far and wide for the solution of our social problems in remote and wholesale panaceas, whereas the true solution is close at hand—in the human individual. Buried within each human being lies concealed a vast store of energy, which awaits release, expression and sublimation. The individual may profitably be considered as the "atom" of society. And the solution of the problems of society and of civilization will be brought about when we release the energies now latent and undeveloped in the individual. Professor Edwin Grant Conklin expresses the problem in another form; though his analogy, it seems to me, is open to serious criticism. "The freedom of the individual man," he writes,[6] "is to that of society as the freedom of the single cell is to that of the human being. It is this large freedom of society, rather than the freedom of the individual, which democracy offers to the world, free societ-

6. [Edwin Grant] Conklin, *The Direction of Human Evolution*, pp. 125, 125.

ies, free states, free nations rather than absolutely free individuals. In all organisms and in all social organizations, the freedom of the minor units must be limited in order that the larger unit may achieve a new and greater freedom, and in social evolution the freedom of individuals must be merged more and more into the larger freedom of society."

This analogy does not bear analysis. Restraint and constraint of individual expression, suppression of individual freedom "for the good of society" has been practised from time immemorial; and its failure is all too evident. There is no antagonism between the good of the individual and the good of society. The moment civilization is wise enough to remove the constraints and prohibitions which now hinder the release of inner energies, most of the larger evils of society will perish of inanition and malnutrition. Remove the moral taboos that now bind the human body and spirit, free the individual from the slavery of tradition, remove the chains of fear from men and women, above all answer their unceasing cries for knowledge that would make possible their self-direction and salvation, and in so doing, you best serve the interests of society at large. Free, rational and self-ruling personality would then take the place of self-made slaves, who are the victims both of external constraints and the playthings of the uncontrolled forces of their own instincts.[7]

Science likewise illuminates the whole problem of genius. Hidden in the common stuff of humanity lies buried this power of self-expression. Modern science is teaching us that genius is not some mysterious gift of the gods, some treasure conferred upon individuals chosen by chance. Nor is it, as Lombroso[8] believed, the result of a pathological and degenerate condition, allied to criminality and madness. Rather is it due to the removal of physiological and psychological inhibitions and constraints which makes possible the release and the channeling of the primordial inner energies of man into full and divine expression. The removal of these inhibitions, so scientists assure us, makes possible more rapid and profound perceptions—so rapid indeed that they seem to the ordinary human being, practically instantaneous, or intuitive. The qualities of genius are not, therefore, qualities lacking in the common reservoir of humanity, but rather the unimpeded release and direction of powers latent in all of us. This process of course is not necessarily conscious.

This view is substantiated by the opposite problem of feeble-mindedness. Recent researches throw a new light on this problem and the contrasting one of human genius. Mental defect and feeble-mindedness are conceived essentially as retardation, arrest of development, differing in degree so that the victim is either an idiot, an imbecile, feeble-minded or a moron, according to the relative period at which mental development ceases.

Scientific research into the functioning of the ductless glands and their secretions throws a new light on this problem. Not long ago these glands were a complete enigma, owing to the fact that they are not provided with excretory ducts. It has just recently been shown that these organs, such as the thyroid, the pituitary, the suprarenal, the parathyroid and the reproductive glands, exercise an all-powerful influence upon the course of individual development or deficiency. Gley,[9] to whom we owe much of our knowledge of glandular action, has asserted that "the genesis and exercise of the higher faculties of men are conditioned by the purely chemical action of the product of these secretions. Let psychologists consider these facts."

These internal secretions or endocrines pass directly into the blood stream, and exercise a dominating power over health and personality. Deficiency in the thyroid secretion, especially during the years of infancy and early childhood, creates disorders of nutrition and inactivity of the nervous system. The particular form of idiocy known as cretinism is the result of this deficiency, which produces an arrest of the development of the brain cells. The other glands and their secretions likewise exercise the most profound influence upon development, growth and assimilation. Most of these glands are of very small size, none of them larger than a walnut, and some—the parathyroids—almost microscopic. Nevertheless, they are essential to the proper maintenance of life in the body, and no less organically related to mental and psychic development as well.

The reproductive glands, it should not be forgotten, belong to this group, and besides their ordinary products, the germ and sperm cells (ova and spermatozoa) form *hormones* which circulate in the blood and effect changes in the cells of distant parts of the body. Through these

7. Editor: Did Sanger really believe conflict between individual and society would disappear when "moral taboos" and "tradition" were done away? Probably, clear thinking was never her strong point. But what would her society do with those who defied her society and insisted on practicing and promoting those old taboos and traditions? *Those* individuals would clearly be in conflict with *her* society. Sanger never grasped that people have a right to think and live in ways she disliked.

8. Editor: Caesare Lombroso (1835–1909) wrote *The Man of Genius* (1891).

9. Editor: Eugène Gley (1857–1930) wrote *The Internal Secretions* (1917).

hormones the secondary sexual characters are produced, including the many differences in the form and structure of the body which are the characteristics of the sexes. Only in recent years has science discovered that these secondary sexual characters are brought about by the agency of these internal secretions or hormones, passed from the reproductive glands into the circulating blood. These so-called secondary characters which are the sign of full and healthy development, are dependent, science tells us, upon the state of development of the reproductive organs.

For a clear and illuminating account of the creative and dynamic power of the endocrine glands, the layman is referred to a recently published book by Dr. Louis Berman.[10] This authority reveals anew how body and soul are bound up together in a complex unity. Our spiritual and psychic difficulties cannot be solved until we have mastered the knowledge of the wellsprings of our being. "The chemistry of the soul! Magnificent phrase!" exclaims Dr. Berman. "It's a long, long way to that goal. The exact formula is as yet far beyond our reach. But we have started upon the long journey, and we shall get there.

The internal secretions constitute and determine much of the inherited powers of the individual and their development. They control physical and mental growth, and all the metabolic processes of fundamental importance. They dominate all the vital functions of man during the three cycles of life. They cooperate in an intimate relationship which may be compared to an interlocking directorate. A derangement of their functions, causing an insufficiency of them, an excess, or an abnormality, upsets the entire equilibrium of the body, with transforming effects upon the mind and the organs. In short, they control human nature, and whoever controls them, controls human nature. . . .

Blood chemistry of our time is a marvel, undreamed of a generation ago. Also, these achievements are a perfect example of the accomplished fact contradicting a prior prediction and criticism. For it was one of the accepted dogmas of the nineteenth century that the phenomena of living could never be subjected to accurate quantitative analysis.

But the ethical dogmas of the past, no less than the scientific, may block the way to true civilization.

HIS HEAD ABOVE THE CLOUDS

Physiologically as well as psychologically the development of the human being, the sane mind in the sound body, is absolutely dependent upon the functioning and exercise of all the organs in the body. The "moralists" who preach abstinence, self-denial, and suppression are relegated by these findings of impartial and disinterested science to the class of those educators of the past who taught that it was improper for young ladies to indulge in sports and athletics and who produced generations of feeble, undeveloped invalids, bound up by stays and addicted to swooning and hysterics. One need only go out on the street of any American city to-day to be confronted with the victims of the cruel morality of self-denial and "sin." This fiendish "morality" is stamped upon those emaciated bodies, indelibly written in those emasculated, underdeveloped, undernourished figures of men and women, in the nervous tension and unrelaxed muscles denoting the ceaseless vigilance in restraining and suppressing the expression of natural impulses.

Birth Control is no negative philosophy concerned solely with the number of children brought into this world. It is not merely a question of population. Primarily it is the instrument of liberation and of human development.

It points the way to a morality in which sexual expression and human development will not be in conflict with the interest and well-being of the race nor of contemporary society at large. Not only is it the most effective, in fact the only lever by which the value of the child can be raised to a civilized point; but it is likewise the only method by which the life of the individual can be deepened and strengthened, by which an inner peace and security and beauty may be substituted for the inner conflict that is at present so fatal to self-expression and self-realization.

Sublimation of the sexual instinct cannot take place by denying it expression, nor by reducing it to the plane of the purely physiological. Sexual experience, to be of contributory value, must be integrated and assimilated. Asceticism defeats its own purpose because it develops

10. *The Glands Regulating Personality: A Study of the Glands of Internal Secretion in Relation to the Types of Human Nature.* By Louis Berman, M.D. Associate in Biological Chemistry, Columbia University; Physician to the Special Health Clinic, Lenox Hill Hospital. New York: 1921.

the obsession of licentious and obscene thoughts, the victim alternating between temporary victory over "sin" and the remorse of defeat. But the seeker of purely physical pleasure, the libertine or the average sensualist, is no less a pathological case, living as one-sided and unbalanced a life as the ascetic, for his conduct is likewise based on ignorance and lack of understanding. In seeking pleasure without the exercise of responsibility, in trying to get something for nothing, he is not merely cheating others but himself as well.

In still another field science and scientific method now emphasize the pivotal importance of Birth Control. The Binet-Simon intelligence tests which have been developed, expanded, and applied to large groups of children and adults present positive statistical data concerning the mental equipment of the type of children brought into the world under the influence of indiscriminate fecundity and of those fortunate children who have been brought into the world because they are wanted, the children of conscious, voluntary procreation, well nourished, properly clothed, the recipients of all that proper care and love can accomplish.

In considering the data furnished by these intelligence tests we should remember several factors that should be taken into consideration. Irrespective of other considerations, children who are underfed, undernourished, crowded into badly ventilated and unsanitary homes and chronically hungry cannot be expected to attain the mental development of children upon whom every advantage of intelligent and scientific care is bestowed. Furthermore, public school methods of dealing with children, the course of studies prescribed, may quite completely fail to awaken and develop the intelligence.

The statistics indicate at any rate a surprisingly low rate of intelligence among the classes in which large families and uncontrolled procreation predominate. Those of the lowest grade in intelligence are born of unskilled laborers (with the highest birth rate in the community); the next high among the skilled laborers, and so on to the families of professional people, among whom it is now admitted that the birth rate is voluntarily controlled.[11]

But scientific investigations of this type cannot be complete until statistics are accurately obtained concerning the relation of unrestrained fecundity and the quality, mental and physical, of the children produced. The philosophy of Birth Control therefore seeks and asks the cooperation of science and scientists, not to strengthen its own "case," but because this sexual factor in the determination of human history has so long been ignored by historians and scientists. If science in recent years has contributed enormously to strengthen the conviction of all intelligent people of the necessity and wisdom of Birth Control, this philosophy in its turn opens to science in its various fields a suggestive avenue of approach to many of those problems of humanity and society which at present seem to enigmatical and insoluble.

Classes and Races Are Unequal

We have, then, pretty good evidence that capacity for intellectual growth is inborn in different degrees, that it is hereditary, and also that it is closely correlated with social status. Further, we have good evidence that different races possess it in widely different degrees; that races differ in intellectual stature, just as they differ in physical stature.[12]

—WILLIAM MCDOUGALL, HARVARD

—§§§—

11. Cf. [Lewis M.] Terman: *Intelligence of School Children.* New York 1919. p. 56. Also, *Is America Safe for Democracy? Six Lectures Given at the Lowell Institute of Boston,* by William McDougall, Professor of Psychology in Harvard College. New York, 1921.

12. William McDougall, *Is America Safe for Democracy?* p. 66–67.

11

Education and Expression

Civilization is bound up with the success of that movement. The man who rejoices in it and strives to further it is alive; the man who shudders and raises impotent hands against it is merely dead, even though the grave yet yawns for him in vain. He may make dead laws and preach dead sermons and his sermons may be great and his laws may be rigid. But as the wisest of men saw twenty-five centuries ago, the things that are great and strong and rigid are the things that stay below in the grave. It is the things that are delicate and tender and supple that stay above. At no point is life so tender and delicate and supple as at the point of sex. There is the triumph of life.—HAVELOCK ELLIS

Our approach opens to us a fresh scale of values, a new and effective method of testing the merits and demerits of current policies and programs. It redirects our attention to the great source and fountainhead of human life. It offers us the most strategic point of view from which to observe and study the unending drama of humanity—how the past, the present and the future of the human race are all organically bound up together. It coordinates heredity and environment. Most important of all, it frees the mind of sexual prejudice and taboo, by demanding the frankest and most unflinching reexamination of sex in its relation to human nature and the bases of human society. In aiding to establish this mental liberation, quite apart from any of the tangible results that might please the statistically minded, the study of Birth Control is performing an invaluable task. Without complete mental freedom, it is impossible to approach any fundamental human problem. Failure to face the great central facts of sex in an impartial and scientific spirit lies at the root of the blind opposition to Birth Control.

Our bitterest opponents must agree that the problem of Birth Control is one of the most important that humanity to-day has to face. The interests of the entire world, of humanity, of the future of mankind itself are more at stake in this than wars, political institutions, or industrial reorganization. All other projects of reform, of revolution or reconstruction, are of secondary importance, even trivial, when we compare them to the wholesale regeneration—or disintegration—that is bound up with the control, the direction and the release of one of the greatest forces in nature. The great danger at present does not lie

with the bitter opponents of the idea of Birth Control, nor with those who are attempting to suppress our program of enlightenment and education. Such opposition is always stimulating. It wins new adherents. It reveals its own weakness and lack of insight. The greater danger is to be found in the flaccid, undiscriminating interest of "sympathizers" who are "for it"—as an accessory to their own particular panacea. "It even seems, sometimes," wrote the late William Graham Sumner, "as if the primitive people were working along better lines of effort in this direction than we are... when our public organs of instruction taboo all that pertains to reproduction as improper; and when public authority, ready enough to interfere with personal liberty everywhere else, feels bound to act as if there were no societal interest at stake in the begetting of the next generation."[1]

Slowly but surely we are breaking down the taboos that surround sex; but we are breaking them down out of sheer necessity. **The codes that have surrounded sexual behavior in the so-called Christian communities, the teachings of the churches concerning chastity and sexual purity, the prohibitions of the laws, and the hypocritical conventions of society, have all demonstrated their failure as safeguards against the chaos produced and the havoc wrought by the failure to recognize sex as a driving force in human nature—as great as, if indeed not greater than, hunger.**[2] Its dynamic energy is indestructible. It may be transmuted, refined, directed, even sublimated, but to ignore, to neglect, to refuse to

---

1. *Folkways*, p. 492.

recognize this great elemental force is nothing less than foolhardy.

Out of the unchallenged policies of continence, abstinence, "chastity" and "purity," we have reaped the harvests of prostitution, venereal scourges and innumerable other evils. Traditional moralists have failed to recognize that chastity and purity must be the outward symptoms of awakened intelligence, of satisfied desires, and fulfilled love. They cannot be taught by "sex education." They cannot be imposed from without by a denial of the might and the right of sexual expression. Nevertheless, even in the contemporary teaching of sex hygiene and social prophylaxis, nothing constructive is offered to young men and young women who seek aid through the trying period of adolescence.

At the Lambeth Conference of 1920, the Bishops of the Church of England stated in their report on their considerations of sexual morality: "Men should regard all women as they do their mothers, sisters, and daughters; and women should dress only in such a manner as to command respect from every man. All right-minded persons should unite in the suppression of pernicious literature, plays and films. . . ." Could lack of psychological insight and understanding be more completely indicated? Yet, like these bishops, most of those who are undertaking the education of the young are as ignorant themselves of psychology and physiology. Indeed, those who are speaking belatedly of the need of "sexual hygiene" seem to be unaware that they themselves are most in need of it. "We must give up the futile attempt to keep young people in the dark," cries Rev. James Marchant in *Birth-Rate and Empire,*[3] "and the assumption that they are ignorant of notorious facts. We cannot, if we would, stop the spread of sexual knowledge; and if we could do so, we would only make matters infinitely worse. This is the second decade of the twentieth century, not the early Victorian period. . . . It is no longer a question of knowing or not knowing. We have to disabuse our middle-aged minds of that fond delusion. Our young people know more than we did when we began our married lives, and sometimes as much as we know, ourselves, even now. So that we need not continue to shake our few remaining

hairs in simulating feelings of surprise or horror. It might have been better for us if we had been more enlightened. And if our discussion of this problem is to be of any real use, we must at the outset reconcile ourselves to the fact that the birth-rate is voluntarily controlled. . . . Certain persons who instruct us in these matter, hold up their pious hands and whiten their frightened faces as they cry out in the public squares against 'this vice,' but they can only make themselves ridiculous."

Taught upon the basis of conventional and traditional morality and middle-class respectability, based on current dogma, and handed down to the populace with benign condescension, sex education is a waste of time and effort. Such education cannot in any true sense set up as a standard the ideal morality and behavior of the respectable middle-class and then make the effort to induce all other members of society, especially the working classes, to conform to their taboos. Such a method is not only confusing, but, in the creation of strain and hysteria and an unhealthy concentration upon moral conduct, results in positive injury. To preach a negative and colorless ideal of chastity to young men  and women is to neglect the primary duty of awakening their intelligence, their responsibility, their self-reliance and independence. Once this is accomplished, the matter of chastity will take care of itself. The teaching of "etiquette" must be superseded by the teaching of hygiene. Hygienic habits are built up upon a sound knowledge of bodily needs and functions. It is only in the sphere of sex that there remains an unfounded fear of presenting without the gratuitous introduction of non-essential taboos and prejudice, unbiased and unvarnished facts.

As an instrument of education, the doctrine of Birth Control approaches the whole problem in another manner. Instead of laying down hard and fast laws of sexual conduct, instead of attempting to inculcate rules and regulations, of pointing out the rewards of virtue and the penalties of "sin" (as is usually attempted in relation to the venereal diseases), the teacher of Birth Control seeks to meet the needs of the people. Upon the basis of their

---

2. Editor: This same argument—that prohibitions don't stop behavior—could be used to call for an end to laws against rape, murder or whatever. And if a "elemental force" causes problems when restricted, good sense suggests that it will cause even more when unleashed. Sanger's own muddled and idiosyncratic mysticism, given on the pages that follow, was certainly no answer to social ills.

3. Editor: Sir James Merchant (1867–1956), published the book in London in 1917.

The Pivot of Civilization in Historical Perspective

interests, their demands, their problems, Birth Control education attempts to develop their intelligence and show them how they may help themselves; how to guide and control this deep-rooted instinct.

The objection has been raised that Birth Control only reaches the already enlightened, the men and women who have already attained a degree of self-respect and self-reliance. Such an objection could not be based on fact. Even in the most unenlightened sections of the community, among mothers crushed by poverty and economic enslavement, there is the realization of the evils of the too-large family, of the rapid succession of pregnancy after pregnancy, of the hopelessness of bringing too many children into the world. Not merely in the evidence presented in an earlier chapter but in other ways, is this crying need expressed. The investigators of the Children's Bureau who collected the data of the infant mortality reports, noted the willingness and the eagerness with which these down-trodden mothers told the truth about themselves. So great is their hope of relief from that meaningless and deadening submission to unproductive reproduction, that only a society pruriently devoted to hypocrisy could refuse to listen to the voices of these mothers. Respectfully we lend our ears to dithyrambs about the sacredness of motherhood and the value of "better babies"—but we shut our eyes and our ears to the unpleasant reality and the cries of pain that come from women who are to-day dying by the thousands because this power is withheld from them.

This situation is rendered more bitterly ironic because the self-righteous opponents of Birth Control practise themselves the doctrine they condemn. The birth-rate among conservative opponents indicates that they restrict the numbers of their own children by the methods of Birth Control, or are of such feeble procreative energy as to be thereby unfitted to dictate moral laws for other people. They prefer that we should think their small number of children is accidental, rather than publicly admit the successful practice of intelligent foresight. Or else they hold themselves up as paragons of virtue and self-control, and would have us believe that they have brought their children into the world solely from a high, stern sense of public duty—an attitude which is about as convincing as it would be to declare that they found them under goose-berry bushes. How else can we explain the widespread tolerance and smug approval of the clerical idea of sex, now reenforced by floods of crude and vulgar sentiment, which is promulgated by the press, motion-pictures and popular plays?

Like all other education, that of sex can be rendered effective and valuable only as it meets and satisfies the interests and demands of the pupil himself. It cannot be imposed from without, handed down from above, super-imposed upon the intelligence of the person taught. It must find a response within him, give him the power and the instrument wherewith he may exercise his own growing intelligence, bring into action his own judgment and discrimination and thus contribute to the growth of his intelligence. The civilized world is coming to see that education cannot consist merely in the assimilation of external information and knowledge, but rather in the awakening and development of innate powers of discrimination and judgment. The great disaster of "sex education" lies in the fact that it fails to direct the awakened interests of the pupils into the proper channels of exercise and development. Instead, it blunts them, restricts them, hinders them, and even attempts to eradicate them.

This has been the great defect of sex education as it has been practised in recent years. Based on a superficial and shameful view of the sexual instinct, it has sought the inculcation of negative virtues by pointing out the sinister penalties of promiscuity, and by advocating strict adherence to virtue and morality, not on the basis of intelligence or the outcome of experience, not even for the attainment of rewards, but merely to avoid punishment in the form of painful and malignant disease. Education so conceived carries with it its own refutation. True education cannot tolerate the inculcation of fear. Fear is the soil in which are implanted inhibitions and morbid compulsions. Fear restrains, restricts, hinders human expression. It strikes at the very roots of joy and happiness. It should therefore be the aim of sex education to avoid above all the implanting of fear in the mind of the pupil.

Restriction means placing in the hands of external authority the power over behavior. Birth Control, on the contrary, implies voluntary action, the decision for one's self how many children one shall or shall not bring into the world. Birth Control is educational in the real sense of the word, in that it asserts this power of decision, reinstates this power in the people themselves.

We are not seeking to introduce new restrictions but greater freedom. As far as sex is concerned, the impulse has been more thoroughly subject to restriction than any other human instinct. "Thou shalt not!" meets us at every turn. Some of these restrictions are justified; some of them are not. We may have but one wife or one husband at a time; we must attain a certain age before we may marry. Children born out of wedlock are deemed "illegitimate"—even healthy children.[4] The newspapers every day are filled with the scandals of those who have leaped over the restrictions or limitations society has written in her sexual code. Yet the voluntary control of the procreative powers, the rational regulation of the number of children we bring into the world—this is the one type of restriction frowned upon and prohibited by law!

In a more definite, a much more realistic and concrete manner, Birth Control reveals itself as the most effective weapon in the spread of hygienic and prophylactic knowledge among women of the less fortunate classes. It carries with it a thorough training in bodily cleanliness and physiology, a definite knowledge of the physiology and function of sex. In refusing to teach both sides of the subject, in failing to respond to the universal demand among women for such instruction and information, maternity centers limit their own efforts and fail to fulfil what should be their true mission. They are concerned merely with pregnancy, maternity, child-bearing, the problem of keeping the baby alive. But any effective work in this field must go further back. We have gradually come to see, as Havelock Ellis has pointed out, that comparatively little can be done by improving merely the living conditions of adults; that improving conditions for children and babies is not enough. To combat the evils of infant mortality, natal and pre-natal care is not sufficient. Even to improve the conditions for the pregnant woman, is insufficient. Necessarily and inevitably, we are led further and further back, to the point of procreation; beyond that, into the regulation of sexual selection. The problem becomes a circle. We cannot solve one part of it without a consideration of the entirety. But it is especially at the point of creation where all the various forces are concentrated. Conception must be controlled by reason, by intelligence, by science, or we lose control of all its consequences.

Birth Control is essentially an education for women. It is women who, directly and by their very nature, bear the burden of that blindness, ignorance and lack of foresight concerning sex which is now enforced by law and custom. Birth Control places in the hands of women the only effective instrument whereby they may reestablish the balance in society, and assert, not only theoretically but practically as well, the primary importance of the woman and the child in civilization.

---

4. Editor: Some feminists wanted the state to subsidize children from superior sorts of women, so they need not bother with marriage—hence Sanger's remark about "healthy children." For an example, see Ellen Key in Chap. 10. In Chap. 5 Sanger made clear her hostility to assisting inferior mothers.

Birth Control is thus the stimulus to education. Its exercise awakens and develops the sense of self-reliance and responsibility, and illuminates the relation of the individual to society and to the race in a manner that otherwise remains vague and academic. It reveals sex not merely as an untamed and insatiable natural force to which men and women must submit hopelessly and inertly, as it sweeps through them, and then accept it with abject humility the hopeless and heavy consequences. Instead, it places in their hands the power to control this great force; to use it, to direct it into channels in which it becomes the energy enhancing their lives and increasing self-expression and self-development. It awakens in women the consciousness of new glories and new possibilities in motherhood. No longer the prostrate victim of the blind play of instinct but the self-reliant mistress of her body and her own will, the new mother finds in her child the fulfilment of her own desires. In free instead of compulsory motherhood she finds the avenue of her own development and expression. No longer bound by an unending series of pregnancies, at liberty to safeguard the development of her own children, she may now extend her beneficent influence beyond her own home. In becoming thus intensified, motherhood may also broaden and become more extensive as well. The mother sees that the welfare of her own children is bound up with the welfare of all others. Not upon the basis of sentimental charity or gratuitous "welfare-work" but upon that of enlightened self-interest, such a mother may exert her influence among the less fortunate and less enlightened.

Unless based upon this central knowledge of and power over her own body and her own instincts, education for woman is valueless. As long as she remains the plaything of strong, uncontrolled natural forces, as long as she must docilely and humbly submit to the decisions of others, how can woman every lay the foundations of self-respect, self-reliance and independence? How can she make her own choice, exercise her own discrimination, her own foresight?

In the exercise of these powers, in the building up and integration of her own experience, in mastering her own environment the true education of woman must be sought. And in the sphere of sex, the great source and root of all human experience, it is upon the basis of Birth Control—the voluntary direction of her own sexual expression—that woman must take her first step in the assertion of freedom and self-respect.

—§§§—

12

Woman and the Future

I saw a woman sleeping. In her sleep she dreamed Life stood before her, and held in each hand a gift—in the one Love, in the other Freedom. And she said to the woman, "Choose!"

And the woman waited long: and she said, "Freedom!"

And Life said, "Thou has well chosen. If thou hadst said, 'Love,' I would have given thee that thou didst ask for; and I would have gone from thee, and returned to thee no more. Now, the day will come when I shall return. In that day I shall bear both gifts in one hand."

I heard the woman laugh in her sleep. —Olive Schreiner

By no means is it necessary to look forward to some vague and distant date of the future to test the benefits which the human race derives from the program I have suggested in the preceding pages. The results to the individual woman, to the family, and to the State, particularly in the case of Holland, have already been investigated and recorded. Our philosophy is no doctrine of escape from the immediate and pressing realities of life. on the contrary, we say to men and women, and particularly to the latter: face the realities of your own soul and body; know thyself! And in this last admonition, we mean that this knowledge should not consist of some vague shop-worn generalities about the nature of woman—woman as created in the minds of men, nor woman putting herself on a romantic pedestal above the harsh facts of this work-aday world. Women can attain freedom only by concrete, definite knowledge of themselves, a knowledge based on biology, physiology and psychology.

Nevertheless it would be wrong to shut our eyes to the vision of a world of free men and women, a world which would more closely resemble a garden than the present jungle of chaotic conflicts and fears. One of the greatest dangers of social idealists, to all of us who hope to make a better world, is to seek refuge in highly colored fantasies of the future rather than to face and combat the bitter and evil realities which to-day on all sides confront us. I believe that the reader of my preceding chapters will not accuse me of shirking these realities; indeed, he may

think that I have overemphasized the great biological problems of defect, delinquency and bad breeding. It is in the hope that others too may glimpse my vision of a world regenerated that I submit the following suggestions. They are based on the belief that we must seek individual and racial health not by great political or social reconstruction, but, turning to a recognition of our own inherent powers and development, by the release of our inner energies. It is thus that all of us can best aid in making of this world, instead of a vale of tears, a garden.

Let us first of all consider merely from the viewpoint of business and "efficiency" the biological or racial problems which confront us. As Americans, we have of late made much of "efficiency" and business organization.[1] Yet would any corporation for one moment conduct its affairs as we conduct the infinitely more important affairs of our civilization? Would any modern stockbreeder permit the deterioration of his livestock as we not only permit but positively encourage the destruction and deterioration of the most precious, the most essential elements in our world community—the mothers and children. With the mothers and children thus cheapened, the next generation of men and women is inevitably below par. The tendency of the human elements, under present conditions, is constantly downward.

---

1. Editor: Sanger used this same argument in a 1925 *Collier's* article. See Chap. XXI.

Turn to Robert M. Yerkes's *Psychological Examining in the United States Army*[2] in which we are informed that the psychological examination of the drafted men indicated that nearly half—47.3 per cent—of the population had the mentality of twelve-year-old children or less—in other words that they are morons. Professor Conklin, in his recently published volume *The Direction of Human Evolution*[3] is led, on the findings of Mr. Yerkes's report, to assert: "Assuming that these drafted men are a fair sample of the entire population of approximately 100,000,000, this means that 45,000,000 or nearly one-half the entire population, will never develop mental capacity beyond the stage represented by a normal twelve-year-old child, and that only 13,500,000 will ever show superior intelligence."

Making all due allowances for the errors and discrepancies of the psychological examination, we are nevertheless face to face with a serious and destructive practice. Our "overhead" expense in segregating the delinquent, the defective and the dependent, in prisons, asylums and permanent homes, our failure to segregate morons who are increasing and multiplying—I have sufficiently indicated,  though in truth I have merely scratched the surface of this international menace—demonstrate our foolhardy and extravagant sentimentalism. No industrial corporation could maintain its existence upon such a foundation. Yet hardheaded "captains of industry," financiers who pride themselves upon their cool-headed and keen-sighted business ability are dropping millions into rosewater philanthropies and charities that are silly at best and vicious at worst. In our dealings with such elements there is a bland maladministration and misuse of huge sums that should in all righteousness be used for the development and education of the healthy elements of the community.

At the present time, civilized nations are penalizing talent and genius, the bearers of the torch of civilization, to coddle and perpetuate the choking human undergrowth,[4] which, as all authorities tell us, is escaping control and threatens to overrun the whole garden of humanity. Yet men continue to drug themselves with the opiate of optimism, or sink back upon the cushions of Christian resignation, their intellectual powers anaesthetized by cheerful platitudes. Or else, even those, who are fully cognizant of the chaos and conflict, seek an escape in those pretentious but fundamentally fallacious social philosophies which place the blame for contemporary world misery upon anybody or anything except the indomitable but uncontrolled instincts of living organisms. These men fight with shadows and forget the realities of existence. Too many centuries have we sought to hide from the inevitable, which confronts us at every step throughout life.

Let us conceive for the moment at least, a world not burdened by the weight of dependent and delinquent classes, a total population of mature, intelligent, critical and expressive men and women. Instead of the inert, exploitable, mentally passive class which now forms the barren substratum of our civilization, try to imagine a population active, resistant, passing individual and social lives of the most contented and healthy sort. Would such men and women, liberated from our endless, unceasing struggle against mass prejudice and inertia, be deprived in any way of the stimulating zest of life? Would they sink into a slough of complacency and fatuity?

No! Life for them would be enriched, intensified and ennobled in a fashion it is difficult for us in our spiritual and physical squalor even to imagine. There would be a new renaissance of the arts and sciences. Awakened at last to the proximity of the treasures of life lying all about them, the children of that age would be inspired by a spirit of adventure and romance that would indeed produce a terrestrial paradise.

Let us look forward to this great release of creative and constructive energy, not as an idle, vacuous mirage, but as a promise which we, as the whole human race, have it in our power, in the very conduct of our lives from day to day, to transmute into a glorious reality. Let us look forward to that era, perhaps not so distant as we believe, when the great adventures in the enchanted realm of the arts and sciences may no longer be the privilege of a gifted few, but the rightful heritage of a race of genius. In such a world men and women would no longer seek

---

2. *Memoirs of the National Academy of Sciences,* Volume XV.

3. [Edwin Grant] Conklin, *The Direction of Human Evolution.* "When it is remembered that mental capacity is inherited, that parents of low intelligence generally produce children of low intelligence, and that on the average they have more children than persons of high intelligence, and furthermore, when we consider that the intellectual capacity or 'mental age' can be changed very little by education, we are in a position to appreciate the very serious condition which confronts us as a nation." p. 108.

4. Editor: Elsewhere Sanger called these people "weeds." See the supplement to Chap. 4.

escape from themselves by the fantastic and the faraway. They would be awakened to the realization that the source of life, of happiness, is to be found not outside themselves, but within, in the healthful exercise of their God-given functions. The treasures of life are not hidden; they are close at hand, so close that we overlook them. We cheat ourselves with a pitiful fear of ourselves. Men and women of the future will not seek happiness; they will have gone beyond it. Mere happiness would produce monotony. And their lives shall be lives of change and variety with the thrills produced by experiment and research.

Fear will have been abolished: first of all, the fear of outside things and other people; finally the fear of one-self. And with these fears must disappear forever all those poisons of hatreds, individual and international. For the realization would come that there would be no reason for, no value in encroaching upon, the freedom of one another.[5] To-day we are living in a world which is like a forest of trees too thickly planted. Hence the ferocious, unending struggle for existence. Like innumerable ages past, the present age is one of mutual destruction. Our aim is to substitute cooperation, equity, and amity for antagonism and conflict. If the aim of our country or our civilization is to attain a hollow, meaningless superiority over others in aggregate wealth and population, it may be sound policy to shut our eyes to the sacrifice of human life—unregarded life and suffering—and to stimulate rapid procreation. But even so, such a policy is bound in the long run to defeat itself, as the decline and fall of great civilizations of the past emphatically indicate. Even the bitterest opponent of our ideals would refuse to sub-scribe to a philosophy of mere quantity, of wealth and population lacking in spiritual direction or significance. All of us hope for and look forward to the fine flowering of human genius—of genius not expending and dissipat-ing its energy in the bitter struggle for mere existence, but developing to a fine maturity, sustained and nourished by the soil of active appreciation, criticism, and recognition.

Not by denying the central and basic biological facts of our nature, not by subscribing to the glittering but false values of any philosophy or program of escape, not by wild Utopian dreams of the brotherhood of men, not by any sanctimonious debauch of sentimentality or religios-ity, may we accomplish the first feeble step toward liber-ation. On the contrary, only by firmly planting our feet on the solid ground of scientific fact may we even stand erect—may we even rise from the servile stooping pos-ture of the slave, borne down by the weight of age-old oppression.

In looking forward to this radiant release of the inner energies of a regenerated humanity, I am not thinking merely of inventions and discoveries and the application of these to the perfecting of the external and mechanical details of social life. This external and scientific perfect-ing of the mechanism of external life is a phenomenon we are to a great extent witnessing today. But in a deeper sense this tendency can be of no true or lasting value if it cannot be made to subserve the biological and spiritual development of the human organism, individual and col-lective. **Our great problem is not merely to perfect machinery, to produce superb ships, motor cars or great buildings, but to remodel the race so that it may equal the amazing progress we see now making in the externals of life.** We must first free our bodies from dis-ease and predisposition to disease. We must perfect these bodies and make them fine instruments of the mind and the spirit.[6] Only thus, when the body becomes an aid instead of a hindrance to human expression may we attain any civilization worthy of the name. Only thus may we create our bodies a fitting temple for the soul, which is nothing but a vague unreality except insofar as it is able to manifest itself in the beauty of the concrete.

Once we have accomplished the first tentative steps toward the creation of a real civilization, the task of free-ing the spirit of mankind from the bondage of ignorance, prejudice and mental passivity which is more fettering now than ever in the history of humanity, will be facili-tated a thousand-fold. The great central problem, and one which must be taken first is the abolition of the shame and fear of sex. We must teach men the overwhelming power of this radiant force. We must make them under-stand that uncontrolled, it is a cruel tyrant, but that con-trolled and directed, it may be used to transmute and sublimate the everyday world into a realm of beauty and joy. Through sex, mankind may attain the great spiritual illumination which will transform the world, which will light up the only path to an earthly paradise. So must we

---

5. Editor: But suppose though some common genetic failing, a feeble-minded woman is born into this ideal world. Would she be free to have children? Or suppose one of this "race of ge-nius" discovers an old and dusty Bible (or Shakespeare as in *Brave New World*) and comes to believe its message. How free would he be to spread its ideas? And how free of "hatred" is a society that has no place for either of these people?

6. Editor: But how many billions of less-than-perfect people would have to be kept from having children to offer even a pos-sibility of achieving this goal? And what kind of civilization would you have if it was dominated by people obsessed with improving the race? Since Sanger wrote this book, the world has had a rather bitter experience with those who wanted "to re-model the race."

necessarily and inevitably conceive of sex-expression. The instinct is here. None of us can avoid it. It is in our power to make it a thing of beauty and a joy forever: or to deny it, as have the ascetics of the past, to revile this expression and then to pay the penalty, the bitter penalty that Society to-day is paying in innumerable ways.

If I am criticized for the seeming "selfishness" of this conception it will be through a misunderstanding. The individual is fulfilling his duty to society as a whole not by self-sacrifice but by self-development. He does his best for the world not by dying for it, not by increasing the sum total of misery, disease and unhappiness, but by increasing his own stature, by releasing a greater energy, by being active instead of passive, creative instead of destructive. This is fundamentally the greatest truth to be discovered by womankind at large. And until women are awakened to their pivotal function in the creation of a new civilization, that new era will remain an impossible and fantastic dream. The new civilization can become a glorious reality only with the awakening of woman's now dormant qualities of strength, courage, and vigor. As a great thinker of the last century pointed out, not only to her own health and happiness is the physical degeneracy of woman destructive, but to our whole race. The physical and psychic power of woman is more indispensable to the well-being and power of the human race than that even of man, for the strength and happiness of the child is more organically united with that of the mother.[7]

Parallel with the awakening of woman's interest in her own fundamental nature, in her realization that her greatest duty to society lies in self-realization, will come a greater and deeper love for all of humanity. For in attaining a true individuality of her own she will understand that we are all individuals, that each human being is essentially implicated in every question or problem which involves the well-being of the humblest of us. So to-day we are not to meet the great problems of defect and delinquency in any merely sentimental or superficial manner, but with the firmest and most unflinching attitude toward the true interest of our fellow beings. It is from no mere feeling of brotherly love or sentimental philanthropy that we women must insist upon enhancing the value of child life. It is because we know that, if our children are to develop to their full capabilities, all chil-dren must be assured a similar opportunity. **Every single case of inherited defect, every malformed child, every congenitally tainted human being brought into this world is of infinite importance to that poor individual; but it is of scarcely less importance to the rest of us and to all of our children who must pay in one way or another for these biological and racial mistakes.**[8] We look forward in our vision of the future to children brought into the world because they are desired, called from the unknown by a fearless and conscious passion, because women and men need children to complete the symmetry of their own development, no less than to perpetuate the race. They shall be called into a world enhanced and made beautiful by the spirit of freedom and romance—into a world wherein the creatures of our new day, unhampered and unbound by the sinister forces of prejudice and immovable habit,[9] may work out their own destinies. Perhaps we may catch fragmentary glimpses of this new life in certain societies of the past, in Greece perhaps; but in all of these past civilizations these happy groups formed but a small exclusive section of the population. To-day our task is greater; for we realize that no section of humanity can be reclaimed without the regeneration of the whole.

I look, therefore, into a Future when men and women will not dissipate their energy in the vain and fruitless search for content outside of themselves, in far-away places or people. Perfect masters of their own inherent powers, controlled with a fine understanding of the art of life and of love, adapting themselves with pliancy and intelligence to the milieu in which they find themselves, they will unafraid enjoy life to the utmost. Women will for the first time in the unhappy history of this globe establish a true equilibrium and "balance of power" in the relation of the sexes. The old antagonism will have disappeared, the old ill-concealed warfare between men and women. For the men themselves will comprehend that in this cultivation of the human garden they will be rewarded a thousand times. Interest in the vague sentimental fantasies of extra-mundane existence, in patholog-

---

7. Editor: It's unlikely that this vague mysticism will "awaken" a willingness to give up motherhood in the hearts of the great majority of women. Instincts are too strong for that. Its greatest appeal is with women who regard themselves as so superior that they assume, as a matter of course, that they will be permitted to have all the (few) children they want.

8. Editor: Notice that, while Sanger admitted that these "tainted human beings" attach "importance" to their own lives, the only importance she was willing to attach to them lay in the burdensome costs the "rest of us" had to pay for their existence.

9. Editor: Unhampered, that is, by any prejudice other than an overwhelming desire to purge humanity of all "biological and racial mistakes." Other prejudices pale in comparison to that. Nor was Sanger's vision limited to one "section of humanity." Much like H. G. Wells (Chap. V), her "regeneration of the whole" would leave no "stagnant ponds of population" free to proliferate anywhere in the world.

ical or hysterical flights from the realities of our earthliness, will have through atrophy disappeared, for in that dawn men and women will have come to the realization, already suggested, that here close at hand is our paradise, our everlasting abode, our Heaven and our eternity. Not by leaving it and our essential humanity behind us, nor by sighing to be anything but what we are, shall we ever become ennobled or immortal. Not for woman only, but for all of humanity is this the field where we must seek the secret of eternal life.[10]

10. Editor: To illustrate a common theme among many of those whose writings are in this book, compare Sanger's closing words here with the 1872 Winwood Reade quote that began Chapter I: "Our religion therefore is Virtue, our Hope is placed in the happiness of our posterity; our Faith in the Perfectibility of Man." The terrible catch to this high vision is that human perfectibility—if such be possible—can only be achieved by dealing ruthlessly with all those who are less than perfect. And it the final analysis that is all of us.

A

Principles and Aims of the American Birth Control League

Principles

The complex problems now confronting America as the result of the practice of reckless procreation are fast threatening to grow beyond human control.

Everywhere we see poverty and large families going hand in hand. Those least fit to carry on the race are increasing most rapidly. People who cannot support their own offspring are encouraged by Church and State to produce large families. Many of the children thus begotten are diseased or feeble-minded; many become criminals. The burden of supporting these unwanted types has to be borne by the healthy elements of the nation. Funds that should be used to raise the standard of our civilization are diverted to the maintenance of those who should never have been born.

In addition to this grave evil we witness the appalling waste of women's health and women's lives by too frequent pregnancies. These unwanted pregnancies often provoke the crime of abortion, or alternatively multiply the number of child-workers and lower the standard of living.[1]

To create a race of well born children it is essential that the function of motherhood should be elevated to a position of dignity, and this is impossible as long as conception remains a matter of chance.

We hold that children should be

1. Conceived in love;
2. Born of the mother's conscious desire;

3. And only begotten under conditions which render possible the heritage of health.[2]

Therefore we hold that every woman must possess the power and freedom to prevent conception except when these conditions can be satisfied.

Every mother must realize her basic position in human society. She must be conscious of her responsibility to the race in bringing children into the world.

Instead of being a blind and haphazard consequence of uncontrolled instinct, motherhood must be made the responsible and self-directed means of human expression and regeneration.

These purposes, which are of fundamental importance to the whole of our nation and to the future of mankind, can only be attained if women first receive practical scientific education in the means of Birth Control. That, therefore, is the first object to which the efforts of this League will be directed.

Aims

The American Birth Control League aims to enlighten and educate all sections of the American public in the various aspects of the dangers of uncontrolled procreation and the imperative necessity of a world program of Birth Control.

The League aims to correlate the findings of scientists, statisticians, investigators, and social agencies in all fields. To make this possible, it is necessary to organize various departments:

---

1. Editor: Note which of the Sanger's two basic arguments—birth control targeted *at* the poor as opposed to birth control *for* the poor—gets the first and longest paragraph. The latter was more an argument of convenience and has not changed as maternal and infant mortality statistics have improved dramatically.

---

2. Editor: The first principle was window dressing, the second directed at superior women under pressure to have larger families, while the third provided the rationale ("responsibility to the race") to keep inferior women from having children.

RESEARCH: To collect the findings of scientists, concerning the relation of reckless breeding to the evils of delinquency, defect and dependence;

INVESTIGATION: To derive from these scientifically ascertained facts and figures, conclusions which may aid all public health and social agencies in the study of problems of maternal and infant mortality, child-labor, mental and physical defects and delinquence in relation to the practice of reckless parentage.[3]

HYGIENIC AND PHYSIOLOGICAL: instruction by the Medical profession to mothers and potential mothers in harmless and reliable methods of Birth Control in answer to their requests for such knowledge.

STERILIZATION: of the insane and feebleminded and the encouragement of this operation upon those afflicted with inherited or transmissible diseases, with the understanding that sterilization does not deprive the individual of his or her sex expression, but merely renders him incapable of producing children.[4]

EDUCATIONAL: The program of education includes: The enlightenment of the public at large, mainly through the education of leaders of thought and opinion—teachers, ministers, editors and writers—to the moral and scientific soundness of the principles of Birth Control and the imperative necessity of its adoption as the basis of national and racial progress.[5]

POLITICAL AND LEGISLATIVE: To enlist the support and cooperation of legal advisers, statesmen and legislators in effecting the removal of state and federal statutes which encourage dysgenic breeding, increase the sum total of disease, misery and poverty and prevent the establishment of a policy of national health and strength.

ORGANIZATION: To send into the various States of the Union field workers to enlist the support and arouse the interest of the masses, to the importance of Birth Control so that laws may be changed and the establishment of clinics made possible in every State.

INTERNATIONAL: This department aims to cooperate with similar organizations in other countries to study Birth Control in its relations to the world population problem, food supplies, national and racial conflicts, and to urge upon all international bodies organized to promote world peace, the consideration of these aspects of international amity.

THE AMERICAN BIRTH CONTROL LEAGUE proposes to publish in its official organ *The Birth Control Review,* reports and studies on the relationship of controlled and uncontrolled populations to national and world problems.

The American Birth Control League also proposes to hold an annual Conference to bring together the workers of the various departments so that each worker may realize the inter-relationship of all the various phases of the problem to the end that National education will tend to encourage and develop the powers of self-direction, self-reliance, and independence in the individuals of the community instead of dependence for relief upon public or private charities.

—§§§—

3. Editor: Notice that both research and investigation focus on the "reckless breeding" and "reckless parentage." Both are assumed and the result cannot be more choices for parents.

4. Editor: Notice the vague categories of people for which sterilization is required or encouraged.

5. Editor: Sanger assumed that "leaders of thought and opinion" would be most receptive to her ideas and that the "public at large" would only gradually be brought around.

Index

CPSIA information can be obtained
at www.ICGtesting.com
Printed in the USA
BVHW010733310122
627588BV00006B/122

9 781587 420047